February 23–25, 2011
San Jose, CA, USA

**Association for
Computing Machinery**

Advancing Computing as a Science & Profession

MMSys'11

Proceedings of the 2011 ACM Conference on
Multimedia Systems

Sponsored by:
ACM SIGMM

In-cooperation with:
ACM SIGCOMM, ACM SIGMOBILE, & ACM SIGOPS

Supported by:
Cisco

Association for Computing Machinery

Advancing Computing as a Science & Profession

The Association for Computing Machinery
2 Penn Plaza, Suite 701
New York, New York 10121-0701

Notice to Past Authors of ACM-Published Articles
ACM intends to create a complete electronic archive of all articles and/or other material previously published by ACM. If you have written a work that has been previously published by ACM in any journal or conference proceedings prior to 1978, or any SIG Newsletter at any time, and you do NOT want this work to appear in the ACM Digital Library, please inform permissions@acm.org, stating the title of the work, the author(s), and where and when published.

ISBN: 978-1-4503-0518-1 (Digital)

ISBN: 978-1-4503-1375-9 (Print)

Additional copies may be ordered prepaid from:

ACM Order Department
PO Box 30777
New York, NY 10087-0777, USA

Phone: 1-800-342-6626 (USA and Canada)
+1-212-626-0500 (Global)
Fax: +1-212-944-1318
E-mail: acmhelp@acm.org
Hours of Operation: 8:30 am – 4:30 pm ET

ACM Order No. 423115

Printed in the USA

Foreword

It gives us great pleasure to welcome you to the second annual ACM Multimedia Systems conference (MMSys). This conference focuses on multimedia computing and networking, lying at the intersection of digital media and the systems (applications, architectures, networking, operating systems) that handle them. The goal is to cut across a diverse set of computer science subfields in order to achieve a longitudinal perspective on the challenges that multimedia data types present. This provides a unique opportunity to view the intersections and interplay of the various approaches and solutions developed across these domains to deal with multimedia data types. Furthermore, MMSys provides an avenue for communicating research that addresses multimedia systems holistically.

Embedded within this year's technical program is a special session on Modern Media Transport (MMT) - Dynamic Adaptive Streaming over HTTP. The papers within the MMT session were chosen from submissions to a separate Call For Papers and selected by a more specialized technical program committee.

Also new in this year's technical program is a Dataset track that encourages and recognizes dataset sharing among researchers from both industry and academia. Papers accepted to the Dataset track have their data hosted by the MMSys organization, making them available as a valuable resource for the MMSys research community.

This year, there were 41 submissions to the main MMSys track. The main program committee accepted 15 (37%) high-quality papers from this pool. There were 12 papers submitted to the Dataset track. The main program committee accepted 5 (42%) papers with the best methodology and most useful data from this pool. Finally, there were 20 papers submitted to the MMT track. The MMT program committee accepted 5 full and 4 short papers (overall, 45%) from this pool.

In order to put together MMSys 2011, a tremendous amount of effort by the collective research community was required. We would like to thank ACM and ACM SIGMM for again supporting and sponsoring the conference. We would also like to thank Cisco for both supporting and hosting the conference. We are also in great debt to the technical program committees for providing thorough, and thoughtful, reviews of each paper in order to select the best papers for the technical program. Lastly, we would like to thank the researchers who contributed papers to the forum, providing material for the excellent technical program presented at this conference. We hope you find the assembled program interesting and thought-provoking, and that you will continue to contribute to the long-term success of this conference. Enjoy the show!

Ali C. Begen
MMSys 2011 General Co-Chair
Cisco, Canada

Ketan Mayer-Patel
MMSys 2011 General Co-Chair
University of North Carolina, USA

Mark Claypool
MMSys 2011 Program Chair
Worcester Polytechnic Institute, USA

Christian Timmerer
MMSys 2011 MMT Program Chair
Klagenfurt University, Austria

Table of Contents

Session 1: Wireless and Mobile
Session Chair: Klara Nahrstedt *(University of Illinois, Urbana-Champaign)*

Session 2: Networking
Session Chair: Roger Zimmerman *(National University of Singapore)*

Session 3: Data Transmission and QoS
Session Chair: Grenville Armitage *(Swinburne University of Technology)*

Session 4: Dataset Track
Session Chair: Michael Zink *(University of Massachusetts, Amherst)*

Session 5: Modern Media Transport 1
Session Chair: Christian Timmerer *(Klagenfurt University)*

Session 6: System Performance
Session Chair: Carsten Griwodz *(University of Oslo)*

Session 7: Encoding and Repair
Session Chair: Wu-chi Feng *(Portland State University)*

Session 8: Modern Media Transport 2

Session Chair: Ali C. Begen *(Cisco, Canada)*

MMSys 2011 Conference Organization

General Chair: Ali C. Begen *(Cisco, Canada)*
Ketan Mayer-Patel *(University of North Carolina, USA)*

Steering Committee: Mark Claypool *(Worcester Polytechnic Institute, USA)*
Wu-Chi Feng *(Portland State University, USA)*
Ketan Mayer-Patel *(University of North Carolina, USA)*

Program Chair – Main Track: Mark Claypool *(Worcester Polytechnic Institute, USA)*

Program Committee – Main Track: Luca Abeni *(University of Trento, Italy)*
Kevin Almeroth *(UC Santa Barbara, USA)*
Grenville Armitage *(Swinburne University of Technology, Australia)*
Azer Bestavros *(Boston University, USA)*
Dick Bulterman *(CWI, The Netherlands)*
Surendar Chandra *(FXPAL, USA)*
Mark Claypool *(Worcester Polytechnic Institute, USA)*
Bruce Davie *(Cisco, USA)*
Wu-Chang Feng *(Portland State University, USA)*
Wu-Chi Feng *(Portland State University, USA)*
Carsten Griwodz *(University of Oslo, Norway)*
Pål Halvorsen *(University of Oslo, Norway)*
Mohamed Hefeeda *(Simon Fraser University, Canada)*
Tristan Henderson *(University of St. Andrews, UK)*
Sugih Jamin *(University of Michigan, USA)*
Charles "Buck" Krasic *(University of British Columbia, Canada)*
Baochun Li *(University of Toronto, Canada)*
Kang Li *(University of Georgia, USA)*
Tom Little *(Boston University, USA)*
Dwight Makaroff *(University of Saskatchewan, Canada)*
Andreas Mauthe *(Lancaster University, UK)*
Ketan Mayer-Patel *(University of North Carolina, USA)*
John Miller *(Microsoft, UK)*
Klara Nahrstedt *(University of Illinois, Urbana-Champaign, USA)*
Wei Tsang Ooi *(National University of Singapore, Singapore)*
Reza Rejaie *(University of Oregon, USA)*
Christoph Rensing *(University of Darmstadt, Germany)*
Larry Rowe *(FXPAL, USA)*
Nabil Sarhan *(Wayne State University, USA)*
Travis Schluessler *(Intel, USA)*
Prashant Shenoy *(University of Massachusetts, Amherst, USA)*
Shervin Shirmohammadi *(University of Ottawa, Canada)*
Michael Vernick *(Avaya, USA)*
Carey Williamson *(University of Calgary, Canada)*
Huahui Wu *(Google, USA)*
Roger Zimmerman *(National University of Singapore, Singapore)*
Michael Zink *(University of Massachusetts, Amherst, USA)*

Program Chair – Modern Media Transport Track: Christian Timmerer *(Klagenfurt University, Austria)*

Program Committee – Modern Media Transport Track: Ali C. Begen *(Cisco, Canada)*
Laszlo Böszörmenyi *(Klagenfurt University, Austria)*
Per Fröjdh *(Ericsson Research, Sweden)*
Pascal Frossard *(EPFL, Switzerland)*
Carsten Griwodz *(University of Oslo, Norway)*
Pål Halvorsen *(University of Oslo, Canada)*
Behnoosh Hariri *(University of Ottawa, Canada)*
Yuwen He *(Dolby, USA)*
Hermann Hellwagner *(Klagenfurt University, Austria)*
Wei Tsang Ooi *(National University of Singapore, Singapore)*
Jörn Ostermann *(Leibniz Universität Hannover, Germany)*
Thomas Schierl *(Fraunhofer/HHI, Germany)*
Thomas Stockhammer *(Nomor Research GmbH, Germany)*
Christian Timmerer *(Klagenfurt University, Austria)*
Ye-Kui Wang *(Huawei, USA)*
Roger Zimmermann *(National University of Singapore, Singapore)*

MMSys 2011 Sponsors & Supporters

Sponsor:

In Cooperation With:

SIGOPS
ACM SIG on Operating Systems

sigmobile

acm sigcomm

Corporate Support:

CISCO

GPS-aided Recognition-based User Tracking System with Augmented Reality in Extreme Large-scale Areas

Wei Guan
Computer Graphics and
Immersive Technologies
Computer Science, USC
wguan@usc.edu

Suya You
Computer Graphics and
Immersive Technologies
Computer Science, USC
suyay@imsc.usc.edu

Ulrich Neumann
Computer Graphics and
Immersive Technologies
Computer Science, USC
uneumann@graphics.usc.edu

ABSTRACT

We present a recognition-based user tracking and augmented reality system that works in extreme large scale areas. The system
will provide a user who captures an image of a building facade
with precise location of the building and augmented information
about the building. While GPS cannot provide information about
camera poses, it is needed to aid reducing the searching ranges
in image database. A patch-retrieval method is used for efficient
computations and real-time camera pose recovery. With the patch
matching as the prior information, the whole image matching can
be done through propagations in an efficient way so that a more
stable camera pose can be generated. Augmented information such
as building names and locations are then delivered to the user. The
proposed system mainly contains two parts, offline database building and online user tracking. The database is composed of images
for different locations of interests. The locations are clustered into
groups according to their UTM coordinates. An overlapped clustering method is used to cluster these locations in order to restrict
the retrieval range and avoid ping pong effects. For each cluster,
a vocabulary tree is built for searching the most similar view. On
the tracking part, the rough location of the user is obtained from
the GPS and the exact location and camera pose are calculated by
querying patches of the captured image. The patch property makes
the tracking robust to occlusions and dynamics in the scenes. Moreover, due to the overlapped clusters, the system simulates the "soft
handoff" feature and avoid frequent swaps in memory resource. Experiments show that the proposed tracking and augmented reality
system is efficient and robust in many cases.

Categories and Subject Descriptors

H.3.3 [**Information Storage and Retrieval**]: Information Search
and Retrieval—*Image Retrieval, Performance Analysis*; I.4.9 [**Image
Processing and Computer Vision**]: Applications—*Scene Recognition, User Tracking*

General Terms

Performance

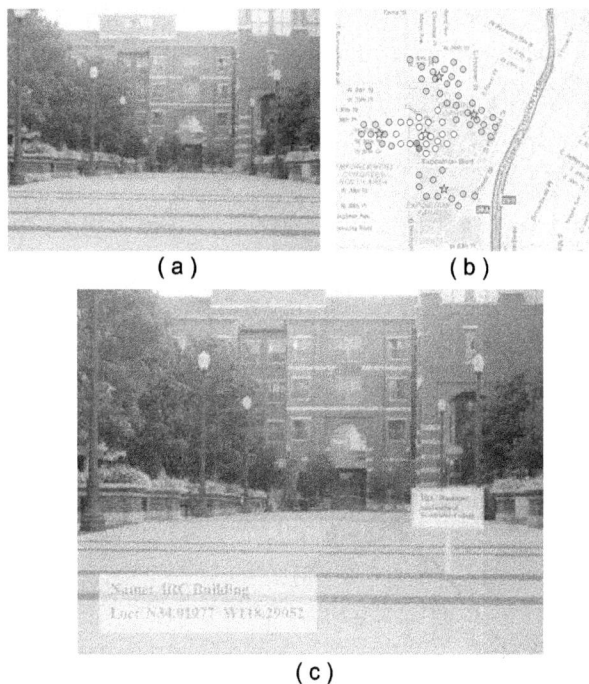

(a)   (b)

(c)

Figure 1: The proposed tracking and augmented reality system. (a) The captured image from the user. (b) The nearest
cluster is selected (yellow dots). The current location is shown
with blue dot and the estimated location is shown with red dot.
(c) The image with augmented information. A 2D annotating
label and 3D annotating sign is embedded in the image.

Keywords

Patch Approach, Real-time Recognition, Augmented Reality

1. INTRODUCTION

The Global Positioning System (GPS) is a space-based satellite
system that can provide location information anywhere where there
is an unobstructed line of sight to more than three satellites. It precisely times the signals sent by GPS satellites and then determines
the distances to these satellites. These distances and the locations of
satellites are used to calculate the position of GPS receivers. While
GPS system is widely used to aid navigation, however, many applications demand more accurate locations and more detailed sensor

information for better environment-interaction capabilities.

Vision sensors provide a tremendous amount of information about the user's environments. They are considered one of the most powerful sources of information among all the sensors. Not only can they be used to provide more accurate location information, they can also provide users with more context-based information such as appearance information about the buildings. However, due to the wealth of information provided by vision sensors, the processing usually takes much longer time than other types of sensors like ultrasound sensors and inertial sensors. Besides, a picture itself provides no information about locations. The location can be estimated by matching images in the database. Therefore, image querying is an essential process, which will consume extra computational resource.

Determining locations from vision-based sensors is a critical problem in the vision and robotics community. When a user obtains information from its optical sensors, the visual information is summarized and compared with the existing landmarks. Point-based features such as SIFT [11] or SURF [3] are usually used in the matching process due to their robustness. However, because of the complexity for such feature generations and matchings, the image retrieval and matching processes are not fast enough for some applications such as real time tracking and augmented reality.

We propose a novel system that can track the user with augmented information in large scale areas. The system can work in real time through speeding up the retrieval and matching processes. With the GPS information, the system first selects the nearest cluster and load the corresponding database. Then for the image captured by the user, the system picks the most promising part of the image and use it to query the best matching patch in the existing database. The query results are used to refine the user's location. The calculated camera pose is still not stable or accurate enough for some applications like augmented reality since the querying features are located in a small area on the image. So in the next step, an algorithm is designed to propagate matchings to the whole image. The searching range for feature matchings is largely limited. Therefore, the speed for matchings will be significantly increased and the calculated camera pose will be more accurate.

Another advantage of our proposed framework is its ability to handle occlusions and dynamics. It is common that the newly captured images are different from existing images in the database due to moving passengers and objects. The proposed algorithm will pick some patches that are from the non-occluded parts and match them in the database. In most cases, the proposed framework is robust to large occlusions and dynamics.

The remainder of this paper presents the proposed system in more details. After discussing some related work in Section 2, we provide an overview of our proposed system in Section 3. The process of building the database is presented in Section 4. Following that, we talk about the recognition-based user tracking in Section 5. In Section 6, we propose a propagation method for camera pose refinement. We show experimental results in Section 7 and conclude the paper in Section 8.

2. RELATED WORK

Over the past years, many vision-based localization systems have been proposed. Depending on the features they use to describe the images and the method they exploit to do the matchings, these systems can be divided into two categories. In the first category [7, 8, 5, 4], simple features like lines and colors are used, but sophistic learning techniques are usually required to locate the users. Horswill [7] extracts features around the environment like walls, doors or openings and identify the robot position according to these fea-

tures. The algorithm is efficient due to its specialization to its task and environment. In [8], the vertical lines are extracted from images and combined with distance information which is obtained from ultrasound sensors. A Bayesian network is used for the combination and estimation of the robot location. Dodds and Hager [5] use a color interest operator consisting of a weighted combination of heuristic scores to identify landmarks. The operator can select regions that are robust representations for scenes recognition. A Bayesian filtering method was proposed in [4]. It uses sampling-based representation method and localizes the robot by using scalar brightness measurement.

In the second category, more sophisticated features are used [15, 16, 19, 9]. In [15], Se et al. propose a vision-based simultaneous localization and mapping (SLAM) system by tracking the SIFT features. SIFT features [11] are robust in scale, orientation and viewpoint variations so they are good natural visual landmarks for tracking over long periods of time from different views. Tamimi et al. [16] propose an approach that reduces the number of features generated by SIFT, and with the help of a particle filter, the robot location can still be estimated accurately. In [19], Wolf et al. use local scale-invariant features and combine with Monte-Carlo localization to estimate robot positions. The system is robust against occlusions and dynamics such as people walking by. In [9], scale-invariant features are also used, and they are combined with a proposed probabilistic environment model in order to locate the robot.

To match images in large-scale database, image retrieval techniques are usually exploited [19, 10, 17, 13]. Wolf et al. [19] make use of image retrieval technique together with sample-based Monte Carlo localization to extract the possible viewpoints for the current image. Krose and Bunschoten [10] describe a vision based localization method that uses principal component analysis on images captured at different locations. In [17], Ulrich and Nourbakhsh propose an efficient approach that uses color histogram matchings for localization. The color images can be classified in real-time based on nearest-neighbor learning and voting scheme. In [13], Nister and Stewenius proposes a recognition scheme that scales to large number of objects. The scheme builds upon indexing descriptors based on SIFT features and efficiently integrates indexing and hierarchical quantization with a vocabulary tree.

Some systems are not specially designed for localization purpose but try to recognize objects with less computational cost. Wagner et al. [18] presents a modified SIFT that is created from a fixed patch size of 15x15 pixels and form a descriptor with only 36 dimensions. The modified feature is used for efficient nature tracking with interactive speed on current-generation phones. Henze et al. [6] combines the simplified SIFT with a scalable vocabulary tree to achieve interactive object recognition on mobile phones. The simplified features consume less computational cost which is necessary for mobile applications. Azad et al. [2] present a combination of the Harris corner detector and the SIFT descriptor, which computes features with a high repeatability and good matching properties. By replacing the SIFT keypoint detector with extended Harris corner detector, the algorithm can generate features in real time.

The techniques described above match images captured by vision sensors with existing landmarks in the database. The goal of this paper is to propose a novel system that can track users in large scale areas and provide with augmented information. We describe how the landmarks are built in the database and how the image can be queried efficiently. In practical experiments we demonstrate that our system is able to locate the user and recover the camera pose at the real time speed and is robust to large occlusions and dynamics.

3. OVERVIEW OF THE SYSTEM

Offline Database Building

| Select locations of interests |
| Take images for each location |
| Generate 3D point cloud |
| Register point cloud in world coordinates |
| Cluster images according to locations |
| Partition images into smaller patches |
| Build a vocabulary tree for each cluster |

☐ Manual Process   ☐ Restrict Searching Range

(a)   Offline Database Building

Online User Tracking

| Capture new image from camera |
| Partition images into smaller patches |
| Obtain rough location from GPS |
| Get the closest cluster |
| Retrieve similar patches in cluster |
| Match two images with propagations |
| Calculate accurate location and camera pose |
| Augment image with 2D and 3D labels |

☐ Fast Retrieval   ☐ Camera Pose Recovery

(b)   Online User Tracking

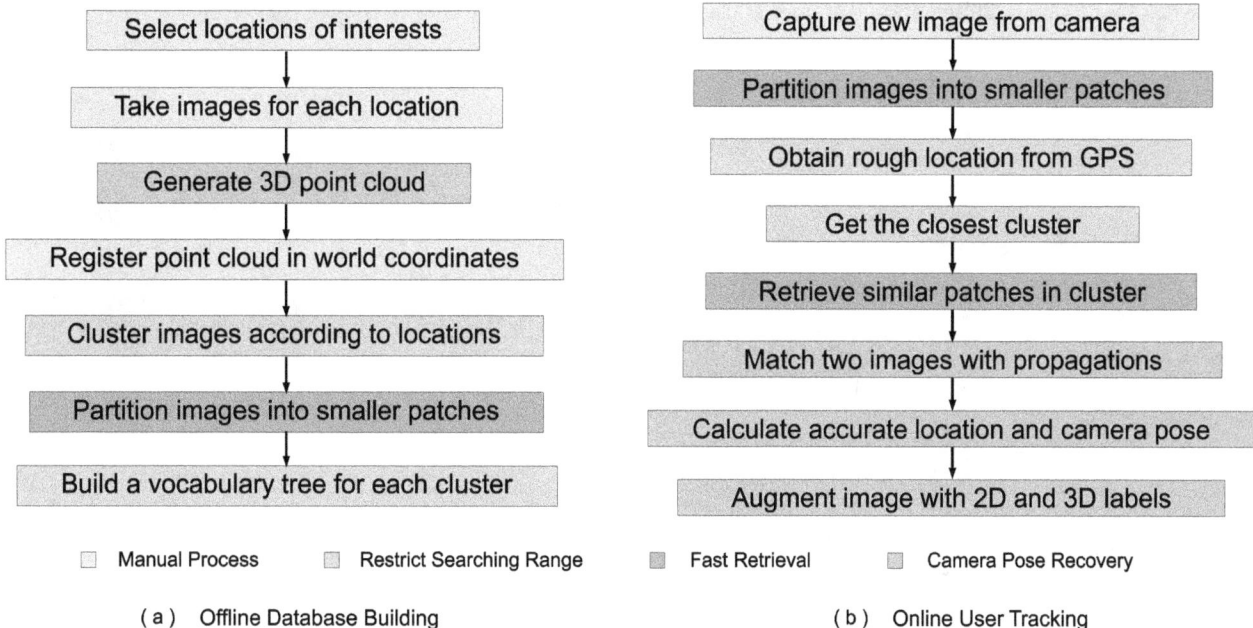

Figure 2: Overview of the system.

The system consists of two main parts, database building and user tracking. As shown in Fig. 2, each part contains several steps. In database building process, first we select locations of interests in the large-scale area and take images from different viewpoints for each location. Then we use the bundler algorithm [1] to build a 3D point cloud per location. The point cloud is manually registered with the world coordinates, i.e. assigning the UTM coordinates, adjusting the scale and orientation. We use overlapped clustering method to cluster these locations so that each cluster contains a few nearby locations. The images are partitioned into smaller patches and the patches in each cluster are put into a vocabulary tree for retrieval in the tracking process.

For the online tracking part, the user's rough location is obtained through GPS device so that the closest cluster is determined. Due to the inaccuracy of GPS devices, the locations that are nearly close to two or more cluster centers will be assigned to these clusters at the same time. An overlapped clustering method that is based on k-means is used. When a user captures a new image, the image is partitioned into patches and the most distinctive patches are used for retrieval through the corresponding vocabulary tree. The more accurate location information and the camera pose can be recovered from 2D to 3D matchings. We will discuss each step in more details in the following sections.

4. DATABASE BUILDING

We use similar method in [1] to build the environment. Instead of obtaining images from the web and cover the whole area, we take images ourselves and only cover the locations of interests such as facades of buildings. At each location, the images are taken from different views at different distances. SURF features [3] are used due to its fast speed and robustness. Moreover, the UTM coordinates and building-related information for each location are also recorded. Such information can be obtained from GPS device or manually input. In our system, 120 locations are recorded. For

each location, we take 10 images from different viewing angles and distances. Therefore, there are totally 1,200 images in our database.

4.1 Overlapped Clustering with K-Means

To reduce the searching range, we cluster the locations of interests into groups. The user is associated with the cluster whose center is nearest to his or her rough location. Such location is represented as the UTM coordinates returned from GPS device, so the retrieval process can be done within the cluster. To build overlapped K clusters, we first use traditional k-means clustering method to get K non-overlapped clusters. For those locations that are at the boundaries, we assign them to all those clusters that are nearly close as the closest one. The steps are shown as follows,

1. Suppose there are N different locations, and the UTM coordinates (easting and northing) for location i are $L_i = (X_i, Y_i)$, $i = 1..N$. Let the maximum error caused by a GPS device be E and the longest distance from which a user is allowed to take pictures for a location be D. Let H be the threshold for handoff (we will discuss in later section). We want to cluster the locations into K groups.

2. (Traditional K-means) Randomly select K locations. We consider these K locations as the centers of K clusters.

3. For each location, assign it to the cluster whose center is nearest to it.

4. For each cluster, recalculate the cluster center. Repeat step 3 and step 4 until it converges. Then goto step 5.

5. (Overlapped assignment) For each location i, let d_i be the distance to the nearest cluster center. Let centers for the K clusters be $C_j = (X_j, Y_j)$, $j = 1..K$. We assign the location i to cluster j if and only if $\|L_i - C_j\|_2 \leq d_i + \max(E, D, H)$.

The step 2 to step 4 are traditional k-means clustering method. We add one more step for overlapped assignment to handle three problems. Firstly, the instability and inaccuracy of GPS. Secondly, the position of the user is usually different from the location of interest. Thirdly, the user may go back and forth within certain areas, which can cause unnecessary swaps of databases in the memory.

In our system, we have $N=120$ locations. We want to cluster them into $K=5$ groups. The clustering results are shown in Fig. 3.

Figure 3: The overlapped clustering with $N=120$ and $K=5$. Only half of the locations are displayed in the figure.

4.2 Image Partitioning

When we build the database, instead of bagging SURF features based on images, we make smaller bags that are based on patches. For a 640 by 480 image, we partition it into 8 by 8 grids. As shown in Fig. 4, there are 4 different patches according to their size. For patches of the same size, the neighboring two patches have an overlap of half size of the patch. For example, in Fig. 4, the two patches of size 1×1 grid have an overlap of half grid size.

For an 8 by 8 partitioning, there are totally $15 \times 15 + 7 \times 7 + 3 \times 3 + 1 = 284$ patches. Therefore, there are totally $1200 \times 284 = 340,800$ patches so on average $340,800/5 = 68,160$ patches for each cluster. Moreover, we will remove those patches that contain too few features since they are not good representations for the locations. After removal, there are around 30,000 to 40,000 patches per cluster.

As we can see, many of the patches have duplicate SURF features. In another word, each SURF feature is contained in many different patches. Therefore, when we calculate the visual words of these features, we need to make sure each feature is only calculated once to avoid overheads caused by partitioning. It is also important to note that we should calculate the SURF features first and then partition them into patches. Otherwise, the features near the patch boundary will not be correctly described.

4.3 Scalable Vocabulary Tree with Patches

Every patch is represented by a bag of SURF features. For a large number of patches, to compare the 64-dimension-vector SURF features for every two images is extremely expensive. Vocabulary tree is usually used to quantize SURF into more compact features. A vocabulary tree is a hierarchical-structured tree that can efficiently integrate quantization and classification. The classification results can be further used as indexing based on well-designed scoring scheme. The quantization is built by hierarchical k-means clustering. The tree can be trained unsupervisely with a large set of

Figure 4: An image is partitioned into 8 by 8 small grids. Four different sizes are used for patches, 1×1 grid, 2×2 grids, 4×4 grids and 8×8 grids (the whole image).

SURF features. In our implementation, the vocabulary tree has 6 levels and each level has 10 branches. So there are 1 million leaf nodes or classes.

A patch usually contains hundreds of features, and each feature generates a visual word by going through the vocabulary tree, so a patch can be represented by the bag of visual words. It can be further described by the frequency or distribution of visual words, and such distribution can be represented by a vector. The length of the vector is the same as the number of leaf nodes. To compare two patches, we only need to compare the two distribution vectors. Though the vector is very high-dimensional, there are only a few non-zero elements, so the comparison can be done in little time. When a new patch is queried, a score is calculated for each comparison with every patch containing the same nodes along the path.

To calculate the distribution vector for a patch, the most time consuming part is the quantization process. Instead of going through the vocabulary tree patch by patch, we first do the quantization for all the features in the image to avoid duplicate quantization. The distribution vectors can be calculated hierarchically in a simple way as follows.

As shown in Fig. 5-(a), let the number of features for these patches be N_1 to N_6. The distribution vectors for patch 7 and patch 8 can be simply calculated as,

$$v_7 = \frac{\sum_{k=1}^{4} v_k N_k}{\sum_{k=1}^{4} N_k}, \qquad v_8 = \frac{\sum_{k=3}^{6} v_k N_k}{\sum_{k=3}^{6} N_k}. \qquad (1)$$

For each image, though we have 284 distribution vectors instead of one vector, the total amount of time used for calculating the vectors is negligible compared to the quantization process. For a 640×480 image on a 4GHz CPU, the total amount of time used for the quantization process is about 70-80ms, and the time to calculate all the vectors is about 2-4ms. Therefore, the overheads for image partitioning are no more than 3 percent.

5. RECOGNITION-BASED TRACKING

For the online stage, we first associate the user with the nearest cluster. The most distinctive patches in the new image will be matched with images in the corresponding database. The over-

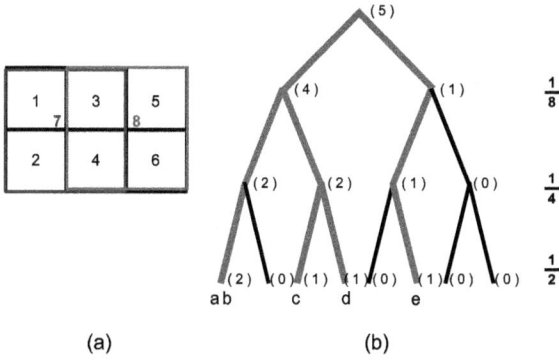

Figure 5: (a) The hierarchical way to calculate the distribution vector. (b) A 3-level vocabulary tree with 5 features (a, b, c, d, e). The weights for level 1 to 3 are $\frac{1}{8}$, $\frac{1}{4}$ and $\frac{1}{2}$. The number in the parenthesis are number of features that going through for each node.

lapped clusters are used to achieve "soft handoff" feature. The use of patches will greatly increase the speed for retrieval thus reduce the localization time. With careful selection of the patch used for retrieval, the performance is still competitive with using the whole image. In the cases that large occlusions exist, the patch-based method can have even better performance.

5.1 Cluster Association and Soft Handoff

With the user's UTM location provided by GPS, the cluster whose center is nearest to the user can be found. The corresponding database will then be loaded to the memory. However, when a user is at some locations that are nearly close to two cluster centers and frequently crosses the boundary, there will be unnecessary swaps of memories. Therefore, we set a handoff threshold H to avoid such overheads.

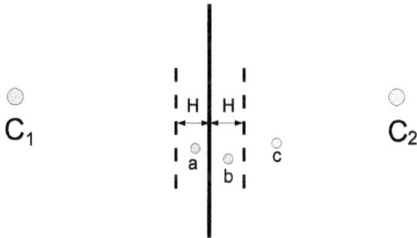

Figure 6: The soft handoff process. H is the threshold.

As shown in Fig. 6, C_1 and C_2 are two clusters. The user is initially at point a, which is closer to cluster C_1. When the user crosses the boundary to point b which is closer to cluster C_2, he or she is still associated with cluster C_1. The association will not change if the user goes back to point a. However, if the user goes further with extra distance H to point c, the association will be changed to cluster C_2. When he or she goes back to b or a, the user is still associated to cluster C_2. In our system, since the GPS has an error E and the user may take pictures with distance D from the location of interest, we will use $\max(E, D, H)$ instead of H.

5.2 Patch Distinctiveness

Similar to the partitioning in database building process, an image is partitioned into 8 by 8 smaller patches. However, in the querying

process, we do not overlap patches so only 64 patches are used.

For each image, the top 5 patches are selected according to the number of features, as shown in Fig. 7. The quantization process for these patches is about 10-20ms, which is 5 to 8 times faster than using the whole image. The patch with the most number of features is considered the one with the wealthiest visual information. However, these features may not be the best for image retrieval because some features may not be as distinct as others to identify the patch. By learning the database images, we can learn about the distinctiveness for the features.

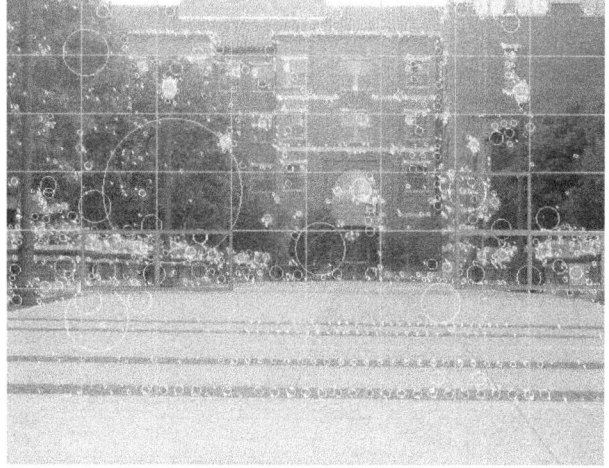

Figure 7: The top 5 patches are selected according to feature numbers. The selected patches are shown in red rectangles.

One way to measure feature distinctness is to calculate the feature frequencies. For a specific feature, the more patches that contain it, the less distinctive the feature is. Reversely, if the feature is contained only in one patch, such feature is considered very distinctive. For any quantized features (visual words), we count the number of patches that contain it. Only the smallest non-overlapping patches in the database are counted.

The process is shown with a simpler vocabulary tree in Fig. 5-(b). Suppose there are 5 patches and each patch contains only one feature. The 5 features are a, b, c, d, e, whose paths are shown in red. As we can see, a and b are quantized to the same value so there are totally 4 different features, and their frequencies are, $f_a = f_b = 2$, $f_c = f_d = f_e = 1$. The distinctiveness weight is then calculated as,

$$w_i = \begin{cases} \frac{1}{f_i} & i=a,b,c,d,e. \\ 0 & \text{other features.} \end{cases} \quad (2)$$

With such weights, features a and b are less distinctive compared to features c, d and e. Features c and d are similar so they should be less distinctive than feature e. However, the above assignment can not distinguish this.

We improve this by assigning weights to nodes along a feature path at different levels. For a n-level vocabulary tree, the weights are $\frac{1}{2^n}$, $\frac{1}{2^{n-1}}$, ..., $\frac{1}{2}$ for nodes at level 1 to level n. For any path in a vocabulary tree, let the number of patches that go through a node in level i be N_i. Then the frequency and weight of the path p can be calculated as,

$$f_p = \sum_{i=1}^{n} \frac{N_i}{2^{n+1-i}}, \quad w_p = \begin{cases} \frac{1}{f_p} & \text{for } f_p \neq 0. \\ 0 & \text{for } f_p = 0. \end{cases} \quad (3)$$

5

With the new weight assignment, frequencies for a to e are calculated as, $f_a = f_b = 2$, $f_c = f_d = 1.5$, $f_e = 0.875$. In this way, e is considered more distinctive than c and d.

With the top 5 patches selected, we will measure the distinctiveness for each patch by summing the weights of all the features in the patch. Then the 5 patches are ranked according to these distinctiveness. The ordered patches are used for querying in the database.

5.3 Querying with Patches

The more distinctive the patch is, the higher probability that the correct patch will be retrieved in the database. Therefore, we start patch retrieval in the order of distinctiveness. In the retrieval process, a similarity score is assigned to each patch in the database that contains same features with the querying patch.

For any two patches, the similarity score can be calculated by multiplying the two distribution vectors of the patches. To consider the distinctiveness for different features, we multiply with the distinctiveness weights in calculating the scores. Let v_1 and v_2 be the two vectors with length n, and $v_1 = (e_{11}e_{12}...e_{1n})$ and $v_2 = (e_{21}e_{22}...e_{2n})$. The score S_{12} is calculated as,

$$S_{12} = \sum_{p=1}^{n} e_{1p}e_{2p}w_p, \tag{4}$$

where w_p is the distinctiveness weight for path p.

For each of the selected 5 querying patches, the top 3 patches in the database with highest scores are returned. As shown in table 1, the top 1 query results are not always reliable. However, the probability is more than 90% that the correct patch is in the top 3 returned patches by querying the best selected patch. The accuracy rate of retrieval can be further increased by querying more patches. From the table, we see that using 3 out of the 5 patches will increase the accuracy to more than 95%, but using all the 5 patches cannot increase further much. Therefore, we will use 3 querying patches which will totally return 9 patches.

	Top 1	Top 2	Top 3
Rank 1	76.1%	85.3%	90.7%
Rank 2	80.4%	89.3%	93.2%
Rank 3	84.2%	91.2%	96.3%
Rank 4	86.3%	92.5%	96.5%
Rank 5	86.5%	93.1%	96.7%

Table 1: The accuracy rate for patch retrieval. The value at ith column, jth row means the probability that the correct patch can be returned by querying j patches with each returning top i results.

To find the correct patch, RANSAC is used to guarantee that the matchings are correct. In our implementation, we set the threshold value for inliers to be 20. On average 4 patch matchings are needed, which cost about 10-15ms.

5.4 More Accurate Locations

When we build the database with method in [1], for each location of interests, a 3D feature point cloud is generated from images at different positions and views. Each 3D feature point corresponds to some 2D features in the database patches. When we match features from the querying patch with the features in the retrieved patch, we also find feature matchings with the 3D points. Therefore, the camera pose can be calculated from the 2D to 3D matchings.

Let camera position for the returned patch be $L'_w = (X'_w, Y'_w, Z'_w)$ in world coordinates. Let the camera pose of returned patch in the camera coordinates be $P'_c = [R'_c|T'_c]$, and the pose of current camera

be $P_c = [R_c|T_c]$. The user's location in the world coordinates is then calculated as,

$$L_w = (X_w, Y_w, Z_w) = L'_w + (T_c - T'_c), \tag{5}$$

where Z_w is set to 0 if the height information is unknown.

6. CAMERA POSE REFINEMENT

The location information is obtained through patch querying and camera pose calculation. However, the calculated pose is not accurate enough for some other applications. For example, many augmented reality applications usually needs high accuracy in order to correctly place the virtual objects into the real scenes. The pose calculated with two patches is not accurate because all the features are located in a small area. With matching propagations, we can obtain a much refined pose.

6.1 Matching Propagations

We can calculate the homography from the matched features in the two patches. This is reasonable because most building facades are more or less planar-like. With the estimated homography transform H_1, we can estimate the locations of the matches for other feature points that lie outside the patch. The procedure is shown in Fig. 8. The red rectangles represent the two matching patches. H_1 is calculated from the matched features, and x_2 is one of feature points that are outside the patch. The location of corresponding point for x_2 can be estimated by $H_1 \cdot x_2$, which is represented by x''_2 in the figure. Therefore, we can find the real match point x'_2 by searching the neighboring area.

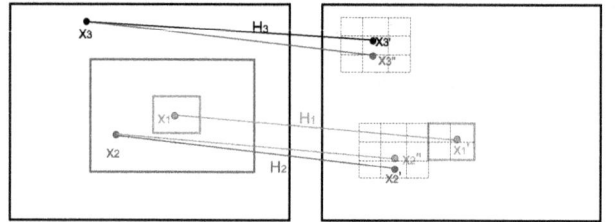

Figure 8: The propagation process. Two propagations are shown in the figure. H_1 is calculated from the matched points in the red area (x_1 and x'_1 are one example matching pair). The corresponding point for x_2 can be estimated by $x''_2 = H_1 \cdot x_2$. The real corresponding point x'_2 can be found nearby x''_2. Then H_2 can be calculated from all matched points within the blue rectangle. Similarly, H_3 can be calculated.

Not all the matches of feature points lie at nearby area. For example, after the first propagation, x'_3, the real match point of x_3 is probably far from the estimated match point x''_3 which is calculated from H_1. This is due to the fact that the further the feature points are from the matched pairs, the larger errors are produced by such homographic transformation. Therefore, one-time propagation is not enough. For an image that is partitioned into a 8 by 8 patches, we use three propagations. The propagation steps are one patch, two patches and four patches, which are shown in Fig. 9.

With the proposed propagations, the searching area for feature matchings can be largely restricted. Another advantage of such matching scheme is that RANSAC process can be simplified. This is because the number of outliers is largely reduced by restriction of searching areas. We randomly select two inliers p_1 and p_2 in the patch, and two matched feature points p_3 and p_4 in the propagation

Figure 9: The 3 propagations in the image matching process. Different colors are used for the correspondence lines in different propagations. The propagation steps are 1 patch, 2 patches and 4 patches for the 1st, 2nd and 3rd propagation.

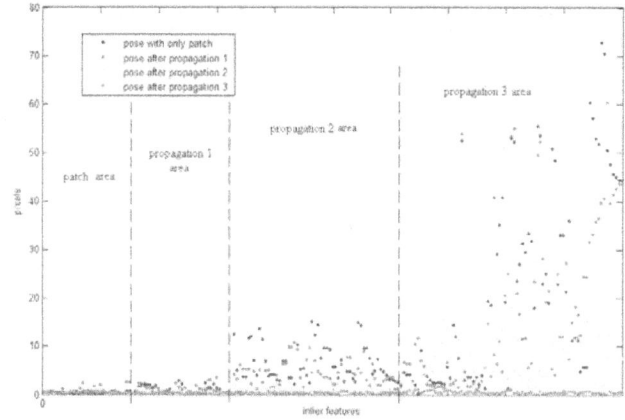

Figure 11: Reprojection errors of the calculated pose after each propagation for Fig. 9. Only the inlier features are displayed. The features are displayed according to order of propagations.

area. The four matching pairs are used to calculate the homography, and it is used to determine the outliers. If there are too many outliers, it is very possible that the selected points p_3 or p_4 is an outlier. In this case, we randomly choose another two points and calculate the pose again. If the number of outliers is small, we remove these outliers and calculate the pose using all the matched points.

The matching time with 3 propagation steps is about 15-25ms, while it usually take 120-160ms without the proposed patch-approach and such propagations.

6.2 Pose Refinement with Propagations

When the camera pose is estimated with features in the patch area, the calculated pose is not accurate. The accuracy can be improved through matching propagations. When the matchings are propagated to the whole image, the calculated pose is accurate enough for most applications. As described in previous section, the propagation method is 5 to 6 times faster than the traditional way of feature matchings.

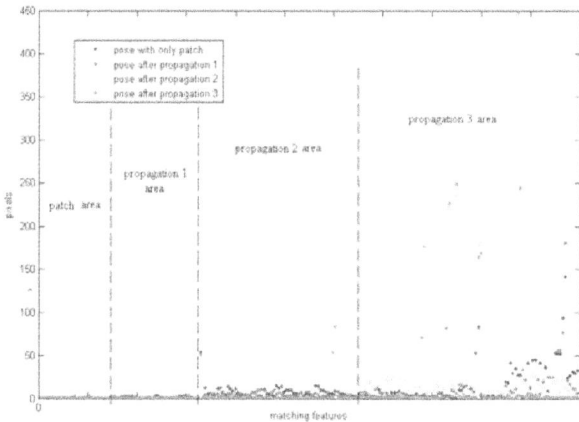

Figure 10: Reprojection errors of the calculated pose after each propagation for Fig. 9. All the matched features are displayed. The features are displayed according to the order of propagations. Those with very large errors are outliers.

As shown in Fig. 10, the reprojection errors of all the matching points are shown. We can see that the errors after the third propagation are the smallest. Without any propagations, the reprojection errors are large for the features that are far from the patch. For example, the errors in the third propagation area are much larger than the errors in the second propagation area, and those errors in the patch area are close to 0. Figure 11 shows similar results but only reprojection errors of the inliers are displayed.

7. EXPERIMENTAL RESULTS

7.1 System Speedup

With the overlapped clustering, we can reduce the database size so that the retrieval performance will not be hurt due to its large scale. The retrieval time is reduced by querying a patch instead of querying the whole image. The matching speed is increased through first matching with a smaller patch and then propagating to the whole image. Therefore, the whole process is speeded up. Table 2 shows the comparisons of computing time between the framework with patch-approach and the one without patch-approach.

	without patch (ms)	with patch (ms)	improved by
Retrieval	70-80	10-20	4-5 times
Matching	120-160	15-25	5-8 times
Total[(1)]	490-540	325-345	40-55%
Total[(2)]	225-275	60-80	200-400%
Total[(3)]	205-255	40-60	300-500%

Table 2: The comparisons between the framework with patch-approach and the one without patch-approach. SURF descriptor (10ms) is employed but different detectors are used. Nearest neighbor method is used for the matching process. (1) SURF detector (300ms) (2) extended Harris corner detector (25ms) (3) FAST corner detector (<5ms).

From the experiments, we conclude that if SURF detector is used, the performance can be increased by up to 50%. If faster detectors such as extended Harris corner detector [12] or FAST corner detector [14] are used, the performance will be increased significantly which can be up to 2 to 5 times. This is because patch retrieval and matching process become the most time consuming parts in the whole system.

7.2 Localization and Augmented Reality

We conduct many experiments for our localization system in the outdoor. Some of the results are shown In Fig. 7.2 and Fig. 7.2. As we can see, the system is demonstrated to be robust for many different cases such as image captured with rotations, at different distances and with large occlusions. The user locations are displayed by red dots in the map. The building names and locations are also displayed with a 2D label and a 3D sign in the captured images.

8. CONCLUSION

We propose an efficient system for user tracking and augmented reality in large scale area. The system is composed of two parts, offline database building process and online user tracking process. The database is built from images captured at many locations with different viewing directions and distances. The locations are clustered with overlaps for limiting the database size. The images are partitioned into patches of different sizes. Each patch is represented by the distribution of visual words, which are generated from the quantization of SURF descriptors. A 3D points cloud is also formed for each location, which is used for pose calculation. At the online stage, the new image is also partitioned into smaller patches. The nearest cluster is selected and the most distinctive patch is used to retrieve the similar patches in the corresponding database for that cluster. The camera pose can be calculated from the 2D to 3D matchings. Since the features are located in a small area, the calculated pose is not accurate enough for augmented reality applications. Therefore, the pose is further refined through matching propagations in an efficient way.

Experiments show that the proposed system works well in large scale areas. Furthermore, the system is demonstrated to be robust to large occlusions and dynamics in the images. Through matching propagations, the pose can be generated with expected accuracies.

9. REFERENCES

[1] S. Agarwal, N. Snavely, I. Simon, S. Seitz, and R. Szeliski. Building rome in a day. In *Proceedings of the International Conference on Computer Vision (ICCV)*, 2009.

[2] P. Azad, T. Asfour, and R. Dillmann. Combining harris interest points and the sift descriptor for fast scale-invariant object recognition. In *EEE/RSJ International Conference on Intelligent Robots and Systems (IROS)*, 2009.

[3] H. Bay, A. Ess, T. Tuytelaars, and L. V. Gool. Speeded-up robust features (surf). *Computer Vision and Image Understanding*, 110(3):346–359, 2008.

[4] F. Dellaert, W. Burgard, D. Fox, and S. Thrun. Using the condensation algorithm for robust, vision-based mobile robot localization. In *IEEE Conference on Computer Vision and Pattern Recognition (CVPR)*, 1999.

[5] Z. Dodds and G. D. Hager. A color interest operator for landmark-based navigation. In *Proceedings of the National Conference on Artificial Intelligence (AAAI)*, pages 655–660, 1997.

[6] N. Henze, T. Schinke, and S. Boll. What is that? object recognition from natural features on a mobile phone. In *Proceedings of the Workshop on Mobile Interaction with the Real World*, 2009.

[7] I. Horswill. Polly: A visisn-based artificial agent. In *Proceedings of the National Conference on Artificial Intelligence (AAAI)*, pages 824–829, 1993.

[8] D. Kortenkamp and T. Weymouth. Topological mapping for mobile robots using a combination of sonar and vision sensing. In *Proceedings of the National Conference on Artificial Intelligence (AAAI)*, pages 1972–1978, 1994.

[9] J. Kosecka, F. Li, and X. Yang. Global localization and relative positioning based on scale-invariant keypoints. *Robotics and Autonomous Systems*, 52(1), 2005.

[10] B. Krose and R. Bunschoten. Probabilistic localization by appearance models and active vision. In *Proceedings of the IEEE International Conference on Robotics and Automation (ICRA)*, 1999.

[11] D. Lowe. Object recognition from local scaleinvariant features. In *Proceedings of the Seventh International Conference on Computer Vision (ICCV)*, 1999.

[12] K. Mikolajcyk and C. Schmid. An affine invariant interest point detector. In *Proceedings of the International Conference on Computer Vision (ICCV)*, 2002.

[13] D. Nister and H. Stewenius. Scalable recognition with a vocabulary tree. In *IEEE Conference on Computer Vision and Pattern Recognition (CVPR)*, 2006.

[14] E. Rosten and T. Drummond. Machine learning for high-speed corner detection. In *Proceedings of the European Conference on Computer Vision (ECCV)*, pages 430–443, 2006.

[15] S. Se, D. Lowe, and J. Little. Vision-based mobile robot localization and mapping using scale-invariant features. In *Proceedings of the IEEE International Conference on Robotics and Automation (ICRA)*, pages 2051–2058, 2001.

[16] H. Tamimi, H. Andreasson, A. Treptow, T. Duckett, and A. Zell. Localization of mobile robots with omnidirectional vision using particle filter and iterative sift. In *Proceedings of the European Conference on Mobile Robots (ECMR)*, 2005.

[17] I. Ulrich and I. Nourbakhsh. Appearance-based place recognition for topological localization. In *Proceedings of the IEEE International Conference on Robotics and Automation (ICRA)*, 2000.

[18] D. Wagner, G. Reitmayr, A. Mulloni, T. Drummond, and D. Schmalstieg. Pose tracking from natural features on mobile phones. In *Proceedings of the International Symposium on Mixed and Augmented Reality (ISMAR)*, 2008.

[19] J. Wolf, W. Burgard, and H. Burkhardt. Robust vision-based localization for mobile robots using an image retrieval system based on invariant features. In *Proceedings of the IEEE International Conference on Robotics and Automation (ICRA)*, 2002.

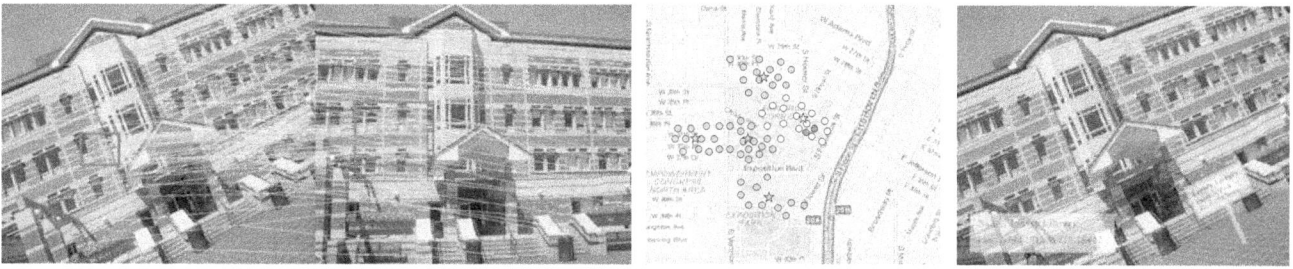

(a)

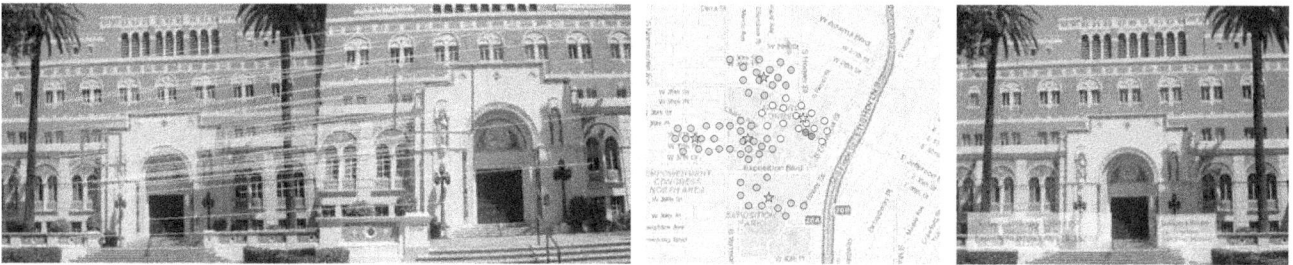

(b)

(c)

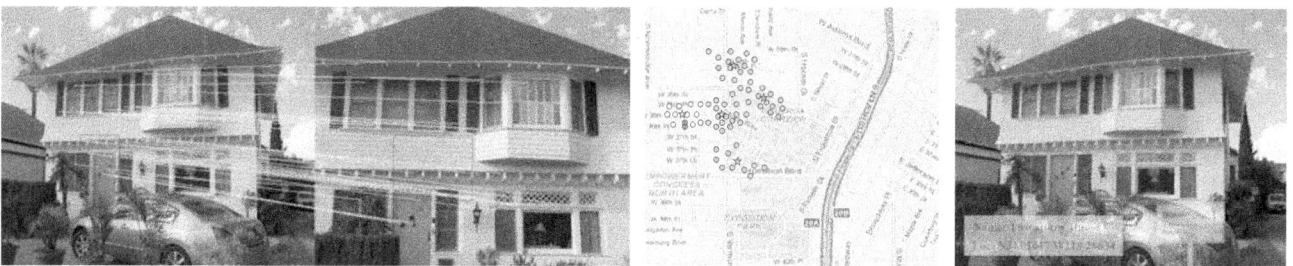

(d)

Figure 12: The localization system and augmented reality. (a) the captured image is rotated. (b) the image is captured at a further distance. (a) and (b) are within the same cluster area. (c) and (d) are two examples captured in other cluster areas.

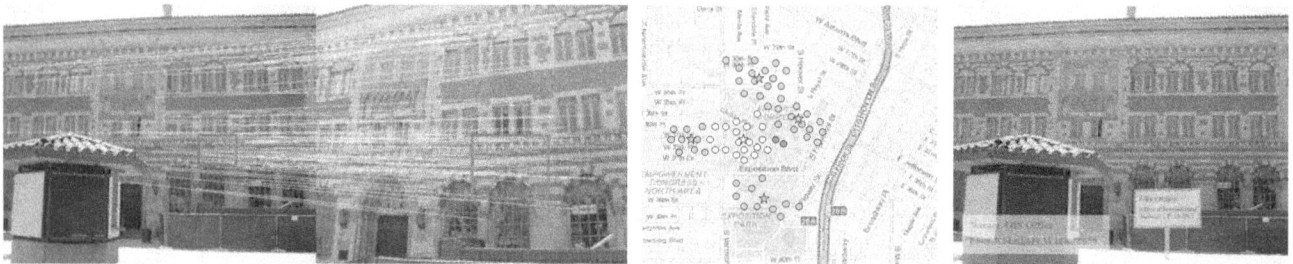

(a)

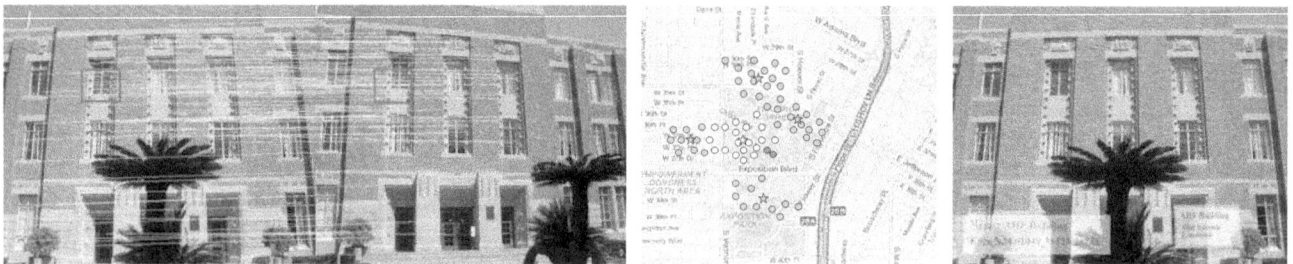

(b)

Figure 13: Occlusions handling of the localization system. Due to its patch property, the proposed system is effective in handling occlusions.

Energy-Efficient Mobile Video Management using Smartphones

Jia Hao[‡], Seon Ho Kim[§], Sakire Arslan Ay[†], Roger Zimmermann[‡]

[‡]School of Computing, National University of Singapore, Singapore 117417

[§]Integrated Media Systems Center, University of Southern California, Los Angeles, CA 90089

[†]Department of Computer Science, University of Southern California, Los Angeles, CA 90089

haojia@comp.nus.edu.sg, seonkim@usc.edu, arslan@usc.edu, rogerz@comp.nus.edu.sg

ABSTRACT

Mobile devices are increasingly popular for the versatile capture and delivery of video content. However, the acquisition and transmission of large amounts of video data on mobile devices face fundamental challenges such as power and wireless bandwidth constraints. To support diverse mobile video applications, it is critical to overcome these challenges. We present a design framework that brings together several key ideas to enable energy-efficient mobile video management applications. First, we leverage off-the-shelf smartphones as mobile video sensors. Second, concurrently with video recordings we acquire geospatial sensor meta-data to describe the videos. Third, we immediately upload the meta-data to a server to enable low latency video search. This last step allows for very energy-efficient transmissions, as the sensor data sets are small and the bulky video data can be uploaded on demand, if and when needed. We present the design, a simulation study, and a preliminary prototype of the proposed system. Experimental results show that our approach substantially prolongs the battery life of mobile devices while only slightly increasing the search latency.

Categories and Subject Descriptors

H.3.4 [**Information Storage and Retrieval**]: Systems and Software—*Distributed Systems*; I.4.8 [**Image Processing and Computer Vision**]: Scene Analysis—*Sensor Fusion*

General Terms

Algorithms, Measurement, Performance

Keywords

Mobile video, geotagging, video search, energy efficiency

1. INTRODUCTION

The influx of affordable, portable, and networked video cameras has made various video applications feasible and practical. Furthermore, the combination of mobile cameras with other sensors has extended plain video sensor networks to wireless multimedia sensor networks. These are expected to manage far more and diverse information from the real world because videos with associated scalar sensor data can be collected, transmitted, and searched to more effectively support a wide range of multimedia applications. These include both conventional and emerging applications such as multimedia surveillance, environmental monitoring, industrial process control, and location based multimedia services [1]. As a result, various mobile devices, sensors, networks, and multimedia search schemes have been designed and tested to implement such systems.

Traditionally, any comprehensive sensor networks that have been constructed with expensive, custom hardware and network architecture work for specific applications only, leading to limited use. However, with rapid advances in communication and cellular phone technologies, smartphones have emerged as a possible off-the-shelf choice of mobile devices since they can satisfy most technical requirements of multimedia sensor networks, such as video capturing with high resolution, meta-data collection from various sensors, communication capabilities with widely available WiFi networks, and true handheld mobility. For example, smartphones such as Apple's iPhone 3GS and 4 and Motorola's Droid have a quality camera, a GPS receiver, a digital compass, an accelerometer, and considerable computing power.

Mobile multimedia applications have inherited the typical challenges of mobile computing such as capacity constraints of the battery and wireless bandwidth bottlenecks. Considering that both the video capture and wireless transmission of large amounts of video data with mobile devices are highly power intensive, it is fundamental to efficiently manage the battery power. Furthermore, mobile video applications introduce new challenges such as the searchability of online videos, especially in large scale applications, because open-domain video content is very difficult to be efficiently and accurately searched.

There are currently two prevalent approaches to make video content searchable. First, there is a significant body of research on content-based video retrieval, which employs techniques that extract features based on the visual signals of a video. While progress has been very significant in this area, the semantic gap between identifying the low-level features and recognizing important semantic themes in the videos, is still wide [14]. Achieving high accuracy with these techniques is often limited to specific domains such as sports or news content, and applying it to large-scale video

Hardware	Description	Parameter	Coefficient (C_j)	Range (of β_j)
CPU	Qualcomm® MSM7201A™, 528 MHz	CPU_hi CPU_lo	$C_{CPU\_hi} = 3.97$ mW/% $C_{CPU\_lo} = 2.79$ mW/%	$\beta_{CPU\_hi} : 0 - 100\%$ $\beta_{CPU\_lo} : 0 - 100\%$
Screen	3.2-inch TFT-LCD flat, touch-sensitive screen with 320×480 (HVGA) resolution	LCD $Brightness$	$C_{LCD} = 150$ mW $C_{br} = 2.07$ mW/step	$\beta_{LCD} : 0, 1$ $\beta_{br} : 0 - 255$ steps
WiFi	Texas Instruments WL 1251B network chipset	$WiFi\_on$ $WiFi\_trf$ $WiFi\_bytes$	$C_{WiFi\_on} = 39$ mW $C_{WiFi\_trf} = 658.93$ mW $C_{WiFi\_bytes} = 0.518$ mW/byte	$\beta_{WiFi\_on} : 0, 1$ $\beta_{WiFi\_trf} : 0, 1$ $\beta_{WiFi\_bytes} :\geq 0$
Storage	MicroSD memory flash card	SD	$C_{SD} = 0.0324$ mW/sector	$\beta_{SD} :\geq 0$
GPS	GPS receiver	GPS	$C_{GPS} = 430$ mW	$\beta_{GPS} : 0, 1$
System	Residual system power consumption in addition to the above components	$System$	$C_{System} = 169.08$ mW	$\beta_{System} : 0, 1$

Table 1: Parameters of the HTC G1 smartphone used in the power model.

repositories creates significant scalability problems. The second approach utilizes searchable text annotations associated with the video content; however high-level concepts must often be added manually, rendering this method ineffective for large video repositories. Furthermore, these text annotations can be ambiguous and subjective.

Recent technological trends have opened another avenue that fuses much more accurate, relevant contextual information with videos: the concurrent collection of sensor-generated geospatial meta-data. The aggregation of multi-sourced geospatial data into a standalone meta-data tag allows video content to be identified by a number of precise, objective geospatial characteristics. For example, current-generation smartphones have GPS receivers, compasses, and accelerometers all embedded into a small, portable, energy-efficient package. When aggregated, the resulting meta-data can provide a comprehensive and easily identifiable model of a video's viewable scene, which can support scalable organization, search, and streaming of large scale video repositories.

In the presence of such meta-data, there are two conventional ways to transmit both meta-data and video jointly from a mobile device: (1) immediate transmission after capturing through wireless network, and (2) delayed transmission when a faster network is available. The former can provide immediate availability of the data to users while consuming lots of battery energy and scarce wireless bandwidth. The latter consumes the minimum power while sacrificing real-time access to the captured videos. Thus, both approaches are not very appealing.

Employing smartphones as the choice of mobile devices, we propose a new framework to support an efficient mobile video capture and their transmission as shown in Figure 3. Based on the important observation that not all collected videos have high priority (i.e., many of them will not be requested and viewed immediately), the core of our approach is to separate the small amount of text-based geospatial meta-data of concurrently captured video content from the large binary-based video content. This small amount of meta-data is then transmitted to a server in real-time, while the video content will remain on the recording device, creating an extensive, resource efficient catalogue of video content, searchable by viewable scene properties established from meta-data attached to each video. Should a particular video be requested, only then will it be transmitted from the camera to the server in an on-demand manner (preferably, only the relevant segments, not the entire videos). The

delivery of unrequested video content to a server can be delayed until a faster connection is available.

This paper presents the design, a simulation study , and a mobile device prototype implementation of an energy efficient mobile video management system. Our simulation results show that the proposed approach can significantly reduce the energy consumption of a smartphone while still providing a satisfactory service latency when videos are requested. Overall, the system achieves a balance between resource demands and quality of service.

The remainder of this paper is organized as follows. In Section 2, we present a mobile device power model. Section 3 describes the system design. In Section 4, a simulator is introduced and we evaluate our system in terms of energy and bandwidth efficiency, query response latency, and result completeness. Section 5 outlines the preliminary implementation of a device acquisition prototype. In Section 6, we summarize the related prior work. Finally Section 7 concludes the paper.

2. POWER MODEL

We define an estimation model to describe the power levels of a mobile device operating under different modes. Our target device is the HTC G1, a smartphone that is based on the open source Google Android mobile device platform [8].

2.1 Modeled Hardware Components

We adapted the power estimation model introduced by Shye et al. [18]. They proposed a linear-regression-based power estimation model, which uses high-level measurements of each hardware component on the mobile device, to estimate the total system power consumption. In our work, we used this model at the device level to understand and evaluate the efficiency and feasibility of our proposed video search technique.

We next describe the relevant details of each hardware component on the target HTC G1 mobile phone. Table 1 lists the G1 hardware components that were considered in the power model and their corresponding parameters. In Table 1, C_j coefficients are the final regression coefficients obtained for the chosen G1 hardware. Our search system incorporates an additional GPS receiver unit to obtain location meta-data. Therefore, we modified the original model and included the power consumption for the GPS receiver. For simplicity, we excluded the power consumption for the Call, EDGE and DSP units.

CPU: The processor supports dynamic frequency scaling

(DFS) and it is rated at 528 MHz, but is scaled down in the platform to run at 124 MHz, 246 MHz, and 384 MHz. The highest frequency of 528 MHz is not used. The lowest frequency is never used on consumer versions of the phone, and is too slow to perform basic tasks. Thus, only the high (384 MHz) and medium (246 MHz) frequencies are considered in the model. CPU power consumption is strongly correlated with the CPU utilization and frequency. In Table 1, the CPU_hi and CPU_lo parameters represent the average CPU utilization while operating at 384 MHz and 246 MHz, respectively.

SCREEN: The display is described by two parameters: a boolean parameter LCD indicating whether the screen is on or off and a $Brightness$ parameter which models the effect of the screen brightness with 256 uniformly spaced levels.

WIFI: The boolean parameter $WiFi\_on$ describes whether the WiFi network interface is turned on or off, while $WiFi\_trf$ and $WiFi\_bytes$ indicate network traffic and the number of bytes transmitted during a particular time interval.

STORAGE: The number of sectors transferred to or from the MicroSD flash memory card per time interval are represented by the parameter SD.

GPS: The boolean parameter GPS denotes the power consumption coefficient when the GPS receiver is on.

SYSTEM: There exists also a residual power consumption parameter $System$. This parameter subsumes all power that is not accounted for the hardware components listed above. We refer to this as the baseline $System$ power in Table 1.

2.2 Analytical Power Model

The described modeling parameters are incorporated into the analytical power model that is utilized in our simulation experiments. The power model determines the relationship between the system statistics (e.g., the value for screen brightness) and the power consumption for each relevant hardware component. The inputs to the model are the statistics collected from the device (β_j values), and the output represents the total power consumption. The overall system power consumption as a function of time t is determined as follows:

$$P(t) = (C_{CPU\_hi} \times \beta_{CPU\_hi}(t)) + (C_{CPU\_lo} \times \beta_{CPU\_lo}(t)) +$$
$$(C_{LCD} \times \beta_{LCD}(t)) + (C_{Brightness} \times \beta_{br}(t)) +$$
$$(C_{WiFi\_on} \times \beta_{WiFi\_on}(t)) + (C_{WiFi\_trf} \times \beta_{WiFi\_trf}(t)) +$$
$$(C_{WiFi\_bytes} \times \beta_{WiFi\_bytes}(t)) + (C_{SD} \times \beta_{SD}(t)) +$$
$$(C_{GPS} \times \beta_{GPS}(t)) + (C_{System} \times \beta_{system}(t))$$

The ranges for the β_j values are listed in Table 1. The overall power consumption is calculated by substituting the statistics for the selected hardware components into $P(t)$.

2.3 Validation of the Power Model

To evaluate the accuracy of our power model, we measured the power consumption of an HTC G1 with $Power$-$Tutor$ [19], an application for Android-based phones that displays the power consumed by major system components such as CPU, network interface, display, and GPS receiver (see Figure 1). According to the authors, PowerTutor was developed on the HTC G1 in collaboration with Google, and its accuracy should be within 5% of actual values for the G1.

With PowerTutor we obtained the various β-statistics for different hardware units. Specifically, we collected logs on a G1 phone for different usage scenarios. For instance, we

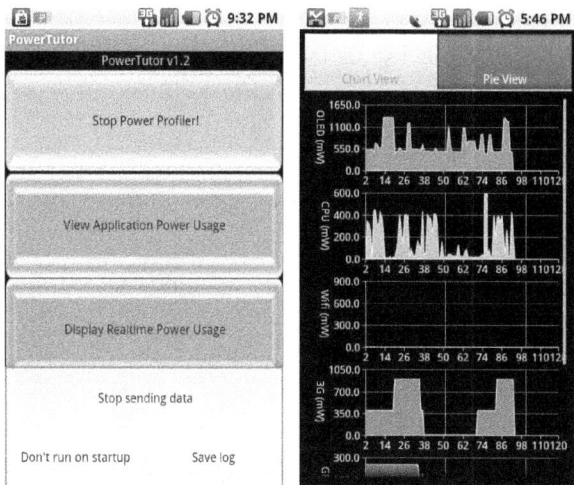

Figure 1: Screenshot of the PowerTutor.

Hardware	Parameter	Video capture	WiFi transmission
CPU	β_{CPU_hi}	77.45	77.33
	β_{CPU_lo}	0	0
LCD	β_{LCD}	1	0
	β_{br}	102	0

Table 2: β-parameters under different operational modes.

captured video for one minute, or uploaded video for one minute, and so on. During these tests, all non-essential processes were disabled. After multiple experiments, we determined the values shown in Table 2.

In the next step, the measured parameters were substituted into our power model. We then performed the same usage scenarios with the Android G1 phone for about two minutes, and collected the trace logs from PowerTutor. We measured the power consumption for various phone usage scenarios such as capture+GPS (capturing video and using GPS to obtain location information), capture+WiFi (capturing video and using WiFi to obtain the location), capture+GSM (capturing video and using GSM to obtain the location), and transmission+WiFi (transmitting data via WiFi). Grouped by usage scenario, the average power consumption obtained from the power model was compared to the power values reported by PowerTutor. The results are shown in Figure 2.

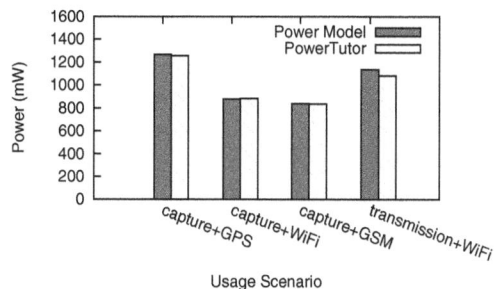

Figure 2: Comparison of the results from the power model with logs from PowerTutor.

The modeled and measured power consumptions match very well for each of the usage scenario. To calculate the accuracy of the model, we used the following error metric e:

$$e = \left| \frac{P_{measured} - P_{modeled}}{P_{measured}} \right| \qquad (1)$$

The results indicate that the power estimation model accurately predicts the system-level power consumption. The error e for each scenario is less than 4.9%, and the average error across all the scenarios is 1.7%.

An important point to note is that capturing video and then transmitting it via WiFi are both very energy-consuming activities. With its standard 1,150 mAh-capacity battery, the G1 phone would last less than three hours in the worst case, when continuously capturing and transmitting video. Our proposal is to extend battery life through more selective transmissions.

3. SYSTEM DESIGN

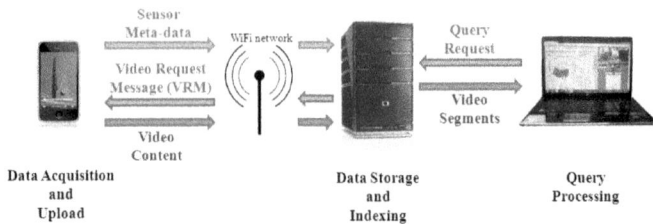

Figure 3: System environment for mobile video management.

Figure 3 shows an overview of the proposed system. Mobile nodes collect the videos and the sensor-associated meta-data such as GPS location, compass direction, capture time and other camera-related information. The video files remain locally on the device until requested while the meta-data are immediately uploaded to the server in real-time where they are stored and indexed in a database. In a typical search scenario, other users (e.g., observers) can query the videos that are being captured from many devices in real-time or near real-time. We assume that a user provides a query as a geographical region of interest. The video meta-data stored on the server are searched to identify and retrieve the video clips that show the requested query region and the search results are presented to the user. During query processing, the video content already available on the server is immediately sent to the user for viewing while the missing video segments are requested *on demand* from the mobile devices that captured the videos. Note that only the precisely delimited parts (i.e., only the video segments that actually overlap with the query region) are retrieved. The complete video content may be uploaded later when the device is in contact with a faster network connection.

The key idea of this approach is to save considerable battery energy by delaying the costly transmission of the large binary video data that have not been requested, especially when the transmission speed is low. We will describe the components of the proposed system next.

3.1 Data Acquisition and Upload

A camera positioned at a given point P in geo-space captures a scene whose covered area is referred to as the camera field-of-view (FOV, also called the *viewable scene*). We adapt the *FOV* model introduced in our prior work [2], which describes a camera's viewable scene in 2D space with four parameters: camera location P, camera orientation α, viewable angle θ and visible distance R (see Eqn. (2)).

$$FOV \equiv \langle P, \alpha, \theta, R \rangle \qquad (2)$$

The camera position P consists of the latitude and longitude coordinates read from a positioning device (e.g., GPS) and the camera direction α is obtained based on the orientation angle provided by a digital compass. R is the maximum visible distance from P at which a large object within the camera's field-of-view can be recognized. The angle θ is calculated based on the camera and lens properties for the current zoom level [9]. The collected meta-data streams are analogous to sequences of $\langle nid, vid, t_{FOV}, t_f, P, \alpha, \theta, R \rangle$ tuples, where nid represents the ID of the mobile device, vid is the ID of the video file and t_{FOV} indicates the time instant at which the FOV is recorded. The timecode associated with each video frame is denoted by t_f.

In 2D space, the field-of-view of the camera at time t_{FOV} forms a pie-slice-shaped area as illustrated in Figure 4.

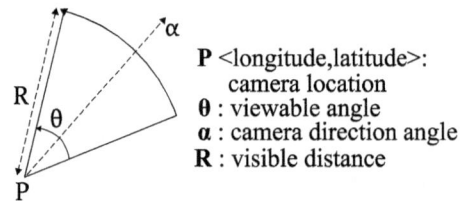

P <longitude,latitude>: camera location
θ : viewable angle
α : camera direction angle
R : visible distance

Figure 4: Illustration of FOV in 2D space.

When a mobile device begins video capture, the GPS and compass sensors are turned on to record the location and orientation of the camera. Our custom-written data-acquisition software fetches such sensor values as soon as new values are available. Video data are processed in real time to extract frame timecodes (t_f). The visible distance R is calculated based on the camera specifications. All collected meta-data (i.e., location, direction, viewable distance, frame timecode and video ID) are combined as a tuple and uploaded to the server.

An appropriate meta-data upload rate should be determined such that the server is updated immediately for real-time video search while the energy consumption for meta-data uploads is minimized. Two policies are possible. First, the system may send the meta-data whenever it is generated. Second, it may buffer the meta-data locally and then send the accumulated data periodically. Such meta-data aggregation and delivery may utilize available network bandwidth more efficiently. For the first policy, since meta-data is always ready to be uploaded, we assume that the WiFi interface is always on when recording. Whereas for the second policy, WiFi will be turned on and off periodically. Some startup energy is consumed when WiFi is turned on. As Cheung *et al.* measured [5], we set the startup energy as 6.47 J. We will further discuss this aspect in Section 4.

Another issue we would like to explore is energy-efficient collection of location meta-data. GPS, WiFi and GSM pose a challenging tradeoff between localization accuracy and energy consumption. While GPS offers good location accuracy of around 10 m, it incurs a serious energy cost that can drain a fully charged phone battery very fast. WiFi and GSM-based schemes are less energy-hungry, however, they incur higher localization errors (approximately 40 m and 400 m, respectively). In our work we employ the GPS-based and GPS-save strategies. GPS-based scheme refers to sampling GPS data periodically, while GPS-save uses a more complicated strategy. When the device orientation change is within a limited range, we assume that the device user does not change his/her moving direction, and the GPS receiver is turned off to save energy. Once the direction changes, the GPS receiver is turned on, reporting the current location. When meta-data with two consecutive GPS data points is uploaded, we can interpolate the device location between the two GPS locations on the server. With this method considerable energy can be saved. More details can be found in Section 4.

3.2 Data Storage and Indexing

This module implements a storage server that manages the video files and the associated meta-data streams. It separately stores the video content and the meta-data. The video files are linked to the the meta-data streams by device ID (nid) and video ID (vid). Each FOV tuple in a meta-data stream includes a frame timecode t_f that points to a particular frame within the video content. This ensures a tight synchronization between the two streams.

The server keeps a data structure $nodeInfo$ for each mobile node, which includes the device MAC address, the unique device ID, and the IP address. While the storage server receives the meta-data from mobile devices, nid is added automatically to each FOV tuple. An additional binary tag ($inServer$) is maintained for each FOV tuple indicating whether the corresponding binary data of the video frame exists or not on the server. Spatial indices are built and maintained to facilitate the efficient search of FOVs.

3.3 Query Processing

When a user issues a query, the video meta-data in the server is searched to retrieve the video segments whose viewable scenes overlap with the geographical region specified in the query. The query region can be a point, a line (e.g., a road), a poly-line (e.g., a trajectory between two points), a circular area (e.g., neighborhood of a point of interest), a rectangular area (e.g., the space delimited with roads) or a polygon area (e.g., the space delimited by certain buildings, roads and other structures). In our initial prototype we only support rectangular queries.

Given a query Q, the query processing module returns a list of the video segments whose corresponding FOVs overlap with the query Q. Each video segment is identified with a tuple $\langle nid, vid, t_{start}, t_{end} \rangle$, where t_{start} and t_{end} are the timecodes for the first and last FOVs.

For each video segment in the query results, the query processor checks for the availability of the corresponding video content on the server. Recall that, the storage server keeps track of which video files are uploaded to the server and what parts of the meta-data they do belong to. For the FOVs with the $inServer$ field set to 1, the corresponding video content is available on the server. And conversely, for those with the $inServer$ field equal to 0 the video content is not available and therefore needs to be requested from the capturing mobile device. To acquire a missing video segment, a Video Request Message (VRM) is sent to the mobile device. A VRM message specifies the IP address of the target mobile device as well as the corresponding video ID and the beginning and ending timecodes for the requested video segment.

If the requested video with video ID vid is still available on the mobile device, the video segment from t_{start} to t_{end} is uploaded to the storage server. The $inServer$ tags for the corresponding FOVs are set to 1. However, if the requested video cannot be located, the mobile device notifies the query processor by sending a Video does not Exist Message ($VNEM$). If no response is received from the device after n trials, the device is assumed to be turned off and the VRM message is dismissed. If the query processor can locate the videos for the search results on the server, it immediately sends the video data to the user. The video segments requested from the mobile devices are sent as soon as they arrive at the server.

4. EXPERIMENTAL EVALUATION

To evaluate our framework we implemented an extensive simulator and executed it on a server with two 4-core Intel(R) Xeon(R) X5450 3.0 GHz CPUs and 16 GB of memory, running Linux 2.6.18.

4.1 Simulator Operation

We first provide an overview of the operation of the simulator before describing its internal details. We assume an urban wireless communication infrastructure where mobile users are moving on the road network of the city of San Francisco. The users capture and transmit videos with predefined simulation models. Similarly, some other users launch queries to retrieve the collected videos from the same region.

The simulated space is approximately 14.3 km × 13.6 km in size. Within this area, N_{node} mobile users and N_{AP} WiFi network access points are distributed. The simulation proceeds in discrete time steps ts (5 s each) for a total duration of T. During T, two types of events occur: video *capture events* and *query events*. In a capture event, each mobile node independently starts to record video and the recording duration follows a log-normal distribution. The capture event arrival rate is λ_c per timestamp ts. Queries are issued by observers and sent to the server with a query event arrival rate of λ_q per timestamp ts. Queries are assumed to be distributed within the simulation space either uniformly random, or skewed with a clustering parameter h ($0 \leq h \leq 1$). When an area is frequently queried, it is regarded as a "popular area". The h parameter represents the popularity of the area. A higher value of h denotes that more queries are requested from that area. The query clustering is designed to emulate areas of interest in the real world. The query size M_q is chosen as a small fraction of the simulation space. The simulation parameters are summarized in Table 3.

Captured videos are either (1) immediately and completely uploaded to the server (Immediate) at a transmission rate that is determined by the mobile node's proximity to an access point, or (2) alternatively, video upload is delayed and only videos where a query request overlaps with the region that was captured in the video will be uploaded in an on-demand manner (OnDemand). Importantly, only the video segments, not an entire video clip, that overlap with the query are transmitted. The query response latency for $L_{Immediate}$ is assumed to be zero (or close to zero), since the data is readily available on the server and can be immediately returned to the observer. With the OnDemand policy,

Module	Parameter	Description	Values
Network Topology Generator	w	WiFi type used	**802.11b**
	N_{AP}	Number of access points	400, 800, **1,000**, 1,200, 1,600, 2,000
		Simulation space	14.295 km × 13.623 km
Node Trajectory Generator	N_{node}	Number of mobile nodes	**2,000**
	T	Simulation time in 1,000s	**150**
	ts	Timestamp in seconds	**5**
Query Generator	λ_q	Query event arrival rate (per timestamp ts)	0.1 − 0.9, **0.5**
	M_q	Mean query rectangle size as a percentage of the map area	0.01 − 0.05, **0.03**
	h	Query rectangle clustering parameter, see Figure 6	0 − 1, **0.5**
FOV Generator	λ_c	Capture event arrival rate (per timestamp ts)	0.01 − 0.04, **0.02**
	D_c	($e^{D_c} \times ts$) is the mean duration of a capture event	0.5 − 2.5, **1.5**
Power Model		Mobile device power parameters	See Table 1

Table 3: Simulation parameters (values in bold are the default settings).

the relevant video segments must be requested and uploaded to the server before the query request is considered satisfied. The worst case response latency of OnDemand, $L_{OnDemand}$, is hence determined by the worst case upload time (we assume that all uploads start concurrently and in parallel from the nodes involved).

Using our simulation testbed we evaluate the Immediate and OnDemand strategies based on following three main metrics: the energy consumption (and hence the lifetime) of mobile nodes, the query response latency, and the total amount of data transmitted to satisfy all queries.

4.2 Simulator Architecture and Modules

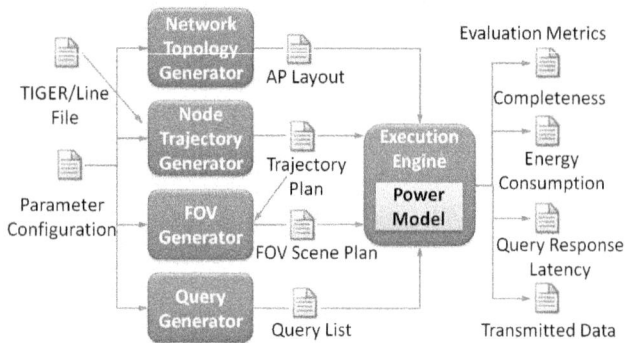

Figure 5: The block diagram of the simulator architecture.

Figure 5 provides a detailed architectural view of the simulator with the following components: generators for (1) the network topology, (2) the node trajectories, (3) FOV viewable scenes, and (4) queries. Additionally, the (5) power model is a part of the (6) execution engine.

NETWORK TOPOLOGY GENERATOR: A number of WiFi access points (N_{AP}) are uniformly distributed in the simulation area and this module emulates the mobile access range with the realistic Auto-Rate Fallback (ARF) mechanism of WiFi, which provides a number of declining transmission rate levels with an increase in the distance between the access point and a mobile client. We implemented and tested both the 802.11b and 802.11g standards for our simulation. However, we found that the results with 802.11g follow the same trend as with the slower standard (i.e., the transmission times are proportionally reduced). Hence we present only the results for 802.11b.

NODE TRAJECTORY GENERATOR: We use the Brinkhoff

generator to produce movements of mobile objects along a road network [3]. The input to the generator consists of a TIGER/Line road network file of the city of San Francisco from the U.S. Census Bureau. The output is a set of objects that move on the road network of the city.

FOV GENERATOR: This module synthesizes the mobile nodes' recording behavior and generates the representations of nodes' viewable scenes. The recording start times follow an exponential distribution based on the capture event arrival rate λ_c (expressed in events per timestamp ts, see Table 3). The duration of recordings is log-normally distributed. The FOV generator obtains the camera location information from the trajectory generator and, for the camera direction, a random orientation is generated for each node's viewable scenes. The maximum visible distance R is set to 200 m.

QUERY GENERATOR: The query workload consists of a list of query rectangles that are mapped to specific locations in the simulation space. The query arrival interval is exponentially distributed with λ_q (measured per timestamp ts, see Table 3). The rectangle size is determined by a normally distributed random variable with the mean value M_q. The parameter h is used to generate different distributions of queries in the given space to evaluate the performance of our proposed system framework and test its robustness with different clusterings, both spatially and temporally. Figure 6 shows three spatial query distributions with different values of h. As can be seen, the larger the value of h, the more clustered the queries are.

POWER MODEL: Power consumption is modeled for each node based on the specifications presented in Section 2. The power model is embedded in the execution engine so that mobile nodes' battery life can be updated during each time step. The power level for the mobile nodes in different states is summarized in Table 1.

EXECUTION ENGINE: The simulation is executed after reading in the access point (AP) layout, the trajectory plan, the FOV scene plan, and the query list. The engine then simulates the movement of the mobile nodes within the simulation space, keeps track of their video recordings, executes the queries, and manages the simulation status. At every timestamp, the engine computes all the evaluation metrics.

4.3 Experiments and Results

The utility of a mobile device depends on the duration of operational hours before its battery needs re-charging. Thus, one of the key metrics we use to evaluate the energy efficiency of our approaches is the expected reduction

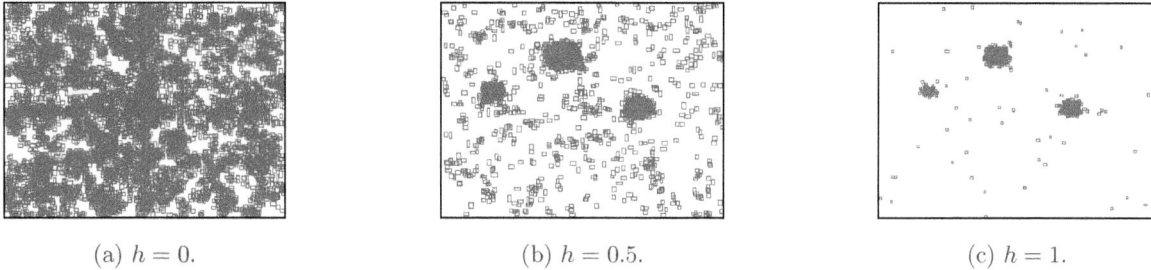

(a) $h = 0$.　　　　　(b) $h = 0.5$.　　　　　(c) $h = 1$.

Figure 6: Spatial query distribution with three different clustering parameter values h.

in power consumption, which directly translates into an extended battery lifetime. We further evaluate the query response latency that a user experiences when searching for real-time mobile video. Finally, mobile bandwidth is still a relatively scarce resource, especially in scenarios where the infrastructure may be limited (e.g., after a disaster). Hence we also calculated the overall size of the video data that must be transmitted to satisfy all queries.

Through simulations our OnDemand approach is compared to Immediate in terms of power-efficiency, latency to obtain the results, overall bandwidth use and result completeness. Recall that using the Immediate approach nodes upload videos without delay, therefore, we assume that the query response latency is zero for this method.

4.3.1 Performance: Without Battery Recharging

In our first experiment we assume a closed system where batteries cannot be recharged. Hence, all the nodes will eventually run out of energy and cease operation. We are interested in the system lifetime and the query completeness under these conditions. The simulation area is populated with $N_{node} = 2,000$ mobile nodes. We track all the nodes' energy consumption and battery levels. The default simulation parameters of Table 3 are used.

Figure 7(a) illustrates that the OnDemand method consumes considerably less energy than the Immediate method, and the lifetime of the last alive node is prolonged from about 84,000 s (≈ 23.3 h) to 120,000 s (≈ 33.3 h). The query workload imposed by the observing users leads to an uneven utilization of the nodes and some deplete their batteries earlier than others.

Once some nodes begin to cease operation, the results of queries may increasingly become *incomplete* because the requested data become unavailable. Figure 7(b) compares the completeness of the query results returned by the two strategies. We compute the completeness of results from both methods every one thousand timesteps using the following fraction: (video segments actually returned)/(video segments that should be returned). To compute the video segments that should be returned, we assume an ideal baseline case in which there are no battery constraints. Hence, all requested video segments are never missed. Figure 7(b) shows that as time advances, the completeness of results of both methods decreases because the number of alive nodes decreases and the number of videos uploaded to the server also declines. However, the downward trend of OnDemand begins later in time because the nodes with OnDemand last longer. This is directly attributable to the energy saved from

fewer unnecessary video transmissions, so mobile nodes retain more battery energy to capture additional videos.

Figure 7(c) shows the worst case query response latency with OnDemand. The average query response latency is 8.08 s while there are some exceptionally long latency. It should be noted that the latency represented here straightforwardly refers to the duration from the time when a query is initiated by a user to the time when the last frame of the latest arriving result video segment has been received. With smarter streaming techniques some of the video segments can be browsed much earlier, which may significantly reduce the effective response latency observed by users. The figure shows some comparatively large values which are due to some "lazy" mobile nodes (a property of the node mobility model). These nodes almost do not move during the simulation, but they keep capturing video and uploading meta-data. For a long time initially, the videos captured by these nodes may not be queried. However, once a query arrives, many videos are to be uploaded consecutively, which causes a considerable delay.

4.3.2 Performance: With Battery Recharging

In some large-scale application scenarios batteries can be recharged or replaced so that the mobile node density will eventually reach a dynamic equilibrium. In the steady state, nodes continuously join and leave (i.e., their batteries run out). We evaluate the Immediate and OnDemand approaches in this scenario using the proposed metrics.

First, we would like to determine the appropriate rate for meta-data uploading. Figure 8 shows the tradeoff between energy consumption over an entire simulation and access latency with varying meta-data rate, λ_s. The access latency represents the average duration from the time meta-data are produced until the time a user is able to search the data (i.e., the meta-data become available on the server). Since the size of the meta-data file is very small, we can effectively ignore its transmission time. When λ_s grows large, the meta-data upload period ($1/\lambda_s$) approaches near zero and the node sends the meta-data whenever it is produced. In this case, the mobile device continuously uploads the meta-data and it will not turn off the WiFi interface. Therefore, the mobile device will continuously consume a certain amount of power (i.e., 658.93 mW) for the meta-data transmission.

In general, the node sends meta-data every $1/\lambda_s$ seconds. To save energy when using WiFi, the mobile device can turn off the WiFi interface while it is not transmitting data. During this transition from the off to the on state, a startup energy of 6.47 J will be consumed. Thus a higher number of meta-data transitions means more startup energy over-

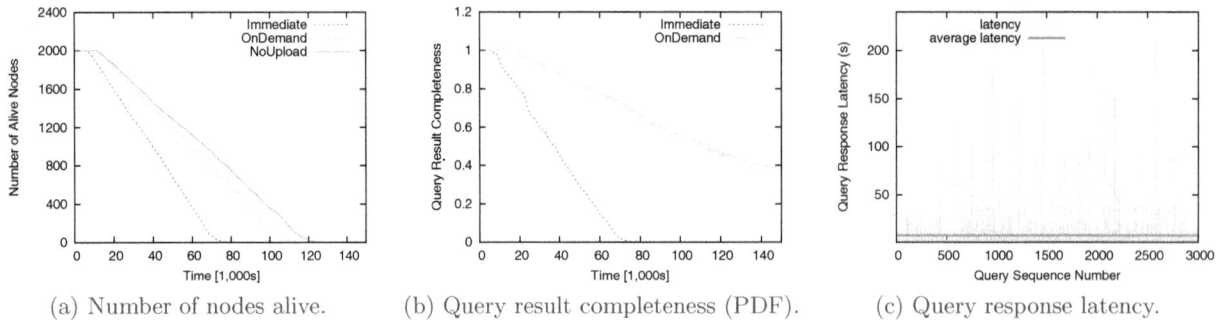

| (a) Number of nodes alive. | (b) Query result completeness (PDF). | (c) Query response latency. |

Figure 7: Node lifetimes (i.e., energy efficiency), result completeness, and query response latency with $N = 2,000$ nodes.

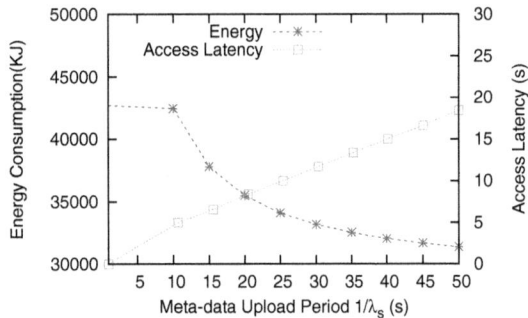

Figure 8: Energy consumption and access latency with varying meta-data upload period ($1/\lambda_s$).

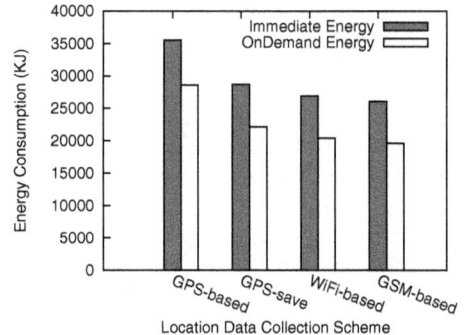

Figure 9: Energy consumption with varying location data collection scheme.

head. The figure shows a tradeoff between access latency and energy-efficiency. As the meta-data upload period increases, the energy consumption decreases while the access latency grows.

Collecting location data itself costs a significant amount of energy so we consider and compare the four different location data collection schemes as mentioned in Section 3.1. With the GPS-based scheme the GPS receiver is always on during recording. The GPS-save scheme means that when the device is not moving or changing direction, GPS sampling is not executed. The WiFi-based and GSM-based schemes are described in [4]. Figure 9 shows a comparison of the energy consumption using these four approaches. The GPS-based scheme consumes the most energy, while the GPS-save scheme indeed saves a significant amount of energy. Also, the energy consumption of the WiFi-based and GSM-based schemes is much less than that of the GPS-based scheme.

Next we evaluate the impact of the capture and network topology parameters on the performance. First, Figure 10(a) shows the trend for an increasing video recording duration, which is log-normally distributed based on parameter D_c. We calculate the average duration with $e^{D_c} \times ts$ (see Table 3). As expected for both Immediate and OnDemand, a longer average recording duration results in a higher energy consumption and a longer query response latency. However, OnDemand consumes less energy, up to 30% less compared to Immediate. Predictably, the query response latency for OnDemand increases as the recording duration increases.

This is because more FOVs are captured in the simulation area. When the same query is executed within a region, mobile nodes will have more video frames to upload, which results in a longer latency. A similar trend can be observed when nodes capture videos more frequently (Figure 10(b)). When the capture event arrival rate λ_c increases, the energy consumption and the latency will increase.

Next we investigate the impact of the number of access points (N_{AP}). APs are uniformly distributed in the simulation area. When more access points are deployed the average available data rate for video transmissions increases, and conversely the average transmission duration decreases. Our simulation results shows that energy consumption is reduced for the Immediate strategy as the number of APs grows (Figure 10(c)). However, with OnDemand the energy usage remains steady while the latency decreases. This indicates that OnDemand is less affected by the number of APs than Immediate, implying that OnDemand utilizes the limited bandwidth more effectively.

We next turn our attention to the impact of the characteristics of queries on the performance metrics. For different query model parameters (i.e., h, λ_q, and M_q), Figure 11 shows how the energy consumption and latency are affected while Figure 12 plots the total amount of transmitted data. Note that the performance of Immediate does not change with the query model parameters because Immediate's behavior determines the data collection and transmission independently from any query models.

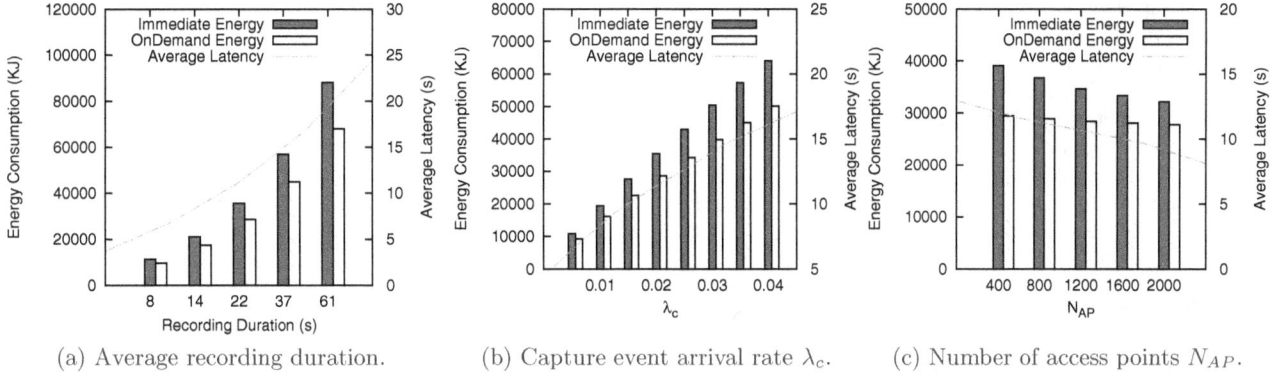

(a) Average recording duration.　　(b) Capture event arrival rate λ_c.　　(c) Number of access points N_{AP}.

Figure 10: Energy consumption and average query response latency with varying FOV and Network topology generator parameters.

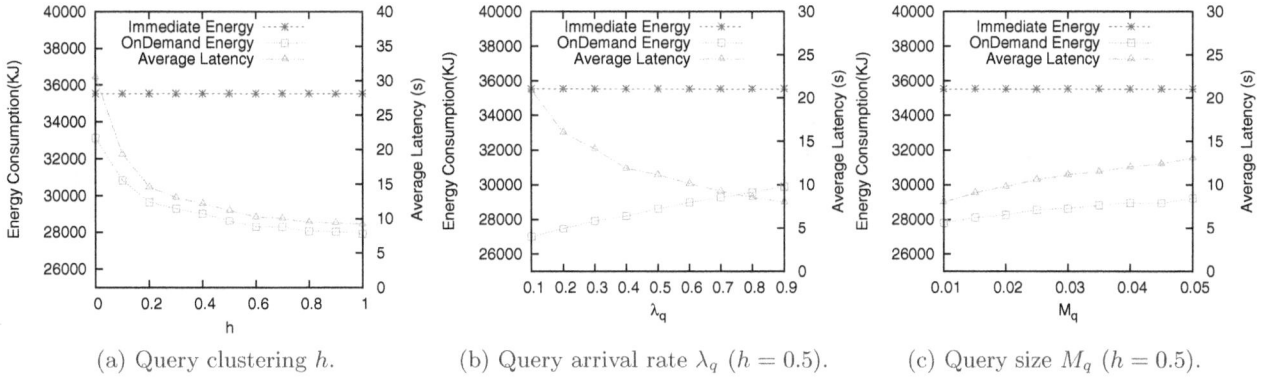

(a) Query clustering h.　　(b) Query arrival rate λ_q ($h = 0.5$).　　(c) Query size M_q ($h = 0.5$).

Figure 11: Energy consumption and average query response latency with varying query model parameters.

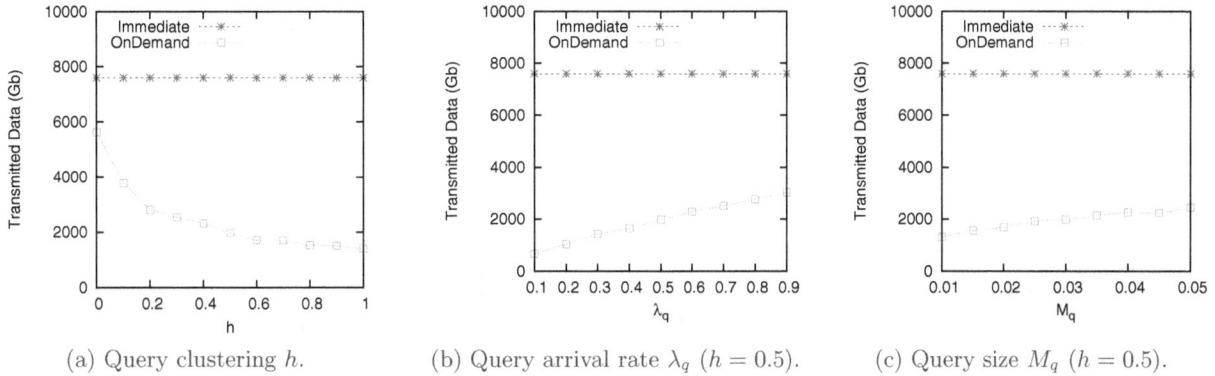

(a) Query clustering h.　　(b) Query arrival rate λ_q ($h = 0.5$).　　(c) Query size M_q ($h = 0.5$).

Figure 12: Total transmitted data size as a function of various query model parameters.

Figure 11(a) illustrates the effects of increased query clustering on the energy consumption and average query response latency. OnDemand's performance significantly improves as the query distribution changes from uniformly random (i.e., $h = 0$) to most clustered ($h = 1$). With $h = 1$ some regions within the simulation space will never be queried, thus the nodes in those areas do not need to transmit collected videos to the server. Consequently, their energy consumption becomes minimal. For popular areas, when a query arrives most of the videos have already been uploaded to the server. Thus, the query response latency can be reduced. Figure 12(a) clearly indicates that the total

amount of video data transmitted is much less with OnDemand than with Immediate. This is especially true when queries are concentrated on some popular hotspots. Our OnDemand strategy clearly demonstrates its strength over Immediate in a highly clustered query distribution which better reflects a realistic situation when user attention focuses on some popular areas.

Figures 11(b) and 12(b) show the trends for an increasing query arrival rate λ_q. As the query frequency increases, the energy consumption and the size of the transmitted video data grow up with OnDemand. However, both metrics still stay well below their corresponding values of Immediate, demonstrating clear benefits. Furthermore, the query response latency also decreases. Intuitively, if a node is in a frequently queried area, the videos captured by the node will be probably uploaded sooner rather than later. Therefore the latency for each query can be reduced substantially. We also evaluate the impact of a varying mean query size M_q on the performance. As expected, Figures 11(c) and 12(c) illustrate that for OnDemand the energy consumption, the query response latency and the total transmitted data all rise gradually with increased M_q.

4.3.3 Hybrid Strategy

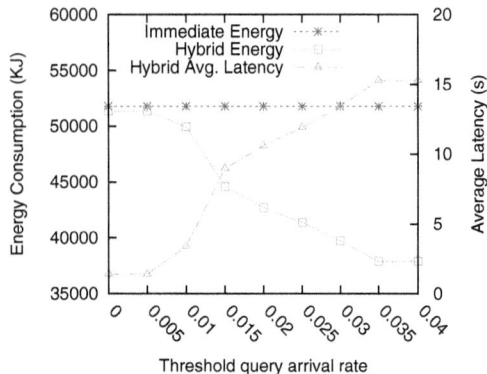

Figure 13: The overall energy consumption and query response latency when using a hybrid strategy with both Immediate and OnDemand as a function of the switching threshold ($h = 0.5$).

As seen in the previous section, the Immediate strategy has an advantage when it comes to query response latency, since videos are always pro-actively uploaded to the server. However, OnDemand has an advantage in power consumption. To get the best combination of response time and battery life one may devise a hybrid strategy that essentially select a method based on the popularity of a region. To achieve this we can divide the map into a grid of small partitions and maintain a popularity threshold for each grid cell. The server continuously computes the query arrival rate λ_q^{est} for each partition per time interval t as $\lambda_q^{est} = \frac{N_q}{t}$. N_q represents the number of queries that are executed during time t. If λ_q^{est} is above the threshold for a partition, the server will mark it as popular and ask the mobile nodes moving in that area to switch to Immediate mode. Figure 13 shows the energy consumption and average query response latency for the hybrid strategy under different threshold values. In the illustrated case, a threshold value in the range of 0.01 to 0.02 may achieve a good compromise in terms of both energy use and query latency.

5. PROTOTYPE

We are currently implementing the proposed system as part of our ongoing project work (hence the reason for presenting simulation results in Section 4). We implemented a prototype geo-referenced video acquisition module on an Android G1 handset, which provides the necessary built-in GPS receiver and compass functionality. Below we describe our current application implementation. Please note that we are just starting to collect real-world data with this platform for further studies.

Parameter	Description
Format	MPEG-4
Format profile	3GPP Media
Overall bit rate	349 Kbps

	Video	Audio
Format	H.263	AMR
Format profile	Baseline@4.0	Narrow band
Bit rate mode	Variable	Constant
Bit rate	334 Kbps	12.8 Kbps
Resolution (pixels)	320 × 240	
Aspect ratio	4:3	
Frame rate	15 fps	
Colorimetry	4:2:0	
Channel(s)		1 channels
Sampling rate		8.0 KHz

Table 4: Android audio/video capture parameters.

5.1 Android Geo-Video Application

Our Geo-Video App was developed with the Google Android SDK v1.5 for Android OS 1.0 or later. The program was written in Java. The Geo-Video App is composed of the following six functional modules: (1) video stream recorder, (2) location receiver, (3) orientation receiver, (4) data storage and synchronization control, (5) data uploader and (6) battery status monitor. Below we will describe each module in more detail.

VIDEO STREAM RECORDER. This module employs the Android MediaRecorder to invoke the built-in camera. On G1, H.263 is the only supported video encoder, together with an AMR_NB encoder for audio. Table 4 summarizes the audio and video acquisition parameters.

LOCATION AND ORIENTATION RECEIVER. Android provides some system services for getting data from the sensors. Available sensors are an accelerometer, magnetic field sensor, and a built-in orientation sensor. To get the camera orientation, one can use either the orientation sensor or compute it using the accelerometer and magnetic field sensor. But the latter is more precise than the former, at the cost of more computation. We choose the latter in our application. The GPS data is straightforwardly provided by location service.

An interesting aspect in sensor data acquisition is the sampling frequency. In our application we set a fixed sampling rate for the location and orientation information. The sampling rate is set to 5 samples per second. Experimentally, with these settings we can discover the changes in the viewable scenes well while saving battery energy as much as possible.

DATA STORAGE AND SYNCHRONIZATION CONTROL. This module manages the storage of the sensor data on the device's flash disk. The goal is to utilize a flexible data format that can be easily ingested at a server. In this situation we choose JSON (JavaScript Object Notation) as the data interchange and storage, since it has the equal descriptive power comparable to XML and an order of magnitude less complexity than XML. The data format consists of four mandatory key attributes:

format_version: The version number of the data format.
video_id: Relevant video id associated with the sensor data.
owner_properties: Associates a user account with the sensor data.
device_properties: Records device dependent information.

sensor_data: Stores raw sensor data collected from a mobile device.

Here is a sample specification of the data format that stores sensor data.

```
{
    "format_version":"0.1",
    "video_id":"a uniquely identifiable video id",
    "owner_properties":{
        "id_type":"google account",
        "id":someone@google.com
    },
    "device_properties":{
        "SIM_id":"an id taken from SIM card",
        "OS":"Android",
        "OS_version":"1.0",
        "firmware_version":"1.0"
    },
    "sensor_data":[
        {
            "location_array_timestamp_lat_long":[
                ["2010-03-18T07:58:41Z",1.29356,103.77],
                ["2010-03-18T07:58:46Z",1.29356,103.78]
            ]
        },
        {
            "sensor_array_timestamp_x_y_z":[
                ["2010-03-18T07:58:41Z",180.00,1.00,1.00],
                ["2010-03-18T07:58:46Z",181.00,1.00,1.00]
            ]
        }
    ]
}
```

To provide synchronization between meta-data and video streams, we extract the duration, encoded date and time from the video. We then add timestamp information to every sensor data record to establish the relationship between a video clip and its corresponding geo-sensor information. Time is represented in Greenwich Mean Time (GMT), to avoid time zone issues. Files include the timestamp as part of their filename to avoid ambiguity..

DATA UPLOADER. This module makes use of open source class *ClientHTTPRequest* written by Vlad Patryshev. This class helps to send POST HTTP requests with various form data to the server, which is not natively supported by Android environment. This third-party class makes some of the more tedious aspects of communicating with web servers easier. The Data Uploader transparently utilizes WiFi, 3G or 2G cellular networks to transmit data files. Importantly, this module implements our two different upload strategies: (1) both video and sensor files are uploaded concurrently and (2) only the sensor files are uploaded first, while the video files may be transmitted later. Video files on the flash disk are tagged whether they still need to be uploaded.

5.2 User Interface

Figure 14 shows two screenshots of our Geo-Video App. When the user launches the software, he or she will first see the main menu (Figure 14(a)). A list of the captured videos is displayed on the screen. The user can choose to continue to upload video clips, whose sensor data was previously uploaded, by choosing name of the needed video file. The main menu consists two tabs: a submit tab for uploading videos, and a query tab for future extension of video query function on mobile device. When the user press **MENU** button, it will show "Record a video" and "Exit". If the user touches the "Record a video" button, a camera viewfinder will be

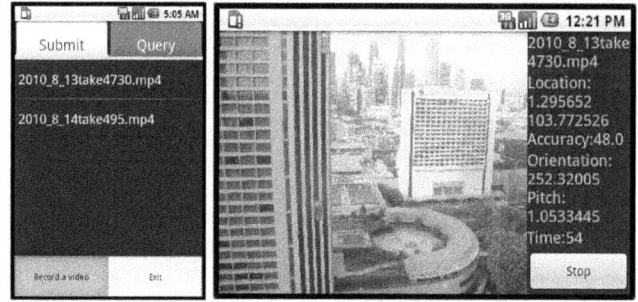

(a) Main menu   (b) Geo-Recorder

Figure 14: Geo-Video Android application prototype.

displayed (Figure 14(b)) and the user can then record, stop, cancel or edit a video clip via this interface just like they usually do in the G1's default camera view. However, our system additionally starts to record geo-referenced information from the GPS and the digital compass and these information is also shown on the phone screen. The sensor data is stored to the device at the time when the video is saved to the camera roll and flash disk. Next, an uploading screen guides the user through the next step. A destination URL is displayed (which can be changed) and either the sensor information only or both the sensor and video files can be uploaded. As mentioned earlier, saved videos can be uploaded at a later point in time directly from the main menu screen.

6. RELATED WORK

There exist only a few systems that associate a large set of sensor values with mobile video. Most of the existing work is limited to images and location coordinates, without considering compass direction. There is no specific work investigating energy issues for mobile video transmissions. Below we provide an overview of some of the existing work.

6.1 Digital Media with Geo-Locations

Associating GPS coordinates with digital photographs has become an active area of research [17]. There has been research on organizing and browsing personal photos according to location and time. Toyama *et al.* [21] introduced a meta-data powered image search and built a database, also known as World Wide Media eXchange (WWMX), which indexes photographs using location coordinates and time. A number of additional techniques in this direction have been proposed [13, 15]. There are also several commercial web sites (e.g., Flickr, Woophy) that allow the upload and navigation of geo-referenced photos. All these techniques use only the camera geo-coordinates as the reference location in describing images. We instead propose a much broader, sensor-based description of video scenes. More related to our work, Ephstein *et al.* [6] proposed to relate images with their view frustum (viewable scene) and used a scene-centric ranking to generate a hierarchical organization of images. Some approaches [20, 11] use location and other meta-data, as well as text tags associated with images, and the images' visual features to generate representative candidates within image clusters. Geo-location is often used as a filtering step. Our work considers a much more comprehensive scenario that is concerned with continuous sensor-streams of mobile videos, which are dynamically changing over time.

6.2 Energy Management on Mobile Devices

Limited battery power has been a fundamental problem in the field of mobile computing. A great deal of work has focused on energy management on mobile devices. Viredaz *et al.* [22] surveyed many energy-saving techniques for handheld devices in terms of improving the design and cooperation of system hardware, software as well as multiple sensing sources. Wang *et al.* [23] proposed a hierarchical approach for managing sensors in order to achieve human state recognition in an energy efficient manner. The SeeMon system [10] is a scalable and energy-efficient context monitoring framework for sensor-rich and resource limited mobile environments. Authors in [16] have drawn attention to the tradeoff between energy and location accuracy. Our work on mobile geo-referenced video management achieves energy efficiency by separating the descriptive sensor information from the bulky video data and by delaying the transmission of the actual video.

6.3 Video Sensor Networks

A few video-based sensor networks have been developed for monitoring and surveillance. Panoptes [7] used a camera device based on a Intel StrongARM PDA platform with a Logitech Webcam as the vision sensor and 802.11b for wireless communication. SensEye [12] is a multi-tier network of heterogeneous wireless nodes and cameras. Low-power cameras, which are capable of taking low-resolution images, form the bottom level. When an object of interest is identified, these sensors trigger cameras at a higher tier on demand to take better images. In contrast, our proposed system uses off-the-shelf mobile devices. This provides mobility and can also simplify the deployment burden.

7. CONCLUSIONS

Capturing video in conjunction with descriptive sensor meta-data allows a new strategy of uploading the sensor information in real-time while transmitting the bulky video data on demand later. This key idea can reduce the transmission of uninteresting videos and hence significantly lower the energy consumption in battery-powered mobile camera nodes. In our study we presented the design and prototype implementation of a mobile video management system that uses smartphones as mobile video sensors. We demonstrated the energy efficiency of our system with simulations and the experimental results showed that our technique can substantially prolong the device usage time, while ensuring a low search latency. We expect this method to be useful for a wide range of novel applications.

Acknowledgments

We acknowledge the support of the Centre of Social Media Innovations for Communities (CoSMIC), sponsored by the Media Development Authority (MDA) of Singapore.

8. REFERENCES

[1] I. Akyildiz, T. Melodia, and K. Chowdhury. A Survey on Wireless Multimedia Sensor Networks. *Computer Networks*, 51, 2007.

[2] S. Arslan Ay, R. Zimmermann, and S. H. Kim. Viewable Scene Modeling for Geospatial Video Search. In *16th ACM Intl. Conference on Multimedia*, pages 309–318, 2008.

[3] T. Brinkhoff. A Framework for Generating Network-Based Moving Objects. *GeoInformatica*, 6(2):153–180, 2002.

[4] Y. Cheng, Y. Chawathe, A. LaMarca, and J. Krumm. Accuracy Characterization for Metropolitan-scale Wi-Fi Localization. In *3rd Intl. Conference on Mobile Systems, Applications, and Services*, page 245. ACM, 2005.

[5] T. Cheung, K. Okamoto, F. Maker III, X. Liu, and V. Akella. Markov Decision Process (MDP) Framework for Optimizing Software on Mobile Phones. In *7rd ACM Intl. conference on Embedded software*, pages 11–20, 2009.

[6] B. Epshtein, E. Ofek, Y. Wexler, and P. Zhang. Hierarchical Photo Organization Using Geo-Relevance. In *15th ACM Intl. Symposium on Advances in Geographic Information Systems (GIS)*, pages 1–7, 2007.

[7] W. Feng, E. Kaiser, W. Feng, and M. Baillif. Panoptes: Scalable Low-power Video Sensor Networking Technologies. *ACM Transactions on Multimedia Computing, Communications, and Applications (TOMCCAP)*, 1(2):151–167, 2005.

[8] I. Google. Android – An Open Handset Alliance Project. http://developer.android.com.

[9] C. H. Graham, N. R. Bartlett, J. L. Brown, Y. Hsia, C. C. Mueller, and L. A. Riggs. *Vision and Visual Perception.* John Wiley & Sons, Inc., 1965.

[10] S. Kang, J. Lee, H. Jang, H. Lee, Y. Lee, S. Park, T. Park, and J. Song. SeeMon: Scalable and Energy-Efficient Context Monitoring Framework for Sensor-Rich Mobile Environments. In *6th Intl. Conference on Mobile Systems, Applications, and Services*, pages 267–280. ACM, 2008.

[11] L. S. Kennedy and M. Naaman. Generating Diverse and Representative Image Search Results for Landmarks. In *WWW '08: 17th Intl. Conference on the World Wide Web*, pages 297–306, New York, NY, USA, 2008. ACM.

[12] P. Kulkarni, D. Ganesan, P. Shenoy, and Q. Lu. SensEye: a Multi-tier Camera Sensor Network. In *13th ACM Intl. Conference on Multimedia*, page 238. ACM, 2005.

[13] M. Naaman, Y. J. Song, A. Paepcke, and H. Garcia-Molina. Automatic Organization for Digital Photographs with Geographic Coordinates. In *4th ACM/IEEE-CS Joint Conference on Digital Libraries*, pages 53–62, 2004.

[14] T. Pavlidis. Why Meaningful Automatic Tagging of Images is Very Hard. In *IEEE ICME 2009*, pages 1432–1435, 2009.

[15] A. Pigeau and M. Gelgon. Building and Tracking Hierarchical Geographical & Temporal Partitions for Image Collection Management on Mobile Devices. In *13th ACM Intl. Conference on Multimedia*, 2005.

[16] M. Ra, J. Paek, A. Sharma, R. Govindan, M. Krieger, and M. Neely. Energy-delay Tradeoffs in Smartphone Applications. In *8th Intl. conference on Mobile systems, applications, and services*, pages 255–270. ACM, 2010.

[17] K. Rodden and K. R. Wood. How do People Manage their Digital Photographs? In *SIGCHI Conference on Human Factors in Computing Systems*, pages 409–416, 2003.

[18] A. Shye and B. Sholbrock. G, M. Into The Wild: Studying Real User Activity Patterns to Guide Power Optimization for Mobile Architectures. Micro, 2009.

[19] B. Tiwana and L. Zhang. Powertutor. 2009.

[20] C. Torniai, S. Battle, and S. Cayzer. *Sharing, Discovering and Browsing Geotagged Pictures on the Web.* 2006.

[21] K. Toyama, R. Logan, and A. Roseway. Geographic Location Tags on Digital Images. In *11th ACM Intl. Conference on Multimedia*, pages 156–166, 2003.

[22] M. Viredaz, L. Brakmo, and W. Hamburgen. Energy Management on Handheld Devices. *Queue*, 1(7):52, 2003.

[23] Y. Wang, J. Lin, M. Annavaram, Q. Jacobson, J. Hong, B. Krishnamachari, and N. Sadeh. A Framework of Energy Efficient Mobile Sensing for Automatic User State Recognition. In *7th Intl. Conference on Mobile Systems, Applications, and Services*, pages 179–192, 2009.

MultiSense: Fine-grained Multiplexing for Steerable Camera Sensor Networks

Navin K. Sharma, David E. Irwin, Prashant J. Shenoy and Michael Zink
University of Massachusetts Amherst
{nksharma,irwin,shenoy}@cs.umass.edu, zink@ecs.umass.edu

ABSTRACT

Steerable sensors, such as pan-tilt-zoom video cameras, expose programmable actuators to applications, which steer them in different directions based on their goals. Despite being expensive to deploy and maintain, existing steerable sensor networks allow only a single application to control them due to the slow speed of their mechanical actuators. To address the problem, we design MultiSense to enable fine-grained multiplexing by (i) exposing a virtual sensor to each application and (ii) optimizing the time to context-switch between virtual sensors and satisfy requests.

We implement MultiSense in Xen and explore how well proportional share scheduling, along with extensions for state restoration and request batching, satisfies the unique requirements of steerable sensors in the form of pan-tilt-zoom video cameras. We present experiments that show MultiSense efficiently isolates the performance of virtual cameras, allowing concurrent applications to satisfy conflicting goals. As one example, we enable a tracking application to photograph an object moving at nearly 3 mph every 23 ft along its trajectory at a distance of 300 ft, while supporting a security application that photographs a fixed point every 3 seconds.

Categories and Subject Descriptors

C.5.0 [**Computer System Implementation**]: General

General Terms

Design, Experimentation, Performance

Keywords

Virtualization, Sensor, Actuator, Pan-Tilt-Zoom

1. INTRODUCTION

Steerable sensor networks allow applications to adjust actuators that control the type, quality, and quantity of data they collect. [1] Steerable pan-tilt-zoom (PTZ) camera networks are an important example of this type of steerable system that are being deployed in

---

[1]This research is supported by NSF grants CNS-0720616, CNS-0720271, EEC-0313747, and CNS-0834243.

a diverse range of settings. For instance, the U.S. Border Patrol is deploying networks of PTZ cameras to continuously monitor the northern border for smugglers [17], and as part of a "virtual fence" on the southern border [8]. Further, networks of traffic cameras that monitor urban environments are now commonplace. Another example of this type of system is steerable radar networks, which are able to improve the accuracy of weather forecasts [20]. While this type of networked cyber-physical system is emerging as a critical piece of society's infrastructure, the deployments are expensive: the hardware cost for the 20-mile prototype of the Border Patrol's "virtual fence" is over $20 million. Further, a key limitation of these systems is that they are not designed for multiplexing. Despite their expense, only a single user, or application, is able to control them.

Supporting concurrent users via fine-grained multiplexing is an important step in providing broader access to these expensive systems. As a simple example, consider using a PTZ camera for both monitoring and surveillance. The monitoring application continuously scans each road at an intersection in a fixed pattern, while the surveillance application intermittently steers the camera to track suspicious vehicles moving through its field of view. Each application alters the setting of three distinct actuators—pan, tilt, and zoom—to satisfy its goals. Conflicts such as these have been cited as one reason multiple government agencies are unable to coordinate control of border cameras for different purposes, including both smuggling and search-and-rescue operations [17]. While simple multiplexing approaches, which schedule control in a coarse-grained batch fashion, are possible [4], they prevent the fine-grained multitasking required for these examples, and, in the camera example, force a choice between either monitoring the intersection or tracking the suspicious vehicle during each coarse-grained time period.

Although many approaches to time-sharing, including proportional share scheduling, have been well-studied for CPUs and other peripheral devices, such as disks and NICs, steerable sensors, such as video cameras, present new challenges because they differ in both their physical attributes and application requirements.

Physical Attributes. Mechanically steerable sensors are both slow and stateful. Since steering latencies are on the order of seconds, the most contentious resource is control of the sensor, and not the aggregate bandwidth of sensed data or the total number of I/Os. Further, since each actuation changes the sensor's physical state, its current state determines the time to transition to a new state, which results in long, highly variable context-switch times.

Application Requirements. Applications control a sensor's actuators directly to drive data collection—often based on past observations. Since real-world events dictate steering behavior, applications may have timeliness constraints, either to sense data at specific locations, e.g., to track a moving object, or to coordinate steering among multiple cameras, e.g., to sense a fixed point from multiple angles.

In general, fine-grained multiplexing benefits any application that values continuous access to data and is willing to tolerate a lower resolution than possible with a dedicated sensor. While the deployment cost of steerable sensors limits their number, it also magnifies the potential benefits of fine-grained sharing. To realize this potential, we design MultiSense, a system for fine-grained multiplexing—at the level of individual actuations—of steerable sensor networks. MultiSense employs a proportional-share scheduler to multiplex multiple virtual sensors on a single physical sensor. While MultiSense is designed to work with a broad range of steerable sensors, we demonstrate its efficacy using pan-tilt-zoom camera sensors that are multiplexed across different applications.

While we could implement sensor multiplexing in numerous ways, MultiSense uses a virtualization-based approach to expose a virtual sensor (*vsensor*) to each application; a vsensor looks no different from the underlying physical sensor in terms of its interface and can be manipulated by an application independently of other vsensors (and applications) that are manipulating the same physical device. Our goal is to extend the benefits of virtual machine performance isolation to include steerable sensor devices. Our hypothesis is that steerable sensors, such as PTZ cameras, are capable of simultaneously tracking multiple real-world events with different sensing modalities, such as a person walking and a building's entry point, and hence, can be shared across concurrent applications. In designing MultiSense, this paper makes the following contributions.

Multiplexing Steerable Sensors. MultiSense employs a finite state machine to track each vsensor's state as it actuates, and uses a request emulation mechanism to buffer actuations until a sense request arrives—similar to a disk that buffers write requests until a read request arrives. We show how MultiSense uses these mechanisms to reduce the significant state restoration overheads incurred from context-switching between vsensors.

Proportional-share Adaptation and Extensions. We introduce Actuator Fair Queuing (AFQ), a proportional share scheduler that can allocate shares of a steerable sensor's time to vsensors, and evaluate a range of extensions and their effect on performance. Our experiments quantify the level of AFQ's isolation and the benefit of each extension.

Implementation and Experimentation. We implement MultiSense in Xen and use it to study multiplexing PTZ video cameras. We present a case study for PTZ video cameras using multiple modalities, including continuous scanning, object tracking, single fixed-point sensing, and multi-sensor fixed-point sensing. Our case studies show that MultiSense is able to satisfy concurrent applications using these sensors. As one example, we enable a tracking application to photograph an object moving at nearly 3 mph every 23 ft along its trajectory at a distance of 300 ft, while supporting a security application that photographs a fixed point every 3 seconds.

In Section 2, we motivate our use of vsensors and present background on multiplexing sensors. Section 3 then discusses MultiSense's basic design, while Section 4 outlines our adaptation of proportional-share and its extensions. Section 5 and Section 6 present MultiSense's implementation and evaluation using pan-tilt-zoom video cameras. Finally, Section 7 puts MultiSense in context with related work, and Section 8 concludes.

2. BACKGROUND

The primary problem addressed in this paper is how to multiplex ("time-share") a steerable sensor, such as a PTZ camera, at a fine time scale across multiple concurrent users with diverse re-

quirements. We chose a virtualization approach for MultiSense to take advantage of the performance isolation capabilities present in modern virtualization platforms. We assume that each sensor node executes a hypervisor (also known as a virtual machine monitor) that hosts multiple virtual machines, one for each user. Each virtual machine exposes a virtual sensor device that appears to be an identical, but slower, version of the physical sensor to the user. A user application can manipulate the virtual sensor independently of other concurrent users; the virtualization layer ensures transparency by hiding the actions of one user from another, thereby providing the appearance of a dedicated sensor to each user. Multiple virtual sensors, one from each virtual machine, are mapped on to the underlying physical sensor and it is the task of the hypervisor to multiplex the virtual sensors onto the physical sensor, akin to time-sharing. Since concurrent requests from multiple users must be serviced by the physical sensor, and since mechanical actuation on steerable sensors is slow, each virtual sensor in MultiSense will appear to be a slower version of the physical sensor. Although MultiSense is capable of supporting a broad range of steerable sensors, in this paper, we focus on Pan-Tilt-Zoom (PTZ) cameras as a representative example of steerable sensors.

2.1 System Model

We assume each steerable sensor exposes one or more programmable actuators that applications control to steer it, and attaches to a node with local processing, storage and communication capabilities that is capable of running modern hypervisors. MultiSense multiplexes requests to steer the sensor across multiple applications, each executing in their own VM on each node. We assume that each application issues a stream of *actuation requests* to steer the sensor, followed by one or more *sense requests* to collect data. Thus, an application's request pattern takes the form:

> $[A_1 A_2 \ldots A_n S_1 S_2 \ldots S_m]^+$, $n \geq 0$, $m > 0$, where A_i and S_i denote an individual actuation and sensing request, respectively.

The request pattern matches low-level sensing device interfaces, where each actuation request A_i alters the setting of only a single actuator. Each actuation A_i takes time t_i to steer the sensor to the specified setting, where t_i is dependent on the actuator's speed and its current setting.

We assume a constant actuator speed, although there may be some mechanical jitter. Sense requests S_i either *capture* data by collecting it using the current setting of the actuators, or *scan* data by collecting it while changing the setting of the actuators. For instance, a monitoring application for a PTZ camera might issue a repeating pattern of *pan* and *tilt* requests, followed by one or more *image capture* requests to retrieve images. We assume that actuation and sense requests from different applications are independent of one another, although a scheduler may take advantage of partial overlaps in requests. To enable fine-grained multiplexing, MultiSense interleaves requests from concurrent applications on the underlying physical sensor.

2.2 Design Challenges

A simple approach for multiplexing multiple users onto a physical sensor is to employ time-sharing and allocate a fixed time slice to each concurrent user in round-robin fashion. However, steerable sensors have actuators that are stateful (e.g, the pan and tilt actuators in a PTZ camera determine where the camera is pointing). Since each user can modify the state of these actuators via actuation commands, naive time sharing can be problematic for such stateful sensor devices.

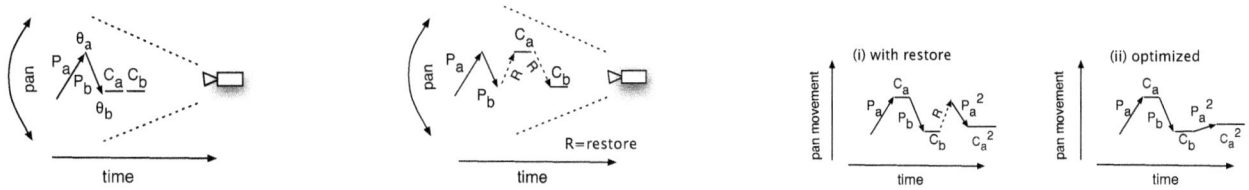

(a) Naïve interleaving $P_a P_b C_a C_b$ yields incorrect results.

(b) Correct interleaving $P_a P_b C_a C_b$ with state restorations.

(c) Optimizing state restoration costs.

Figure 1: Examples showing why request interleaving is challenging for steerable sensors.

We highlight the challenges in multiplexing stateful steerable sensors using a simple example.

Example 1: Consider two users—Alice and Bob—sharing control of a single PTZ camera. Assume that Alice first issues a pan, followed by a capture, denoted by $P_a C_a$ while Bob issues a similar sequence $P_b C_b$, where the subscripts a and b denote Alice and Bob, respectively. Consider naïve time-sharing that interleaves these requests in the following order on the camera: $P_a P_b C_a C_b$. In this case, the camera pans to position θ_a, as requested by Alice, and then pans to a position θ_b, as requested by Bob (see Figure 1(a)).

As a result of the ordering, executing Alice's capture request C_a next results in an inconsistent picture, since *the camera's lens is at pan position θ_b when Alice expects the camera's lens to be at pan position θ_a*. Since the camera is stateful, Bob's actuation leaves the camera in a different state than Alice left it. As a result, naïve time-slicing using time quanta is inappropriate, since Alice and Bob would have no guarantee of the camera's state at the beginning of any time-slice.

Example 2: A straightforward solution is to *restore* Alice's state before context-switching back to her, similar to a CPU scheduler that restores the state of a thread's program counter and registers prior to scheduling it for execution. However, unlike CPUs and other peripheral devices, state restoration for mechanically steerable sensors is *slow*, and can be more expensive than the execution time of actuation requests.

For instance, the PTZ camera we use for our experiments takes nearly 9 seconds to pan from $0°$ to $340°$, nearly 4 seconds to tilt from $0°$ to $115°$, and over 2 seconds to zoom from 1x to 25x. Naïve state restoration can also exacerbate a sensor's slowness by executing wasteful actuations. In our example, restoring Alice's state to position θ_a is wasteful, since it requires re-executing the P_a pan request (Figure 1(b)). Better interleavings, such as $P_a C_a P_b C_b$, still pose a problem for a naïve strategy, since it is often more efficient to steer the sensor directly from θ_b to the position of Alice's next request P_a^2, rather than directly restoring her previous state (Figure 1(c)).

These simple examples motivate two basic elements of our approach. First, we maintain the correct vsensor state for each user to ensure their sensing requests are consistent. Second, we automatically group together requests of the form $A_i^* S_i$ to prevent wasteful actuations, since interleaving actuation requests from other vsensors within a group results in unnecessary state restoration. Despite these elements, context-switches between groups inevitably require some state restoration, making them inherently slow. Since Multi-Sense does not know each user's request pattern in advance, these context-switch times are also unpredictable.

Users will notice unpredictable context-switch times if they have strict timeliness requirements, and will perceive them as changes in vsensor actuation speed. For example, rather than maintaining a stable vsensor speed of v degrees/second, an application may observe a speed of $\frac{v}{2}$ degrees per second for one sensing request, and then a speed of $2v$ for the subsequent one. One option for reducing this variability is to require all applications to reveal their desired request pattern and timeliness requirements at allocation time, and then decide whether to insert the request pattern into a fixed, repeating schedule of actuator movements, similar to Rialto's approach to hard real-time CPU scheduling [13]. This type of scheduling is difficult even on a dedicated sensor since, similar to a disk head, the mechanical steering mechanism has inherent jitter.

Real-time scheduling similar to Rialto also requires strict admission control policies that limit the number of simultaneous users a system supports, and is problematic because sensing applications generally do not know their request patterns or requirements in advance, since real-world events may occur anywhere at anytime. Ultimately, some uncertainty is inherent if we allow each application the freedom to determine what actuation requests to issue and when to issue them. As a result, in our design of MultiSense, we explore how well proportional-share scheduling and its extensions isolate vsensor performance and meet the practical timeliness requirements of representative applications. Share-based scheduling is appropriate for allocating a resource whose supply varies over time. Since the time the physical sensor spends context-switching is dependent on the request patterns of its applications, the time available to control the sensor has the effect of a resource with varying supply.

3. MULTISENSE DESIGN

MultiSense extends traditional hypervisors by adding support to multiplex steerable sensors using a virtual sensor abstraction. A vsensor behaves like a slower version of the physical sensor that has identical functionality: an application designed to interface with the physical sensor should also interface with the corresponding vsensor. MultiSense resides in the hypervisor or a privileged control domain—e.g., Domain-0 in Xen—and interleaves requests from each vsensor on the underlying physical sensor, as shown in Figure 2. We separate MultiSense's functions into three categories described below. The goal of this decomposition is to reduce context-switch overheads while preserving a level of performance isolation.

1. **State Restoration**. MultiSense tracks the state of the physical sensor and each vsensor using finite state machines (FSM), and restores state whenever it detects a state mismatch at context-switch time.

2. **Request Groups**. MultiSense prevents wasteful context-switches by automatically grouping together requests from each vsen-

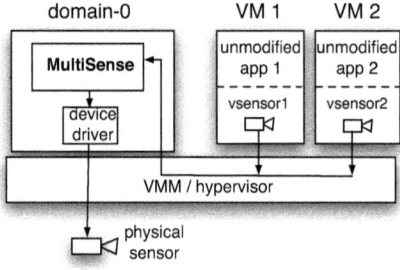

Figure 2: MultiSense Architecture Overview

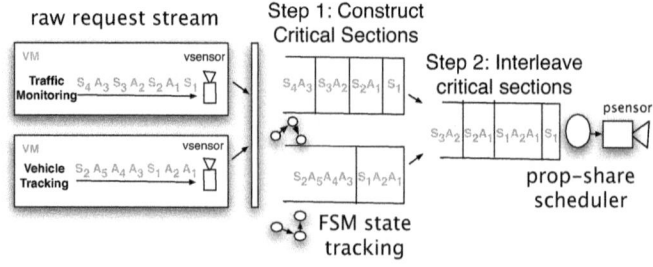

Figure 3: Constructing and interleaving request groups

sor of the form $A_i^* S_i$ and atomically issuing them to the sensor.

3. **Scheduling**. MultiSense employs a proportional-share scheduler and extensions at the granularity of request groups to determine an ordering that balances fair access to the sensor with its efficient use.

We describe MultiSense's FSMs, and their use in restoring state and inferring atomic request groups in this section, and discuss scheduling in Section 4. We use the term actuator broadly to include both mechanical actuators, as well as non-mechanical settings of interest. For instance, a PTZ camera's state includes both the pan, tilt, and zoom position of its lens, as well as the image resolution and shutter speed settings. Pan and tilt are true mechanical actuators that require a motor to alter, while zoom, shutter speed, and image resolution are settings of the lens, camera, and CMOS sensor, respectively. Each actuation modifies the state of one or more of these parameters, causing the sensor to transition from one state to another.

3.1 Sensor State Machines

Finite state machines track the state of each physical and virtual sensor, where a state is an n-tuple that represents a setting for each of n actuators. Each state transition has a cost that denotes the time the sensor takes to complete the transition. MultiSense employs a virtual state machine (VSM) to track the current state of each virtual sensor and a physical state machine (PSM) to track the state of the physical sensor. The state of a virtual sensor (and hence the VSM) changes only when the corresponding user actuates its vsensor. In contrast, the state of the physical sensor (and the PSM) depends on which vsensor request is currently executing on the physical sensor. Thus, the PSM and VSM state machines allow MultiSense to track the state expected by each user, as well as the current state of the underlying physical sensor.

3.2 Intelligent State Restoration

Whenever MultiSense context-switches from one vsensor to another, it compares the state of the currently executing vsensor state machine (VSM) and the physical sensor's state machine (PSM). As with a CPU, if there is a state mismatch, MultiSense performs state restoration by automatically issuing requests for each out-of-sync state parameter to synchronize the vsensor's state with the physical sensor's state. As an example, assume that Alice's VSM is in state $pan = \theta_a \; tilt = \phi_a \; zoom = Z_a$, and the PSM is in state $pan = \theta_b \; tilt = \phi_a \; zoom = Z_b$. The two state machines are out-of-sync along the pan and zoom dimensions but in-sync along the tilt dimension. MultiSense synchronizes Alice's VSM state with

the PSM by issuing a pan request to move the camera from θ_b to θ_a and a zoom request to move from Z_b to Z_a. No synchronization action is necessary along the tilt dimension.

We refer to this simple state restoration strategy as the eager strategy, since it eagerly synchronizes states with a past state on every context-switch. For steerable sensors, the eager strategy imposes a higher overhead than necessary, since it ignores actuation requests queued by each vsensor. Recall the example from Section 2.2, where Alice issues $P_a C_a$ followed by $P_a^2 C_a^2$, and the P_a request causes the camera to move to pan position θ_a. Now suppose that Bob's request $P_b C_b$ executes next, and the camera pans to position θ_b. Before executing Alice's next request, the eager strategy restores the pan state of the camera by moving it from the current position θ_b to position θ_a. As depicted in Figure 1(c), the approach is wasteful, since Alice's queued pan request P_a^2 intends to pan to position θ_a^2, making it more efficient to move the camera directly from θ_b to θ_a^2. To see why, suppose $\theta_b = 50°$, $\theta_a = 30°$ and $\theta_a^2 = 75°$. Eager restoration pans from $50° \rightarrow 30° \rightarrow 75° = 65°$, while a direct pan from $50°$ to $75°$ requires only a $25°$ movement. For the PTZ camera we use, an additional $40°$ pan movement wastes more than 1 second.

MultiSense avoids this overhead using a lookahead strategy that does not restore state parameters that queued vsensor acutations will subsequently modify. For example, let VSM_{prev} denote the VSM state prior to a context-switch, and let VSM_{next} denote the VSM state that would result from executing requests queued after the last context-switch. $VSM_{prev} \cap VSM_{next}$ now denotes the set of state parameters not modified by these requests. The lookahead strategy only restores the states in $VSM_{prev} \cap VSM_{next}$. In the Alice and Bob example, $VSM_{prev} \cap VSM_{next}$ includes the parameters zoom and tilt, but not pan, since Alice's queued request will modify the pan parameter.

3.3 Grouping Requests via Request Emulation

To eliminate wasteful state restoration overheads, MultiSense automatically groups requests from each vsensor that the physical sensor should execute atomically. Each group includes a sequence of zero or more actuation requests, followed by a sense request from a single vsensor. Request groups prevent interference from the actuation requests of competing vsensors. However, since sensing and actuation requests are often blocking calls executed synchronously on the underlying physical sensor, vsensors only see a single request at a time, which does not permit grouping. To group requests, MultiSense enables asynchronous execution of blocking requests by emulating the execution of requests on the vsensor and deferring their actual execution on the physical sensor.

Request emulation allows the vsensor to behave as if the request actually executed on the sensor, allowing the blocking call to com-

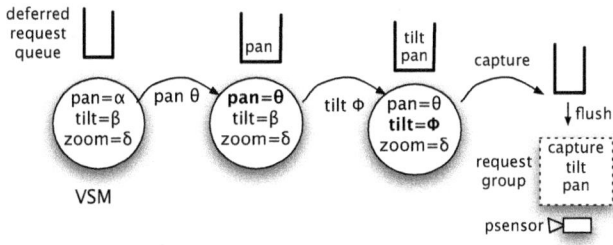

Figure 4: Request emulation and request groups

plete and the vsensor to continue execution. The vsensor's VSM tracks the state changes that result from any emulated requests, and defers their execution until the vsensor context-switches in. To ensure correctness, we only emulate actuation requests, since they do not return data that alters an application's control flow. Since sense requests return real-world data, MultiSense cannot emulate them, but must execute them using the physical sensor in the appropriate state to return a correct result. When a sense request arrives, MultiSense flushes the queue of deferred actuation requests to its scheduler, which then schedules the request group as a single atomic unit. The sense request blocks until the result returns.

As an example, consider how Alice's virtual camera maps onto a physical camera. Assume that Alice issues an actuation request P_a to pan to position θ_a. Request emulation triggers a VSM state transition to a new pan position θ_a, as shown in Figure 4. The figure also shows that MultiSense queues the request for deferred execution. Once the blocking pan completes, Alice's application continues execution and issues an actuation request to tilt to position ϕ_a, causing request emulation to continue by triggering another state transition in the VSM. Finally, Alice issues a capture request C_a, which MultiSense groups with the two pending actuation requests in the vsensor's queue and flushes it to the scheduler for execution on the physical sensor. Alice blocks until the group executes and returns the appropriate image.

One consequence of request emulation is that applications do not immediately perceive errors from actuations. We report any errors as a result of an actuation when its corresponding sense request executes, similar to any write-back cache that will defer reporting hardware errors until after a write executes. Note that this change affects neither application correctness nor device safety. MultiSense delays reporting actuation errors to the time of an application's next sense request. Since sensor data dictates an application's control flow, the application will observe errors prior to making control flow decisions. Likewise, since MultiSense controls the issuing of requests to the physical sensor, it is capable of preventing cascading errors from unknowing applications that may damage the sensor.

4. PROPORTIONAL-SHARE FOR STEERABLE SENSORS

MultiSense flushes request groups to a proportional-share scheduler that decides when to execute them. We design Actuator Fair Queuing (AFQ) by modifying the standard Start-time Fair Queuing (SFQ) algorithm, originally designed for NICs [3] and CPUs, to schedule steerable sensors [9].

As background, we provide a brief summary of SFQ. SFQ assigns a weight w_i to each vsensor and allocates $w_i/\sum_j w_j$ of the physical sensor's time to vsensor i. Controlling the weight assignment alters the share and performance of a vsensor's acuators: a

smaller weight results in a smaller share and slower actuation. For example, a weight assignment in a 1:2 ratio for Alice and Bob results in an allocation of $1/3$ and $2/3$ of the physical sensor's time, respectively. An ideal fair scheduler guarantees that over any time interval $[t_1, t_2]$, the service received by any two vsensors i and j is in proportion to their weights, assuming continuously backlogged requests at each vsensor during the interval. Thus, $\frac{W_i(t_1,t_2)}{W_j(t_1,t_2)} = \frac{w_i}{w_j}$, or equivalently, $\frac{W_i(t_1,t_2)}{w_i} - \frac{W_j(t_1,t_2)}{w_j} = 0$, where W_i and W_j denote the aggregate service each vsensor receives over the interval $[t_1, t_2]$. In our case, the aggregate service denotes the total time the (dedicated) physical sensor consumes scheduling a vsensor's request during the interval.

We define the SFQ algorithm for scheduling critical sections in MultiSense as follows. For ease of exposition, we will use the terms critical sections and requests interchangeably: SFQ maintains a queue of pending requests for each vsensor.

- Upon arrival, the scheduler assigns each request r_i^k with a start tag $S(r_i^k)$, where $S(r_i^k) = max(v(A(r_i^k)), F(r_i^{k-1}))$, r_i^k denotes the kth request of vsensor i, $F(r_i^{k-1})$ denotes the finish time of the previous request, $v(t)$ represents virtual time, described below, and $A(t)$ represents the actual arrival time of the request. The start tag of a request is the maximum of the virtual time at arrival or the finish tag of the previous request.

- The finish tag of a request is $F(r_i^k) = S(r_i^k) + \frac{l_i^k}{w_i}$, where l_k^k denotes the length of the kth request and w_i denotes the weight assigned to vsensor i. Intuitively, the finish tag of a request is its start tag incremented by the length of time required to execute the entire critical section, normalized by the vsensor's weight. To enable precise computation of l_k^k, SFQ computes the finish tag *after* the request/critical section completes execution. Once SFQ computes a request's finish tag, it computes the start tag of the next request in its queue.

- The scheduler starts at virtual time 0. During a busy period—when the scheduler is continuously scheduling requests on the physical sensor—SFQ defines the virtual time at time t, $v(t)$, to be the start tag of the request currently executing. At the end of a busy period, SFQ sets the virtual time to the maximum finish tag of any request completed during this busy period. The virtual time does not increment when the physical sensor is idle.

- The scheduler always schedules the request with the minimum start tag next, ensuring that it schedules the vsensor with the minimum weighted service thus far. This is the key property that ensures each vsensor receives its fair share of the psensor over time. Note also that scheduling the request with the minimum start tag implies that the virtual time during a busy period is always equal to the minimum start tag of any request in the system.

4.1 Actuator-Fair Queuing

AFQ differs from SFQ by setting the length of a request equal to the time it would take to execute on the dedicated sensor, and introducing batch-based reordering, discussed in the following subsection, that address scheduling issues specific to steerable sensors. As with other proportional-share schedulers, AFQ associates a weight w_i with each vsensor and allocates $w_i/\sum_k w_k$ of the physical sensor's time to vsensor i. Lowering a vsensor's weight assignment affects its performance by slowing down its actuation speed. In

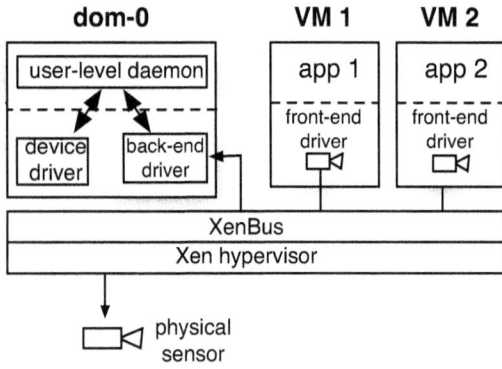

Figure 5: MultiSense uses Xen's split-driver framework for communication, and a user-level daemon in Domain-0 to maintain vsensor VSMs and execute scheduling policies. Each request passes from application → front-end driver → back-end driver → daemon → device.

From	→ To	Latency	Percentage
application	→ front-end	0.24 μsecs	$7.1x10^{-8}$
front-end	→ back-end	6.35 μsecs	$1.9x10^{-4}$
back-end	→ listener	286 μsecs	$8.51x10^{-3}$
listener	→ camera	274 μsecs	$8.15x10^{-3}$
camera	→ listener	3.35 secs	99.7
listener	→ back-end	17 μsecs	$5.1x10^{-4}$
back-end	→ front-end	27 μsecs	$8.0x10^{-4}$
front-end	→ application	229 μsecs	$6.8x10^{-3}$
total		**3.36** secs	**100**

Table 1: Latency breakdown for a sample vsensor actuation of the Sony PTZ camera in our Xen implementation. The dominant factor in the request latency ($>$ 99.7%) is the time to actuate the camera. Our implementation imposes comparatively little overhead ($<$ 0.3%).

work-conserving mode, actuation speeds may also become faster if any vsensor is not using its share by being passive.

The ideal is only possible if the physical sensor is able to divide each actuation into infinitesimally small time units. Since actuations are of variable length and MultiSense schedules at the granularity of request groups, enforcing the ideal is not possible. We chose SFQ as our foundation because it bounds the resulting unfairness due to this discrete granularity by ensuring that $|\frac{W_i(t_1,t_2)}{w_i} - \frac{W_j(t_1,t_2)}{w_j}| \leq (\frac{l_i^{max}}{w_i} + \frac{l_j^{max}}{w_j})$ for all intervals $[t_1, t_2]$, where l_i^{max} is the maximum length of a request group from vsensor i. Intuitively, this bound is a function of the largest possible request group, which for our PTZ camera is an actuation, from $pan = -170°$ $tilt = -90°$ $zoom = 1x$ to $pan = 170°$ $tilt = 25°$ $zoom = 25x$. Since this worst-case scenario takes nearly 16 seconds for our camera, one goal of our evaluation is to explore performance in the common, rather than the worst, case for representative applications.

4.2 Batching

SFQ ignores the actuation costs from context-switching between request groups, causing significant overheads. As an example, consider three users Alice, Bob and Carol sharing a PTZ camera. Assume that the camera is currently at position $25°$, and Alice, Bob and Carol have start tags of 10, 11 and 12, respectively, when Alice issues a pan request for position $30°$ and Bob and Carol issue pan requests for positions $75°$ and $40°$. SFQ services these requests in order of the start tags—Alice, then Bob, and finally Carol—and triggers pans from $25° \rightarrow 30° \rightarrow 75° \rightarrow 40° = 85°$. However, since Alice and Carol's requests are close to each other, servicing the requests in the order Alice, then Carol, and finally Bob lowers the overhead to $25° \rightarrow 30° \rightarrow 45° \rightarrow 75° = 50°$. For our PTZ camera, this results in nearly a 1 second reduction in overhead. We address this issue in AFQ by selecting the k pending request groups with the smallest start tags, one from each vsensor, instead of selecting only the request group with the minimum start tag.

Given a batch of k request groups, we reorder them to minimize the physical sensor's total actuation time. In our example, this strategy selects the more efficient Alice → Carol → Bob ordering. For a single actuator, the batching strategy is similar to proportional-share disk schedulers that use an elevator algorithm

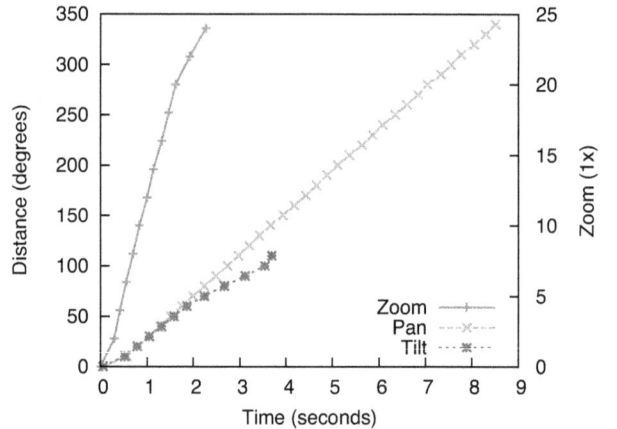

Figure 6: Time benchmarks for the pan, tilt, and zoom actuators of Sony SNC-SRZ30N Network Camera that show the distance moved by the actuator is roughly linear to the time and energy required to complete the actuation.

to reorder batched requests [6]. Since our sensors have multiple actuators, minimizing actuation time is an instance of the NP-hard Traveling Salesman Problem. We use a greedy heuristic that always executes the next closest request in the batch. For small values of k, a brute force search that tries all permutations is also feasible. Introducing the parameter k defines a new tradeoff: the higher the value of k the more efficient, but less fair, the schedule. In Section 6.2, we show that a value of k that is close to half the number of vsensors N in the system strikes a good balance between fairness and efficiency for our examples.

5. MULTISENSE IMPLEMENTATION

Although MultiSense is designed to support a range of steerable sensor, here we focus on supporting PTZ camera sensors. Our MultiSense prototype is implemented in the Xen virtual machine and integrates with Xen's virtual device framework. Our PTZ camera sensors are implemented as character devices that transfer streams of data serially to applications. In Linux, applications typically interface with sensors through character device files using the open, close, read, write, and ioctl system calls. To support devices, Xen uses a split-driver approach that divides conventional driver functionality into two halves: a front-end driver that runs in each VM

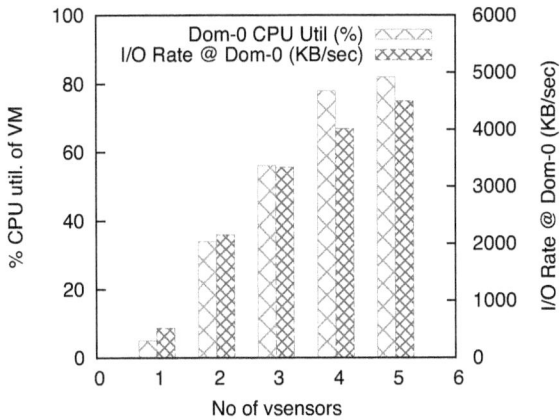

Figure 7: Utilization of Domain-0's 40% CPU share and I/O rate for streaming data. The number of vsensors vary from 1 to 5, where the first vsensor is a PTZ camera and the remaining vsensors are streaming data.

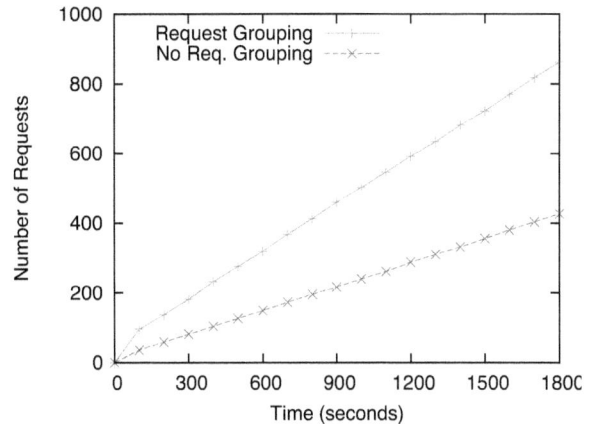

Figure 8: Request grouping improves performance 2x.

and a back-end driver that typically runs in Domain-0, a privileged management domain. Details of the split-driver approach can be found in [2]. Figure 5 depicts MultiSense's Xen implementation using a generic front-end character driver that passes the front-end's open, close, read, write, and ioctl requests to the back-end driver, which executes them and returns the response.

As with other character drivers, the front-end/back-end communication channel supports multiple threads to permit asynchronous interactions. In our current implementation the back-end driver passes requests to a user-level daemon running in Domain-0 using the back-end's read and write system calls. This daemon includes the logic to maintain and restore state, group requests, and schedule groups using a sensor's conventional application-level interface. Implementing MultiSense at user-level has two advantages beyond simplifying debugging. First, manufacturers often release binary-only drivers for Linux that are only accessible from user-level, necessitating user-level integration. Second, the user-level daemon decouples our implementation from a specific virtualization platform, allowing us to switch to alternatives, e.g., Linux VServers, if necessary. Since the dominant performance cost for steerable sensors is actuation time and not data transfer, as we show in Section 5.2, the overhead of moving data between kernel-space and user-space in our case is insignificant. For sensors where data transfer is the dominant cost, we could integrate the functions of this daemon into the back-end driver.

MultiSense's front-end/back-end drivers are reusable with different types of sensors since they only serve as a communication channel for requests. The user-level daemon maintains a vector and queue for each vsensor that stores the current setting of its actuators and its backlog of deferred actuation requests, respectively. The daemon also manages VSMs and state restoration as well as our extensions, such as request batching. When an actuation request arrives, the daemon associates a start tag with it, places it at the end of its vsensor's queue, sends back a response, and changes the actuator's vector entry. When a sense request arrives, the daemon batches it with any deferred requests in order of their minimum start tag, assigns the start tag of batch as the start tag of the sense request, and flushes the batch to the common queue used by the AFQ scheduler. As soon as k request batches arrive or time t passes from the last scheduling opportunity, the scheduler reorders

the request batches in the common queue using our greedy heuristic and issues them to physical sensor, as described in Section 3.3.

5.1 PTZ Camera

We evaluate MultiSense for PTZ cameras using the Sony SNC-RZ50N PTZ Network Camera. Beyond the three actuators we focus on, the camera has many non-obvious actuators, including resolution setting, shutter speed, backlight compensation, night vision, and electronic stabilization, that influence an image's fidelity. The camera is capable of panning between $-170°$ and $170°$ and tilting between $-90°$ and $25°$ of center, while supporting 25 different optical zoom settings (1x to 25x). The camera's direct drive motor allows control of pan and tilt increments as small as $1/3°$. We benchmarked the speed of each of the camera's actuators independently (Figure 6). The camera is capable of panning at $40°$/sec, tilting at $30°$/sec, and zooming at 12x/sec, although shorter movements are slower due to the acceleration/deceleration of the motor, which accounts for a major fraction of overall actuation time in case of shorter movements.

5.2 Benchmarks

Before evaluating MultiSense, we benchmark its implementation overhead. Our experiments run on our testbed nodes which each use a 2.00 Ghz Intel Celeron CPU, 1GB RAM, and an 80GB SCSI disk running version 3.2 of the Xen hypervisor with Ubuntu Linux using kernel version 2.6.18.8-xen in both Domain-0 and each guest VM. Each guest uses a file-backed virtual block device to store its root file system image. Each node consists of a Sony RZ50N PTZ camera sensor. Using the camera, Table 1 reports the overhead MultiSense imposes on a single vsensor actuation request and its response as it flows from the application to the device and then back to the application. Xen adds two additional layers in the flow—the front-end and back-end device driver—while MultiSense adds one layer by using a user-level daemon in Domain-0. As Table 1 shows, the overhead of these additional layers is minimal compared (order of μseconds) to the actuation times (order of seconds). We also benchmark the maximum aggregate I/O that MultiSense is able to support, and its CPU overhead.

For these experiments, we use Xen's proportional-share credit scheduler to allocate Domain-0 40% of the CPU and each VM 10% of the CPU. Domain-0 requires some CPU to process vsensor I/O requests and execute MultiSense's scheduler. We vary the number

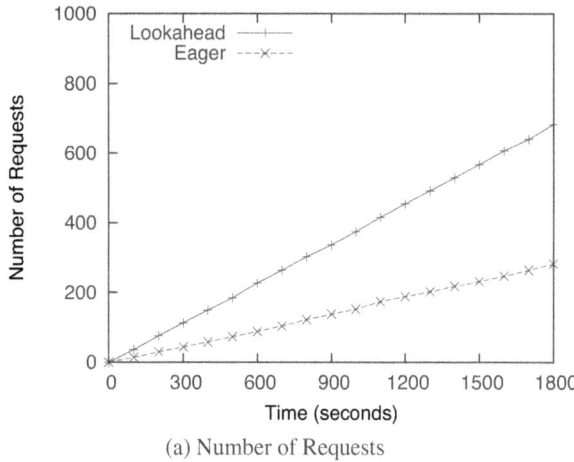

(a) Number of Requests

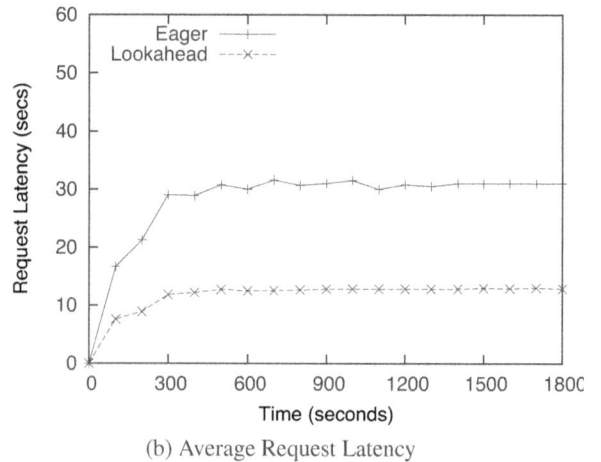

(b) Average Request Latency

Figure 9: The lookahead state restoration strategy outperforms the eager approach in our sample workloads. The number of requests completed (a) is 2x more and the average latency to satisfy each request (b) is 2x less using the lookahead approach.

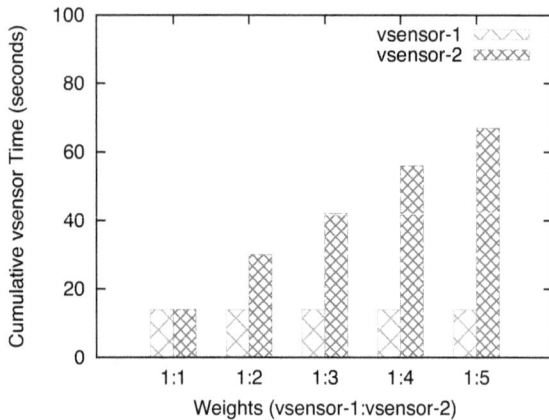

Figure 10: AFQ enforces performance isolation over large numbers of requests. The ratio of the total vsensor time for the two continuous scan workloads is in proportion to the assigned weights.

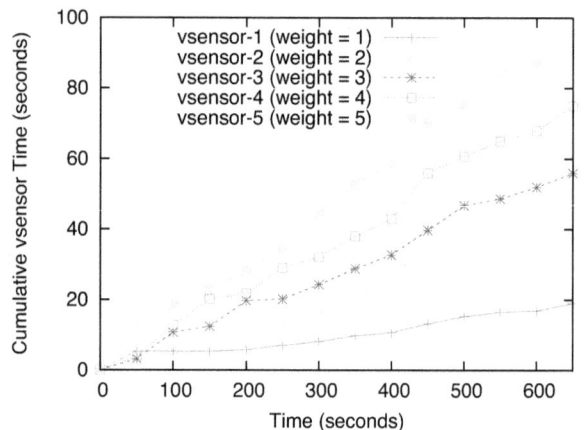

Figure 11: While AFQ enforces performance isolation over many requests, it may diverge slightly, due to high state restoration costs, over short intervals of time.

of VMs from 1 to 5, where the first VM controls the PTZ camera and the other VMs are streaming data continuously to stress I/O request processing. Figure 7 shows the maximum achievable I/O rate that MultiSense is able to deliver to each vsensor when cameras produce data as fast as possible. The result demonstrates that MultiSense is able to handle an I/O rate of 4.6 MBps of streaming data in this extreme case without overloading the CPU allocated to Domain-0, as shown by the Domain-0 CPU utilization in the figure. For reference, Netflix's watch instantly feature has a bit rate 5 MBps using the VC-1 codec [1].

6. EXPERIMENTAL EVALUATION

We first evaluate the impact of MultiSense's strategies for state restoration, request groups, and scheduling individually using synthetic workloads. The experiments demonstrate the extent to which these optimizations improve request throughput and latency. MultiSense's primary metric for success is whether or not it accommodates real concurrent applications. We present a case study for the camera that demonstrates the application-level performance and timeliness requirements MultiSense can achieve using our example sensors. We use both deterministic and random synthetic workloads to benchmark MultiSense's functions.

For the camera, the deterministic workload performs continuous scans using a single actuator in a single direction interspersed with sense requests, while the random workload repeatedly issues requests for a random setting of the actuators followed by a sense request. Each scan issues a sense request every $10°$ starting at one extreme and moving to the other. We intend these synthetic workloads to be conservative, since they force MultiSense to steer to extreme points in a sensor's state space, while also satisfying randomly generated requests. We describe the workloads for the applications in our case study in Section 6.3.

6.1 State Restoration and Request Groups

We demonstrate the impact of state restoration and request grouping, independently of our scheduling policy, on throughput—the

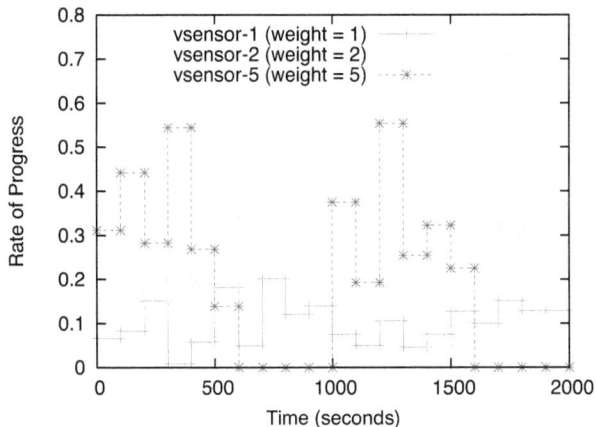

Figure 12: AFQ maintains the work-conserving property when applied to actuators.

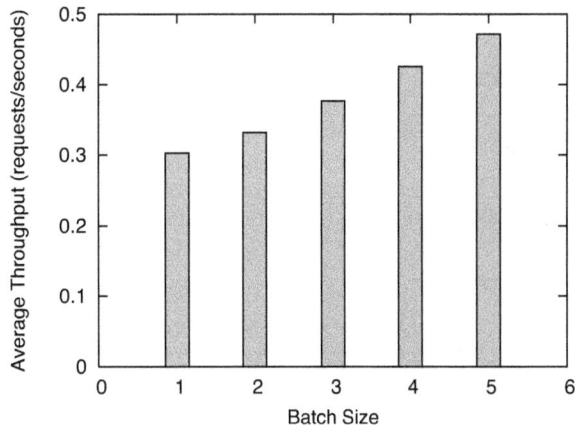

Figure 13: AFQ shows better global performance in terms of average throughput in requests/seconds as batch size increases. For this experiment, each increment in the batch size results in roughly a 10% improvement.

number of requests a sensor is able to satisfy per time interval. We first compare the eager approach to state restoration, described in Section 3.2, with our lookahead approach. Figure 9 shows results from an experiment using five vsensors, with batch size of 3, executing the random workloads described above. Figure 9(a) shows the progress of completed requests on the physical camera for both approaches, while Figure 9(b) plots the average latency to satisfy each request.

The lookahead approach is significantly more efficient: it is able to satisfy nearly 2x as many requests during the same 30 minute time period with 2x less latency on average per request. We also demonstrate the impact of request grouping by running the same experiments above with and without grouping. In this case, we use a group size of 5. Figure 8 shows the results. Using request groups, the camera is able to satisfy 2x more requests than without request groups. Our result highlights the importance of optimizing state restoration and grouping requests for efficiency, since a poor strategy may cancel any benefits from better scheduling. The consequences for an application are significant. For our camera case study (Figure 16), a 2x increase in request latency would mean capturing an image every 6 seconds, versus capturing it every 3 seconds.

6.2 AFQ Scheduling

The goal of AFQ is to enforce performance isolation between vsensors—each vsensor should receive performance in proportion to its weight (Figure 11). While AFQ bounds the maximum unfairness within any time interval, our extensions relax this bound to increase efficiency. We first demonstrate AFQ's strengths and limitations when scheduling steerable sensors, and then present results that show the performance gains, as well as the impact on fairness, for each of our extensions.

AFQ advances virtual time in relation to the time each actuation consumes on the dedicated sensor, which we denote as vsensor time. The more vsensor time each actuation consumes the slower the actuator. Figure 10 shows the total vsensor time of two vsensors with different weight assignments using AFQ, where each vsensor executes the continuous scan workload. The figure demonstrates that a straightforward adaptation of SFQ for actuators isolates vsensor performance: the cumulative vsensor time it allocates is in proportion to the assigned weights. As shown in Figure 12, AFQ proportionally distributes shares of the passive vsensor

(vsensor-5's share during time interval 500-1000 and 1500-2000 seconds) among active vsensors (vsensor-1 and vsensor-2). However, while SFQ enforces performance isolation over large numbers of requests, high context-switch costs cause it to perform unfairly over short intervals.

To demonstrate the point, Figure 11 shows how the cumulative vsensor time progresses over the course of an experiment. Since each workload includes 100 requests, at any point in time the cumulative vsensor time for each vsensor should be in proportion to the assigned weights. The experiment uses five vsensors—four running the continuous scan workload (1-4) and one running the random workload (5). The result demonstrates that over short time periods SFQ is not always fair: during the period 0-100 seconds both vsensor-3/vsensor-4 and vsensor-1/vsensor-2 receive similar performance that is not in proportion to their weights. Further, vsensor-1/vsensor-2 receive similar performance by time 200 and vsensor-3/vsensor-2 receive similar performance up to time 400, which diverges from the weight assignments. However, as before, as MultiSense services larger numbers of requests, performance converges to the assigned weights by 550 seconds.

6.2.1 Request Batching

Figure 13 demonstrates the performance improvement from batching for the camera. The experiment uses random workloads from 5 vsensors to stress actuation, and shows that the average throughput increases as the batch size increases—each increment in batch size results in roughly a 10% improvement. However, the improvement comes at a cost: the scheduler diverges from strict fairness. Figure 14(a) shows the cumulative request latency for each of the five vsensors as a function of batch size, using the same five vsensors and workloads as Figure 13. The cumulative request latency is the sum of the latencies to satisfy all requests at each vsensor, which is equivalent to each vsensor's makespan.

Figure 14(b) plots the cumulative vsensor time over the course of the experiment for a batch size of 4. Comparing the result with Figure 11 in the previous section emphasizes the decrease in performance isolation. As expected, SFQ, which corresponds to a batch size of 1, exhibits strong performance isolation. As the batch size increases, though, performance isolation decreases, causing the height of the bars to approach each other. For these workloads,

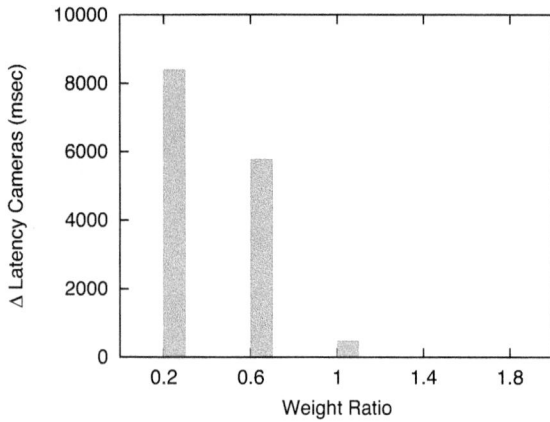

Figure 15: The difference in latency when coordinating multiple vsensors on different nodes to sense the same point.

a batch size of 3 exhibits an appropriate balance by increasing performance by 20% while achieving similar fairness properties. In practice, we have found that a batch size of roughly half the number of active vsensors strikes the appropriate balance.

6.3 Case Studies for PTZ Camera Sensors

Our case study explores MultiSense's use for the camera with four example applications with specific performance metrics. We use the lookahead state restoration approach, request groups, and AFQ.

- **Continuous Monitoring**. Continuously pan in increments of $65°$—nearly one-fifth of the possible pan range—and capture an image. The performance metric is the time to cover the sensor's entire range.

- **Fixed-point Sensing**. Pan, tilt, and zoom the lens to a fixed point and repeatedly capture images at a regular interval. The performance metric is the sensing rate.

- **Object Tracking**. Periodically track a pre-defined path along both the pan and tilt axes and capture images every $10°$. The performance metrics are both the latency between sensing requests, and the minimum overall latency necessary to keep up with the moving object.

- **Multi-sensor Fixed Point Sensing**. For two cameras, pan, tilt, and zoom the lens to a fixed point and repeatedly capture images at a regular interval. The sensor must also satisfy competing applications. The performance metric is the rate at which both sensors capture the fixed-point, which is equivalent to the minimum sensing rate of the two sensors.

With a dedicated camera, fixed-point sensing has near video quality. The sensing rate is 11 images/second with an average inter-image interval of 0.09 seconds. However, even on a dedicated sensor, actuation does have a significant effect on performance. Executing our random workload, reduces the rate to 0.3 images/second with an average inter-image interval of 3.35 seconds. Similarly, two fixed-point sensing applications—at a distance of $180°$—are both able to capture 0.2 images/second with an average inter-image interval of 4.65 seconds.

We first execute both continuous monitoring (Figure 16(a)) and object tracking (Figure 16(b)) concurrently with the fixed-point sensing application for the camera. We maintain a weight of 1 for fixed-point sensing, while varying the weights assigned to continuous monitoring and object tracking. Figure 16 shows the results for the camera, where the left y-axis plots the application's performance metric, the right y-axis plots sensing rate for fixed-point sensing, and the dotted line depicts performance on a dedicated sensor. The results show that MultiSense is able to satisfy the conflicting demands of concurrent applications. Of course, the applications must be able to tolerate less performance than possible with the dedicated sensor, which in these examples ranges from 1.5x to 8x less performance for the different weight assignments. Since weight dictates performance, some applications may need a minimum weight to satisfy their requirements.

Consider continuous monitoring for the camera with a 1:30 weight ratio, the application is able to pan all $340°$ in 20 seconds. Thus, in the real-world, the monitoring application is able to capture 5 distinct points 113 feet apart, e.g. four doorways, at distance of 100 feet from the camera every 4 seconds. The example assumes the points are along a circle with radius 100 feet with camera's lens as its center. Simultaneously, fixed-point sensing maintains an average sensing rate of nearly 0.2 images/second, allowing it to continuously capture a single point, such as a nearby intersection. Likewise, for a 1:3 weight ratio, the object tracking application is able to scan a pre-defined path every $10°$ and capture images at least every 6 seconds, which is suitable for tracking a moving object at a distance of 300 feet moving at 2.66 miles/hour, e.g., a person walking, for up to 1779 feet (over 1/3 mile) of the object's motion with 25x zoom. Both the specific speed and the total distance tracked are dependent on the object's trajectory, its distance from the camera, and the camera's optical zoom and resolution settings. Our example assumes that the object's trajectory is along a circle of radius 300 feet with the camera's lens as its center. During tracking, the fixed-point sensing application maintains a sensing rate of 0.3 images/second.

We also ran an experiment for a networked multi-sensor scenario where the application coordinates multiple sensors to sense a fixed point, while competing with continuous monitoring on one sensor and fixed-point sensing on the other. The experiment demonstrates the extent to which MultiSense satisfies timeliness requirements. Figure 15 shows the results. The x-axis shows experiments with different weight ratios assigned to the competing applications on each sensor, while the y-axis plots the average difference in latency between two requests. The magnitude of this difference determines how close in time the two sensors are able to capture data for the same point. As the graph shows, higher weight assignments decrease the difference, and provide near (< 1 second) simultaneous sensing. Even with a low relative weight assignment the sensors sense the same point within 2 seconds of each other, which is suitable for a range of scenarios, such as estimating the pedestrian entry/exit points for cameras. We are exploring other challenges that arise in distributed multi-sensor scheduling as part of future work, including applications with tighter time constraints.

7. RELATED WORK

MultiSense adapts existing techniques from many different areas, including sensor networks, platform virtualization, and proportional share scheduling, to virtualize stateful sensors with actuators. We briefly review important topics in each of these areas.

Mote-class sensor networks primarily use virtualization as a mechanism for safe execution and reprogramming, as demonstrated by Maté [11], since motes are generally not powerful enough to execute multiple applications concurrently. While some recent mote-class OSes incorporate threads and time-sharing [5], the energy constraints of motes prevent them from using high-power sensors

(a) Fairness vs. Batch Size

(b) Unfairness with Batch Size=4

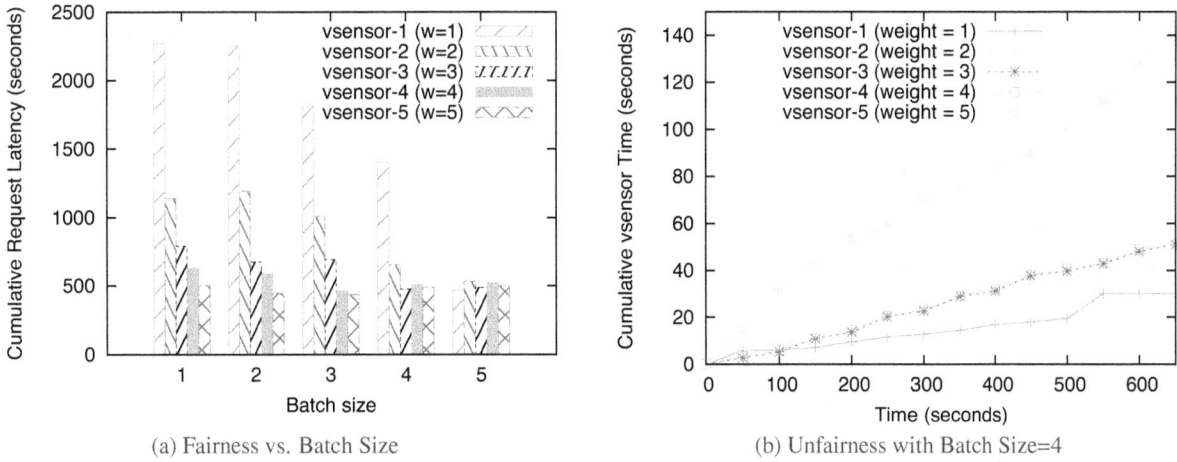

Figure 14: AFQ exhibits less fairness as the batch size increases (a) in terms of the average latency per request. For this experiment, batch sizes of 4 and greater are unfair, and exhibit much less performance isolation (b) than SFQ.

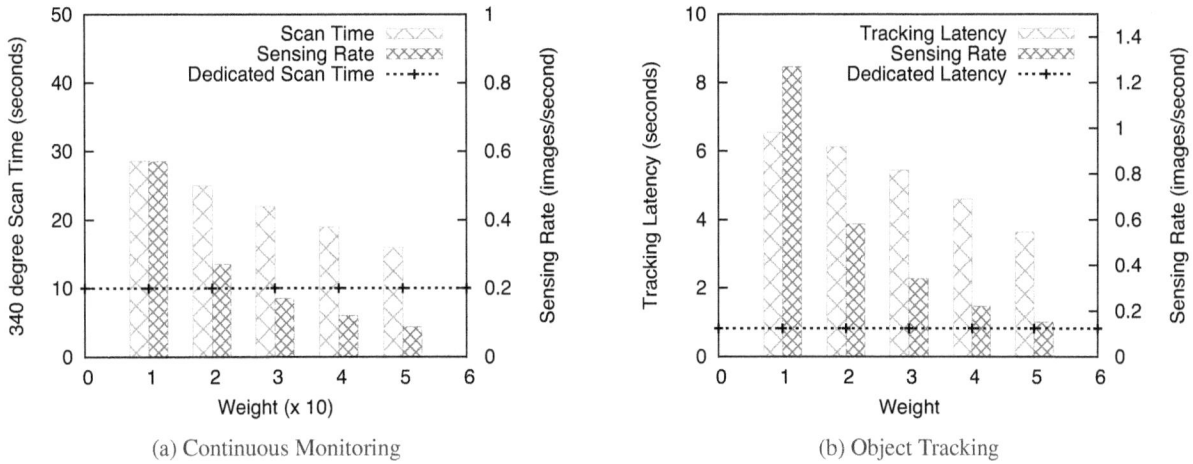

(a) Continuous Monitoring

(b) Object Tracking

Figure 16: For the camera, MultiSense is able to serve concurrent sensing applications. A continuous monitoring application (a) and an object tracking application (b) both maintain tolerable performance for varying weight assignments, while competing with a fixed-point sensing application with weight 1.

with rich programmable actuators, such as PTZ cameras or steerable weather radars. PixieOS [14] uses proportional-share scheduling techniques (in the form of *tickets*) to enable explicit conventional resource control (CPU, memory, bandwidth, energy) by individual mote applications; we extend similar proportional-share scheduling techniques to the equally important actuation "resources" of high-power sensors. Finally, ICEM also encounters a problem with blocking calls to peripheral devices when abstracting devices [10]; ICEM solves the problem for mote power management by exposing concurrency to drivers through power locks. In contrast, MultiSense does not change the application/device interface to support unmodified applications, and, instead, characterizes actuations as either safe or unsafe and uses request emulation to "complete" blocking calls asynchronously.

MultiSense uses Xen's [2] basic abstractions for multiplexing I/O devices [19]. Other frameworks, including VMedia [22], use Xen for coordinating shared access to peripheral devices. As with other device virtualization frameworks, VMedia focuses on stationary devices, e.g., web-based cameras and microphones, but does not extend the paradigm to steerable devices. Modern VMMs, in-

cluding Xen and VMware, focus on virtualizing the hardware at the lowest layer possible, e.g., the PCI bus, the USB controller, etc., to support unmodified device drivers. However, virtualizing at this layer requires the physical device to attach to a single VM and "pass-through" device requests to the physical bus [23]. We virtualize at the protocol layer—the character device file interface—so MultiSense can interpret each vsensor request and control their submission to the physical sensor. Our choice to implement sensor multiplexing and proportional-share scheduling in Xen is a result of our broader goal of lowering the barrier to experimenting with these systems from the ground up. Xen and other virtualization platforms offer the low-level fault, resource, and configuration isolation that we require. MultiSense's FSM that tracks the state of each vsensor is similar to shadow drivers [18], but we use them to ensure correct operation and enforce performance isolation and do not focus on reliability. Many prior approaches structure device drivers as state machines; the technique is natural for stateful devices [15].

MultiSense applies the proportional-share paradigm, which has been well-studied in other contexts, to multiplex control of steerable sensors. SFQ was originally prototyped for multiplexing packet streams and later extended to CPUs [9]. More recently, there has been work on proportional-share scheduling for energy—another non-traditional resource—using virtual batteries [7]. We extend the paradigm to the actuation resources of steerable sensors. Perhaps most related to MultiSense is past work on proportional-share scheduling for disks. Disk schedulers incorporate a similar batching technique [6] and often group together write requests and flush them to disk after a read request occurs. However, there are fundamental differences in the relative speed of actuators and their use, as well as workload characteristics, that present different trade-offs for steerable sensors. Rather than modeling the shared resource as I/O bandwidth or aggregate number of I/Os, which is often the case for disks [16], we use total time controlling the sensor, since this determines when and what applications are able to sense. We also introduce and evaluate new extensions for scheduling steerable sensors and evaluate their impact on applications. As with disk scheduling, other optimizations, such as Anticipatory Scheduling, may further improve performance [12].

8. CONCLUSION

MultiSense extends proportional-share scheduling to multiplex the resource of controlling a sensor's actuators. For steerable sensors, control of the actuators is the most important resource since it determines the type of data the sensor collects. This is the first work, to the best of our knowledge, to multiplex this important, but often overlooked, class of sensors. One reason multiplexing is critical for steerable sensor networks is their high deployment costs. In this paper, we demonstrate techniques for enabling multiplexing and proportional-share scheduling, and evaluate our techniques on synthetic workloads, as well as four real applications, that demonstrate their effectiveness for PTZ cameras.

9. REFERENCES

[1] Netflix Watch Instantly. http://www.netflix.com/WiMessage?msg=59. Retrieved September, 2010.

[2] P. Barham, B. Dragovic, K. Fraser, S. Hand, T. L. Harris, A. Ho, R. Neugebauer, I. Pratt, and A. Warfield. Xen And The Art Of Virtualization. In *Proceedings of the Symposium on Operating Systems Principles*, Bolton Landing, NY, October 2003.

[3] J.C.R. Bennett and H. Zhang. Wf2q: Worst-case Weighted Fair Queuing. In *Proceedings of the IEEE International Conference on Computer Communications*, June 2002.

[4] K. Binsted, N. Bradley, M. Buie, S. Ibara, M. Kadooka, and D. Shirae. The Lowell Telescope Scheduler: A System To Provide Non-Professional Access To Large Automatic Telescopes. In *Proceedings of the Internet and Multimedia Systems and Applications Conference*, Grindelwald, Switzerland, August 2005.

[5] Q. Cao, T. Abdelzaher, J. Stankovic, and T. He. The LiteOS Operating System: Towards Unix-like Abstractions For Wireless Sensor Networks. In *Proceedings of the International Conference on Information Processing in Sensor Networks*, April 2008.

[6] J. Bruno, J. Brustoloni, E. Gabber, B. Ozden, and A. Silberschatz. Disk Scheduling With Quality Of Service Guarantees. In *Proceedings of the International Conference on Multimedia Computing and Systems*, Florence, Italy, July 1999.

[7] Q. Cao, D. Fesehaye, N. Pham, Y. Sarwar, and T. Abdelzaher. Virtual Battery: An Energy Reserve Abstraction For Embedded Sensor Networks. In *Proceedings of the Real-time Systems Symposium*, San Diego, CA, November 2008.

[8] A. Francoeur. Border Patrol Goes High Tech. photonics.com, August 2009.

[9] P. Goyal, H. Vin, and H. Cheng. Start-time Fair Queueing: A Scheduling Algorithm For Integrated Services Packet Switching Networks. In *Proceedings of SIGCOMM*, Stanford, CA, August 1996.

[10] K. Klues, V. Handziski, C. Lu, A. Wolisz, D. Culler, D. Gay, and Philip Levis Integrating Concurrency Control and Energy Management in Device Drivers. In *Proceedings of the Symposium on Operating Systems Principles*, October 2007.

[11] P. Levis and D. Culler. Maté: A Tiny Virtual Machine For Sensor Networks. In *Proceedings of the International Conference on Architectural Support for Programming Languages and Operating Systems*, October 2002.

[12] S. Iyer and P. Druschel. Anticipatory Scheduling: A Disk Scheduling Framework To Overcome Deceptive Idleness In Synchronous I/O. In *Proceedings of the Symposium on Operating Systems Principles*, Banff, Canada, October 2001.

[13] M. Jones, D. Rosu, and M. Rosu. CPU Reservations And Time Constraints: Efficient, Predictable Scheduling Of Independent Activities. In *Symposium on Operating Systems Principles*, Saint-Malo, France, October 1997.

[14] K. Lorincz, B. Chen, J. Waterman, G. Werner-Allen, and M. Welsh. Resource Aware Programming In The Pixie Operating System. In *Conference on Embedded Networked Sensor Systems*, November 2008.

[15] T. Nelson. The Device Driver As State Machine. *C Users Journal*, 10(3), March 1992.

[16] P. Shenoy and H. Vin. Cello: A Disk Scheduling Framework For Next Generation Operating Systems. In *Proceedings of the International Conference on Measurement and Modeling of Computer Systems*, Madison, WI, June 1998.

[17] S. Magnuson. New Northern Border Camera System To Avoid Past Pitfalls. National Defense Magazine, September 2009.

[18] M.M. Swift, M. Annamalai, B.N. Bershad, and H.M. Levy. Recovering Device Drivers. In *Symposium on Operating System Design and Implementation*, December 2004.

[19] A. Warfield, S. Hand, K. Fraser, and T. Deegan. Facilitating The Development Of Soft Devices. In *USENIX Annual Technical Conference*, Anaheim, CA, April 2005.

[20] M. Zink, E. Lyons, D. Westbrook, J. Kurose, and D. Pepyne. Meteorological Command & Control: Closed-loop Architecture for Distributed Collaborative Adaptive Sensing of the Atmosphere. *International Journal for Sensor Networks*, 7(1).

[21] D. McLaughlin, D. Pepyne, V.Chandrasekar, B. Philips, J. Kurose, M. Zink. Short-Wavelength Technology and the Potential for Distributed Networks of Small Radar Systems. *Bulletin of the American Meteorological Society*, April 2009.

[22] H. Raj, B. Seshasayee and K. Schwan. VMedia: Enhanced Multimedia Services in Virtualized Systems. In *Multimedia Computing and Networks Conference*, San Jose, CA, January 2008.

[23] L. Xia and J. Lange. Towards Virtual Passthrough I/O On Commodity Devices. In *Workshop on I/O Virtualization*, December 2008.

Multimedia-unfriendly TCP Congestion Control and Home Gateway Queue Management

Lawrence Stewart, David A. Hayes,
Grenville Armitage
Centre for Advanced Internet Architectures,
Swinburne University of Technology
Melbourne, Australia
{lastewart, dahayes,
garmitage}@swin.edu.au

Michael Welzl, Andreas Petlund
Department of Informatics,
P.O. Box 1212, University of Oslo
University of Oslo, Norway
{michawe, apetlund}@ifi.uio.no

ABSTRACT

Consumer broadband services are increasingly a mix of TCP-based and UDP-based applications, often with quite distinct requirements for interactivity and network performance. Consumers can experience degraded service when application traffic collides at a congestion point between home LANs, service provider edge networks and fractional-Mbit/sec 'broadband' links. We illustrate two key issues that arise from the impact of TCP-based data transfers on real-time traffic (such as VoIP or online games) sharing a broadband link. First, well-intentioned modifications to traditional TCP congestion control can noticeably increase the latencies experienced by VoIP or online games. Second, superficially-similar packet dropping rules in broadband gateways can induce distinctly different packet loss rates in VoIP and online game traffic. Our observations provide cautionary guidance to researchers who model such traffic mixes, and to vendors implementing equipment at either end of consumer links.

Categories and Subject Descriptors

C.2.0 [**Computer-Communication Networks**]: General—*Data communications*; C.2.5 [**Computer-Communication Networks**]: Local and Wide-Area Networks

General Terms

Algorithms, Experimentation, Performance

Keywords

Broadband, Congestion Control, Queue Management, Real-time Traffic, TCP

1. INTRODUCTION

Most home Internet users connect to their Internet Service Provider (ISP) through asymmetric consumer broadband links. These links experience a mixture of traffic generated by latency-tolerant applications (such as web browsing, streaming multimedia, and peer-to-peer content transfer) and latency-sensitive applications (such as voice over IP (VoIP) and online interactive games). For latency-sensitive applications, transmissions are usually triggered by interactions between users (or users and a system). The result of such interaction patterns is that many streams produced by interactive applications show very small packet sizes and (relatively) high interarrival times between packets. Table 1 shows examples of such thin-stream applications and how their packet size and interarrival times compare.

Greedy traffic sources tend to probe and utilise as much path capacity as they can get away with. Consequently their behaviour "on the wire" can involve wide variations in inter-arrival times, even down to sequences of back to back packets, and packet sizes are often distributed bi-modally between pathMTU and smallest IP packet size.

Loss of packets will in many cases reduce the experience of the interactive application e.g. introduce noise into a VoIP conversation [1]. In other applications, like online games, congestion-induced latency can delay response time for the game enough to significantly reduce game performance[1].

Many consumer modems provide minimal configuration controls for upstream quality of service (QoS) at the home end, and non-existent end-user control of QoS in the downstream (as the bottleneck queuing occurs in the service provider's equipment, such as a Digital Subscriber Line Access Multiplexer, DSLAM).

Latency-tolerant applications often utilise the Transmission Control Protocol (TCP) to provide a reliable end-to-end data transport that adapts to available network capacity between sender and receiver [3]. TCP's congestion control (CC) algorithms have evolved over time, usually to provide improved performance in terms of usable throughput (or goodput) for high speed network connections; one notable example of a new, experimental TCP variant is CUBIC [4], which is the default mechanism in Linux at the time of writing.

---

[1]Latencies of 100 ms, 500 ms and 1000 ms are enough to degrade the experience for first person shooters, massively multiplayer online games and real-time strategy games, respectively [2].

Application	Payload size (bytes)			Interarrival time (ms)						Average bandwidth	
	avg	min	max	avg	med	min	max	1%	99%	(pps)	(bps)
Windows remote desktop	111	8	1417	318	159	1	12254	2	3892	3.145	4497
VNC (from client)	8	1	106	34	8	< 1	5451	< 1	517	29.412	17K
G.711 RTP VoIP	180	180	180	20	20	19	21	19	21	50	64K
Skype (2 users) (UDP)	111	11	316	30	24	< 1	20015	18	44	33.333	37K
Skype (2 users) (TCP)	236	14	1267	34	40	< 1	1671	4	80	29.412	69K
World of Warcraft	26	6	1228	314	133	< 1	14855	< 1	3785	3.185	2046
Quake 3 (from server)	80	40	300	50	50	30	70	35	65	20	25K

Table 1: Examples of thin stream traffic characteristics from time-dependent applications. All traces are one-way (no ACKs are recorded) packet traffic.

What all currently deployed TCP CC algorithms have in common is that they cause a cyclical filling and draining of the queues at the path's bottleneck link. This in turn induces fluctuating latency and periodic packet loss to all traffic sharing the link.

Consumers with fractional- and multiple-Mbps "broadband" links to the Internet often find their home broadband connection is the bottleneck link for individual communication sessions (for example, the data rates of ADSL 1 or ADSL 2 are dwarfed by today's 100 Mbps and 1 Gbps home LANs and service providers' edge network speeds). It would then seem natural to give users full control over what happens on their home connection — but in reality, such control is quite limited, and where it is available, there is a lack of guidance. By showing the impact of a normally "invisible" parameter (a detail in the drop behavior of the simple, and most commonly used, FIFO queue), and comparing the likely collateral damage caused by NewReno [5] and CUBIC on interactive real-time traffic like VoIP, we intend to fill this gap. Our observations also provide cautionary guidance to researchers who model such traffic mixes, and to vendors implementing equipment at either end of consumer links.

Section 2 introduces the relevant parts of TCP behavior, and lists three superficially-similar packet dropping rules that may be encountered in live and testbed networks. Our technique for simulating and experimentally verifying some typical home broadband scenarios is described in Section 3. Section 4 presents the impact on latency of choosing CUBIC versus NewReno, and the dramatic impact on packet loss rates caused by particular definitions of 'queue full' events. Our paper concludes with Section 5.

2. BACKGROUND

In this section we review TCP congestion control, the types of packet drop rules one might encounter, and the importance of testing the collateral impact of TCP flows on latency-sensitive non-TCP flows.

2.1 TCP Congestion Control

The Internet's IP-based network and underlying infrastructure has grown beyond initial architectural design assumptions and expectations in a number of areas. Since TCP congestion control (CC) was first proposed [6] and subsequently mandated [7], there has been significant ongoing research to ensure CC addressed these changes, efficiently utilising the available capacity and protecting the network from congestion collapse.

TCP dynamically adjusts its transmission speed to balance multiple competing goals – maximise the use of available network capacity, share network capacity with other users, and do not overrun the receiver with packets. A TCP sender constrains the number of unacknowledged packets in flight to the smaller of the receiver's advertised window ($rwnd$) and the congestion window ($cwnd$). TCP receivers keep senders informed of rwnd by placing a copy in each TCP ACK (acknowledgment) packet. Assuming the receiver's buffer is large enough, the TCP flow control window is usually constrained by cwnd.

Typically cwnd will start at a small value and grow incrementally (*additive increase*) as packets are successfully acknowledged, effectively increasing the sender's transmission rate over time. This will also tend to increase the number of packets buffered in any bottleneck queue between sender and receiver. When a packet is detected as lost, the sender responds by reducing cwnd to some fraction of its previous value (*multiplicative decrease*) before restarting the growth cycle. TCP presumes that packet loss means a queue overflowed somewhere between sender and receiver. Dropping cwnd causes a reduction in the sender's average transmission rate, protecting the network from congestion collapse (and allowing packets belonging to other flows to utilise the bottleneck link).

Most TCP CC schemes differ in their specific algorithms for *additive increase multiplicative decrease* (AIMD) control of cwnd and their detection of congestion. Traditional NewReno flows have trouble with wireless links (where packet losses are frequently unrelated to congestion) and paths with large bandwidth-delay product (BDP) (it can take multiple minutes to re-probe network capacity after a single packet loss [8]).

Using a simulated ADSL 1 link with a 20 000 byte bottleneck queue and 100ms baseline round trip time (RTT), Figure 1 illustrates how a single downstream flow's cwnd fluctuation over time is cyclical and yet can be quite different depending on one's choice of CC algorithm.

Figure 1(a) and 1(b) show a ten second sample of cwnd and induced queuing delay associated with a single NewReno and CUBIC flow respectively.

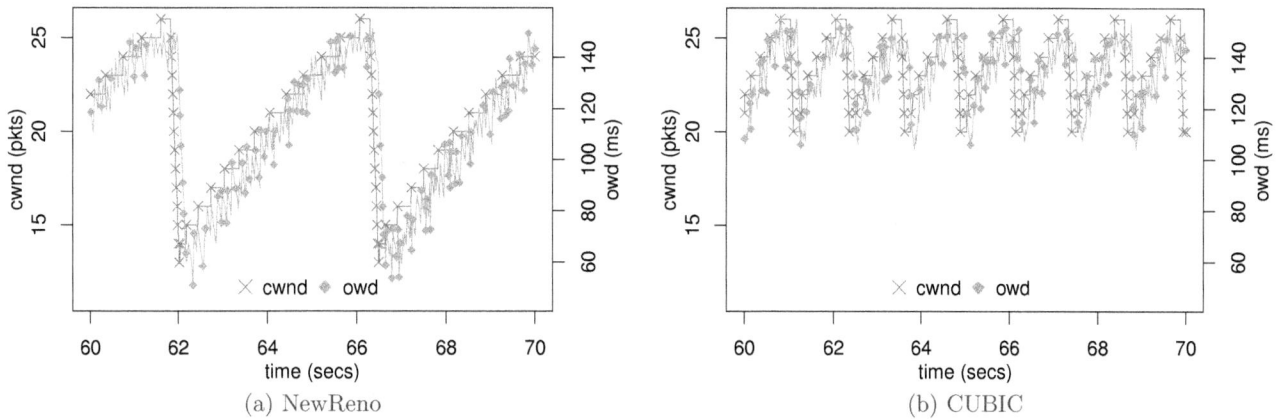

Figure 1: TCP congestion window oscillation coupled with the induced queueing delay. ADSL1 type link: 1.5 Mbps/256 kbps, with a minimum 100ms RTT and 20 000 byte queue.

The one way delay (OWD) experienced by a constant bit rate VoIP-like traffic source sharing the bottleneck link is intuitively proportional to and driven by the fluctuation of cwnd.

CUBIC's aggressiveness compared to NewReno is clearly visible, both in terms of growing cwnd at a faster rate and backing off less on congestion. The lower-bound base OWD of 50ms (100ms path RTT divided by two) grows by up to 107ms to a maximum of 157ms when the queue is full. By backing off less on congestion, CUBIC does not give the queue time to drain as much as with NewReno, and therefore the queuing delay is consistently higher. Regardless of the TCP algorithm, a real VoIP session sharing this link with a TCP session would clearly experience substantial fluctuations of OWD above the path's 50ms minimum.

2.2 Choosing when to drop packets

Buffering at bottleneck links is often implemented (and modeled in research papers) as a first-in first-out (FIFO) drop-tail queue – a newly arrived packet is dropped rather than queued if it arrives when the queue is full. Although the notion of 'being full' might seem obvious, we identify three superficially-similar ways to define when a queue is full:

- **PS**: The queue is *packet* (*slot*) based, and the maximum queue length is specified as an integer number of packets:
  ```
  if (NumPktsInQ ≥ PktQueueLength)
    drop incoming packet
  ```

- **FB-strict**: A *fixed* length *byte*-based queue where the current queue length + new packet length must not exceed a specified number of bytes:
  ```
  if ((NumBytesInQ + InPktLength)
                  > ByteQueueLength)
    drop incoming packet
  ```

- **FB-loose**: A *fixed* length *byte*-based queue where the current queue length must not exceed a fixed number of bytes before adding the new packet:
  ```
  if (NumBytesInQ > ByteQueueLength)
    drop incoming packet
  ```

Network devices, simulators and emulators may implement one or more of the preceding packet drop rules, without necessarily making the actual rule clear to their users. For example, FreeBSD's *dummynet* [9] (a tool used by many researchers to emulate various network conditions in small testbeds[2]) uses PS by default but silently switches to FB-loose if the queue size is configured in bytes. Commercial equipment and network simulators (such as ns-2 [10]) often implement PS or FB-strict.

Our experiments reveal that one's choice of PS, FB-strict or FB-loose packet drop rule can have significantly different impacts on what we predict or expect to see when TCP and non-reactive flows share a bottleneck.

2.3 Interactions between application flows

Community evaluation of new TCP CC schemes has tended to focus on aspects such as intra-protocol fairness, inter-protocol fairness with NewReno, maximising throughput and speeding convergence to a fair transmission rate [11]. Although broad consensus has yet to be reached, NewReno has already been replaced by CUBIC as the default CC algorithm in recent releases of Linux, and Microsoft is migrating to the use of *CompoundTCP* [12].

However, most consumers will experience a mixture of entertainment, information access and communication services over a single (often asymmetric) broadband IP service to their homes. To date, we have found very little prior work [13, 14, 15] investigating home broadband scenarios and the behaviour of emerging TCPs, or TCPs interacting with non-congestion reactive, latency-sensitive traffic in this environment. The continuing convergence towards IP based entertainment, information access and communication service delivery ensures this is an area of increasing importance. Consequently it is crucial to properly model and understand the likely behavior of different TCP CC schemes when interacting with non-congestion reactive, latency-sensitive traffic in such a consumer environment.

Online multiplayer games and VoIP are two examples of latency-sensitive consumer applications that do not typically react to congestion in the network. Online multiplayer com-

---

[2]http://citeseerx.ist.psu.edu/ lists 311 citations (accessed 13 April 2010) of [9] for dummynet

puter games, and the popular first person shooter genre in particular, have well known latency sensitivity requirements for effective game play [16]. Voice telephony is another real-time service with well characterised latency tolerances (see [17, 18]). Markopoulou et al. [19] look at these performance issues over IP backbone. Such applications typically generate relatively constant streams of UDP packets in the 80 to 300+ byte range (small in comparison to typical TCP data packets).

In the rest of this paper we explore how such applications are likely to be impacted by sharing a home broadband link with NewReno and CUBIC TCP flows. In particular we focus on the case where TCP-based content is being delivered into a home, cyclically congesting the downstream link shared with a VoIP-like flow.

3. EVALUATION METHODOLOGY

Our evaluation follows on from our previous work in [15] by exploring a significantly wider range of more realistic scenarios including asymmetric bandwidth and variable queue size. We utilise both an experimental testbed (Figure 2) and ns-2 [10] simulating the same network topology. The testbed's FreeBSD router uses dummynet [9] to emulate the bottleneck drop-tail queues and RTT/2 of delay in each direction[3]. Hosts A (TCP sender) and C (TCP receiver) run Debian Linux[4]. The other communicating endpoints (hosts B and D) run FreeBSD 7.0.

While not topologically equivalent to real network paths, our simple *dumbbell* testbed focuses on emulating a consumer's asymmetric ADSL-style bottleneck link combined with realistic end-to-end RTT characteristics.

For clarity we evaluated the interaction between a single downstream TCP flow and a bi-directional non-reactive constant bit rate (CBR) flow under the following scenarios:

- Typical consumer ADSL 1 and high-end ADSL 2 speeds of 1500/256 kbps and 24/1 Mbps respectively.

- Byte-based queues of length 10 000, 20 000, 40 000, 60 000, and 100 000 bytes[5]

- Slot-based queues of length 7, 14, 20, 27, 34, 40, 47, 54, 60 and 67 slots

- Round trip time (RTT) delays of 24, 50, 100, and 200 ms.

- PS and FB-loose packet dropping in the testbed

- PS, FB-strict and FB-loose in ns-2[6].

---

[3]Configured latency is accurate to within 0.5ms as the router's kernel was set to tick at 2000Hz ($kern.hz = 2000$). FreeBSD 7.0-RC1 on a 2.80 GHz Intel Celeron D (256K L2 Cache), 512 MB PC3200 DDR-400 RAM, with two Intel PRO/1000 GT 82541PI PCI gigabit Ethernet cards as forwarding interfaces

[4]A 2.6.25 kernel ticking at 1000 Hz, each one a 1.86 GHz Intel Core2 Duo E6320 (4 MB L2 Cache) CPU, 1 GB PC5300 DDR2 RAM and Intel PRO/1000 GT 82541PI PCI gigabit Ethernet NIC. Load-time tunable variables of the Linux CUBIC implementation were left at their default values.

[5]Sizes are based on previously published estimations of buffering in consumer routers [20, 21]

[6]ns-2, version 2.33 had to be modified slightly to ensure the FB-strict implementation properly accounted for the length of the packet in the front of the queue.

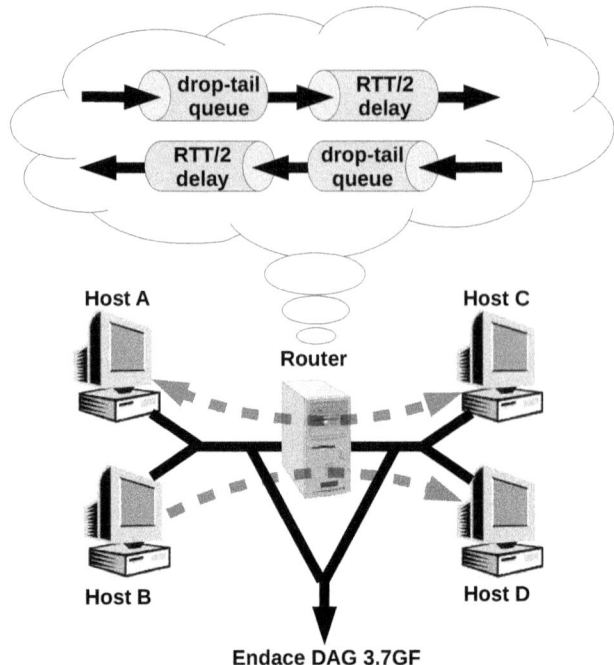

Figure 2: Testbed for investigation of TCP interaction with non-reactive CBR traffic

For PS packet dropping the slot-based queue limit was calculated as the number of 1500 byte packets that fit into the equivalent byte-based queue lengths, rounded up to the nearest slot.

3.1 Testbed traffic generation

Bulk TCP traffic was generated using Iperf [22], with data flowing from Host A to C and ACKs from Host C to A. Non-reactive CBR UDP traffic was emulated using tcpreplay[23] to send two uni-directional streams of 186 byte UDP packets from Hosts B to D and D to B. The UDP packets are sent on average every 20 ms, with a normally distributed jitter with a standard deviation of 1 ms.

3.2 Measurements

Trials were run five times for each combination of TCP algorithm, ADSL speed, queue size, and RTT. Trials lasted for at least five minutes. Where applicable, graphs plot the median with error bars spanning the range of results from the repeated trials.

We used Web100 [24] on testbed Hosts A and C to enable polling of *cwnd* every 1ms over the lifetime of each TCP session. Two Endace DAG 3.7GF gigabit Ethernet capture ports were used for precision traffic capture to calculate delays through the router.

4. RESULTS

For home users, TCP performance is not substantially impacted by the choice of NewReno or CUBIC. However, CUBIC induces noticably higher additional latency than NewReno, and the FB-loose packet drop scheme creates much higher packet losses than PS or FB-strict.

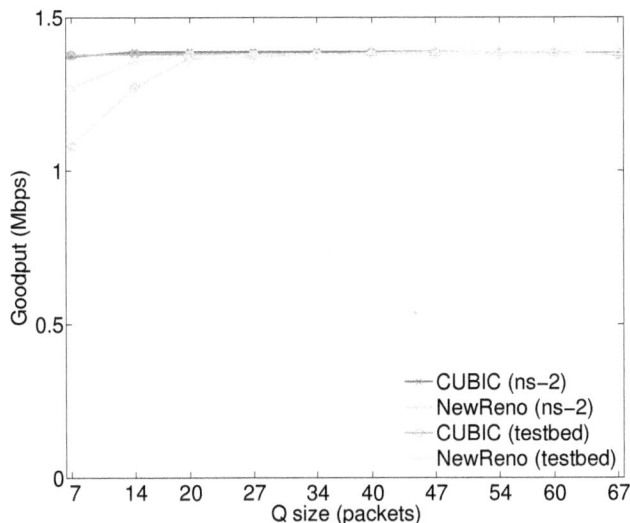

(a) ADSL1 TCP Goodput – 1.5 Mbps/256 kbps

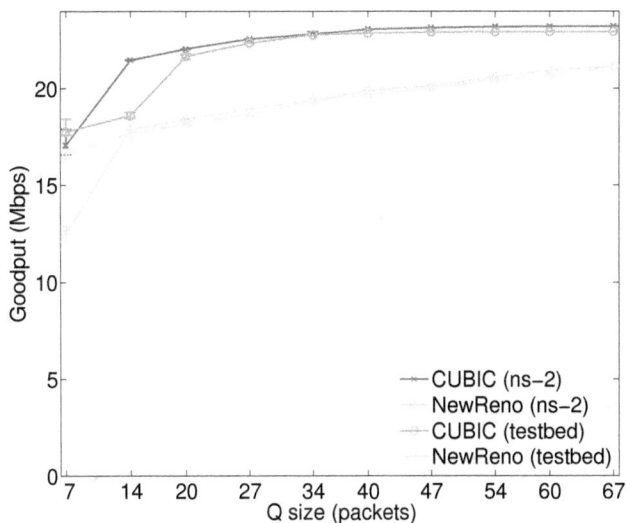

(b) ADSL2 TCP Goodput – 24 Mbps/1 Mbps

Figure 3: Downstream TCP goodput vs PS queue length – measured (testbed) and simulated (ns-2) for a 1.5 Mbps/256 kbps link and 24/1 Mbps link, 100 ms minimum RTT.

4.1 TCP Goodput

A useful indication of TCP performance is *goodput* – the usable throughput experienced by an application (i.e. not counting retransmitted packets). As noted in Figure 1, cwnd cycles as TCP probes for available capacity and regularly hits a bottleneck queue's limit. Larger queues lead to more time with larger cwnd, and hence higher goodput.

Figure 3(a) shows TCP goodput for various bottleneck queue sizes (in units of 1500 byte packets) for a 1.5Mbps/256kbps link and 100ms base RTT. CUBIC was able to fully utilise the bandwidth with the smallest tested queue size of 7 packets, while NewReno required 20 packets.

Figure 3(b) shows goodput for a 24/1 Mbps link and 100ms base RTT. CUBIC and NewReno both fail to fully utilise the bandwidth at queue sizes below 40 packets. NewReno was unable to drive the link at full capacity even with the largest queue size we tested with. It follows in the subsequent sections that the marginally better goodput achieved by CUBIC comes at a price. In our view, that cost outweighs the benefit in a home environment, where absolute performance is less important than the full range of services in use working adequately "out of the box" without specialised configuration.

The testbed and ns-2 simulations compare well, except when the buffer size is very small. Small buffer sizes tend to magnify the discrepancies between the ns-2 model and the real Linux TCP stack, with the cwnd increase and backoff oscillations occuring more rapidly on the testbed (see section 4.2.1 for more discussion).

4.2 CBR packet loss: results of trial runs

The proportion of CBR packets lost due to bottleneck queue congestion is very sensitive to the choice of queue full packet drop mechanism (Section 2.2). Figure 4(a) shows the proportion of CBR packets lost on the downstream of a 1500/256 kbps bottleneck link, assuming the TCP flow experiences a minimum RTT of 100ms.

4.2.1 FB-loose

FB-loose allows overfilling by at most one packet. Since TCP data packets are typically much larger than a VoIP packet and arrive at the queue more frequently, the TCP data packet is more likely to overfill the queue (and when this happens the queue remains full for longer). Figure 4(a) illustrates that FB-loose consequently introduces much higher CBR loss rate than PS or FB-strict.

Figure 4(b) shows that our NewReno simulation and testbed results are very close, although the simulation results tend to underestimate real CBR packet loss for CUBIC. (Wei and Cao [25] find that the ns-2 CUBIC cwnd oscillation and congestion epochs differ in their own Linux/dummynet testbed trials. The ns-2 CUBIC model has less congestion epochs than the real Linux implementation, resulting in a smaller number of CBR packets being lost.)

Although the general CBR loss rate trends down as the queue size increases, it also depends on how the actual packet sizes fit into the queue. Both the testbed and ns-2 simulations highlight this especially for CUBIC in Figure 4(b) for queue sizes which are multiples of TCP's 1500 byte packets.

There is a stark difference in the proportion of CBR packets lost between FB-loose and FB-strict (explained in section 4.3). This should be of interest to researchers using dummynet to emulate typical in-network queues, as dummynet's use of FB-loose may not be representative of FB-strict implementations in deployed equipment.

4.2.2 FB-strict

When a FB-strict queue approaches full there can be room at the end for one or more of our 186 byte CBR packets even when there is no room for a 1500 byte TCP data packet. This leads to a bias toward accepting smaller packets when the link's capacity is primarily being consumed by large TCP packets.

As shown in Figure 4(a), FB-strict saw almost 0 % loss of CBR packets. ISPs who configure their down link queues to be byte based with the FB-strict drop policy can expect

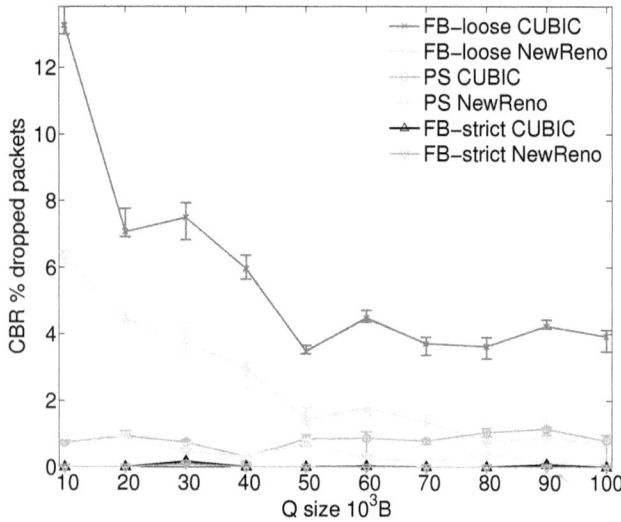

(a) CBR packet loss for FB-loose, PS and FB-strict packet drop schemes (simulated with ns-2)

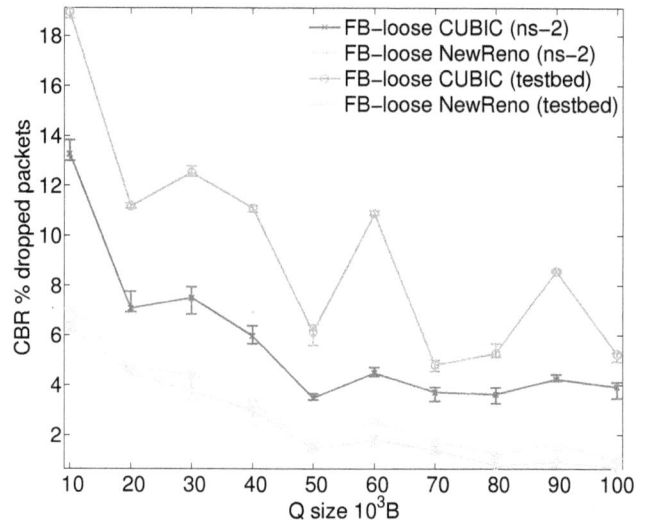

(b) Comparison of CBR packet loss for FB-loose – measured (testbed) and simulated (ns-2).

Figure 4: Proportion of CBR packets lost on the downstream for different packet drop mechanisms – 1500/256 kbps link, 100ms minimum RTT.

to provide their customers with better VoIP or online game play experience in terms of minimising packet loss.

4.2.3 PS

PS treats all packets equally, regardless of size, resulting in a moderate CBR packet loss. This queue drop mechanism also provides a degree of robustness to the overall fairness between reactive and non-reactive flows when the non-reactive flows have much smaller packets than the reactive flows (though this may well be a non-goal).

4.2.4 ADSL2

Our equivalents of Figures 4(a) and 4(b) using a 24/1 Mbps link revealed that relative CBR loss rates were similarly impacted by the choice of FB-loose, PS or FB-strict packet drop scheme. However, we have not included a graph as the absolute CBR loss rates were exceedingly low (about 1 % and 0.4 % for CUBIC and NewReno respectively with FB-loose) and relatively insensitive to queue size.

4.2.5 CUBIC's Fast Convergence Heuristic

During TCP's congestion avoidance phase, CUBIC uses its *fast convergence* heuristic to detect competition for bottleneck resources and more aggressively backoff to allow new flows to gain their share of the available bandwidth [4]. When a congestion event occurs, the heuristic compares the value of cwnd from the previous congestion event against the current cwnd and backs off more aggressively if the current cwnd is smaller. The reasoning for this behaviour is that if a new flow begins competing for buffer space, the buffer will fill sooner and our flow's cwnd will not have grown as much when the next congestion event occurs.

We frequently observed single flow CUBIC trials operating in either *fast convergence* or regular congestion avoidance mode exclusively. All other parameters being the same, operating exclusively in the *fast convergence* mode results in fewer congestion epochs compared to operating exclusively in regular congestion avoidance mode. Figure 5 shows

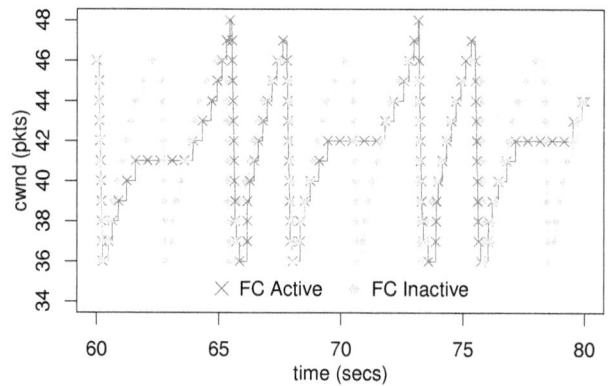

Figure 5: Comparison of CUBIC flows from separate but identical trials showing the effect of the fast convergence heuristic – single CUBIC TCP vs single CBR flow, 50ms RTT, 1.5Mbps/256kbps link, 60000 byte queue.

the phenomenon using representative twenty second samples from two otherwise identical, three minute long trials. The "FC Active" flow became synchronised with the CBR flow after the first congestion event in such a way that it continually triggered the fast convergence heuristic. In contrast, the "FC Inactive" flow reached the same cwnd value every congestion event and never triggered the heuristic.

Fewer congestion epochs induces lower CBR loss rates, making comparison of data between such tests misleading. By jittering the interarrival times of the CBR UDP packets using a normal distribution (mean: 20ms, stddev: 1ms), we reduced the probability of the phenomenon occurring to the point where we did not observe it in any of our subsequent tests.

It is unlikely that this phenomenon would be induced by flows interacting in the wider Internet where jitter is natu-

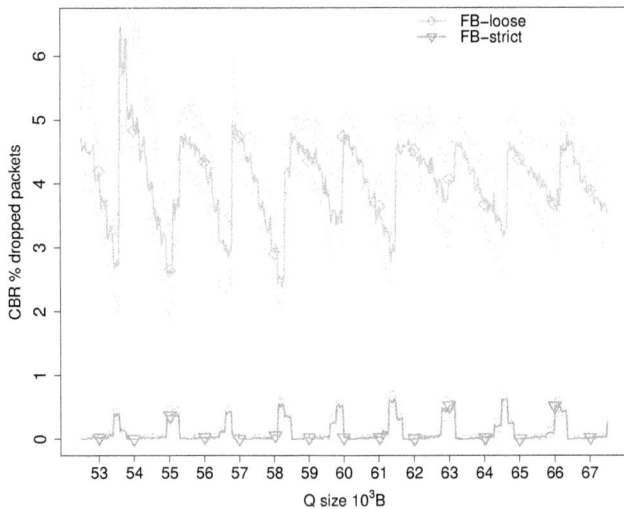

(a) CBR packet loss for FB-loose and FB-strict queues. TCP stream uses CUBIC CC.

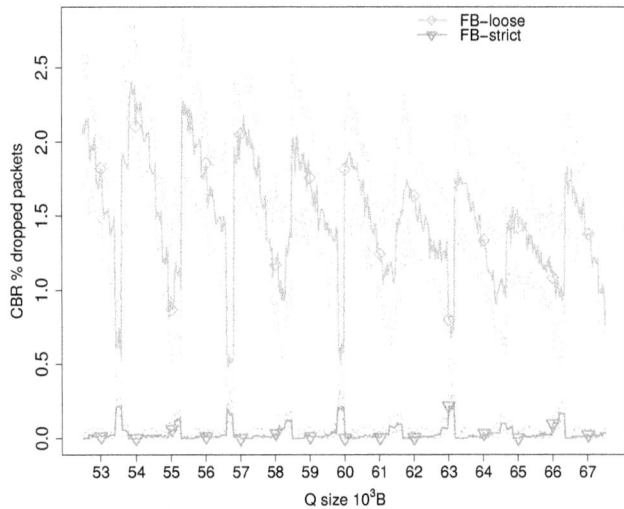

(b) CBR packet loss for FB-loose and FB-strict queues. TCP stream uses NewReno CC.

Figure 6: More detailed simulation based on Figure 4, with queue sizes ranging from 52500 bytes to 67500 bytes – 1500/256 kbps link, 100ms minimum RTT, 30 byte queue increments. The dashed line envelope represents the 5% and 95% confidence intervals for the plot data.

rally added by shared networking devices along a path. However, the potential for it to occur in home networks where there is often very little cross-traffic and small numbers of TCP flows sharing a bottleneck link requires further investigation.

4.3 CBR packet loss: analysis

The significant difference in loss between the PS queue and either of the byte-based queues in the previous section is to be expected because of the difference in TCP and CBR packet sizes. What is surprising is the large difference in loss produced by the two different byte based queue drop rules and counter-intuitive relationship between loss rate and queue size (the peaks around queue sizes 30, 60 and 90 kbyte in Figure 4(b)).

When a queue is close to full, a 1500 byte TCP packet will have a significantly smaller chance to fit in than a 186 byte CBR packet. CBR packets arrive at the queue relatively infrequently (based on the VoIP encoding clock), while the TCP packets dominate the queue at times of congestion because of TCP's bandwidth probing behaviour. For the following discussion, we therefore assume that there are only TCP packets and no CBR packets in the queue (the existence of CBR packets in the queue, the probability of which depends on the queue length, would modulate the numbers discussed below but leave the described effect intact).

In an almost full FB-strict queue, TCP packets will be dropped most of the time, while there will usually be room for a CBR packet, e.g. a queue of size $(n \times 1500 + 1499)$ bytes would always leave room for $int(1499/186) = 8$ CBR packets, irrespective of the value of n and the amount of greedy traffic which arrives. This behaviour makes the FB-strict queue friendlier towards the CBR traffic in most configurations of queue size. Based on the dynamics and parameters of a particular test, we expect there to be a range of queue sizes that, when unable to accept additional TCP packets, will also have insufficient room to accommodate any extra CBR packets. We would expect the range to be about 186

bytes (size of a CBR packet) and expect a queue of such size to induce higher CBR losses than usual.

In an almost full FB-loose queue, the ability to overfill the queue shifts the friendliness of the scheme towards the TCP sender. Since TCP packets flow at a much faster rate than CBR packets, the chance that a TCP packet will overfill the queue is greater. The increased probability of a large TCP packet overfilling the queue results in higher CBR loss waiting for the queue to drain. By allowing the queue to overflow by an entire packet, the behaviour of an FB-loose queue is very dependent on the exact contents of the queue and timing between flows. The interaction of CBR and TCP interarrival times with the path RTT determines if the queue overflows by a small or large amount.

We performed an additional set of simulations to explore these queue effects more closely. Thirty, 180 second trials were run for each permutation of TCP (CUBIC and NewReno), FB queue-drop type (FB-loose and FB-strict) and queue size (52500 to 67500 bytes in 30 byte increments).

Figure 6 plots the results, with each point on each line representing the median of all thirty trials for that permutation. The 5% and 95% confidence intervals are given by the dashed line envelope around the median value plot. Figure 6 is effectively zooming in on Figure 4(a) and providing more visibility between the coarsely-grained data points.

Starting with the FB-strict plot, the periodic peaks correspond with queue sizes in the 186 byte "sweet spot" that cause significantly increased CBR loss. For this set of trial parameters, the peaks occur at queue sizes just below an integer multiple of 1500 byte packets (e.g. 57000, 58500, 60000 bytes).

In contrast, the FB-loose plot's minima are complex and not amenable to being described by a simple mathematical model. Under the conditions shown in Figure 6, the queue overfills by a large (1500 bytes worst case) amount at queue sizes slightly larger than an integer multiple of the TCP packet size. This observation directly relates to the CBR vs TCP occupancy of the queue at the time of congestion.

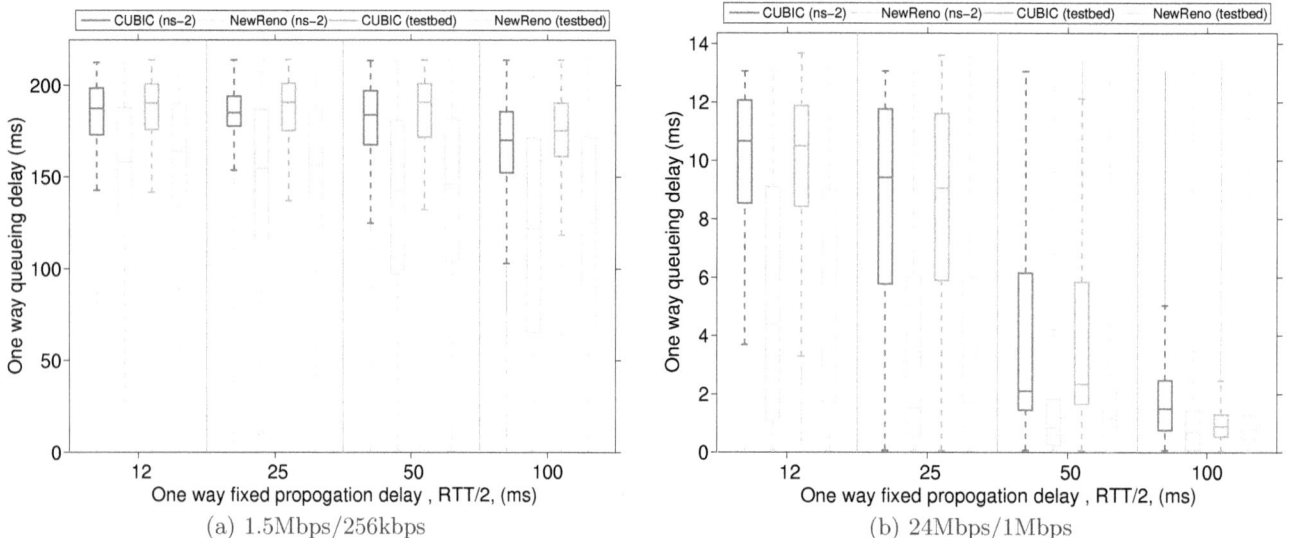

Figure 7: Additional downstream CBR queuing delay experienced on a link shared with a CUBIC or NewReno TCP flow – measured (testbed) and simulated (ns-2), 40 000 byte FB-loose queue.

Changing the RTT or intearrival times would shift the plot along the x-axis, changing the locations of the loss minima.

The behaviour demonstrated in Figure 6 clearly accounts for the counter-intuitive FB-loose CBR loss figures seen in Figure 4.

4.4 CBR latency

The latency experienced by CBR packets is important for real-time applications such as VoIP and online games. Figure 7 uses box-and-whisker plots to summarise the additional queuing delay experienced by CBR packets on the downstream (total one way delay is queuing delay plus RTT/2). Box-and-whisker plots are shown for CUBIC and NewReno (ns-2 simulation and testbed) for each minimum RTT/2 (minimum one way delay) used in the experiments, with a queue size of 40×10^3 bytes.

The spread of delays experienced by CBR packets is driven by the TCP CC sawtooth, which in turn depends on the RTT – how fast it can probe, and how long it takes for TCP to react to congestion. As the propagation delay increases, TCP's probing and response to congestion becomes slower, and the variation in delay increases. Notice that CUBIC's aggressive congestion control ensures that the bottleneck queue stays fuller, resulting in a higher median latency and tighter variance than NewReno.

At 24/1 Mbps link speed the total additional latency is lower, but CUBIC still induces noticeably higher latency than NewReno. The maximum additional queuing delay is about 13 ms. Median delay introduced by CUBIC and NewReno is about 11 ms and 5 ms respectively when RTT/2 is 12 ms, and 9 ms and 1 ms respectively when RTT/2 is 25 ms. (As RTT increases further neither CUBIC nor NewReno could saturate the link, resulting in median additional delays under 2 ms for both.)

5. CONCLUSION

We have specifically considered the impact of reactive TCP-based data transfers on non-reactive real-time traffic (such as VoIP) sharing the downstream of an asymmetric consumer broadband link. Modifications to the traditional NewReno TCP congestion control algorithm to better utilise high bandwidth links can noticeably increase the typical latencies experienced by other traffic (particularly at common ADSL 1 link speeds). Second, superficially-similar packet dropping rules on the consumer and ISP sides of a home Internet connection can induce distinctly different packet loss rates in non-reactive real-time type traffic. These increases in loss and latency significantly degrade the quality of service of non-reactive real-time services.

Our observations suggest that a less aggressive form of TCP, such as NewReno, may be a better choice for delivering content toward consumers than CUBIC if one wishes to minimise additional latency induced by TCP traffic. We also observe that both researchers and implementors must pay close attention to how their simulation of a network device defines a queue being 'full'. In particular, fixed byte-length queues that allow themselves to overfill by 'one more packet' can induce substantially higher packet loss rates than queues bounded (regardless of packet lengths) by strict byte lengths or integer numbers of packets. Finally, we believe our observations may be applied to selection of packet drop mechanisms on both the upstream and downstream sides of consumer broadband modems.

Acknowledgment

This work has been made possible in part by a grant from the Cisco University Research Program Fund at Community Foundation Silicon Valley.

6. REFERENCES

[1] A. Petlund, K. Evensen, C. Griwodz, and P. Halvorsen, "Tcp mechanisms for improving the user experience for time-dependent thin-stream applications," in *33rd IEEE Conference on Local Computer Networks, 2008.*, oct. 2008, pp. 176 –183.

[2] G. Armitage, M. Claypool, and P. Branch, *"Networking and Online Games - Understanding and Engineering Multiplayer Internet Games"*. UK: John Wiley & Sons, April 2006.

[3] M. Allman, V. Paxson, and W. Stevens, "TCP Congestion Control ," RFC 2581 (Proposed Standard), Apr. 1999, updated by RFC 3390. [Online]. Available: http://www.ietf.org/rfc/rfc2581.txt

[4] L. X. I. Rhee and S. Ha, "CUBIC for fast long-distance networks," North Carolina State University, Tech. Rep., Aug. 2008. [Online]. Available: http://tools.ietf.org/id/draft-rhee-tcpm-cubic-02.txt

[5] S. Floyd, T. Henderson, and A. Gurtov, "The NewReno Modification to TCP's Fast Recovery Algorithm," RFC 3782 (Proposed Standard), Apr. 2004. [Online]. Available: http://www.ietf.org/rfc/rfc3782.txt

[6] V. Jacobson, "Congestion avoidance and control," in *SIGCOMM '88: Symposium proceedings on Communications architectures and protocols*. New York, NY, USA: ACM, 1988, pp. 314–329.

[7] R. Braden, "Requirements for Internet Hosts - Communication Layers," RFC 1122 (Standard), Oct. 1989, updated by RFC 1349. [Online]. Available: http://www.ietf.org/rfc/rfc1122.txt

[8] S. Floyd, "HighSpeed TCP for Large Congestion Windows," RFC 3649 (Experimental), Dec. 2003. [Online]. Available: http://www.ietf.org/rfc/rfc3649.txt

[9] L. Rizzo, "Dummynet: a simple approach to the evaluation of network protocols," *ACM SIGCOMM Computer Communication Review*, vol. 27, no. 1, pp. 31–41, 1997.

[10] "The network simulator - ns-2," accessed 19 Nov 2007. [Online]. Available: http://www.isi.edu/nsnam/ns/

[11] L. Andrew, C. Marcondes, S. Floyd, L. Dunn, R. Guillier, W. Gang, L. Eggert, S. Ha, and I. Rhee, "Towards a common TCP evauation suite," in *Sixth International Workshop on Protocols for Fast Long-Distance Networks*, Manchester, GB, Mar. 2008.

[12] D. B. M. Sridharan, K. Tan and D. Thaler, "Compound TCP: A new TCP congestion control for high-speed and long distance networks," Microsoft, Tech. Rep., Nov. 2008. [Online]. Available: http://www.ietf.org/internet-drafts/draft-sridharan-tcpm-ctcp-02.txt

[13] L. Andrew, I. Atov, D. Kennedy, and B. Wydrowski, "Evaluation of FAST TCP on low-speed DOCSIS-based access networks," in *IEEE TENCON 05*, Melbourne, Australia, Nov. 2005.

[14] G. Armitage, L. Stewart, M. Welzl, and J. Healy, "An independent H-TCP implementation under FreeBSD 7.0: Description and observed behaviour," *SIGCOMM Comput. Commun. Rev.*, vol. 38, no. 3, pp. 27–38, 2008.

[15] L. Stewart, G. Armitage, and A. Huebner, "Collateral damage: The impact of optimised TCP variants on real-time traffic latency in consumer broadband environments," in *Proceedings of IFIP/TC6 NETWORKING 2009*, Aachen, Germany, May 2009.

[16] G. Armitage, "An Experimental Estimation of Latency Sensitivity in Multiplayer Quake 3," in *11th IEEE International Conference on Networks (ICON 2003)*, Sydney, Australia, Sep. 2003, pp. 137–141.

[17] G. K. Helder, "Customer evaluation of telephone circuits with transmission delay," *Bell System Technical Journal*, vol. 45, pp. 1157–1191, Sep. 1966.

[18] N. Kitawaki and K. Itoh, "Pure delay effects on speech quality in telecommunications," *Selected Areas in Communications, IEEE Journal on*, vol. 9, no. 4, pp. 586–593, May 1991.

[19] A. Markopoulou, F. Tobagi, and M. Karam, "Assessing the quality of voice communications over internet backbones," *Networking, IEEE/ACM Transactions on*, vol. 11, no. 5, pp. 747–760, Oct. 2003.

[20] M. Claypool, R. Kinicki, M. Li, J. Nichols, and H. Wu, "Inferring queue sizes in access networks by active measurement," in *Passive and Active Measurement Workshop*, Antibes Juan-les-Pins, France, Apr. 2004. [Online]. Available: http://www.pamconf.org/2004/papers/209.pdf

[21] M. Dischinger, A. Haeberlen, K. P. Gummadi, and S. Saroiu, "Characterizing residential broadband networks," in *IMC '07: Proceedings of the 7th ACM SIGCOMM conference on Internet measurement*. New York, NY, USA: ACM, 2007, pp. 43–56.

[22] "Iperf - the TCP/UDP bandwidth measurement tool," May 2005, accessed 19 Nov 2007. [Online]. Available: http://dast.nlanr.net/Projects/Iperf/

[23] A. Turner, "Tcpreplay," accessed 4 Dec 2008. [Online]. Available: http://tcpreplay.synfin.net/

[24] M. Mathis, J. Heffner, and R. Reddy, "Web100: extended TCP instrumentation for research, education and diagnosis," *SIGCOMM Comput. Commun. Rev.*, vol. 33, no. 3, pp. 69–79, 2003.

[25] D. X. Wei and P. Cao, "Ns-2 tcp-linux: an ns-2 tcp implementation with congestion control algorithms from linux," in *WNS2 '06: Proceeding from the 2006 workshop on ns-2: the IP network simulator*. New York, NY, USA: ACM Press, 2006, p. 9.

Effects of Internet Path Selection on Video-QoE

Mukundan Venkataraman and Mainak Chatterjee
School of EECS
University of Central Florida
Orlando, FL, 32826
{mukundan, mainak}@eecs.ucf.edu

ABSTRACT

This paper presents large scale Internet measurements to understand and improve the effects of Internet path selection on perceived video quality. We systematically study a large number of Internet paths between popular video destinations and clients to create an empirical understanding of location, persistence and recurrence of failures. We map these failures to perceptual quality by reconstructing video clips obtained from the trace to quantify both the perceptual degradations from these failures as well as the fraction of such failures that can be recovered.

We then investigate ways to recover from QoE degradation by choosing one-hop detour paths that preserve application specific policies. We seek simple, scalable path selection strategies *without* the need for background path monitoring or apriori path knowledge of any kind. To do this, we deployed five measurement overlays: one each in the US, Europe, Asia-Pacific, and two spread across the globe. We used these to stream IP-traces of a variety of clips between source-destination pairs while probing alternate paths for an entire week. Our results indicate that a source can recover from upto 90% of the degradations by attempting to restore QoE with any five *randomly* chosen nodes in an overlay. We argue that our results are robust across datasets.

Finally, we design and implement a prototype packet forwarding module called source initiated frame restoration (SIFR). We deployed SIFR on PlanetLab nodes, and compared the performance of SIFR with the default Internet routing. We show that SIFR outperforms IP-path selection by providing higher on-screen perceptual quality.

Categories and Subject Descriptors

J [**Computers Applications**]: Miscellaneous
; J.7 [**Computers in Other Systems**]: Real Time

General Terms

Internet, Quality of Experience, Multimedia

Permission to make digital or hard copies of all or part of this work for personal or classroom use is granted without fee provided that copies are not made or distributed for profit or commercial advantage and that copies bear this notice and the full citation on the first page. To copy otherwise, to republish, to post on servers or to redistribute to lists, requires prior specific permission and/or a fee.
MMSys'11, February 23–25, San Jose, California, USA
Copyright 2011 ACM 978-1-4503-0517-4/11/02 ...$10.00.

1. INTRODUCTION

Multimedia streaming over IP networks is poised to be the dominant Internet traffic in the coming decade. Industry forecasts already predict that more than 90% of the Internet traffic will carry multimedia content by 2012 [6]. As multimedia service providers deploy services on top of packet switched networks that compete with cable based content providers, there is an ever growing need to provide superior *Quality of Experience* (QoE) [5, 13, 14, 21].

Quality of Service (QoS) has been proposed to meet customer service level agreement (SLA) for streaming services over the Internet. QoS provides *statistical* guarantees on parameters that are known to hamper video quality such as loss, delay and jitter [2, 25]. However, QoS ignores an important dimension in assessing quality: that of subjective perception. The recognition of subjective perception as an important dimension in assessing quality has led to investigations into QoE. Providing superior QoE on top of Internet's best-effort service, however, is non-trivial. The effects of Internet path selection on video QoE, as well as the goodness of an Internet path, are not very well understood.

There are various reasons to expect current Internet path selection policies to be sub-optimal in assuring superior QoE. Current wide area routing protocols choose paths solely based on hop count and autonomous system (AS) connectivity, and are as such not optimized for QoE. For reasons of scalability, connectivity information between AS's is further filtered during routing advertisements. As a result, a video source has limited routing options when sending its packets, especially during times of an outage. However, the Internet itself is comprised of billions of interconnections, and the probability that there are alternate paths which can perform better are high [1, 12, 22]. An empirical understanding of QoE degradations along an Internet path, and simple alternative path selection strategies that go beyond default IP-routing, would help us overcome some of these limitations.

This paper presents a large scale measurement based study on the effects of Internet path selection on video-QoE, and investigates ways to improve it using application specific policies and redundant Internet paths. We seek answers to the following questions: (i) What *degrades* video QoE in the Internet and *where* in the path do these outages frequent?, (ii) How does an Internet outage *effect* video-QoE?, (iii) What fraction of these outages are *addressable* by using redundant alternative Internet paths?, and (iv) How can a source select the right alternative path to improve Internet video-QoE *without* having to perform any prior path quality measurements?

(a)   (b)

Figure 1: QoE v/s QoS: While both clips experienced the same loss rate (QoS), the perceived quality can be very different.

To answer the first question, we probe 1000+ popular Internet video destinations from 62 geographically diverse PlanetLab [29] vantage points for seven consecutive days. Our probing mimics "fetching" streaming content from each destination for a variety of low and high motion clips. Our destination set includes the 200 most popular IPTV/VoD servers, and a set of 1,200 IP addresses from crawls of popular P2PTV providers. We discovered a significant number of path outages that led to complete loss in path connectivity, while we characterize the frequency and duration of such outages. We find that outages occur in various points in a path and vary significantly between paths to servers and P2P hosts. Of the outages on a round trip path to servers, we found that only 11% of these occur on the last hop, and therefore cannot be corrected by alternate routing; the remaining 89% are potentially recoverable by Internet re-routing. For P2P hosts, we found that over 40% of the outages are last hop, which indicates that alternate paths can potentially recover upto 60% of these outages.

To measure the perceptual degradation resulting from these outages, we reconstructed a variety of MPEG video samples using the IP-traces collected from every destination set. We create a comprehensive list of 54 video clips that mirror the most commonly occurring loss patterns. We asked 77 subjects to review these clips to gain a deeper understanding of perceptual degradations. Network anomalies typically manifest as a video *artifact*, which is a visible distortion during playout that persists for a certain duration. These artifacts could range from slicing to freezing to extreme pixellation [9, 10]. These artifacts and their on-screen duration depend on the type of frame impacted (see Figs. 1(a), 1(b)), the motion complexity inherent in the clip (low v/s high), and encoding bitrate. Using the survey, we outline application specific policies that can improve perceptual quality.

Perceptual quality can be raised by path selection strategies which preserve these application specific policies in times of QoE degradations. To make our results more generally applicable, we seek path selection strategies that *do not* require background monitoring of alternative routes or any apriori path quality information. We analyze a large number of Internet path measurements derived from five different overlays built using PlanetLab. Our datasets include week-long measurements taken from overlays of: (i) 21 nodes in United States, (ii) 19 nodes in Europe, (iii) 22 nodes in Asia, and (iv) two different overlays (22 and 32 nodes each) spread across the globe. Using these datasets, we compare the per-

formance of the "default" Internet path and other alternate paths derived by synthetically combining path metrics of disjoints nodes. Similar in spirit to randomized load allocation [7, 8, 12], we show that attempting to route key frames following a degradation using a random subset of 5 nodes is sufficient to recover from upto 90% of failures. We argue that are results are robust across datasets.

Finally, we design and implement a prototype forwarding module in PlanetLab called source initiated frame restoration (SIFR). We evaluate the effectiveness of SIFR in improving video-QoE against the default IP-path. We show that we can minimize and recover quickly from perceptual degradations and preserve interactivity, thereby raising perceptual quality on top of the best effort Internet.

2. PROBING INTERNET DESTINATIONS

Streaming content on the Internet today is most commonly disseminated by VoD/IPTV service providers or by peer-to-peer (p2p) streaming (e.g., Joost, BBC iPlayer, PPLive etc.). Hence, we begin by measuring the round trip path to these destinations from geographically diverse client locations. We analyze outages on these paths, their recurring frequency, as well as their location along the path. We provide upper bounds on the fraction of outages that occur on the last hop, which cannot be recovered by using alternate paths. Overall, results presented in this section are crucial to understanding paths used to disseminate streaming content from popular sites/hosts all over the Internet. We map the perceptual degradation caused by these outages in Section 3.

2.1 Vantage Points and Destination Sets

Vantage Points: IP-based streaming services are currently popular in Germany, France, Belgium, United States, Korea, and China among other nations. Hence, we select vantage points that have a presence in these countries and are generally placed in United States, Europe and Asia. We initially began with a list of 70 vantage points[1]. However, we removed data from 8 vantage points which had more than 24 hours worth of data loss due to downtimes, effectively reducing our vantage points to 62 nodes.

Destination Sets: To create our destination set, we gathered a list of the 200 most popular IPTV/VoD service providers from various Internet sources. To create a destination set for P2P video sharing hosts, we used 1,200 IP addresses of broadband hosts obtained from crawls of TVUNetworks and PPLive. In the end, our source-destination pairs are representative of typical round trip paths on the Internet used to disseminate streaming content.

2.2 Probing Methodology

Between January 08 and 14, 2010, we systematically studied paths between our vantage points and destination sets. We probed the destinations from our vantage points mimicking a "fetch" operation of streaming content using UDP probes of 1024 bytes. To do this, we timed our probes according to the IP-level trace of a variety of low and high motion clips. We use three representative low motion clips (*Foreman, Akiyo, Coastguard*) and two high motion clips (*Football, Tennis*) to obtain IP-level traces. The IP-level

---

[1] All our vantage points and destination sets, and additional discussion, can be found at [31]

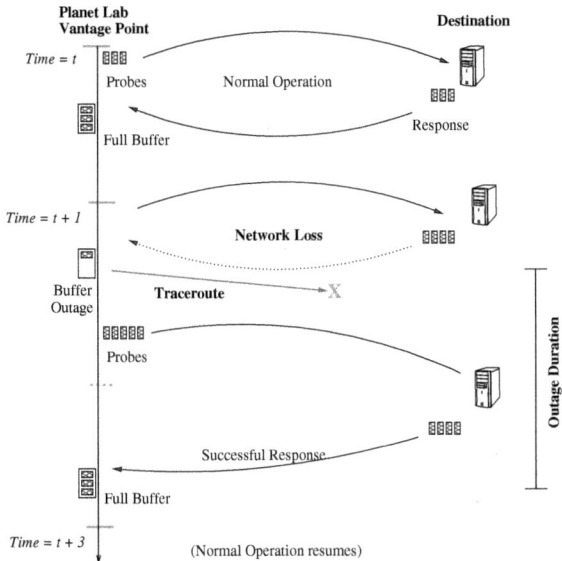

Figure 2: Overview of probing methodology. At time $t + 1$, a failure event is observed. With the ensuing traceroute failure, an outage is declared. The path returns to normal with the reception of an intact buffer of information.

Event	Servers	P2P hosts
paths probed	18,600	62,000
Failure Events	4,181	16,724
Path failures	1829	6743
Classifiable path failures	915	3439
Last hop failures	101 (11%)	1308 (38%)
Non last hop failures	814 (89%)	2131 (62%)
Unclassifiable	914	3304

Table 1: Overview of outage locations for paths to servers and P2PTV hosts observed from 62 vantage points in a one week period.

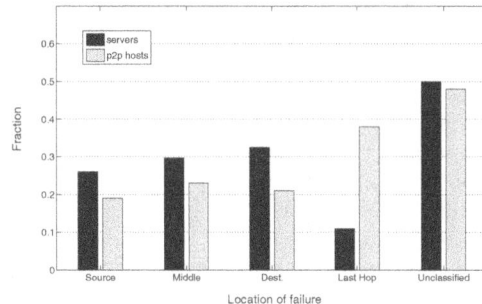

Figure 3: Fraction of location failures for classifiable failures; the last column shows fraction of unclassifiable failures observed for all path failures.

trace of these clips were recorded using an Ineoquest Singulus digital media analyzer [28] with a fragmentation limit of 1024 bytes. We use a 15:2 GOP at 30 frames per second to encode a given clip, with most clips encoded within 10 seconds of sending time.

Every 5 minutes, each vantage point selects the IP-trace of a randomly chosen clip to probe a randomly chosen destination from its destination set. The destination's response to these probes enables us to create an IP-level trace of the chosen clip at the receiver, which we use to infer path quality. We partitioned the destination sets across our vantage points ensuring an even mix of servers and P2P hosts.

Failures v/s outages: While even a single packet loss can potentially induce perceptual degradation, we strive to distinguish between short lived congestion drops and a true path outage in this round of study. We declare a path to experience a *failure event* if three or more consecutive probe packets fail to receive a response. As soon as this happens, we issue a traceroute from the vantage point to that destination. If the first traceroute after a failure event *also* fails, we declare a destination *outage* (see Figure 2). Upon detecting an outage, we send a continuous stream of probes to the destination until the path return to normal. The path is deemed normal with the first incident of successfully receiving 10 probe responses. In the end, any definition of an outage based on probe loss patterns is arbitrary.

Traceroutes: When a path experiences a *failure event*, we used TCP traceroutes to determine the possible *location* of the failure. TCP traceroute return results faster than the standard ICMP based traceroute to determine failure location within milliseconds of its happening [12]. From our experience, we found TCP-traceroute to be a better alternative than standard traceroute. We broadly classify failure locations as source side, destination side, last hop, or middle core (backbone) [12, 24].

2.3 Outage Locations

We begin with characterizing failure locations summarized in Table 1. A 'failure event' is the loss of three consecutive probe packets. A 'path failure' is the additional failure of the first traceroute issued. Likewise, a 'classifiable' failure is when we can potentially isolate the location of failure from traceroute. We group the classifiable failures as either a 'last hop' failure or failures occurring elsewhere. Last hop failures are failures that happen on the last hop to the destination, and are very hard to recover from using alternate Internet paths. Lastly, we group outages as 'unclassified' if we cannot infer the location of failure from traceroute.

Of the classifiable failures, we observe that on paths to servers, only 11% of the failures happen at the last hop. This both indicates that servers are well provisioned and server side path outages are less frequent. This also implies that it is possible to potentially recover from 89% of outages on a path to a server. The last hop failure rate for broadband hosts is quite high (38%). This implies that routing around failures can potentially solve upto 62% of the outages. This has further implications for content providers: while a providers "walled garden network" may be well provisioned, performance is bound by the quality of their clients last hop links. Finally, failure events whose ensuing traceroute did not fail are grouped as 'unclassified'. Even though we issue a TCP-traceroute immediately *after* a failure, the failure has to be long enough for its location to be detectable by traceroute. We believe these failures were a result of transient load fluctuations that resulted in packet drops, and

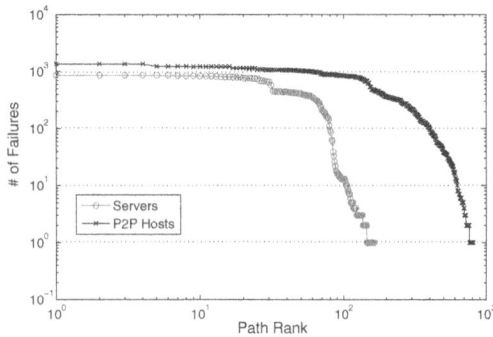

Figure 4: Failure rate (log-log scale) of individual paths to servers and broadband hosts.

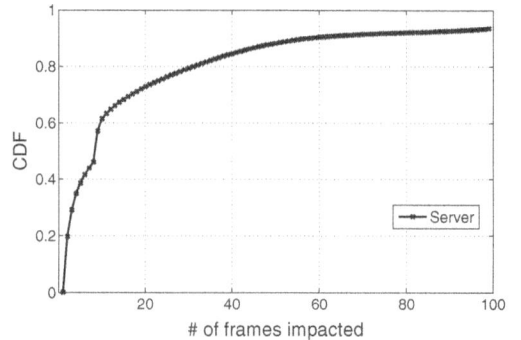

Figure 5: Failure duration: number of consecutive frames impacted during outages.

were recovered soon enough to remain unclassified by the ensuing traceroute.

Of the classifiable failures, we present in Figure 3 the ratio of failures observed on each path segment to the total number of classifiable failures. To better group failure location, we divide a path into four segments [12]: *Last hop* failures are either the last access link failure or a 'destination unreachable' failure of traceroute, *Middle* failures occur in the backbone network (Tier-1 ISPs) that peer with a POP at the source's ISP [24]. We infer a middle failure by checking the router addresses to infer a backbone link. Likewise, *Source* and *Destination* are the path segments before and after *Middle*. The plot shows that failures to servers and P2P hosts are equally likely at 'source' and 'destination'. However, paths to servers experience lower last hop failures.

2.4 Failure Rate

We also measure the number of failures observed by *each* path over the seven day period (Figure 4), which represents failure rate for the seven day observation period. Paths are ranked by the number of failures they encountered sorted by highest to lowest. We observe that a fraction of the total paths measured in each destination set experience a majority of the failures observed, with few paths registering loss free incidents. Paths to servers observe relatively lesser failures than paths to P2P hosts. Most paths that observe failures share similar number of failures.

2.5 Failure Duration

Also of interest is the duration of an outage, which gives us a measure of failure persistence. We report on failure duration in terms of the number of *consecutive* MPEG-2 frames impacted due an outage. We count a frame corrupt if at least one packet loss is observed in a given frame, and we continue counting corrupt frames until an intact frame reception is inferred.

Figure 5 shows the CDF of the number of consecutive frames impacted as a result of network induced degradation. In more than 50% of the case, more than 10 frames that are impacted during an outage. The probability that a key frame is lost increases with the number of frames impacted per outage. Also, 20% of the outages result in the corruption of more than 50 frames. This strongly brings out the need to quickly detect and recover from degradations.

2.6 Summarizing

The above results make a strong case for Internet redirection. Of the classifiable failures, upto 89% of paths to servers and 62% of paths to broadband hosts potentially recoverable by timely routing redirections; the few paths that observe very high failure rates would almost certainly benefit from redirections. A majority of the paths that evenly observe failures would benefit from timely redirections when outages start occurring. Since BGP convergence times are high and Internet paths are not chosen based on QoE, route selection will not discover new paths to switch to until the outage continues to corrupt multiple frames. In general, outages that do not occur at last hops can potentially be alleviated by using alternate routes, provided the detection of QoE degradation and path switching happen in a timely fashion.

3. IMPACT ON PERCEPTUAL QUALITY

This section analyzes the *perceptual* degradations caused by packet drops resulting from network anomalies in the IP-traces obtained from the previous round of study. We begin with a brief overview of the MPEG-2 encoding scheme, and discuss our methodology of reconstructing MPEG-2 video clips using the IP-traces. These clips were used to conduct a survey with human subjects to better understand perceptual degradations, the factors that affect it, and user preferences. Finally, we summarize our key finding from this round of study to derive application specific parameters that can help preserve QoE.

3.1 MPEG-2 Overview

Streaming content in IP networks is commonly transported as a data stream encoded using the MPEG standard and transported via the real time protocol (RTP) over a UDP/IP stack. MPEG encodes video streams as a series of Intra (I), Predictive (P) and Bidirectional (B) frames. I-frames carry a complete video picture, and as such provide reference to the following B- and P-frames for decoding an MPEG stream. P-frames predict the frames to be coded using a preceding I or P-frame.

Lastly, B-frames use the previous or next I-frame for motion compensation. Each frame is typically fragmented into multiple IP packets for transport over the Internet. The frames are packed into a group of pictures (GOP), where

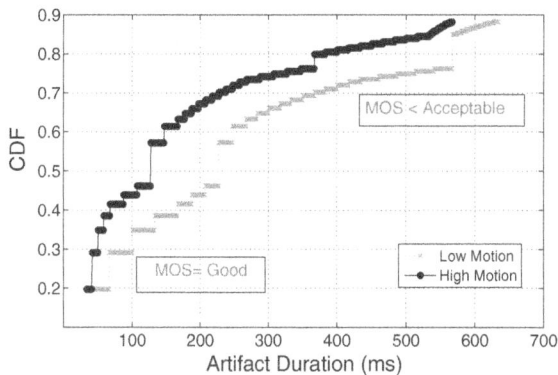
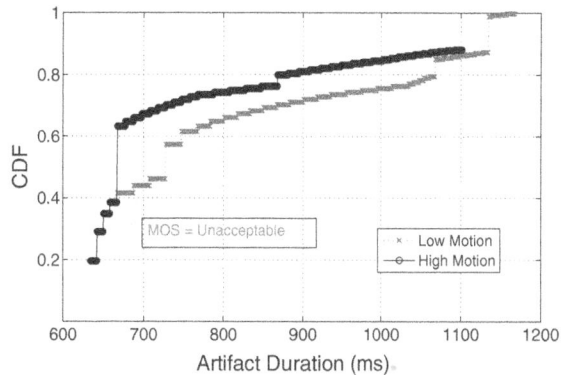

(a)   (b)

Figure 6: Outages and their impacts on paths to servers: (a) Best case video artifact durations for low and high motion clips, and (b) Corresponding worst case artifact durations.

each GOP consists of an I-frame at the start and a series of B and P-frames which use it as a reference. Depending upon the motion complexity inherent in a clip, the structure of a GOP can be very different: low motion clips (like a news program) have larger I-frames and a handful of P and B-frames to complete a GOP, while high motion (sports clip) clips have smaller I-frames and relatively larger P-frames for motion compensation.

3.2 Video Buffering v/s Interactivity

Streaming services over the Internet present the opportunity of significant user interaction, perhaps more than cable based services. For example, users could go beyond channel changes to participate in opinion polls or providing feedback. Network anomalies that degrade video quality are loss and jitter. Loss directly contributes to missing information. Jitter can cause packets to arrive out of order, sometimes enough to render a received packet useless. Almost all receivers implement a playout buffer to counter network jitter, stalling playback until a buffer worth of information is received. The size of the playout buffer can have a significant impact on user interactivity: each time a user flips a channel or requests new material (forwarding, rewinding etc), the buffer contents are flushed and information from the new stream is re-buffered before playout. Channel changes apart, real time streaming (live broadcasts) necessarily requires smaller buffer sizes to preserve a near real-time viewing experience.

For services such as IPTV or VoD, interactivity is mostly presented as end user "zapping", which include channel changes, forwarding, rewinding, etc. Zapping delays of more than 2 seconds are perceived as poor by end users. Network service providers typically target round trip delays of less than 500 ms [9, 10]. Zapping behavior is closely tied with user attention span and browsing habits. A recent investigation into six months of end-user browsing habits reveals that user attention span can be quite low: over 60% of channel changes happen within 10 seconds, and that a users favorite channels are non-sequential but browsing habits are predominantly sequential [4]. This means that the amount of interactivity presented by the average user can be significant, and a con-

sistent loss in interactivity can lead to the user perceiving a service to be poor. On the same lines, users who perceive zapping times to be too high show an unwillingness to switch channels, which further degrades their perception of quality. Hence, an ability to provide consistent zapping experience is crucial to prevent subscriber churn.

3.3 Outage Impact on Perceived Quality

Since destinations were probed using the IP-trace of a given clip, the probe responses create an IP-trace at the receiver which contains round trip times and sequence numbers. We analyze this trace to look for missing information caused by network level degradations. Missing sequence numbers directly capture network drops. To account for jitter, we mark a received probe response as lost if the round trip time exceeds 1 second (typical playout buffer sizes for VLC [30]). Hence, after this process, we have an IP-level trace of packet reception for a given video clip.

A popular way to report QoE is a mean opinion score (MOS). However, unlike the R-Score in VoIP, there is no consensus on a standard QoE scoring methodology. Instead, we quantify the *type* of visual impairment and its *expected* duration within a playout by observing the instantaneous contents in a 1 second playout buffer and discuss user perception of these impairments from our survey. We make a distinction between the *actual* failure observed on a path and the *perceived* failure. The actual failure is measure of the number of packets lost. However, the perceived failure is the severity of perceptual degradation and its on-screen persistent caused by the actual failure. A *worst case* degradation is when the loss corrupts an I-frame. Likewise, *best case* degradation happen when a loss does not impact an I-frame.

While relative priorities of MPEG frames have been emphasized in the past, we seek to characterize the persistence of on-screen degradation that we infer from the IP-traces. The best case on-screen artifact duration as a result of the corrupted frames for different motion clips is shown in Figure 6(a). We note that the on-screen persistence can range from less than 100 ms to about 700 ms. Best case artifacts can range from minor glitches to frozen frames. The worst case artifact duration for the same number of corrupted frames is very different (Figure 6(b)). Worst case degradation occur when the loss surely corrupts an I-frame, manifesting pixellization, ghosting, and extreme distortions. In this case, the remaining frames cannot quite reconstruct the scenes and depending upon motion complexity, the persistence of on screen is longer. Even a *single* corrupt I-frame (10ms loss) results in impairments that persist for over 600 ms.

3.4 Reconstructing Video Clips for Survey

To better understand the *perceptual* experience of viewing clips with the aforesaid loss patterns and artifacts, we decided to recreate a set of clips that are representative of the most commonly occurring loss patterns. From our traces, we observed loss rates of less than 0.1 in a majority of cases, with typical loss rates crowding at around 0.01, 0.05 and 0.1. Loss rate occasionally reached 0.5 and above. We reconstructed video clips at various bitrates using these loss rates. To do this, we manually edited the IP-trace of the low and high motion clips originally obtained to induce these loss rates in a variety of frames. We consider two possibilities of loss impacting an MPEG frame: (i) loss in key frames (or worst case losses), and (ii) loss in non-key frames (best case losses). We consider an I-frame as a key frame for all clips. We used three encoding bitrates of 800, 3200 and 6400 kbps to reconstruct the video clips. In summary, we recreated a set of 54 unique combinations of losses impacting key frames of high and low motion clips at three encoding bitrates[2].

3.5 Survey with Subjects

The reconstructed video clips were used to conduct a survey with an initial set of 80 human subjects in an indoor lab environment. Subjects were shown the original video sequences, and were asked to rate the distorted sequences on a scale of 1 to 5. Subjects were chosen with sufficient diversity in age, gender, and expertise in subject matter. Care was taken to identify outliers who tend to give erroneous ratings to video sequences. To do this, we interspersed a random video clip from our set multiple times during the survey: subjects who gave different ratings to the same interspersed video were marked as outliers. We identified a total of 3 outliers in the lab environment, effectively reducing our survey strength to 77. A typical survey included a brief orientation followed by the actual survey with video clips, all of which lasted less than half an hour.

We observed many interesting patterns in subjective perception of these video clips with artifacts. For a given loss rate, the perceptual quality can *vary significantly* depending on the motion complexity of the clip and the type of frames impacted during loss. Subjects were less irritated with best case artifacts for low motion clips, and generally rate the clips as "good" (between 3 and 4.2). When rating clips as good, subjects ratings varied between 3 and 4. However, subjects were more irritated with increased P-frame losses in high motion clips, and rate the clips as just about "acceptable". Subjects consistently rated worst case degradations as "unacceptable" with very little or no variance. Low motion clips have larger proportion of I-frames, hence it is more likely that an I-frame is impacted during a loss. Also, because of the longer sizes of GOPs for low motion clips, the

persistence of playout distortion tends to be longer. Though greater perceptual loss due to an I-frame over other frames is not a new result, this process helps us assign a perceptual rat3333ing to various combinations of frame losses and motion-complexities.

Interestingly, once the playout reaches "below acceptable" perception, subjects seemed to hardly react any further with continued losses within that GOP. Subjects also tend to "forgive" the degradation if the on-screen artifact suddenly heals with the new arrival of an intact I-frame.

3.6 Summarizing

Video-QoE is known to be multidimensional, and the overall perceived quality of a service provider depend on parameters that go beyond network efficiency. In this paper, we focus on discovering *network* induced degradations that are addressable by using alternate paths in the Internet.

We summarize our basic assumptions about QoE that we use for the rest of this paper as follows. For each instance of a corrupted frame in a GOP, an artifact is produced. Not all artifacts induce the same user reaction. Subjective perception degrades to "below acceptable" when key frames are corrupted within a GOP. For low motion clips, we mark the I-frame as a key frame. For high motion clips, we mark both I- and P-frames as key frames. While subjective perception degrades with the loss of key frames, immediate restoration of key frames following a degradation induce a "forgiveness" effect. Interactivity delay of more than 500 ms network round trip time degrades QoE.

4. USING ROUTING REDIRECTIONS

We investigate frame preserving policies and path selection strategies that can raise perceptual quality. We observe that a strategy of preserving key frames following a degradation can instantly convert worst case degradations to a best case degradation and raise perceptual experience. Given a degradation on an Internet path, however, we need a deeper understanding on how long an outage persists when a frame is corrupted, how soon should one switch paths, and what is the best strategy to utilize redundant Internet paths without the need for background monitoring. Choosing paths without background monitoring allows overlays to scale to large number of nodes. It also makes such strategies generally applicable in a wide variety of streaming services without burdening the existing infrastructure.

The Internet by default returns one path for a given destination to the source. Alternative paths can be derived by creating an *overlay* network. Overlays are not a new concept to computer networking: the Internet itself was built as an overlay on top of the telephone network [1, 12]. Current examples of overlays built on top of the Internet include: P2P networks, content delivery networks or CDNs (like Akamai [27]), multicast networks [15], OverQoS [25] etc. These networks often have a multitude of nodes in different ASs that can likely provide redirections around outages.

4.1 Methodology

We analyze five different datasets that contain weeklong measurements of a large number of Internet paths all over the world. We streamed packets using IP-traces of a variety of low motion and high clips between source destination pairs. When transmitting key frames from the clip, we *simultaneously* probe every intermediary which indirectly

---

[2]All our clips can be examined at [31]

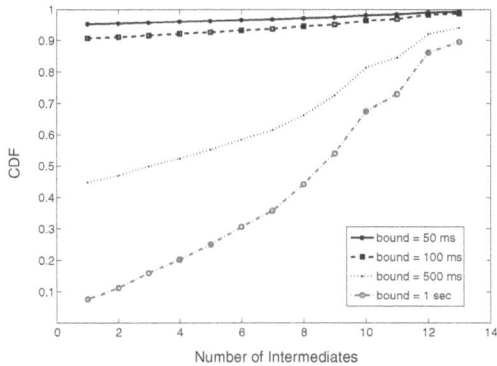

Figure 7: CDF of number of useful intermediaries as a function of the upper bound on tolerable delay.

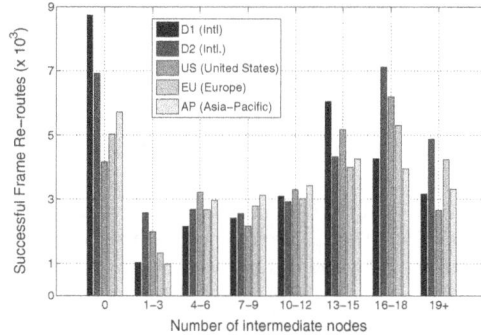

Figure 8: Number of intermediaries that offered a better path in times of failures.

probes the destination. We record the receiver trace at the destination, and the probe responses from the intermediaries at source to analyze offline the suitability of alternate paths during outages. We then derive ways to select alternate paths while preserving zapping delays *without* the need to perform background monitoring of any kind. We only consider *one* hop redirections to recover from perceptual degradations. It has been shown that additional redirections often provide marginal additional gains [19].

Datasets: We created five measurement overlays in different parts of the world, both within a continent and across continents. We created one overlay each within United States (US), Europe (EU) and Asia-Pacific (AP) consisting 21, 19, and 22 nodes respectively. In addition, we created two international overlays D1 and D2 consisting of 22 and 32 nodes *evenly* spread across the U.S., Europe and Asia-Pacific.

Experimental Setup and Video Clips: Between January 22 to 29, 2010, every node streamed 1024 byte UDP packets every 5 minutes to a randomly selected destination. The stream mimics the IP-packet trace of a randomly selected high or low motion clip from a set of five clips used in the previous round of study. We passed the name of the clip and the type of frame the packet carries in the packet payload, creating an IP-trace of the clip at the receiver. For any of our overlay with N nodes, the source indirectly probed the destination via the $N - 2$ other intermediaries while streaming packets to the destination. This probing is performed only when transmitting key frames within the clips.

4.2 What kind of paths help QoE?

In general, preserving key frames and providing consistent zapping times are excellent network level support to raise perceptual quality. Hence, paths that can re-route subsequent key frames *and* ensure that zapping times don't exceed a given bound are excellent candidates for selection in times of an outage.

By "bound", we mean that the difference in RTTs of the new path and the default IP path is within a given threshold, i.e., $RTT_{new} < RTT_{Default-IP} + bound$. Choosing a bound assures that the interactivity resulting from the new path is also bounded. As a result, not all intermediaries can be of use if they exceed this bound even if they are determined to be loss free.

4.3 Suitability of Intermediaries

For a default IP-path from source (S) to destination (D), an intermediary (I) is considered "useful" when the alternative route stitched together by combining paths of (S,I) and (I,D) is loss free *and* whose round trip time is bounded by a given value. The choice of this bound limit can have a significant effect in the choice of intermediaries that can be considered useful.

Shown in Figure 7 are the number of useful intermediaries each time a frame was corrupt at the receiver as a function of the delay bound. When bounds are tight (50 ms), the number of useful intermediaries in times of an outage are low. In fact, the same chosen few nodes tend to help recovery and the probability of finding newer nodes are low. When the bound is loosened to around 1 second, we see an even likelihood of finding a varying number of useful intermediaries for every instance of an outage. We also observed (not shown in the plot) that the number of useful intermediaries tend to be more when the overlay is confined to a geographical area, largely because of the availability of paths with round trip times within the defined tolerable bounds. Note that this plot reports data from dataset D2, which is spread all over the world. We observed that the number of useful intermediaries is higher with global overlays than overlays confined to a geographical location (like US, EU or AP).

From our survey in the previous round, we note that worst case degradations often persist between 600 ms to 1 second. Also, subjective perception does not degrade any further for the entire GOP given an impaired I-frame. Hence, given the duration of on-screen artifact persistence and subjective perception, we choose an upper bound for RTT as 500 ms to choose suitable intermediaries.

4.4 Useful Intermediaries

For every instance of a corrupt frame at the receiver, we analyze the number of useful intermediaries that can help preserve subsequent frames with a bound of 500 ms. Figure 8 shows the fraction of times the number of intermediaries (in bins of 3) were determined useful each time a frame was corrupt. We observe that few failures could be exclusively addressed by a small number of nodes (bin [1-3]). A large number of failures could find many intermediate nodes that prove helpful. We also observe that a fraction of these failures could not be recovered by any alternate route (the left most bar). This number seems to be relatively higher for international datasets (D1 and D2) than datasets derived from within a geographical area.

4.5 Choosing Intermediaries

Given the number of useful intermediaries in times of an outage, we now look at path selection strategies that can improve perceived quality. Our key requirements in designing a path selection strategy is twofold: (i) path selection is done *without* the need for background monitoring or apriori path quality knowledge of any kind, and (ii) the approach is simple, lightweight and adds negligible computational overhead at the sender. We assume that the receiver can provide a feedback to source informing an outage whenever key frames are corrupt.

Similar in spirit to randomized load allocation [7, 8, 12], we employ a strategy of *randomly* selecting any k intermediate nodes in times of an outage, and simultaneously attempting to transmit the subsequent key frames through them. The first such intermediate node of the chosen k which is loss free and whose RTT is bounded is chosen as the best alternative and we continue streaming via that node. A subsequent failure on that path again triggers the random-k strategy until a new path is found. In case of finding no paths, we re-invoke random-k until we find a suitable intermediary or if the IP-path self repairs. By sending the next set of key frames of multiple paths, we maximize the chances of at least one of the paths to deliver the frames that help restore quality.

A natural question then is the what value of k presents a reasonable tradeoff between reducing the number of nodes to be simultaneously attempted for recovery while maximizing gains in the resulting perceived quality. To answer this, we measure the fraction of outages recovered by various values of k across all our datasets. An outage is considered recovered if the subsequent key frames are corrupted in the default IP-path while the path through the intermediary was both loss free and within a desired round trip delay bounds.

Figure 9 shows this for all our five datasets, and additionally shows the results for different delay bounds with dataset D2. Each datapoint was obtained by calculating the recovery percentage using that value of k for the entire trace period on a given dataset. We observe that for all datasets, the value of $k = 5$ presents a reasonable tradeoff in selecting intermediaries. Beyond $k = 5$, we observe the law of diminishing results: attempting to recover from more number of intermediaries results in little gain. For datasets confined to a geographical area (US, EU, or AP) we observe that the value of $k = 4$ provides comparable gains owing to more intermediaries within the desired RTT bounds. For smaller RTT bounds, we observe that the gains hit a ceiling after a small number of intermediaries because only a few select intermediaries out of the available ones can help recover from outages.

4.6 Path Switching with random-5

Path switching is performed when the destination reports a degradation which impairs perceptual quality. We now investigate the following question: how soon should a receiver inform of a degradation, and what are the benefits of switching paths early.

We begin by looking at the typical loss patterns in key frames that were corrupt at the receiver. For dataset D2,

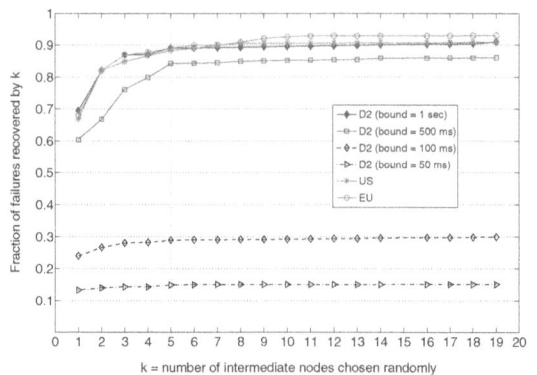

Figure 9: Fraction of outages recovered by transmitting the next GOP to k-intermediate nodes; for dataset *D2*, we additionally plot success for different delay bounds.

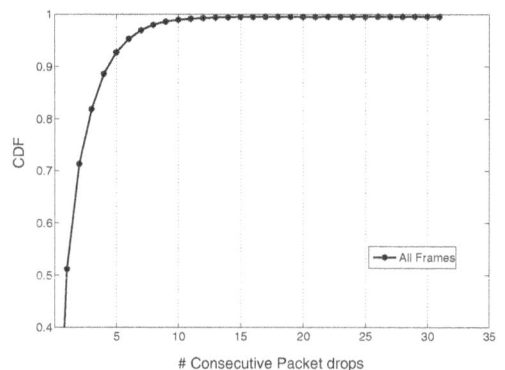

Figure 10: CDF of packet loss distributions in key frames.

Figure 10 shows the typical number of consecutive packet drops observed in key frames for low and high motion clips. The plot shows that reception is void of any losses 51% of the time. Consecutive losses of 2 or more packets are only seen in 29% of the cases. We argue that the receiver should inform source to switch paths after a single packet loss in a key frame.

The benefits of switching paths early are further shown in Figure 11. This plot shows the probability of the next key frame being received successfully *after* observing a certain number of consecutive drops in a key frame. We plot this probability for upto 6 consecutive packet losses observed for $k = (1, 5, 10)$ alongwith the performance of the default IP-path. After only two successive drops, the probability of the default IP-path restoring the next key frame seem to diminish to around 0.42. Both random-5 and random-10 maintain a higher recovery probability of more than 80% for upto 5 consecutive drops. Once again, the additional gains by selecting 10 nodes over 5 for transmitting key frames are marginal. This leads us to believe that paths should indeed be switched early. The plot also shows that even random-1 is able to provide higher returns than the default IP-path when 3 or more packets are lost in succession.

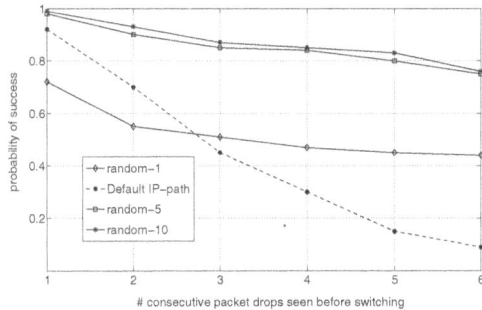

Figure 11: Benefits of switching early: probability of recovery after consecutive packet losses in key frames.

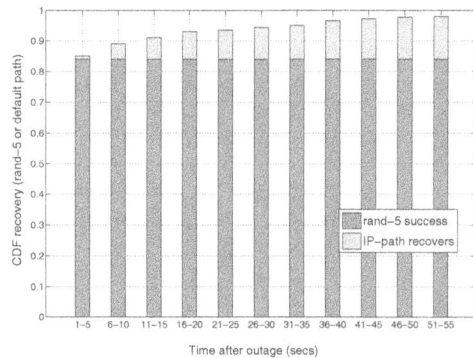

Figure 12: Resilience of random-5 recovery time over IP-path self repairing itself.

4.7 Robustness

We further elucidate the robustness of random-5 by next looking at the probability of recovering from a perceptual degradation either due to random-5 recovering from an outage or the IP-path self-repairing itself when random-5 cannot solve the problem after persistent efforts. Figure 12 shows the CDF of all degradations recovered from either due to random-5 or the IP-path self repairing itself as a function of time elapsed since the destination reported a degradation. In effect, the plot shows the *combined* recovery due to random-5 and default-IP for a source that uses this strategy. The success probability of random-5 continues to be 0.84 irrespective of the time elapsed since the degradation was reported. The IP-path, however, repairs itself with an increasing probability with elapsed time since an outage. The mean time to recover from outages for the default IP-path is typically 30 seconds. The plot highlights the ability of random-5 to recover quickly from perceived degradations to restoring playout within the first few seconds.

4.8 Preserving Interactivity

When a source selects a path using the random-5 strategy, it automatically ensures two things: (i) the key frames make it to the destination in the *least* time possible using any of the five alternate paths, and (ii) the selection of the path with the minimum delay within specified maximum bounds ensures round trip times do not exceed the stated bound. Figure 13 shows the difference between the mean round trip time of the default IP-path and paths due to random-5 between all source destination pairs for all our datasets. While it is easy to observe that the additional round trip delay by choosing alternate paths is bounded (because the source will not consider a path successful until the round trip is within bounds), what is interesting to observe is the occasion *improvement* in round trip time. An improvement in RTT results could be either due to: (i) the alternate path having a round trip time that is indeed lesser than the default IP-path, and (ii) during times of an outage, the round trip path to the source increases and the alternate paths which do not experience that outage have a smaller RTTs. We observe that the difference is smaller for overlays confined to a geographical area compared to overlays spanning multiple continents. This is largely because of the higher availability of alternate paths with desired RTT bounds within a continent.

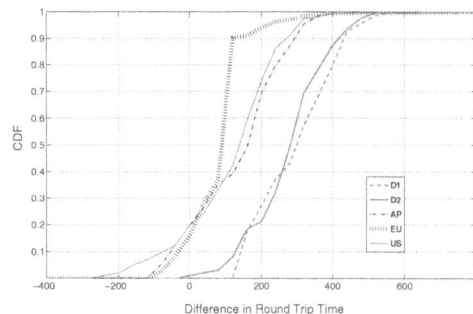

Figure 13: Difference in round trip times resulting from random-5 path selection with bound = 500ms.

4.9 Summarizing

Though a number of intermediaries have loss free paths to the destination in times of a perceptual degradation, not all of them can be a viable alternative if the desired round trip delay is bounded to preserve interactivity. Using a bound of 500 ms, we investigated ways to restore perceptual quality by attempting to preserve key frames following an outage using intermediate nodes. Our results indicate that a source can restore perceptual quality by simultaneously transmitting key frames to five randomly chosen intermediaries following a degradation. We observe that random-5 is robust across all our datasets.

5. PROTOTYPE EVALUATION

Using the insights from the previous section, we now design and implement a prototype called SIFR, or source initiated frame restoration. SIFR employs frame preserving policies coupled with a random-5 path selection strategy for improving perceptual quality of streaming content. We deploy SIFR on 32 PlanetLab nodes which were used to obtain dataset D2. We evaluate the effectiveness of SIFR over the default IP-path in restoring and improving perceptual quality for three source-destination pairs, one each in the United States, Europe, and Asia-Pacific.

5.1 Prototype description

SIFR requires deployment at source, destination, and intermediate nodes. SIFR at source applies application specific policies to packet generation following a degradation, and chooses intermediate paths based on the random-5 strategy to restore key frames. The receiver takes ingress packets and counts the number of correctly received frames in a 1 second playout buffer. When losses that manifest in perceptual degradation are observed, the destination issues an "outage" feedback to the source. Upon reception of this, the source tries to recover from the degradation by sending the next set of key frames simultaneously through five randomly chosen intermediaries. When the destination receives an intact GOP from a path after an outage, it reports of this successful reception using this path back to the source. We use a custom header to capture feedback from the destination. Finally, the intermediaries simply forward ingress packets to the announced destination.

5.2 Methodology

We select three pairs of PlanetLab nodes to act as a source, with one pair each in the US, Germany and Korea. Each pair of nodes in a country belong to the same site (university) that hosts them, and are as such geographically co-located (i.e., within the same campus); one runs SIFR while the other uses the default IP path to reach destinations. We verify that the source pairs take similar ASs to reach a variety of destinations to eliminate bias in our results. Our destination and intermediary set consists of 32 PlanetLab nodes used in the previous round to obtain dataset D2. Our goal is to compare the perceptual quality of video streams that use SIFR over using the default IP-path. Note that SIFR at intermediate nodes was deployed at all 32 nodes used in dataset D2. Though we focus on UDP/RTP, our solution generally applies to any sender-receiver pair on the Internet that relies on IP-path selection. SIFR offers an alternative path selection strategy that is irrespective of the transport layer protocols used (e.g., HTTP over TCP).

Every minute, each source pair cycles through a list of five low and high motion clips used in our previous rounds to stream to a destination. The destination is likewise cycled through each of the 32 intermediaries every instance. Using the IP packet trace of the clip, each source pair generate packets with a fragmentation limit of 1024 bytes to the destination. The destination records the packet trace received from each pair of source, which enables us to compare the performance of our prototype over the default IP-path in recovering from outages. We ran this experiment for a little over 48 hours starting Feb 08, 2010.

5.3 Results

Table 2 summarizes a comparison of receiver traces of source nodes that implement SIFR against source nodes that only used the default IP path. We report the number of events when playout 'degraded' to "below acceptable" (MOS < 3, typically due to a corrupt I-frame), the number of 'episodes' where the degradation persisted on screen, the percentage of times playout could be restored in the very next GOP, and the mean time to restore on screen perceptual quality.

A GOP is considered 'degraded' when a key frame is corrupt within a GOP, which manifest artifacts resulting in strong user dissatisfaction. We observed a total of 303 such

Performance Metric	SIFR	Default IP-path
total # of GOP degradations	303	779
# of degradation "episodes"	251	293
Mean # of corrupt GOP per episode	1.167	2.65
% of times episodes were limited to one GOP	96%	82%
Mean time to restore quality	< 1 sec	5.23 secs

Table 2: Comparing perceptual quality of SIFR against default IP-routing.

instances on source nodes that implement SIFR and 779 degraded GOPs using the default IP-path. Overall, this indicates that SIFR could preserve about 61% of GOPs that the default IP-path could not. Since SIFR reroutes key frames *after* the destination reports of a degradation, a fraction of degradations cannot be prevented. To further elucidate this, we analyze the number of degradation '*episodes*'. A degradation episode begins with a degraded GOP and lasts until the first arrival of an intact GOP. We observe that on paths using SIFR, there were 251 episodes of degradation. For every such episode, the destination would have sent a feedback to source requesting a route change. The default IP-path registers about 293 degradations, which seems to indicate that the combination of alternative paths used by SIFR were marginally better in terms of episodes observed.

Of interest then is the mean number of degraded GOPs per episode, which dictates the mean on screen degradation time. For SIFR, we observe that this amounts to 1.2, which indicates that SIFR is able to restore a GOP on most occasions following a degradation. For the default IP-path the mean is about 2.65, which indicates that SIFR could improve episode duration by about 55%.

To better estimate recovery using SIFR, we measure the percentage of times the degradation episode was limited to one GOP. Our results indicate that 96% of the time, SIFR could restore playout following a degradation using alternate paths. For default IP-paths this is around 82%, which in a way reflects on the IP-path in self healing itself. In effect, the availability of higher on screen perceptual quality benefits by 14% with SIFR. We also measure the mean time to restore quality when it degrades. The mean time for IP-path to recover is around 5.23 seconds, while SIFR takes less than one second on average.

The perceptual benefits of preserving key frames is substantive. To better illustrate the perceptual benefits of restoring frames, consider the screenshots in Figure 14(a) and Figure 14(b). After an degradation on the default IP-path, the quality of playout degraded to below acceptable. SIFR successfully restored playout by quickly rerouting frames (Figure 14(b)), while the IP-path continued to experience a longer episode of degradation (Figure 14(a)).

6. RELATED RESEARCH

Internet pathologies have been well investigated in the past [17, 20]. Researchers have consistently found that Internet outages are unpredictable, and worse, can go undetected for a while [1, 22, 25]. BGP convergence times and IP-rerouting following a path outage can take of the order of minutes, while streaming services demand path switch-

| (a) | (b) |

Figure 14: (a) Default IP-path v/s (b) SIFR, following a degradation: SIFR recovers from perceptual degradation by restoring key frames.

ing in the order of milliseconds. Overlay networks have been proposed as a solution to many of Internet's problems: from resilience in recovering from outages using RON [1] to multicasting [15] to providing higher QoS [25]. Improving web-browsing experience using randomized load allocation to choose alternate paths was studied in [12]. However, the ensuing perceptual benefits for web-browsing was determined to be negligible.

Internet QoS was aimed at enabling streaming services [2, 25]. QoS mechanisms operate with a notion of providing service guarantees to enhance application performance. However, service guarantees alone are not sufficient to raise *perceptual* quality. Our experiments demonstrate and validate that QoS alone cannot guarantee perceptual quality. For the same given loss rate, the perceptual quality can vary dramatically between "good" and "unacceptable" depending upon what was impacted. Perceptual quality is best characterized by QoE, which attempts to infer quality from a user's perspective. QoS based quality assessments have often found to be grossly inaccurate at predicting user experience, and as such are not applicable in evaluating video quality [5, 13, 14, 21].

Quality of Experience (QoE) has been investigated in the recent past with different propositions from various researchers to estimate quality degradation, ranging from transcoding losses to network induced degradations. Mapping network degradations to perceptual quality for H.323 traffic was investigated in [3]. NTUStreaming, which integrates multiple description coding with P2P networking to build IPTV services, was investigated in [18]. That QoE can be raised when QoS and its interaction with the network and application layer are considered a whole rather than separate entities was proposed in [23]. Work by Tasaka *et. al.* focus on receivers, where the proposed SCS strategy switches from error concealment to frame skipping based on a threshold of error concealment. The effects of packet loss on perceptual quality of MPEG video streams was studied in [9, 10].

We believe our work compliments much of prior Internet based measurement studies and directions towards improving Internet video-QoE. Our measurements of popular Internet destinations and the benefits of using alternative routes can provide valuable insights to service providers and ISPs with major commercial and technical implications.

7. CONCLUSIONS

This paper presented large scale Internet measurements to understand the effects of Internet path selection on perceptual quality of MPEG-2 video and investigates ways to improve it. We began by performing repeated video "fetching" acts from top IPTV/VoD providers, PPLive hosts and random Internet destinations for one week from geographically diverse PlanetLab nodes. We mapped the probe responses to perceptual quality by reconstructing numerous representative low and high motion video sequences and conducted subjective surveys using them. Consistent with recent research, our finding indicate that degradation depend upon motion complexity and type of frame impacted among other things. High level results also indicate that upto 89% of paths to servers and 62% of paths to broadband are recoverable by using alternate paths.

To understand the benefits of using alternate paths, we collected weeklong measurements from five different datasets that both confine to and span multiple continents with a dominant presence of online streaming services. We observe that not all alternative paths can be useful even if they are loss free, and that a large fraction of degradations could be overcome by a large number of alternate paths. We investigated ways to restore quality by attempting to route successive key frames through k random intermediate nodes *without* relying on any kind of background path monitoring or apriori path knowledge. Our results indicate that $k = 5$ provides a reasonable tradeoff between minimizing k and maximizing gains, and we argue that our results are consistent across datasets. Finally, we designed a prototype called SIFR for choosing intermediate nodes in a simple, lightweight, yet efficient manner to improve perceptual quality. SIFR outperforms default IP-routing over a 2 day period across wide-area links on the Internet.

We believe our results have implications for any video source that streams content across the Internet. A technique of randomly choosing intermediaries requires little overhead. This promises large, scalable overlays to be easily build, deploy and maintain. We show that it is possible to achieve substantive gains in perceptual quality using our prototype on top of todays best effort Internet.

8. REFERENCES

[1] D. G. Andersen, H. Balakrishnan, M. F. Kaashoek, R. Morris, "Resilient Overlay Networks", *Proc. 18th ACM Symp. on Operating System Principles (SOSP)*, Banff, Canada, pp. 131–145. Oct 2001.

[2] S. Blake, D. Black, M. Carlson, E. Davies, Z. Wang, and W. Weiss, "An Architecture for Differentiated Services", IETF RFC# 2475. Dec. 1998.

[3] P. Calyam, M. Sridharan, W. Mandrawa, and P. Schopis, "Performance Measurement and Analysis of H.323 Traffic", *Passive and Active Measurements (PAM)*, Antibes Juan-les-Pins, France, pp. 137-146. April 2004

[4] M. Cha, P. Rodriguez, J. Crowcroft, S. Moon, and X. Amatriain, "Watching television over an IP network", *Proc. ACM Internet Measurement Conference (IMC)*, Vouliagmeni, Greece, pp. 71–84. Oct. 2008.

[5] K. Chen, C. Wu, Y. Chang, and C. Lei, "A Crowdsourceable QoE Evaluation Framework for Multimedia Content", . *ACM Multimedia (MM)*, Beijing, China, pp. 491–500. Oct. 2009.

[6] Cisco White Paper, "Cisco Visual Networking Index: Forecast and Methodology, 2008–2013", Cisco Inc. Available: www.cisco.com. July 2009.

[7] A. Czumaj and V. Stemann, "Randomized Allocation Processes", *Symp. on Foundations of Computer Science*, Miami, FL. Oct. 1997.

[8] D. Eager, E. Lazowska, and J. Zahorjan, "Adaptive load sharing in homogeneous distributed systems", *IEEE Trans. on Software Engg.*, vol. 12(5), pp. 747–760. May 1986.

[9] J. Greengrass, J. Evans, and A. C. Begen, "Not All Packets Are Equal, Part I: Streaming Video Coding and SLA Requirements", *IEEE Internet Computing*, vol. 13(1), pp. 70–75. March 2009.

[10] J. Greengrass, J. Evans, and A. C. Begen, "Not All Packets Are Equal, Part II: The Impact of Network Packet Loss on Video Quality", *IEEE Internet Computing*, vol. 13(2), pp. 74–82. March 2009.

[11] M. Goodman, "Internet Video Forecast: Broadband Emerges as an Alternative Channel for Video Distribution" *Yankee group*, 2006.

[12] K. Gummadi, H. Madhyastha, S. Gribble, H. Levy, and D. Wetherall, "Improving the reliability of internet paths with one-hop source routing", *Proc. Operating System Design and Implementation (OSDI)*, San Fransico, CA, pp. 13–26. Dec. 2004.

[13] International Telecommunication Union, "Subjective video quality assessment methods for multimedia applications", Rec. ITU-T P.910, Sept. 1999.

[14] R. Jain, "Quality of Experience", *IEEE Multimedia*, vol. 11(1), pp. 95–96, March 2004.

[15] J. Jannotti, D. Gifford, K. Johnson, M. F. Kaashoek, and J. O'Toole, "Overcast: Reliable Multicasting with an Overlay Network", *Proc. Operating System Design and Implementation (OSDI)*, San Diego, CA, pp. 14–27. Oct. 2000.

[16] S. Kanumuri, P. C. Cosman, A. R. Reibman, and V. A. Vaishampayan, "Modeling packet-loss visibility in MPEG-2 video", *IEEE Trans. on Multimedia*, vol. 8(2), pp. 341–355, April 2006.

[17] C. Labovitz, R. Malan, and F. Jahanian, "Internet Routing Instability", *IEEE/ACM Trans. on Networking*, vol. 6(5), pp. 515–528, Oct. 1998.

[18] M. Lu, J. Wu, K. Peng, P. Huang, J. Yao, and H. Chen, "Design and Evaluation of a P2P IPTV System for Heterogeneous Networks", *IEEE Trans. on Multimedia*, vol. 9(8), pp. 1568–1579, Dec. 2007.

[19] C. Lumezanu, D. Levin, and N. Spring, "PeerWise Discovery and Negotiation of Faster Paths", *ACM HotNets*, Atlanta, GA. Nov. 2007.

[20] V. Paxson, "End-to-end routing behavior in the Internet", *IEEE/ACM Trans. on Networking*, 5(5), pp. 601–615, 1997.

[21] M. H. Pinson and S. Wolf, "A New Standardized Method for Objectively Measuring Video Quality", *IEEE Trans. on Broadcasting*, vol. 50(3), pp. 312–322 . Sept 2003.

[22] S. Savage *et. al.*, "Detour: A Case for informed internet routing and transport", *IEEE Micro*, vol. 19(1), pp. 50–59. Jan. 1999.

[23] M. Siller and J. Woods, "QoS arbitration for improving the QoE in multimedia transmission", *Proc. Intl. Conf. on Visual Information Engineering (VIE)*, Guildfor, UK, pp. 238–241. July 2003.

[24] L. Subramanian, S. Agarwal, J. Rexford, and R. H. Katz, "Characterizing the Internet hierarchy from multiple vantage points", *IEEE Infocom*, New York, NY, pp. 618–627. June 2002.

[25] L. Subramanian, I. Stoica, H. Balakrishnan, and R. Katz, "OverQoS: An Overlay Based Architecture for Enhancing Internet QoS", *Usenix Network System Design and Implementation (NSDI)*, San Fransisco, CA, pp. 4–17. March 2004.

[26] S. Tasaka, H. Yoshimi, A. Hirashima, and T. Nunome, "The Effectiveness of a QoE-Based Video Output Scheme for Audio-Video IP Transmission", *ACM Multimedia (MM)*, Vancouver, Canada, pp. 259–268. Oct. 2008.

[27] Akamai Inc., http://www.akamai.com

[28] Ineoquest Singulus G1-T Equipment. www.ineoquest.com/singulus-family

[29] PlanetLab Consortium. http://www.planet-lab.org/

[30] VLC Media Player, http://www.videolan.org/vlc

[31] Video Clips and PlanetLab Vantage points used in this paper. http://sites.google.com/site/anonqoe/

Improving the Performance of Quality-Adaptive Video Streaming over Multiple Heterogeneous Access Networks

Kristian Evensen[1], Dominik Kaspar[1], Carsten Griwodz[1,2], Pål Halvorsen[1,2],
Audun F. Hansen[1], Paal Engelstad[1]

[1]Simula Research Laboratory, Norway [2]Department of Informatics, University of Oslo, Norway

{kristrev, kaspar, griff, paalh, audunh, paale}@simula.no

ABSTRACT

Devices capable of connecting to multiple, overlapping networks simultaneously are becoming increasingly common. For example, most laptops are equipped with LAN- and WLAN-interfaces, and smart phones can typically connect to both WLANs and 3G mobile networks. At the same time, streaming high-quality video is becoming increasingly popular. However, due to bandwidth limitations or the unreliable and unpredictable nature of some types of networks, streaming video can be subject to frequent periods of rebuffering and characterised by a low picture quality.

In this paper, we present a client-side request scheduler that distributes requests for the video over multiple heterogeneous interfaces simultaneously. Each video is divided into independent segments with constant duration, enabling segments to be requested over separate links, utilizing all the available bandwidth. To increase performance even further, the segments are divided into smaller subsegments, and the sizes are dynamically calculated on the fly, based on the throughput of the different links. This is an improvement over our earlier subsegment approach, which divided segments into fixed size subsegments.

Both subsegment approaches were evaluated with on-demand streaming and quasi-live streaming. The new subsegment approach reduces the number of playback interruptions and improves video quality significantly for all cases where the earlier approach struggled. Otherwise, they show similar performance.

Categories and Subject Descriptors

C.2.4 [**Computer-Communication Networks**]: Distributed Systems - Client/Server

General Terms

Performance

1. INTRODUCTION

Streaming high-quality video is rapidly increasing in popularity. Video aggregation sites, like YouTube and Vimeo, serve millions of HD-videos every day, various events are broadcasted live over the Internet and large investments are made in video-on-demand services. One example is Hulu [1], which is backed by over 225 content companies and allows users to legally stream popular TV-shows like Lost, Glee, and America's Got Talent.

However, high-quality video has a high bandwidth requirement. For example, the bitrate of H.264-compressed 1080p video is usually around 6-8 Mbit/s. This might not be a problem in areas with a highly developed broadband infrastructure, but a single, average home connection to the Internet might not be able to support this quality. For example, the average broadband connection in the US is about 4 Mbit/s [2]. Due to bandwidth limitations or the unreliable and unpredictable nature of some types of networks, for example WLAN and HSDPA, streaming video can be subject to frequent periods of rebuffering, characterised by a low picture quality and playback interruptions.

Today, devices capable of connecting to multiple, overlapping networks simultaneously are common. For example, most laptops are equipped with LAN- and WLAN-interfaces, and smart phones can often connect to both WLANs and HSDPA-networks. One way to alleviate the bandwidth problem, is to increase the available bandwidth by aggregating multiple physical links into one logical link. By dividing the video into segments, parts can be requested/sent over independent links simultaneously, achieving bandwidth aggregation. An example of a popular, commercial streaming system which can be extended to support bandwidth aggregation, is Microsoft's HTTP-based Smooth-Streaming [15]. Videos are encoded at different fixed quality levels and divided into independent segments. The quality level is chosen once for every segment by the client, using the previously observed bandwidth to make the decision.

We have previously developed and presented a client-side request scheduler that retrieves video segments in several encodings over multiple heterogeneous network interfaces simultaneously [5]. To improve performance even further, the segments are divided into smaller logical subsegments, and the request scheduler performed well in our experiments. It reduced the number of playback interruptions and increased the average video quality significantly. However, this subsegment approach has a weakness - segments are divided into fixed-sized subsegments which, in combination with lim-

---

[1]http://www.hulu.com/about

ited receive buffers, have a significant effect on multilink-performance. Unless the buffer is large enough to compensate for the link heterogeneity, this static approach is unable to reach maximum performance. Increasing the size of the receive buffer alleviates the problem. However, it might not be acceptable, desirable or even possible with a larger buffer, as it adds delay and requires more memory.

In this paper, we present an improved subsegment approach. Subsegment sizes are dynamic and calculated on the fly, based on the links' performance. By doing this, the request scheduler avoids idle periods by allocating the ideal amount of data (at that time) to each link. The request scheduler and both subsegment approaches were implemented as extensions to the DAVVI [7] streaming platform. The approaches were evaluated with on-demand streaming and live streaming with and without buffering, in a controlled network environment and with real world wireless links. In the context of this paper, live is liveness, where we have defined liveness to be how much the stream lags behind the no-delay broadcast. The dynamic subsegment approach significantly reduces the number of playback interruptions, and improves the video quality when multiple links are used. When the buffer is large enough to compensate for the link heterogeneity, both the old and new subsegment approach show similar performance.

The rest of the paper is organized as follows. Section 2 contains a presentation of related work, while section 3 describes DAVVI and our modifications. Our testbed setup is introduced in section 4, and the results from our experiments are discussed in section 5. Finally, we give the conclusion and prospects for future work in section 6.

2. RELATED WORK

HTTP is currently one of the, if not the, most common protocol used to stream video through the Internet, and multi-quality encoding and file segmentation is a popular way to allow quality adaptation and increase performance. By picking the quality most suited to the current link performance, a smoother playback can be achieved. Also, file segmentation allows content providers to build more scalable services that offer a better user experience due to increased capacity. Commercial examples of HTTP-based streaming solutions built upon segmentation of the original content, include Move Networks [10], Apple's QuickTime Streaming Server [1] and Microsoft's SmoothStreaming [15].

Picking the most appropriate server is a non-trivial problem that has been studied extensively. Parallel access schemes, like those presented in [12] and [14], try to reduce the load on congested servers by automatically switching to other servers for further segment requests. These parallel access schemes assume that excessive server load or network congestion create the throughput bottleneck. We assume that the bottleneck lies somewhere in the access network. However, the scheduling problem is similar - either the client or server has more available bandwidth than the other party can utilize.

Parallel access schemes are not suitable for achieving live or quasi-live streaming (sometimes referred to as "progressive download"), as they have no notion of deadlines. Also, the additional complexity introduced by automatically adapting the video quality is not solved by these parallel access schemes. Still, with some modifications, the techniques developed within the field of parallel access can be applied to

multilink streaming. Our earlier subsegment approach was inspired by the work done in [9], where the authors divide a complete file into smaller, fixed-size subsegments. The new, dynamic subsegment approach uses some of the ideas found in [6], most notably using the current throughput to calculate the size of the subsegments.

Although our solution can be extended to support multiple servers, our current research focuses on client-based performance improvements of using multiple network interfaces simultaneously. Wang et al. pursued a similar goal in [13], where the server streams video over multiple TCP connections to a client. However, such push-based solutions have limited knowledge about the client-side connectivity, and introduce a significant delay before detecting if a client's interface has gone down or a device has lost the connection with its current network. Also, push-based solutions, for example [3], cannot easily be extended to support multiple servers. Since we assume that the bottleneck is in the access network, we favour a pull-based scheme, allowing the client to adjust the quality and subsegment-request schedule.

3. SYSTEM COMPONENTS

Streaming high-quality video is bandwidth intensive, as discussed earlier. In many cases, for example with wireless networks, a single link is often insufficient. To show how multiple independent links can be used to achieve a higher video quality, we extended the DAVVI streaming system [7] with support for more than a single network interface. This section describes DAVVI in more detail, as well as the improvements we made to the data delivery subsystem.

3.1 Video streaming

DAVVI is an HTTP-based streaming system where each video is divided into fixed length, independent (closed-GOP) segments with constant duration (two seconds). A video is encoded in multiple qualities (bitrates), and the constant duration of the segments limits the liveness of a stream - at least one segment must be ready and received by the client before playback can start.

DAVVI stores video segments on regular web servers. A dedicated streaming server is not needed, the video segments are retrieved using normal HTTP GET-requests. Because no additional feedback is provided by the server and the client monitors the available resources, the client is responsible for prefetching, buffering, and adapting video quality. The quality can be changed whenever a new segment is requested, but the user can not see the change immediately. In our case, each segment contains two seconds of video, which has been shown to be a good segment length. According to the work done in [11], changing video quality more frequently than every 1-2 seconds annoys the user. However, the two second segment length is a limit imposed by DAVVI, in our future work, we plan to look at how the duration of a segment affects the subsegment approaches and thereby performance. For example, one possibility would be to use H.264 SVC-encoding and allow changing quality immediately, but then forbid a new change within one second.

For this paper, we look at three types of streaming, on-demand streaming, live streaming with buffering and live streaming without buffering. **On-demand streaming** is the most common type of streaming and used as our base case, it assumes "infinite" receive buffers and is only limited by network bandwidth. Because the entire video is available in advance, segments are requested as soon as there is room in the receive buffer. We use an alternative encoding and linear download, so we do not have the common concept of a base layer that could be downloaded first with quality improvements as time permits. On-demand streaming is used together with full-length movies and similar content, meaning that video quality and continuous playback are the most important metrics.

Live streaming with buffering is very similar to on-demand streaming, except that the whole video is not available when the streaming starts. As defined in the introduction, live in the context of this paper is liveness, and by delaying playback by a given number of segments (the startup delay), a trade off between liveness and smoothness is made. Provided that all requested segments are received before their playout deadline, the total delay compared to the no-delay broadcast is *startup_delay + initial_segments_transfer_time*. Any errors occurring during transfer cause a further reduction in liveness.

Live streaming without buffering has liveness as the most important metric and is the opposite of on-demand streaming. Segments (requests) are skipped if the stream lags too far behind the broadcast, and a requirement for being as live as possible is that the startup delay is the lowest that is allowed by the streaming system. In our case, this limit is two seconds (one segment), so the client lags *2s + initial_segment_transfer_time* behind the no-delay broadcast when playback starts, and skips segments if the lag exceeds the length of one segment. This limitation can be overcome by for example using x264-encoding with the zerolatency option. However, this would involve abandoning the standard web server and the creation of new request schedulers and subsegment approaches, and has been left for future work.

3.2 Multilink support

Several changes were made to the DAVVI streaming system to support multiple links. We implemented our multilink HTTP download and pipelining mechanisms [8], as well as the request scheduler and subsegment approaches described in section 3.3. The scheduler is responsible for distributing segment requests among the links efficiently, while the subsegment approaches try to make sure that each link is used to its full capacity.

The routing table on the client must be configured properly to allow DAVVI, or any other application, to use multiple links simultaneously. The network subsystem must be aware of the default interface and know how to reach other machines in the connected networks, and packets must be sent through the correct interfaces. Once the routing table is correct, multilink-support in the application is enabled by binding network sockets to the desired interfaces. This is supported by all major operating systems.

3.2.1 Subsegments of varying size

Even though DAVVI divides the video into segments, the segments can still be large. Therefore, they are divided into smaller logical subsegments to reduce latency, increase the granularity of the request scheduler and allow the transfer of video over multiple interfaces simultaneously. Using the *range retrieval request*-feature of HTTP/1.1, it is possible to request a specific part of a file (a subsegment). For example, if the first 50 kB of a 100 kB large file are requested, bytes 0 - 49 999 are sent from the server. There are other techniques

to request/send data over multiple links simultaneously, see for example the transparent network-layer proxy presented in [4]. However, they are outside the scope of this paper.

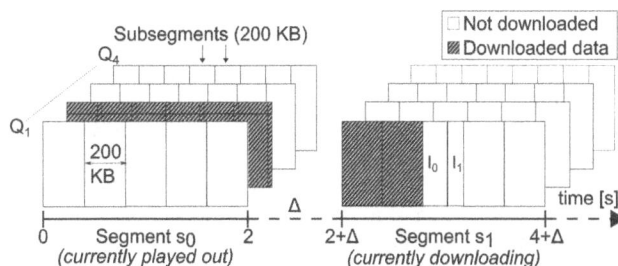

Figure 1: In this example, two interfaces I_0 and I_1 have finished downloading segment s_0 of quality Q_2. As the throughput dropped, the links currently collaborate on downloading the third subsegment of a lower quality segment.

The subsegment approach decides how complete segments are divided into subsegments, and how the links are allocated their share of the data. For example, figure 1 shows how a 200kB subsegment would be divided between two links with a bandwidth ratio of 3:2, according to the dynamic subsegment approach presented in section 3.3. Interface zero requests 120 kB and interface one 80 kB.

3.2.2 Request pipelining

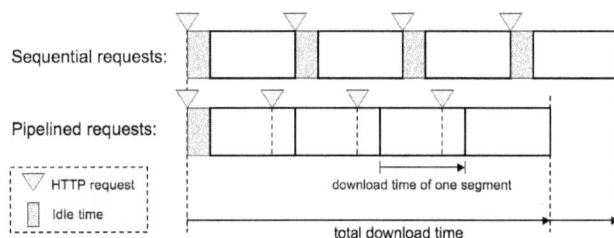

Figure 2: From a client-side perspective, HTTP pipelining eliminates the time overhead incurred by a sequential processing of requests and replies.

Dividing segments into subsegments introduces two challenges. First, subsegments cause an increase in the number of HTTP GET-requests. This reduces performance, as the client spends more time idle waiting for responses. HTTP pipelining, illustrated in figure 2, is used to reduce both the number and duration of these idle periods. Initially, two subsegments are requested on every interface, and then, a new subsegment is requested for each one received. This ensures that the server always has a request to process, and that there is always incoming data.

The second challenge is related to the size of the subsegments, and only applies when fixed size subsegments are used. If they are too small, an entire subsegment might have been sent from the server before the next is requested, causing interfaces to become idle. This can be alleviated by having a fixed subsegment size. For example, our earlier work [8] has shown that 100 kB is well suited, as it allows sufficient flexibility for the request scheduler, and is large enough to take advantage of HTTP pipelining.

The reason the subsegment size challenge does not apply to subsegment approaches that calculate the size dynamically, is that the size of the subsegments matches the links' performance. Thus, the size of the subsegment is equal to what the link can transfer.

3.3 Quality adaptation and request schedulers

To use multiple links efficiently, segments must be requested according to the available resources. If a slow interface is allocated a large share of a segment, the performance of the whole application might suffer. For example, the segment may not be ready when it is supposed to be played out, causing a deadline miss and an interruption in playback.

The request scheduler is responsible for distributing requests and adjusting the desired video quality, and, in combination with the subsegment approaches, is the most important part of our multilink streaming approach. Without a good scheduler and subsegment approach, adding multiple interfaces can cause a drop in performance and have a significant effect on the user experience. For example, the quality adaptation might be too optimistic and select a higher quality than the links can support, or links are not used to their full capacity.

In this paper, we compare the performance of two subsegment size approaches. The underlying request scheduler is identical for both approaches, i.e., the same technique is used to measure the link characteristics (throughput and RTT) and adjust the video quality. The video quality adaptation is outlined in algorithm 1. First, the client calculates how much content it has already received and is ready for playout (*transfer_deadline*), and estimates how long it takes to receive already requested data (*pipeline_delay*). The *pipeline_delay* is subtracted from the *transfer_deadline* to get an estimate of how much time the client can spend receiving new data without causing a deadline miss. This estimate is then compared against estimates of the time it takes to receive the desired segment in the different qualities, and the most suited quality is selected.

Algorithm 1 Quality adaptation mechanism

$transfer\_deadline = time\_left\_playout + (segment\_length * num\_completed\_segments)$
$pipeline\_delay = requested\_bytes\_left / aggregated\_throughput$
for $quality\_level$ = "super" to "low" **do**
   $transfer\_time = segment\_size[quality\_level] / aggregated\_throughput$
   if $transfer\_time < (transfer\_deadline - pipeline\_delay)$ **then**
     return $quality\_level$
   end if
   reduce $quality\_level$
end for

The two approaches differ in how they divide segments. The **static subsegment approach**, which is the one that was used in [5], divides each segment into fixed-sized 100KB subsegments. Requests for subsegments are distributed among the links, and provided that there are more subsegments available, new requests are pipelined as soon as possible.

However, our earlier work did not sufficiently consider the challenges introduced by limited receive buffers and timeliness. In addition to the *last segment problem* [8], caused by clients having to wait for the slowest interface to receive the last subsegment of a segment, the static subsegment approach is unable to reach maximum performance unless the receive buffer is large enough to compensate for the link

heterogeneity. This problem is discussed in more detail in section 3.4.

Increasing the buffer size is in many cases not acceptable, desirable or even possible. We therefore decided to improve on our old subsegment approach by allocating data to the links in a more dynamic fashion. The segments are now divided into subsegments of *number_of_interfaces* * 100kB (or as big as possible), where 100kB is a well suited share of data to request over one link, as discussed earlier and presented in [8]. These subsegments are divided into even smaller subsegments that are requested over the interfaces, and the size of each requested subsegment is calculated based on the monitored throughput of the current interface. Pipelining is still done as soon as possible, and the algorithm is outlined in algorithm 2.

Algorithm 2 Dynamic subsegment approach *[simplified]*

$share\_interface = throughput\_link / aggregated\_throughput$
$size\_allocated\_data = share\_interface * subsegment\_length$
if $size\_allocated\_data > left\_subsegment$ **then**
   $size\_allocated\_data = left\_subsegment$
end if
update $left\_subsegment$
request new Subsegment($size\_allocated\_data$)

By allocating the data dynamically based on performance, the need for a big buffer is removed, and the effect of the *last segment problem* is reduced. The problem can still occur, but because the performance of the links is used when allocating data, it has a smaller effect. When dividing segments dynamically, the performance for a given buffer size should ideally be the same for all link heterogeneities. This approach is hereby referred to as the **dynamic subsegment approach**.

3.4 Considerations: Static vs. Dynamic

The switch from a static to a dynamic subsegment approach was motivated by the buffer requirement imposed by the *static* subsegment approach. Unless the buffer is large enough to compensate for the link heterogeneity, the client is unable to reach maximum performance. With a short startup delay and small buffer, the request scheduler is only allowed a little slack when requesting the first segment after the playout has started. Assuming that the links are heterogeneous and none exceed the bandwidth requirement for the stream by a wide margin, this forces the scheduler to pick a segment of lower quality. Smaller segments consist of fewer subsegments, so the slowest link is allocated a larger share of the data, and has a more significant effect on throughput. This continues until the throughput and quality stabilizes at a lower level than the links might support. In other words, the request scheduler is caught in a vicious circle. Furthermore, increasing the receive buffer size and startup delay improves the situation. A larger receive buffer allows the scheduler more slack, so the first segment after the startup delay is requested in a higher quality than with a small buffer. Larger segments consist of more subsegments than smaller ones, so the slowest interface is made responsible for less data. Provided that the buffer is large enough, the links are allocated their correct share of subsegments (or at least close to). Thus, throughput measurements are higher and a better video quality distribution is achieved.

On the other hand, when dividing the segments into subsegments *dynamically*, the buffer size/startup delay problem is avoided. Each link is allocated their correct share of a segment (at that time), so the slower links are made responsible for less data. However, there are challenges when dividing segments dynamically as well. In the first version of the dynamic subsegment approach, we used the size of the segment to determine a link's share. As it turned out, the performance of this approach suffers when faced with dynamic network environments. Links are often allocated too much data, making the approach vulnerable to throughput and delay variance. Therefore, we limited the amount of data used for calculating a link's share to $number\_of\_interfaces * 100kB$, as presented earlier.

4. EXPERIMENTAL SETUP

To evaluate the performance of the two request schedulers, two testbeds were created. We wanted to measure the performance in the real world and in a controlled environment, to fully control all parameters.

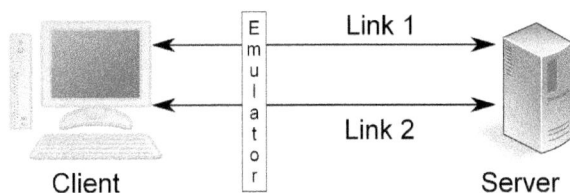

Figure 3: Our controlled environment-testbed.

The controlled environment-testbed, shown in figure 3, consists of a client and a server (Apache 2) connected using two independent 100 Mbit/s Ethernet links. Both client and server run Linux 2.6.31, and to control the different link characteristics, the network emulator *netem* is used with a hierarchical token bucket queueing discipline. For measuring the real world performance, we made experiments in a wireless scenario where the client was connected to one public WLAN (IEEE 802.11b) and an HSDPA network. The characteristics of these networks are summarized in table 1, and the reason we choose wireless networks is that they present a more challenging environment than fixed links.

	WLAN	HSDPA
Average experienced throughput	287 KB/s	167 KB/s
Average RTT for header-only IP packets	20 ms	100 ms
Average RTT for full-size IP packets	30 ms	220 ms

Table 1: Observed Characteristics of used Links

To get comparable results, the same video clip was used in all the experiments. The clip shows a football match, has a total playout duration of 100 minutes (3127 segments of two seconds) and was available in four qualities. We chose a subset of 100 segments, and the bandwidth requirements are shown in table 2.

Quality level	Low	Medium	High	Super
Minimum bitrate (Kbit/s)	524	866	1491	2212
Average bitrate (Kbit/s)	746	1300	2142	3010
Maximum bitrate (Kbit/s)	1057	1923	3293	4884

Table 2: Quality levels and bitrates of the soccer movie

5. RESULTS AND DISCUSSION

When evaluating the performance of the two subsegment approaches, we measure the video quality and deadline misses.

The video quality is dependent on the bandwidth aggregation, i.e., an efficient aggregation results in a higher throughput. Thus, the quality increases. Deadline misses are of highest importance from a user's perspective, with respect to perceived video quality. The number of deadline misses depend on the subsegment approach. A poor approach allocates too much data to slower interfaces, causing data to arrive late and segments to miss their deadlines.

In our earlier work [5], we compared the single-link and multilink performance of the static subsegment approach, as well as the performance of the request scheduler. In this paper, the focus is on the differences between the two subsegment approaches in a multilink scenario. With multiple links, bandwidth and latency heterogeneity are the two most significant challenges, so we decided to look at their effect on performance, both in a completely controlled environment, with emulated network dynamics and in a real-world wireless environment. Multilink request schedulers and subsegment approaches have to take heterogeneity into account, otherwise the performance is less than ideal, and sometimes worse than when only a single link is used [5].

The combined bandwidth of the emulated links was always 3 Mbit/s, which is equal to the average bandwidth requirement for the highest quality of the video clip used in our experiments. The startup delay was equal to the buffer size in all the experiments, forcing the application to fill the buffer completely before starting playback.

5.1 Bandwidth heterogeneity

For measuring how bandwidth heterogeneity affects the performance of the two subsegment approaches, the controlled testbed was used and configured to provide different levels of bandwidth heterogeneity. The goal with using multiple links simultaneously, was that the performance should match that of a single 3 Mbit/s link, in other words, the aggregated logical link should perform just as well as an actual 3 Mbit/s link.

5.1.1 On-demand streaming

For an on-demand scenario, figure 4 shows the video quality distribution for a buffer size of two segments (four second delay). The bandwidth ratio is shown along the x-axis, and the X:Y notation means that one link was allocated X % of the bandwidth, while the other link was allocated Y %. The bars represents the four video qualities, and the y-value of each bar is its share of the received segments. The reason we did not divide the y-axis into the four quality-levels and plot the average quality, is that the y-value of a bar would end up between qualities. As the quality level "Medium.5" (or similar) does not exist, we decided to plot the quality distributions instead.

When a single link was used, the expected behavior can be observed. As the available bandwidth increased, so too did the video quality. Also, the static and dynamic subsegment approaches achieved more or less the same video quality.

However, the situation was different with multiple links. The dynamic subsegment approach adapted to the heterogeneity, the performance was close to constant irrespective of link heterogeneity, and significantly better than when a single link was used. However, the performance never reached the level of a single 3 Mbit/s link (even though the difference was small), due to the additional overhead introduced when using multiple links.

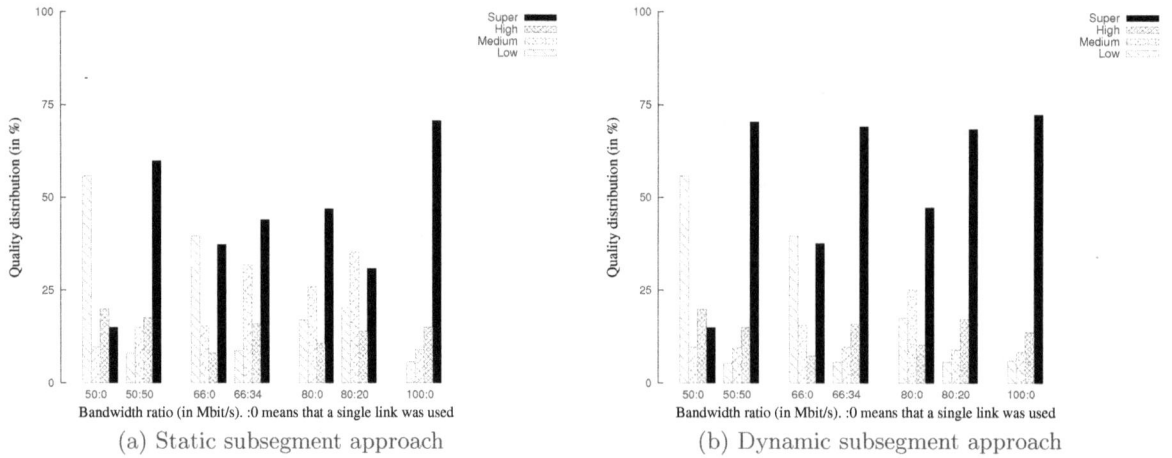

(a) Static subsegment approach   (b) Dynamic subsegment approach

Figure 4: Video quality distribution for different bandwidth heterogeneities, buffer size/startup delay of two segments (4 seconds) and on-demand streaming.

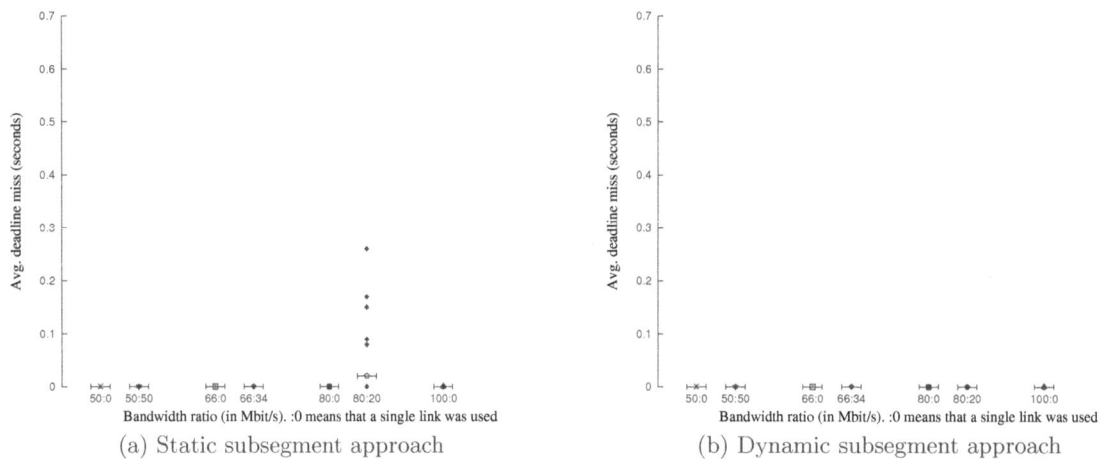

(a) Static subsegment approach   (b) Dynamic subsegment approach

Figure 5: Deadline misses for different levels of bandwidth heterogeneity with on-demand streaming, buffer size/startup delay of two segments (4 seconds).

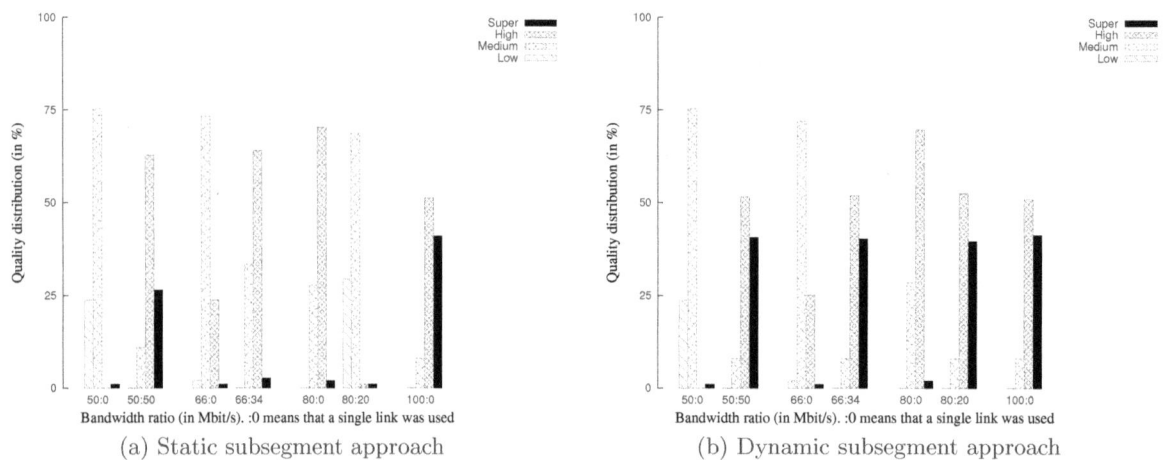

(a) Static subsegment approach   (b) Dynamic subsegment approach

Figure 6: Video quality distribution for different levels of bandwidth heterogeneity, buffer size/startup delay of one segment (2 second startup delay) and live streaming with buffering.

The static subsegment approach, on the other hand, suffered from the problem discussed in section 3.4, when the heterogeneity increased, the achieved video quality decreased. When the bandwidth ratio was 80:20, the single link performance exceeded multilink.

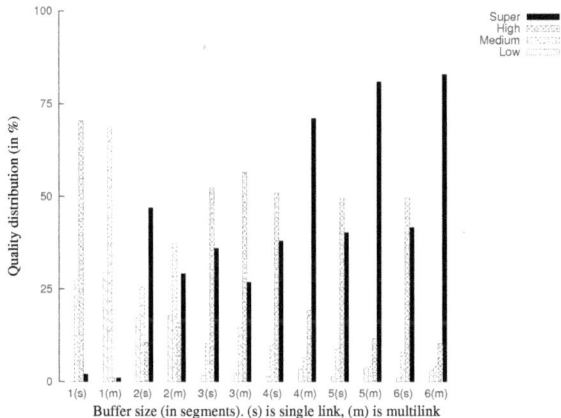

Figure 7: Quality distribution plotted against the startup delay/buffer size for a bandwidth ratio of 80:20, on-demand streaming and static subsegment approach.

As discussed in [5], the static subsegment approach requires the buffer to be large enough to compensate for the bandwidth heterogeneity. A rule of thumb is that the buffer size shall be equal to the ratio between the links. For example, with a bandwidth ratio of 80:20, the ideal buffer size is five segments, because the fast interface can receive four segments for every one segment over the slow interface. However, this is only correct with a CBR-encoded video. With a VBR-encoded video, the segments are of different sizes and have different bandwidth requirements. The latter explains why a buffer size of four segments was sufficient for the multilink performance to exceed that of a single link with a bandwidth ratio of 80:20, as seen in figure 7. This figure shows how increasing the startup delay and buffer size improved the video quality when the bandwidth ratio was 80:20.

Figure 5 shows the average number of deadline misses for the bandwidth ratios. As expected when faced with static links, both subsegment approaches performed well. The bandwidth measurements and quality adaption were accurate, there were close to no deadline misses, except for when the buffer was unable to compensate for heterogeneity. The deadline misses when the bandwidth ratio was 80:20 were caused by the slow interface delaying the reception and thereby playback of some segments. However, all deadline misses were significantly lower than the segment length, the worst observed miss was only ~0.3 seconds.

5.1.2   Live streaming with buffering

When live streaming with buffering was used, the experimental results were similar to those of the on-demand streaming tests. The single link performance of the two subsegment approaches was more or less the same, and when multiple links were used, the dynamic subsegment approach showed similar performance irrespective of bandwidth heterogeneity, while the performance of the static subsegment approach suffered from the buffer being to small to compensate for the link heterogeneity. The number of deadline

misses were also the same as with on-demand streaming. The reason for these similar results, is that segments were always ready also when live streaming with buffering was used. The client was never able to fully catch up with the no-delay broadcast.

With on-demand streaming, it makes no sense to talk about liveness. However, in live streaming with buffering, liveness is one of the most important criteria. With a startup-delay/buffer size of two segments, the static subsegment approach added an additional worst-case delay of 4 s compared to the no-delay broadcast. The dynamic subsegment approach caused an additional worst-case delay of 2.5 s.

Figure 6 shows the effect of increasing the liveness to the maximum allowed by DAVVI. Both the startup delay and buffer size was set to one segment (two second delay). The dynamic subsegment approach was able to cope well with the increased liveness requirement, and showed a significant increase in performance compared to using a single link. Also, the performance was independent of the bandwidth heterogeneity. The static subsegment approach, on the other hand, struggled because of the small buffer. In addition to pipelining loosing almost all effect, it only worked within a segment, the problem discussed in section 3.4 came into play. The performance hit was reflected in the deadline misses, shown in figure 8. While the dynamic subsegment approach was able to avoid almost all deadline misses, the static subsegment approach caused several misses. When the dynamic subsegment approach was used, a worst-case additional delay of 2.3 seconds was observed, compared to 6 seconds with the static subsegment approach.

5.1.3   Live streaming without buffering

The goal with skipping segments is that the stream shall be as live as possible, the client chooses not to request old segments. Skipping leads to interruptions in playback, but did not affect the video quality, as shown in figure 9. The results were the same as for live streaming with buffering and a buffer size/startup delay of one segment - the dynamic subsegment approach improved the performance significantly, while the static subsegment approach suffered from the problem discussed in section 3.4. The deadline misses were similar to figure 8, in other words, the dynamic subsegment approach was able to avoid most deadline misses, unlike the static subsegment approach.

However, the number of skipped segments were the same for both subsegment approaches, with a worst case of two segments. This was because of the first segment, which is requested in the highest quality to get the most accurate measurements. The approaches assume that all links are equal and initially allocates the same amount of data to each. If the links are not homogeneous, which was the case in almost all of our experiments, or able to support the quality, the segment takes longer than two seconds to receive and one or more segments are skipped. The deadline misses and initial segment transfer time with the static subsegment approach caused a worst case additional total delay of 1.86 seconds, which is less than the length of a single segment, and explains why the static subsegment approach did not skip more segments than the dynamic subsegment approach.

5.2   Latency heterogeneity

When measuring the effect of latency heterogeneity on video quality and deadline misses, we used one link that had

(a) Static subsegment approach

(b) Dynamic subsegment approach

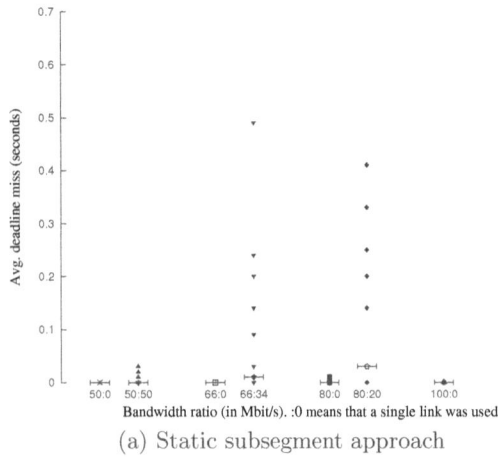

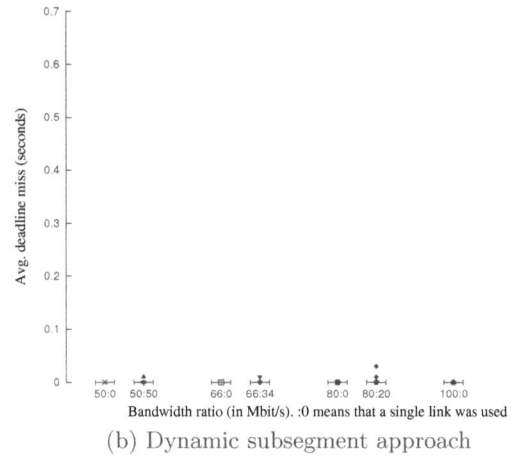

Figure 8: Deadline misses for a buffer size of one segment (2 second startup delay) and various levels of bandwidth heterogeneity, live streaming with buffering.

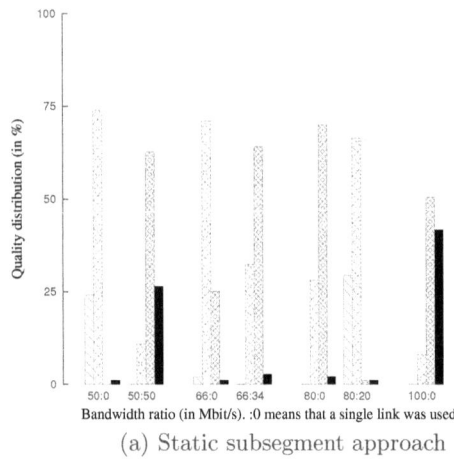

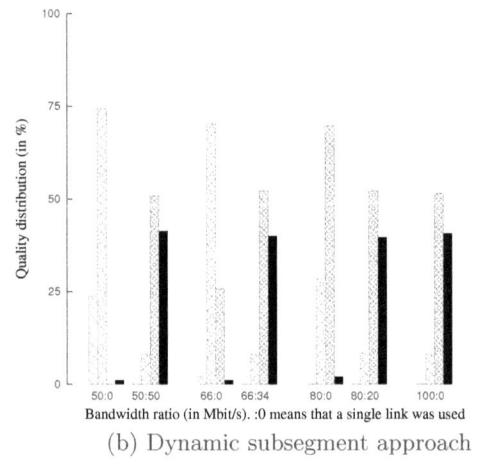

(a) Static subsegment approach

(b) Dynamic subsegment approach

Figure 9: Video quality distribution for a buffer size of one segment (2 second startup delay), live streaming without buffering and bandwidth heterogeneity.

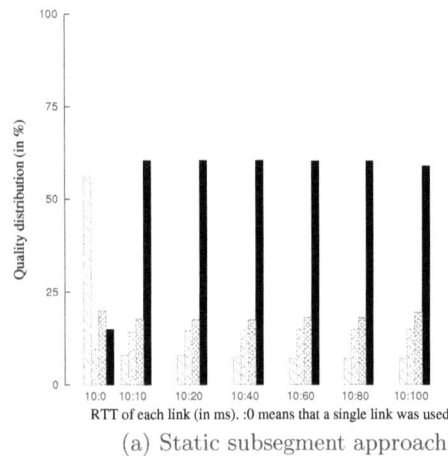

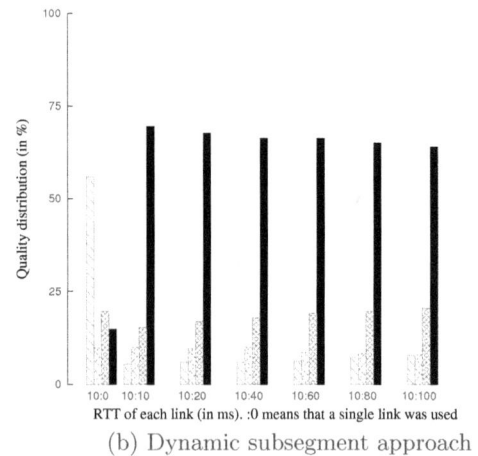

(a) Static subsegment approach

(b) Dynamic subsegment approach

Figure 10: Video quality distribution for two-segment buffers and various levels of latency heterogeneity.

a constant RTT of 10 ms. The other link was assigned an RTT of r ms, with $r \in \{10, 20, \ldots, 100\}$. The bandwidth of each link was limited to 1.5 Mbit/s, and a buffer size of two segments was used (according to the rule of thumb presented earlier and [5]).

5.2.1 On-demand streaming

Figure 10 depicts the video quality distribution for different levels of latency heterogeneity. As shown, RTT heterogeneity did not have a significant effect on video quality, independent of subsegment approach. The bandwidth ratio was 50:50, and both subsegment approaches achieved close to the same quality distribution as in the on-demand bandwidth heterogeneity experiments (for a 50:50 bandwidth ratio), shown in figure 4, for all latency heterogeneities. The reason for the performance difference between the two approaches, is that the dynamic subsegment approach is able to use the links more efficiently.

For both subsegment approaches, a slight decrease in quality as the heterogeneity increased can be observed, indicating that the RTT heterogeneity at some point will have an effect. The reason for the quality decrease, is that it takes longer to request, and thereby receive, each segment. The approaches measure a lower throughput, and potentially reduces the quality of the requested segments.

HTTP pipelining is used to compensate for high RTT and RTT heterogeneities. However, pipelining is not possible when the buffer is full and the next segment can't be requested immediately. Also, TCP throughput is lower for short transfers and high delay.

The deadline misses were also similar to the 50:50-case in the bandwidth heterogeneity experiments, shown in figure 5. As expected in a static environment, both subsegment approaches made accurate decisions and no deadline misses were observed.

5.2.2 Live streaming with buffering

As with bandwidth heterogeneity, the results when measuring the effect of latency heterogeneity on live streaming with buffering were very similar to those with on-demand streaming. The quality distribution and deadline misses were not affected for the levels of heterogeneity we have used. However, a slight decrease in video quality as the RTT heterogeneity increases can be seen also here. The worst case observer additional delay compared to the no-delay broadcast was 2 s for both subsegment approaches.

Reducing the buffer size/startup delay to one, caused a similar reduction in performance to the ones seen in figures 6 and 8 (for a 50:50 bandwidth ratio). However, as for a buffer size of two segments, the latency heterogeneity did not affect the quality distribution or deadline misses. Both subsegment approached caused a worst additional case additional delay of 2.5 s.

5.2.3 Live streaming without buffering

The observed video quality and deadline misses using live streaming without buffering, were similar to the earlier latency heterogeneity experiments. RTT heterogeneity did not have a significant impact on video quality, however, a slight decrease can be observed, indicating that the RTT heterogeneity will affect the performance of the approaches at some point. As in the bandwidth heterogeneity experiments for live streaming without buffering, the number of

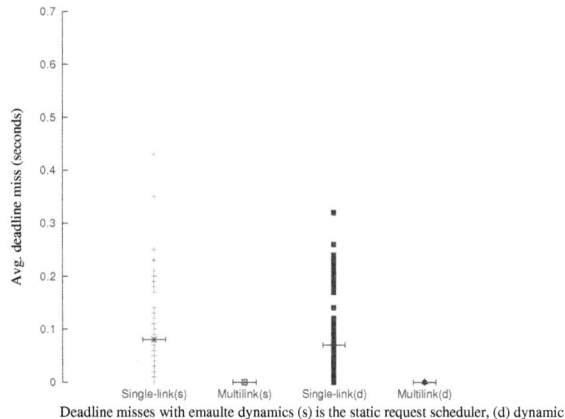

Figure 14: Deadline misses with on-demand streaming and emulated dynamics.

skipped segments and the total delay compared to the no-delay broadcast were the same for both approaches. When multiple links were used, zero segments were skipped, and a worst case additional delay of 1.86 seconds was observed for both subsegment approaches, caused by the first segment. Even though the initial assumptions that both links are homogeneous were correct, the links were unable to support the bandwidth requirement for this segment.

5.3 Emulated dynamics

Dynamic links impose different challenges than static links, the scheduler has to adapt to often rapid changes in the network. To expose the two subsegment approaches to dynamic links while still having some control over the parameters, we created a script which emulates our observed real-world network behavior. The sum of the bandwidth of the two links was always 3 Mbit/s, but at random intervals of t seconds, $t \in \{2, \ldots, 10\}$, the bandwidth bw Mbit/s, $bw \in \{0.5, \ldots, 2.5\}$ of each link was updated. The RTT of link 1 was normally distributed between 0 ms and 20 ms, while the RTT of link 2 was uniformly distributed between 20 ms and 80 ms. A buffer size of six segments was used to compensate for the worst case bandwidth heterogeneity, according to the rule of thumb presented earlier and in [5], except for in the live streaming without buffering experiments. Each subsegment approach was tested 30 times for each type of streaming, and the results shown are the averages of all measurements.

5.3.1 On-demand streaming

The aggregated throughput when combining emulated link dynamics with on-demand streaming, is shown in figure 11. With both subsegment approaches, adding a second link gave a significant increase in throughput, and thereby achieved video quality. Also, as in the other experiments where the buffer size was large enough to compensate for link heterogeneity, both approaches gave close to the same video quality distribution, with a slight advantage to the dynamic subsegment approach. The average aggregated throughput oscillated between the average bandwidth requirement for "High" and "Super" quality, the quality distribution is presented in table 3.

In terms of deadline misses, shown in figure 14, both approaches were as accurate. When a single link was used, misses occurred, however, none were severe. The worst case

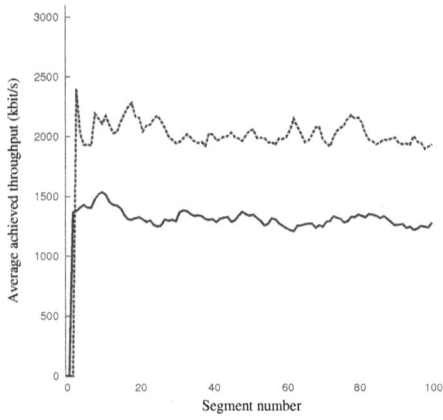

(a) Static subsegment approach (b) Dynamic subsegment approach

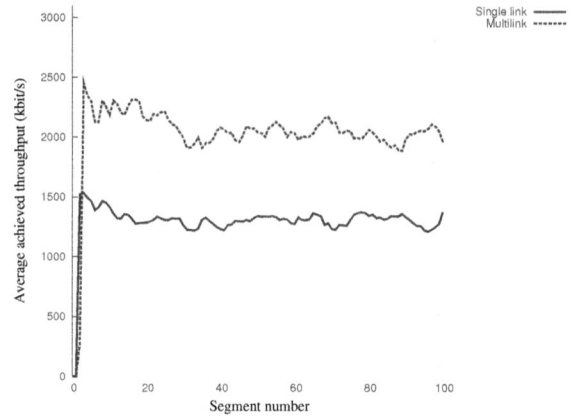

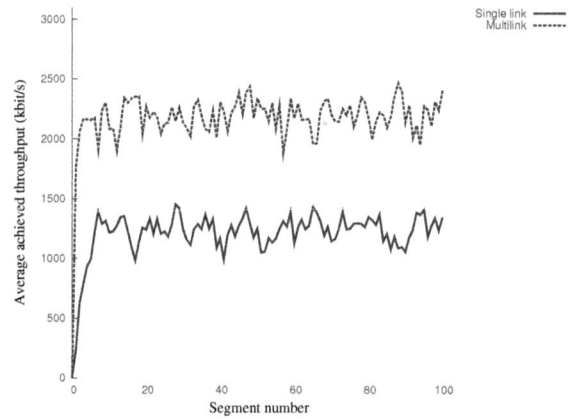

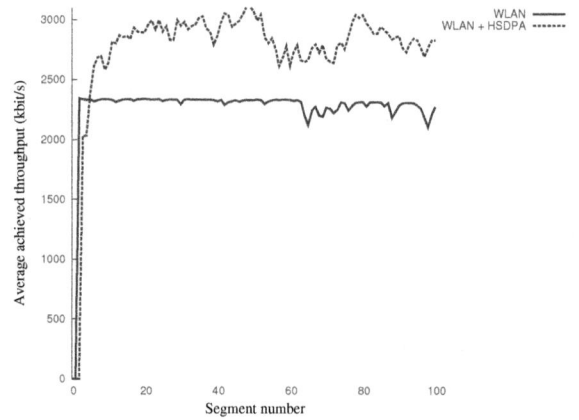

Figure 11: Average achieved throughput of the schedulers with emulated dynamic network behaviour, on-demand streaming.

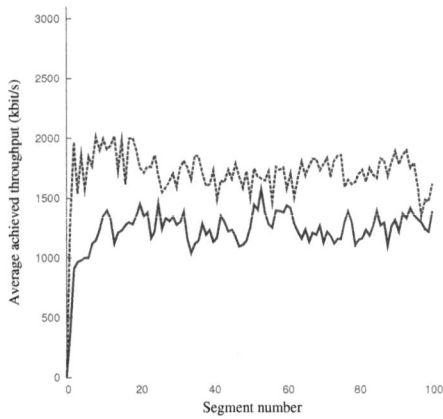

(a) Static subsegment approach (b) Dynamic subsegment approach

Figure 12: Average achieved throughput of the schedulers with emulated dynamic network behaviour, live streaming without buffering.

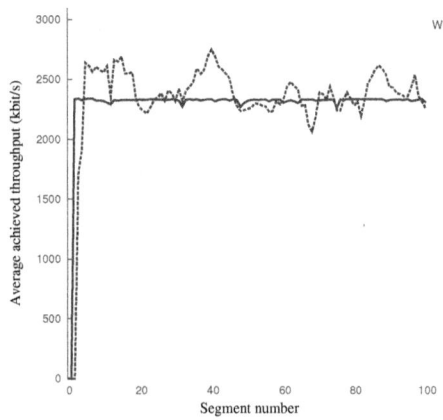

(a) Static subsegment approach (b) Dynamic subsegment approach

Figure 13: Average achieved throughput of the schedulers with real-world networks, on-demand streaming.

Subsegment approach	Low	Medium	High	Super
Static, single-link	31%	27%	28%	15%
Static, multilink	4%	4%	11%	81%
Dynamic, single-link	30%	26%	29%	15%
Dynamic, multilink	3%	3%	10%	83%

Table 3: Quality distribution, emulated dynamics and on-demand streaming

observed miss for both approaches was less than 0.5 seconds. With multiple links, both approaches avoided all deadline misses.

5.3.2 Live streaming with buffering

As with both bandwidth and latency heterogeneity, the performance of live streaming with buffering was similar to the on-demand streaming experiments, seen in figure 11. A significant increase in performance was seen when a second link was added, and the quality distributions are found in table 4. The deadline misses were also the same as in the on-demand experiments (figure 14), when multiple links were used no misses occurred. The worst-case additional delay compared to the no-delay broadcast was 2.3 s, caused exclusively by the initial segment transfer time.

Subsegment approach	Low	Medium	High	Super
Static, single-link	30%	26%	28%	16%
Static, multilink	4%	4%	11%	81%
Dynamic, single-link	29%	26%	29%	15%
Dynamic, multilink	3%	3%	11%	82%

Table 4: Quality distribution, emulated dynamics and live streaming with buffering

5.3.3 Live streaming without buffering

The live streaming without buffering experiments were performed with the same settings as the other emulated dynamics experiments, except that a buffer size and startup delay of one segment was used. This was, as discussed earlier, done to increase the liveness to the maximum that DAVVI allows (one segment).

As in the earlier live streaming without buffering experiments, the two subsegment approaches performed differently, the static approach was outperformed by the dynamic approach. This was because the dynamic subsegment approach adapts better to smaller buffers, and the performance difference is reflected in the quality distribution, presented in table 5, and seen in figure 12. While the static subsegment approach most of the time achieved a throughput that exceeded the average requirement for "Medium" quality, the dynamic subsegment approach exceeded the requirement for "High" quality.

Subsegment approach	Low	Medium	High	Super
Static, single-link	41%	44%	14%	1%
Static, multilink	15%	45%	35%	5%
Dynamic, single-link	44%	41%	14%	1%
Dynamic, multilink	2%	28%	55%	15%

Table 5: Quality distribution, emulated dynamics and live streaming without buffering

However, both subsegment approaches experienced deadline misses, as shown in figure 15. None were severe, as earlier, the worst case observed miss was around 0.5 second. However, if continuous playback had been important, a bigger buffer and startup delay should have been used. This, of course, would involve making a trade-off between liveness and quality of the user experience. The deadline misses are also reflected in the number of skipped segments, on average both subsegment approaches skipped five segments.

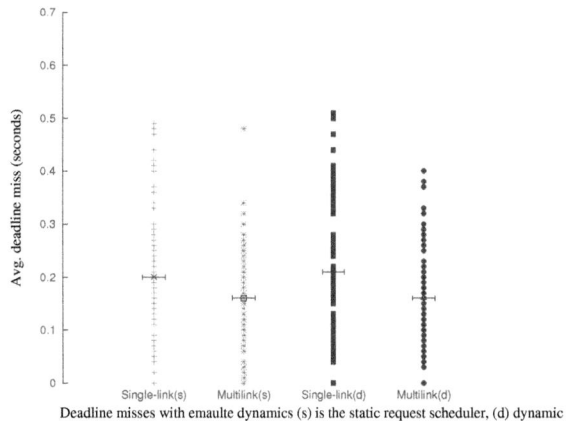

Figure 15: Deadline misses with live streaming without buffering and emulated dynamics.

5.4 Real world networks

Our real world experiments were conducted with the networks described in table 1, and a buffer size of three was used to compensate for the worst-case measured bandwidth heterogeneity (except when measuring the performance for live streaming without buffering). The tests were run interleaved to get comparable results, and the experiments were performed during peak hours (08-16) to get the most realistic network conditions. I.e., we did not want to have the full capacity of the networks to ourself.

5.4.1 On-demand streaming

The average aggregated throughput for on-demand streaming and real world networks can be found in figure 13. There was a significant difference in performance between the two subsegment approaches. While the dynamic subsegment approach showed an increase in performance when a second link was added, the static subsegment approach did not benefit that much. In fact, sometimes the aggregated throughput was less than when a single link was used. The reason for the performance difference was, as earlier, that the dynamic subsegment approach is able to utilize the links more efficiently, it adapts better to the buffer size. The performance difference is also reflected in the quality distribution, shown in table 6.

Subsegment approach	Low	Medium	High	Super
Static, single-link	1%	8%	51%	40%
Static, multilink	5%	6%	10%	79%
Dynamic, single-link	3%	11%	46%	41%
Dynamic, multilink	3%	2%	9%	86%

Table 6: Quality distribution, real world networks and on-demand streaming

In terms of deadline misses, both subsegment approaches performed equally. Except for some outliers caused by significant and rapid changes in the network conditions, like congestion and interference, both approaches were able to avoid all misses when multiple links were used.

5.4.2 Live streaming with buffering

The performance with live streaming with buffering was, as in the other live streaming with buffering experiments, similar to the on-demand performance. The quality distribution is shown in table 7, and both approaches avoided

67

almost all deadline misses when multiple links were used. A worst-case additional delay compared to the no-delay broadcast of 4 s was observed for both subsegment approaches.

Subsegment approach	Low	Medium	High	Super
Static, single-link	1%	10%	49%	40%
Static, multilink	5%	4%	7%	84%
Dynamic, single-link	1%	9%	49%	41%
Dynamic, multilink	3%	2%	5%	91%

Table 7: Quality distribution, real world networks and live streaming with buffering

5.4.3 Live streaming without buffering

When live streaming without buffering was combined with our real world networks, the performance was similar to that presented in section 5.3.3. The static subsegment approach struggled with the small buffer, while the dynamic approach adapts better, which resulted in a significantly improved performance. The only significant difference compared to the results in section 5.3.3, is that the quality distribution for both approaches were better due to more available bandwidth and more stable links, as can be seen in table 8. This was also reflected in the deadline misses and a lower number of skipped segments.

Subsegment approach	Low	Medium	High	Super
Static, single-link	0%	27%	68%	5%
Static, multilink	10%	12%	45%	32%
Dynamic, single-link	0%	27%	68%	5%
Dynamic, multilink	1%	10%	35%	55%

Table 8: Quality distribution, real world networks and live streaming without buffering

6. CONCLUSION

In this paper, we have presented and evaluated two different subsegment approaches. The approaches were implemented in the DAVVI streaming system together with a request scheduler which retrieve video segments in several different bitrates for quality adaption over multiple heterogeneous network interfaces simultaneously. The static subsegment approach was based on our earlier work, presented in [5], and divides the segments into smaller fixed-sized subsegments to achieve efficient bandwidth aggregation. This increases performance compared to a single link, but for the client to reach maximum performance with this approach, the buffer size has to be large enough to compensate for link heterogeneity.

To avoid the buffer requirement and allow quasi-live streaming at high quality, we developed a subsegment approach which calculates the sizes of the subsegments dynamically, based on the current interfaces' throughput. The two approaches were evaluated in the context of on-demand and live streaming with and without buffering (startup delay) over both emulated and real networks. Only when the buffers were large enough to compensate for link heterogeneity, the static and dynamic subsegment approaches performed the same. In all the other scenarios, the dynamic subsegment approach was able to alleviate the buffer problem and showed similar performance independent of link heterogeneity for a given buffer size.

In our future work, we plan to analyze how increasing or decreasing the duration of a segment affects quality decisions and the performance of the subsegment approaches. In addition, we want to look into tweaking the dynamic subsegment approach, e.g., by adding weights to different measurements and calculations, and experimenting with x264-encoding and live streaming without buffering.

7. REFERENCES

[1] Apple Inc. Mac OS X Server – QuickTime Streaming and Broadcasting Administration, 2007.

[2] ars technica. US broadband's average speed: 3.9Mbps. Online: http://bit.ly/6TQROA.

[3] E. Biersack and W. Geyer. Synchronized delivery and playout of distributed stored multimedia streams. *Multimedia Syst. J.*, 7(1):70–90, 1999.

[4] K. Evensen, D. Kaspar, P. Engelstad, A. F. Hansen, C. Griwodz, and P. Halvorsen. A network-layer proxy for bandwidth aggregation and reduction of IP packet reordering. In *IEEE Conference on Local Computer Networks (LCN)*, pages 585–592, October 2009.

[5] K. R. Evensen, T. Kupka, D. Kaspar, P. Halvorsen, and C. Griwodz. Quality-adaptive scheduling for live streaming over multiple access networks. In *The 20th International Workshop on Network and Operating Systems Support for Digital Audio and Video (NOSSDAV)*, pages 21–26, 2010.

[6] J. Funasaka, K. Nagayasu, and K. Ishida. Improvements on block size control method for adaptive parallel downloading. *Distributed Computing Systems Workshops, International Conference on*, 5:648–653, 2004.

[7] D. Johansen, H. Johansen, T. Aarflot, J. Hurley, A. Kvalnes, C. Gurrin, S. Zav, B. Olstad, E. Aaberg, T. Endestad, H. Riiser, C. Griwodz, and P. Halvorsen. DAVVI: A prototype for the next generation multimedia entertainment platform. In *Proc. ACM MM*, pages 989–990, 2009.

[8] D. Kaspar, K. Evensen, P. Engelstad, and A. F. Hansen. Using HTTP pipelining to improve progressive download over multiple heterogeneous interfaces. In *Proc. IEEE ICC*, pages 1–5, 2010.

[9] A. Miu and E. Shih. Performance analysis of a dynamic parallel downloading scheme from mirror sites throughout the internet. Technical report, Massachusetts Institute of Technology, 1999.

[10] Move Networks. Internet television: Challenges and opportunities. Technical report, Move Networks, Inc., November 2008.

[11] P. Ni, A. Eichhorn, C. Griwodz, and P. Halvorsen. Fine-grained scalable streaming from coarse-grained videos. In *Proc. ACM NOSSDAV*, pages 103–108, 2009.

[12] P. Rodriguez and E. W. Biersack. Dynamic parallel access to replicated content in the internet. *IEEE/ACM Trans. Netw.*, 10(4):455–465, 2002.

[13] B. Wang, W. Wei, Z. Guo, and D. Towsley. Multipath live streaming via TCP: Scheme, performance and benefits. *ACM Trans. Multimedia Comput. Commun. Appl.*, 5(3):1–23, 2009.

[14] F. Wu, G. Gao, and Y. Liu. Glitch-Free Media Streaming. Patent Application (US2008/0022005), January 24 2008.

[15] A. Zambelli. IIS Smooth Streaming technical overview. Technical report, Microsoft Corporation, 2009.

SyncCast: Synchronized Dissemination in Multi-site Interactive 3D Tele-immersion

Zixia Huang, Wanmin Wu, Klara Nahrstedt, Raoul Rivas and Ahsan Arefin
Department of Computer Science
University of Illinois at Urbana-Champaign
{zhuang21, wwu23, klara, trivas, marefin2}@illinois.edu

ABSTRACT

An ideal interactive 3D tele-immersion (3DTI) system is expected to disseminate and synchronize multi-streams with a shortest-possible latency among participating sites, achieve *inter-stream synchronization*, and bound both *inter-sender* and *inter-receiver* skews. This is, however, a key challenge because of (1) the coexistence of multi-modal, correlated, bandwidth-savvy streams from multiple source media, (2) the bounded bandwidth resources at each site, (3) the heterogeneous transmission end-to-end delays (EED) between sites and (4) the diversity of 3D views requested by multiple users. Our study of the existing content dissemination topologies reveals their inadequacy of handlings the complication and dynamics present in 3DTI systems.

In this paper, we propose SyncCast, a multi-stream multicast dissemination scheme that takes into account the bandwidth constraint, as well as the inter-stream, inter-sender and inter-receiver synchronization. We classify the 3DTI media streams into different service classes based on the users' visual interests. SyncCast is designed to address the interactions among EED, synchronization and bandwidth in the real-world Internet settings. We compare SyncCast and our previous ViewCast algorithm [20]. The simulation results show the improvement in the synchronization performance and the implementation feasibility of SyncCast in supporting the multi-site interactive 3DTI system.

Categories and Subject Descriptors

H.5.1 [**Multimedia Information Systems**]: Video; C.2.1 [**Network Architecture and Design**]: Network communications

General Terms

Design, Performance, Experimentation

Keywords

SyncCast, 3D tele-immersion, synchronization

1. INTRODUCTION

Interactive 3D tele-immersion (3DTI) (Fig. 1) is an application in which geographically distributed users can achieve realistic collaborations in a joint virtual space. Some useful applications are medical consultation, remote education and collaborative entertainment. The characteristics of 3DTI include photorealistic video capturing of the participants, real-time dissemination of the media data, and multi-view rendering of the aggregated video. Users can thus interact seamlessly with remote peers in a joint virtual environment with auditory and visual feedback.

In a two-party interactive 3DTI system, synchronization of multiple sensory streams is already a big challenge. The system needs to synchronize the audio streams with multiple highly correlated video streams (e.g., the streams sent from site A to B in Fig. 2(a)). The correlation of video streams results from the deployment of 3D cameras in different positions around the stage to capture multiple views of the same scene. The timing synchronization of these different sensory streams is complicated by the fact that they have heterogeneous end-to-end delay (EED) between the *sender site* (i.e., the site which generates sensory streams) and the *receiver site* (i.e., the site which renders/plays sensory streams) [6] (Fig. 3). The reason is that different sensory streams employ their own protocols and adaptation algorithms in response to the bandwidth dynamics according to their diverse quality-of-service (QoS) requirements. The EED heterogeneity can impact the *inter-stream synchronization*. In addition, Internet dynamics (e.g. jitters) must be taken into account, and timely scheduling of audio playout and video rendering at the receivers thus becomes a key issue. Though this can be achieved by the receiver-side buffering, the buffer size can contribute to the overall EED, and a long EED can decrease the interactivity of the 3DTI system and may reduce the overall user satisfaction [15].

The extension of the 3DTI system for multi-site support creates increased complications to multi-stream dissemination and synchronization due to the following reasons.

(1) *Prolonged EED*: the possible relays though some *intermediate sites* (IS) (i.e., sites that relay media streams to other sites in Fig. 3[1]) in the application-layer overlay [20] can contribute to a prolonged EED between two sites. To improve the interactivity, a good 3DTI system should be able to minimize its *average system EED* (i.e., the average EED between all sender and receiver sites in the system). In addition, the aggregate jitter effects over multiple links can contribute to the latency variations which will further

---

[1]An intermediate site can also be a receiver site.

Figure 1: Collaborative 3DTI with 3 sites

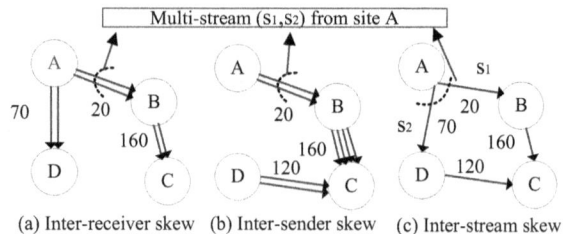

Figure 2: Synchronization Skews. Number presents the link latency (msec).

impact the synchronization. To simplify the problem in this paper, we do not consider the jitter impacts and assume the fixed receiver-side buffer can smooth the Internet jitters. We use the equal buffer size for all receivers and do not include the buffer size in the EED computation.

(2) *Inter-receiver skew*: multiple receiver sites can experience different perceptions of the same 3DTI activity due to the heterogenous EEDs from a same sender site (of which the maximum EED difference is called *inter-receiver skew*). For example, in Fig. 2(a), site A is sending streams to all other sites. The maximum EED (A → C) is 180 msec while the minimum (A → B) is 20 msec, so the inter-receiver skew is 160 msec. The inter-receiver skew can cause unfairness when multiple people at different receiver sites require a timing privilege to conduct an activity. For example in a remote education application, students at different receiver sites (B, C, D) are racing to answer a question asked by an instructor at site A. In case of a double-talk when two or more people are talking at the same time, the third-party people at different receivers can also perceive the double-talks with different timing characteristics [14].

(3) *Inter-sender skew*: from an audience's perspective, some people in the 3DTI activity may be more distant or respond slower than others because of the heterogenous EEDs from multiple senders to a same receiver site (of which the maximum latency difference is called *inter-sender skew*). For instance in Fig. 2(b), site C is receiving the streams from A,B and D. The maximum EED (A → C) is 180 msec while the minimum (D → C) is 120 msec, so the skew is 60 msec. The inter-sender skew may lead to the misunderstanding of the audience located at the receiver site in a highly collaborative activity. An example is a collaborative basketball scenario, where a defensive player (site C in Fig. 2(b)) is interacting with two offensive players (site A and D). The temporal synchrony between player A and D can be seriously broken as perceived by player C if the inter-sender skew is large.

(4) *Inter-stream skew*: multi-streams from the same sender may follow different paths to reach the same receiver site [20]. The heterogeneity of EED incurred on multiple paths can further increase the *inter-stream skew*. For example in Fig. 2(a), site A has two streams s_1 and s_2 which follow two paths to site C. The incurred EED of s_1 is 180 msec while the latency of s_2 is 190 msec. So the skew is 10 msec. It is recommended in the 3DTI that the correlated video streams from the same site should be synchronized before they are sent to the renderer [6], and the audio-visual skew should fall within a 80-msec threshold [17] for lip synchronization. There has been a large body of work on the audio-visual synchronization [6, 11, 12, 17].

(5) *Bandwidth constraint*: Unlike the dissemination of the spatial audio [23] or VoIP, where data rate is usually small and audio signals can be mixed together when bandwidth is inadequate, the transmission of multiple 3D video streams can overload a site and 3D video mixing is often not accessible in real time due to the huge computation overhead.

(6) *Diversity of user interests*: multiple users can request different 3D video views and hence only a subset of video streams may be required [20] at each receiver site.

Note that even in an interactive 3DTI virtual environment (or a gaming system) with hundreds of active participants (or avatars), previous studies [22, 23] have shown that these active participants/avatars tend to communicate within a certain small-scale group, called *activity region*. Hence, it is more interesting and important to study the stream dissemination within a group of active participants/avatars.

Most of the previous studies working on application-layer centralized/distributed overlays or multicast trees are aimed at minimizing the delay or delay variation with or without bandwidth constraints [3, 7, 8, 13, 14, 23]. However they oversimplify the problem by either overlooking the combined impact of bandwidth overhead at each site caused by the co-existence of multiple overlays/trees for multi-stream dissemination of heterogeneous senders in the content dissemination topology, or by assuming the homogeneity of the media data requested at different sites. Therefore, their work cannot directly apply to our multi-site 3DTI system.

In our previous study, we have proposed ViewCast [20] algorithm which can effectively disseminate multiple video streams and allow cross-tree adjustment under bandwidth constraints and user view heterogeneity. But ViewCast does not take into account the interactivity and synchronization of the dissemination problem. [19, 2] have proposed multi-stream synchronization with bounded delay and delay variations. However, the two papers do not consider the constraints of the bandwidth and the inter-sender skew. In addition, [19, 2] only focus on the dissemination of video streams and do not take into account the audio's nature and impact on 3DTI synchronization.

In [6], we have also proposed a synchronization framework called TSync, which only operates under single-sender scenarios. TSync can bound the inter-stream skew within the recommended 80-msec threshold via the decision of the *dominant stream* (i.e., the view-central video stream in the *multi-stream bundle* [1] that is used for audio-visual synchronization), the implementation of timed synchronization points at multiple locations, the cooperative frame rate allocation for Internet bandwidth adaptation at the sender site, and the proper audio playout scheduling to synchronize to the 3D videos at the receiver site.

In this paper we propose SyncCast, a synchronized dissemination framework for multi-site interactive 3DTI with

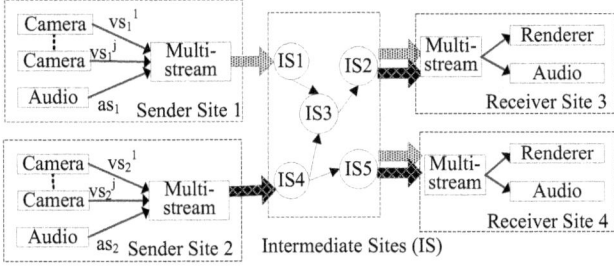

Figure 3: Multi-site 3DTI architecture.

Table 1: Notations and definitions

Notations	Definitions
n_i	The i-th participating site in 3DTI
$\mathcal{E}^{snd}$, $\mathcal{E}^{rcv}$	Set of sender or receiver sites in the system
E_i^{snd}, E_k^{rcv}	The i-th sender site or k-th receiver site
$\mathcal{E}^{snd(k)}$, $E_i^{snd(k)}$	Set of/i-th sender sites for E_k^{rcv}
$\mathcal{E}^{rcv(i)}$, $E_k^{rcv(i)}$	Set of/k-th receiver sites for E_i^{snd}
$L_{n_i \to n_k}$	One-way latency from n_i to n_k
$P_{i \to k}^s$	Dissemination path of stream s from E_i^{snd} to $E_k^{rcv(i)}$
$\mathcal{PS}_{i \to k}^s$	Set of all path options for stream s from E_i^{snd} to $E_k^{rcv(i)}$
$\text{EED}[P_{i \to k}^s]$	EED for $P_{i \to k}^s$
$B_{n_i}^{in}$, $B_{n_i}^{out}$	Incoming/outgoing bandwidth overhead at n_i
$\mathcal{S}_i$	Media stream set from E_i^{snd}
$\mathcal{AS}_i$, $\mathcal{VS}_i$	Audio or video stream set from E_i^{snd}
vs_i^j	j-th video stream from camera j of E_i^{snd}
as_i	Audio stream from E_i^{snd}
$DS_{i \to k}$	Video DS from E_i^{snd} to $E_k^{rcv(i)}$
$\mathcal{S}_{i \to k}^{NDS}$, $\mathcal{S}_{i \to k}^{NUS}$	Set of video NDS and NUS from E_i^{snd} to $E_k^{rcv(i)}$
$\mathcal{RS}_{i \to k}$	Set of all streams requested at $E_k^{rcv(i)}$ from E_i^{snd}
$\text{CF}_{i \to k}^s$	Contribution factor of stream s from E_i^{snd} at $E_k^{rcv(i)}$
$\Delta T_{i \to k}^{vs}$	Inter-video skew from E_i^{snd} to $E_k^{rcv(i)}$
$\Delta T_{i \to k}^{avs}$	Audio-visual sync skew from E_i^{snd} to $E_k^{rcv(i)}$
$\Delta T_{i \to k}^s$	Inter-stream skew from E_i^{snd} to $E_k^{rcv(i)}$
ΔT_k^{snd}	Inter-sender skew at E_k^{rcv}
ΔT_i^{rcv}	Inter-receiver skew of E_i^{snd}

multiple senders and receivers. The contributions are as follows. (1) We generalize the concept of synchronization in the multi-site interactive multimedia system, and model different synchronization aspects (inter-stream, inter-sender and inter-receiver synchronization) used in the real application. (2) We study the interactions of media data dissemination EED, synchronization and bandwidth overhead, and propose a multi-sender multi-receiver dissemination topology based on the interactions. The topology can minimize the average dissemination EED, bound inter-sender and inter-receiver skews, and guarantee inter-stream synchronization given the bandwidth constraint. (3) We take into account the diversity of user interests, and propose the concept of *global contribution factor* and *local contribution factor* which can describe the visual contribution of a certain video stream to all or only a subset of receiver sites respectively. We guarantee all receiver sites can receive the audio stream and the video streams containing the most important visual information relevant to the user view at each site respectively. (4) We bound the bandwidth overhead at each site either by reselecting the alternative dissemination paths, or by applying cooperative bandwidth allocation at an overloaded site. (5) We evaluate SyncCast and several existing topologies based on the real Internet statistics collected in PlanetLab.

2. 3DTI SYSTEM MODEL

We present in this section the 3DTI system model (Fig. 3). A list of symbols and denotations is shown in Table 1. Throughout this paper, we use sites to represent nodes or vertices, and links to represent edges between two *neighboring sites* (i.e., sites that can connect each other).

2.1 Topology Model

We are given a set of N sites $(n_1, n_2, \ldots, n_N)$ in the 3DTI system. Each of the N sites can be classified as a sender or/and a receiver [2]. We let $\mathcal{E}^{snd}$ and $\mathcal{E}^{rcv}$ denote the set of sender and receiver sites in the system, and E_i^{snd}, E_k^{rcv} are the i-th sender site/k-th receiver site in $\mathcal{E}^{snd}$, $\mathcal{E}^{rcv}$. For each E_i^{snd}, it has a set of receiver sites $\mathcal{E}^{rcv(i)} = \{E_k^{rcv(i)}\}$, where $E_k^{rcv(i)}$ is the k-th receiver site in $\mathcal{E}^{rcv(i)}$. In this paper, we assume that for each sender site E_i^{snd}, all other sites are receiver sites of E_i^{snd} (i.e., $\mathcal{E}^{rcv(i)} = \{n_1, n_2, \ldots, n_N\} \backslash E_i^{snd}$) [3]. For each E_k^{rcv}, it has a set of sender sites $\mathcal{E}^{snd(k)} = \{E_i^{snd(k)}\}$, where $E_i^{snd(k)}$ is the i-th sender site in $\mathcal{E}^{snd(k)}$.

---

[2] A sender site can also be a receiver.

[3] A 3DTI sender site also receives and renders its own video streams. Because there is no transmission EED introduced over the Internet, we do not consider it as a receiver of its own streams in this paper.

We use the one-way latency $L_{n_i \to n_k}$ to describe the link cost between two neighboring sites. Note that there may not be a direct link between two sites (section 4.1). A path of a media stream s from E_i^{snd} to its receiver $E_k^{rcv(i)}$ is denoted as $P_{i \to k}^s$ [4]. $P_{i \to k}^s = \langle E_i^{snd}, n_1^{IS}, n_2^{IS}, \ldots, n_m^{IS}, E_k^{rcv(i)} \rangle$, may be routed through several IS (i.e., $n_1^{IS}, n_2^{IS}, \ldots, n_m^{IS}$) in the application-layer overlay or multicast tree. The total cost of the path $P_{i \to k}^s$ (i.e., EED) is denoted as $\text{EED}[P_{i \to k}^s]$. $\text{EED}[P_{i \to k}^s]$ can be computed by summing up all the link costs on the path and the processing latencies incurred on sender, intermediate and receiver sites. In this paper, we assume all the processing latencies are negligible. Note that there can be be multiple path options from E_i^{snd} to $E_k^{rcv(i)}$ for stream s, and we denote the set of path options $\mathcal{PS}_{i \to k}^s$.

Each site n_i has an in-degree and out-degree bandwidth upper bound (i.e., max $B_{n_i}^{in}$ and max $B_{n_i}^{out}$) to constrain the bandwidth overhead $B_{n_i}^{in}$ and $B_{n_i}^{out}$. We assume the bandwidth consumption of the audio streams is negligible compared to the videos.

2.2 Stream Model

As Fig. 3 shows, each sender site E_i^{snd} contains M 3D cameras and one audio microphone component. The M cameras at E_i^{snd} produce a video *stream bundle* $\mathcal{VS}_i = \{vs_i^j\}$ [1] with stream vs_i^j from camera j. Each vs_i^j consists of a sequence of frames $\{f_i^j(t)\}$ captured at time t. $\mathcal{VS}_i$ can also be represented as a sequence of video *macroframes* $mf_i(t)$ (i.e., $\mathcal{VS}_i = \{mf_i(t)\}$), where a macroframe $mf_i(t)$ is a set of video frames taken from different cameras at E_i^{snd} at the same time t, i.e., $mf_i(t) = \{f_i^1(t), \ldots, f_i^M(t)\}$. Each audio microphone can produce one audio stream $\mathcal{AS}_i = as_i$

---

[4] Throughout this paper, $i \to k$ denotes E_i^{snd} to $E_k^{rcv(i)}$.

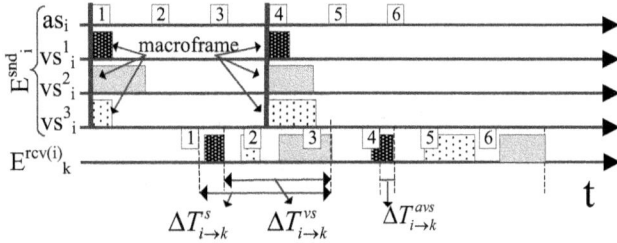

Figure 4: Inter-stream skew, Inter-video skew, and audio-visual skew from E_i^{snd} to $E_k^{rcv(i)}$. vs_i^1 is the DS.

(i.e., $\|\mathcal{AS}_i\| = 1$) consisting of periodic audio frames [14]. The set of all sensory streams from E_i^{snd} are denoted as $\mathcal{S}_i = \{\mathcal{AS}_i, \mathcal{VS}_i\}$.

Each receiver site $E_k^{rcv(i)}$ contains one renderer (display)[5] and one audio speaker component. We define the concept of a *dominant stream* (DS) $DS_{i\to k}$ within a bundle $\mathcal{VS}_i$ to be the most important video stream for the display from E_i^{snd}. It is the stream with the maximum *contributing factor* (CF) which represents the contribution of the stream's 3D image pixels to the user view. CF is determined using (a) camera orientation of a video stream $s = vs_i^j$, $\vec{O}_s$, and (b) the desired user view orientation $\vec{O}_{u_k^i}$ at $E_k^{rcv(i)}$ from site E_i^{snd} [21]: $CF_{i\to k}^s = \vec{O}_s \cdot \vec{O}_{u_k^i}$. Other video streams in the correlated 3D video bundle that are not DS but satisfy $CF > CF_0$ are called *non-dominant streams* (NDS), where CF_0 is the lower bound of CF which has the visual contribution [20]. Streams whose CF is less than CF_0 are called *non-use streams* (NUS). A receiver site E_k^{rcv} may only request a subset in the video stream bundle from E_i^{snd}, and this subset is denoted as $\mathcal{RS}_{i\to k}$. Note that the concept of $\mathcal{RS}$ also extends to the audio stream and in this paper, all receiver sites always request the audio.

2.3 Synchronization Model

Multiple video streams from the same sender can arrive at a receiver at different time. We define the *inter-video skew* to denote this difference. The skew $\Delta T_{i\to k}^{vs}$ of the video stream from E_i^{snd} to $E_k^{rcv(i)}$ can be computed by:

$$\Delta T_{i\to k}^{vs} = \max_{s,\ s'\in\mathcal{RS}_{i\to k}\setminus as_i} |EED_{i\to k}^s - EED_{i\to k}^{s'}| \quad (s \neq s') \quad (1)$$

Because it is impossible to synchronize the audio to all video streams in the bundle, we also define the *audio-visual skew* $\Delta T_{i\to k}^{avs}$ to describe the EED difference between the audio and video DS from the same sender site, i.e.,

$$\Delta T_{i\to k}^{avs} = |EED_{i\to k}^{as} - EED_{i\to k}^{DS_{i\to k}}| \quad (2)$$

The audio-visual skew is important because it can cause lip asynchrony which will degrade human subjective perceptions. We compare the audio with the video DS because video DS contains the most important visual information.

The inter-stream skew, on the other hand, is defined as the maximum EED difference among all audio and video streams from a sender site to a receiver. It is denoted as $\Delta T_{i\to k}^s$:

$$\Delta T_{i\to k}^s = \max_{s,\ s'\in\mathcal{RS}_{i\to k}} |EED_{i\to k}^s - EED_{i\to k}^{s'}| \quad (s \neq s') \quad (3)$$

Fig. 4 shows the relationship between $\Delta T_{i\to k}^s$, $\Delta T_{i\to k}^{vs}$ and $\Delta T_{i\to k}^{avs}$. Note that $\Delta T_{i\to k}^{vs} \leq \Delta T_{i\to k}^s$.

In order to facilitate audio-visual synchronization, in this paper we prescribe that the audio stream as_i from sender

---

[5]We assume there is only one display at each receiver site.

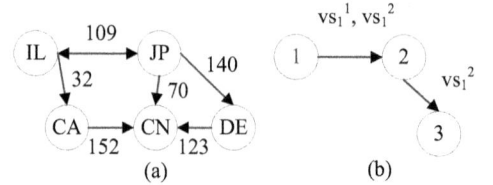

Figure 5: (a) Illustration of problem formulation, numbers are delays in msec. (b) Unfair routing.

site E_i^{snd} and its corresponding video DS ($DS_{i\to k}$) to a receiver site $E_k^{rcv(i)}$ follow the same transmission path to minimize the EED difference. We call the audio stream and video DS *audio-visual dominant stream* (AVDS).

The inter-receiver skew ΔT_i^{rcv} of E_i^{snd} is defined as the difference in EED of the video DS to multiple receiver sites, i.e.,

$$\Delta T_i^{rcv} = \max_{k,\ k'\in\mathcal{E}^{rcv(i)}} |EED_{i\to k}^{DS_{i\to k}} - EED_{i\to k'}^{DS_{i\to k'}}| \quad (k \neq k') \quad (4)$$

The inter-sender skew ΔT_k^{snd} of E_k^{rcv} is defined as the difference in EED of the video DS from multiple sender sites.

$$\Delta T_k^{snd} = \max_{i,\ i'\in\mathcal{E}^{snd(k)}} |EED_{i\to E_k^{rcv}}^{DS_{i\to E_k^{rcv}}} - EED_{i'\to E_k^{rcv}}^{DS_{i'\to E_k^{rcv}}}| \quad (i \neq i')$$
$$(5)$$

There are several things to note here. First, due to the space limit, we assume that all receiver sites are using the fixed jitter buffer with the same buffer size for all media streams, so we do not take into account the impact of jitters on synchronization skews. Second, we compute the inter-sender and inter-receiver skews based on the timing information of the AVDS, because AVDS contains the most important audio-visual information, and is thus given top priority for dissemination in our paper (section 5). Most of the receiver sites can receive multiple AVDS from different sender sites, and can play the 3D videos with high quality even though they do not receive any video NDS. Last, only the AVDS's arrival timing information at the receiver affects the audio playout and 3D multi-view rendering time, which is the deterministic factor deciding the interactivity of the multi-site 3DTI. We will show in section 5 that inter-stream and inter-video skews do not affect the multi-site interactions using our algorithm.

3. PROBLEM FORMULATION

As discussed in Section 1, the goal of our paper is to develop an interactive multi-site 3DTI system which can minimize the average system EED under both synchronization and bandwidth constraints, and each receiver site should be given the top priority to receive the AVDS in order to guarantee the audio-visual rendering quality.

An illustration of our problem is shown in Fig. 5(a) where IL and JP are the sender sites, and all sites are receivers (sender sites do not receive streams from themselves). There are a total of 8 sender-receiver pairs in the graph. Each sender site has two streams (i.e., s_{IL}^1, s_{IL}^2, s_{JP}^1, s_{JP}^2). Each receiver site requests one DS and one NDS from each sender site. We assume that s_{IL}^1 and s_{JP}^1 are DS for all receivers, and the other two streams are NDS. For each sender-receiver pair, there can be one or multiple path options. For example, between IL and CN there are three path options for all streams $\mathcal{PS}_{IL\to CN}[0] = \langle IL,JP,CN\rangle$, $\mathcal{PS}_{IL\to CN}[1] = \langle IL,CA,CN\rangle$ and $\mathcal{PS}_{IL\to CN}[2] = \langle IL,JP,DE,CN\rangle$, and different paths lead to different costs (EEDs). Our goal is to select a path, for each stream of each sender-receiver pair, from a list of path options, and to combine the selected paths of all the sender-receiver pairs into an dissemination overlay such that (1) in the sub-overlay disseminating only AVDS, the resulting average system EED is minimized; (2) synchronization metrics (inter-sender, inter-receiver and inter-stream skews) and incoming/outgoing bandwidth overhead are bounded.

The problem can be formulated in a general form as follows. δ_s, δ_{src} and δ_{rcv} are the upper bounds of inter-stream, inter-sender and inter-receiver synchronization.

- **Minimizing average system EED of AVDS paths:**

$$\text{Min} \quad \frac{1}{\sum_i^{|\mathcal{E}^{snd}|} |\mathcal{E}^{rcv(i)}|} \sum_{E_i^{snd}} \sum_{E_k^{rcv(i)}} \text{EED}[P_{i \to k}^{DS_{i \to k}}]$$

- **Synchronization constraint :**

$$\forall\, E_i^{snd}, E_k^{rcv} : \qquad \Delta T_{i \to k}^{vs} \leq \Delta T_{i \to k}^{s} < \delta_s$$
$$\Delta T_k^{snd} < \delta_{snd}, \quad \Delta T_i^{rcv} < \delta_{rcv}$$

- **Bandwidth constraint :**

$$\forall\, n_i : \; B_{n_i}^{in} < \max B_{n_i}^{in}, \quad B_{n_i}^{out} < \max B_{n_i}^{out}$$

Note that because of bandwidth and synchronization constraints, some receiver sites may not receive the AVDS from one or multiple sender sites. We call these receiver sites *victim sites*, which are sites that cannot receive at least one AVDS. In this situation, we are aimed at first maximizing the number of *successfully*-received AVDS and given the successful AVDS, then minimizing their average system EED.

In a multi-site 3DTI system, there are several application-specific factors that affect the construction and optimization of the content dissemination scheme.

First, due to the diversity of user views, different receivers may request different video DS and NDS. Previous studies [3, 7, 8, 13] assume the multi-stream homogeneity from the same sender, and hence it is possible that some IS may have to relay some video streams which are of no use (i.e., NUS) to them. For example, in Fig. 5(b), site 2 has to relay vs_1^2 even though it does not request the stream. This will cause an *unfair routing* in the transmission topology. A good scheme should be able to achieve *fair routing* in which the IS only relay streams that they themselves may request.

Second, in a dissemination scheme with multiple multi-cast trees, cross-tree adjustment [10, 20] is not the only feasible solution to satisfy the bandwidth constraint. The characteristics of 3DTI multi-streams can allow adaptations at an overloaded site by cooperative bandwidth allocation to more important streams and achieve frame rate allocation [6]. However, it may degrade the overall visual quality due to the motion jerkiness due to the reduced frame rate.

To sum up, the overall problem can be divided into two parts. The first part only considers multi-stream homogeneity, and minimize average system EED given the synchronization and bandwidth constraints. We use the real link costs by collecting the one-way latencies between different sites in the real Internet settings (section 4). There have been numerous existing studies constructing dissemination topologies aimed at minimizing delay related metrics [3, 7, 8, 13]. We evaluate these studies in section 4. The second part focuses on 3DTI-specific multi-stream heterogeneity in deciding the topology. We will consider both parts in designing our own algorithm (section 5).

4. EVALUATION OF DELAY-SENSITIVE TOPOLOGIES

Previous studies on delay-sensitive topologies [3, 7, 13, 19, 23] conducted evaluations based upon link costs which are randomly selected within a certain range, computed by propagation delays in a wireless setting, or obtained in the virtual gaming environment. Due to the delay correlations over the Internet, their results can neither describe a real network environment for multi-site 3DTI, nor can they present real EED heterogeneity, synchronization behaviors, bandwidth overhead and their interactions. In this section, we collect the one-way latency statistics from PlanetLab to simulate a real Internet setting. We construct dissemination topologies based on real link costs between sites, and study the interactions of EED, synchronization and bandwidth overhead resulting from the Internet delay distributions. Based on their timing and bandwidth consumption characteristics, we design our own algorithm in section 5.

4.1 Network Environment

We present the one-way latencies (link costs) collected from PlanetLab in Table 2 and 3 to simulate both 5-site and 9-site real 3DTI settings. We sent UDP packets from each site to all others at the same time and computed the one-way latency by halving the round-trip time information. The size of the packets was smaller than the maximum transmission unit (MTU) in order to avoid fragmentation. Because different sites can exhibit different latency variations, we consider both 5-site and 9-site communications and classify the network environment into three scenarios based on their geographical locations: (1) all sites in US (represented as 5A and 9A), (2) sites in both US and Europe (5B and 9B), and (3) sites in US, Europe and Asia (5C and 9C). In addition, widely-deployed firewall and poor link conditions (high loss rate, large jitter or low data rate) can impede the direct connections and transmissions of real-time traffic between certain sites. Hence, we remove some of the links and represent the new network environment as 5D-5F and 9D-9F (shown in the grey boxes in Table 2 and 3) to simulate the firewall-blocked connection (e.g. the link between IL and IN in Table 2(a)) or poor link conditions (e.g., links between Beijing and all sites outside China in Table 3(c)). So there are total of 12 environment for evaluation.

Table 2 and 3 show the correlations of one-way latency in the real Internet environment. First, sites that are close in the geographical locations usually exhibit similar latency distributions. For example, IL1 and IL2 in Table 3 have similar one-way latencies to other sites. Second, there are correlations among the links shared by a same site. For instance, the delays from BJ to all sites outside China are greater than 180 msec possibly due to the poor International connections there. We will show in section 4.3 the impact of latency correlations on the existing content dissemination schemes.

4.2 Classification of Content Dissemination Schemes

We classify the existing content dissemination schemes into four categories. These schemes are designed not for specific applications and do not take into account the heterogeneity within the multi-stream bundle (i.e., inter-stream synchronization skew).

(1) A *full-mesh scheme* requires each sender site to send

Table 2: One-way delay (msec) for 5 nodes. (a) in US, (b) in US and Europe, (c) in US, Europe and Asia.

Table 3(a): 5 nodes in US (5A,5D)

5A	CA	IL	FL	IN	NY
CA	0	32	35	33	43
IL	32	0	28	10	21
FL	35	28	0	24	24
IN	33	10	24	0	18
NY	43	21	24	18	0

Table 3(b): 5 nodes in US and Europe (5B,5E)

5B	CA	IL	UK	DE	NY
CA	0	32	80	88	43
IL	32	0	72	75	21
UK	80	72	0	18	53
DE	88	75	18	0	52
NY	43	21	53	52	0

Table 3(c): 5 nodes in US, Europe and Asia (5C,5F)

5C	CA	IL	DE	JP	CN
CA	0	32	88	70	152
IL	32	0	75	109	178
DE	88	75	0	140	123
JP	70	109	140	0	34
CN	152	178	123	34	0

Table 3: One-way delay (msec) for 9 nodes. (a) in US, (b) in US and Europe, (c) in US, Europe and China.

Table 4(a): 9 nodes in US (9A,9D)

9A	CA1	CA2	IL1	IL2	IL3	FL	IN	NY	TX
CA1	0	2	32	31	32	35	33	43	18
CA2	2	0	31	35	32	35	20	46	19
IL1	32	31	0	1	2	28	10	21	19
IL2	31	35	1	0	1	28	11	21	19
IL3	30	32	2	1	0	28	11	21	20
FL	35	35	28	28	28	0	24	24	27
IN	33	20	10	11	11	24	0	18	21
NY	43	46	21	21	21	24	18	0	31
TX	18	19	19	19	20	27	21	31	0

Table 4(b): 9 nodes in US and Europe (9B,9E)

9B	CA	IL1	IL2	FL	IN	UK	DE1	DE2	IT
CA	0	32	31	35	33	80	88	90	102
IL1	32	0	1	28	10	72	75	81	95
IL2	31	1	0	28	11	74	72	85	98
FL	35	28	28	0	24	85	86	82	92
IN	33	10	11	24	0	70	71	76	93
UK	80	72	74	85	70	0	18	18	24
DE1	88	75	72	86	71	18	0	6	17
DE2	90	81	85	82	76	18	6	0	21
IT	102	95	98	92	93	24	17	21	0

Table 4(c): 9 nodes in US, Europe and China (9C,9F)

9C	CA	IL1	IL2	UK	DE1	DE2	SH	BJ	HK
CA	0	32	31	80	88	90	152	193	167
IL1	32	0	1	72	75	81	178	204	179
IL2	31	1	0	74	72	85	175	203	182
UK	80	72	74	0	18	18	155	187	160
DE1	88	75	72	18	0	6	143	181	152
DE2	90	81	85	18	6	0	140	180	153
SH	152	178	175	155	143	140	0	61	55
BJ	193	204	203	187	181	180	61	0	87
HK	167	179	182	160	152	153	55	87	0

multiple streams directly to the receiver sites via unicasts. This scheme usually results in the small EED, inter-sender and inter-receiver synchronization skews, but it is bottle-necked at the bandwidth availability of each sender. In addition, because of the firewall-blocked connections and poor link conditions, a full-mesh scheme may not always be accessible in the 3DTI system.

(2) A *centralized scheme* requires an intermediate dedicated server/site to relay the multi-streams from the senders to the receivers. This scheme is usually adopted in the multi-party VoIP (e.g., Skype[6] and QQ[7]) due to the low bandwidth demand of the audio streams and the feasibility of mixing audio signals. Although it increases the EED compared to a full-mesh topology, a centralized scheme can avoid the blocked connection due to the firewall deployment or prevent transmissions over poor links. The 3DTI however cannot use this scheme due to the huge network and computation demand of video streaming and processing.

(3) An extension of the centralized scheme is a *hybrid scheme* (usually an overlay network) in which there can be more than one IS to relay the media data. Each site communicates with the nearest IS in the overlay. One example of a hybrid scheme is proposed in [14]. Compared to a centralized scheme, the increased number of IS can reduce the chances of bandwidth overload. But it further increases the EED and can degrade both inter-sender and inter-receiver synchronization. The construction of an overlay can vary depending on different optimization goals. For example, the algorithm in [14] is aimed at minimizing the maximum EED in the overlay.

(4) An application-layer *multicast tree* in essence is another type of overlay in which the number of IS is usually not bounded or preset, and multiple streams from the same/different sender sites may follow different trees. The coexistence of multiple trees rooted at the same/different senders forms a multicast forest. The EED, inter-sender and

inter-receiver skews can vary depending on tree construction algorithms. Multiple trees used for multi-stream dissemination from the same sender can create a multi-stream skew. Given the bandwidth constraint at each site, the tree construction algorithms can be generally divided into three layers. The bottom layer is the multicast tree construction with certain optimization goals (e.g., reducing the average EED and/or bounding EED variations, etc.). Some examples are the minimum spanning tree (MST) [8], minimal diameter spanning tree (MDST) [4], the shortest path tree (SPT) [23] or the DVMA algorithm with bounded delay and delay variations [13]. The medium layer is the bandwidth adjustment within the tree. For each tree constructed in the bottom layer, the algorithms [10, 20] reduce the overloaded sites either by pruning (sacrificing some victims) or by intra-tree adjustment achieved via removing some descendants of the overloaded sites to those that have more bandwidth availability. However, these problems have been proven to be NP complex [9, 18]. Hence, most of those adjustment algorithms are quite heuristic and their effectiveness can vary, depending on specific applications. In addition, adjustment can be difficult for a tree with a large number of sites, so there are some algorithms that combine the bottom and medium layers together into a single layer and directly construct a multicast tree with a bounded incoming/outgoing degree [16]. The top layer is the bandwidth adjustment across the trees (within a forest) [10, 20], because multiple trees can share some sites which may cause the bandwidth overload at these sites. Just as the medium layer, adaptation across multiple trees can also vary at different applications.

---

[6]Skype: http://www.skype.com
[7]QQ: http://www.qq.com

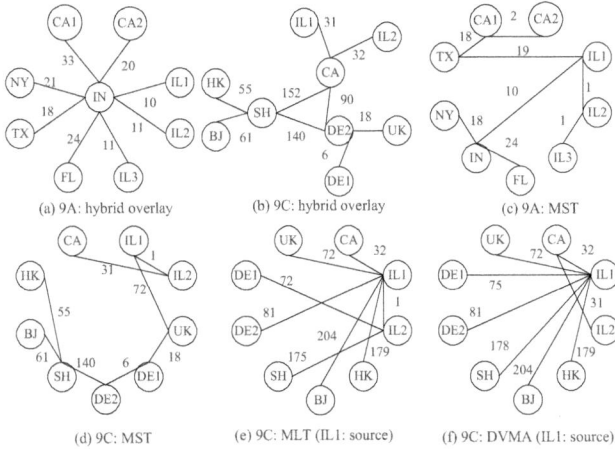

(a) 9A: hybrid overlay   (b) 9C: hybrid overlay   (c) 9A: MST

(d) 9C: MST   (e) 9C: MLT (IL1: source)   (f) 9C: DVMA (IL1: source)

Figure 6: Resulting content distribution topologies based on the Internet data in Table 2 and 3. Number by the links are the one-way latency (in msec).

4.3 Evaluation of Five Topologies

We evaluate the following five topologies typically used in content dissemination. In this section, we assume all sites in the topology are both senders and receivers. We do not consider factors that are specific to 3DTI applications.

(1) Full-mesh topology.

(2) Hybrid overlay [14] which uses a greedy approach to increase the number of intermediate sites in order to minimize the maximum EED in the overlay.

(3) Minimum spanning tree (MST) based on Kruskal's Algorithm [8] which finds the cheapest unmarked edges (links) that does not form a marked loop.

(4) Minimum latency tree (MLT) [23] which is constructed by combining all shortest paths from the senders to their receiver sites using the Dijkstra's Algorithm.

(5) Delay variation multicast algorithm (DVMA) [13] which constructs a tree with bounded delay and delay variation based on k-shortest paths from the sender sites to the receivers.

Table 4 presents the simulation results for the five topologies under network environment 5A-5F and 9A-9F. Note that both full-mesh network and hybrid overlay are not available under network environment 5D-5F and 9D-9F because they require the link latency information between every two neighboring sites in the topology. Several observations are presented as follows.

EED. Table 4 shows that MST leads to the largest average and maximum EED, due to the largest number of IS introduced in the topology (e.g., four IS on the path from CA2 to FL in Fig. 6(c)). The EED can be further increased if the processing latencies on these IS are not negligible. On the contrary, all other topologies can achieve relatively small EED, of which MLT leads to the minimum EED.

Inter-sender and inter-receiver skews. Due to the EED variations across different sites, MST results in the largest inter-sender and inter-receiver skews. The EED variations in the full-mesh, hybrid overlay and MLT are comparatively small, but still their topologies may exceed the upper bound of both synchronization skews (say, 200 msec). DVMA is constructed based on MLT by keeping the path with the largest EED in the topology and replace the shortest path with other alternatives in order to reduce the syn-

chronization skews. E.g., in Fig. 6(f), IL1 sends media data to IL2 via CA instead of direct communication as in MLT in Fig. 6(e). This can increase the latency between IL1 and IL2 from 1 msec to 63 msec, and thus reduce the maximum synchronization skew from 203 msec to 175 msec. Note that DVMA may not always be effective if there is no alternative path (e.g. the connection between IL1 and IL2 network environment 9F in Table 4(b)).

Bandwidth overhead. Bandwidth availability is an issue in all algorithms. In a full-mesh topology, each sender site needs to send multiple copies of media streams to its receivers. A hybrid overlay can lead to a centralized topology which will overwhelm the central site when delay variation is small (e.g., network environment 9A in Fig. 6(a)). In MST, many sites (e.g., UK, DE1, and etc. in Fig. 6(d)) need to relay all streams to other sites even though they only need a subset of these streams. MLT and DVMA can create multiple trees in the topology rooted at different sender sites, but none of them considers the bandwidth constraints within/across trees (e.g., site IL1 in Fig. 6(e) and (f)).

Interactions of different metrics. Those network-layer quality metrics exhibit strong interactions. First, the topology may not lead to the smallest average system EED if we want to reduce the synchronization skews by replacing the paths with the shortest EED with k-shortest alternatives (as in DVMA), or to satisfy the bandwidth constraints by preventing the stream dissemination being routed through the shortest paths. Second, due to the Internet delay correlations, media data from a sender site can be routed through a geographically close intermediate sites for the shortest paths (e.g., IL1 uses IL2 as an intermediate site in Fig. 6(e)). If IL2 is not a sender site, the routing paths via IL2 can effectively reduce the bandwidth overhead at IL1. However, IL1 will use the bandwidth resources at IL2 if IL2 itself is a sender site.

Of all the five topologies, DVMA can lead to a topology with the smallest EED given the constraint of the inter-receiver skew compared to other algorithms. Unfortunately, none of the existing topologies has studied the interactions among EED, synchronization and bandwidth metrics in a real Internet setting. Nor do these studies consider the heterogeneity within a multi-stream bundle. Hence, based upon DVMA, we design SyncCast to address these issues in section 5.

5. DESIGN OF SYNCCAST

We design SyncCast based on the multi-stream heterogeneity and the interactions of EED, synchronization and bandwidth metrics in the real Internet settings. We adopt a multi-tree structured scheme rooted at different sender sites because of its flexibility to both Internet dynamics and synchronization/bandwidth adaptations. We compare Sync-Cast with ViewCast [20] during our discussions. We study the design of receiver-side buffer and its impact on synchronization in SyncCast at the end of this section.

5.1 Design Rationale

This type of optimization problems has been proven to be NP hard [9, 18], and an optimal solution is inaccessible without introducing some heuristics. Here, we discuss the rationale behind the design of our SyncCast algorithm.

1. **Stream prioritization.** We prioritize multi-streams from different sender sites because of the limited amount

Table 4: Minimum and maximum inter-sender/inter-receiver skew (msec) as well as average and maximum EED (msec) for the 5 topologies under 12 network environment (5A-5F,9A-9F in Table 2 and 3).

Table 4(a)			Full-mesh	Hybrid	MST	MLT	DVMA
5A	Skew	min	11	23	24	11	11
		max	25	33	42	25	25
	EED	avg	26.8	34	35.6	26.8	26.8
		max	43	57	66	43	43
5B	Skew	min	32	31	49	32	32
		max	70	53	105	70	70
	EED	avg	53.4	67.6	63.8	53.4	53.4
		max	88	105	123	88	88
5C	Skew	min	65	88	75	65	65
		max	146	152	177	106	106
	EED	avg	100.1	135.8	104.8	90.4	90.4
		max	178	240	211	140	140
9A	Skew	min	11	23	35	11	11
		max	44	33	71	43	43
	EED	avg	23.1	32.9	31.9	22.5	22.5
		max	46	57	73	45	45
9B	Skew	min	67	84	95	67	67
		max	97	103	130	95	95
	EED	avg	55.7	69.4	70.3	55.4	55.4
		max	102	127	147	102	102
9C	Skew	min	123	129	195	121	123
		max	203	213	298	203	175
	EED	avg	114.2	140.6	152.4	113.7	115.5
		max	204	245	329	204	204

Table 4(b)			MST	MLT	DVMA
5D	Skew	min	35	11	11
		max	71	41	41
	EED	avg	45.8	33.3	33.3
		max	95	59	59
5E	Skew	min	49	32	32
		max	105	86	86
	EED	avg	63.8	56.8	56.8
		max	123	104	104
5F	Skew	min	75	65	65
		max	177	106	106
	EED	avg	104.8	90.4	90.4
		max	211	140	140
9D	Skew	min	42	12	12
		max	100	50	50
	EED	avg	40.4	27.2	27.2
		max	102	52	52
9E	Skew	min	81	64	64
		max	172	82	82
	EED	avg	87.7	59.2	59.2
		max	189	104	104
9F	Skew	min	195	124	124
		max	297	239	239
	EED	avg	152.4	119.5	119.5
		max	329	240	240

of network resources. The dissemination of 3DTI streams can be divided into three service classes: (1) AVDS from the sender sites to their corresponding receivers; (2) streams that have been disseminated as AVDS, but can also serve as NDS for other receivers; and (3) streams that have never been serviced, and can only serve as NDS for all receiver sites (sole-NDS). In our design, we give top priority to all AVDS streams, and last priority to the sole-NDS.

Streams within the same class can also be prioritized. We propose two concepts based on the tree-structured multicast topology: *global contribution factor* (GCF) and *local contribution factor* (LCF). The GCF of a stream s in the the j-th class (GCF_j^s) is defined as the accumulative CF to all designated receiver sites within the class. A formal definition is as follows.

$$\text{GCF}_1^s = \sum_{i,k} CF_{i \to k}^s \qquad s = DS_{i \to k}$$

$$\text{GCF}_2^s = \sum_{i,k} CF_{i \to k}^s \quad s \in \mathcal{S}_{i \to k}^{NDS} \,\&\, \exists\, k' \neq k, s = DS_{i \to k'} \qquad (6)$$

$$\text{GCF}_3^s = \sum_{i,k} CF_{i \to k}^s \quad s \in \mathcal{S}_{i \to k}^{NDS} \,\&\, \nexists\, k' \neq k, s = DS_{i \to k'}$$

The metrics GCF describes a stream's overall contribution to all receiver sites in each stream class. A stream with a larger GCF is more visually important to whole system compared to other streams within the same class.

The LCF of a stream s at a node n_i ($\text{LCF}_{n_i}^s$), on the other hand, is defined as the accumulative CF for all n_i's descendants in the tree (i.e., nodes that receive s through the relay of n_i). The metrics LCF describes the overall contribution of relaying each stream at an intermediate node. A stream with a larger LCF at a node should be given higher priority.

In comparison, ViewCast does not prioritize streams within the same service class. Its prioritization is only based on the CF and it uses preemption for service differentiation. CF alone however can only tell the contribution of a stream to a single receiver, and does not describe its importance to the whole system. This can create an issue when two streams (one with a small CF and a large GCF, and the other with a large CF and a small GCF) competing for the

limited resources. ViewCast in this case will prefer the second stream, and thus can increase the likelihood of victim sites and *victim streams* (i.e., the number of DS/NDS not received).

2. **Path prioritization**. A stream from a sender site to a receiver can follow multiple paths. Both EED and fairness impact the path prioritization. To evaluate the fairness of a path, we compute on each path $\mathcal{PS}_{i \to k}^s[j]$ (i.e., the j-th path in path options $\mathcal{PS}_{i \to k}^s$ for stream s) the number of IS where s has no contributions, and denote the number as $Q[j]$. Suppose $\mathcal{PS}_{i \to k}^s[j]$ has M IS, i.e., $\mathcal{PS}_{i \to k}^s[j] = \{E_i^{snd}, n_1^{IS}, n_2^{IS}, \ldots, n_M^{IS}, E_k^{rcv(i)}\}$, $Q[j]$ can be computed by

$$Q[j] = \sum_{m=1}^{M} I\,\{CF_{E_i^{snd} \to n_m^{IS}}^s \leq \text{CF}_0\} \qquad (7)$$

Here $I\{\cdot\}$ is the indicator function.

To improve the fairness of the dissemination topology and prevent nodes relay NUS which otherwise would waste their own network resources, while preserving the interactivity, we prioritize path candidates based on a *fairness-first, latency-next* policy in our system, meaning that the paths with a smaller $Q[j]$ are always placed at a higher priority, and that the path with a $Q[j]$ and a shorter EED is better than those with the same $Q[j]$ and a longer EED.

By contrast, fairness is also guaranteed in ViewCast because the receiver sites only request a stream from the sender site and those that have already requested and received the streams. However, multiple DS can compete for bandwidth resources at a site, and thus may cause a degradation of audio/visual quality in ViewCast.

3. **Bandwidth preservation policy**. The 3DTI system has a very high demand of bandwidth for multi-stream dissemination. To provide the shortest dissemination paths in the real Internet setting and offer resilience to the user view changes, we prescribe in our system that: unless a site needs to relay a stream which is a DS for other sender-receiver pair and their is no alternative path available for this DS,

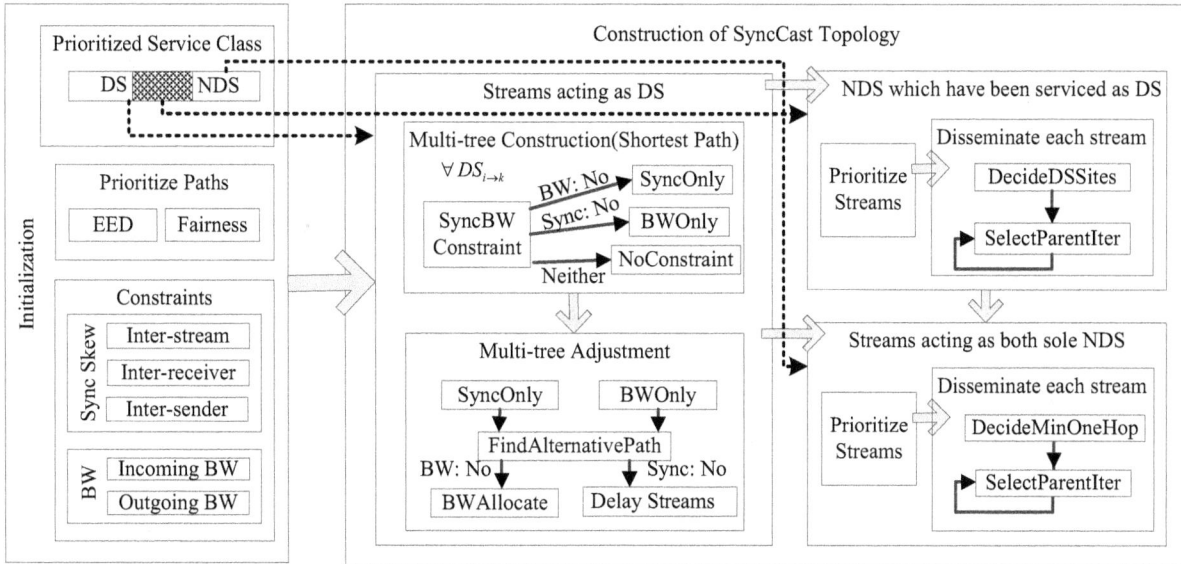

Figure 7: An overview of SyncCast.

• no site is responsible for relaying its NUS (which can be DS/NDS to other receivers) from the senders;
• no sender site should relay its NDS from other senders.

The ViewCast algorithm does not have this layer of bandwidth preservation because of a lack in the service class differentiation.

5.2 SyncCast Design Details

Based on the design rationale, we propose SyncCast. Fig. 7 shows its framework. We use GCF to prioritize the streams within each service class.

5.2.1 An Overview

SyncCast first determines the dissemination topology for all AVDS (class 1). The algorithm can be divided into two parts: multi-tree construction and multi-tree adjustment. In the multi-tree construction, SyncCast uses an approach similar to DVMA. It tries to find the latency/fairness prioritized path that satisfies both synchronization and bandwidth constraints. If there is no successful path, the algorithm relaxes the constraints (section 5.2.2). In the multi-tree adjustment, SyncCast seeks alternative paths for previous successfully assigned paths on the purpose of reducing the synchronization skews and/or the bandwidth overhead within the bounded allowance (section 5.2.2). After that, it either achieves cooperative bandwidth allocation (**BWAllocate**) at each site based on the LCF if the bandwidth constraint (section 5.2.3) is not satisfied, or delays the stream with the shortest EED before it is sent to the receiver-side buffer (section 5.3) if the synchronization constraints are violated.

Next, SyncCast decides all NDS which have been requested as AVDS (class 2). In order to reduce the bandwidth overhead at the sender sites, an option is to let these NDS receivers only request from the *serviced* sites (i.e., sites that have already received a stream as either DS or NDS). SyncCast determines all serviced sites in the AVDS topology (**DecideDSSites**) before it seeks by iteration the immediate best serviced parent site for each *unserviced* receiver (i.e. site that has not received a stream) in **SelectParentIter**.

Last, SyncCast finds possible dissemination paths for all sole-NDS (class 3). To maximize the dissemination of sole-NDS (which are usually bottlenecked at the sender sites due to the inadequate bandwidth unavailability), an option of the algorithm is to iteratively locate the closest single-hop unserviced receiver site (which is not itself a sender) to the original sender (**DecideMinOneHop**). Through the relay of each selected single-hop receiver, the algorithm then determines the dissemination paths for the rest of unserviced receivers in **SelectParentIter**.

By contrast, ViewCast only sets an upper bound on the EED and does not take synchronization into account. The algorithm simply picks a site with the least bandwidth overhead among the sender and the sites which have already received the stream. Hence, multiple streams belonging to the same sender-receiver pair can follow paths with huge EED difference and thus cause noticeable inter-stream (or inter-video) skew. Both inter-sender and inter-receiver skews, on the other hand, can only be constrained within the EED upper bound.

5.2.2 Dissemination of AVDS (class 1)

In the multi-tree construction stage, SyncCast finds the best prioritized path for each sender-receiver pair which satisfies the bandwidth constraints and the inter-sender/ inter-receiver synchronization (**SyncBW**), i.e., a successful path. If there is no successful path available, SyncCast considers three cases.

(1) If there are paths with only synchronization constraints, SyncCast selects the sync-constrained path with the least number of overloaded sites on the path (**SyncOnly**).

(2) If there are paths satisfying only bandwidth constraints, SyncCast selects the bandwidth-constrained path with the smallest inter-sender or inter-receiver synchronization skew (**BWOnly**).

(3) If there is no path satisfying either constraints, SyncCast selects the bandwidth-unconstrained path with the smallest synchronization skew (**NoConstraint**).

We call the paths assigned in the three cases above *unsuccessful* paths.

In the multi-tree adjustment stage, the function **FindAlternativePath** seeks the alternative path for the affected successfully assigned paths in order to remove/reduce the synchronization skew or bandwidth bottleneck. It takes into account the following two situations.

(1) If there is an inter-sender/inter-receiver skew violating the synchronization upper bound, SyncCast picks the successful path (and its corresponding sender and receiver) which results in the largest synchronization skew, and seeks the alternatives to the reduce the skew. This can be done via iteration until either the synchronization is constrained or no alternative path can be found.

(2) If there are sites bottlenecked at the incoming/outgoing bandwidth, SyncCast picks the successful paths which pass through the sites, and finds the alternatives by iteration until either the site is not overloaded, or no alterative path can be found.

After **FindAlternativePath** returns, if there are still unsuccessful paths violating synchronization constraints, SyncCast delays the AVDS with the shortest EED (section 5.3). If some sites are still overloaded, the algorithm applies cooperative bandwidth allocation scheme.

5.2.3 Cooperative Bandwidth Allocation

SyncCast applies the cooperative bandwidth allocation scheme to reduce the incoming/outgoing bandwidth overhead to the overloaded sites shared by multiple AVDS. We guarantee the best audio quality because users are usually more sensitive to the degradation of the audio signals. But because the bandwidth overhead of audio signals is negligible compared to the huge amounts of 3D visual information, we only discuss the video streams here.

Suppose there are L DS ($s_1, \ldots, s_L$) that need to be relayed by an overloaded site n_i and their corresponding LCF are ($\mathrm{LCF}_{n_i}^{s_1}, \ldots, \mathrm{LCF}_{n_i}^{s_L}$), the outgoing bandwidth $B_{n_i}^{\mathrm{out}}(l)$ allocated for stream s_l at n_i can be computed as:

$$B_{n_i}^{\mathrm{out}}(l) = \frac{\mathrm{LCF}_{n_i}^{s_l}}{\sum_{m=1}^{L} \mathrm{LCF}_{n_i}^{s_m}} \times (\max B_{n_i}^{\mathrm{out}}) \qquad (8)$$

Based upon the allocated bandwidth, we then decide the frame rate of each stream by its estimated frame size which can be obtained using the linear prediction approach [6].

For the sites bottlenecked at the incoming bandwidth, we apply the same strategy by considering the LCF of the streams that are disseminating over the links between each overloaded site and its immediate parent node.

5.2.4 Dissemination of NDS (class 2 and 3)

The pseudocode of **SelectParentIter** is shown in Code 1. For each stream s in either class (from a sender site E_i^{snd}) requested by a receiver site $E_k^{rcv(i)}$, the input of the function $\mathcal{S}^{IS}$ (the set of serviced receiver sites of s) is determined by **DecideDSSites** or **DecideMinOneHop**. SyncCast searches in $\mathcal{S}^{IS}$, and picks a site n_{best}^{IS} with the smallest bandwidth overhead that satisfies the inter-stream (or inter-video) skew (**DecideBestSync**). n_{best}^{IS} then becomes the immediate parent site of $E_k^{rcv(i)}$. The new receiver site is added to the serviced set.

5.3 Receiver-side Buffering

Receiver-side buffering is important in SyncCast because it can (1) smooth jitters and conceal losses for audio sig-

---

Code 1 Function SelectParentIter($\mathcal{S}^{IS}$)

```
1: 𝒮^rcv ← All unserviced receiver sites requesting s
2: for all E_k^{rcv(i)} ∈ 𝒮^rcv do
3:     n_best^IS ← DecideBestSync(𝒮^IS, E_k^{rcv(i)})
4:     𝒮^rcv ← 𝒮^rcv − E_k^{rcv(i)}
5:     𝒮^IS ← 𝒮^IS + E_k^{rcv(i)}
6: end for
```

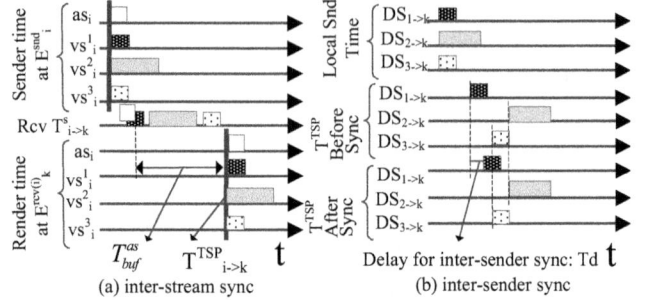

Figure 8: Receiver site buffering.

nals, (2) synchronize the video multi-stream bundle from the same sender site before it is sent to the 3D video renderer (inter-video synchronization), (3) synchronize the audio with the corresponding video DS or multi-stream bundle sharing the same sender (audio-visual or inter-stream synchronization). We call the moment *timed synchronization point* (TSP) at a receiver site of the multi-stream bundle, which is the time that the sender's video macroframe is sent to the renderer and the synchronous audio frame to the speaker. A TSP sequence at a receiver includes all TSP for different macroframes (in time) of the same sender. Note that there can be multiple TSP sequences at a receiver site with each TSP sequence corresponding to one individual sender.

In this paper, we set each TSP based on the fact that audio signals usually require $T_{buf}^{as} = 60 - 80$ msec buffering time to smooth 98% of the audio jitters [5]. For each new video macroframe from a sender site E_i^{snd}, SyncCast searches the corresponding audio frame nearest in time (suppose the audio frame is captured at t_0 local time at E_i^{snd}). At each receiver site $E_k^{rcv(i)}$, we set the TSP for this video macroframe to $T_{i \to k}^{TSP} = T_{i \to k}^{as}(t_0) + T_{buf}^{as}$ (Fig. 8(a)), where $T_{i \to k}^{as}(t_0)$ is the expected arrival time at $E_k^{rcv(i)}$ of an audio frame captured at t_0 from E_i^{snd}, and T_{buf}^{as} is set to be 80 msec in our system. Because the video DS follow the same dissemination path as the audio signal, it can arrive within T_{buf}^{as} (audio-visual synchronization). If we set $\delta_s = T_{buf}^{as}$, all video NDS from E_i^{snd} can also arrive within the inter-stream (inter-video) synchronization constraint.

To achieve the inter-sender and inter-receiver synchronization across different sender/reciever sites, all sites periodically probe for EED from every other sites. If the inter-sender or inter-receiver synchronization skew is larger than the upper bound δ_{snd} or δ_{rcv}, we delay the AVDS with the shortest EED (by a period of T_d) before it is sent to the receiver buffer, so that both inter-sender and inter-receiver synchronization can be satisfied. Fig. 8(b) shows the example of delaying $DS_{1 \to k}$ (the path with the shortest EED to E_k^{rcv}) in order to reduce the inter-sender skew below δ_{snd} while guaranteeing inter-receiver synchronization. Note that we take T_d in the computation of EED in section 6.

6. EVALUATION RESULTS

We evaluate SyncCast using the one-way latency statistics in Table 2 and 3. We also compare SyncCast with ViewCast.

- **Experiment Setup**

We develop a multi-party 3DTI simulator for the evaluation of SyncCast. We consider both 5-site and 9-site cases, and simulate all the 12 Internet environment in Table 2 and 3. We use the link costs in the two tables to represent the latencies between the corresponding two sites in the simulator. Due to the space limit, we only consider the situation that there are roughly 50% of the sites are sender sites (i.e., 2 sender sites in the 5-site case and 4 sender sites in the 9-site case), and the senders are randomly selected in each Internet environment.

We suppose each sender site outputs 1 audio stream and 8 video streams from 8 3D cameras placed evenly (in a separation of 45-degree angle) in a 360-degree circle around a scene [20]. These cameras can capture the 3D images of the same scene from different views. From each sender site, a receiver requests 1 audio stream, 1 video DS and 2 video NDS (which are the two neighboring streams of the video DS). To simulate a real multi-site collaboration scenario, we suppose 50% of the receiver sites share the same video DS, and the other 50% of the receiver sites request different video DS. The audio streams are always requested by the receivers.

For simplicity, we represent in evaluation the incoming and outgoing bandwidth overhead as the number of 3D video streams. We assume that the bandwidth demand of audio streams is negligible compared to that of the video streams. In this paper, we set both incoming and outgoing bandwidth upper bound to be 10 video streams at each site (i.e., max $B^{in} = 10$, max $B^{out} = 10$). We prescribe the inter-stream skew bound δ_s be 80 msec (as discussed in section 5.3). We use an equal value for inter-sender and inter-receiver skew upper bound ($\delta_{snd} = \delta_{rcv}$). To simulate different application demand, the upper bound varies from 100 msec to 300 msec (in a separation of 100 msec).

To compare SyncCast with ViewCast, we also constrain the ViewCast's inter-sender and inter-receiver synchronization skews within the same upper bound as SyncCast, by assigning the value of δ_{snd} (or δ_{rcv}) to the EED upper bound in ViewCast.

- **Simulation Results**

Victims. Fig. 9(a) shows the number of victim sites in ViewCast. The victims are incurred due to the fact that (1) ViewCast does not take into account service class differentiation, so the limited bandwidth resources can be used to transmit less visually-important NDS; and that (2) a small EED upper bound can reduce AVDS path availability, so the number of victim sites increases as the EED upper bound decreases. By contrast, there are no victim sites introduced by SyncCast because of the service class differentiation, cooperative bandwidth allocation and AVDS path delaying policy to satisfy the inter-sender/inter-receiver synchronization constraints. Fig. 9(b) shows the number of delayed AVDS paths. As the inter-sender/inter-receiver synchronization upper bound decreases, more AVDS paths with short EED will create an unbounded synchronization skew and thus need to be delayed. Fig. 10(a)-(b) show that the number of victim streams are consistently lower than ViewCast due

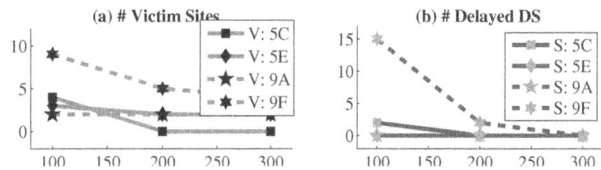

Figure 9: SyncCast/ViewCast. X-axis is δ_{snd} (δ_{rcv}).

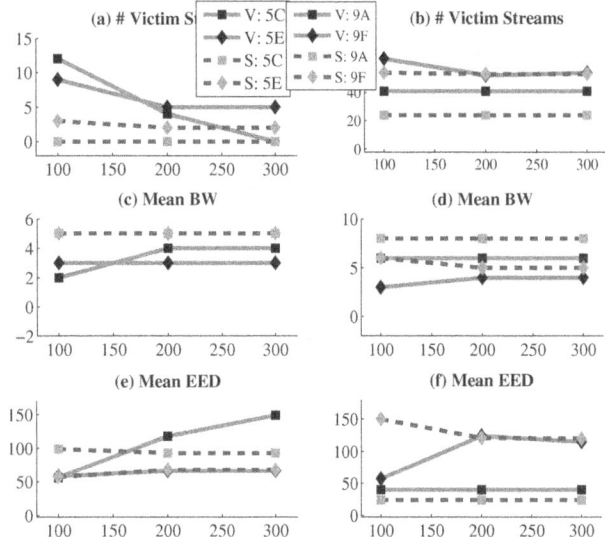

Figure 10: SyncCast/ViewCast. X-axis is δ_{snd} (δ_{rcv}).

to the combined impact of the service class differentiation, routing fairness and bandwidth preservation policies.

Bandwidth overhead. The average incoming and outgoing bandwidth overhead should be equal because we assume there is no broken link in this paper. Fig. 10(c)-(d) demonstrate that SyncCast boasts a high bandwidth utilization than ViewCast and thus a smaller number of victim streams/sites.

Average EED of AVDS paths. Fig. 10(e)-(f) show the average system EED of all AVDS paths of the two algorithms. When $\delta_{snd} = \delta_{rcv} = 200$ or 300 msec, SyncCast's results are comparable to or smaller than ViewCast's data. This shows the effectiveness of SyncCast algorithm based on DVMA. When $\delta_{snd} = \delta_{rcv} = 100$ msec, due to huge amounts of unsuccessful transmissions of AVDS (victim sites) in ViewCast, the remaining successful AVDS paths with short EED can lead to an average smaller than Sync-Cast's results. As mentioned in Section 3, the minimization of the number of victim sites is placed at the top priority in the 3DTI system in order to guarantee AVDS's audio-visual contributions.

Inter-stream skew. We compare the inter-stream skews in Fig. 11(a)-(b). We show that SyncCast can consistently achieve the inter-stream synchronization within the preset 80 msec constraint by dropping streams which will cause unbounded skew. On the other hand, ViewCast exhibits randomness of the inter-stream skews which can exceed the constraint, because it only sets the EED upper bound.

Inter-sender and inter-receiver skews. Fig. 11(c)-(f) show the maximum inter-sender and inter-receiver skews. They show that both ViewCast and SyncCast can successfully limit all the skews within the prescribed upper bound. Note that because the two protocols are using different ap-

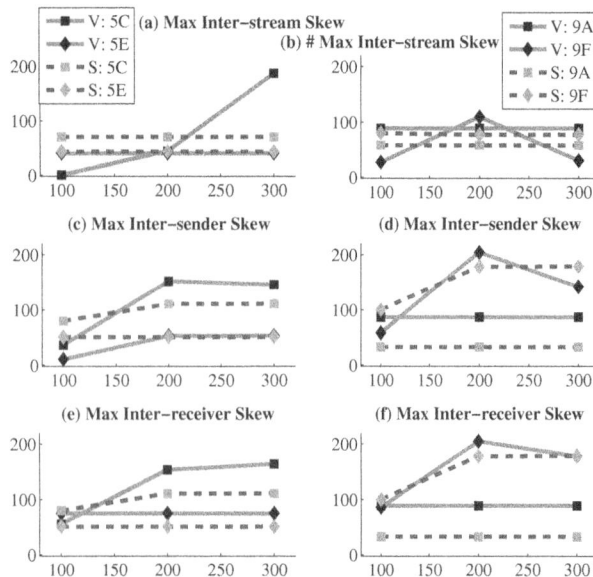

Figure 11: SyncCast/ViewCast. X-axis is δ_{snd} (δ_{rcv}).

proaches to achieve the synchronization, the resulting skews of SyncCast do not have to be smaller than those of View-Cast. In addition, the synchronization upper bound of View-Cast depends on its preset EED upper bound. Hence, more victim sites/streams (due to a lack of paths with bounded EED) can be introduced under the circumstance of a tight timing synchronization constraint.

7. CONCLUSION

In conclusion, compared to ViewCast, SyncCast can successfully reduce the number of victim sites and victim streams, minimize the average system EED of all DS paths, achieve the bandwidth and synchronization constraints. Our new disseminations scheme is not limited to the 3DTI application. It can be extended to any delay-sensitive online gaming systems when each avatar can output more than one correlated media streams, and the timing synchronization is critical.

We would like to acknowledge all constructive comments from the reviewers. This research study is supported by NSF CNS 0720702 and 0834480, by UPCRC grant from Intel and Microsoft, and by Grainger Grant.

8. REFERENCES
[1] P. Agarwal, R. Rivas, W. Wu, and K. Nahrstedt. Bundle of streams: Concept and evaluation in distributed interactive multimedia environments. In *Proc. of IEEE Int'l Symposium on Multimedia*, 2010.
[2] A. Bhattacharya and Z. Yang. Dvbmn-l: delay variation bounded multicast network with multiple paths. In *Proc. of IEEE Int'l Conference on Multimedia and Expo*, pages 762–765, 2009.
[3] E. Brosh, A. Levin, and Y. Shavitt. Approximation and heuristic algorithms for minimum-delay application-layer multicast trees. *IEEE/ACM Transaction on Networking*, 15(2):473–484, 2007.
[4] R. Hassin and A. Tamir. On the minimum diameter spanning tree problem. *Information Processing Letters*, 53:109–111, 1997.
[5] Z. Huang, B. Sat, and B. W. Wah. Automated learning of play-out scheduling algorithms for improving the

perceptual conversational quality in multi-party VoIP. In *Proc. IEEE International Conference on Multimedia and Expo*, pages 493–496, July 2008.
[6] Z. Huang, W. Wu, K. Nahrstedt, A. Arefin, and R. Rivas. Tsync: A new synchronization framework for multi-site 3d tele-immersion. In *Proc. ACM Workshop on Network and Operating Systems Support for Digital Audio and Video*, June 2010.
[7] S. Khuller, B. Raghavachari, P. State, and N. Young. Balancing minimum spanning trees and shortest-path trees. *Algorithmica*, 14:305–321, 1995.
[8] J. Kruskal. On the shortest spanning subtree of a graph and the traveling salesman problem. *American Mathematical Society*, 7(1):48–50, 1956.
[9] F. A. Kuipers. An overview of constraint-based path selection algorithms for qos routing. *IEEE Communications Magazine*, pages 50–56, 2002.
[10] K. Liang and R. Zimmermann. Cross-tree adjustment for spatialized audio streaming over networked virtual environments. In *Proc. ACM Workshop on Network and Operating Systems Support for Digital Audio and Video*, pages 73–78, 2009.
[11] T. Little. A framework for synchronous delivery of time-dependent multimedia data. *Multimedia Systems*, 1(2):87–94, 1993.
[12] H. Liu and M. Zarki. An adaptive delay and synchronization control scheme for Wi-Fi based audio/video conferencing. *Springer Wireless Networks*, 12(4):511–522, July 2006.
[13] G. N. Rouskas and I. Baldine. Multicast routing with end-to-end delay and delay variation constraints. *IEEE Journal on Selected Areas in Communications*, 15(3):346–356, Apr. 1997.
[14] B. Sat, Z. Huang, and B. W. Wah. The design of a multi-party VoIP conferencing system over the Internet. In *Proc. IEEE Int'l Symposium on Multimedia*, pages 3–10, Taichung, Taiwan, Dec. 2007.
[15] B. Sat and B. W. Wah. Playout scheduling and loss-concealments in VoIP for optimizing conversational voice communication quality. In *Proceedings of ACM Multimedia*, pages 137–146, Sept. 2007.
[16] S. Y. Shi, J. S. Turner, and M. Waldvogel. Dimensioning server access bandwidth and multicast routing in overlay networks. In *Proc. of ACM International Workshop on Network and Operating System Support for Digital Audio and Video*, pages 83–92, 2001.
[17] R. Steinmetz. Human perception of jitter and media synchronation. *IEEE Journal on Selected Areas in Communications*, 14(1):61–72, 1996.
[18] Z. Wang and J. Crowcroft. Quality of service routing for supporting multimedia applications. *IEEE Journal on Selected Areas in Communications*, 14:1228–1234, 1996.
[19] Z. Yang. Multi-stream synchronization for 3d tele-immersive and collaborative environment. In *Proc. of ICST Conference on Immersive Telecommunications*, 2009.
[20] Z. Yang, W. Wu, K. Nahrstedt, G. Kurillo, and R. Bajcsy. Enabling multi-party 3d tele-immersive environments with viewcast. *ACM Transactions on Multimedia Computing, Communications, and Applications*, 6(2), 2010.
[21] Z. Yang, B. Yu, K. Nahrstedt, and R. Bajcsy. A multi-stream adaptation framework for bandwidth management in 3D tele-immersion. In *Proc. ACM Workshop on Network and Operating Systems Support for Digital Audio and Video*, 2006.
[22] K. Yasumoto and K. Nahrstedt. Ravitas: Realistic voice chat framework for cooperative virtual spaces. In *Proc. of IEEE 2005 International Conference on Multimedia and Expo*, 2005.
[23] R. Zimmermann and K. Liang. Spatialized audio streaming for networked virtual environments. In *Proc. of ACM Int'l Conference on Multimedia*, pages 299–308, 2008.

Quantifying QoS Requirements of Network Services: A Cheat-Proof Framework

Kuan-Ta Chen[1], Chen-Chi Wu[2], Yu-Chun Chang[12], and Chin-Laung Lei[2]

[1]Institute of Information Science, Academia Sinica
[2]Department of Electrical Engineering, National Taiwan University

ABSTRACT

Despite all the efforts devoted to improving the QoS of networked multimedia services, the baseline for such improvements has yet to be defined. In other words, although it is well recognized that better network conditions generally yield better service quality, the exact minimum level of network QoS required to ensure satisfactory user experience remains an open question.

In this paper, we propose a general, cheat-proof framework that enables researchers to systematically quantify the minimum QoS needs for real-time networked multimedia services. Our framework has two major features: 1) it measures the quality of a service that users find intolerable by intuitive responses and therefore reduces the burden on experiment participants; and 2) it is cheat-proof because it supports systematic verification of the participants' inputs. Via a pilot study involving 38 participants, we verify the efficacy of our framework by proving that even inexperienced participants can easily produce consistent judgments. In addition, by cross-application and cross-service comparative analysis, we demonstrate the usefulness of the derived QoS thresholds. Such knowledge will serve important reference in the evaluation of competitive applications, application recommendation, network planning, and resource arbitration.

Categories and Subject Descriptors

C.4 [**Performance of Systems**]: Measurement techniques; H.1.2 [**Models and Principles**]: User/Machine Systems—*Human factors*; H.4.3 [**Information Systems Applications**]: Communications Applications—*Computer conferencing, teleconferencing, and videoconferencing*

General Terms

Human Factors, Measurement, Performance

Keywords

Psychophysics, Method of Limits, Quality of Experience, Crowdsourcing, Comparative Analysis

1. INTRODUCTION

Currently, it is not possible to guarantee the quality of packet delivery over the Internet because of unavoidable network impairment events, such as queuing delay, packet dropping, and packet reordering. Despite the Internet's unpredictable nature, researchers endeavor to design networked multimedia services that can always provide satisfactory user experience whatever level of network QoS (Quality of Service)[1] is provided. The research efforts sit from the core to the end-points, and address issues ranging from the packet level to the media level. For example, on the policy level, IntServ [5] attempts to guarantee the performance of mission-critical and real-time services, and DiffServ [2] is designed to provide differentiated quality levels for different needs. At the network layer, a number of router scheduling algorithms and their variants [20] try to provide prioritized and fair packet delivery. Meanwhile, at the application layer, numerous studies focus on the control of source traffic [10,27], the adjustment of VoIP playout buffer [21,29,32], and the concealment of information loss [13,14,28] to cope with the chaotic network impairments and provide the best possible service quality at their best.

Despite all the efforts devoted to improving the QoS of networked multimedia services, the *baseline* for such improvements has yet to be clearly defined. In other words, although it is widely recognized that better network conditions generally yield better service quality, *the exact minimum level of network QoS required to ensure user satisfaction remains an open question.*

For example, if network bandwidth is "insufficient," the quality of a VoIP call would degrade and the call parties would experience lower satisfaction. Normally a VoIP call requires tens of Kbps of bandwidth for the transmission of audio packets. However, the minimum bandwidth required by a particular VoIP service to barely ensure an "acceptable" degree of user satisfaction is undefined. This is also true in network gaming. Although short network delay is critical for interactive gaming, the exact minimum requirement of such delay (i.e., the longest acceptable delay) for gaming is unknown. In addition, the difference between the longest

---

[1]Here by network QoS we refer to the service level of network data delivery, including network bandwidth, network delay, packet loss rate, to name a few.

acceptable delay for slow-paced games, e.g., RPG (Role-Playing Games), and that for fast-paced gaming, e.g., FPS (First-Person Shooter) games, has yet to be determined.

We define the "minimum QoS needs" of a networked multimedia service as the minimum level of QoS that will yield an acceptable level of service quality from the user's perspective. In this case, users may feel that, although the service quality is far from perfect, it is acceptable so they will continue using the service. Quantifying the minimum QoS requirements for networked multimedia services is essential for the following tasks:

- **Network planning**: If the minimum QoS requirements for a networked multimedia service can be determined, networks can be planned accordingly. For example, if the longest acceptable delay for FPS games is 200 ms, an FPS game provider can ensure that game play is at least tolerable by hosting its game servers within 200 ms network delay from the majority of the players' locations.

- **Resource arbitration**: When network resources are limited, arbitration between different needs is necessary to avoid congestion collapse and subsequent service quality degradation. For example, suppose that the minimum bandwidth required for conference calls is 80 Kbps. To guarantee the quality of such calls, we can allocate at least 80 Kbps of bandwidth to each call, as long as other simultaneous needs do not have stricter real-time requirements.

We define an "intolerance threshold" as *the minimum level of a QoS factor that yields acceptable service quality from the user's perspective*. By definition, this threshold is not derivable by pure mathematical axioms and deductions; rather, it has to be extracted from users' opinions. The *de facto* subjective method for measuring the quality of a networked multimedia service is the MOS (Mean Opinion Score) rating test [15]. In an MOS test, subjects are asked to rate the quality level from Bad (the worst) to Excellent (the best), and the overall rating is obtained by averaging the scores from repeated tests. MOS scoring is widely used because it is simple and intuitive; however, it is not suitable for detecting the intolerance threshold for the following reasons.

1. The rating standard is somewhat obscure to experiment participants. As the concepts of the five scales, i.e., Bad, Poor, Fair, Good, and Excellent, cannot be concretely defined and explained, subjects may be confused about which scale they should give in each test.

2. In MOS tests, participants are asked to grade the MOS scores for stimuli; however, we do not know whether they pay full attention to the scoring procedures, or whether they just give ratings in a perfunctory manner. There is no established methodology for verifying the authenticity of a participant's ratings, and the measurement accuracy may be degraded due to untrustworthy participants [12].

3. Since the range of an MOS score is from 1 to 5, it is difficult to define an appropriate threshold that represents "the barely acceptable user experience." It may seem reasonable to take either 2 (Poor) or 3 (Fair) as the threshold. In VoIP quality tests, an MOS score of 4.0 is usually considered as the toll quality, but it

does not represent the threshold for the barely tolerable service quality.

In this paper, using a psychophysical approach [30], *we propose a general, cheat-proof framework that enables researchers to systematically quantify the minimum QoS requirements for real-time networked multimedia services*. The framework not only enables us to measure the intolerance thresholds for QoS factors of interest, but also addresses the disadvantages of the MOS rating test mentioned earlier. In our experiments, a participant is simply asked to use the networked multimedia service under investigation. We adjust the service quality systematically over time, and the user clicks a dedicated button whenever he feels that the quality is intolerable. Obviously, the decision-making process here is simpler than that in the MOS test, since the five-scale rating is reduced to a dichotomous choice (i.e., whether or not the current service quality is acceptable). The features of the proposed framework are as follows:

1. It is *generalizable* across a variety of networked multimedia services. Thus, it can be applied to compare the resource demands of various services and a service's different implementations.

2. The participants do not have to describe the intensity of their sensations on a categorical or numerical scale. They only need to decide whether or not the current service quality is acceptable; thus, the burden on participants is much less than in the MOS rating experiments.

3. The framework is cheat-proof in that *the experiment results can be verified*. The verification relies on the consistency of each participant's inputs; that is, the service quality that a participant finds intolerable should be at similar levels in repeated tests. By employing this property, we can detect inconsistent judgments and remove problematic data before performing further analysis and modeling.

To evaluate the proposed framework, we conducted a pilot study that targeted three real-time networked multimedia services, namely, VoIP, video conferencing, and network gaming, including six applications that provide those services. In the study, the minimum network bandwidth, as well as the maximum packet loss rate and network delay, for the applications were assessed based on $1,037$ experiments involving 38 participants and $13,184$ click actions. The results show that the judgments made by different participants were highly consistent with one another, which confirms the reliability of our framework and validates the derived QoS needs of networked multimedia services. We also provide cross-application and cross-service comparative analyses and discuss their implications.

Our contribution in this work is three-fold:

1. We propose a general, cheat-proof framework for quantifying the minimum QoS needs of real-time networked multimedia services. The most important features of the framework are that i) the experiment procedure is simple, so even inexperienced participants can make consistent judgments easily; ii) it enables us to employ crowdsourcing strategy because it supports systematic verification of the participants' inputs [3, 31]; and iii) its measures the quality of a service that users find

intolerable in a natural way instead of relying on artificial thresholds.

2. The framework enables *cross-application comparative analysis* of applications' minimum network QoS needs. Therefore, it can be used to compare the design and implementation of an application with competing applications in terms of their resource demands. It can also be used to recommend the most suitable networked multimedia application to end-users based on the capacity and congestion level of their access networks (cf. Section 4.3).

3. The framework also allows us to perform *cross-service comparative analysis* of networked multimedia services' resource demands. Thus, it can be used to quantify the intrinsic discrepancy of QoS needs between different services, e.g., between VoIP and video conferencing (cf. Section 4.4). Moveover, the quantification results provide information that is essential to network planning and resource arbitration for the provision of quality services.

The remainder of this paper is organized as follows. Section 2 contains a review of related works. We elaborate on our proposed framework in Section 3. In Section 4, we discuss the pilot study conducted on three real-time networked multimedia services to validate the framework's ability to derive minimum QoS needs and demonstrate its use. Finally, in Section 6, we present our conclusions and consider future research directions.

2. RELATED WORK

Although a great deal of effort has been devoted to improving the quality of networked multimedia services, relatively little research has been done to understand the minimum QoS needs of such services. According to [17] and the ITU-T E-model [16], the maximum allowable end-to-end delay for a satisfactory VoIP conversation is 150 ms, but it is not clear how this value was derived. While the subjective experiments for constructing the E-Model training data were based on the MOS rating test, the threshold is specified by setting a certain MOS score as the intolerance threshold, which may not faithfully reflect users' intolerance levels.

In [23], it is suggested that the intolerable packet loss rate should be 1% for high-quality audio-video streaming, and 2–3% for two-way interactive conferencing based on the recommendations of the Study Group 12 of ITU-T. Once again, how these thresholds were derived is not reported. Moreover, the thresholds ignore the discrepancies between applications, each of which may have a distinct intolerable loss rate due to different codec choices and data transmission strategies (which we will show by experiments in Section 4.3). Therefore, the applicability of the thresholds is questionable.

In [4], Bouch et al. proposed an experiment design for assessing the minimum QoS needs of network audio applications. In the experiments, two participants were asked to play a word-guessing game where they could only communicate with each other via VoIP and adjust the network quality by using a software slider at the same time. The participants were expected to find the lowest network quality that provided the least acceptable voice quality for game play, but there was no mechanism for validating whether

participants followed the guidelines. Hence, careless or untrustworthy participants could skew the experiment results by, for example, focusing on the word-guessing game and randomly dragging the slider backwards and forwards.

A few studies have proposed to adopt the psychophysical approach [30] to understand the acceptability of certain multimedia content in terms of users' perceptions [1, 19, 22]. For instance, in [22], McCarthy et al. asked participants to watch 210-second test clips in which the video quality is increased or decreased every 30 seconds and report whenever they feel the quality acceptable or unacceptable. The authors varied the degree of quantization and/or the frame rate, and measured the perceived quality by calculating the ratio of time the video quality is acceptable by users. The experiment results indicated that users prefer high resolution over high frame rates.

This work also adopts the psychophysical approach; however, it differs significantly from previous studies (e.g., [1, 19, 22]) in a number of ways:

1. Rather than using the traditional "Method of Limits" test [30] for merely a study on the factors that may affect multimedia content quality, we extend the test with a more careful control of factor magnitude (c.f., Section 3.1) and a cheat proof mechanism (c.f., Section 3.2). We intend to make the proposed framework as general as possible so that researchers and practitioners can base on the framework for further studies.

2. We focus on the minimum acceptable level of QoS that should be provided for a networked multimedia service, rather than on the quality of source multimedia content.

3. Our framework is unique in that it supports the verification of users' inputs, which may be untrustworthy if a user experiment is outsourced or even crowdsourced [9, 11][2]. We believe this feature makes the proposed framework particularly useful as crowdsourcing is now gradually adopted in the research community [24].

3. THE PROPOSED FRAMEWORK

In this section, we describe our framework for assessing the intolerance thresholds of network QoS factors from the user's perspective. First, we consider the design of the experiments in which participants are asked to click a dedicated button whenever the service quality becomes intolerable. Second, we explain how we identify inconsistent judgments provided by malicious or perfunctory participants. We conclude this section with the derivation of the intolerance threshold of the QoS factor of interest.

In our framework, each experiment configuration focuses on one QoS factor for a service. Hereafter, we refer to the target networked multimedia service as "the service," and the target network QoS factor as "the QoS factor."

3.1 Experiment Design

Our framework basically adopts and extends the "Method of Limits" approach from Psychophysics [30] by a more careful control of QoS factors and cheat proof support. In our

---

[2]A cheat-proof framework for QoE evaluation has been proposed in [9] and [8], but it is targeted at a different goal, that is, to quantify the QoE of multimedia content, rather than to find the minimum QoE levels of network systems.

experiment, we systematically alter the quality of the networked multimedia service by controlling the QoS factor while the participants use the service. Participants are asked to press a dedicated button whenever they feel that the degradation in quality is unacceptable. This design is simple and intuitive in that the participants do not need to be well-trained to make a simple dichotomous decision (i.e., decide whether the current service quality is tolerable), and the click action is straightforward. When a participant clicks the button, we record the current magnitude of the QoS factor, and designate it as the intolerance threshold sample (ITS) generated by the click.

The rationale behind our experiment design is simple. Provided that a participant's click decisions are based purely on his perceptions of the service quality, and his intolerance threshold samples are self-consistent, the average of those samples can be treated as the intolerance threshold of the QoS factor from the participant's perspective. However, this raises two major issues in the experiment design: 1) *How should we ensure that a participant makes click decisions based purely on his perceptions*; i.e., how can we prevent a participant from "predicting" the magnitude of the QoS factor and making click decisions accordingly? 2) *How should we judge the consistency of a participant's intolerance threshold samples?* We discuss the first issue below and consider the second in Section 3.2.

During an experiment, we systematically vary the magnitude of the QoS factor, which determines the service quality, to "explore" a participant's intolerance threshold for that factor. Meanwhile, we have to ensure that the participant cannot predict the magnitude of the QoS factor; otherwise, he could report that the quality is intolerable based on timing predictions and still remain highly consistent with his intolerance threshold samples. An experiment is comprised of a number of cycles, each of which contains two stages, *the plateau stage* and *the probing stage*, and one operation called *quality boosting*. Basically, we maintain the service quality for an unspecified period (the plateau stage), and gradually degrade the service quality until the participant becomes intolerant of the quality and clicks the button (the probing stage). Then, we raise the service quality to a certain level (quality boosting) and proceed to the next cycle. Figure 1 illustrates the evolution of the service quality over time. Without loss of generality, we assume that the QoS factor and the service quality are positively correlated; that is, the higher the QoS factor, the better the service quality. If a QoS factor, e.g., the network loss rate, correlates negatively with the service quality, we simply reverse the direction of changes; in other words, to degrade the service quality, we tune the QoS factor higher rather than lower. Next, we consider the design of the plateau stage, the probing stage, and the quality boosting operation.

3.1.1 Plateau Stage

The plateau stage has two functions. One is to remind the participants how the reasonable service quality should be; thus, occasionally we need to reinforce the point by providing a reasonable service quality for a certain period. The second is to prevent the participants from predicting the degradation pattern of the service quality; therefore, the process of the quality degradation must include a certain amount of randomness. This explains why we use a variable-length plateau stage before the probing stage. To achieve a balance

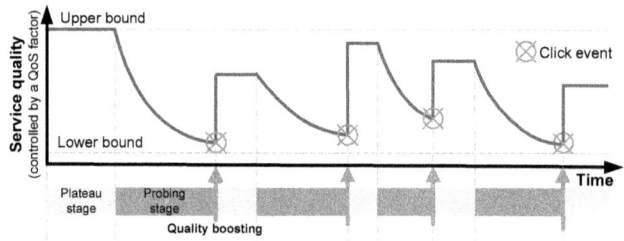

Figure 1: An evolution of the service quality over time. Each cycle starts with a plateau stage, which is followed by a probing stage, and terminates with a quality boosting.

between the experiment's efficiency and the predictability of quality degradation, we choose a random period between 2 and 6 seconds for each plateau stage.

3.1.2 Probing Stage

The probing stage is designed to discover a participant's intolerance threshold for a QoS factor by gradually degrading the service quality. The procedure needs to be planned carefully because there is a response delay between a participant's perception and his click action. The delay is unavoidable since a participant needs time to assess the current service quality and react to it accordingly. Suppose that a participant clicks the button at time t_x, his response delay is t_{delay}, and the magnitude of the QoS factor at time t is $Q(t)$. Then, we would obtain an intolerance threshold sample $Q(t_x)$. However, if we consider the response delay, the exact time that the participant feels intolerant should be $t_x - t_{delay}$, and the magnitude of the actual intolerance threshold sample should be $Q(t_x - t_{delay})$. Since the response delay of each click action is neither constant nor measurable, we can only compensate for it by reducing the difference between $Q(t_x)$ and $Q(t_x - t_{delay})$. In other words, to ensure that the measured intolerance threshold sample is close to the actual sample, the service quality should not degrade too rapidly. On the other hand, if the service quality degrades too slowly, it will elongate the experiment time and lower the data collection efficiency.

To achieve a balance between the experiment's efficiency and the accuracy of intolerance threshold samples, we devised a strategy that degrades the service quality at an inconstant rate. Specifically, the quality degradation in the experiments follows a parameterized exponential decay function. The unit exponential decay function is defined as

$$N(t) = N_0 e^{-\lambda t}, \qquad (1)$$

where $N(t)$ denotes the quantity at time t, N_0 is the initial quantity, i.e., the quantity at time $t = 0$, and λ is the decay constant. The function describes how a variable declines from N_0 to 0 over time, where the rate of decline is decided by λ. We extend the function by adding three parameters: an upper bound, a lower bound, and the time allowed for decline. The extended function allows us to compute the magnitude of the QoS factor at time t by

$$Q(t) = Q_{lb} + e^{-\lambda t/T}(Q_{ub} - Q_{lb}), \qquad (2)$$

where $Q(t)$ denotes the magnitude of the QoS factor at time t; Q_{ub} and Q_{lb} denote the upper bound and lower bound of

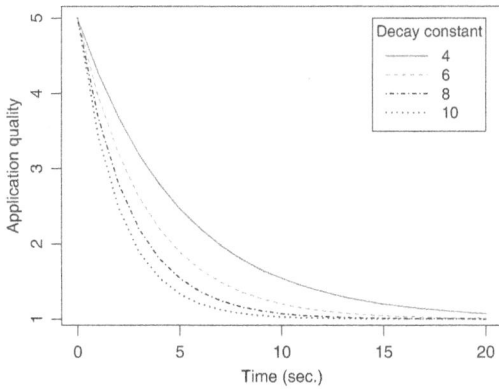

Figure 2: Exponential decay process of an application's quality with decay constants of 4, 6, 8, and 10 within a 20-second period

the QoS factor respectively; and T is the time required for the QoS factor to decline from Q_{ub} to Q_{lb}. Figure 2 illustrates the exponential decay process of the service quality, where the probing range of the QoS factor is between 1 and 5. The QoS factor decreases from the upper bound (5) to the lower bound (1) in 20 seconds, while λ equal 4, 6, 8, and 10 for the respective bounds. As shown on the graph, if a larger decay constant is used, the QoS factor will decline more rapidly toward the lower bound.

By adopting the exponential decay strategy, the service quality will decline rapidly initially, and slow down as the QoS factor approaches the lower bound. The upper bound and the lower bound of the QoS factor must be chosen carefully based on the guidelines: 1) the upper bound should yield a satisfactory service quality; and 2) the lower bound should yield a clearly intolerable service quality. A participant is more likely to feel dissatisfied with the quality when the QoS factor is closer to the lower bound; therefore, we can ensure the experiment's efficiency and the accuracy of the intolerance threshold samples by adopting a rapid decline followed by a gradual decline during the probing process. Based on our experience, setting λ between 2 and 6 is a reasonable choice.

The parameter T also needs to be randomized to reduce the predictability of the magnitude of the QoS factor. Considering the balance between the efficiency and the predictability, we set T uniformly distributed between 15 and 25 seconds. If the QoS factor reaches the lower bound, it will not change until the participant clicks the button. However, this is unlikely to happen if the lower bound is chosen properly, since the service quality at that point should be much worse than "barely acceptable."

3.1.3 Quality Boosting

Each time a participant clicks the button, a probing period terminates and a quality boosting operation is performed immediately; that is, the service quality is increased by a certain amount (i.e., by controlling the QoS factor). The mechanism serves two purposes. First, it provides prompt feedback on a participant's click action. This makes the action worthwhile because it seems to "rescue" the service from serious quality degradation. It also facilitates interaction and adds fun to the experiments. Second, since the

quality boosting operation raises the QoS factor toward the upper bound, the experiment process can transit smoothly to the plateau stage in the next cycle.

The amount of quality boosting is not constant. We cannot always reset the QoS factor to its upper bound because a participant may get used to the pace of quality degradation and detect its regularity. Therefore, in each quality boosting operation, the QoS factor is raised to a random level between the current value and its upper bound. As long as the length of the plateau stage, the degradation rate of the service quality, and the amount of quality boosting are unpredictable, the participant has no choice but to pay full attention to the varying service quality if he is to make consistent judgments.

3.2 Cheat Proof Mechanism

In each experiment, we collect the intolerance threshold samples generated by the participants' click actions. If the click actions are made randomly, either unintentionally or mischievously, they will lead to inaccurate assessment of the intolerance threshold; therefore, methods must be devised to detect such inputs. In addition, punishment and reward rules can be set to encourage participants to provide quality judgments. For example, participants who provide problematic feedback do not get rewards.

Suppose a participant has made n click actions in an experiment and produced intolerance threshold samples $\mathbf{v} = (v_1, v_2, ..., v_n)$, where v_i denotes the magnitude of the QoS factor when he made the i-th click. We assume that v_i are independent and identically distributed random variables. This is reasonable because a participant's assessments of intolerable quality each time should be independent and his standard should not change over time. Thus, if we randomly split $\mathbf{v}$ into two disjoint sets $\mathbf{v_a}$ and $\mathbf{v_b}$, they are likely to have statistically identical distributions. Based on the rationale, we apply the Wilcoxon rank-sum test [31] to determine the consistency of a participant's intolerance threshold samples by testing if $\mathbf{v_a} \sim \mathbf{v_b}$ holds. Specifically, we randomly and divide $\mathbf{v}$ into two equal[3] disjoint sets $\mathbf{v_a}$ and $\mathbf{v_b}$. Then we perform a Wilcoxon rank-sum hypothesis test on the two subsets with the null hypothesis that the distributions of $\mathbf{v_a}$ and $\mathbf{v_b}$ are drawn from a single population. If the computed p-value is above the desired significance level, it means that we cannot reject the null hypothesis. In this case, we consider that the participant's intolerance threshold samples are consistent; otherwise, we deem that his judgments are not trustworthy.

As the above hypothesis test can be biased by how $\mathbf{v}$ is divided into two sets, we extend it to an m-fold version to enhance its robustness; that is, we perform the test m times. Since we perform a total of m hypothesis tests in parallel, the desired significance level in each fold must be corrected, or the overall confidence will be not equal the expected $(1 - \alpha)$, assuming that the desired significance level is α. Thus, we apply the Bonferroni method [3] so that the significant level in each fold is α/m. Then, if all the p-values from the m tests are above α/m, we conclude that the participant's judgments are self-consistent; otherwise they are considered inconsistent. From our data set, we find that setting m to 30 is sufficient to achieve a reliable result when testing the consistency of a participant's behavior.

---

[3]If the size of $\mathbf{v} = n$ is odd, we split $\mathbf{v}$ into two sets where the size of one set is $(n-1)/2$ and that of another is $(n+1)/2$.

3.3 Intolerance Threshold Estimation

Suppose that n_p participants have conducted a total of n_{exp} experiments ($n_{exp} \geq n_p$); for each participant i, we have collected a set of intolerance threshold samples $\mathbf{v}_i$. The estimation of the intolerance threshold begins by applying the behavior consistency test on $\mathbf{v}_i$, $1 \leq i \leq n_p$, and removing the participants whose behavior is not self-consistent. Then, for each of the remaining participants, we compute the average intolerance threshold as $IT_i = mean(\mathbf{v}_i)$, where $mean(\cdot)$ is the function of the arithmetic mean. Finally, we calculate the intolerance threshold of the QoS factor by taking the average of the intolerance thresholds of the behavior-consistent participants as $mean(\{IT_i\}), i \in$ the set of behavior-consistent participants.

4. PILOT STUDY

In this section, we present a pilot study of three real-time networked multimedia services based on the proposed framework. The purpose of the study is four-fold:

1. To show that even inexperienced participants can produce consistent judgments easily, i.e., intolerance threshold samples (ITS), if they stay focused on the experiments.

2. To show that the intolerance threshold samples of different participants are mutually consistent. This confirms the robustness of our framework and validates the derived minimum QoS needs of networked multimedia services.

3. To demonstrate that the framework facilitates comparisons of the QoS needs of *different implementations* that provide identical networked multimedia services. For example, we compare four VoIP products, namely, AIM, MSN Messenger, Skype, and Google Talk, in terms of their minimum QoS demands.

4. To demonstrate that the framework facilitates comparisons of the QoS needs of *different networked multimedia services*, and provide quantitative results that are essential to network planning and resource arbitration. For example, we compare the minimum bandwidth requirements of VoIP, video conferencing, and network gaming.

We begin with a description of the experiment setup and a summary of the collected data. Then, we verify the consistency of the measured intolerance threshold samples from several aspects, and examine the derived intolerance thresholds for the compared applications and services. Finally, based on the results, we perform cross-application and cross-service comparative analysis of their minimum QoS requirements.

4.1 Experiment Description

4.1.1 Studied Services and Applications

We consider three real-time networked multimedia services, namely, VoIP, video conferencing (referred to as conferencing hereafter), and network gaming. For VoIP, we select four popular applications for investigation: AOL Instant Messenger 6.9 (AIM), MSN Messenger 2008 build 8.5, Skype 3.8, and Google Talk 1.0. In addition, we conduct conferencing experiments on the first three applications because Google Talk does not support conferencing. For network

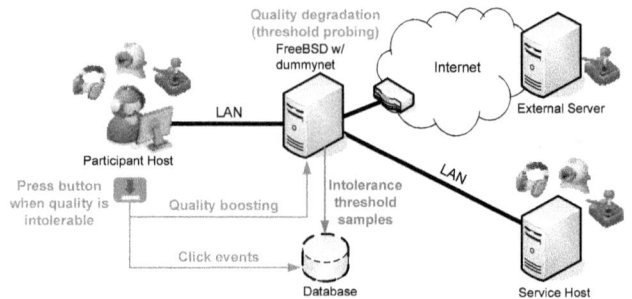

Figure 3: The environment setup for the VoIP, video conferencing, and network gaming experiments conducted in the pilot study

gaming, we select two genres, FPS (First-Person Shooter) games and RPG (Role-Playing Games). We consider three games: Unreal Tournament 3 (UT), which is an FPS game; and Lineage 2 (Lineage) and World of Warcraft (WoW), which are RPGs. The selection of games enables us to perform both intra-genre and cross-genre analysis of the games' QoS demands.

4.1.2 Environment Setup

We use three computers in a LAN to conduct the experiments for assessing the QoS needs of the three services. The first computer, the "participant host," is designated for the experiment participants; the second, the "service host," provides the content of the investigated service; and the third, the "router," connects the participant host and the service host to control the traffic between the two hosts. We run `dummynet` on the router to control the delay, bandwidth, and packet drop rate of the traffic passing through the router. Some applications have a centralized server-client architecture, so we have to connect to an external server instead of using our own service host. In these cases, the traffic from the participant host will flow through the router before reaching the external server, and vice versa. The setup of the network and facilities is illustrated in Figure 3.

In each VoIP experiment, we establish a VoIP call between the participant host and the service host. A two-minute song is played as the audio input on the service host, and the participants hear it from the participant host because of the VoIP connection. The participants are asked to listen to the VoIP-relayed song and click the button whenever the music quality (amount of degradation) becomes unacceptable. Similar settings are used in conferencing experiments, except that the song is replaced by a video clip, and the participants are asked to watch the network-relayed video (with sound tuned mute) instead of listening to music.

In the FPS game experiments, UT is configured in the Deathmatch mode, which means that each player must kill as many characters as possible, or his characters will be endangered. To induce more interaction, we put six bots in the game, so a participant will always encounter six opponents. In the RPG game experiments, external servers hosted by the game operators are used in place of the service host. Because the Internet induces additional latency, we compute the overall round-trip time (RTT) as the sum of the `dummynet`-injected RTT and the Internet RTT, which are derived from on the respective timestamps and sequence numbers of TCP packets. In the experiments, the partic-

Table 1: Summary of the experiment results in the pilot study

Service	QoS Factor	Application	# Users	# Exp.	# Clicks	Inter-click Time (secs)	Average ITS	95% Confidence Band of ITS	Lower Bound	Upper Bound
VoIP	Loss rate (%)	AIM	16	74	1,059	8	9.2	(9.0, 9.4)	0	20
		MSN Messenger	15	69	824	9	10.8	(10.5, 11.1)	0	20
		Skype	15	66	898	8	8.2	(7.9, 8.5)	0	20
		Google Talk	15	62	985	7	8.1	(7.9, 8.3)	0	20
	Bandwidth (Kbps)	AIM	15	41	462	10	27.3	(26.4, 28.2)	10	80
		MSN Messenger	15	40	626	7	39.6	(38.5, 40.6)	10	80
		Skype	14	40	688	7	43.5	(42.6, 44.5)	10	80
		Google Talk	15	42	481	10	29.3	(28.1, 30.4)	10	80
Conferencing	Loss rate (%)	AIM	12	42	529	9	11.4	(11.1, 11.7)	0	20
		MSN Messenger	11	35	552	7	8.9	(8.6, 9.1)	0	20
		Skype	11	38	381	11	12.8	(12.4, 13.2)	0	20
	Bandwidth (Kbps)	AIM	11	36	413	10	60.5	(58.4, 62.6)	30	200
		MSN Messenger	11	43	490	10	80.6	(77.2, 84.0)	30	280
		Skype	11	33	302	12	78.9	(73.7, 84.2)	30	350
Gaming	RTT (sec)	Lineage	21	74	1,080	19	0.77	(0.75, 0.79)	0	0.80
		WoW	19	68	681	27	0.93	(0.91, 0.96)	0	0.80
		UT	21	72	925	21	0.79	(0.77, 0.81)	0	0.80
	Bandwidth (Kbps)	Lineage	16	53	681	22	6.2	(6.0, 6.5)	1	15
		WoW	16	56	503	30	9.2	(8.9, 9.5)	5	25
		UT	16	53	624	23	16.9	(16.6, 17.1)	15	30
Overall			38	1,037	13,184	13				

ipants are asked to continuously interact with other characters and the environment, such as by fighting monsters, picking up items on ground, or interacting with NPCs (non-player characters), because network impairments only affect gaming experience during such interaction. In addition, to make the game play environment comparable, the participants were asked to operate their characters in a region where there were about 20 monsters and several NPCs that they could interact with.

4.1.3 Data Summary

We hired 38 part-time employees to conduct experiments on an overall of 20 service-application-QoS-factor configurations. The participants performed 1,037 experiments and 13,184 click actions, which took 47.6 hours in total. Table 1 summarizes the experiments and the collected intolerance threshold samples.

4.2 Consistency Checks

Next, we examine whether our framework yields consistent intolerance threshold estimates contributed by the experiment participants.

4.2.1 Consistency of Individual Participants

We begin by assessing the consistency of each participant's judgments (c.f., Section 3.2). The results show that 97% (245 out of 253) of experiment-participant pairs passed the test with a significance level of 0.05. We believe this rate satisfactory given that all the participants are regular computer users without specialized training in network or multimedia QoS. The only guideline given to the participants before the experiments began was "click the dedicated button whenever you find the service quality intolerable."

4.2.2 Consistency of Overall Inputs

Next, we examine the consistency of the overall intolerance threshold samples (ITS) that comprise the ITS contributed by all participants with the same experiment setting. Figure 4 shows the distributions of the overall ITS. Samples provided by a participant have a distinct color and mark. Clearly, the ITS for an application generally cluster

around a certain value, even if they are from different participants. Moreover, the dispersion of the clusters varies across services and QoS factors. We believe that the variability in the overall ITS is caused by two factors. 1) Participants may use different criteria for an "acceptable quality." This explains the disagreements between the ITS from different participants. 2) Applying identical network impairments to a service does not necessarily lead to the same quality degradation because of *the variation in the service's workload*, mostly *the multimedia content*. For example, the impact of insufficient bandwidth on conferencing may vary because the service's bandwidth requirement is highly dependent on the complexity of the video frames, which may vary significantly over time. This property explains why the effect of bandwidth on VoIP/conferencing and the effect of network delay on gaming induce more variability in the overall ITS than the other experiments. Specifically, the impact of packet loss on VoIP/conferencing is relatively stable, since the router always drops a certain proportion of packets regardless of the service's current workload; however, this is not the case with insufficient network bandwidth. In addition, the games' bandwidth usage is more constant [7], so the impact of network bandwidth on gaming is relatively stable, as shown in Figure 4. On the other hand, the impact of delay on gaming is highly dependent on the workload, i.e., the action that a game character is performing or trying to perform.

4.2.3 Consistency across Participants

Our last check assesses the consistency of different participants' judgments. It is expected that the consistency between different participants would be lower than that of a single participant. However, it is a challenge to pinpoint what degree of consistency could be considered "reasonable." Since our experiments evaluate several applications for each service, and the applications' QoS needs are usually different, we adopt a "relative comparison" approach. That is, if the ITS of an application from several participants is more consistent than that of different applications from individual participants, we consider that the judgments on intolerable thresholds are consistent across the experiment participants.

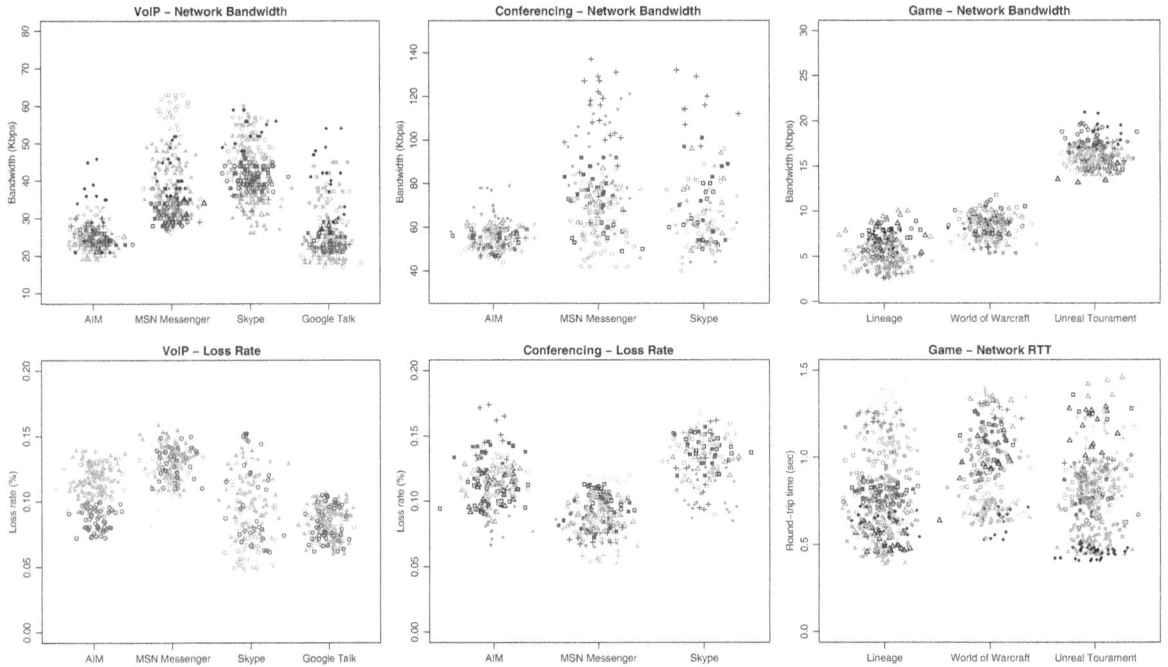

Figure 4: The scatter plots of the collected intolerance threshold samples in the pilot study

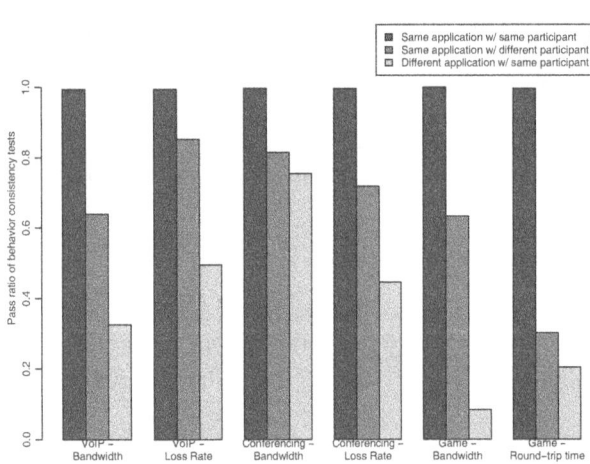

Figure 5: Behavior consistency tests across participants and applications

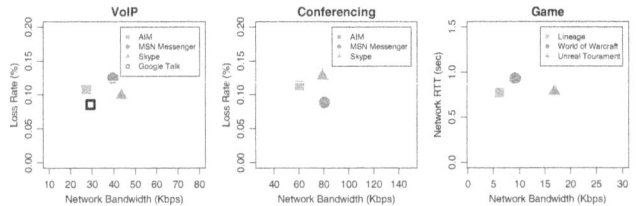

Figure 7: Comparison of the minimum QoS needs for applications that provide the same service

group of untrained participants with different backgrounds can achieve a consensus about the minimum QoS needs of an application. Furthermore, it validates our derivation of the intolerance threshold by taking an average of the participants' judgments.

4.3 Intra-Service Application Assessment

In this subsection, we discuss the intolerance thresholds derived from the experiment results. Figure 6 shows the intolerance threshold for each network QoS factor in each application, where the vertical bars represent the factors' 95% confidence bands. The summarized version is shown in Figure 7, where the x-axis and y-axis represent the intolerance thresholds of the two QoS factors we examine for each networked multimedia service.

4.3.1 VoIP

Figure 6 shows that different VoIP applications have different requirements in terms of network bandwidth and packet loss rate, even though they all provide VoIP services. In terms of bandwidth, Skype is the most demanding because it requires at least 42 Kbps to ensure an acceptable voice quality. In contrast, 27 Kbps bandwidth is sufficient for Google

To perform this check, we apply the behavior consistency test for cheat proof (Section 3.2) in three cases: 1) the ITS of an application from a single participant; 2) the ITS of an application from different participants; and 3) the ITS of different applications from a single participant. Figure 5 shows the proportion of tests that passed the consistency test with a significant level of 0.05 in each case. On the graph, nearly all the pass ratios of case 1 reach 1 because the participants' judgments were generally consistent. We compare the pass ratios of case 2 and case 3, and find that, for each service-QoS-factor combination, the pass ratio of case 2 is always higher than that of case 3. The result indicates the robustness of our experiment design in that a

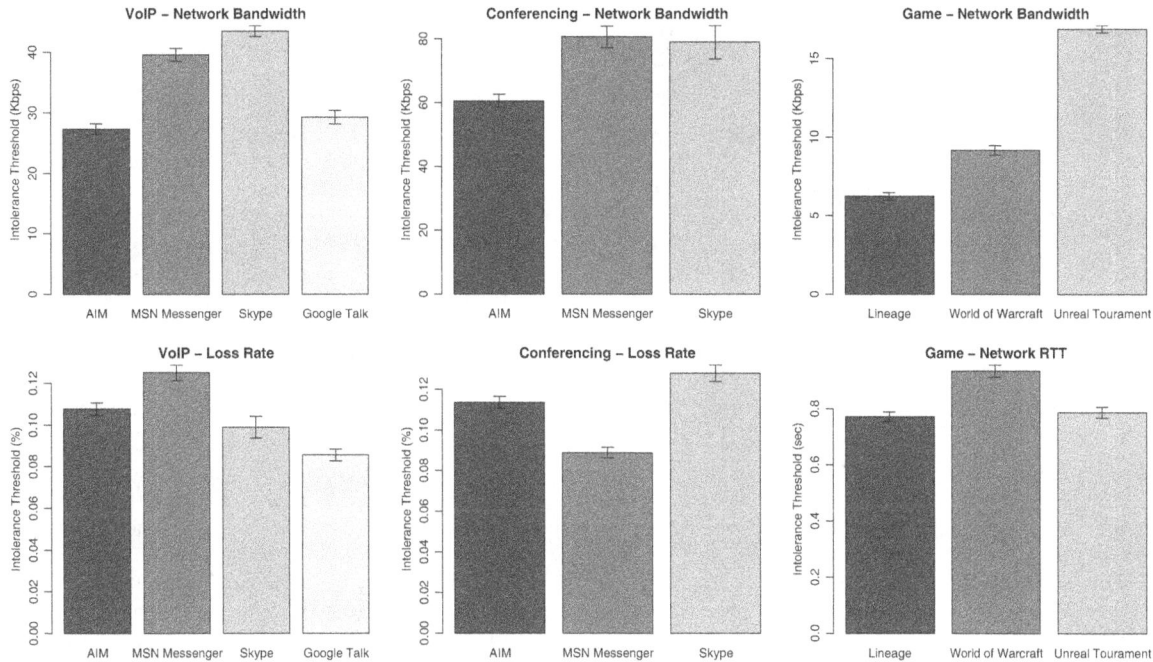

Figure 6: The derived intolerance thresholds for all the applications and services in the pilot study

Talk to provide a tolerable quality. In terms of packet loss rate, however, Google Talk is the most demanding application (8.5%), and MSN Messenger exhibits the strongest resilience against packet loss (12.5%).

We also compare the QoS needs of four VoIP applications when both QoS factors are considered, as shown in Figure 7. Among the four VoIP applications, MSN Messenger and Skype can be classified in one group, and AIM and Google Talk can be placed in another. The first group is more demanding in terms of network bandwidth, but relatively more robust in terms of packet loss. On the other hand, the second group requires less bandwidth to maintain an acceptable quality, but is relatively more sensitive to network loss. We believe that the chart provides useful information for network planning and application selection. For example, if network bandwidth is a concern, then AIM and Google Talk would be the preferred choices; otherwise, MSN Messenger and Skype may be considered because they are relatively more robust against packet loss.

4.3.2 Video Conferencing

According to Figure 6, MSN Messenger and Skype are similar in terms of their minimum bandwidth requirement (80 Kbps), while AIM's requirement is much lower (60 Kbps). On the other hand, AIM and Skype are more resilient in terms of packet loss ($\geq$ 11%) compared to MSN Messenger whose tolerable loss rate is 9%. The comparative analysis in Figure 7 shows that none of the applications excels in all aspects. However, if the bandwidth is of the major concern, Skype and MSN Messenger would be the best choices; otherwise, AIM is preferred as its minimum bandwidth requirement is relatively low at 60 Kbps.

4.3.3 Network Gaming

In this subsection, we present an intra-genre analysis of

the two RPG games [6]. The inter-genre analysis is presented in Section 4.4. Figure 6 shows that Lineage has a slightly stricter demand in terms of network delay than WoW. We confirm this difference by independent experiments in which the magnitude of the network delay is fixed and known to players. According to the players, when the RTT is large, it causes perceivable lag in the characters' movements in Lineage, but it has little impact on WoW. Given the same large RTT in the game play, Lineage players can sense the movement delay, whereas WoW players barely notice the difference if they are not interacting with other players or the environment. We attribute the cause to the fact that WoW game clients support local simulations, which allow players to control their characters without step-by-step acknowledgement from the server unless any form of interaction is performed. Moreover, WoW implements dead reckoning [25], so other characters would continue to move on the screen even if the communications with the server are cut temporarily.

By contrast, WoW requires a higher bandwidth than Lineage to support unobstructed gaming. We believe this is because WoW supports a higher degree of local simulations and dead reckoning, both of which require more game states to be transmitted by the server in real time. In addition, WoW's graphical effects are richer and more sophisticated than those of Lineage, so the states of more game objects have to be transmitted over the Internet. To name a few, the flying of weapons, such as axes being thrown, and the environmental updates, such as the debris resulting from bomb explosions.

4.4 Cross-Service Assessment

We now present a cross-service assessment of the QoS

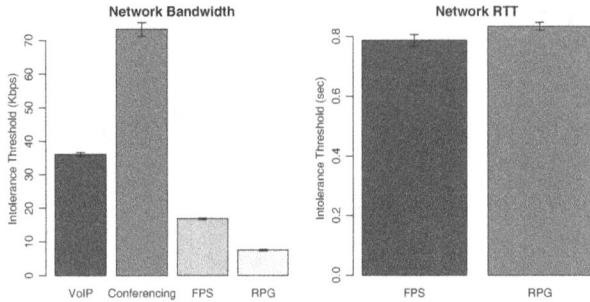

Figure 8: Comparison of intolerance thresholds of different networked multimedia services

needs of the four compared networked multimedia services[4]. Figure 8 summarizes the minimum QoS needs of each service. They are computed by averaging the needs of the applications that provide the same service. In terms of network bandwidth, the results are not surprising. Conferencing is the most demanding in terms of network bandwidth, and VoIP, FPS games, and RPG games rank 2nd, 3rd, and 4th respectively. It has been observed that FPS games require more bandwidth than RPG games because they are fast-paced, i.e., players only have sub-seconds to react at any time [7].Coincidentally, the relative bandwidth requirements of conferencing, VoIP, FPS games, and RPG games are roughly 8 : 4 : 2 : 1 (70 Kbps, 35 Kbps, 17 Kbps, and 8 Kbps) respectively. Although this may be a coincidence, it can serve as a handy guideline for network planning and resource arbitration purposes. For instance, the ratios indicate that the bandwidth required for one FPS game session can be alternatively used to serve two RPG game sessions at the minimum acceptable level of gaming experience.

To our surprise, the network delay requirements for FPS and RPG games are similar. We discovered that, although UT is a fast-paced FPS game, it supports a high degree of local simulations, which can reduce the impact of large delays unless character interactions are involved. The result indicates that local simulations can be very helpful in reducing the impact of network latency, even in fast-paced games like FPS games. Moreover, even if local simulations and dead reckoning are implemented, 0.8 seconds might be the longest tolerable round-trip time for FPS and RPG games. This is plausible because interaction between game characters always involves data exchange between game peers, such as actions performed by other players and environmental updates of the game world. We plan to conduct more studies to verify the observations regarding the games' delay requirements.

5. DISCUSSION

During the development and pilot study of our framework, we have identified the following issues worth to be discussed and investigated further.

5.1 Comparison to Mean Opinion Scores

A common, intuitive interpretation of the proposed framework is that it gives an alternative approach for assessing

the quality of multimedia systems. Thus, one may wonder how the framework performs compared with the traditional MOS method. However, as we have explained in Section 1, the framework is not designed to replace MOS. Rather, we expect it works a *complementary* methodology to MOS, that is, while the MOS method is used to quantify the QoE provided by a system, the proposed framework is used to measure the system's *minimum QoS requirements* with which the QoE it provides would be satisfactory. In other words, MOS cannot be used to detect such requirements, and our framework is not designed to quantify the QoE levels of multimedia systems. This is the reason why we do not provide a comparison of the proposed framework and MOS.

5.2 Interpretation of Intolerance Threshold

The interpretation of "barely acceptable" quality may vary across different participants. While most users may be moderately aware of service quality degradation, some may be more tolerant and avoid clicking until the quality becomes worse than unacceptable. However, all the users can pass the behavior consistency tests as long as they maintain their own standards. To address this problem, a more sophisticated design that can detect such differences may be required.

5.3 Mapping to QoE

The "barely acceptable" quality defined by users may be *relative* rather than *absolute* compared to the QoE (Quality of Experience) users actually perceive. For example, users can easily become annoyed with quality degradation if an application provides a high quality experience under perfect network conditions, even if the current quality in an absolute sense is still considered good. The phenomenon is called the "expectation effect" [26]. We plan to explore this issue by mapping the derived intolerable quality onto the QoE scale [18].

5.4 Content-dependent Measurements

From Section 4.2.2, we can see that the minimum QoS needs may be significantly affected by the service's instantaneous workload and/or multimedia content offered. Therefore, the inferred QoS needs may be inconsistent if different multimedia content is being transmitted or the involving parties have different levels of interaction. In view of the purpose of this paper, the workload variation is not a serious issue because we care about the minimum QoS needs of a networked multimedia or a particular application rather than that of a particular content.

The proposed framework can be further extended to take the variability of workload and content complexity into account by treating the workload intensity as a parameter in addition to network QoS factors. By so doing, we can then quantify the minimum acceptable QoS needs for a networked multimedia service under any specific workload.

5.5 Multi-dimensional QoS

In our pilot study, we assumed that only one QoS factor is variable while other factors are kept constant; however, QoS degradation in real networks is multi-dimensional and correlated, i.e., insufficient bandwidth and high packet loss rates usually go hand in hand. For a multi-dimensional extension of the proposed framework, an intuitive approach is to focus on a dimension at a time while treating the other dimensions invariant. Assume that we have n QoS factors

---

[4]Here the RPG and FPS games are treated as different services.

in total and the magnitude of each factor is quantified by m levels, we have to repeat the experiments $(n-1)^m$ times in order to obtain the intolerance thresholds of a certain factor in different scenarios. In other words, the number of experiments required would grow exponentially as the number of QoS factors increases. Therefore, a more efficient approach is needed to address this problem. We plan to consider the extension of multi-dimension QoS factors in our future work.

5.6 Extension to Non-networking Factors

We note that though we focus on the minimum level of network QoS for real-time networked multimedia services in the pilot study, our framework is not limited to such scenarios. By replacing the network QoS factors with non-networking factors such as compression level, quantization degree, frame rate, screen size, audio volume, and so on, the framework can be easily extended to evaluate the minimum needs of non-networking QoS factors without any changes.

5.7 Crowdsourcing Support

Since subjective QoE experiments is costly, we believe that crowdsourcing [8, 11] will be a good strategy to conduct such experiments. Our framework supports the behavior consistency tests of participants' judgements, which is the key to crowdsourcing the experiments. However, if network factors are to be evaluated, since such experiments rely on an exact control of network quality, how to make the experiments crowdsourceable so that participants can perform experiments via their own computers at their places remains a challenge. We believe that the rich media technologies, such as Flash and Silverlight, and virtualization technologies, such as Xen and VMWare, may be keys to the crowdsourcing of network experiments.

6. CONCLUSION

In this paper, we have proposed a general, cheat-proof framework that can quantify the minimum QoS needs of real-time networked multimedia services. We have intended to make the framework general so that network and multimedia researchers and practitioners can utilize it to measure the QoS needs of their own systems; the cheat proof support of the framework is also essential since not every decision from every experiment participant is trustworthy: participants may make wrong judgements any time due to tiredness, carelessness, or even deliberate willfulness. We have shown that, with our framework, even untrained, inexperienced participants can produce consistent judgments. In addition, the derived QoS needs can serve important reference and have numerous applications in the evaluations of competitive applications, application recommendation, network planning, and resource arbitration.

7. REFERENCES

[1] F. Agboma and A. Liotta. User centric assessment of mobile contents delivery. In *Proceedings of the 6th Advances in Mobile Multimedia*, pages 121–130, Dec. 2006.

[2] S. Blake, D. Black, M. Carlson, E. Davies, Z. Wang, and W. Weiss. An architecture for differentiated services. RFC 2475, 1998.

[3] J. M. Bland and D. G. Altman. Multiple significance tests: the Bonferroni method. *British Medical Journal*, 310:170–170, 1995.

[4] A. Bouch and M. A. Sasse. Network quality of service: What do users need? In *Proceedings of the 4th International Distributed Conference*, pages 21–23, 1999.

[5] R. Braden, D. Clark, and S. Shenkar. Integrated services in the Internet architecture: an overview. RFC 1633, 1994.

[6] Y.-C. Chang, K.-T. Chen, C.-C. Wu, C.-J. Ho, and C.-L. Lei. Online game QoE evaluation using paired comparisons. In *Proceedings of IEEE CQR 2010*, June 2010.

[7] W. chang Feng, F. Chang, W. chi Feng, and J. Walpole. A traffic characterization of popular on-line games. *IEEE/ACM Transactions on Networking*, 13(3):488–500, June 2005.

[8] K.-T. Chen, C.-J. Chang, C.-C. Wu, Y.-C. Chang, and C.-L. Lei. Quadrant of Euphoria: A crowdsourcing platform for QoE assessment. *IEEE Network*, 2010.

[9] K.-T. Chen, C.-C. Wu, Y.-C. Chang, and C.-L. Lei. A crowdsourceable QoE evaluation framework for multimedia content. In *Proceedings of ACM Multimedia 2009*, 2009.

[10] P. de Cuetos and K. W. Ross. Adaptive rate control for streaming stored fine-grained scalable video. In *Proceedings of ACM NOSSDAV'02*, pages 3–12, 2002.

[11] J. Howe. The rise of crowdsourcing. *Wired Magazine*, 14(6):176–183, 2006.

[12] P. Hsueh, P. Melville, and V. Sindhwani. Data quality from crowdsourcing: a study of annotation selection criteria. In *Proceedings of the NAACL HLT 2009 Workshop on Active Learning for Natural Language Processing*, pages 27–35. Association for Computational Linguistics, 2009.

[13] T.-Y. Huang, K.-T. Chen, and P. Huang. Tuning the redundancy control algorithm of Skype for user satisfaction. In *Proceedings of IEEE INFOCOM 2009*, April 2009.

[14] T.-Y. Huang, P. Huang, K.-T. Chen, and P.-J. Wang. Can Skype be more satisfying? – a QoE-centric study of the FEC mechanism in the internet-scale VoIP system. *IEEE Network*, 2010.

[15] ITU-T Recommandation P. 800. Methods for subjective determination of transmission quality, 1996.

[16] ITU-T Recommendation G.107. The E-model, a computational model for use in transmission planning, 2005.

[17] ITU-T Recommendation G.114. General recommendations on the transmission quality for an entire international telephone connection - one-way transmission time, 2003.

[18] R. Jain. Quality of experience. *IEEE Multimedia*, 11(1):96–97, Jan.-March 2004.

[19] J. K. Kies. A psychophysical evaluation of frame rate in desktop video conferencing. In *Proceedings of the Human Factors and Ergonomics Society 41st Annual Meeting*, pages 310–314, 1997.

[20] Y. Lee, J. Lou, J. Luo, and X. Shen. An efficient packet scheduling algorithm with deadline guarantees for input-queued switches. *IEEE/ACM Transactions on Networking*, 15(1):212–225, 2007.

[21] Y. J. Liang, N. Farber, and B. Girod. Adaptive playout scheduling and loss concealment for voice communication over IP networks. *IEEE Transactions on Multimedia*, 5:532–543, 2003.

[22] J. D. McCarthy, M. A. Sasse, and D. Miras. Sharp or smooth?: Comparing the effects of quantization vs. frame rate for streamed video. In *Proceedings of CHI 2004*, pages 535–542, Mar. 2004.

[23] D. Miras. A survey of network QoS needs of advanced internet applications. Technical report, Internet2 QoS Working Group, 2002.

[24] S. Nowak and S. Rüger. How reliable are annotations via crowdsourcing: a study about inter-annotator agreement for multi-label image annotation. In *Proceedings of the international conference on Multimedia information retrieval*, pages 557–566. ACM, 2010.

[25] L. Pantel and L. C. Wolf. On the suitability of dead reckoning schemes for games. In *Proceedings of ACM NetGames'02*, 2002.

[26] A. Parasuraman, V. A. Zeithaml, and L. L. Berry. Alternative scales for measuring service quality: a comparative assessment based on psychometric and diagnostic criteria. *Journal of Retailing*, 70(3):201–230, 1994.

[27] Z. Qiao, L. Sun, N. Heilemann, and E. Ifeachor. A new method for VoIP quality of service control use combined adaptive sender rate and priority marking. In *Proceedings of IEEE ICC'04*, pages 1473–1477, 2004.

[28] B. Sat and B. W. Wah. Playout scheduling and loss-concealments in VoIP for optimizing conversational voice communication quality. In *Proceedings of ACM Multimedia'07*, pages 137–146, 2007.

[29] C. J. Sreenan, J.-C. Chen, P. Agrawal, and B. Narendran. Delay reduction techniques for playout buffering. *IEEE Transactions on Multimedia*, 2:88–100, 2000.

[30] S. Stevens. Mathematics, measurement, and psychophysics. *Handbook of experimental psychology*, pages 1–49, 1951.

[31] F. Wilcoxon. Individual comparisons by ranking methods. *Biometrics*, 1:80–83, 1945.

[32] C.-C. Wu, K.-T. Chen, C.-Y. Huang, and C.-L. Lei. An empirical evaluation of VoIP playout buffer dimensioning in Skype, Google Talk, and MSN Messenger. In *Proceedings of ACM NOSSDAV 2009*, 2009.

Efficient Data Transmission Between Multimedia Web Services via Aspect-Oriented Programming

Dominik Seiler
Information Systems Institute
University of Siegen
Hölderlinstr. 3
D-57068 Siegen, Germany
d.seiler@fb5.uni-
siegen.de

Ernst Juhnke
Dept. of Math. and Comp. Sci.
University of Marburg
Hans-Meerwein-Str. 3
D-35032 Marburg, Germany
ejuhnke@informatik.uni-
marburg.de

Ralph Ewerth
Dept. of Math. and Comp. Sci.
University of Marburg
Hans-Meerwein-Str. 3
D-35032 Marburg, Germany
ewerth@informatik.uni-
marburg.de

Manfred Grauer
Information Systems Institute
University of Siegen
Hölderlinstr. 3
D-57068 Siegen, Germany
grauer@fb5.uni-
siegen.de

Bernd Freisleben
Dept. of Math. and Comp. Sci.
University of Marburg
Hans-Meerwein-Str. 3
D-35032 Marburg, Germany
freisleb@informatik.uni-
marburg.de

ABSTRACT

The number of web services capable of processing multimedia data is growing. Typically, a multimedia web service realizes only a specific algorithmic processing step, such as video decoding. Thus, it is desirable to compose several web services hosted on different sites into a new value-added workflow. However, the transfer of large amounts of multimedia data within workflows based on SOAP as the prevalent communication paradigm between web services induces redundant data transfers. In previous work, we have presented a reference technique called Flex-SwA that solves this problem. However, its usage is accompanied by additional software development efforts that have to be repeated when a new service or client is implemented. In this paper, we present an aspect-oriented programming approach that significantly reduces these software development efforts. The solution allows developers to easily extend existing multimedia web services with the capability of efficient data transmission without modifying the implementations of the original services, while at the same time the advantages of SOAP web services are still maintained. Experimental results for a distributed video analysis workflow demonstrate the feasibility of the presented approach.

Categories and Subject Descriptors

C.2.4 [**Distributed Systems**]: Distributed applications; D.4.8 [**Performance**]: Measurements

General Terms

Design, Measurement, Performance

Keywords

Distributed multimedia analysis, aspect-oriented programming, web services, service-oriented architecture, BPEL

1. INTRODUCTION

Increased hard disk capacities, improved network bandwidth and mobile multimedia devices have fostered an enormous growth of multimedia data. People increasingly maintain private archives of homemade digital content or expose their images and videos on Web 2.0 platforms. For example, the popular social network *Facebook* stated that over 15 Billion images were uploaded by its users until the middle of 2009 [36].

Furthermore, not only multimedia data are available in the World Wide Web (WWW), but also services that are capable of processing these data. Such multimedia web services range from video editing and video conversion to pattern recognition and object detection. Popular services in this field are Flickr, YouTube, Hey!Watch (video encoding, [20]), face.com (face detection and recognition, [15]), or WiseTREND (optical character recognition, [38]). Along with the increasing number of available multimedia web services, there is the possibility and an increasing need to build new value-added applications by composing existing multimedia services into a new workflow. For example, one could use YouTube as a data source and apply the content analysis services mentioned above in order to recognize faces and superimposed text in the video frames. The recognized content can be stored as metadata and thus allows a developer to create applications for content-based search in multimedia data. Existing multimedia services are often realized as RESTful services [16]. They support a straightforward integration into an existing application, since they only use HTTP mechanisms. However, when RESTful services are used in more sophisticated scenarios, such as the orchestration of several services, they suffer from their lack of standardization.

On the other hand, web services based on SOAP [41] are often used to realize a service-oriented architecture (SOA). SOAP-based web services offer standardized interfaces, industrial-strength tools and a supporting community in the research area as well as in the commercial field. They can be used in a transparent manner by both service developers and service consumers. Furthermore, SOAP web services enable users to access distributed resources, including cluster, Grid or Cloud computing resources. In this respect, they are also interesting for data-intensive and compute-intensive multimedia applications. In addition, external third-party services can be included easily in an application. The technical service interface is defined via the Web Services Description Language (WSDL, [42]). The communication is handled according to the request/response message exchange pattern via SOAP.

In a SOA, applications may be composed of existing components (i.e., web services), which leads to higher reusability, faster development and reduced costs. The Business Process Execution Language for Web Services (BPEL, [3]) is the de facto standard for service composition in business applications; it has emerged from the earlier proposed XLANG [25] and Web Service Flow Language (WSFL, [21]). BPEL is widely used in industry as well as in academia to support large-scale applications while being a research topic itself. This lead to a broad variety of tools that support the development and the execution layer of BPEL processes. BPEL enables the construction of complex web services composed of other web services that act as the basic activities in the process model of the newly constructed service. Access to a process is exposed by the execution engine through the web service interface, allowing the process to be accessed by web service clients or to be used as a basic activity in other processes. This allows developers to model complex applications using basic reusable services.

While several issues such as the problem of long-running services are addressed by the WS-* stack (cf., Section 2), SOAP is disadvantageous in the context of multimedia data due to its extensive encoding based on XML schema [43]. This means that all transmitted data are encoded in an XML structure. Especially for array-like structures, e.g., video frames, this leads to a significant increase in size. If multiple services are orchestrated and operate on the same set of large data, a bottleneck within the service orchestrator may occur, due to the forwarding of incoming data. Forwarding a message means that it has to be deserialized, an object representation in memory has to be built and eventually this representation must be serialized again in order to transmit it to the next service. Even SOAP with Attachments [40] or MTOM [39] only optimize the encoding of the binary data within the SOAP message, but the data must still pass through the orchestrator.

In previous work, we have proposed the Flex-SwA framework for modeling binary data transmission between multimedia services in BPEL workflows [34] to avoid the arising bottleneck at the service orchestrator. However, this was achieved at the expense of additional software development efforts. On the other hand, efficient data transmission is a non-functional application requirement that can be considered as a cross-cutting concern, since it cannot be cleanly separated from the rest of the system. Aspect-oriented programming (AOP) is a paradigm that is aimed at increasing the modularity of software by encapsulating cross-cutting concerns in aspects [23]. AOP enables a developer to integrate modularized cross-cutting concerns into existing applications via join points.

In this paper, we present an approach to modularize efficient data transmission for distributed service-oriented multimedia applications via *request/response aspects*. The name request/response aspects recurs to the request/response pattern used by SOAP message communication. Furthermore, it indicates that aspects operate on the message level and do not need to interfere with the actual service logic or implementation, respectively. The presented solution allows developers to easily extend existing multimedia web services with the capability to efficiently transmit data *without* modifying the implementations of the original services. An additional advantage is the reduced effort for maintaining the service-oriented application as a whole. One of the main contributions of this paper is to provide SOAP web services with a flexible and transparent reference mechanism for the transmission of large binary data. In other words, the advantages offered by RESTful services by means of data transmission are realized for SOAP web services by using references, while at the same time service developers can benefit from the advantages offered by SOAP-based web services, such as standardized interfaces, industrial-strength tools, and the wide support by both research and industrial communities. Experimental results for the example of distributed content-based video analysis demonstrate the advantages of the proposed approach.

The paper is organized as follows. Section 2 summarizes related work. In Section 3, we discuss workflows for multimedia web services and the problem of the corresponding data handling. Section 4 describes the proposed aspect-oriented approach for efficient data transmission in multimedia web service workflows. Experimental results for the example of video analysis are presented in Section 5. Section 6 concludes the paper and outlines areas for future research.

2. RELATED WORK

In this section, an overview of related work is given. First, we introduce and discuss the communication model of both RESTful and SOAP-based web services in the context of our work. Next, other work on service-oriented video analysis is reviewed. Then, existing approaches that integrate AOP in a service-oriented environment are presented.

RESTful services [16] can be used for providing multimedia services. They utilize the HTTP protocol as the communication protocol to execute remote procedures. A call is simply represented by opening an URL. In this way, RESTful services represent a different architectural style of invoking services [31] compared to SOAP. When using RESTful services, the existing HTTP infrastructure in which they are hosted is utilized to exchange binary data. This is achieved by copying the data into an accessible folder of the HTTP container. Then, a reference to this data is created and in turn the data is passed to the successor service or client. An example for such a reference from Hey!Watch can be seen in Listing 1. Next, the successor can load the binary data stream via a HTTP connection.

RESTful services do not have a strict communication pattern, they rely only on HTTP and utilizes the common operations of HTTP (*GET, POST* etc.) as an interaction model. Furthermore, they do not have a (standardized) interface description (like WSDL). The interface is described more or less formally in a human-readable manner on a web page (cf., `http://www.flickr.com/services/api/`). Nevertheless, most services use XML as the common exchange format without being restricted to use XML schema or similar standards. Bulk data are not directly included into the exchanged XML, but referenced via an HTTP link (as shown in Listing 1). This supports seamless handling of large binary data in the HTTP context.

Despite the advantages of RESTful services, there is a lack of a common agreement when different services are composed in a workflow. A developer has to handle (very) different interfaces and has to deal with format conversions since the absence of standardization leads to a high degree of freedom. In practice, workflow developers have to deal with an uncontrolled growth of message and interface definitions.

In contrast to RESTful services, SOAP-based web services realize communication in a different way. SOAP uses a standardized message format. Every message is contained in a SOAP envelope that in turn comprises the XML encoded method invocation. Data types are also converted into a XML representation based on the XML Schema definition [43]. Typically, bulk data is contained in the aforementioned data types and thus, bulk data is also represented as XML fragments and, finally, part of the SOAP envelope.

```
<encoded-video>
  <title>YouTube - Mel Gibson on Grey's ↘
  →Anatomy</title>
  <job-id>20960</job-id>
  <specs>
    <format-name>Mobile MP4</format-name>
    <audio channels="" sample_rate="24000"
      codec="aac" stream="" bitrate="0"/>
    <format-id>15</format-id>
    <video height="144" aspect="1.22"
      length="77" container="mov" width="176"
      codec="mpeg4" fps="15.0" stream=""
      bitrate="216"/>
    <size>2037</size>
    <mime-type>video/mp4</mime-type>
    <thumb>http://static-1.heywatch.com/thumb↘
    →/623207/MNmQyOlDZ4/NMZMG.jpg</thumb>
  </specs>
  <link>http: //static-1.heywatch.com/683072/↘
  →zYWzTZB3kD/YouTube_-↘
  →_Mel_Gibson_on_Grey_s_Anatomy.mp4</link>
  <id>508</id>
  <created-at>Fri Oct 27 01:08:17 CEST 2006</↘
  →created-at>
</encoded-video>
```

Listing 1: Example response of Hey!Watch

Using SOAP, a developer does not have to deal with different interface formats and is enabled to easily integrate services into a value-added workflow. SOAP offers several advantages, such as its foundation on the WS-* protocol stack, providing specifications and implementations for metadata, transactions, addressing stateful resources, semantics etc. [44]. One of the main benefits is that SOAP is independent of the underlying transport mechanism. Typically, SOAP uses HTTP as a transport protocol, but also message bus systems like the Java message service [22] can be used. Furthermore, SOAP supports communicating in a synchronous as well as in an asynchronous manner. The latter one is

especially important when it comes to long-running tasks, because synchronous communication would lead to timeout problems due to the typical configuration of SOAP communication. Notifications, as provided by the WS-* stack, can help to avoid this problem. They are able to provide a distributed observer pattern and prevent a client of cyclic polling when it comes to long-running and/or asynchronous invocations. In combination with the contribution presented in this paper, SOAP services will provide a flexible and transparent reference mechanism for large binary data. In other words, we realize the advantages offered by RESTful services for SOAP web services by means of using references, but also maintain the advantages of SOAP-based web services such as standardized interfaces, industrial-strength tools, and the wide support by both research and industrial communities.

The CASSANDRA framework [28] is a distributed multimedia content analysis system that is based on a service-oriented architecture and is aimed at facilitating the composition of applications from distributed components on a network of cooperating devices. The individual analysis components are encapsulated into functional units, called service units. All units on one particular device are managed by a local component repository that is synchronized by a master repository. Service composition is initiated by a special coordination component. Each service unit has a control and a data streaming interface. The control interface is based on UPnP, while the streaming interface is based on TCP/IP. This framework does not use web services to build a SOA, neither for service definition nor for workflow composition. In general, the expressiveness of BPEL and the flexibility of Flex-SwA are not utilized. The data transport is fixed to TCP/IP; an adaptation to support other transport protocols requires additional development efforts.

With a large scale content analysis engine, Gibbon et al. [17] have built a distributed system to assist content-based video retrieval and related applications. The system consists of multiple specialized servers with a centralized database. Video data is ingested through acquisition servers and delegated to certain processing servers. The system relies on the MPEG-7 standard to store and distribute metadata. It makes use of web services to expose processing operations, but the task of data transport is delegated to a subsystem. Thus, the data transfer is performed outside of the web service scope. Furthermore, the system does not rely on standardized workflow systems.

AO4BPEL [10] is an extension for BPEL to improve modularity and to support dynamic adaptation of the composition logic. AO4BPEL provides support for the dynamic weaving of aspects, such that the activation and deactivation of aspects at execution time of a BPEL process is possible. This does not only support the modularization of crosscutting concerns in a BPEL process, but also enables the modification or adaptation of the business logic itself. AO4BPEL and our approach complement each other: AO4BPEL modularizes at the orchestration level, whereas our approach modularizes at the service level.

DJCutter [29] is a framework that provides remote pointcuts as a new language construct for distributed aspect-oriented programming. The architecture of DJCutter is based on a central aspect server on which the code for all remote aspects is hosted and which is notified in case a remote join point is activated. In this way, state information

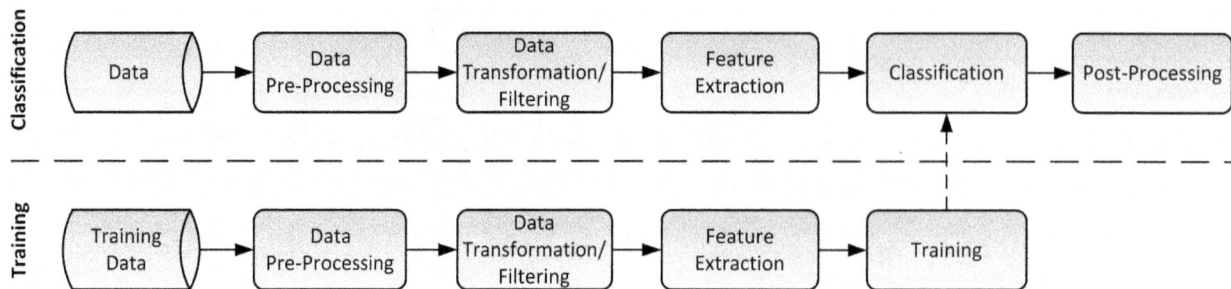

Figure 1: Common multimedia analysis workflow

can be shared across host boundaries. The central server is a drawback of this approach. Referring to the data transfer example again, this means that the data has to be transferred to the aspect server to process it. This will certainly undo the desired performance gain. Furthermore, the language for describing aspects operates on the Java syntax, and this assumption is not fulfilled in general in web service environments.

Binder et al. [8] have introduced Service Invocation Triggers, a lightweight infrastructure that routes messages and thereby optimizes the data transfer when workflows are orchestrated. To attain this goal, the authors introduce a proxy layer that is in charge of routing messages. Thus, the exchange of messages is not controlled by the orchestration engine anymore, and the latter is not able to control the invocation of the services, because this task is performed by the proxy layer. The proxies themselves can be located on different machines within the distributed architecture. If they are located on the same host as the service, a comparable situation to Flex-SwA is achieved. In contrast, in our approach the control flow remains at the orchestration engine.

Baligand and Monfort [7] present a framework to separate crosscutting concerns within the service implementation, but do not deal with crosscutting concerns over multiple services or hosts. They focus on the weaving into the (Java) byte code of the service implementation. Thus, they pin the presented framework to Java web services, whereas request/response aspects operate on the message level, which allows them to be independent of the concrete implementation language of a service.

Approaches in the field of multimedia streaming address issues like jitter and protocol-dependent APIs and foster an explicit handling of communication channels in order to be able to address QoS issues (e.g., [18, 9, 27]). But streaming approaches do not allow to centralize the control flow and often are not able to build a loosely-coupled analysis system.

Ecklund et al. [12] present a management protocol that addresses functional and non-functional requirements in multimedia database management systems. The proposed protocol deals with changes of the runtime requirements. However, the authors neither address a consistency model if QoS requirements have to be enrolled on different administrative domains, nor they propose an approach to deploy QoS enforcements during runtime. In other words, their middleware is only capable of mediating between QoS requirements that are already available at the affected communication partner, whereas our system is also capable of deploying new aspects during runtime.

3. WORKFLOWS FOR MULTIMEDIA SERVICES

In this section, a typical workflow for distributed multimedia analysis and the modeling of data flows in BPEL processes are described. Then, it is explained how the Flex-SwA framework supports efficient data transmission between web services and how it interacts with BPEL workflows. In addition, general implementation efforts that are needed for realizing efficient data transmission using Flex-SwA are discussed.

3.1 Workflows for Multimedia Analysis

Most approaches for multimedia content analysis are built in a monolithic fashion following a sequential structure (see Eide et al. [13]). In case of supervised learning algorithms, this structure can be divided into two phases: training and classification (see Figure 1). In general, preparatory tasks are executed to first generate the smallest entities of interest needed to solve the problem in question, e.g., retrieving images from a database, decoding frames of a video or decompressing audio signals. Next, some pre-processing such as transforming or filtering of image data is done. Then, feature extraction is performed, followed by the actual classification. Sometimes, a post-processing step is needed, e.g., generating a representation of the analysis results. The training phase is similar, but a learning step instead of a classification step is performed. In addition, the classification step can be considered as a feature extraction step offering the opportunity to combine it with other features for building more complex analysis approaches.

The abstract workflow mentioned above performs a generalized analysis in a supervised learning environment. In the sequel, we will use a concrete workflow that performs face detection based on the Viola-Jones algorithm [37]. More precisely, we have modeled a BPEL workflow that calls web services that represent the different tasks of the analysis. Since BPEL is an orchestration approach, users can benefit from the centralized control flow, enabling easy control and sophisticated runtime decisions while at the same time keeping the services loosely-coupled. This workflow allows us to identify typical problems arising in a service-oriented multimedia architecture. More details about the actual workflow can be found in Section 5.

3.2 Data Flow and BPEL

BPEL as an orchestration language for business processes defines a workflow as a set of activities. These activities are divided into two groups: basic and structured. The basic activities describe single steps for the interaction with a service and/or the manipulation of data passing the engine. With the help of structured activities, the order of activity execution is defined. BPEL offers a rich vocabulary of control mechanisms to express sequences of activities like *receive*, *invoke* and *reply*, parallel execution, loops, error handling as well as compensation mechanisms to perform roll-back actions. The *invoke* activity is used to model the invocation of external services; it is the most error-prone BPEL activity. Fault handlers may be described either on the process level or for each scope (scopes are hierarchically organized parts in which a process can be divided). The *faultHandlers* element contains an arbitrary number of *catch* (and optionally one *catchAll*) elements that define fault types to react to (comparable to a *switch-case* construct in other programming languages).

Thus, BPEL provides a rich set of elements to explicitly model the control flow, whereas the data flow is only modeled implicitly by the manipulation and assignment of data encapsulated in request/response messages. For example, the normal way of modeling the data exchange between two web services is as follows: invoke the first service with a request message, wait for the corresponding response from the service, assign all needed data to the input variable of the second service, invoke it with a request message encapsulating the data, and finally wait for the response. For highly frequent data exchanges and transfers of large amounts of data, this way of modeling the data flow is not efficient and does not support the requirements of workflows for multimedia content analysis.

3.3 Flex-SwA

The Flex-SwA architecture [19] provides a flexible way to handle bulk data in service-oriented environments. It differs from SOAP Messages with Attachments by offering message forwarding and demand-driven evaluation and transmission of binary data. A reference builder is used to create an XML description that refers to the actual location of a file used to transmit the binary data objects. The service provider uses a reference to retrieve the data directly from a remote server (on a client computer or anywhere else in the web) instead of transferring data from a remote server to the client and from the client to the next service provider. References do not need to be handled by a service provider directly but can be forwarded to other service providers with negligible additional communication cost.

From an application developer's point of view, service invocation and data transmission remain coupled in a single service invocation operation. A service developer can choose between different communication patterns to configure how the Flex-SwA platform should handle the referenced data, e.g., if the data should be completely transferred before the service is executed or if the transmission should overlap with the service execution.

3.4 Data Transmission in BPEL via Flex-SwA

In previous work [34], we have proposed to use references based on the Flex-SwA framework to avoid the mentioned load at the orchestration point, i.e., the BPEL engine. A reference points to a resource location in memory or to a file. The service can then directly pull the data from the resource location. The data do not have to be sent to the

BPEL engine, but only references. Since references are very small, the load at the BPEL engine is very small, too.

When services are used to which data is sent repetitively (for example, video frames are sent repetitively), then it can be modeled in the following way: For each resulting processing unit (video part, frame, audio sample, ...), a reference passes the BPEL engine and in turn is sent to the subsequent service. This way, the BPEL engine keeps full control over the data flow, while the control flow resides at the engine. This is necessary since web services are by definition loosely-coupled and do not have any information about their environment. Therefore, a web service does not have any information about predecessors and successors. By locating the control flow at the workflow engine, it is possible to model conditional elements in reaction to the responses sent by the services, while failure and compensation handling can be realized in the workflow as well.

Figure 2 a) shows the typical sequence of service invocations and the corresponding – schematic – data flow. For example, first the workflow engine invokes service 1. The service sends its results to the workflow engine that delegates them to the subsequent consumer service 2. It is clear that the data are transferred twice in this scheme. In Figure 2 b), the workflow as well as the services make use of references. Service 1 responds a reference to the workflow engine, which in turn sends this reference to service 2. It receives this reference, resolves it via the Flex-SwA framework that transfers the data from service 1 directly to service 2. This scheme can lead to a significant speedup if the data payload from service 1 to service 2 is larger than the data volume of the messages that have to be exchanged for the delegation of the references.

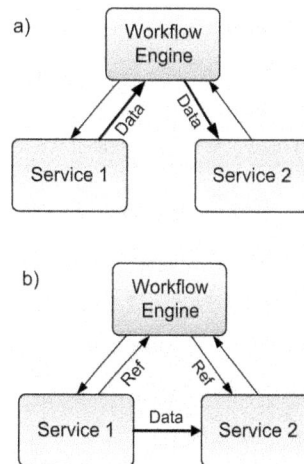

Figure 2: Schematic data flow via a BPEL engine

To gain the mentioned benefit of the Flex-SwA framework, the software developer has to consider several preparatory tasks. First, the Flex-SwA framework must be available within the context of the application container. This means that a special handler component has to be plugged into the handler chain of the web service stack (this step has to be performed once per container). Afterwards, the software developer has to ensure that each method of each service that is supposed to exchange data by using Flex-SwA exposes this usage via its signature, i.e., the signature of the method contains a reference instead of the actual data type.

Furthermore, the developer must ensure that the implementation resolves the reference and retrieves the actual data, when a method of a service is called. After retrieving the data, they have to be casted into the actual format as used within the method. If the data should also be returned as a reference, the same effort has to be done. This procedure has to be performed for each method's argument that should be replaced by a reference.

4. EFFICIENT DATA TRANSMISSION USING ASPECT-ORIENTED PROGRAMMING

The realization of optimized data transmission as described above requires several code modifications at the client and the service. This holds for Flex-SwA as well as for SOAP with attachments (or any other transport optimization). Apart from the needed middleware, clients and web services must be able to explicitly deal with references in request messages and to build new references for response messages. Hence, if existing web services should be enabled to efficiently transmit data using Flex-SwA, additional software development efforts have to be made. On the other hand, the requirement of efficient data transmission between web services can be viewed as a cross-cutting concern and solved using aspect-oriented programming.

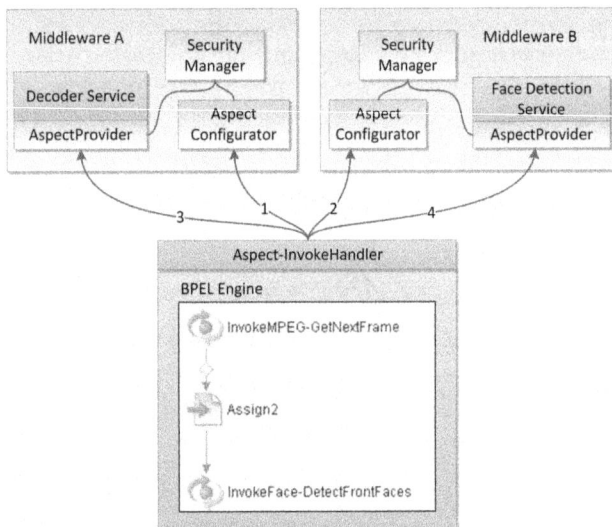

Figure 4: Excerpt of a face detection workflow within our aspect framework

In this section, we present a solution for efficient data transmission for multimedia web services using *request/response aspects* to reduce the development efforts significantly, while at the same time leaving the web service implementation unchanged. The proposed aspect-oriented framework is able to weave non-functional aspects, such as efficient data transmission, into web services at the message exchange level.

4.1 Aspect-Oriented Programming

The paradigm of aspect-oriented programming provides a high benefit for software developers in the modularization of crosscutting concerns [24]. In aspect-oriented software development (AOSD), crosscutting concerns are identified and

realized as *advice*. The *pointcut language* defines a set of *join points* where these advice are integrated. In this manner, aspect-oriented programming eases the development of reusable and maintainable code.

According to Kiczales et al. [23], aspect-oriented programming (AOP) has the same significance for crosscutting concerns that object-oriented programming (OOP) has for encapsulation and inheritance. They argue that crosscutting concerns can be programmed in a modular way and one can benefit from this modularity by "simpler code that is easier to develop and maintain, and that has greater potential for reuse" [23]. Modularized crosscutting concerns are called *aspects*. AOP distinguishes two approaches. *Static crosscutting* affects the static type signature of a program, whereas *dynamic crosscutting* allows to intercept a program at well-defined points in its execution trace. This work only focuses on the latter approach.

Dynamic crosscutting consists of several parts. *Join points* are well-defined points within an execution trace of a program. *Pointcuts* are sets of join points and *advices* are method-like constructs that define the behavior of these join points.

4.2 Design Considerations

The execution of web services requires some middleware, such as a web service container and a SOAP processing engine. The underlying idea of the proposed framework is to weave aspects into the processing chain of SOAP messages to remain independent of web service implementation details. In advance, it is necessary to add an aspect configurator to the existing middleware that allows the weaving of aspects and the checking whether it is allowed and possible to weave an aspect into a service.

If the aspect configurator permits the weaving of an aspect, the aspect is persisted within a data structure in the aspect provider. The aspect provider queries this data structure every time a web service is invoked (therefore, we use a lightweight map-like data structure to perform this lookup) and if an aspect is found, the aspect is applied to the corresponding request or response message.

In a service-oriented multimedia architecture, two main objectives hold. First, services are loosely-coupled, i.e., services are not aware of the context they are executed in. Second, services are defined in a contract-first manner, which means that interfaces are defined and are not subject to change. Both objectives have to be respected not only by the service developer but also by any employed aspect. Especially, aspects modifying the data payload must be aware of the second objective. Furthermore, such aspects must be employed not only on the service that sends the data but also on the service that finally receives these (modified) data, i.e., an atomic employment of aspects is crucial.

4.3 Framework Implementation

The proposed aspect framework is based on Apache Tomcat 6 [5] in combination with Apache Axis 1.4 [4] as the SOAP engine and web service execution environment. On the caller's side, the client libraries of Apache Axis are used. The orchestration engine for composing web services is ActiveBPEL [1], an implementation of BPEL.

The activation of (web service) aspects is realized as an AspectJ aspect [6, 23], the so called "Aspect-Provider". It is woven into the handler chain of Apache Axis (see Figure 3).

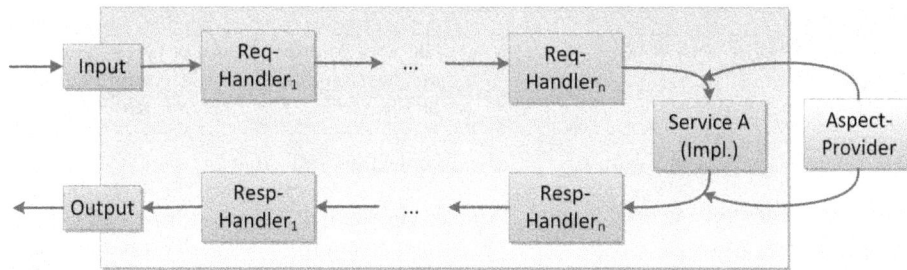

Figure 3: Web service invocations with aspects

A service-oriented environment is based on the exchange of XML documents. These documents represent the request and response messages of a web service invocation. Request/response aspects take advantage of this communication pattern, because the exchanged documents are independent of any service implementation. Consequently, the aspects are applied to these messages. A request/response aspect defines a pointcut that specifically describes at which part of such a message an advice should be applied to (cf., Listing 2). Hence, any dependency on the service implementation can be avoided. Furthermore, the implementation of a service remains unchanged (see Figure 3). To prevent a misuse of our framework, a security manager utilizes a public key infrastructure to secure the configurator service and to validate the aspect signature.

In particular, the request/response aspect based on Flex-SwA substitutes a field within a SOAP message. In case of a response message, the request/response aspect based on Flex-SwA takes the original data, creates a reference to it and encodes this reference into the actual data field. Subsequently, on the receiving side the request/response aspect decodes the reference and puts the resolved data into that corresponding data field.

The combination of a web service and an invocation handler supports the scenario shown in Figure 4. Considering the previously mentioned use case, request/response aspects are used in the video analysis workflow as follows: First, the video decoder is called and then face detection is performed. If no aspects are available, each video frame is passed through the BPEL engine and the engine can become a bottleneck due to high network traffic. Request/response aspects together with Flex-SwA are able to prevent this situation (see Section 3.4). They are woven into the services (step 1 and 2 in Figure 4) and realize the optimization of the data transfer (more details are presented in Section 5). Afterwards, the actual services are called (step 3 and 4). Instead of the binary data of the decoded frame, the request/response aspect based on Flex-SwA transparently encodes a reference into the returned value that is decoded in the same transparent manner at the face detection service.

The weaving of aspects is initiated by the Aspect-Invoke-Handler (AIH, see Figure 4). The AIH is called every time the workflow engine performs a web service invocation. To register and use the AIH, we utilize extension mechanisms provided by the workflow engine itself. Thus, we do not need to modify any implementation of the workflow engine. When the AIH is called, it checks whether the actual web service should use an aspect. If this is the case (this information is provided by the workflow developer during design time of the workflow), the AIH deploys the aspect to the ac-

tual web service and – depending on the type of the aspect – also deploys it to subsequent web services. In order to call to Aspect Configurator, the AIH constructs the aspects correspondingly based on supplied information (an example can be seen in Listing 2). An aspect includes the qualified name of the service (see line 2 of that Listing), the operation to be called (3) as well as a XPath expression (4)that describes particularly the part of the message the advice (6) is applied to.

```
  Aspect serviceaAspect = new Aspect(
2    new QName("http://www.fb12.de/videana/↘
     →MpegDecoderService", "MpegDecoder"),
     "getNextFrame",
4    "/0/imageData",
     Aspect.AOP_RESPONSE_MODE,
6    "FlexSwAPlugIn")
```

Listing 2: Java bean constructor of an aspect

When the AIH has successfully woven an aspect into a service, e.g., the decoder service and this service is called by this AIH in the next step, the AspectProvider extracts part of the message that is specified by the aspect, as shown in Listing 2. It describes that the FlexSwAPlugin should be applied on the response of the MpegDecoder and, more precisely, on the imageData element. The implementation of the FlexSwA advice (see Listing 3) first creates a reference for the return object (lines 12 – 17) that in the next step is converted into the same syntactical data structure the service actually returns (lines 30 – 51). The aspect on the receiver's side operates accordingly, it extracts the encoded reference. Then, it acquires the actual data, converts it into the expected data format and eventually passes it to the service implementation.

```
  @Override
2 public Object handleResponse(Object value) ↘
   →throws Exception {

4 if (value == null) {
    return value;
6 }

8 Reference reference = new Reference();

10 bufferSize = ...

12 OutputStream os = reference.↘
   →requestMemoryOutputStream(bufferSize, false↘
   →);
   ObjectOutputStream oos = new ↘
   →ObjectOutputStream(os);
14 oos.writeObject(value);
   oos.close();
```

```
16
   String referenceString = JSONSerializer.\
   →toJSON(reference);
18
   Object result = null;
20 if (value.getClass().isArray()) {
   result = convertReferenceToReturnValue(\
   →value, referenceString);
22 } else if (value instanceof String) {
   result = referenceString;
24 } ...

26   return result;

28 }

30 private Object convertReferenceToReturnValue(
   Object value,
32 String refString) {

34 Class<?> arrayClass = value.getClass();
   Class<?> componentClass =
36  arrayClass.getComponentType();

38 Object result = null;

40 if (componentClass.isPrimitive()) {
   if (componentClass.equals(byte.class)) {
42 byte[] temp=new byte[refString.length()];
   for (int i = 0;
44  i < refString.length(); i++) {
   temp[i] = (byte) refString.charAt(i);
46 }
   result = temp;
48 } ...

50  return result;
   }
```

Listing 3: Response handling of the efficient data transmission aspect

5. EVALUATION

This section describes the experimental setup used to evaluate the proposed approach. Then, experimental runtime results are presented and discussed.

5.1 Web Services and Workflow

To evaluate the proposed approach, we use an implementation for face detection that is integrated in our video analysis toolkit Videana [14]. This implementation can be divided into three main components. First, for a given input video, an MPEG decoder sequentially produces a series of frames. After a frame has been decoded, it is processed by the face detection algorithm (mainly consisting of feature extraction and classification). For face detection, the well known approach proposed by Viola and Jones [37] provided by the "Open Source Computer Vision Library" (OpenCV, [30]) is used. The results of this algorithm are bounding boxes that are stored in a simple list. After the whole input video has been processed in this manner, the final list is given to a component that uses this information to build an MPEG-7 result file [26, 32]. The MPEG-7 standard is commonly used to save meta-information for multimedia data.

A straightforward decomposition of this implementation is realized by wrapping each of the components as a web service, resulting in three services: an MPEG decoder service, a face detection service, and a MPEG-7 converter service.

The purpose of the MPEG-7 converter service is to collect the coordinates of detected faces and to integrate them into an existing MPEG-7 file containing the shot segmentation of the video. The decoded frames produced by the MPEG decoder service are represented as integer arrays along with some meta-information such as frame number, width and height. Operating on the level of single frames supports achieving a high level of interoperability with other services and clients from different scenarios. All three services were deployed into an Apache Axis 1.4 SOAP processing engine that runs within an Apache Tomcat 6. Using these services, a BPEL workflow has been modeled. It processes a complete video file by calling the services sequentially for all frames. For simplicity, it is assumed that the decoder resides on the machine hosting the video file. The workflow was modeled using an Eclipse-based visual BPEL editor called DAVO [11], which offers easy and wizard-based development of BPEL workflows (see Figure 5).

To utilize the proposed solution, a user only has to graphically annotate the given multimedia workflow once. That is, the data flow that should be optimized by the aspect for efficient data transfer is simply marked by the user. This information is saved within the BPEL process. If this process is then executed by the BPEL engine, the AIH interprets this information and performs the corresponding calls to the Aspect Configurator. In our use case, this call takes the aspect description of Listing 2 as its input. This is repeated at all services that should use the data transfer optimization. After this configuration phase, the aspects are woven and the workflow can be executed without any modification. Sometimes, it is not necessary to use annotations to weave aspects, since for other scenarios it is also possible to explicitly use a Java library that provides an API for weaving request/response aspects. In particular, this is a again a web service call of the Aspect Configurator taking the Aspect Bean as an input argument.

Referring to Figure 1, the decoder service corresponds to the data pre-processing step. An actual data transformation is not necessary in the presented setup, because the decoded frames can be directly processed by the face detection service. Thus, this step can be omitted. Both feature extraction and classification are performed by the face detection service relying on OpenCV's face detector. Finally, as the post-processing step all meta-information generated by the face detection service are aggregated by the MPEG-7 service.

One of the basic problems to be solved in this scenario is the sequential invocation of two subsequent services in the workflow, one of which produces (large amounts of) data and the other one consumes it. The available network bandwidth of the machine hosting the BPEL engine that invokes the services can very quickly become a bottleneck. To avoid the transfer of huge data via the BPEL engine, the proposed aspect framework is used.

5.2 Experimental Setup and Results

All tests were performed in the Amazon Elastic Compute Cloud (EC2, [2]) which allowed us to easily setup a homogeneous environment to perform our analyses. Although other authors have made negative experiences with the reliability of their EC2 computing resources [33], our results show a low standard deviation. The tests were performed on two or three EC2 machines of the type High-CPU Medium In-

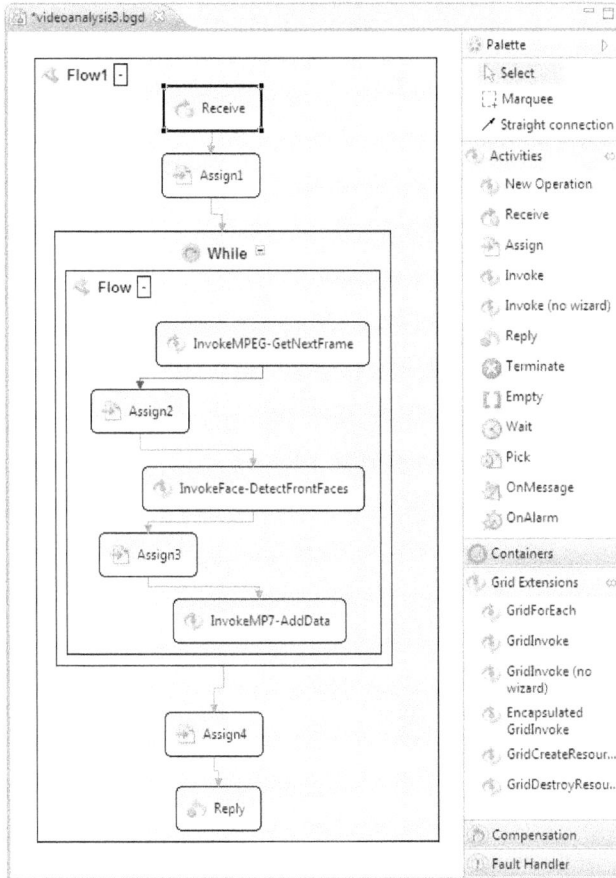

Figure 5: Modeling the face detection workflow with DAVO

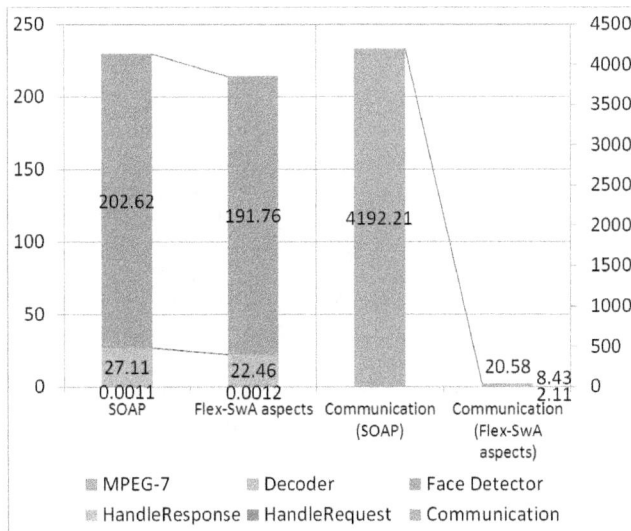

Figure 6: Runtime separated into computational and data communication effort; left y-axis: service runtime without data communication, right y-axis: runtime of data communication (orange bars)

stances that have a guaranteed interconnection rate of 250 Mbits/sec. Each of those instance types comes along with 1.7 GB of memory, 5 EC2 compute units, 350 GB storage and a 32-bit platform. At the time the tests were performed, an EC2 compute unit is proclaimed to provide the same CPU capacity as a 1.0–1.2 GHz 2007 Opteron or 2007 Xeon processor. To determine the overall runtime, the client records the overall process runtime, and the aspect framework records the actual execution time of the service's logic. The difference between these two values (minus possible runtimes for aspect handling) is the communication time.

In the first scenario, no aspects were used. The data exchange between the BPEL engine and the service were plain SOAP messages. Thus, only two machines were used, one hosting the BPEL engine, and the other one hosting the three services.

In the second scenario, our aspect framework was used. Three EC2 instances were used per run, one for the BPEL engine and two as worker nodes. One worker hosts the decoder service, while the other one hosts the face detector and the MPEG-7 converter service. On both worker nodes, the aspect framework as well as the Flex-SwA aspect were available. Since the decoder and the face detection service have the biggest fraction of data exchange, the request/response aspect based on Flex-SwA was woven into this communication. It substitutes the array containing the frame data returned by the decoder through a reference. This setup leads to the highest number of data transfers, because each service invocation requires a new data transmission between different hosts.

In each scenario, one news video (approx. 100 MB, 2005-1209_125800_CNN_LIVEFROM_ENG.mpg) from the TREC-VID 2006 test set [35] was analyzed. Our measurements are shown in Figure 6. Each value represents the average of 35 runs that were made for both scenarios. With respect to the three considered web services, the face detector service has the longest runtime, with 202.62 seconds in the first and 191.76 seconds in the second scenario, followed by the MPEG decoder service with 27.11 seconds and 22.46 seconds, respectively. With respect to the accuracy of measurements, no difference can be seen for the runtime of the MPEG-7 collector service (1.1 milliseconds to 1.2 milliseconds). Nevertheless, the client runtimes differ significantly. When using plain SOAP communication, the runtime is 4421.94 seconds, whereas the runtime in the second scenario is only 245.34 seconds (see Table 1). Whereas the service runtime are nearly comparable, the time needed for communication differs significantly. This leads to an average speed-up compared to the average SOAP runtime of approximately 18.02 and of 15.98 and 18.85 in the worst case and best case, respectively. When using SOAP, the communication took 4192.21 seconds, whereas the use of the request/response aspect reduced the communication overhead to 20.58 seconds. The use of request/response aspects results in an overhead of 10.5 seconds: 2.1 seconds for the request message and 8.4 seconds for the corresponding response message. The standard deviation in the SOAP setup was approximately 3.3% and 5.2% in the other case for our runtime measurements, therefore the EC2 has proven reliable with respect to the computational resources for the given scenarios.

The huge difference between the time needed for communication of the plain SOAP scenario compared to the aspect

	Plain SOAP	Flex-SwA aspects
Video Decoder	27.1	22.4
Face Detector	202.6	191.7
Mpeg7 Converter	0.001	0.001
Communication	4192.2	20.5
Client	4421.9	245.3

Table 1: Runtimes in seconds

scenario is mainly caused by two reasons. The first reason is the doubling of the transfer of the data array (from the decoder to the workflow engine and from the workflow engine to the face detector) when using plain SOAP communication. The second reason is the serialization and deserialization of the data array. Since video frames encoded as an array contain usually many items/elements (several 100.000 entries that represent the encoded pixels of each frame), this is a time-consuming task. However, the overhead using request/response aspects (2.1 seconds on the request side and 8.4 seconds on the response side, respectively) is negligible due to the massive runtime improvements introduced by the request/response aspects (245.34 seconds compared to 4421.94 seconds).

The proposed system allows to reduce the communication overhead. This is caused by two reasons. 1.) The absolute number of large data transmissions is reduced, and 2.) the type of transmitted data has changed. To be more precise: if we assume a system in which the response of the decoder service is processed by multiple post-processors (e.g., face detection and text detection/text recognition), its response must be sent to several services. While the proposed approach reduces to number of transmitted message from $(n+1)$ (from the decoder via the BPEL engine to the n successor services) to n, the overhead for serialization and deserialization is reduced significantly, too. In the original case, the XML representation must be serialized and deserialized by the decoder and the BPEL engine, respectively. As a result, the data are transmitted over the network in this memory and bandwidth consuming representation (the same is true for transmitting the data from the BPEL engine to the successor services), whereas in the proposed aspect-oriented solution only the (relatively) small reference has to be transferred and the bulk data are then directly transferred from the decoder service to its successors in a streaming-like approach.

6. CONCLUSIONS

In this paper, we have presented an aspect-oriented solution for realizing efficient data transmission between multimedia web services. The proposed request/response aspects are woven into the message handler chain of web services and leave the web service implementation unchanged. Our solution uses references for orchestrating data between multimedia services and is based on the Flex-SwA framework in conjunction with the BPEL workflow language. The proposed aspect-oriented solution significantly reduces the required software development efforts for implementing efficient data transmission between web services. Hence, it allows software developers of multimedia applications to benefit from the advantages that are offered by service-oriented environments. Experimental results for a video analysis workflow

showed a significant speedup for the data transfer between services when using the presented approach.

In future work, we plan to investigate, model and evaluate further aspects and their applicability to the domain of distributed service-oriented multimedia content analysis. Thus, one of our targets is to automatically integrate crosscutting concerns such as reliable messaging and profiling. Another field of future work are aspects that aggregate two or more services into a new one to reduce communication costs. This approach will utilize the principle of locality in service-oriented environments.

7. ACKNOWLEDGMENTS

This work is supported by the German Research Foundation (DFG, PAK 509, Project MT) and by the German Ministry of Education and Research (BMBF, D-Grid Initiative, Project MediaGrid).

8. REFERENCES

[1] ActiveEndpoints. ActiveBPEL Business Process Execution Engine. http://www.activebpel.org.

[2] Amazon. Amazon Web Services LLC, Amazon Elastic Compute Cloud (EC2). http://aws.amazon.com/ec2/.

[3] T. Andrews, F. Curbera, H. Dholakia, Y. Goland, J. Klein, F. Leymann, K. Liu, D. Roller, D. Smith, S. Thatte, I. Trickovic, and S. Weerawarana. *Business Process Execution Language for Web Services Version 1.1*. Microsoft, IBM, Siebel, BEA und SAP, 1.1 edition, May 2003.

[4] Apache Foundation. Apache Axis. http://ws.apache.org/axis/.

[5] Apache Foundation. Apache Tomcat. http://tomcat.apache.org/.

[6] AspectJ. http://eclipse.org/aspectj/.

[7] F. Baligand and V. Monfort. A Concrete Solution for Web Services Adaptability Using Policies and Aspects. In *Proceedings of the 2nd International Conference on Service Oriented Computing*, pages 134–142. ACM, 2004.

[8] W. Binder, I. Constantinescu, and B. Faltings. Service Invocation Triggers: A Lightweight Routing Infrastructure for Decentralized Workflow Orchestration. *International Conference on Advanced Information Networking and Applications*, 2:917–921, 2006.

[9] A. Black, J. Huang, and J. Walpole. Reifying communication at the application level. In *Proceedings of the 2001 international workshop on Multimedia middleware*, pages 32–35. ACM, 2001.

[10] A. Charfi and M. Mezini. Aspect-oriented Web Service Composition with AO4BPEL. In *Proceedings of the European Conference on Web Services*, pages 168–182. Springer, 2004.

[11] T. Dörnemann, M. Mathes, R. Schwarzkopf, E. Juhnke, and B. Freisleben. DAVO: A Domain-Adaptable, Visual BPEL4WS Orchestrator. In *Proceedings of the 23rd IEEE International Conference on Advanced Information Networking and Applications (AINA)*, pages 121–128. IEEE, 2009.

[12] D. Ecklund, V. Goebel, T. Plagemann, and E. Ecklund Jr. Dynamic end-to-end QoS management

middleware for distributed multimedia systems. *Multimedia Systems*, 8(5):431–442, 2002.

[13] V. S. W. Eide, F. Eliassen, O.-C. Granmo, and O. Lysne. Scalable Independent Multi-level Distribution in Multimedia Content Analysis. In *Proceedings of the Joint International Workshops on Interactive Distributed Multimedia Systems and Protocols for Multimedia Systems (IDMS/PROMS)*, pages 37–48. Springer-Verlag, 2002.

[14] R. Ewerth, M. Mühling, T. Stadelmann, J. Gllavata, M. Grauer, and B. Freisleben. Videana: A Software Tool for Scientific Film Studies. *Digital Tools in Media Studies – Analysis and Research*, pages 145–160, 2007.

[15] Face.com – Face recognition for the masses. http://face.com/.

[16] R. Fielding. *Architectural styles and the design of network-based software architectures*. PhD thesis, University of California, Irvine, 2000.

[17] D. Gibbon and Z. Liu. Large Scale Content Analysis Engine. In *Proceedings of the First ACM Workshop on Large-scale Multimedia Retrieval and Mining*, pages 97–104, New York, NY, USA, 2009. ACM.

[18] C. Griwodz and M. Zink. Dynamic data path reconfiguration. In *Proceedings of the 2001 international workshop on Multimedia middleware*, pages 72–75. ACM, 2001.

[19] S. Heinzl, M. Mathes, T. Friese, M. Smith, and B. Freisleben. Flex-SwA: Flexible Exchange of Binary Data Based on SOAP Messages with Attachments. In *Proceedings of the IEEE International Conference on Web Services (ICWS)*, pages 3–10. IEEE Press, 2006.

[20] Hey!Watch – Video encoding web service. http://heywatch.com/page/home.

[21] IBM. Web Services Flow Language, 2001.

[22] Java Message Service. http://www.oracle.com/technetwork/java/index-jsp-142945.html.

[23] G. Kiczales, E. Hilsdale, J. Hugunin, M. Kersten, J. Palm, and W. Griswold. An Overview of AspectJ. *Proceedings of the 15th European Conference on Object-Oriented Programming*, pages 327–353, 2001.

[24] H. Masuhara and G. Kiczales. Modeling Crosscutting in Aspect-Oriented Mechanisms. In *Proceedings of the 17th European Conference on Object-Oriented Programming*, pages 2–28. Springer-Verlag, 2003.

[25] Microsoft. XLANG – Web Services for Business Process Design, 2001.

[26] MPEG-7 Overview. http://mpeg.chiariglione.org/standards/mpeg-7/mpeg-7.htm.

[27] H. Naguib and G. Coulouris. Towards automatically configurable multimedia applications. In *Proceedings of the 2001 international workshop on Multimedia middleware*, pages 28–31. ACM, 2001.

[28] J. Nesvadba, P. Fonseca, A. Sinitsyn, F. de Lange, M. Thijssen, P. van Kaam, H. Liu, R. van Leeuwen, J. Lukkien, A. Korostelev, J. Ypma, B. Kroon, H. Celik, A. Hanjalic, U. Naci, J. Benois-Pineau, P. de With, and J. Han. Real-Time and Distributed AV Content Analysis System for Consumer

Electronics Networks. In *Proceedings of Int. Conf. on Multimedia and Expo*, pages 1549–1552. IEEE, 2005.

[29] M. Nishizawa, S. Chiba, and M. Tatsubori. Remote Pointcut: A Language Construct for Distributed AOP. In *Proceedings of the 3rd International Conference on Aspect-Oriented Software Development*, pages 7–15. ACM, 2004.

[30] OpenCV. http://www.intel.com/technology/computing/opencv/.

[31] C. Pautasso, O. Zimmermann, and F. Leymann. Restful web services vs. "big" web services: making the right architectural decision. In *WWW '08: Proceeding of the 17th international conference on World Wide Web*, pages 805–814, New York, NY, USA, 2008. ACM.

[32] P. Salembier. Overview of the MPEG-7 Standard and of Future Challenges for Visual Information Analysis. *EURASIP Journal on Signal Processing*, 2002(1):343–353, 2002.

[33] J. Schad, J. Dittrich, and J. Quiane-Ruiz. Runtime Measurements in the Cloud: Observing, Analyzing, and Reducing Variance. *Proceedings of the VLDB Endowment*, 3(1), 2010.

[34] D. Seiler, S. Heinzl, E. Juhnke, R. Ewerth, M. Grauer, and B. Efficient Data Transmission in Service Workflows for Distributed Video Content Analysis. In *Proceedings of the 6th International Conference on Advances in Mobile Computing and Multimedia*, pages 7–14. ACM, 2008.

[35] A. F. Smeaton, P. Over, and W. Kraaij. Evaluation campaigns and trecvid. In *MIR '06: Proceedings of the 8th ACM International Workshop on Multimedia Information Retrieval*, pages 321–330, New York, NY, USA, 2006. ACM Press.

[36] P. Vajgel. Needle in a haystack: efficient storage of billions of photos. http://www.facebook.com/note.php?note_id=76191543919, 2009.

[37] P. Viola and M. J. Jones. Robust Real-Time Face Detection. *International Journal of Computer Vision*, 57(2):137–154, 2004.

[38] WiseTrend – OCR, Document Conversion, Data Capture & Form Processing. http://www.wisetrend.com/.

[39] World Wide Web Consortium (W3C). SOAP Message Transmission Optimization Mechanism. http://www.w3.org/TR/soap12-mtom/.

[40] World Wide Web Consortium (W3C). SOAP Messages with Attachments. http://www.w3.org/TR/SOAP-attachments.

[41] World Wide Web Consortium (W3C). W3C SOAP Specification. http://www.w3.org/TR/soap/.

[42] World Wide Web Consortium (W3C). Web Services Definition Language (WSDL) 1.1. http://www.w3.org/TR/wsdl.

[43] World Wide Web Consortium (W3C). XML Schema. http://www.w3.org/XML/Schema.html.

[44] Web Service Specifications. http://en.wikipedia.org/wiki/List_of_web_service_specifications.

Network Traces of Virtual Worlds: Measurements and Applications

Yichuan Wang[*]
Department of Computer Science
University of California
Davis, CA
yicwang@ucdavis.edu

Cheng-Hsin Hsu
Deutsche Telekom Inc.
R&D Laboratories USA
Los Altos, CA
cheng-hsin.hsu@telekom.com

Jatinder Pal Singh
Deutsche Telekom Inc.
R&D Laboratories USA
Los Altos, CA
j.singh@telekom.com

Xin Liu
Department of Computer Science
University of California
Davis, CA
xinliu@ucdavis.edu

ABSTRACT

Although network traces of virtual worlds are valuable to ISPs (Internet service providers), virtual world software developers, and research communities, they do not exist in the public domain. In this work, we implement a complete testbed to efficiently collect and analyze network traces from a popular virtual world: Second Life. We use the testbed to gather traces from 100 regions with diverse characteristics. The network traces represent more than 60 hours of virtual world traffic and the trace files are created in a well-structured and concise format. Our preliminary analysis on the collected traces is consistent with previous work in the literature. It also reveals some new insights: for example, local avatar/object density imposes clear implications on traffic patterns. The developed testbed and released trace files can be leveraged by research communities for various studies on virtual worlds. For example, accurate traffic models can be derived from our trace files, which in turn can guide developers for better virtual world designs.

Categories and Subject Descriptors

H.5.1 [**Information Systems Applications**]: Multimedia Information Systems

General Terms

Measurement

1. INTRODUCTION

Virtual worlds, such as *Second Life* [18], *Habbo Hotel* [4], and *Playstation Home* [15], are computer-simulated environments that

---

[*]This work was done when Y. Wang was an intern at Deutsche Telekom R&D Labs USA.

allow many users to interact with each other via graphical avatars. Virtual worlds enable a plethora of interesting applications spanning entertainments, 3D shopping malls, immersive distance learning, virtual workspace, and online art galleries, and are thus becoming increasingly popular. For example, Linden Research reports that there were more than a million users logged in to Second Life in July 2010 [16].

While most online games distribute game data to users using optical media such as DVDs, virtual worlds consist of user-generated and dynamic in-world objects that can only be downloaded on-demand. The bandwidth requirements of virtual worlds, therefore, are significantly higher than online games [6]. The high-volume real-time traffic generated by virtual worlds imposes great challenges to the best-effort Internet. Hence, network traces of virtual worlds are very valuable to ISPs (Internet service providers) for better network planning [1] and software developers for better virtual world design [12].

To the best of our knowledge, there exists no publicly available network traces of virtual worlds. Research groups resort to building their own utilities to capture traces, which is a tedious and time consuming task. In this work, we conduct extensive experiments in a popular virtual world to collect network traces in different environments (e.g., diverse avatar and object density) and with various avatar actions (e.g., walk and run). Most importantly, we share the resulting traces with research communities to stimulate the future research on virtual worlds [17].

Our main contributions are summarized as follows:

- A fully automated testbed is developed for efficient and large-scale virtual world traffic analysis.
- We collect Second Life traces from 100 diversified regions. The total length of our traces is over 60 hours, and the resulting trace files are over 3 GB in size.
- We validate previous work in this area, and provide new insights. For example, local avatar/object density has strong correlation with traffic patterns, which was never reported in the literature.

The rest of this paper is organized as follows. We review related work in Sec. 2. We give an overview of virtual worlds in Sec. 3. Sec. 4 describes our measurement methodology. We present the network traces in Sec. 5. Sec. 6 briefly discusses some potential applications and Sec. 7 concludes the paper.

2. RELATED WORK

Two types of traces have been collected from virtual worlds: (i) traces of the locations and movements of avatars/objects and (ii) traces of timestamped network packets. Traces of avatars/objects are usually gathered by crawlers that traverse through many regions of a virtual world. For example, Varvello et al. [20] build a crawler that collects information about avatars, objects and server status from $\sim$ 13,000 regions. La and Michiardi [7] and Liang et al. [9] also build crawlers to derive mobility models for avatars. Some avatar/object traces are made publicly available [11], which are complementary to the network traces we collected.

Network traces from virtual worlds have also been collected in various studies [1–3, 5, 8, 12]. Liang et al. [8] implement a Second Life proxy to collect network packets exchanged between clients and servers. Fernandes et al. [2] use packet sniffer to capture packets from/to an official Second Life client. Kinicki and Claypool [5] conduct a similar, but more comprehensive measurement study. Ferreira and Morla [3] develop a Second Life testbed to systematically collect network traces resulted by various avatar actions. Oliver et al. [12] collect network traces from real Second Life users: 30 users participating in a virtual conference. They also gather network traces from controlled avatar actions in two regions. To the best of our knowledge, unlike our work, none of the network traces used in [1–3, 5, 8, 12] is publicly available.

3. SECOND LIFE: AN OVERVIEW

In this section, we give a high-level overview on Second Life, which is a popular virtual world. Second Life follows the client-server network model. Companies such as Linden Research [18], and non-profit organizations such as OSgrid [14] host Second Life servers, and users (or *residents*) use Second Life clients (called *viewers*) to connect to these servers. The viewers support various in-world actions, including stand, walk, run, fly, and teleportation. *Teleportation* refers to an instant change of an avatar's location. In general, user commands are sent from viewers to servers for processing and the results are transmitted back to viewers for rendering and displaying. Second Life is built and customized by users, and users create new 3D structures using *primitives* (or prims, which are basic 3D objects) as building blocks, and upload image files as textures for these 3D structures. These 3D objects are distributed to viewers *on-demand*, i.e., the servers transmit a 3D object to a viewer once the object is visible to that viewer. Viewers usually cache recently downloaded 3D objects.

Multiple servers are used in Second Life, and they can be classified into two groups: simulation and administration servers. Simulation servers run the logics to simulate physics in the virtual world, and execute user scripts written in Linden script language (LSL). LSL allows users to programmatically control objects' behavior. As simulating physics is computationally intensive, the virtual world is divided into more than 30,000 *regions*, where a typical region has a size of 256x256 m^2 and is managed by a simulation server. Each viewer is connected to one or more simulation servers, and is handed over to other simulation servers once the avatar moves into different regions.

Administration servers include login, user, space, data, and utility servers. Before participating in the virtual world, a viewer sends the avatar's username and password to the login server. Upon authentication, the login server determines the start location of the avatar and directs the viewer toward the simulation server manging that location. During simulation, the user server routes instant messages, and the space server coordinates all the simulation servers for a seamless, unified virtual world. The data server is essentially a central database used by other servers, and the utility servers handle miscellaneous tasks.

4. METHODOLOGY

4.1 Region Classes

Earlier works on Second Life consider very few regions. For example, Kinicki and Claypool [5] and Liang et al. [8] only consider three regions. While these studies reveal the implications of avatar/object density on network traffic, the number of regions is too small to *interpolate* the traffic patterns in regions other than those chosen ones. To address this limitation, we choose many regions with diverse avatar/object density as follows. We obtained the complete region list from an online database[1] on Aug 20, 2010, which contains 31,543 regions. We implement a region crawler, which iteratively teleports an avatar to each region and gathers the number of avatars/objects in it.

We successfully collected avatar/object density from 22,717 regions. Missed regions are either too busy, private, or with adult contents. The maximum number of avatars is 93, but most regions have very few avatars, e.g., 57% of regions have only one avatar. The maximum number of objects is 15,000, and the distribution is more uniform compared to that of avatars. We divide the regions into 25 *classes*. We let $\boldsymbol{X} = \{1, 2, 4, 8, 16, \infty\}$ and $\boldsymbol{Y} = \{0, 3000, 6000, 9000, 12000, \infty\}$, and define class $\boldsymbol{C}_{i,j}$ $(1 \leq i, j \leq 5)^2$ be all regions with number of avatars $x \in [X_i, X_{i+1})$ and number of objects $y \in [Y_i, Y_{i+1})$. In our experiment, we collect network traces from four random regions in each class. Although excluding private or adult regions, the selected regions are statistically representative in terms of object and avatar numbers. The collected trace shows statistics similarity to previous work in which adult and private regions were considered [20].

4.2 Actions and Scripts

Users interact with the virtual world through various *actions*, such as stand, rotation (yaw, pitch, roll), walk, run, jump, fly, teleportation, and grab. We consider the following actions in our experiments.

1. **Stand:** Stay in the current location. This can happen, e.g., when users chat by typing or speaking.

2. **Walk:** Walk straight, which can be due to keyboard inputs or LSL scripts. The default walking speed is around 2 m/sec, which may be changed through LSL scripts or affected by other factors such as terrains.

3. **Yaw:** Change the avatar's orientation. This occurs when users check the surroundings through avatar's eyes. Yawing 360 degrees takes about 5 secs.

4. **Run:** Run straight. This is similar to walk, except a different avatar animation is rendered. The running speed is around 5 m/sec.

5. **Fly:** Take off from the ground, fly straight, and land on the ground again. The flying speed is about 15 m/sec. Therefore, avatars can fly across a 256x256 m^2 region in 17 to 25 secs.

6. **Teleportation:** Change location instantaneously.

With these actions, we define several *scripts*. Each script starts at a random location and runs for one minute. We program the viewer to deliberately prevent avatars from crossing region boundaries. We consider the following scripts.

---

[1] http://www.gridsurvey.com.

[2] In this paper, we use bold symbols to represent vectors.

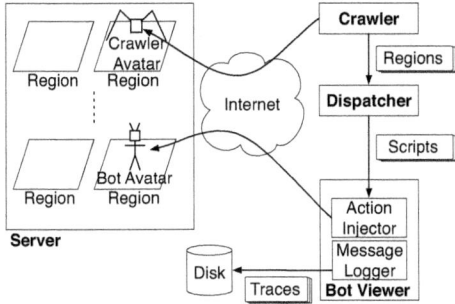

Figure 1: Second Life testbed setup.

1. **Stand:** Stand for one minute.

2. **Yaw:** Rotate avatar's orientation for 12 secs, and repeat this 5 times.

3. **Walk:** Walk in a random direction for 12 secs, and repeat this 5 times.

4. **Run:** Run in a random direction for 12 secs, and repeat this 5 times.

5. **Fly:** Fly in a random direction for 12 secs, and repeat this 5 times.

6. **Teleportation:** Teleport to a random location in the same region, wait for 12 secs, and repeat this 5 times.

7. **YWRFT:** Sequentially perform four actions: yaw, walk, run, and fly, each for 12 secs. Then teleport to a random location in the same region and wait for 12 secs.

8. **TFRWY:** Reversed YWRFT script.

For scripts other than Yaw, we turn an avatar's direction by directly setting its orientation, which takes virtually no time to complete.

4.3 Testbed Implementation

We design and build a testbed to collect Second Life network traces. We make the following decisions:

1. **Modifying a GUI viewer.** Viewers can be categorized into two classes: GUI viewers and text-based chat clients. We have augmented both a GUI viewer (Snowglobe [19]) and a chat client (TestClient of LibOpenMetaverse [10]), and used them to collect network traces. Our experimental results indicate that chat clients ignore several multimedia packet types, and may lead to unrepresentative traffic patterns.

2. **Logging packets at the viewer.** Packets can be logged: (i) at a viewer, (ii) at a proxy, and (iii) with a packet sniffer, such as Wireshark [21]. While using a proxy (or a packet sniffer) is easier than modifying a viewer to log network traces, additional networking and processing latency may result in deviated packet timestamps.

3. **Using official Linden servers.** While private servers can be set up using the open-source OpenSim [13] implementation, doing so prevents us from capturing the actual traffic patterns in live Second Life networks.

Following these design decisions, we implement our testbed as illustrated in Fig. 1. Our testbed contains two parts: Server on the left, and the measurement tools, including Crawler, Dispatcher, and Bot Viewer, on the right. We run the tools on a PC with 2.4 GHz Intel processor, which is connected to the Internet via a dedicated link with 10 Mbps bandwidth in both directions. The same link is shared with common office applications such as emails and web browsing. Next, we present our measurement tools in details.

1: Crawler collects avatar/object density of all regions and categorizes them into 25 classes
2: **for all** Class $C_{i,j}$, where $1 \leq i, j \leq 5$ **do**
3:     Let C' be four random regions from $C_{i,j}$
4:     **for all** Region r in C' **do**
5:         Dispatcher compiles eight scripts S_r
6:         **for all** script s in S_r **do**
7:             Bot Viewer performs s
8:             Bot Viewer saves traces of s into files
9:         **end for**
10:     **end for**
11: **end for**

Figure 2: Pseudocode to collect network traces.

Table 1: Packet trace format

Field	Example	Description
Timestamp	12834907204	Unix Time in usec
Protocol	UDP	Transport protocol
Direction	in	Downlink or uplink
Remote IP	216.82.23.202	IP address
Remote Port	13001	TCP/UDP port
Packet Type	LayerData	Second Life packet type
Payload Size	81	Second Life packet size

Crawler. We implement Crawler based on TestClient of LibOpenMetaverse [10]. Crawler first logins to the virtual world with a starting region. It then checks its current location and aborts if it's not in the specified starting region. Last, Crawler sends a query packet to Server for the number of avatars/objects in that region. The regions are then classified into 25 classes (see Sec. 4.1 for details).

Dispatcher. Dispatcher is implemented in Python and Bourne shell. Dispatcher first generates the eight scripts mentioned above for each considered region. The avatar starts at random location in each script. All the scripts are saved for future reference. Dispatcher then calls Bot Viewer to follow each script and collect network traces.

Bot Viewer. We implement the Bot Viewer by adding two new components: Action Injector and Message Logger, to Snowglobe [19]. After logging in a region, Action Injector reads the script created by Dispatcher, and injects actions into Bot Viewer. Since we are doing this in the core engine of Bot Viewer, we can accurately control the action time and collect exact location information among other useful statistics. Bot Viewer exits after each script is finished. We perform several sanity checks in Bot Viewer, e.g., we rerun a script if a teleportation gets rejected or a login authentication fails. Message Logger logs all network packets, including their timestamp, size, type, and remote address. It also logs the avatar's location and surrounding avatar/object density.

4.4 Trace Collection

We systematically collect network traces of eight scripts from 100 regions with diverse characteristics. Fig. 2 shows the high-level steps used in trace collection. The for-loop starting from lines 2, 4, and 6, iterate through the considered region classes, random regions, and action scripts, respectively.

We collect network traces in two setups: *uncached* and *cached*. We consider both cases because viewer cache can significantly reduce network traffic amount [6]. For uncached experiments, we

Table 2: Script record format

Field	Example	Description
Type	Script	Record type
No. Actions	5	No. actions
Action 1	Walk 10	Action
Action 2	Stand 20	Action
...	...	...

Table 3: Location record format

Field	Example	Description	Field	Ex.	Description
Type	Location	Record type	Local Objects	185	Object density
Timestamp	12543524234	Unix time	Local Avatars	3	Avatar density
Region	Morris	Region name	Global Objects	949	Object density
Global Pos.	912,834,1	Pos. vector	Global Avatars	7	Avatar density
Local Pos.	22,127,2	Pos. vector			

Table 4: Action record format

Field	Example	Description
Type	Action	Record type
Timestamp	12543524234	Unix time
Action	Walk 10	Action

Table 5: Statistics trace format

Field	Example	Description
Region	Morris	Name of the region
Crawled Object Density	9484	Object density from Crawler
Crawled Avatar Density	10	Avatar density from Crawler
Global Object Density	9730.5	Mean global object density from Bot Viewer
Global Avatar Density	14.9	Mean global avatar density from Bot Viewer
Local Object Density	181.5	Mean local object density from Bot Viewer
Local Avatar Density	3.6	Mean local avatar density from Bot Viewer

instruct the viewer to clean its cache before running each script. For cached experiments, we only clean the cache before running the first script in a region, and for each region, we repeat the eight scripts twice without cleaning the cache. The first run of the eight scripts warms up the cache, and we collect network traces during the second run. We started the trace collection on Aug 25, 2010.

5. TRACES

5.1 Format

To assist readers better utilizing the traces, we processed the raw trace files into a well-structured and concise format. The trace files contain lines of *fields* separated by a pipe character (|). We define the fields in the following.

Packet trace. Packet trace files log the traffic to and from the Bot Viewer during each script execution. Each line represents a Second Life packet, and lines are sorted based on timestamp. Table 1 lists the fields of packet traces.

Location trace. Location trace file contains three types of *records*: script, position, and action. Each record is saved in a line. Script record appears at the beginning of each location trace file, and indicates the planned actions of every script. Table 2 shows its format. Location records are periodically saved with 1-sec interval. As presented in Table 3, a location record indicates region name, global/local position of our bot avatar, global avatar/object density in the region, and local avatar/object density at the current location. Action records are saved whenever the bot avatar performs a new action. The timestamps, actions, and action parameters are saved in action records, as illustrated in Table 4.

Statistics trace. Statistics trace reports avatar/object density of each region. The numbers are computed across all experiments, which provide readers the ground truth of the region characteristics. Table 5 lists its fields.

5.2 Analysis

We report the characterizing statistics of the collected traces. We consider three metrics: throughput, packet size, and interarrival time. We consider six scripts (YWRFT and TFRWY are skipped due to the space limitations). We first report the statistics of a randomly chosen region *Tokugawa*. This region has 2531 objects and 1 avatar, and our bot avatar encountered 93 local objects and 1 local avatar on average during the time of the trace collection.

Downlink traffic, uncached, Tokugawa. We show the Cumulative Distribution Function (CDF) of downlink traffic for uncached experiments in Fig. 3. Fig. 3(a) illustrates the correlation between avatar action and downlink traffic, which is also observed in several previous work, including [5]. Fig. 3(b) reveals that packets can be categorized into two groups: ~200 bytes and ~1000 bytes. We found that packets with size ~1000 bytes are mostly multimedia packets, such as texture packets. Fig. 3(c) shows that actions impose insignificant impacts on interarrival time.

Uplink traffic, uncached, Tokugawa. We plot the CDF curves of uplink traffic for uncached experiments in Fig. 4. Fig. 4(a) reveals that the uplink throughput is lower by an order of magnitude comparing to downlink throughput (see Fig. 3(a)). Fig. 4(b) shows that about 95% of the uplink packets are smaller than 200 bytes. Fig. 4(c) shows that uplink interarrival time is higher than downlink, and Stand and Teleport have higher interarrival time.

Cached, Tokugawa. We plot sample CDF curves for cached experiments in Fig. 5. In Figs. 5(a) and 5(b), we observe a throughput reduction of about 50% in both downlink and uplink, compared to results from the uncached experiments (see Figs. 3(a) and 4(a)). Fig. 5(c) shows that the number of packets with size ~1000 bytes are significantly reduced when cache is used, which indicates a decent amount of multimedia data were retrieved from the cache.

Downlink traffic, uncached, aggregated. Next, we report the aggregated statistics across 100 regions. We plot the CDF curves of downlink traffic for uncached experiments in Fig. 6. Uplink and cached results are omitted due to the page limitations; interested readers can generate them from our trace files [17]. The CDF curves in Figs. 6(b) and 6(c) are aligned with those in Figs. 3(b) and 3(c). However, comparing Fig. 6(a) against Fig. 3(a), we found that the correlation between action and throughput is *weaker* in aggregated form: the CDF curves in Fig. 6(a) are quite close to each other. This observation implies that avatar action may not be the strongest factor affecting the traffic pattern.

Correlation between avatar/object density and traffic pattern. To evaluate other factors affecting traffic patterns, we compute the mean throughput, packet size, and interarrival time across all action scripts of individual regions. We tried three types of density: crawled, global, and local, and found that local density has the strongest correlation with the traffic pattern. We then plot a few sample figures in Fig. 7 to illustrate how local avatar/object density affects downlink traffic patterns in uncached experiments.

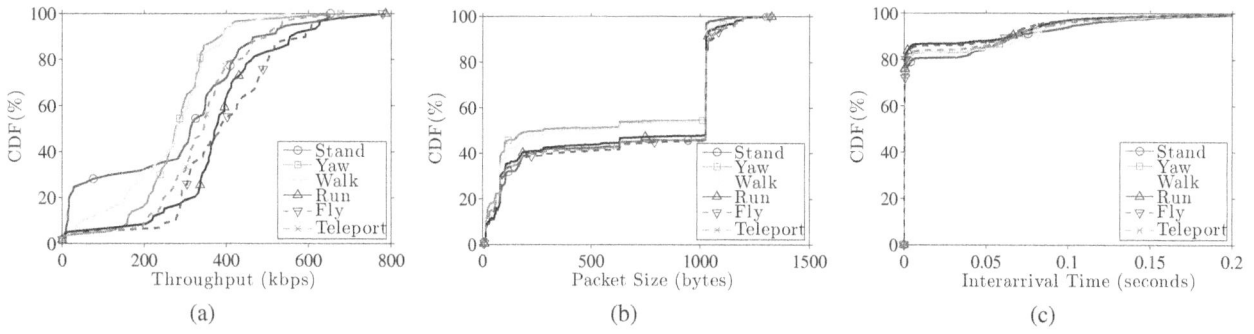

Figure 3: Downlink statistics of an uncached region: (a) throughput, (b) packet size, and (c) interarrival time.

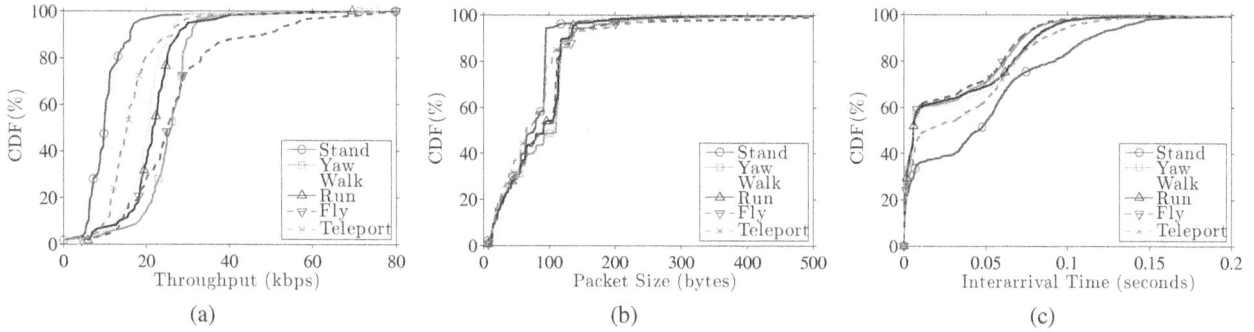

Figure 4: Uplink statistics of an uncached region: (a) throughput, (b) packet size, and (c) interarrival time.

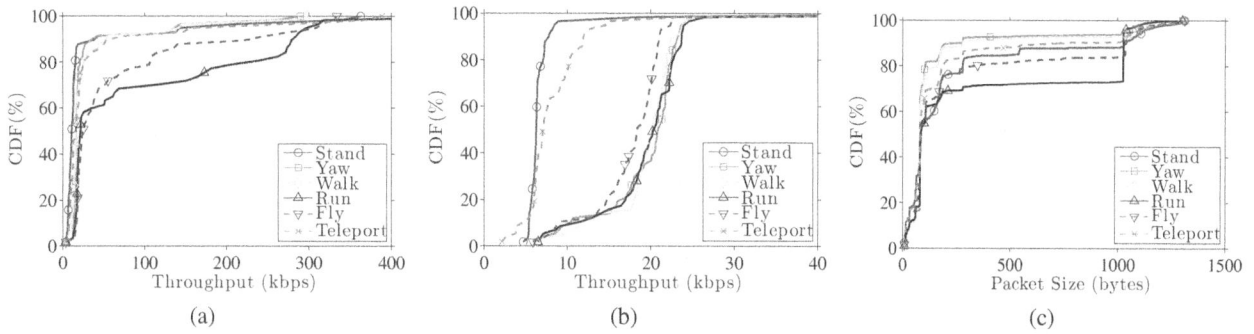

Figure 5: Statistics of a cached region: (a) downlink throughput, (b) uplink throughput, and (c) downlink packet size.

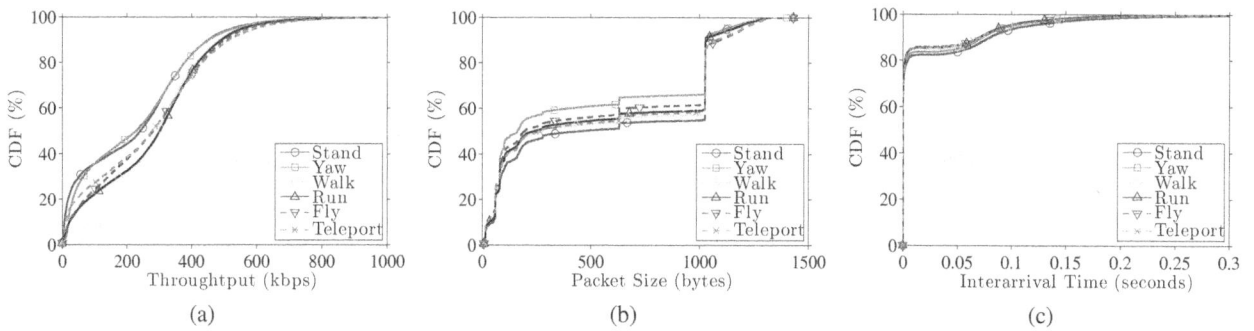

Figure 6: Aggregated uncached downlink statistics: (a) throughput, (b) packet size, and (c) interarrival time.

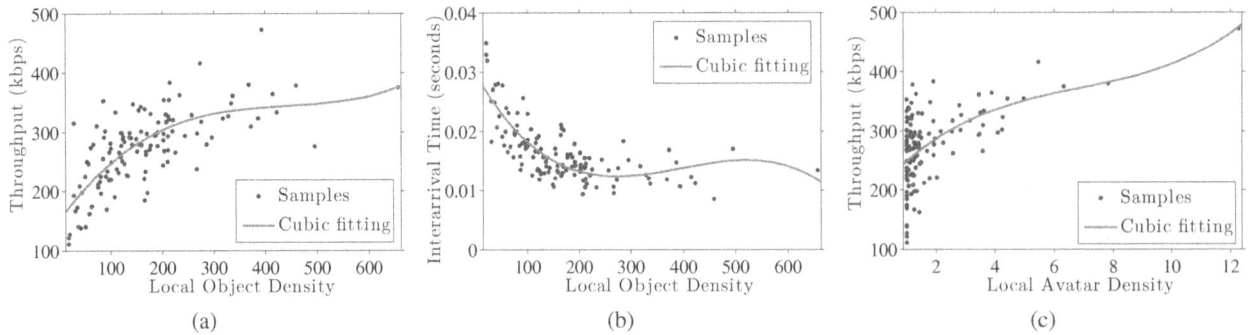

Figure 7: Correlation between avatar/object density and traffic pattern: (a) throughput vs. local object density, (b) interarrival time vs. local object density, and (c) throughput vs. local avatar density.

Fig. 7(a) shows a strong correlation between throughput and local object density, which can be modeled by a cubic function. Similarly, Fig. 7(b) reveals the correlation between interarrival time and local object density, and Fig. 7(c) illustrates the correlation between throughput and local avatar density.

6. APPLICATIONS

Traffic modeling in virtual worlds. Several research groups [1, 3] have pointed out that modeling network traffic of virtual worlds is valuable for: (i) ISPs to configure their networks, (ii) virtual world developers to achieve better Quality-of-Service (QoS), and (iii) research communities to generate synthetic traffic for simulations. Antonello et al. [1] model packet size and interarrival time using several common distributions such as beta, gamma, and lognormal. Ferreira and Morla [3] argue that there is a strong correlation between packet size and interarrival time, and propose to categorize the packets into multiple groups based on their sizes and then model packets in each group with a separate distribution.

A few approaches can be applied to refine the existing models in the literature. For example, packets of each packet type can be modeled with a different distribution. In addition, as showed in Sec. 5.2, region characteristics, such as avatar/object density, can be considered as *parameters* in traffic models. These extensions may not be possible without our extensive network traces.

Improving Quality-of-Service. Oliver et al. [12] observe that some packet types are very sensitive to packet loss and delivery delay, while others are more loss and delay tolerant. This leads to a possible QoS mechanism that prioritizes packets on their packet types for better user experience. Designing and evaluating such QoS mechanisms heavily rely on our network traces and the traffic models derived from them.

7. CONCLUSIONS

We implemented an automated testbed to systematically collect network traces from virtual worlds. We used the testbed to gather extensive traces from 100 diverse Second Life regions, which result in more than 60 hour traffic trace and more than 3 GB trace files. In comparison, most previous studies only consider a few regions, and more importantly, they did not make their traces public. We analyzed the virtual world traffic patterns using the collected traces. Our results are consistent with work in the literature, and also reveal new insights, e.g., local avatar/object density imposes clear implications on the downlink throughput. Our network traces [17] can stimulate the research on virtual worlds.

8. REFERENCES

[1] R. Antonello, S. Fernandes, J. Moreira, P. Cunha, C. Kamienski, and D. Sadok. Traffic analysis and synthetic models of Second Life. *Multimedia Tools and Applications*, 15(1):33–47, February 2009.

[2] S. Fernandes, F. Antonello, J. Moreira, D. Sadok, and C. Kamienski. Traffic analysis beyond this world: the case of Second Life. In *Proc. of ACM International Workshop on Network and Operating Systems Support for Digital Audio and Video (NOSSDAV'07)*, Urbana-Champaign, IL, June 2007.

[3] M. Ferreira and R. Morla. Second Life in-world action traffic modeling. In *Proc. of ACM International Workshop on Network and Operating Systems Support for Digital Audio and Video (NOSSDAV'10)*, pages 3–8, Amsterdam, The Netherlands, June 2010.

[4] Habbo Hotel official site, August 2010. http://www.habbo.com.

[5] J. Kinicki and M. Claypool. Traffic analysis of avatars in Second Life. In *Proc. of ACM International Workshop on Network and Operating Systems Support for Digital Audio and Video (NOSSDAV'08)*, pages 69–74, Braunschweig, Germany, May 2008.

[6] S. Kumar, J. Chhugani, K. Changkyu, D. Kim, A. Nguyen, P. Dubey, C. Bienia, and Y. Kim. Second Life and the new generation of virtual worlds. *IEEE Computer*, 41(9):46–53, September 2008.

[7] C. La and P. Michiardi. Characterizing user mobility in Second Life. In *Proc. of ACM Workshop on Online Social Networks (WOSN'08)*, pages 79–84, Seattle, WA, August 2008.

[8] H. Liang, M. Motani, and W. Ooi. Textures in Second Life: Measurement and analysis. In *Proc. of IEEE International Conference on Parallel and Distributed Systems (ICPADS'08)*, pages 823–828, Melbourne, Australia, December 2008.

[9] H. Liang, R. Silva, W. Ooi, and M. Motani. Avatar mobility in user-created networked virtual worlds: Measurements, analysis, and implications. *Multimedia Tools and Applications*, 45(1-3):163–190, October 2009.

[10] LibOpenMetaverse official site, August 2010. http://www.libsecondlife.org.

[11] Measurement and analysis of large distributed virtual environments, August 2010. http://nemesys.comp.nus.edu.sg/projects/secondlife.

[12] I. Oliver, A. Miller, and C. Allison. Virtual worlds, real traffic: Interaction and adaptation. In *Proc. of ACM conference on Multimedia systems (MMSys'10)*, pages 305–316, Scottsdale, AZ, February 2010.

[13] OpenSimulator official site, August 2010. http://opensimulator.org.

[14] OSgrid official site, August 2010. http://www.osgrid.org.

[15] Playstation Home official site, August 2010. http://us.playstation.com/psn/playstation-home.

[16] Second Life economic statistics, August 2010. http://secondlife.com/statistics/economy-data.php.

[17] Second Life network traces, September 2010. http://12.71.54.173/sl.

[18] Second Life official site, August 2010. http://secondlife.com.

[19] Snowglobe official site, August 2010. http://snowglobeproject.org.

[20] M. Varvello, F. Picconi, C. Diot, and E. Biersack. Is there life in Second Life? In *Proc. of ACM International Conference on Emerging Networking Experiments and Technologies (CoNEXT'08)*, Madrid, Spain, December 2008.

[21] Wireshark official site, August 2010. http://www.wireshark.org.

End-to-End and Network-Internal Measurements of Real-Time Traffic to Residential Users

Martin Ellis
School of Computing Science
University of Glasgow
ellis@dcs.gla.ac.uk

Colin Perkins
School of Computing Science
University of Glasgow
csp@csperkins.org

Dimitrios P. Pezaros
School of Computing Science
University of Glasgow
dp@dcs.gla.ac.uk

ABSTRACT

Little performance data currently exists for streaming high-quality Internet video to residential users. Data on streaming performance will provide valuable input to the design of new protocols and applications, such as congestion control and error-correction schemes, and sizing playout buffers in video receivers. This paper presents measurements of streaming real-time UDP traffic to a number of residential users, and discusses the basic characteristics of the data.

Categories and Subject Descriptors

C.2.3 [**Computer Communication Networks**]: Network Operations; C.4 [**Performance of Systems**]: Measurement Techniques

General Terms

Experimentation, Measurement

Keywords

Internet Measurement, Streaming Video, DSL, Cable

1. INTRODUCTION

Streaming video now comprises a significant fraction of Internet traffic [6]. Modern Internet streaming video systems are generally built using either ISP-managed intradomain UDP/IP multicast, or unmanaged interdomain HTTP streaming. Interdomain UDP streaming can potentially offer improved performance compared to HTTP streaming, since it doesn't have to fight TCP dynamics, however traversal of CPE NAT devices has limited its deployability. With the recent publication of ICE [9], NAT traversal has become more manageable and so we revisit the issue of interdomain UDP streaming performance.

In this paper, we present data showing packet level characteristics of synthetic end-to-end UDP traffic transmitted over the open Internet from a well-connected server to residential hosts connected via a number of ISPs, using both

ADSL and cable modem connections, in the UK and Finland. We provide an initial summary of the data, highlighting some of the differences between access technologies and ISPs, and due to sending rates and time of day. We further report on TTL-limited probes used to capture hop-by-hop performance characteristics, and on packet-pair capacity estimates of the paths. The data and scripts can be downloaded at http://csperkins.org/research/adaptive-iptv/.

These measurements provide insight into the performance of multimedia streaming from the perspective of the home user, and by using TTL-limited probing, we also expose details of the network-internal performance. This insight into the loss and delay characteristics may inform the design of new error-correction schemes and receiver playout buffers.

The remainder of this paper is structured as follows. We outline experimental rationale and methodology in §2 and §3. The format of the data is described in §4. Initial analysis and summary statistics are presented in §5 and §6. We conclude with a discussion of results and related work.

2. RATIONALE

Over-the-top (interdomain) streaming video services generally use HTTP. As a result, they suffer from high latency, due to buffering to compensate for TCP dynamics disrupting packet timing. To achieve low-latency at high quality and data rates, traffic will need to move to non-TCP transport. Accordingly, we study UDP-based interdomain streaming.

We use an active measurement approach, using synthetic RTP traffic [10] running over UDP/IP. This gives us precise control of packet size and timing, allowing us to generate traffic patterns that match commonly used video formats (standard- and high-definition MPEG-2).

We have chosen to implement our measurements using a dedicated platform that can be deployed into residential networks. This platform is built using Soekris net5501 single-board computers running FreeBSD 7 with a custom measurement application. These devices are low-power, easily transported, and can be connected to a home network with zero configuration, providing an environment with known timing behaviour and alleviating the vagaries in performance of home computers administered by unskilled users.

We focus primarily on end-to-end performance, since this is what applications experience, and what drives user perception of the video quality. We also conduct limited hop-by-hop probing, using low-rate TTL-limited packets to solicit ICMP responses from intermediate routers, to attempt to give some insight into the location of loss events, and how timing disruptions evolve across a network path.

Dates 2009	Link	Rate Mb/s	Time				Len mins
06/27- 07/18	adsl1 8Mb/s	1	Hourly at :50				1
		2	03:15	10:15	15:15	20:15	10
		4	05:15	12:15	17:15	22:15	10
		6	05:35	12:35	17:35	22:35	10
07/07- 07/13	adsl2 2Mb/s	1	Hourly at :30				1
		2	04:15	11:15	16:15	21:15	10
06/27- 07/04	cable1 2Mb/s	1	Hourly at :30				1
		2	04:15	11:15	16:15	21:15	10
07/16- 07/22	cable2 10Mb/s	1	Hourly at :05				1
		2	04:10	11:10	16:10	21:10	5
		4	04:20	11:20	16:20	21:20	5
		6	04:30	11:30	16:30	21:30	5
		8.5	04:40	11:40	16:40	21:40	5
09/12- 09/18	adsl1 8Mb/s	1	Hourly at :50				1
		2	03:12	10:12	15:12	20:12	5
		4	03:20	10:20	15:20	20:20	5
		6	03:32	10:32	15:32	20:32	5
09/12- 09/18	adsl3 2Mb/s	1	Hourly at :05				1
		2	04:12	11:12	16:12	21:12	5
09/22- 09/28	adsl4 8Mb/s	1	Hourly at :05				1
		2	04:12	11:12	16:12	21:12	5
		4	04:20	11:20	16:20	21:20	5
		6	04:32	11:32	16:32	21:32	5
10/07- 10/13	adsl5 24Mb/s	1	Hourly at :50				1
		2	03:12	10:12	15:12	20:12	5
		4	03:20	10:20	15:20	20:20	5
		6	03:32	10:32	15:32	20:32	5
10/07- 10/13	adsl6 8Mb/s	1	Hourly at :05				1
		2	04:12	11:12	16:12	21:12	5
		4	04:20	11:20	16:20	21:20	5
		6	04:32	11:32	16:32	21:32	5

Table 1: Measurement schedule: *dset-A*

Dates 2010	Link	Rate Mb/s	Time	Len mins
04/25- 05/01	adsl5 24Mb/s	1	2,5,8,11AM/PM at :22	4
		2	2,5,8,11AM/PM at :28	4
		5	2,5,8,11AM/PM at :34	4
	adsl6 8Mb/s	1	2,5,8,11AM/PM at :40	4
		2	2,5,8,11AM/PM at :46	4
		5	2,5,8,11AM/PM at :52	4
05/13- 05/19	finadsl0 8Mb/s	1	2,5,8,11AM/PM at :04	4
		2	2,5,8,11AM/PM at :10	4
		5	2,5,8,11AM/PM at :16	4
	cable2 10Mb/s	1	2,5,8,11AM/PM at :22	4
		2	2,5,8,11AM/PM at :28	4
		5	2,5,8,11AM/PM at :34	4
05/25- 05/31	cable3 20Mb/s	1	2,5,8,11AM/PM at :22	4
		2	2,5,8,11AM/PM at :28	4
		5	2,5,8,11AM/PM at :34	4
06/12- 06/18	fincable0 5Mb/s	1	2,5,8,11AM/PM at :04	4
		2	2,5,8,11AM/PM at :10	4
		5	2,5,8,11AM/PM at :16	4
	cable4 20Mb/s	1	2,5,8,11AM/PM at :22	4
		2	2,5,8,11AM/PM at :28	4
		5	2,5,8,11AM/PM at :34	4
	cable5 20Mb/s	1	2,5,8,11AM/PM at :40	4
		2	2,5,8,11AM/PM at :46	4
		5	2,5,8,11AM/PM at :52	4
08/01- 08/07	adsl4 8Mb/s	1	2,5,8,11AM/PM at :22	4
		2	2,5,8,11AM/PM at :28	4
		5	2,5,8,11AM/PM at :34	4
08/28- 09/04	adsl7 8Mb/s	1	2,5,8,11AM/PM at :22	4
		2	2,5,8,11AM/PM at :28	4
		5	2,5,8,11AM/PM at :34	4

Table 2: Measurement schedule: *dset-B*

Rate (Mb/s)	1	2	4	5	6	8.5
Size (bytes)	1316	1316	1128	1316	752	1128
Spacing (ms)	10	5	2	2	1	1

Table 3: Sending rates, packet sizes and spacings

Finally, we implement one-way packet-pair probing to estimate the available capacity of the network path. Packet pair has well-known limitations [2], but because of its ease of implementation, it has been widely deployed in some commercial streaming systems. We explore the accuracy of its results on paths where we know the edge link capacity.

3. METHODOLOGY

We describe two datasets, collected between July 2009 and September 2010. The same general methodology was used for each, although specific details evolved over time. Tables 1 and 2 show the residential links hosting receivers, the rates measured, trace schedules, and durations. Link *adsl5* is the same physical link as *adsl1*, but was upgraded by the ISP during the course of the study; the others are distinct links. The server is a well-connected machine at our university.

Measurement traffic is constant bit rate RTP/UDP flows where the RTP sequence number and logical timestamp are augmented with accurate transmission timestamps. Transmission and reception times are logged at the receiver for later analysis. Sender and receiver clocks are synchronised using NTP, allowing us to measure one-way delay variation, but not accurate one-way delay, as discussed in Section 5.

Most of the volunteers hosting our measurement devices have monthly-limited or time-of-day-capped bandwidth usage quotas imposed by their ISPs. Extreme connection throttling (to a few kb/s) and excess use fees are possible on exceeding the quota. While we did not consider this in *dset-A*, in *dset-B* we limited the bandwidth consumption of our traces to around 2GB per day for each link, a value that avoids exceeding our volunteers' quotas. Given the video rates we wish to simulate, the total bandwidth consumed per day B_{day} may be calculated as $B_{day} = N \times L \times (B_{1Mb/s} + B_{2Mb/s} + B_{5Mb/s})$, where N is the number of traces per rate per day, and L is trace length.

To give a snapshot of activity at each time, and allow us to capture the variation over different times of day, N was chosen to be 8; this allows L to be as long as 240 seconds. The eight traces per-day capture enough of the diurnal variation seen in the short, hourly traces used previously, and their increased length gives better insight into packet delay distributions. However, we note that even longer traces may also be useful, allowing in-depth time-series analysis of the characteristics within a trace; at the time of writing, such measurements are also being conducted.

Both datasets used a range of transmission rates, chosen

to be representative of both standard-definition and high-definition content. Due to limited scheduling granularity in the measurement system, different packet sizes were required to achieve certain transmission rates (see Table 3). In *dset-A* we used rates chosen to cover the full bandwidth of the links; *dset-B* used a more limited set of rates, matching common MPEG-2 TS packetization rates, that were achievable with fixed packet size. This gives less coverage of the extremes of link capacity, but removes the influence of packet size. Similarly, trace lengths are also standardised in *dset-B*.

TTL-limited hop-by-hop probes and packet pair measurements were taken as part of *dset-B*; *dset-A* is end-to-end only. Logs of which packets were sent with reduced TTL were kept by the sender, along with records of the timing of the corresponding ICMP responses. The TTL-limited packets are sent at a rate of once per second to each of the responsive routers on the path (determined by probing each of the routers on the path before starting the measurement). This low rate was chosen to avoid overloading routers, and to ensure that only one ICMP response was outstanding at any time, to ease matching of response to probe.

The packet-pairs are sent every ten seconds, by generating two packets back-to-back, then leaving a gap of twice the usual interval before the next packet to maintain the average sending rate. The server logs the times both packets were sent, as well as the logical RTP timestamps of each of the packets; these are combined with the arrival timestamps to estimate the path capacity [2].

4. TRACE FORMATS

The datasets are arranged hierarchically, with a directory for each link, and within these, a directory for each rate. The log files are found within these "rate" directories. Reception log files are named according to the time at which they were captured (e.g., `20100501-0222.log` was captured on May 1st 2010, at 02:22am). For each trace, another file shows the anonymised output of a traceroute from the receiver to the sender, taken at the end of the trace. These are named according to the time of capture, with suffix `.rs.traceroute` (e.g., `20100501-0222.rs.traceroute`).

In *dset-B*, the sender also generates log files, named similarly based on the start time of the trace. The file extension represents the type of file (either `.path`, `.pathprobes`, `.packetpairs`, or `.icmp`). Additionally, *dset-B* includes traceroutes from sender to receiver, stored with file extension `.sr.traceroute`.

The format of the packet trace files captured at the receiver and present in both datasets is shown in Figure 1. Each line begins with the capture timestamp (all timestamps measure seconds since 1970). The first line is a header line. The following (`rtp ...`) lines report capture of each RTP packet, giving the decimal values of the RTP header fields [10] with a 1MHz RTP timestamp clock. The `sender_ts` fields is the transmission time inserted by the sender.

Figure 2 shows the format of the additional trace files present in *dset-B* relating to packet-pair and hop-by-hop probing. In particular:

- Before the start of the trace, the sender sends five RTP packets to each hop in turn, checking for multiple IPs per hop, logging the IP addresses of the responses, and timing out if no response is received after one second. Files with the `.path` extension show this mapping from

TTLs to (anonymised) router IP addresses; this is used to match the received ICMP messages to the correct TTL-limited packets, as discussed in Section 5.2.

- Files with the `.icmp` extension contain a line for each of the ICMP messages received by the sender within the trace. The 3rd field shows the receive timestamp (seconds since 1970). The 5th field shows the anonymised address of the router that generated the ICMP packet.

- Files with the `.pathprobes` extension contain a line for each of the TTL-limited packets sent within the trace. The 3rd field shows the timestamp (seconds since 1970) just before the TTL-limited packet was sent. The 5th field shows the RTP timestamp ([10], Section 5.1). The 7th field shows the TTL with which the packet was sent. When processing the receiver log file, this log file is consulted to make sure the TTL-limited packets (which stop at the designated router rather than reaching the receiver) are not counted as lost. It is also processed to calculate per-hop loss rates and round-trip times for TTL-limited probes.

- Files with the `.packetpairs` extension contain a line for each of the packet-pairs sent within the trace. The 3rd and 5th fields show the sender and RTP timestamps of the first packet in the pair, and the 7th and 9th fields show the sender and RTP timestamps of the second packet in the pair.

To anonymise the trace files, we process them through a script which replaces IP addresses and hostnames with a token; these have been selected to distinguish, but not identify, the ISPs. The home routers have been named according to the link ID to which they correspond.

5. POST-PROCESSING

This section describes some of the post-processing applied to the traces to extract metrics of interest, including how clock skew is removed from the traces, how one-way delay is calculated, how the logs of TTL-limited packets and received ICMP messages are processed to produce round-trip times, and how the packet-pair measurements are used to estimate capacity. The processed data discussed in this section are also available in the dataset; each of the following sections describe the processing and file formats used. Figure 3 shows an example of these output files.

5.1 Skew Removal / One-way Delay

Conceptually, one-way delay is obtained by simply subtracting send timestamp from receive timestamp; this approach assumes that both clocks are running at the same constant rate, and have zero relative offset. In reality, these assumptions are typically not true, and therefore some external clock synchronisation mechanism is required (as considered in [1]). Although our clients and server are synchronised using NTP, their clocks are still subject to an unknown relative offset β (the difference between the values of the clocks), and relative skew α (the ratio of the rates of the clocks).

End-to-end delays are made up of propagation (fixed), serialisation and queueing (variable) components. The true end-to-end delay of a packet i, d_i (which includes all three components), is the difference between the sender and receiver timestamps (t_i^s and t_i^r) calculated with perfect knowledge of the relative clock offset and skew between sender and

```
dataset-B/adsl5/cbr1.0/20100501-0222.log:
  1272676920.206448 (airmtrecv (version 4.0.1) (build r1000))
  1272676921.297392 (rtp (v 2) (p 0) (x 1) (cc 0) (m 0) (pt 1 unknown) (seq 44954) (ts 0) (ssrc 475832294) (sender_ts 1272676921.276892))
  1272676921.307410 (rtp (v 2) (p 0) (x 1) (cc 0) (m 0) (pt 1 unknown) (seq 44955) (ts 10000) (ssrc 475832294) (sender_ts 1272676921.287114)
  ...
```

Figure 1: Format of Receiver Trace Files

```
dataset-B/adsl5/cbr1.0/20100501-0222.path:
  Hop  1 :   glasgowuni-3    glasgowuni-3    glasgowuni-3    glasgowuni-3    glasgowuni-3
  Hop  2 :   glasgowuni-4    glasgowuni-4    glasgowuni-4    glasgowuni-4    glasgowuni-4
  ...

dataset-B/adsl5/cbr1.0/20100501-0222.icmp:
  icmp  recv_ts 1272676921.340018 icmp_src glasgowuni-3
  icmp  recv_ts 1272676921.408699 icmp_src glasgowuni-4
  ...

dataset-B/adsl5/cbr1.0/20100501-0222.pathprobes:
  pathprobe   send_ts 1272676921.337370 rtp_ts  60000 ttl 1
  pathprobe   send_ts 1272676921.407785 rtp_ts 130000 ttl 2
  ...

dataset-B/adsl5/cbr1.0/20100501-0222.packetpairs:
  packetpair  send_ts1 1272676932.024460 rtp_ts1 10690000 send_ts2 1272676932.024508 rtp_ts2 10700000
  packetpair  send_ts1 1272676942.783357 rtp_ts1 21390000 send_ts2 1272676942.783403 rtp_ts2 21400000
  ...
```

Figure 2: Format of Sender Trace Files (*dset-B* only)

receiver. However, since we have only the measured timestamps $\tilde{t}_i^r$ and $\tilde{t}_i^s$ and don't know the offset or skew, we must use the *measured* end-to-end delay $\tilde{d}_i$.

This $\tilde{d}_i$ is subject to the relative offset (β) and skew (α) between receiver and sender clocks. Since α and β are unknown, they need to estimated from the data; to do this, we followed the approach proposed by Moon *et al.* [8] and implemented by Kohno *et al.* [5], using a linear programming technique to generate estimates for the clock skew and offset, $\hat{\alpha}$ and $\hat{\beta}$. Using these estimates, we were able to correct for skew as shown in (1), producing the *corrected* end-to-end delay $\hat{d}_i$ as an approximation of d_i:

$$\hat{d}_i = \tilde{d}_i - (\hat{\alpha} - 1)\tilde{t}_i^s + \hat{\beta} \tag{1}$$

Assuming the minimum observed delay $\hat{d}_{min}$ corresponds to a packet which experienced minimal queueing delays at the routers along the path, the variation of other packets above $\hat{d}_{min}$ can be seen as a measure of the extent of queueing these packets experienced. We therefore subtract $\hat{d}_{min}$ from the other $\hat{d}_i$ values to approximate queueing delay:

$$DQ_i = \hat{d}_i - \hat{d}_{min} \tag{2}$$

The output of this process is logged in files with the .qdelay extension, as shown in Figure 3. The first shows the relative arrival time (in seconds, since the start of the trace); the second shows DQ_i, calculated as described in (2).

5.2 Matching ICMP Responses

The timestamp and target hop of each TTL-limited probe are obtained from the .pathprobes file. The timestamp of each received ICMP message is obtained from the .icmp file, and the .path file is consulted to identify the hop number of the sending router. Using these, each probe is matched to its ICMP response by checking the timestamps of messages received from the router being probed. Since the probes are spaced at 1 second intervals (larger than the highest observed RTT), the ICMP message following a probe is counted as its response, and the RTT is calculated from the send and receive timestamps. We identify losses when a sent probe is not followed by an ICMP response.

The output of this process is logged in files with the .pathprobe_rtt extension, as shown in Figure 3. Each line in

```
dataset-B-proc/adsl4/cbr1/20100801-0222.qdelay:
  0.009468 0.00241679
  0.021026 0.00401279
  ...

dataset-B-proc/adsl4/cbr1/20100801-0222.pathprobe_rtt
  1 1280625722.579040 1280625722.580453 0.00141287
  1 1280625723.704560 1280625723.708295 0.00373507
  ...

dataset-B-proc/adsl4/cbr1/20100801-0222.packetpair_dispersion:
  10.747899 0.001209 0.000040 8.303
  21.496965 0.000985 0.000044 10.192
  ...
```

Figure 3: Format of Processed Trace Files

this file represents a sent probe and ICMP response. The 1st field shows the hop number, and the 2nd and 3rd fields show the send and receive timestamps, respectively. The 4th field contains the RTT for this probe.

5.3 Calculating Capacity with Packet-Pairs

As described in [2], the estimate of capacity is obtained by dividing packet size (in this case, 1316 bytes) by the arrival dispersion between the packets in the pair.

The output of this processing is contained in files with the .packetpair_dispersion extension, as shown in Figure 3. The 1st field shows the arrival time of the second packet in the pair (in seconds since the start of the trace). The 2nd and 3rd fields show the dispersion in seconds between the arrival and departure times, respectively. The 4th field shows the capacity estimate from this pair, in Mb/s.

6. STATISTICS

During the measurement campaign, over 230×10^6 packets were received in roughly 3800 traces while a very low fraction of packets were dropped (0.39%). Reordering was rare, with only 243 packets arriving out of sequence. Our traceroute and ICMP logs indicate the paths we measure are stable, with very few route changes over the measurement period. The following sections describe some of the basic statistics in more detail, including end-to-end packet loss and queueing delay, followed by an analysis of packet-pair and intermediate path measurements.

6.1 End-to-End Packet Loss

Packet loss rates over the traces are typically very low, with many of the traces showing no loss at all. Some vari-

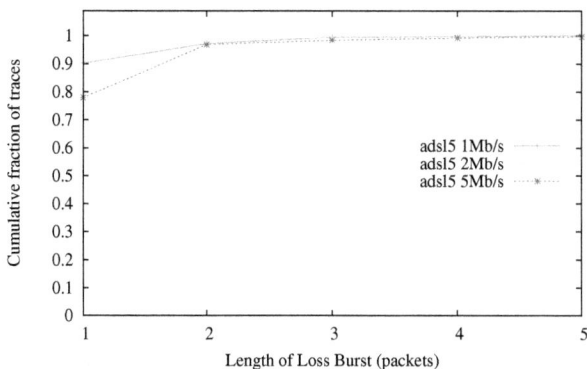

Figure 4: Cumulative Distribution of Loss Bursts (from *dset-B*, link *adsl5*)

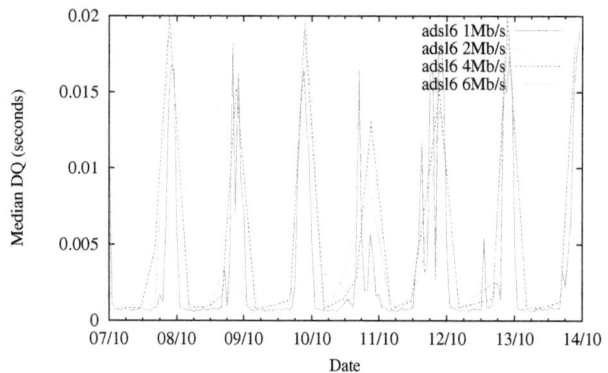

Figure 6: Example of Diurnal Variation in Median Queueing Delay (from *dset-A*, link *adsl6*)

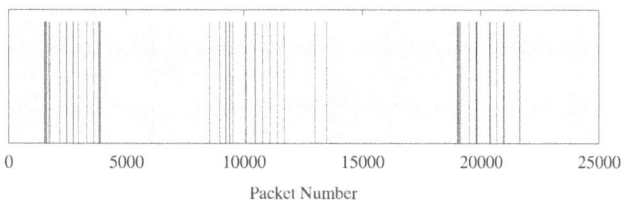

Figure 5: Example of Clustering in Loss Bursts (from *dset-B*, link *adsl5*, 2Mb/s, 2010/04/26, 08:28)

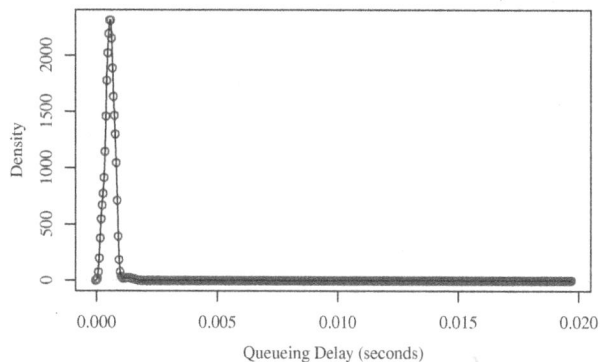

Figure 7: Example of Queueing Delay Distribution (from *dset-A*, link *adsl4*, 4Mb/s, 2009/09/28, 21:20)

ation is present over times of day, albeit the loss rates are low enough that there is not an obvious trend.

Loss burstiness (i.e., whether they occur closely together in time or randomly spaced out) is more interesting. Figure 4 shows the cumulative distribution of loss burst lengths for *adsl5* (other links are similar). From the CDF, it appears that most bursts consist of a single packet; however, closer inspection reveals that these short loss bursts are clustered together in time. Figure 5 demonstrates the clustering in loss bursts for one trace.

These results show that while overall loss rates are low, the bursty nature of the loss (with groups of bursts clustered together) means that sophisticated error correction and recovery mechanisms may be needed for Internet video systems across these networks.

6.2 End-to-End Queueing Delay

The queueing delay experienced by packets across the dataset varies greatly, between times of day, and between links (with different ISPs showing different behaviours).

Figure 6 shows an example of diurnal variation in queueing delay; half of the links measured (both ADSL and Cable) show this type of behaviour, while the other half show more consistent behaviour over time.

As shown in Figure 7 the queueing delay values tend to cluster around a single mode, with a long right tail (representing large-valued outliers). While only a small proportion of packets show these large delays, their impact may be large since they can disrupt the decoding process.

Previous work [7] found evidence of *heavy-tailed* behaviour in delay on dial-up links, indicating that the values in the tail of the distribution may be extremely large. In order to investigate whether similar behaviour is present for ADSL and Cable links, our ongoing work focuses on tail index estimation and classification.

6.3 Intermediate Path RTTs

Across the traces, the RTT values produced by each router have a similar clustering; however, there are outliers present, consistent with the right-skewed distribution seen for end-to-end queueing delay. For example, in Figure 8, the distribution of the RTTs can be seen in the boxplot for each hop; routers 7-10 show a significant number of large values. Since the large values are present on these routers, but not on subsequent ones, the variation may be due to the ICMP processing delay. Ongoing work is seeking to determine the effect of each of these components. Using a combined approach, examining these per-hop delay distributions alongside the end-to-end distributions, we hope to model the behaviour of the various parts of the network, and determine the effect of the various parts of the end-to-end path (e.g., core vs. edge networks) on the delay experienced by the receiver.

6.4 Packet-pair Capacity Estimation

Initial investigation of the capacity estimates from the packet-pairs show an interesting difference between ADSL and Cable. Figure 9 shows the distributions of capacity estimates obtained from *adsl6* and *cable2* (each are representative of the other ADSL/Cable links). The ADSL estimate is bimodal (between 10-20Mb/s); this seems consistent with the rated capacity for this link. However, the Cable estimate (around 50Mb/s) is much higher than the speed provided by the ISP (10Mb/s), instead matching the highest rate offered by this Cable ISP. Since Cable uses a time-shared downstream channel, we believe that the estimates of 50Mb/s are

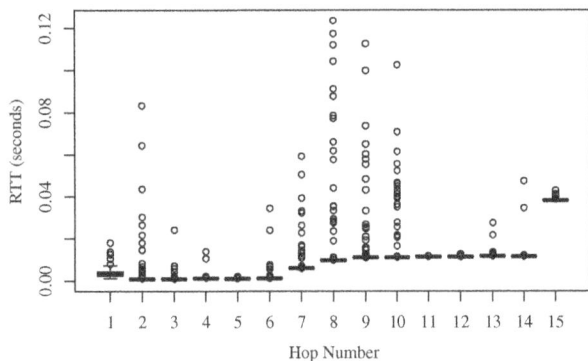

Figure 8: Example of End-to-Middle RTTs
(from *dset-B*, link *adsl5*, 1Mb/s, 2010/05/01, 14:22)

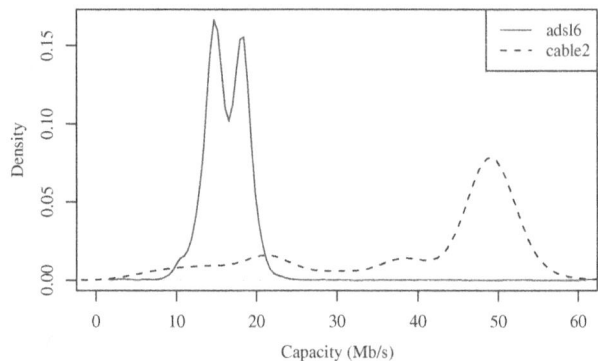

Figure 9: Capacity Estimate Distribution
(from *dset-B*, links *adsl6*, *cable2*)

due to both packets in the pair passing through in a single time slice. Further investigation supports this conjecture; using longer trains of packets, we were able to force a pair to be split across a time-slice, producing a lower capacity estimate. Although this technique fails to accurately measure capacity for the Cable links, it might instead be used for link-type classification.

7. RELATED WORK

Prior work has focused on studying peer-to-peer TV [3], backbone performance of IPTV traffic [4], UDP streaming over dial-up links [7] or TCP streaming to broadband users [12]. However, only the data from [4] is publicly available. We publish our measurements of UDP streaming over ADSL and Cable networks, applying similar analyses as [7].

8. DISCUSSION AND CONCLUSIONS

We have presented a dataset of containing measurements of UDP-based streaming to residential Internet users, looking at the loss, reordering, and delay characteristics of these streams. We have also presented intermediate path measurements that aim to correlate end-to-end behaviour and packet-pairs to estimate the capacity of the path.

The clustered bursty loss behaviour we have seen means that simple error correction techniques (such as parity FEC) will be insufficient to mask packet losses: Using retransmissions or more complex FEC techniques will therefore be required to provide acceptable video quality. The queueing delay behaviour we see provides insight into the design of receiver playout buffers for streaming video systems. The distribution of delay does not show tight bounds on the range of expected delays, implying that buffers cannot be optimised in this way. Instead, the receivers will need to cope with occasional highly delayed packets, possibly requiring larger playout buffers.

The differences observed in capacity estimation between packet-pair measurements on ADSL and Cable links pose an interesting question for further work; namely, whether receivers can determine their access type from the incoming video stream (compared with [11], which uses upstream characteristics to distinguish Cable links). This technique would allow the video sender to adapt the stream for each receiver, tuning for their particular access network type.

Future work will include further analysis of the queueing behaviour experienced by the data traffic, using both end-to-end queueing delay and intermediate path RTT measurements. This will inform the design of new protocols and applications for streaming. Development of a link-type classifier based on dispersion of downstream traffic, and effective capacity estimation for these links will also be useful for Internet video systems.

Acknowledgements

This work was supported by Cisco Research and the UK EPSRC. Thanks to Jörg Ott and Alex Koliousis for helpful suggestions, and to the volunteers for hosting measurements.

9. REFERENCES

[1] L. De Vito et al. One-Way Delay Measurement: State of the Art. *IEEE Trans. Instrum. Meas.*, 57(12), 2008.

[2] C. Dovrolis et al. Packet-Dispersion Techniques and a Capacity-Estimation Methodology. *IEEE/ACM Trans. Networking*, 12(6), 2004.

[3] X. Hei et al. Measurement Study of a Large-Scale P2P IPTV System. *IEEE Trans. Multimedia*, 9(8), 2007.

[4] K. Imran et al. Measurements of Multicast Television over IP. In *Proc. IEEE LANMAN*, 2007.

[5] T. Kohno et al. Remote Physical Device Fingerprinting. *IEEE Trans. Dependable Secure Comput.*, 2(2), 2005.

[6] C. Labovitz et al. Internet Inter-Domain Traffic. In *Proc. ACM SIGCOMM*, 2010.

[7] D. Loguinov and H. Radha. End-to-End Internet Video Traffic Dynamics: Statistical Study and Analysis. In *Proc. IEEE INFOCOM*, 2002.

[8] S. B. Moon et al. Estimation and Removal of Clock Skew from Network Delay Measurements. In *Proc. IEEE INFOCOM*, 1999.

[9] J. Rosenberg. ICE: A Protocol for NAT Traversal for Offer/Answer Protocols. RFC 5245, April 2010.

[10] H. Schulzrinne et al. RTP: A Transport Protocol for Real-Time Applications. RFC 3550, July 2003.

[11] W. Wei et al. Clarification of Access Network Types: Ethernet, Wireless LAN, ADSL, Cable Modem or Dialup? *Computer Networks*, 52(17), 2008.

[12] Y. Won et al. Measurement of Download & Play and Streaming IPTV Traffic. *IEEE Comm.*, 46(10), 2008.

The Stanford Mobile Visual Search Data Set

Vijay Chandrasekhar
Stanford University, CA

David M. Chen
Stanford University, CA

Sam S. Tsai
Stanford University, CA

Ngai-Man Cheung
Stanford University, CA

Huizhong Chen
Stanford University, CA

Gabriel Takacs
Stanford University, CA

Yuriy Reznik
Qualcomm Inc., CA

Ramakrishna Vedantham
Nokia Research Center, CA

Radek Grzeszczuk
Nokia Research Center, CA

Jeff Bach
NAVTEQ, Chicago

Bernd Girod
Stanford University, CA

ABSTRACT

We survey popular data sets used in computer vision literature and point out their limitations for mobile visual search applications. To overcome many of the limitations, we propose the Stanford Mobile Visual Search data set. The data set contains camera-phone images of products, CDs, books, outdoor landmarks, business cards, text documents, museum paintings and video clips. The data set has several key characteristics lacking in existing data sets: rigid objects, widely varying lighting conditions, perspective distortion, foreground and background clutter, realistic ground-truth reference data, and query data collected from heterogeneous low and high-end camera phones. We hope that the data set will help push research forward in the field of mobile visual search.

Categories and Subject Descriptors

C.3 [**Computer Systems Organization**]: Special Purpose and Application Based Systems—*Signal Processing Systems*

General Terms

Algorithms,Design

Keywords

mobile visual search, data sets, CHoG, content-based image retrieval

1. INTRODUCTION

[1] Mobile phones have evolved into powerful image and video processing devices, equipped with high-resolution cameras, color displays, and hardware-accelerated graphics. They

---

[1]Contact Vijay Chandrasekhar at vijayc@stanford.edu.

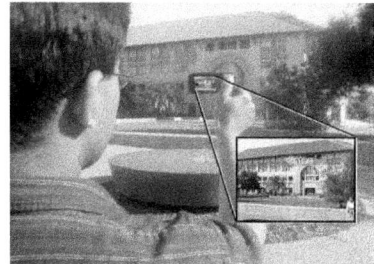

Figure 1: A snapshot of an outdoor visual search application. The system augments the viewfinder with information about the objects it recognizes in the camera phone image.

are also equipped with GPS, and connected to broadband wireless networks. All this enables a new class of applications which use the camera phone to initiate search queries about objects in visual proximity to the user (Fig 1). Such applications can be used, e.g., for identifying products, comparison shopping, finding information about movies, CDs, buildings, shops, real estate, print media or artworks. First commercial deployments of such systems include Google Goggles, Google Shopper [11], Nokia Point and Find [21], Kooaba [15], Ricoh iCandy [7] and Amazon Snaptell [1].

Mobile visual search applications pose a number of unique challenges. First, the system latency has to be low to support interactive queries, despite stringent bandwidth and computational constraints. One way to reduce system latency significantly is to carry out feature extraction on the mobile device, and transmit compressed feature data across the network [10]. State-of-the-art retrieval systems [14, 22] typically extract 2000-3000 affine-covariant features (Maximally Stable Extremal Regions (MSER), Hessian Affine points) from the query image. This might take several seconds on the mobile device. For feature extraction on the device to be effective, we need fast and robust interest point detection algorithms and compact descriptors. There is growing industry interest in this area, with MPEG recently launching a standardization effort [18]. It is envisioned that the standard will specify bitstream syntax of descriptors, and parts of the descriptor-extraction process needed to ensure interoperability.

Next, camera phone images tend to be of lower quality compared to digital camera images. Images that are degraded by motion blur or poor focus pose difficulties for visual recognition. However, image quality is rapidly improving with higher resolution, better optics and built-in flashes on camera phones.

Outdoor applications pose additional challenges. Current retrieval systems work best for highly textured rigid planar objects taken under controlled lighting conditions. Landmarks, on the other hand, tend to have fewer features, exhibit repetitive structures and their 3-D geometric distortions are not captured by simple affine or projective transformations. Ground truth data collection is more difficult, too. There are different ways of bootstrapping databases for outdoor applications. One approach is to mine data from online collections like Flickr. However, these images tend to be poorly labelled, and include a lot of clutter. Another approach is to harness data collected by companies like Navteq, Google (StreetView) or Earthmine. In this case, the data are acquired by vehicle-mounted powerful cameras with wide-angle lenses to capture spherical panoramic images. In both cases, visual recognition is challenging because the camera phone query images are usually taken under very different lighting conditions compared to reference database images. Buildings and their surroundings (e.g., trees) tend to look different in different seasons. Shadows, pedestrians and foreground clutter are some of the other challenges in this application domain.

OCR on mobile phones enables another dimension of applications, from text input to text-based queries to a database. OCR engines work well on high quality scanned images. However, the performance of mobile OCR drops rapidly for images that are out of focus and blurry, have perspective distortion or non-ideal lighting conditions.

To improve performance of mobile visual search applications, we need good data sets that capture the most common problems that we encounter in this domain. A good data set for visual search applications should have the following characteristics:

- Should have good ground truth reference images
- Should have query images with a wide range of camera phones (flash/no-flash, auto-focus/no auto-focus)
- Should be collected under widely varying lighting conditions
- Should capture typical perspective distortions, motion blur, foreground and background clutter common to mobile visual search applications.
- Should represent different categories (e.g., buildings, books, CDs, DVDs, text documents, products)
- Should contain rigid objects so that a transformation can be estimated between the query and reference database image.

We surveyed popular data sets in the computer vision literature, and observed that they were all limited in different ways. To overcome many of the limitations in existing data sets, we propose the Stanford Mobile Visual Search (SMVS) data set that we hope will help move research forward in this field. In Section 2, we survey popular computer vision data sets, and point out their limitations. In Section 3, we propose the SMVS data set for different mobile visual search applications.

2. SURVEY OF DATA SETS

Popular computer vision data sets for evaluating image retrieval algorithms consist of a set of query images and their ground truth reference images. The number of query images typically range from a few hundred to a few thousand. The scalability of the retrieval methods is tested by retrieving the query images in the presence of "distractor" images, or images that do not belong to the data set [14, 22]. The "distractor" images are typically obtained by mining Flickr or other photo sharing websites. Here, we survey popular data sets in computer vision literature and discuss their limitations for our application. See Fig. 2 for examples from each data set, and Tab. 1 for a summary of the different data sets.

ZuBuD.

The Zurich Building (ZuBuD) dataset [12] consists of 201 buildings in Zurich, with 5 views of each building. There are 115 query images which are not contained in the database. Query and database images differ in viewpoint, but variations in illumination are rare because the different images for the same building are taken at the same time of day. The ZuBuD is considered an easy data set, with close to 100% accuracy being reported in several papers [13, 24]. Simple approaches like color histograms and descriptors based on DCT [24] yield high performance for this dataset.

Oxford Buildings.

The Oxford Buildings Datset [22] consists of 5062 images collected from Flickr by searching for particular Oxford landmarks. The collection has been manually annotated to generate a comprehensive ground truth for 11 different landmarks, each represented by 5 possible queries. This gives only a small set of 55 queries. Another problem with this data set is that completely different views of the same building are labelled by the same name. Ideally, different facades of each building should be distinguished from each other, when evaluating retrieval performance.

INRIA Holidays.

The INRIA Holidays dataset [14] is a set of images which contains personal holiday photos of the authors in [14]. The dataset includes a large variety of outdoor scene types (natural, man-made, water and fire effects). The dataset contains 500 image groups, each of which represents a distinct scene or object. The data set contains perspective distortions and clutter. However, variations in lighting are rare as the pictures are taken at the same time from each location. Also, the data set contains scenes of many non-rigid objects (fire, beaches, etc), which will not produce repeatable features, if images are taken at different times.

University of Kentucky.

The University of Kentucky (UKY) [20] consists of 2550 groups of 4 images each of objects like CD-covers, lamps, keyboards and computer equipment. Similar to ZuBuD and INRIA data sets, this data set also offers little variation in lighting conditions. Further, there is no foreground or background clutter with only the object of interest present in each image.

Image Net.

The ImageNet dataset [6] consists of images organized by nouns in the WordNet hierarchy [8]. Each node of the hierarchy is depicted by hundreds and thousands of images. E.g.,

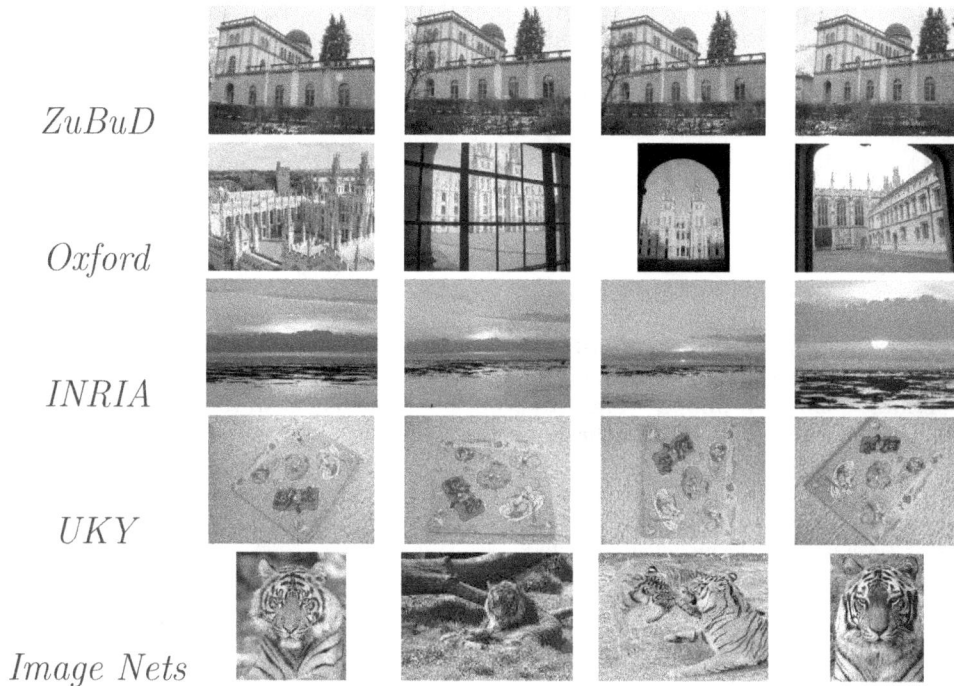

Figure 2: Limitations with popular data sets in computer vision. The left most image in each row is the database image, and the other 3 images are query images. ZuBuD, INRIA and UKY consist of images taken at the same time and location. ImageNets is not suitable for image retrieval applications. The Oxford dataset has different faades of the same building labelled with the same name.

Fig. 2 illustrates some images for the word "tiger". Such a data set is useful for testing classification algorithms, but not so much for testing retrieval algorithms.

We summarize the limitations of the different data sets in Tab. 1. To overcome the limitations in these data sets, we propose the Stanford Mobile Visual Search (SMVS) data set.

3. STANFORD MOBILE VISUAL SEARCH DATA SET

We present the SMVS (version 0.9) data set in the hope that it will be useful for a wide range of visual search applications like product recognition, landmark recognition, outdoor augmented reality [26], business card recognition, text recognition, video recognition and TV-on-the-go [5]. We collect data for several different categories: CDs, DVDs, books, software products, landmarks, business cards, text documents, museum paintings and video clips. Sample query and database images are shown in Figure 4. Current and subsequent versions of the dataset will be available at [3].

The number of database and query images for different categories is shown in Tab. 2. We provide a total 3300 query images for 1200 distinct classes across 8 image categories. Typically, a small number of query images ($\sim$1000s) suffice to measure the performance of a retrieval system as the rest of the database can be padded with "distractor" images. Ideally, we would like to have a large distractor set for each query category. However, it is challenging to collect distractor sets for each category. Instead, we plan to release two distractor sets upon request: one containing Flickr images, and the other containing building images from Navteq. The distractor sets will be available in sets of 1K, 10K, 100K and 1M. Researchers can test scalability using these distractor data sets, or the ones provided in [22, 14]. Next, we discuss how the query and reference database images are collected, and evaluation measures that are in particular relevant for mobile applications.

Reference Database Images.

For product categories (CDs, DVDs and books), the references are clean versions of images obtained from the product websites. For landmarks, the reference images are obtained from data collected by Navteq's vehicle-mounted cameras. For video clips, the reference images are the key frame from the reference video clips. The videos contain diverse content like movie trailers, news reports, and sports. For text documents, we collect (1) reference images from [19], a website that mines the front pages of newspapers from around the world, and (2) research papers. For business cards, the reference image is obtained from a high quality upright scan of the card. For museum paintings, we collect data from the Cantor Arts Center at Stanford University for different genres: history, portraits, landscapes and modern-art. The reference images are obtained from the artists' websites like [23] or other online sources. All reference images are high quality JPEG compressed color images. The resolution of reference images varies for each category.

Query Images.

We capture query images with several different camera phones, including some digital cameras. The list of companies and models used is as follows: Apple (iPhone4), Palm (Pre), Nokia (N95, N97, N900, E63, N5800, N86), Motorola (Droid), Canon (G11) and LG (LG300). For product cate-

Data Set	Database (#)	Query (#)	Classes (#)	Rigid	Lighting	Clutter	Perspective	Camera Phone
ZuBuD	1005	115	200	$\checkmark$	–	$\checkmark$	$\checkmark$	–
Oxford	5062	55	17	$\checkmark$	$\checkmark$	$\checkmark$	$\checkmark$	$\times$
INRIA	1491	500	500	–	–	$\checkmark$	$\checkmark$	–
UKY	10200	2550	2550	$\checkmark$	–	–	$\checkmark$	–
ImageNet	11M	15K	15K	–	$\checkmark$	$\checkmark$	$\checkmark$	–
SMVS	1200	3300	1200	$\checkmark$	$\checkmark$	$\checkmark$	$\checkmark$	$\checkmark$

Table 1: Comparison of different data sets. "Classes" refers to the number of distinct objects in the data set. "Rigid" refers to whether on not the objects in the database are rigid. "Lighting" refers to whether or not the query images capture widely varying lighting conditions. "Clutter" refers to whether or not the query images contain foreground/background clutter. "Perspective" refers to whether the data set contains typical perspective distortions. "Camera-phone" refers to whether the images were captured with mobile devices. SMVS is a good data set for mobile visual search applications.

gories like CDs, DVDs, books, text documents and business cards, we capture the images indoors under widely varying lighting conditions over several days. We include foreground and background clutter that would be typically present in the application, e.g., a picture of a CD would might other CDs in the background. For landmarks, we capture images of buildings in San Francisco. We collected query images several months after the reference data was collected. For video clips, the query images were taken from laptop, computer and TV screens to include typical specular distortions. Finally, the paintings were captured at the Cantor Arts Center at Stanford University under controlled lighting conditions typical of museums.

The resolution of the query images varies for each camera phone. We provide the original JPEG compressed high quality color images obtained from the camera. We also provide auxiliary information like phone model number, and GPS location, where applicable. As noted in Tab. 1, the SMVS query data set has the following key characteristics that is lacking in other data sets: rigid objects, widely varying lighting conditions, perspective distortion, foreground and background clutter, realistic ground-truth reference data, and query images from heterogeneous low and high-end camera phones.

Category	Database	Query
CD	100	400
DVD	100	400
Books	100	400
Video Clips	100	400
Landmarks	500	500
Business Cards	100	400
Text documents	100	400
Paintings	100	400

Table 2: Number of query and database images in the SMVS data set for different categories.

Evaluation measures.

A naive retrieval system would match all database images against each query image. Such a brute-force matching scheme provides as an upper-bound on the performance that can be achieved with the feature matching pipeline. Here, we report results for brute-force pairwise matching for different interest point detectors and descriptors using the ratio-test [16] and RANSAC [9]. For RANSAC, we use

affine models with a minimum threshold of 10 matches post-RANSAC for declaring a pair of images to be a valid match.

In Fig. 3, we report results for 3 state-of-the-art schemes: (1) SIFT Difference-of-Gaussian (DoG) interest point detector and SIFT descriptor (code: [27]), (2) Hessian-affine interest point detector and SIFT descriptor (code [17]), and (3) Fast Hessian blob interest point detector [2] sped up with integral images, and the recently proposed Compressed Histogram of Gradients (CHoG) descriptor [4]. We report the percentage of images that match, the average number of features and the average number of features that match post-RANSAC for each category.

First, we note that indoor categories are easier than outdoor categories. E.g., some categories like CDs, DVDs and book covers achieve over 95% accuracy. The most challenging category is landmarks as the query data is collected several months after the database.

Second, we note that option (1): SIFT interest point detector and descriptor, performs the best. However, option (1) is computationally complex and is not suitable for implementation on mobile devices.

Third, we note that option (3) performs comes close to achieving the performance of (1), with worse performance (10-20% drop) for some categories. The performance hit is incurred due to the fast Hessian-based interest point detector, which is not as robust as the DoG interest point detector. One reason for lower robustness is observed in [25]: the fast box-filtering step causes the interest point detection to lose rotation invariance which affects oriented query images. The CHoG descriptor used in option (3) is a low-bitrate 60-bit descriptor which is shown to perform on par with the 128-dimensional 1024-bit SIFT descriptor using extensive evaluation in [4]. We note that option (3) is most suitable for implementation on mobile devices as the fast hessian interest point detector is an order-of-magnitude faster than SIFT DoG, and the CHoG descriptors generate an order of magnitude less data than SIFT descriptors for efficient transmission [10].

Finally, we list aspects critical for mobile visual search applications. A good image retrieval system should exhibit the follow characteristics when tested on the SMVS dataset.

- High Precision-Recall as size of database increases
- Low retrieval latency

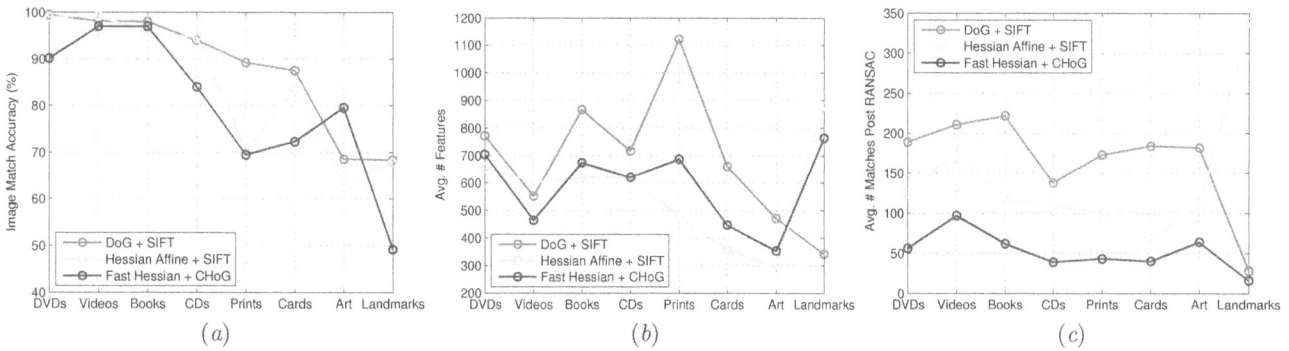

(a) (b) (c)

Figure 3: Results for each category (PR = Post RANSAC). We note that indoor categories like CDs are easier than outdoor categories like landmarks. Books, CD covers, DVD covers and video clips achieve over 95% accuracy.

- Fast pre-processing algorithms for improving image quality
- Fast and robust interest point detection
- Compact feature data for efficient transmission and storage

4. SUMMARY

We survey popular data sets used in computer vision literature and note that they are limited in many ways. We propose the Stanford Mobile Visual Search data set to overcome several of the limitations in existing data sets. The SMVS data set has several key characteristics lacking in existing data sets: rigid objects, several categories of objects, widely varying lighting conditions, perspective distortion, typical foreground and background clutter, realistic ground-truth reference data, and query data collected from heterogeneous low and high-end camera phones. We hope that this data set will help push research forward in the field of mobile visual search.

5. REFERENCES

[1] Amazon. *SnapTell*, 2007. http://www.snaptell.com.
[2] H. Bay, T. Tuytelaars, and L. V. Gool. SURF: Speeded Up Robust Features. In *Proc. of European Conference on Computer Vision (ECCV)*, Graz, Austria, May 2006.
[3] V. Chandrasekhar, D.M.Chen, S.S.Tsai, N.M.Cheung, H.Chen, G.Takacs, Y.Reznik, R.Vedantham, R.Grzeszczuk, J.Back, and B.Girod. *Stanford Mobile Visual Search Data Set*, 2010. http://mars0.stanford.edu/mvs_images/.
[4] V. Chandrasekhar, G. Takacs, D. M. Chen, S. S. Tsai, R. Grzeszczuk, Y. Reznik, and B. Girod. Compressed Histogram of Gradients: A Low Bitrate Descriptor. In *International Journal of Computer Vision, Special Issue on Mobile Vision*, 2010. under review.
[5] D. M. Chen, N. M. Cheung, S. S. Tsai, V. Chandrasekhar, G. Takacs, R. Vedantham, R. Grzeszczuk, and B. Girod. Dynamic Selection of a Feature-Rich Query Frame for Mobile Video Retrieval. In *Proc. of IEEE International Conference on Image Processing (ICIP)*, Hong Kong, September 2010.
[6] J. Deng, W. Dong, R. Socher, L. Li, K. Li, and L. Fei-Fei. Imagenet: A large-scale hierarchical image database. In *Proc. of IEEE Conference on Computer Vision and Pattern Recognition (CVPR)*, Miami, Florida, June 2009.
[7] B. Erol, E. Antúnez, and J. Hull. Hotpaper: multimedia interaction with paper using mobile phones. In *Proc. of the 16th ACM Multimedia Conference*, New York, NY, USA, 2008.
[8] C. Fellbaum. *WordNet: An Electronic Lexical Database*. Bradford Books, 1998.
[9] M. A. Fischler and R. C. Bolles. Random Sample Consensus: A paradigm for model fitting with applications to image analysis and automated cartography. *Communications of ACM*, 24(6):381–395, 1981.
[10] B. Girod, V. Chandrasekhar, D. M. Chen, N. M. Cheung, R. Grzeszczuk, Y. Reznik, G. Takacs, S. S. Tsai, and R. Vedantham. Mobile Visual Search. In *IEEE Signal Processing Magazine, Special Issue on Mobile Media Search*, 2010. under review.
[11] Google. *Google Goggles*, 2009. http://www.google.com/mobile/goggles/.
[12] L. V. G. H.Shao, T. Svoboda. Zubud-Zürich buildings database for image based recognition. Technical Report 260, ETH Zürich, 2003.
[13] S. J. Matas. Sub-linear indexing for large scale object recognition. In *Proc. of British Machine Vision Conference (BMVC)*, Oxford, UK, June 2005.
[14] H. Jegou, M. Douze, and C. Schmid. Hamming embedding and weak geometric consistency for large scale image search. In *Proc. of European Conference on Computer Vision (ECCV)*, Berlin, Heidelberg, 2008.
[15] Kooaba. *Kooaba*, 2007. http://www.kooaba.com.
[16] D. Lowe. Distinctive image features from scale-invariant keypoints. *International Journal of Computer Vision*, 60(2):91–110, 2004.
[17] K. Mikolajczyk. *Software for computing Hessian-affine interest points and SIFT descriptor*, 2010. http://lear.inrialpes.fr/~jegou/data.php.
[18] MPEG. Requirements for compact descriptors for visual search. In *ISO/IEC JTC1/SC29/WG11/W11531*, Geneva, Switzerland, July 2010.
[19] Newseum. *Newseum*. http://www.newseum.org/todaysfrontpages/hr.asp?fpVname=CA_MSS&ref_pge=gal&b_pge=1.
[20] D. Nistér and H. Stewénius. Scalable recognition with a vocabulary tree. In *Proc. of IEEE Conference on Computer Vision and Pattern Recognition (CVPR)*, New York, USA, June 2006.
[21] Nokia. *Nokia Point and Find*, 2006. http://www.pointandfind.nokia.com.
[22] J. Philbin, O. Chum, M. Isard, J. Sivic, and A. Zisserman. Object Retrieval with Large Vocabularies and Fast Spatial Matching. In *Proc. of IEEE Conference on Computer Vision and Pattern Recognition (CVPR)*, Minneapolis, Minnesota, 2007.
[23] W. T. Richards. *William Trot Richards: The Complete Works*. http://www.williamtrostrichards.org/.
[24] J. M. S.Obdrzalek. Image retrieval using local compact dct-based representation. In *Proc. of the 25th DAGM Symposium*, Magdeburg, Germany, September 2003.
[25] G. Takacs, V. Chandrasekhar, H. Chen, D. M. Chen, S. S. Tsai, R. Grzeszczuk, and B. Girod. Permutable Descriptors for Orientation Invariant Matching. In *Proc. of SPIE Workshop on Applications of Digital Image Processing (ADIP)*, San Diego, California, August 2010.
[26] G. Takacs, V. Chandrasekhar, N. Gelfand, Y. Xiong, W. Chen, T. Bismpigiannis, R. Grzeszczuk, K. Pulli, and B. Girod. Outdoors augmented reality on mobile phone using loxel-based visual feature organization. In *Proc. of ACM International Conference on Multimedia Information Retrieval (ACM MIR)*, Vancouver, Canada, October 2008.
[27] A. Vedaldi and B. Fulkerson. VLFeat: An open and portable library of computer vision algorithms, 2008. http://www.vlfeat.org/.

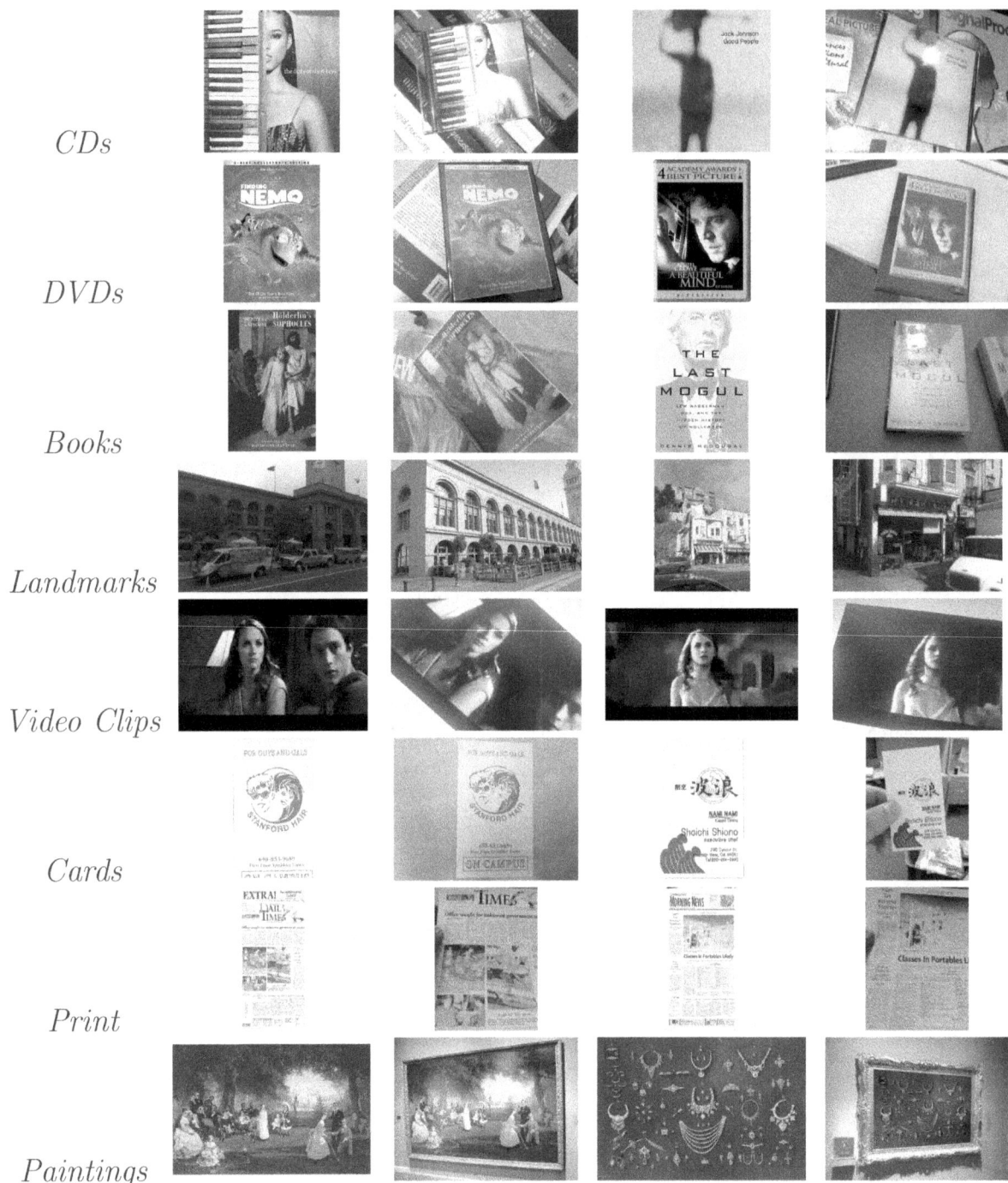

CDs

DVDs

Books

Landmarks

Video Clips

Cards

Print

Paintings

Figure 4: Stanford Mobile Visual Search (SMVS) data set. The data set consists of images for many different categories captured with a variety of camera-phones, and under widely varying lighting conditions. Database and query images alternate in each category.

World of Warcraft Avatar History Dataset

Yeng-Ting Lee
Department of Electrical
Engineering, National Taiwan
University
Taipei, Taiwan
habamhabam@gmail.com

Kuan-Ta Chen
Institute of Information
Science, Academia Sinica
Taipei, Taiwan
swc@iis.sinica.edu.tw

Yun-Maw Cheng
Department of Computer
Science and Engineering,
Tatung University
Taipei, Taiwan
kevin@ttu.edu.tw

Chin-Laung Lei
Department of Electrical
Engineering, National Taiwan
University
Taipei, Taiwan
lei@cc.ee.ntu.edu.tw

ABSTRACT

From the perspective of game system designers, players' behavior is one of the most important factors they must consider when designing game systems. To gain a fundamental understanding of the game play behavior of online gamers, exploring users' game play time provides a good starting point. This is because the concept of game play time is applicable to all genres of games and it enables us to model the system workload as well as the impact of system and network QoS on users' behavior. It can even help us predict players' loyalty to specific games. In this paper, we present the World of Warcraft Avatar History (WoWAH) dataset, which comprises the records of 91,065 avatars. The data includes the avatars' game play times and a number of attributes, such as their race, profession, current level, and in-game locations, during a 1,107-day period between Jan. 2006 and Jan. 2009. We believe the WOWAH dataset could be used for various creative purposes, now that it is a public asset of the research community. It is available for free download at http://mmnet.iis.sinica.edu.tw/dl/wowah/.

Categories and Subject Descriptors

H.1.2 [**Models and Principles**]: User/
Machine Systems—*Human factors*; K.8.0 [**Personal Computing**]: General—*Games*

General Terms

Human Factors, Measurement

Keywords

Game session, MMOG, MMORPG, User behavior

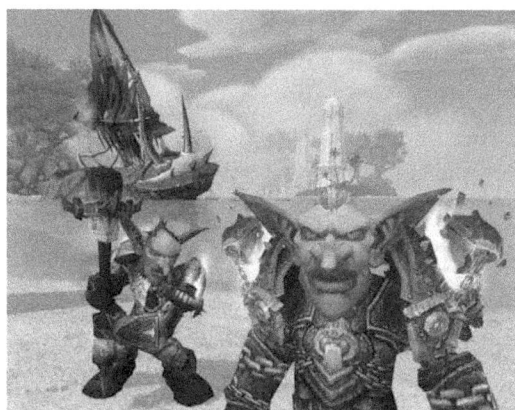

Figure 1: A screenshot of World of Warcraft.

1. INTRODUCTION

Massively multiplayer online games (MMOGs) are a popular type of entertainment on the Internet. In [26], it is reported that over 55% of Internet users are also online gamers, while the number of MMOG subscribers worldwide grew to 21 million in 2010. For the popular game StarCraft II[1], one of the biggest real-time strategy (RTS) titles in 2010, the average number of active players is 500,000 per day; while the number of players listed on the Battle.net scoreboard[2] is around 1.7 million [1].

Among the various types of MMOGs, massively multiplayer online role-playing games (MMORPGs) are the most popular genre, with a 95% share of the MMOG market [22]. According to [25], the MMORPG market is currently worth in excess of US$6 billion worldwide, with an anticipated value of US$8 billion by 2014.

From the perspective of game system designers, players' behavior is one of the most important factors they must consider when designing game systems. However, understanding player behavior is not a trivial task because there are so many types of player behavior to be considered, and the behavior is usually game-dependent. For example, how

---

[1]http://us.battle.net/sc2/en/
[2]http://www.sc2ranks.com/ranks/

players control troop movements in real-time strategies and how players interact with each other (e.g., chatting, trading, or fighting) in role-play games may be important issues in some game genres, but not in others. Moreover, some types of player behavior are more general than others. For example, how players react to imperfect network conditions is a general problem in all real-time network games, so it is a concern for all game designers.

To gain a fundamental understanding of users' online game play behavior, we believe that exploring *users' game play time* provides a good starting point because game play time is the most general type of player behavior; thus, it is applicable to all genres of games. Game play time refers to all the information related to the time between when a player logs into a game and the time he logs out. How can information about game play time benefit the research community? The following list describes some of the uses of such information.

1. **System workload modeling/prediction**: The arrival and departure process of game players determines the workload of game systems [7,9]. Thus, if we could model and even predict game players' arrival and departure events, we could improve the provisioning and allocation of system resources, and simultaneously maintain satisfactory QoS (Quality of Service) levels [3,5].

2. **System QoS modeling/prediction**: The early departure of game players may indicate that a game system is providing less-than-satisfactory QoS. By combining the information about system- and network-level QoS with game play time data, we can model the impact of QoS factors on player departure processes and improve system designs based on such models [4].

3. **Player loyalty modeling/prediction**: Players may quit a game because they are dissatisfied with the game's design or content, or possibly due to cheating by other players. In other words, to some degree, quitting behavior may indicate low user satisfaction. Thus, we may infer a player's loyalty to a particular game based on his game play history [18, 19].

In this paper, we present the World of Warcraft Avatar History (WoWAH) dataset, which provides information about the game play time of 91,065 avatars and a number of their attributes. We focus on the World of Warcraft (WoW) because it is the most popular MMORPG in the world (as of December 2010). According to MMOData.net [8], the game's 12 million subscribers accounted for 62% of the MMOG market in March 2010 [14]. Because of the game's popularity, it has motivated studies by researchers in various academic fields, such as psychology [24], social interaction [6, 15], and game play behavior [2,9,10,11,16].

The WoWAH dataset comprises continual observations of the status of 91,065 avatars over a 3-year period (Jan. 2006 to Jan. 2009). During each observation we recorded the names of the avatars that were online and their respective attributes, including their current levels and in-game locations. Observations were made at 10-minute intervals; hence, during the 3-year period, we made approximately 157,680 observations (samples) on a WoW server. Because the samples are dense, we can extract the avatars' game play history from the 10-minute observations (i.e., if an avatar appeared in one sample but not in the subsequent one, we

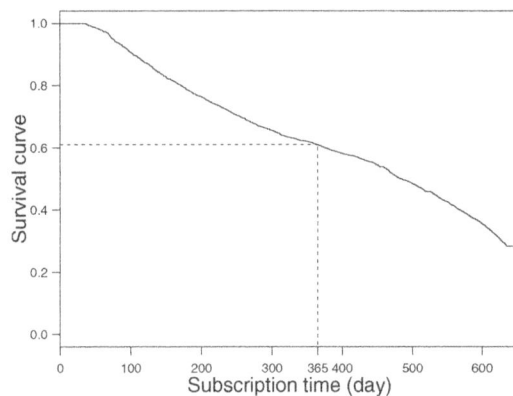

Figure 2: The survival curve of players' subscription times.

assumed it had logged out in the time between the two samples).

The WOWAH dataset is now publicly available at http://mmnet.iis.sinica.edu.tw/dl/wowah/. Researchers are free to download it for their own research purposes. In the remainder of the paper, we explain how we compiled the dataset in Section 2, and discuss its basic statistics in Section 3. We present two sample studies based on the dataset in Section 4, and then summarize our conclusions in Section 5.

2. DATASET DESCRIPTION

In this section, we explain how we collected the avatars' game play history in an automated fashion. After describing the data collection methodology, we discuss the naming and format of log files, and conclude with a summary of the traces.

2.1 Data Collection Methodology

We used the `who` command to collect the trace at regular intervals. The command, which asks the game server to provide a list of avatars in the same faction that are currently online, is available to every player in the game; hence, anyone can obtain the game play history of all the avatars in the same faction from the server.

To collect the trace, we created a character in a World of Warcraft realm (the Light's Hope realm in Taiwan) and kept it online throughout the 3-year study period. The character was controlled by a program written in the Lua scripting language [23], which World of Warcraft uses for interface customization. Our program automatically collected a list of the online avatars every 10 minutes. If an avatar logins and logouts within 10 minutes, we may not be able to observe his re-login activity in consecutive snapshots. However, we do not think this is a significant problem because most World of Warcraft sessions are much longer than 10 minutes [17].

Because of scalability considerations, World of Warcraft servers restrict the number of avatars returned in response to a query to a maximum of 50. Thus, we have to narrow down our query ranges by dividing all the avatars into different races, professions, and levels. For example, in the initial query, we need to ask the server to list all the avatars in the Fighter class whose levels are between level 1 and level 20. Then, in the second query, we ask the server to list all the avatars in the Fighter class whose levels are between level 21 and level 40, and so on. This technique allows us to systematically list the entire set of online avatars despite the restriction of the query function.

2.2 Log File Naming

The directory structure of the dataset archive comprises two levels of sub-directories. Each sub-directory in the first level represents the traces in a season with the directory name format `yyyy-fm-lm`, where `fm`, `lm`, and `yyyy` refer, respectively, to the first month, last month, and year of the traces in the sub-directory. For example, for the traces in 2006, there are four first-level directories, namely, `2006-01-03`, `2006-04-06`, `2006-07-09`, and `2006-10-12`. Each of the second-level sub-directories contains the traces collected in a day with the directory name format `yyyy-mm-dd`, where `mm` denotes the month and `dd` denotes the day of the month of the traces in the directory. With a few exceptions, which we discuss shortly, there are 144 files in each second-level sub-directory. Each file contains all the information observed about the avatars online during the sampling period. The reason for 144 files is that there are 1,440 minutes in a day and we make observations every 10 minutes. The name format of the log files is `hh-mm-ss`, where `hh`, `mm`, and `ss` represent, respectively, the hour, minute, and second of the sampling time.

2.3 Log Format

A log file is composed of two arrays: `Persistant_Storage` and `RoundInfo`. All the information collected about the avatars' history is stored in the `Persistant_Storage` array. Each element stores the information about an avatar observed during the sampling period; thus, the number of elements is equal to the number of avatars online in that sampling interval. An element is a string that contains 11 fields separated by commas. The 11 fields are `dummy`, `query time`, `query sequence number`, `avatar ID`, `guild`, `level`, `race`, `class`, `zone`, `dummy`, `dummy`. The meanings and valid values of the fields are detailed in Table 2. We also provide three sample records in Table 3. The first record, which relates to the initial query, indicates that we observed an avatar with ID 467 at 23:59:39 on 01/01/2006, and the avatar was a level-1 non-guilded Orc Warrior in Orgrimmar.

2.4 Data Summary

We collected the data over 1,107 days between Jan. 2006 and Jan. 2009. During the monitored period, 91,065 avatars, and 667,032 sessions associated with the avatars were observed. Because the sampling interval was 10 minutes, there should have been 159,408 samples, each providing the status of all the avatars online during the sampling period. However, 21,324 samples were missing due to server maintenance[3] and occasional client compatibility problems. As a result, the total number of samples was 138,084. In the dataset archive, the details of the missing samples are stored in the `missingdata` directory. To protect players' privacy, we mapped the avatars' names and guild names randomly as positive integers with a consistent mapping (i.e., the same names were always mapped to the same integers). A summary of the dataset is presented in Table 1.

[3] 4am to 12pm every Thursday is a weekly maintenance down time.

Table 1: Dataset Summary

Realm	TW-Light's Hope
Faction	Horde
Start date	2006-01-01
End date	2009-01-10
Duration	1,107 days
Sampling rate	144 samples per day
# of samples	159,408
# of missing samples	21,324
# of avatars	91,065
# of sessions	667,032

Table 2: Field Description

Field	Valid Values
Query Time	Between Jan. 2006 and Jan. 2009
Query Seq. #	An integer ≥ 1
Avatar ID	An integer ≥ 1
Guild	An integer within $[1, 513]$
Level	An integer within $[1, 80]$
Race	Blood Elf, Orc, Tauren, Troll, Undead
Class	Death Knight, Druid, Hunter, Mage, Paladin, Priest, Rogue, Shaman, Warlock, Warrior
Zone	One of the 229 zones in WoW world

3. BASIC STATISTICS

In this section, we present some basic statistics derived from the dataset. By assuming that each avatar is played by one game player, we can analyze the subscription length and daily game play behavior of World of Warcraft players. We also examine the variability and regularity of the number of avatars online because the information is an important indicator of the workload on game servers.

3.1 Subscription Time

A player's subscription time denotes the length of time since he became a member of the game to the time of his last login, i.e., the player has not logged in since then. Figure 2 shows the survival function [5] of players' subscription times. According to the statistics, 60% of users will subscribe for longer than one year after their first visit, and 50% will subscribe for longer than 500 days. These figures indicate that the game is indeed very attractive, and most players seem to become addicted to its fantasy world once they are immersed in it.

3.2 Daily Game Play Activities

We also investigate gamers' daily play behavior, including the average daily play time, average daily session count, and average session play time. Note that if a gamer does not play the game for some days, we do not include those days in his average daily play time. For example, if a gamer's subscription period was one year, but he only played for 200 days, then his average daily play time was his overall play time divided by 200 days.

The cumulative distribution functions (CDFs) of the av-

Table 3: Example Avatar Observation Records

Query Time	Seq. #	Avatar ID	Guild	Level	Race	Class	Zone
01/01/06 23:59:39	1	467		1	Orc	Warrior	Orgrimmar
01/01/06 23:59:39	1	921	19	1	Orc	Shaman	Orgrimmar
01/02/06 00:03:31	45	1367	8	60	Undead	Warrior	Arashi Mountain

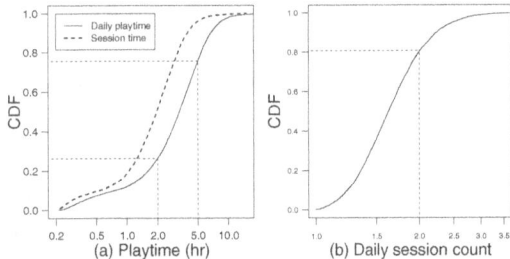

Figure 3: CDF of daily play time and session times.

Table 4: Summary of daily game play activities

	(Mean, SD)	Quantiles (5%, 25%, 50%, 75%, 95%)
Session time (hr)	(2.8, 1.8)	(0.4, 1.0, 1.8, 3.0, 5.5)
Daily session count	(1.7, 0.9)	(1.0, 1.1, 1.4, 2.1, 3.3)
Daily play time (hr)	(3.7, 2.8)	(0.5, 1.6, 3.1, 5.1, 8.8)

erage daily play time and the average session play time are shown in Figure 3(a). We find that 75% of gamers play longer than 1.9 hours per day on average, and 25% play longer than 4.9 hours per day, which again indicates that the game is very attractive to the gamers. If we analyze the average session play time, we find significant "knee" around 1 hour and 5 hours, which indicate that after logging into the game, there is a high probability that players will stay for at least one hour, but usually no longer than 5 hours. Because of the long session property, players probably do not login into the game too many times a day; hence, the daily session count is not large, as shown in Figure 3(b), where more than 80% of gamers have less than 2 session counts per day on average. We summarize the quantiles and averages of the average daily play time, average session play time, and average daily session count in Table 4.

3.3 Variations in the Number of Avatars Online

In this subsection, we consider how the number of avatars online evolves over time. We begin by plotting the average maximum, mean, median, and minimum numbers of avatars in different time scales, as shown in Figure 4. The top graph in the Figure 4 shows that, except for daily variations, there are no obvious systematic variations at larger time scales. By contrast, the middle graph shows that daily variations dominate the variability in the evolution of the number of avatars. The blackout period on Thursday morning is due to weekly maintenance downtime scheduled by the operator. The bottom graph plots daily variations in the number of avatars. Clearly, there are large fluctuations in the number of avatars (between 0 and 600) in a 24-hour period. On average, the quietest period is around 7am and the busiest period is around 11pm. This finding shows that many peo-

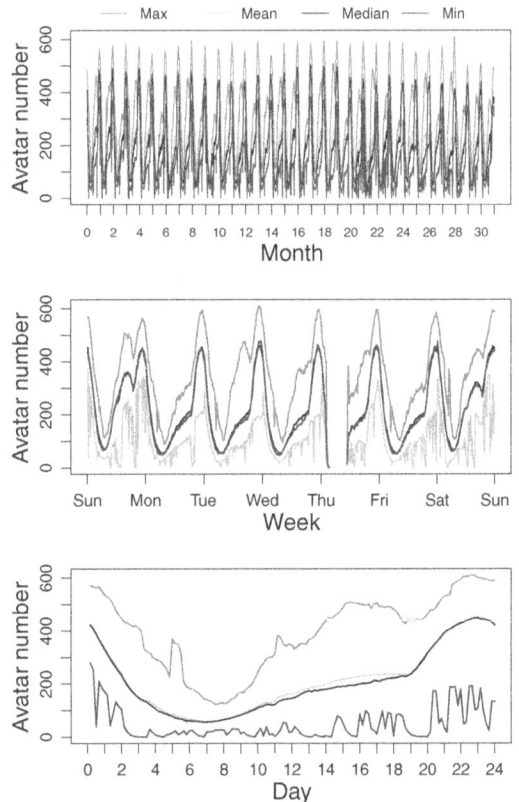

Figure 4: The averaged avatar number process shown in different time scales. The top two graphs are plotted based on daily averages and the bottom one is plotted based on the hourly averages.

ple play all night, and therefore implies that the game is addictive.

We also consider the distribution of the number avatars in consecutive periods for different time scales, as shown in Figure 5. The left-hand graph in the figure shows that the number of avatars in different months are similar with a slightly decreasing trend over the 9-month period. The only exception is January, which we suspect is a consequence of the Chinese New Year vacation. During such vacations, Chinese people gather with their families, play mahjong, and travel; thus, in our trace, the number of avatars in January was slightly lower than in February. The middle graph in Figure 5 shows that, as expected, the distribution of the number of avatars in different weeks is similar. Meanwhile, in the right-hand graph, the distribution of avatars on each day of the week indicates that the overall game play time is significantly different on weekdays and weekends, with Sunday attracting more gamers than Saturday. The distribution curve of Thursday is due to the scheduled weekly

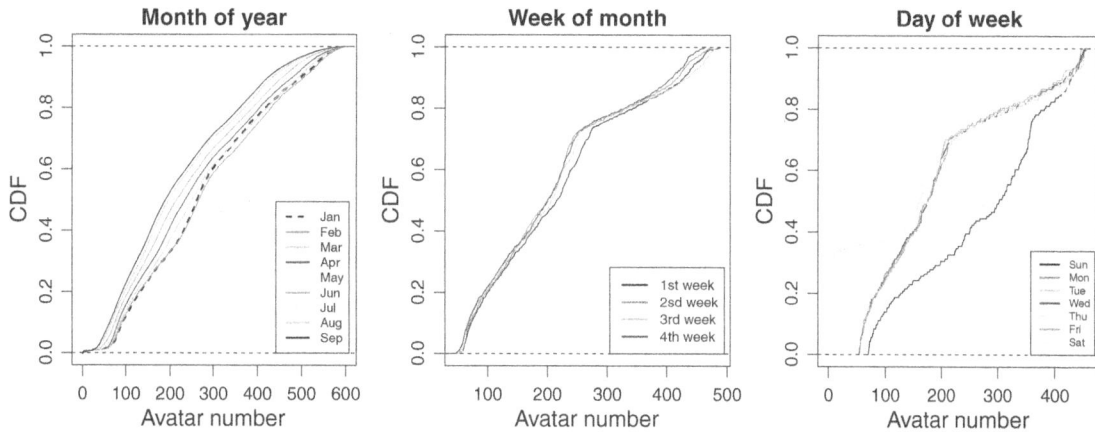

Figure 5: The cumulative distribution functions of averaged avatar numbers in different time scales. The leftmost graph is based on monthly averaged numbers; the middle graph is based on weekly averaged numbers; the rightmost graph is based on daily averaged numbers.

maintenance. The deviation of the curve from those of other weekdays implies that gamers return immediately after the maintenance period without "wasting" off-game time, which again reveals the addictiveness of the game.

3.4 Regularity of the Number of Avatars Online

The strong regularity over consecutive weeks and days and the strong variability within a 24-hour period can be further examined by auto-correlation function (ACF) plots on corresponding time scales, as shown in Figure 6. The top graph in the figure exhibits strong weekly regularity, while the middle graph exhibits strong daily regularity in the evolution of the number of avatars. The ACF of the number of avatars over the number of hours in the bottom graph shows that there is no regularity within a 24-hour period; however, the large coefficients with a lag of less than 2 hours indicate the potential for accurately predicting the number of avatars in the next few hours.

4. SAMPLE USES OF THE DATASET

We consider two sample studies that examine different aspects of the WoWAH dataset. The first study tries to model and predict the subscription time of game players and the usage time of avatars; and the second uses the WoWAH dataset to evaluate the effectiveness of a server consolidation strategy designed for MMORPGs. We present the studies here in the hope of motivating potential users of the dataset to find other creative uses.

4.1 Player Unsubscription Prediction

In [19], based on the WoWAH dataset, the authors presented a prediction model of online gamers' intentions that takes a player's game hours as input and predicts whether or not the player will decide to continue in the game once his current subscription expires. Predictions about players' non-renewal decisions are important to game operators because the decisions affect the operators' revenue directly. The rationale of the scheme is that, if the intentions of players can be predicted before they actually leave a game, the game operator can take remedial action to prevent the players' departure and improve the game based on feedback provided

by those players. The authors developed a scheme to predict a gamer's departure [19]. For hardcore players, the scheme enables game operators to predict players' non-renewal decisions two months prior to expiry of their membership with a compound accuracy of over 80%. In addition, the authors conducted a generalizability analysis, which showed that the scheme is generalizable across different MMORPGs and that it can be applied to both game play and avatar usage predictions.

4.2 Server Consolidation Techniques

With the advent of virtualization technology [20], consolidation of MMORPG servers [13] is now possible, even though various system architectures may be involved. By using an appropriate server consolidation strategy, an operator can reduce investments in hardware (by consolidating different game servers on a physical computer) and energy consumption (by putting idle servers into the sleep mode whenever appropriate), while maintaining user-perceived service quality. In [12], the authors proposed using a zone-based server consolidation strategy for MMORPGs to reduce the considerable investments in hardware and the energy consumption. Based on the WoWAH dataset, they implemented the proposed zone-based server consolidation algorithm, which reallocates zones among a set of server clusters regularly. The algorithm's impact in terms of the number of servers required and the energy consumption was also evaluated. Moreover, the authors presented a technique to upscale the number of avatars based on the avatars' game play history observed on a single server from the WoWAH dataset. Specifically, they modeled the number of avatars in a realm as a normal distribution with mean $2,640$ and standard deviation $1,500$ (derived from the data in the Warcraft Census[4] and WoW Database[5]) assuming that the maximum number of avatars per realm was $7,500$. After obtaining the number of avatars in each realm (with the above normal distribution), they computed the number of avatars in each zone based on the relative number of avatars in each zone in the WoWAH trace.

---

[4] http://www.warcraftrealms.com/census.php
[5] http://www.hotwow.com/

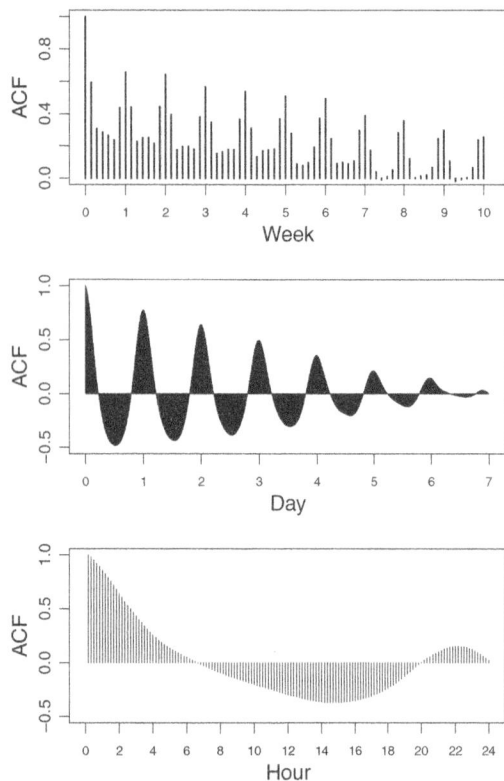

Figure 6: The auto-correlation functions of the avatar number process in different times scales. The top graph is based on daily averaged numbers; the middle graph is based on hourly averaged numbers; and the bottom graph is based on the avatar number observed at each 10 minutes.

5. CONCLUSION

In this paper, we have presented the WoWAH dataset, a three-year trace of avatars' game play history in World of Warcraft. We believe the trace is of value and could benefit the research community for the following reasons:

1. World of Warcraft, which currently has 12 million subscribers, has been the most popular MMORPG in the world since 2006 [21].

2. The dataset comprises avatars' game play records for a three-year period from Jan. 2006 to Jan. 2009. During that time, game designers released two important expansions, namely, The Burning Crusade and Wrath of the Lich King.

3. The value of the dataset has been demonstrated in studies of user behavior and game server clouds, as mentioned in Section 4.

In addition to the presented sample studies, we believe that game designers and researchers will find further creative uses for the dataset now that it is a public asset of the research community. The dataset is available for free download at `http://mmnet.iis.sinica.edu.tw/dl/wowah`.

6. REFERENCES

[1] Starcraft 2 Rankings, 2010. http://www.sc2ranks.com.
[2] C. Chambers, W. chang Feng, S. Sahu, and D. Saha. Measurement-based characterization of a collection of online games. *IMC'05*, pages 1–14, 2005.
[3] K.-T. Chen, P. Huang, and C.-L. Lei. How sensitive are online gamers to network quality? *Communications of the ACM*, 49(11):34–38, Nov 2006.
[4] K.-T. Chen, P. Huang, and C.-L. Lei. Effect of network quality on player departure behavior in online games. *IEEE Trans.*, pages 593–606, 2009.
[5] K.-T. Chen, P. Huang, G.-S. Wang, C.-Y. Huang, and C.-L. Lei. On the sensitivity of online game playing time to network QoS. In *Proceedings of IEEE INFOCOM'06*, Barcelona, Spain, Apr. 2006.
[6] V. H. H. Chen and H. B.-L. Duh. Understanding social interaction in World of Warcraft. *ACE'07*, pages 21–24, 2007.
[7] C. Francis and F. Wu-Chang. Modeling player session times of on-line games. In *Proceedings of the 2nd workshop on Network and system support for games*, NetGames'03, pages 23–26, 2003.
[8] I. V. Geel. MMOG subscriptions with a peak between 1,000,000 and 12,000,000. http://users.telenet.be/mmodata/Charts/Subs-1.png.
[9] T. Henderson and S. Bhatti. Modeling user behaviour in networked games. *Proceedings of ACM Multimedia'01*, pages 212–220, 2001.
[10] J. Kim, J. Choi, D. Chang, T. Kwon, Y. Choi, and E. Yuk. Traffic characteristics of a massively multi-player online role playing game. *ACM NetGames'05*, pages 1–8, 2005.
[11] M. Kwok and G. Yeung. Characterization of user behavior in a multi-player online game. *ACE'05*, pages 69–74, 2005.
[12] Y.-T. Lee and K.-T. Chen. Is server consolidation beneficial to MMORPG? a case study of World of Warcraft. *IEEE Cloud'10*, 0:435–442, 2010.
[13] D. A. Menascé. Virtualization: Concepts, applications, and performance modeling. In *Int. CMG Conference*, pages 407–414, 2005.
[14] MMORPGRealm. World of Warcraft Statistic in 2010, 2010. http://www.mmorpgrealm.com/world-of-warcraft-statistic-in-2010/.
[15] B. Nardi. Collaborative play in World of Warcraft. *LA-WEB'06*, page 3, 2006.
[16] D. Pittman and C. GauthierDickey. A measurement study of virtual populations in massively multiplayer online games. *ACM NetGames'07*, pages 25–30, 2007.
[17] P. Svoboda, W. Karner, and M. Rupp. Traffic analysis and modeling for World of Warcraft. *ICC'07*, pages 1612–1617, 2007.
[18] P.-Y. Tarng, K.-T. Chen, and P. Huang. An analysis of WoW players game hours. In *Proceedings of ACM NetGames'08*, 2008.
[19] P.-Y. Tarng, K.-T. Chen, and P. Huang. On prophesying online gamer departure. In *Proceedings of ACM NetGames 2009 (poster)*, 2009.
[20] VMware. Virtualization overview. http://www.vmware.com/pdf/virtualization.pdf.
[21] Voig, Inc. MMOGData: Charts, subscriptions. http://mmogdata.voig.com/.
[22] B. S. Woodcock. Market share by genre. http://www.mmogchart.com/Chart8.html.
[23] WoWWiki. Lua. http://www.wowwiki.com/Lua.
[24] R. Wright. Expert: 40 percent of World of Warcraft players addicted, 2006.
[25] J. Wu. The world of MMORPG: a tale of two regions.
[26] Z. Z. Eric Wan and X. Xu. 2006 online game report, 2006. In Pacific Epoch Red Innovation Report Series.

Affect Corpus 2.0: An Extension of a Corpus for Actor Level Emotion Magnitude Detection

Ricardo A. Calix
Louisiana State University
3128 Patrick F. Taylor Hall
Baton Rouge, LA, 70803
(225) 315 5655

rcalix1@lsu.edu

Gerald M. Knapp
Louisiana State University
3128 Patrick F. Taylor Hall
Baton Rouge, LA, 70803
(225) 578 5374

gknapp@lsu.edu

ABSTRACT

Improvement in human computer interaction requires effective and rapid development of multimedia systems that can understand and interact with humans. These systems need resources to train and learn how to interpret human emotions. Currently, there is a relative small number of existing resources such as annotated corpora that can be used for affect and multimodal content detection. In this paper, an extension of an existing corpus is presented. The corpus includes new annotations for affect magnitude detection and anaphora resolution. The format of the collected data is presented, along with the annotation methodology, basic statistics, suggestions for possible uses, and future work. This corpus is an extension of the UIUC Affect corpus of children's stories. The corpus includes new automatic annotations using Natural Language Processing toolkits as well as new manual annotations for affect magnitude detection and anaphora resolution. Results of inter-annotator agreement analysis on a subset of the corpus are also presented.

Categories and Subject Descriptors

I.2.7 [**Artificial Intelligence**]: Natural Language Processing

General Terms

Experimentation, Human Factors, Standardization

Keywords

Social Mining, Affect Detection, Sentient Nominal Entity Detection, Text-to-Scene processing.

1. INTRODUCTION

Advances in multimedia semantic analysis require rapid analysis and implementation of new tools and methodologies for information understanding. Currently, there is a relative small number of existing annotated corpora for affect and multimodal content detection. This in turn means that new ideas and implementations can take a long time to bring to fruition. To address this issue, affect and multimodal corpora needs to be created or extended and made available.

Advances in Human Computer Interaction will benefit from multimodal resources that link Natural Language Processing (NLP) approaches in both text and speech to multimedia synthesis in speech and computer graphics. Automatic virtual world synthesis or text-to-speech implementations are examples of areas that need these multimodal resources.

The annotations presented in this paper are an extension of work started at UIUC (University of Illinois at Urbana-Champaign) [1-3]. This new extended corpus, the Affect Corpus 2.0 [16], includes automatic annotations using new NLP toolkits as well as manual annotations for affect magnitude detection and anaphora resolution. Human annotations are specific to the areas of affect detection, sentient nominal entity recognition and anaphora resolution.

2. LITERATURE REVIEW

2.1 State of the Art in Corpora Development

Affect detection is the process of inferring emotion states through automated learning approaches from multimedia inputs (e.g. text or speech). Previous implementations for affect detection corpora include MPQA [14], Movie Reviews [11], and the UIUC affect corpus [1-3]. These are good implementations of affective corpora which have been used for machine learning methodologies such as in Calix et al. [4]. One problem with some of these corpora, however, is that they have focused mainly on sentence level emotion annotation and classification. In order to know who experiences an emotion and who produces it, annotation needs to be at the actor level. This means that actors and their respective referring expressions must be identified before emotions can be annotated. This combination of annotations requires a corpus that includes actors per story, referring expressions and their location in a story, and emotion magnitudes per actor to determine evolving emotional state of actors.

There are some corpora that have addressed the issue of anaphora resolution such as Ace [10], MUC-6 [8], and MUC-7 [9]. These corpora are very important in the field but do not combine annotations on anaphora, actors and emotions. A good annotation means using good NLP tools and annotating methodologies. Important annotating tools include NLTK [7], BART [12], GATE [5], Nuance Dragon Audio Mining SDK [15], and various other standalone parsing algorithms. Multimodal corpora include two or more modes of information such as text and speech. Corpora such as the TIMIT corpus, the Switchboard corpus, and the Buckeye corpus [6] are good examples of this type of corpus. They include the text transcript of the audio recordings. For speech extensions to text corpora, Librivox [17] is a good source to obtain audio recordings of public domain texts.

3. METHODOLOGY

The UIUC affect corpus of children's stories is used as a base for this work. This corpus uses sentence level annotations for emotion classification [1-3]. The UIUC corpus consists of 176 children's stories by three authors which are the Brothers Grimm, H. C. Andersen, and B. Potter. In this work, the corpus has been automatically and manually extended for emotion magnitude detection. While the annotations in 3.1 and 3.2 are not linear or connected, they are complementary. Both types of annotations can be used for machine learning methodologies. The magnitudes can be used as classes or predicted values (outputs) and the XML annotations as features for a learning methodology (inputs).

3.1 Automatic Annotation

The BART toolkit [12] was used to produce XML mark-up versions of each story in the corpus. The XML mark-up provides a simple data structure which can be used to automatically extract the features. Using this approach, all additional NLP information about each story is contained in the XML mark-up. This includes the sentence parse for each sentence, POS tags, enamex tags for actors, tags for semantic classes about each actor, and other useful tags. Additionally, referring expressions (pronouns) and their sentence position for each story were extracted.

3.2 Manual Annotation

In this step, human annotators read, identified, and recorded actor level emotion magnitudes in text. The UIUC corpus was extended by manually extracting the actors in each story and annotating them with their evolving emotional state. Three human annotators (two males and a female) used a new annotation tool to select actors, annotate their presence in a sentence, and assign evolving emotional state of actors throughout the story. The annotators were undergraduate and graduate students from the college of engineering at Louisiana State University (LSU). The structure of the output frame for each actor-emotion annotation pair is as follows:

AE (SentenceNum, Actor, HappyMagnitude, AngerMagnitude, SadMagnitude, SurpriseMagnitude, AfraidMagnitude, Presence).

Annotation of actors was performed assuming that the stories were acted out as plays to simplify the annotation process. The annotator was free to assign the name to be used for the actor but had to use the same name throughout the story.

Whenever an actor was present in a sentence, the annotator had to select the actor name to indicate presence. References to the actor can be made by name, referring expression, or implied in the context of each sentence. The ID used for each actor is the name, if available, or a description of the actor (e.g. the old miller).

3.3 Annotation Tool

For the purposes of this work, a new VB.NET based annotation tool was developed [16]. The annotating tool has two main sections (Figure 1). One section displays the story and highlights the current sentence being annotated. The second section displays the actors in the story. This area can be considered the stage where the actors will interact. In this section, each actor has five

scroll bars which are used to adjust the magnitude of each of the emotion classes. The score for each emotion is from 0.0 to 1.0. The annotating application records the annotator's user name and relevant statistics. Each session, the annotator proceeds to select one of the stories he or she is responsible for. The annotator loads the story into the system by searching for the story's name in the stories directory. When the user clicks on the "begin annotation" button, the first sentence of the story is highlighted.

Each sentence in the story is highlighted as the user annotates it. As the user is reading each sentence, he or she will identify actors in the story and determine if they have already been added to the list of actors. If the actor is not on the list, the annotator will click a button to add the actor to the actor's list section. Once the actor is on the list, the annotator can select the actor and adjust emotional state at the given sentence position in the story. This process is repeated for each sentence until the story is completed.

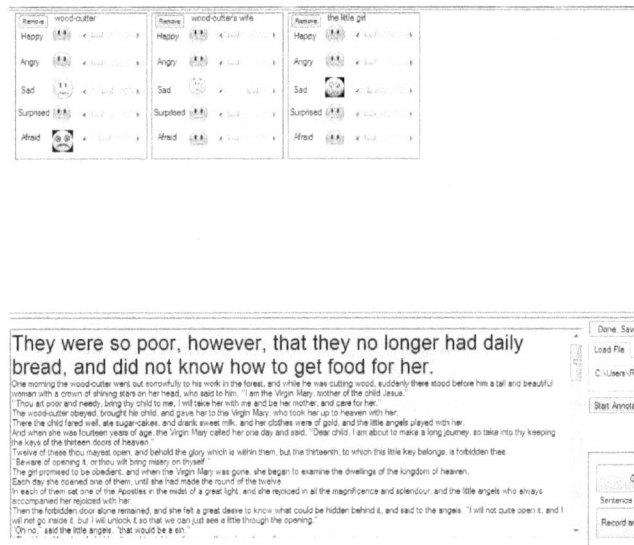

Figure 1. Annotation tool

Each annotation produces vectors with the actor name, emotional states, and the position of the actor's in the story. Emotional states per actor need to be adjusted only if the states change. Otherwise, the previous states are recorded for the current sentence. Once the actor leaves the scene, the emotion states are reset to zero.

4. CORPUS CHARACTERISTICS

4.1 Corpus Format

The corpus includes a file of actors per story, and a file of actor-emotion-magnitude vectors for each story. The list of actors is a simple ASCII format file containing the names for each sentient actor in the story. An example is provided in Figure 2.

poor man
poor man's son
The king
King's daughter
the snake
second snake
the servant
the skipper

Figure 2. Actors for "Three snake leaves" by the brothers Grimm

130

For the actor-emotion vectors, information on sentence position, actor name (ID), and emotion magnitudes are provided. Each vector includes a presence feature which indicates if an actor is present in the sentence. Here, an actor could be referred to by name, a referring expression or implied by story context.

```
[84,mrs. rebeccah puddle-duck,0,0,0,0,0,0,Jemima became much alarmed.]
[84,jemima puddle-duck,0,0,0,0,42,66,1,Jemima became much alarmed.]
[84,Kep,0,0,0,0,0,0,Jemima became much alarmed.]
[84,gentleman with sandy whiskers,0,0,0,0,0,1,Jemima became much alarmed.]
```

Figure 3. Emotion vectors with emotion magnitudes

The emotion vectors are very important because they can provide information about sentiment flow per actor in the story. This can allow sentiment flow to be represented as an emotion signal over time (Figure 4).

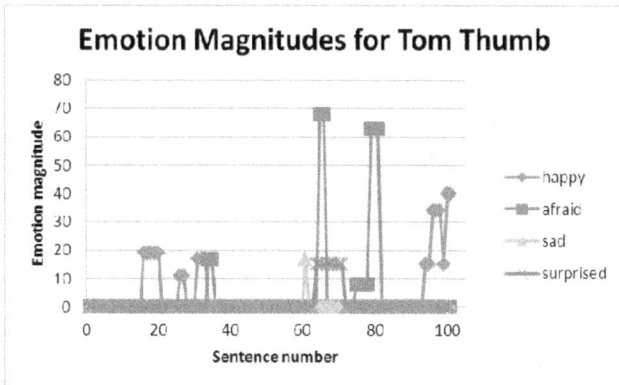

Figure 4. Emotion magnitudes for Thomas Thumb throughout the story "Tom Thumb" by the Brothers Grimm

Several important aspects of the stories such as correlation between actors and actor emotions can be visualized with the emotion magnitude vectors. For example, in Figure 4, the evolving emotional state of Tom Thumb in the story can be visualized. Here it can be seen, without reading the story, that Tom Thumb started out happy but then something happened that caused him sadness, surprise and a lot of fear.

```
0 1:0 2:0 3:0 4:0 5:1 6:0 7:0 8:0 9:0 he \Potter ginger_and_pickles.bart.xml 11
0 1:0 2:0 3:0 4:0 5:0 6:0 7:1 8:0 9:0 it \Potter ginger_and_pickles.bart.xml 11
0 1:1 2:0 3:0 4:0 5:0 6:0 7:0 8:0 9:0 I \Potter ginger_and_pickles.bart.xml 12
0 1:0 2:0 3:0 4:0 5:1 6:0 7:0 8:0 9:0 he \Potter ginger_and_pickles.bart.xml 12
0 1:0 2:0 3:0 4:0 5:0 6:0 7:0 8:0 9:1 them \Potter ginger_and_pickles.bart.xml 12
0 1:1 2:0 3:0 4:0 5:0 6:0 7:0 8:0 9:0 I \Potter ginger_and_pickles.bart.xml 13
0 1:0 2:0 3:0 4:0 5:0 6:0 7:1 8:0 9:0 it \Potter ginger_and_pickles.bart.xml 13
0 1:0 2:0 3:0 4:0 5:0 6:0 7:0 8:0 9:1 they \Potter ginger_and_pickles.bart.xml 13
```

Figure 5. PRP Referring Expression vectors

These problems, however, seem to have been resolved because the final emotion state is happy. The referring expressions are provided in a text file for the entire corpus. The list includes the pronoun, sentence position, story, author, and some syntactic and knowledge features. An example is provided in Figure 5.

4.2 Corpus Statistics

The corpus has 15,302 sentences with an average of 10 words per sentence. There are 176 stories by 3 authors. The emotion magnitude classes included happy, sad, angry, surprised, and afraid. The neutral class was represented when all emotion class magnitudes were set to zero. From a syntactic parse analysis it was observed that the corpus contains 45,120 NPs with Nouns as constituents. Additional, statistics about the corpus can be found in [1-4].

4.3 Inter-annotator Agreement

To evaluate the reliability of the annotation scheme, a subset consisting of 19 stories from the corpus was double annotated. This subset was analyzed in two different ways. The first approach included all emotion magnitude assignments including neutral emotional states. Including all the data helped to evaluate emotion class assignment between the five classes and the neutral state. The second approach limited the sample to annotations where the actor received at least one emotion magnitude assignment other than zero. This second approach was used to evaluate annotator agreement on emotion magnitude assignment.

The metrics used to evaluate inter-annotator agreement included Average observed agreement, Pi, alpha, S, and Kappa [13]. In their simplest form, these metrics (e.g. Avg_Ao) serve to determine the percentage of samples that were equally annotated by two or more annotators. Other metrics like Kappa, consider expected chance agreement in the calculations. By knowing these rates, theoretical upper bounds on expected accuracy can be determined for automatic systems trained on annotated data [18].

Table 2. Inter-annotator metrics for emotion class assignment

	Happy	Angry	Sad	Surprised	Afraid
Avg_Ao	0.897	0.867	0.872	0.794	0.742
π	0.222	0.463	0.280	0.086	0.089
S	0.863	0.823	0.829	0.725	0.657
Kappa	0.223	0.464	0.289	0.128	0.129
Alpha	0.222	0.463	0.280	0.086	0.089

Since most main agreement metrics in the literature use categorical label assignments, the magnitude data presented here was categorized into four groups. Magnitudes between 0-25 were designated as low, 26-50 as medium low, 51-75 as medium high, and 76-100 as high. The inter-annotator metrics are shown in Table 2 and 3.

Table 3. Inter-annotator agreement for emotion magnitude

	Happy	Angry	Sad	Surprised	Afraid
Avg_Ao	0.586	0.412	0.555	0.551	0.475
π	0.090	0.164	0.318	0.126	0.139
S	0.448	0.216	0.407	0.402	0.300
Kappa	0.096	0.186	0.332	0.186	0.182
Alpha	0.091	0.166	0.321	0.128	0.141

From the results, it can be seen that class assignment had higher inter-annotator agreement than emotion magnitude assignment. This reflects the fact that emotion magnitude assignment is a subjective task because what is very happy to one person may just be average to another.

4.4 Applications

This corpus can be used for many types of applications. Important areas to note include: Text-to-Scene processing, Text-to-Speech processing, calibration of emotion recognition within multimedia systems, social media content analysis and Twitter dialog censoring of inappropriate language. In the field of forensic science, the corpus could be useful for email content analysis, speech analysis of emotional cues, antiterrorism, and hate speech detection. As an example of text-to-scene processing, a 3-D rendering is provided to illustrate that with the current annotations, 3-D scenes could be generated from the corpus stories. The colors and type of mesh can be selected based on the actors and emotion magnitudes. The background as can be seen in the image provides a "dark forest" which can indicate that fear is present in the scene.

Figure 6. 3-D rendering of a scene with emotion context and actors

5. CONCLUSION

In conclusion, new annotations for a beloved set of children's stories are provided with the intention that future research will be able to focus on developing applications instead of resources. The corpus provides new annotations for emotion magnitude per actor, actor detection, and anaphora resolution. Inter-annotator agreement metrics compared annotation of emotion categories vs. annotation of emotion magnitudes.

6. FUTURE WORK

Most of the future work on the corpus will be focused on the speech extension. Roughly about half of the stories are already recorded and available from Librivox. Each speech recording per story ranges from two to five megabytes and is in MP3 format. Future versions will include annotations for sentence boundary in the audio recordings. Praat and other tools will be used to manually perform sentence breaks.

7. ACKNOWLEDGMENTS

The authors would like to thank Brandon Pitts, Denis Daly, Heather Dylla, and Leili Javadpour for their help in developing the new extensions of the corpus.

8. REFERENCES

[1] Alm, C. O., Roth, D., Sproat, R., 2005, Emotions from text: Machine Learning for text-based emotion prediction. *In proceedings of Human Language Technology Conference and Conference on Empirical Methods in Natural Language Processing*, pp. 579-586

[2] Alm, C. O., Affect data, DOI = http://lrc.cornell.edu/swedish/dataset/affectdata/index.html

[3] Alm, C. O., 2008, Affect in Text and Speech, PhD Dissertation, University of Illinois at Urbana-Champaign

[4] Calix, R., Mallepudi, S., Chen, B., Knapp, G., 2010, Emotion Recognition in Text for 3-D Facial Expression Rendering, *IEEE Transactions on Multimedia,* Special Issue on Multimodal Affective Interaction, Volume 12, Issue 6, pp. 544-551

[5] Cunningham, H., Maynard, D., Bontacheva, K., Tablan, V., 2002, GATE: A framework and graphical development Environment for robust NLP tools and applications, *Proceedings of the 40th anniversary meeting of the association for computational linguistics (ACL '02),* Philadelphia

[6] Jurafsky, D., Martin, J., 2008, Speech and Language Processing, 2nd ed. New Jersey: Prentice Hall

[7] Loper, E., Bird, S., 2002, NLTK: The Natural Language Toolkit, *Proceedings of the ACL Workshop on Effective Tools and Methodologies for Teaching Natural Language Processing and Computational Linguistics*, Philadelphia, Association for Computational Linguistics, pp. 62-69

[8] MUC-6, 1995, Co-reference task Definition, *In Proceedings of the Sixth Message understanding Conference*, San Francisco, California, pp. 335-344

[9] MUC-7, 1997, Co-reference task Definition, *In Proceedings of the Seventh Message Understanding Conference*

[10] NIST, 2004, *The ACE Evaluation Plan,* NIST

[11] Pang, B., Lee, L., 2008, Opinion Mining and Sentiment Analysis, *Foundations and Trends in Information Retrieval*, Vol. 2, No.1-2, pp.1-135

[12] Versley, Y., Ponzetto, S. P., Poesio, M., Eidelman, V., Jern, A., Smith, J., Yang, X., Moschitti, A., 2008, BART: A Modular Toolkit for Co-reference Resolution, *Language Resources and Evaluation Conference (LREC).*

[13] Artstein, R., Poesio, M., 2008, Inter-Coder Agreement for Computational Linguistics, *Computational Linguistics*, Volume 34, Issue 4, pp. 555-596

[14] Wiebe, J., Wilson, T., Cardie, C., 2005, Annotating Expressions of Opinions and Emotions in Language, *Language Resources and Evaluation*, Volume 39, Issue 2-3, pp. 165-210

[15] Nuance Dragon, [Date: Sept, 2010], DOI = http://nuance.com/dragon

[16] LSU-NLP, [Date: Sept, 2010], DOI = http://nlp.lsu.edu

[17] Librivox, [Date: Sept, 2010], DOI = http://librivox.org/

[18] Bird, S., Klein, E., Loper, E., 2009, Natural Language Processing with Python, 1st ed., *O'Reilly Media*

Dynamic Adaptive Streaming over HTTP – Standards and Design Principles

Thomas Stockhammer
Qualcomm Incorporated
c/o Nomor Research
Brecherspitzstraße 8
81541 Munich, Germany
+49 89 978980 02

stockhammer@nomor.de

ABSTRACT

In this paper, we provide some insight and background into the Dynamic Adaptive Streaming over HTTP (DASH) specifications as available from 3GPP and in draft version also from MPEG. Specifically, the 3GPP version provides a normative description of a Media Presentation, the formats of a Segment, and the delivery protocol. In addition, it adds an informative description on how a DASH Client may use the provided information to establish a streaming service for the user. The solution supports different service types (e.g., On-Demand, Live, Time-Shift Viewing), different features (e.g., adaptive bitrate switching, multiple language support, ad insertion, trick modes, DRM) and different deployment options. Design principles and examples are provided.

Categories and Subject Descriptors

H.4.m [**Information Systems Applications**]: Miscellaneous.

General Terms

Standardization.

Keywords

3GPP, video, mobile video, standards, streaming.

1. INTRODUCTION

Internet access is becoming a commodity on mobile devices. With the recent popularity of smart phones, smartbooks, connected netbooks and laptops the Mobile Internet use is dramatically expanding. According to recent studies [7], expectations are that between 2009 and 2014 the mobile data traffic will grow by a factor of 40, i.e., it will more than double every year. Figure 1 shows that the video traffic will by then account for 66% of the total amount of the mobile data. At the same time mobile users expect high-quality video experience in terms of video quality, start-up time, reactivity to user interaction, trick mode support, etc., and the whole ecosystem including content providers, network operators, service providers, device manufacturers and technology providers need to ensure that these demands can be

met. Affordable and mature technologies are required to fulfil the users' quality expectations. One step into this direction is a common, efficient and flexible distribution platform that scales to the rising demands. Standardized components are expected to support the creation of such common distribution platforms.

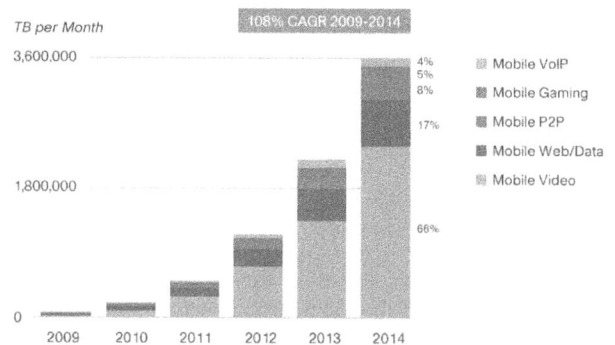

Figure 1 Video Will Account for 66 Percent of Global Mobile Data Traffic by 2014 (Source [7], Figure 2)

Traditional streaming generally uses a stateful protocol, e.g., the Real-Time Streaming Protocol (RTSP): Once a client connects to the streaming server the server keeps track of the client's state until the client disconnects again. Typically, frequent communication between the client and the server happens. Once a session between the client and the server has been established, the server sends the media as a continuous stream of packets over either UDP or TCP transport. In contrast, HTTP is stateless. If an HTTP client requests some data, the server responds by sending the data and the transaction is terminated. Each HTTP request is handled as a completely standalone one-time transaction.

Alternatively to streaming, progressive download may be used for media delivery from standard HTTP Web servers. Clients that support HTTP can seek to positions in the media file by performing byte range requests to the Web server (assuming that it also supports HTTP/1.1 [4]). Disadvantages of progressive download are mostly that (i) bandwidth may be wasted if the user decides to stop watching the content after progressive download has started (e.g., switching to another content), (ii) it is not really bitrate adaptive and (iii) it does not support live media services. Dynamic Adaptive Streaming over HTTP (DASH) addresses the weaknesses of RTP/RTSP-based streaming and progressive download.

2. DESIGN PRINCIPLES

HTTP-based progressive download does have significant market adoption. Therefore, HTTP-based streaming should be as closely aligned to HTTP-based progressive download as possible, but take into account the above-mentioned deficiencies.

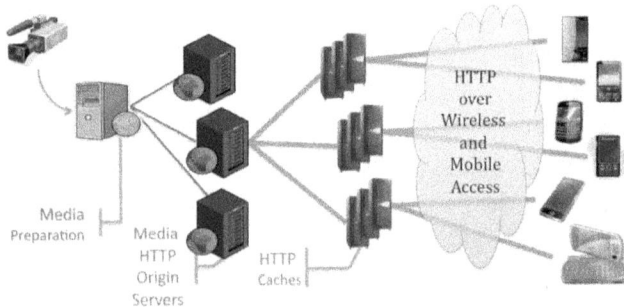

Figure 2 Example Media Distribution Architecture

Figure 2 shows a possible media distribution architecture for HTTP-based streaming. The media preparation process typically generates segments that contain different encoded versions of one or several of the media components of the media content. The segments are then hosted on one or several media origin servers typically, along with the media presentation description (MPD). The media origin server is preferably an HTTP server such that any communication with the server is HTTP-based (indicated by a bold line in the picture). Based on this MPD metadata information that describes the relation of the segments and how they form a media presentation, clients request the segments using HTTP GET or partial GET methods. The client fully controls the streaming session, i.e., it manages the on-time request and smooth playout of the sequence of segments, potentially adjusting bitrates or other attributes, for example to react to changes of the device state or the user preferences.

Massively scalable media distribution requires the availability of server farms to handle the connections to all individual clients. HTTP-based Content Distribution Networks (CDNs) have successfully been used to serve Web pages, offloading origin servers and reducing download latency. Such systems generally consist of a distributed set of caching Web proxies and a set of request redirectors. Given the scale, coverage, and reliability of HTTP-based CDN systems, it is appealing to use them as base to launch streaming services that build on this existing infrastructure. This can reduce capital and operational expenses, and reduces or eliminates decisions about resource provisioning on the nodes. This principle is indicated in Figure 2 by the intermediate HTTP servers/caches/proxies. Scalability, reliability, and proximity to the user's location and high-availability are provided by general-purpose servers. The reasons that lead to the choice of HTTP as the delivery protocol for streaming services are summarized below:

1. HTTP streaming is spreading widely as a form of delivery of Internet video.

2. There is a clear trend towards using HTTP as the main protocol for multimedia delivery over the Open Internet.

3. HTTP-based delivery enables easy and effortless streaming services by avoiding NAT and firewall traversal issues.

4. HTTP-based delivery provides reliability and deployment simplicity due as HTTP and the underlying TCP/IP protocol are widely implemented and deployed.

5. HTTP-based delivery provides the ability to use standard HTTP servers and standard HTTP caches (or cheap servers in general) to deliver the content, so that it can be delivered from a CDN or any other standard server farm.

6. HTTP-based delivery provides the ability to move control of "streaming session" entirely to the client. The client basically only opens one or several or many TCP connections to one or several standard HTTP servers or caches.

7. HTTP-based delivery provides the ability to the client to automatically choose initial content rate to match initial available bandwidth without requiring the negotiation with the streaming server.

8. HTTP-based delivery provides a simple means to seamlessly change content rate on-the-fly in reaction to changes in available bandwidth, within a given content or service, without requiring negotiation with the streaming server.

9. HTTP-based streaming has the potential to accelerate fixed-mobile convergence of video streaming services as HTTP-based CDN can be used as a common delivery platform.

Based on these considerations, 3GPP had identified the needs to provide a specification for a scalable and flexible video distribution solution that addresses mobile networks, but is not restricted to 3GPP radio access networks (RANs). 3GPP has taken the initiative to specify an Adaptive HTTP Streaming solution in addition to the already existing RTP/RTSP-based streaming solutions and the HTTP-based progressive download solution.

Specifically the solution is designed

- to support delivery of media components encapsulated in ISO base media file format box structure,

- to address delivery whereas presentation, annotation and user interaction is largely out-of-scope,

- to permit integration in different presentation frameworks.

The 3GPP sub-group SA4 working on codecs and protocols for media delivery started the HTTP streaming activity in April 2009 and completed the Release-9 specification work early March 2010. The 3GPP Adaptive HTTP Streaming (AHS) has been integrated into 3GPP Transparent end-to-end Packet-switched Streaming Service (PSS). Specifically, 3GPP TS 26.234 [1] (PSS Codecs and Protocols) clause 12 specifies the 3GPP Adaptive HTTP Streaming solution, and 3GPP TS 26.244 [2] (3GP File Format) clauses 5.4.9, 5.4.10, and 13 specify the encapsulation formats for segments. The Release-9 work is now under maintenance mode and some minor bug fixes and clarifications were agreed during the year 2010 and have been integrated into the latest versions of 3GPP TS 26.234 and 3GPP TS 26.244.

The solution supports features such as

- fast initial startup and seeking,

- bandwidth-efficiency,

- adaptive bitrate switching,

- adaptation to CDN properties,

- re-use of HTTP-server and caches,

- re-use of existing media playout engines,

- support for on-demand, live and time-shift delivery services,

- simplicity for broad adoption.

3GPP has also sought alignment with other organizations and industry fora that work in the area of video distribution. For example, as the Open IPTV Forum (OIPF) based their HTTP Adaptive Streaming (HAS) solution [13] on 3GPP. 3GPP recently also addressed certain OIPF requirements and integrated appropriate features in the Release-9 3GPP Adaptive HTTP Streaming specification. Also MPEG's draft DASH solution is heavily based on 3GPP's AHS. Finally, 3GPP has ongoing work in Release-10, now also referred to as DASH. This work will extend the Release-9 3GPP AHS specification in a backward-compatible way. Close coordination with the ongoing MPEG DASH activities is organized.

3. 3GPP Adaptive HTTP Streaming
3.1 Overview
3GPP Adaptive HTTP Streaming, since Release-10 referred to as as 3GP-DASH, is the result of a standardization activity in 3GPP SA4 Figure 3 shows the principle of the 3GP-DASH specification. The specification provides

- a normative definition of a Media Presentation, with Media Presentation defined as a structured collection of data that is accessible to the DASH Client through Media Presentation Description,
- a normative definition of the formats of a Segment, with a Segment defined as an integral data unit of a media presentation that can be uniquely referenced by a HTTP-URL (possibly restricted by a byte range),
- a normative definition of the delivery protocol used for the delivery of Segments, namely HTTP/1.1,
- an informative description on how a DASH client may use the provided information to establish a streaming service for the user.

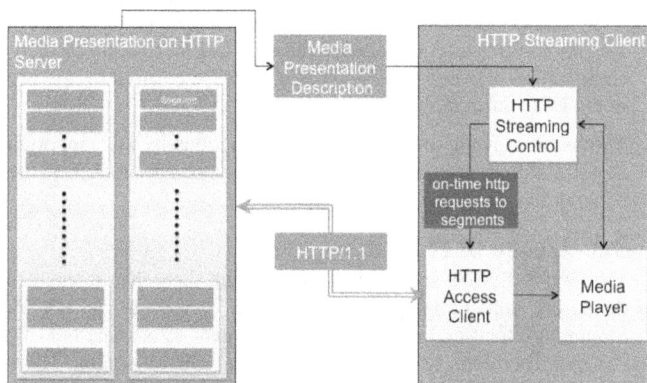

Figure 3 Solution overview – 3GP-DASH

DASH in 3GPP is defined in two levels:

1. Clause 12.2 in TS 26.234 [1] provides a generic framework for Dynamic Adaptive Streaming independent of the data encapsulation format for media segments.
2. Clause 12.4 in TS 26.234 [1] provides a specific instantiation of this framework with the 3GP/ISO base media file format by specifying the segment formats, partly referring to the formats in TS 26.244 [2].

This approach makes the framework defined in 3GPP extensible, for example to any other segment formats, codecs and DRM solutions.

3G-DASH supports multiple services, among others:

- On-demand streaming,
- Linear TV including live media broadcast,
- Time-shift viewing with network Personal Video Recording (PVR) functionalities.

Specific care was taken in the design that the network side can be deployed on standard HTTP servers and distribution can be provided through regular Web infrastructures such as HTTP-based CDNs. The specification also leaves room for different server/network-side deployment options as well as for optimized client implementations.

The specification also defines provisions to support features such as

- Initial selection of client- and/or user-specific representations of the content,
- Dynamic adaptation of the played content to react to environmental changes such as access bandwidth or processing power,
- Trick modes such as seeking, fast forward or rewind,
- Simple insertion of pre-encoded advertisement or other content in on-demand and live streaming services,
- Efficient delivery of multiple languages and audio tracks,
- Content protection and content security, etc.

The remainder of this section provides further background information on the concept of a Media Presentation, the usage of HTTP, as well as segment types and formats in the 3GPP instantiation. A summary of the normative specification is also provided.

3.2 Media Presentation
The concept of a Media Presentation is introduced in TS 26.234 [1], clause 12.2. A Media Presentation is a structured collection of encoded data of some media content, e.g., a movie or a program. The data is accessible to the DASH Client to provide a streaming service to the user. As shown in Figure 4:

- A Media Presentation consists of a sequence of one or more consecutive non-overlapping Periods.
- Each Period contains one or more Representations from the same media content.
- Each Representation consists of one or more Segments.
- Segments contain media data and/or metadata to decode and present the included media content.

Period boundaries permit to change a significant amount of information within a Media Presentation such as server location, encoding parameters, or the available variants of the content. The Period concept has been introduced among others for splicing of new content, such as ads, and for logical content segmentation. Each Period is assigned a start time, relative to start of the Media Presentation.

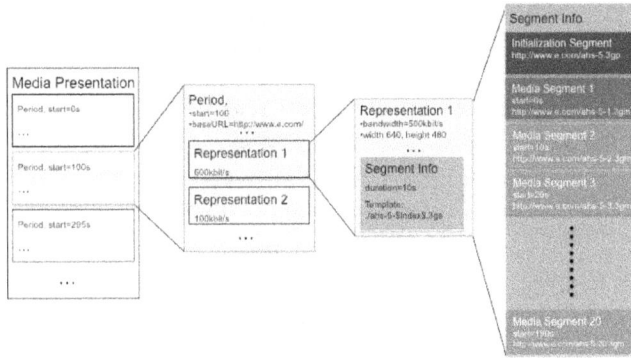

Figure 4 Media Presentation Data Model

Each Period itself consists of one or more Representations. A Representation is one of the alternative choices of the media content or a subset thereof typically differing by the encoding choice, e.g., by bitrate, resolution, language, or codecs.

Each Representation includes one or more media components, where each media component is an encoded version of one individual media type such as audio, video or timed text. Each Representation is assigned to a group. Representations in the same group are alternatives to each other. The media content within one Period is represented by either one Representation from group zero, or the combination of at most one Representation from each non-zero group.

A Representation consists of at most one Initialisation Segment and one or more Media Segments. Media components are time-continuous across boundaries of consecutive Media Segments within one Representation. Segments represent a unit that can be uniquely referenced by an HTTP-URL (possibly restricted by a byte range). Thereby, the Initialisation Segment contains information for accessing the Representation, but no media data. Media Segments contain media data and must fulfil some further requirements, namely:

- Each Media Segment is assigned a start time in the media presentation to enable downloading the appropriate Segments in regular play-out mode or after seeking. This time is generally not accurate media playback time, but only approximate such that the client can make appropriate decisions on when to download the Segment such that it is available in time for play-out.
- Media Segments may provide random access information, i.e., presence, location and timing of Random Access Points (RAPs).
- A Media Segment, when considered in conjunction with the information and structure of the MPD, contains sufficient information to time-accurately present each contained media component in the Representation without accessing any previous Media Segment in this Representation provided that the Media Segment contains a RAP. The time-accuracy enables seamlessly switching Representations and jointly presenting multiple Representations.
- Media segments may also contain information for randomly accessing subsets of the Segment by using partial HTTP GET requests.

A Media Presentation is described in a Media Presentation Description (MPD), and MPDs may be updated during the lifetime of a Media Presentation. In particular, the MPD describes accessi-

ble Segments and their timing. The MPD is a well-formatted XML document and the 3GPP Adaptive HTTP Streaming specification defines an XML schema to define MPDs. An MPD may be updated in specific ways such that an update is consistent with the previous instance of the MPD for any past media. A graphical presentation of the XML schema is provided in Figure 5. The mapping of the data model to the XML schema is highlighted. For the details of the individual attributes and elements please refer to TS 26.234 [1], clause 12.2.5.

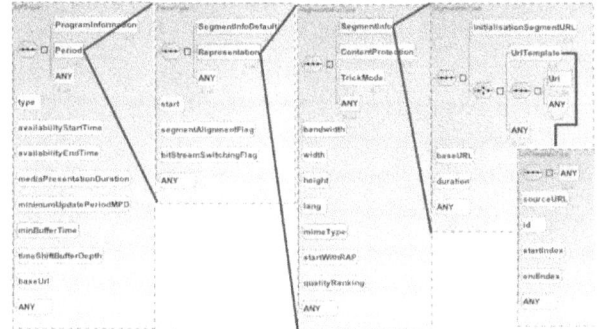

Figure 5 MPD XML-Schema

DASH also supports live streaming services. In this case, the generation of segments typically happens on-the-fly. Due to this clients typically have access to only a subset of the Segments, i.e., the most recent MPD describes a time window of accessible Segments for this instant in time. By providing updates of the MPD, the server may describe new Segments and/or new Periods such that the updated MPD is compatible with the previous MPD.

Therefore, for live streaming services a Media Presentation is typically described by the initial MPD and all MPD updates. To ensure synchronization between client and server, the MPD provides access information in Universal Time Clock (UTC) time. As long as server and client are synchronized to UTC time, the synchronization between server and client can be ensured by the use of the UTC times in the MPD.

Time-shift viewing and network PVR functionality are supported in a straightforward manner, as segments may be accessible on the network over a long period of time.

3.3 Usage of HTTP

The 3GPP DASH specification is written such that it enables delivering content from standard HTTP servers to an HTTP-Streaming client and enables caching content by standard HTTP caches. Therefore, the streaming server and streaming client comply to HTTP/1.1 as specified in RFC2616 [7] and HTTP-Streaming Clients are expected to use the HTTP GET method or the partial GET method for downloading media segments. No further details on caches and proxies are specified, as they are transparent to protocol.

3.4 Segments based on 3GP File Format

Beyond the general adaptive streaming framework, 3GPP DASH specifies an instantiation that uses segment formats based on the 3GP file format as specified in TS 26.244 [2]. Each Representation may either consist of

- one Initialisation Segment and at least one Media Segment, but typically a sequence of Media Segments, or
- one self-Initialising Media Segment.

An *Initialisation Segment* provides the client with the metadata that describes the media content and is basically a file conformant with the 3GPP file format without any media data. An Initialisation Segment consists of the "ftyp" box, the "moov" box, and optionally the "pdin" box. The "moov" box contains no samples. This reduces the start-up time significantly as the Initialisation Segment needs to be downloaded before any Media Segment can be processed, but may be downloaded asynchronously before the Media Segments.

Self-Initialising Media Segments comply with the 3GP Adaptive-Streaming Profile as specified in TS 26.244, clause 5.4.9. For 3GP files conforming to this profile the 'moov' box is in the beginning of the file after the 'ftyp' and a possibly present 'pdin' box, all movie data is contained in Movie Fragments, and the 'moov' box is followed by one or more 'moof' and 'mdat' box pairs. In addition 3GP files conforming to this profile may contain any of the new boxes specified in TS 26.244 [2], clause 13, namely the segment type ('styp') box, the track fragment adjustment ('tfad') box and the segment index ('sidx') box. Self-Initialising media segments are assigned start time 0 relative to the Period start time, so no additional information is necessary for each segment. However, the additional boxes 'tfad' and 'sidx' may be used for accurate timing of each component within the 3GP file after random access and seeking within the 3GP file. More details on the boxes for DASH are provided further below.

A *Media Segment* may start with a 'styp' box and a sequence of one or more whole self-contained movie fragments. The 'styp' box is used for file branding of segments. In addition, each 'traf' box may contain a 'tfad' box for track alignment to permit random access to the start of the segment or any fragment within the segment. Furthermore, each Media Segment may contain one or more 'sidx' boxes. The 'sidx' provides global timing for each contained track, time/byte range offsets of the contained movie fragments, as well as time offsets of random access points, if any.

Note that the codecs in 3GPP AHS are identical to 3GPP PSS codecs as specified in TS 26.234, clause 7.2 for speech, 7.3 for audio, 7.4 for video and 7.9 for timed text. However, there is no restriction for use of any other codecs as long as the codecs can be encapsulated in ISO base media file format.

3.5 Segment Indexing

Segment Indexing is an important concept to permit byte range access to subsets of segments. This permits fast access to sub-structures in the segment for fast switching, simple random access, etc. Each segment index 'sidx' box documents a sub-segment defined as one or more consecutive movie fragments, ending either at the end of the containing segment, or at the beginning of a subsegment documented by the next 'sidx'.

The 'sidx' contains timing information to place the segment into the global time line of the media presentation. Beyond, it contains a loop that provides an index of the subsegment, i.e., the duration of each sub-segment and the offset from the first byte following the enclosing 'sidx', to the first byte of the referenced box.

By downloading only a small portion in the beginning of the media segment, e.g., by using a byte range request, the segment index boxes may be fetched. Segment index boxes may be used for several purposes:

1. To provide a mapping of each track contained in the media segment to the media presentation timeline, such that synchronous playout of media components within

and across Representations is enabled as well as to permit switching across Representations.

2. To enable fast navigation through segments, possibly using byte range requests and to minimize the download of media data during a seeking process.

3. To locate the position of random access points within segments without downloading unnecessary media data before the random access point.

Figure 6 shows a simple example of a single segment index. In this case, the first loop of the segment index box provides the exact timing for each media component starting in fragment F1. Furthermore, the second loop provides time-byte offset information as well as random access information for selected fragments, namely fragment F1, F3, and F5.

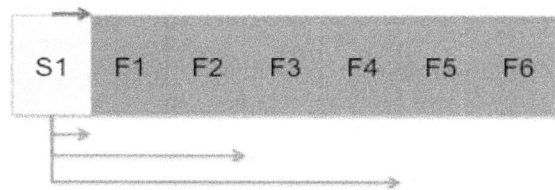

Figure 6 A Simple Example of Segment Index (Legend: S, in yellow is a segment index box; F, in blue, is a movie fragment with its data; The arrows, in red above, shows the fragment documented by the first loop; Blue arrows below show the second-loop time-byte index pointers)

As Segments may be of very different size, the first 'sidx' box may or may not describe all details of the following movie fragments in this segment. To avoid large 'sidx' boxes in case of large segments, the information may be provided in a nested manner, in such a way that 'sidx' boxes may reference not only the start of a movie fragment, but also other 'sidx' boxes.

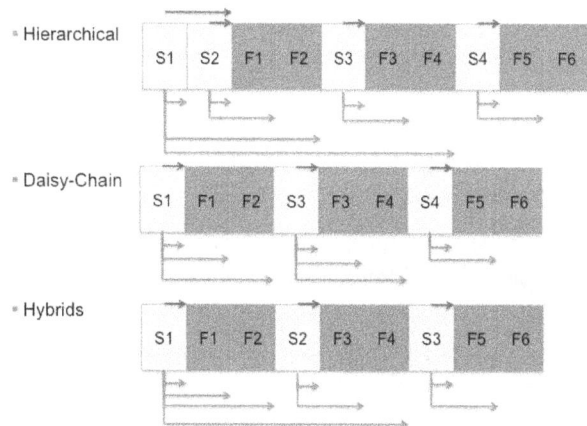

Figure 7 Nested Segment Indices (same legend as in Figure 6)

Several examples for nested segment indices are provided in Figure 7. In the 'hierarchical' case, the first loop for S1 points to the first movie fragment, but the first pointer in the second loop for S1 references a 'sidx' box. Also, any other pointer in the second loop for S1 references a 'sidx' box. Only the second level (S2/3/4) points directly to movie fragments. Therefore, with downloading the 'sidx' box S1, fast coarse navigation through the segment is enabled. Further refinements are done in the lower level. In the daisy chain case, S1 and S3 reference both movie fragments and other 'sidx' boxes: Such a construction enables fast navigation to the initial fragments of the segments, whereas later fragments may require some sequential resolution. The syntax is flexible enough to also support any hybrids of strictly hierarchical and daisy-chain constructions.

3.6 Summary

The 3GP-DASH specification provides a universal and flexible solution for Adaptive HTTP Streaming. The solution is based on existing technologies, including codecs, encapsulation formats, content protection and delivery protocols. 3GP-DASH focuses on the specification of the interface between standard HTTP servers that host media presentations and the HTTP Streaming client. Specifically, 3GPP AHS specifies

- syntax and semantics of Media Presentation Description,
- format of Segments, and
- the delivery protocol for segments.

3GP-DASH also provides an informative overview on how a DASH Client may use the provided information to establish a streaming service to the user.

However, 3GP DASH permits flexible configurations to address different use cases and delivery scenarios. Among others, 3GP-DASH does not specify

- Details on content provisioning, for example
  - o Size and duration of segments can be selected flexibly and individually for each Representation,
  - o Number of Representations and the associated bitrates can be selected based on the content requirements,
  - o Frequency and position of random access points are not restricted by the streaming solution,
  - o Other attributes and encoding parameters of each Representation, etc, are not restricted.
  - o Multiplexed components and individual component may be used.
- Normative client behaviour to provide streaming service, e.g.
  - o Prescriptions of how and when to download segments
  - o Representation selection and switching procedures among different Representations
  - o Usage of HTTP/1.1 on how to download segments, etc
- The transport of MPD, while being possible through HTTP, may also be delivered by other means.

To emphasize the flexibility in terms of use cases and deployment options, some example deployments are provided in section 4.

4. DEPLOYMENT OPTIONS

3GP-DASH provides a significant amount of options and flexibility for deploying Adaptive HTTP Streaming services on both, the service provisioning end as well as the client side. Figure 8 shows a possible deployment architecture. Content preparation is done offline and ingested into an HTTP-Web serving cloud with origin and cache servers. The ingestion tool may adapt to specifics of CDNs, for example adapt the segment duration/size to CDN properties, use load-balancing and geo-location information, etc. By providing access to the MPD, the access client can access the streaming service through any IP network that enables HTTP connections. The network may be managed or unmanaged, wired or wireless, and multiple access networks may even be used in parallel. The major intelligence to enable an efficient and high-quality streaming service is in the HTTP Streaming client. With the access to the MPD, the client is able to issue requests to seg-

ments at the appropriate times and provide the media player with data for best user experience.

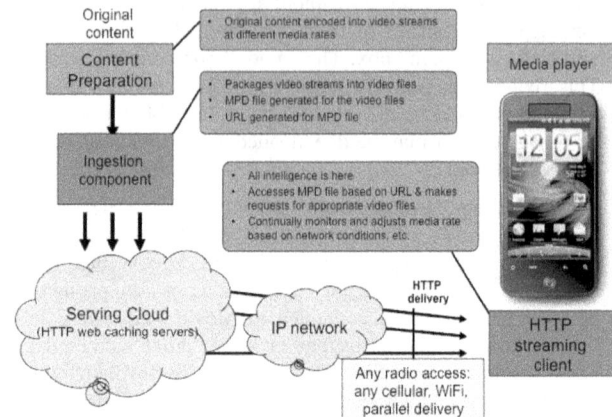

Figure 8 Example Deployment Architecture

3GP-DASH provides flexibility and options such that on the content preparation and ingestion side, the service may be optimized to support different delivery and/or user experience aspects, such as

- minimization of service access time, i.e., to ensure that the client have fast access after tune-in and after any seeking operations.
- minimization of the end-to-end delay in live services, e.g., by the adaptation of segment durations.
- maximization of delivery efficiency, e.g., by ensuring that the client has options for close-to-playout time downloading, or by providing appropriate bandwidth Representations, etc.
- adjustment to CDN properties, for example the desired file sizes, the amount of files, the handling of HTTP requests, etc.
- the reuse of encoded legacy content, for example media stored in MP4 files, media encoded with/without coordination between encoders of different bitrates, coordinated random access point placement, etc.

The 3GP-DASH solution includes some of the design options from proprietary Adaptive HTTP Streaming solutions, in particular Apple HTTP Live Streaming [8] and Microsoft Smooth Streaming [10]. For example, Apple HTTP Live Streaming configuration may typically be mapped to

- Constant segment duration of roughly 10 seconds for each Representation,
- Each segment is provided in one fragment so only the first loop in the 'sidx' box of the segment may be provided,
- Each Representation is complete and assigned to group 0, i.e., typically audio and video are multiplexed within a single segments,
- Playlist-based segment lists with regularly updated MPDs to address the live generation and publishing of segments,

Typical MS SmoothStreaming deployments may be mapped to the 3GPP AHS specification by providing

- constant segment size of roughly 1 or 2 seconds for each Representation,

- each Segment is represented by one movie fragment, and only the first loop of the 'sidx' is used to provide the media presentation time of each segment,

- media components are provided in separate Representations with alternatives in same group and complementary components in separate groups,

- a template-based segment list generation is applied to support compact MPD/manifest representation.

Additional design principles results from from implementation experience of progressive download services, especially the reuse of existing media content, or DFSplash [9] for which segments may be easily accessed with HTTP partial GET requests for optimized user experience, bandwidth efficiency and CDN adaptation.

Table 1 provides a comparison of adaptive streaming solutions based on a collection in [11]. 3GP-DASH is added to the row. It is obvious that the flexibility of 3GP-DASH can address the features of proprietary adaptive streaming solutions.

Table 1 Adaptive Streaming Comparison, based on collection in [11]

Feature	MS IIS [10]	Apple [8]	3GP- DASH
On-Demand & Live	Yes	yes	Yes
Live DVR	Yes	no	Yes
Delivery Protocol	HTTP	HTTP	HTTP
Scalability via HTTP Edge Caches	Yes	yes	Yes
Origin Server	MS IIS	HTTP	HTTP
Stateless Server Connection	Yes	yes	yes
Media Container	MP4	MP2 TS	3GP/MP4
DRM Support for Live and VOD	PlayReady	no	OMA DRM
Add Insertion Support	Yes	no	yes
Supported Video Codecs	Agnostic	H.264 BL	Agnostic
Default Segment Duration	2 sec	10 sec	flexible
End-to-End Latency	>1.5sec	30sec	flexible
File Type on Server	contiguous	fragmented	both
3GPP Adaptation	No	No	in work
Specification	proprietary	proprietary	standard

A few service examples are provided in section 5.

5. SERVICE EXAMPLES

5.1 On-Demand Adaptive Streaming Service

Assume that a streaming service provider offers a popular piece of content as on-demand streaming. The content has duration of around 1 hour and 30 minutes and one video and one audio component. The on-demand content is accessible for a long time. The service is deployed on a CDN that is optimized to file sizes of around 2MByte.

The media content is offered for different access bitrates with video resolution 320x240 with H.264/MPEG AVC baseline profile with level 1.3 and low-complexity AAC audio in a 3GP container. The service offering should permit seeking and fast for-

ward. It is especially important to support fast start-up at the beginning of the service or after seeking.

An example for a valid MPD for this service offering is provided below:

```
<?xml version="1.0" encoding="UTF-8"?>
<MPD
 type="OnDemand"
 mediaPresentationDuration="PT1H27M48.2S"
 minBufferTime="PT3S"          availabilityStartTime="1971-03-
06T23:36:47+01:00"
 availabilityEndTime="2051-03-06T09:30:47Z"

xsi:schemaLocation="urn:3GPP:ns:PSS:AdaptiveHTTPStreamingMPD:
2009 3GPP-MPD.xsd"
 xmlns:xsi="http://www.w3.org/2001/XMLSchema-instance"
 xmlns="urn:3GPP:ns:PSS:AdaptiveHTTPStreamingMPD:2009">
  <ProgramInformation                          moreInfor-
mationURL="http://www.example.com">
   <Title>Example 2: Adaptive On-Demand Streaming</Title>
  </ProgramInformation>
  <Period start="PT0S">
   <SegmentInfoDefault              sourceUrlTemplatePeri-
od="http://www.example.com/rep-$RepresentationID$/seg-
$Index$.3gs"/>
   <Representation  mimeType='video/3gpp;  codecs="avc1.42E00C,
mp4a.40.2"' bandwidth="96000" width="320" height="240">
    <SegmentInfo duration="PT160S">
     <InitialisationSegmentURL
sourceURL="http://www.example.com/rep-96/seg-init.3gs"/>
     <UrlTemplate id="96"/>
    </SegmentInfo>
    <TrickMode alternatePlayoutRate="8.0"/>
   </Representation>
   <Representation  mimeType='video/3gpp;  codecs="avc1.42E00C,
mp4a.40.2"' bandwidth="192000" width="320" height="240">
    <SegmentInfo duration="PT80S">
     <InitialisationSegmentURL
sourceURL="http://www.example.com/rep-192/seg-init.3gs"/>
     <UrlTemplate id="192"/>
    </SegmentInfo>
   </Representation>
   <Representation  mimeType='video/3gpp;  codecs="avc1.42E00C,
mp4a.40.2"' bandwidth="256000" width="320" height="240">
    <SegmentInfo duration="PT62.5S">
     <InitialisationSegmentURL
sourceURL="http://www.example.com/rep-256/seg-init.3gs"/>
     <UrlTemplate id="256"/>
    </SegmentInfo>
   </Representation>
   <Representation  mimeType='video/3gpp;  codecs="avc1.42E00C,
mp4a.40.2"' bandwidth="320000" width="320" height="240">
    <SegmentInfo duration="PT50S">
     <InitialisationSegmentURL
sourceURL="http://www.example.com/rep-320/seg-init.3gs"/>
     <UrlTemplate id="320"/>
    </SegmentInfo>
   </Representation>
   <Representation  mimeType='video/3gpp;  codecs="avc1.42E00C,
mp4a.40.2"' bandwidth="384000" width="320" height="240">
    <SegmentInfo duration="PT40S">
     <InitialisationSegmentURL
sourceURL="http://www.example.com/rep-384/seg-init.3gs"/>
     <UrlTemplate id="384"/>
    </SegmentInfo>
   </Representation>
  </Period>
</MPD>
```

The Segments for each representation are encoded according to the Initialisation Segment and Media Segment Format of 3GP DASH. The 'sidx' is provided to permit accurate seeking by the use of byte range requests. Fragments within the Media Segments are typically of 1 second duration, but not each fragment starts at a RAP.

A typical message flow is shown in Figure 9. It is assumed that the client has access to the MPD. Then according to the client behavior specified in [1] the client may parse the MPD and may create a list of accessible Segments for each Representation as defined in Table 2 - **Table 6**.

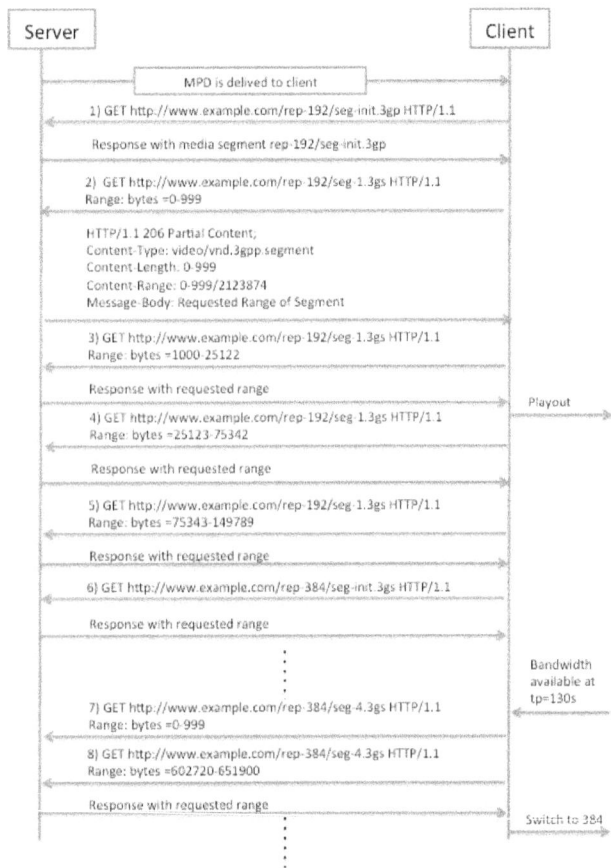

Figure 9 Message flow for Adaptive On-Demand Service

Table 2 Segment list for Representation with Id=96

Index	Start Time	URL
1	0s	http://www.example.com/rep-96/seg-1.3gs
2	160s	http://www.example.com/rep-96/seg-2.3gs
3	320s	http://www.example.com/rep-96/seg-3.3gs
...	...	....
33	5120s	http://www.example.com/rep-96/seg-33.3gs

Table 3 Segment list for Representation with Id =192

Index	Start Time	URL
1	0s	http://www.example.com/rep-192/seg-1.3gs
2	80s	http://www.example.com/rep-192/seg-2.3gs
3	160s	http://www.example.com/rep-192/seg-3.3gs
...	...	....
66	5200s	http://www.example.com/rep-192/seg-66.3gs

Table 4 Segment list for Representation with Id =256

Index	Start Time	URL
1	0s	http://www.example.com/rep-256/seg-1.3gs
2	62.5s	http://www.example.com/rep-256/seg-2.3gs
3	125s	http://www.example.com/rep-256/seg-3.3gs
...	...	....
85	5250s	http://www.example.com/rep-256/seg-85.3gs

Table 5 Segment list for Representation with Id=320

Index	Start Time	URL
1	0s	http://www.example.com/rep-320/seg-1.3gs
2	160s	http://www.example.com/rep-320/seg-2.3gs
3	320s	http://www.example.com/rep-320/seg-3.3gs
...	...	....
106	5250s	http://www.example.com/rep-320/seg-106.3gs

Table 6 Segment list for Representation with Id=384

Index	Start Time	URL
1	0s	http://www.example.com/rep-384/seg-1.3gs
2	40s	http://www.example.com/rep-384/seg-2.3gs
3	80s	http://www.example.com/rep-384/seg-3.3gs
...	...	....
132	5240s	http://www.example.com/rep-384/seg-132.3gs

An example message flow is provided in Figure 9.

1) The client initially requests the Initialisation Segment for the 192 kbit/s Representation.

2) The client also requests the first 1000 bytes of the first Media Segment of this Representation and after receipt it analyses the 'sidx' box and finds out the size and duration of the first fragment.

3) The client requests the first fragment by using byte ranges and starts play-out of the sequence.

4) The client requests a larger chunks of the segments with possible multiple fragments to gradually fill the buffer, but ensuring the continuous playout. The same may be achieved by parallel requests to multiple byte ranges.

5) The client continues to fill the data until the buffer is sufficiently filled by requesting possibly larger pieces of segment.

6) Once in stable buffer mode, the client prepares in parallel for switching representations, for example by downloading Initialisation Segment for Representation with id=384.

7) Once the client discovers that sufficient bandwidth is available, e.g., at tp=130s, it prepares to switch to a new representation by first identifying the segment that contains a possible switch time, in this case http://www.example.com/rep-384/seg-4.3gs, and downloads the 'sidx' box for scheduling further downloads.

8) A suitable byte range containing a RAP is chosen to start downloading the new Representation and eventually switch to the new Representation.

The message flow does not address fast seeking, but seeking would be performed in a similar manner as at start-up with the difference that the accessible bandwidth is known and search for a RAP using the 'sidx' box is necessary.

5.2 Adaptive Live Streaming Service

Assume that a service provider offers a popular live program as linear TV. The service is deployed on a CDN with an end-to-end delay being in a range of around 30 seconds. The media content is typically offered for different access bitrates and different device capabilities. The live service is typically split into Periods where live content is distributed and Periods during which pre-canned program is inserted, for example for ad insertion.

The program is available with a maximum time shift buffer of 90 minutes. More concrete the meeting starts at 9am at the West Coast, but the service is up from 8:45 showing a black screen only. At 9am, the live session is started which is interrupted by a canned ad starting at 11:01:22.12 seconds. After 15 minutes, the live session will restart. Further details are not known and the MPD is continuously updated. At some time before lunch break, the exact timing for the next ad break is scheduled. The duration of this break is unknown at this time. In the evening the session will terminate.

An example for a valid MPD for this service offering at time NOW of 2010-04-26T08:53:00-08:00 is provided below:

```xml
<?xml version="1.0" encoding="UTF-8"?>
<MPD
 type="Live"
 minBufferTime="PT3S"
 availabilityStartTime="2010-04-26T08:45:00-08:00"
 minimumUpdatePeriodMPD="PT5M0S"
 timeShiftBufferDepth="PT1H30M0S"

xsi:schemaLocation="urn:3GPP:ns:PSS:AdaptiveHTTPStreamingMPD:
2009 3GPP-MPD.xsd"
 xmlns:xsi="http://www.w3.org/2001/XMLSchema-instance"
 xmlns="urn:3GPP:ns:PSS:AdaptiveHTTPStreamingMPD:2009">
 <ProgramInformation                             moreInfor-
mationURL="http://www.example.com">
  <Title>Example 3: 3GPP SA4 Meeting in Vancouver as Live
Broadcast</Title>
  <Source>3GPP</Source>
 </ProgramInformation>
 <Period start="PT0S">
  <Representation mimeType='video/3gpp; codecs="avc1.42E00B"'
bandwidth="10000" width="320" height="240">
   <SegmentInfo duration="PT60S">
    <InitialisationSegmentURL        sourceURL="http://www.ad-
server.com/1-day-black/QVGA/0.3gp"/>
    <UrlTemplate     sourceURL="http://www.ad-server.com/1-day-
black/QVGA/$Index$.3gs"/>
   </SegmentInfo>
  </Representation>
 </Period>
 <Period start="PT15M0S">
  <SegmentInfoDefault duration="PT10S" sourceUrlTemplatePeri-
od="http://www.example.com/Period-2010-04-26T08-45-00/rep-
$RepresentationID$/seg-$Index$.3gs"/>
  <Representation mimeType='video/3gpp; codecs="avc1.42E00C,
mp4a.40.2"' bandwidth="192000" width="320" height="240">
   <SegmentInfo>
    <InitialisationSegmentURL
sourceURL="http://www.example.com/rep-QVGA-LQ/seg-init.3gp"/>
    <UrlTemplate id="QVGA-LQ"/>
   </SegmentInfo>
  </Representation>
  <Representation mimeType='video/3gpp; codecs="avc1.42E00C,
mp4a.40.2"' bandwidth="384000" width="320" height="240">
   <SegmentInfo>
    <InitialisationSegmentURL
sourceURL="http://www.example.com/rep-QVGA-HQ/seg-init.3gp"/>
    <UrlTemplate id="QVGA-HQ"/>
   </SegmentInfo>
  </Representation>
  <Representation mimeType='video/3gpp; codecs="avc1.64001E,
mp4a.40.2"' bandwidth="512000" width="640" height="480">
   <SegmentInfo>
    <InitialisationSegmentURL
sourceURL="http://www.example.com/rep-VGA-LQ/seg-init.3gp"/>
    <UrlTemplate id="VGA-LQ"/>
   </SegmentInfo>
  </Representation>
  <Representation mimeType='video/3gpp; codecs="avc1.64001E,
mp4a.40.2"' bandwidth="1024000" width="640" height="480">
   <SegmentInfo>
    <InitialisationSegmentURL
sourceURL="http://www.example.com/rep-VGA-HQ/seg-init.3gp"/>
    <UrlTemplate id="VGA-HQ"/>
   </SegmentInfo>
  </Representation>
 </Period>
 <Period start="PT2H01M22.12S">
  <SegmentInfoDefault duration="PT10S" sourceUrlTemplatePeri-
od="http://www.ad-server.com/15min-
Ads/$RepresentationID$/$Index$.3gs"/>
```

```xml
  <Representation mimeType='video/3gpp; codecs="avc1.42E00C,
mp4a.40.2"' bandwidth="256000" width="320" height="240">
   <SegmentInfo>
    <InitialisationSegmentURL        sourceURL="http://www.ad-
server.com/15min-Ads/QVGA/0.3gp"/>
    <UrlTemplate id="QVGA"/>
   </SegmentInfo>
  </Representation>
  <Representation mimeType='video/3gpp; codecs="avc1.64001E,
mp4a.40.2"' bandwidth="512000" width="640" height="480">
   <SegmentInfo>
    <InitialisationSegmentURL        sourceURL="http://www.ad-
server.com/15min-Ads/VGA/0.3gp"/>
    <UrlTemplate id="VGA"/>
   </SegmentInfo>
  </Representation>
 </Period>
 <Period start="PT2H16M22.12S">
  <SegmentInfoDefault duration="PT10S" sourceUrlTemplatePeri-
od="http://www.example.com/Period-2010-04-26T11-01-22/rep-
$RepresentationID$/seg-$Index$.3gs"/>
  <Representation mimeType='video/3gpp; codecs="avc1.42E00C,
mp4a.40.2"' bandwidth="192000" width="320" height="240">
   <SegmentInfo>
    <InitialisationSegmentURL
sourceURL="http://www.example.com/rep-QVGA-LQ/seg-0.3gp"/>
    <UrlTemplate id="QVGA-LQ"/>
   </SegmentInfo>
  </Representation>
  <Representation mimeType='video/3gpp; codecs="avc1.42E00C,
mp4a.40.2"' bandwidth="384000" width="320" height="240">
   <SegmentInfo>
    <InitialisationSegmentURL
sourceURL="http://www.example.com/rep-QVGA-HQ/seg-0.3gp"/>
    <UrlTemplate id="QVGA-HQ"/>
   </SegmentInfo>
  </Representation>
  <Representation mimeType='video/3gpp; codecs="avc1.64001E,
mp4a.40.2"' bandwidth="512000" width="640" height="480">
   <SegmentInfo>
    <InitialisationSegmentURL
sourceURL="http://www.example.com/rep-QVGA-LQ/seg-0.3gp"/>
    <UrlTemplate id="VGA-LQ"/>
   </SegmentInfo>
  </Representation>
  <Representation mimeType='video/3gpp; codecs="avc1.64001E,
mp4a.40.2"' bandwidth="1024000" width="640" height="480">
   <SegmentInfo>
    <InitialisationSegmentURL
sourceURL="http://www.example.com/rep-QVGA-LQ/seg-0.3gp"/>
    <UrlTemplate id="VGA-HQ"/>
   </SegmentInfo>
  </Representation>
 </Period>
</MPD>
```

At time 2010-04-26T12:26:00-08:00 the client has accesses to an updated MPD as follows:

```xml
<?xml version="1.0" encoding="UTF-8"?>
<MPD
 type="Live"
 minBufferTime="PT3S"
 availabilityStartTime="2010-04-26T08:45:00-08:00"
 minimumUpdatePeriodMPD="PT5M0S"            timeShiftBuffer-
Depth="PT1H30M0S"

xsi:schemaLocation="urn:3GPP:ns:PSS:AdaptiveHTTPStreamingMPD:
2009 3GPP-MPD.xsd"
 xmlns:xsi="http://www.w3.org/2001/XMLSchema-instance"
 xmlns="urn:3GPP:ns:PSS:AdaptiveHTTPStreamingMPD:2009">
 <ProgramInformation                             moreInfor-
mationURL="http://www.example.com">
  <Title>Example 3: 3GPP SA4 Meeting in Vancouver as Live
Broadcast</Title>
  <Source>3GPP</Source>
 </ProgramInformation>
 <Period start="PT2H01M22.12S">
  <SegmentInfoDefault duration="PT10S" sourceUrlTemplatePeri-
od="http://www.ad-server.com/15min-
Ads/$RepresentationID$/$Index$.3gs"/>
  <Representation mimeType='video/3gpp; codecs="avc1.42E00C,
mp4a.40.2"' bandwidth="256000" width="320" height="240">
   <SegmentInfo>
    <InitialisationSegmentURL        sourceURL="http://www.ad-
server.com/15min-Ads/QVGA/0.3gs"/>
    <UrlTemplate id="QVGA"/>
   </SegmentInfo>
  </Representation>
  <Representation mimeType='video/3gpp; codecs="avc1.64001E,
mp4a.40.2"' bandwidth="512000" width="640" height="480">
   <SegmentInfo>
    <InitialisationSegmentURL        sourceURL="http://www.ad-
server.com/15min-Ads/VGA/0.3gs"/>
    <UrlTemplate id="VGA"/>
```

```
    </SegmentInfo>
   </Representation>
  </Period>
  <Period start="PT2H16M22.12S">
   <SegmentInfoDefault duration="PT10S" sourceUrlTemplatePeri-
od="http://www.example.com/Period-2010-04-26T11-01-22/rep-
$RepresentationID$/seg-$Index$.3gs"/>
   <Representation mimeType='video/3gpp; codecs="avc1.42E00C,
mp4a.40.2"' bandwidth="192000" width="320" height="240">
    <SegmentInfo>
     <InitialisationSegmentURL
sourceURL="http://www.example.com/rep-QVGA-LQ/seg-0.3gs"/>
     <UrlTemplate id="QVGA-LQ"/>
    </SegmentInfo>
   </Representation>
   <Representation mimeType='video/3gpp; codecs="avc1.42E00C,
mp4a.40.2"' bandwidth="384000" width="320" height="240">
    <SegmentInfo>
     <InitialisationSegmentURL
sourceURL="http://www.example.com/rep-QVGA-HQ/seg-0.3gs"/>
     <UrlTemplate id="QVGA-HQ"/>
    </SegmentInfo>
   </Representation>
   <Representation mimeType='video/3gpp; codecs="avc1.64001E,
mp4a.40.2"' bandwidth="512000" width="640" height="480">
    <SegmentInfo>
     <InitialisationSegmentURL
sourceURL="http://www.example.com/rep-VGA-LQ/seg-0.3gs"/>
     <UrlTemplate id="VGA-LQ"/>
    </SegmentInfo>
   </Representation>
   <Representation mimeType='video/3gpp; codecs="avc1.64001E,
mp4a.40.2"' bandwidth="1024000" width="640" height="480">
    <SegmentInfo>
     <InitialisationSegmentURL
sourceURL="http://www.example.com/rep-VGA-HQ/seg-0.3gs"/>
     <UrlTemplate id="VGA-HQ"/>
    </SegmentInfo>
   </Representation>
  </Period>
  <Period start="PT4H15M18.3S">
   <SegmentInfoDefault duration="PT10S" sourceUrlTemplatePeri-
od="http://www.ad-server.com/120min-
Ads/$RepresentationID$/$Index$.3gs"/>
   <Representation mimeType='video/3gpp; codecs="avc1.42E00C,
mp4a.40.2"' bandwidth="256000" width="320" height="240">
    <SegmentInfo>
     <InitialisationSegmentURL       sourceURL="http://www.ad-
server.com/15min-Ads/QVGA/0.3gs"/>
     <UrlTemplate id="QVGA"/>
    </SegmentInfo>
   </Representation>
   <Representation mimeType='video/3gpp; codecs="avc1.64001E,
mp4a.40.2"' bandwidth="512000" width="640" height="480">
    <SegmentInfo>
     <InitialisationSegmentURL       sourceURL="http://www.ad-
server.com/15min-Ads/VGA/0.3gs"/>
     <UrlTemplate id="VGA"/>
    </SegmentInfo>
   </Representation>
  </Period>
 </MPD>
```

At time 2010-04-26T18:45:00-08:00 the client has access to another update of the MPD as follows:

```
<?xml version="1.0" encoding="UTF-8"?>
<MPD
 type="Live"
 minBufferTime="PT3S"
 availabilityStartTime="2010-04-26T08:45:00-08:00"
 mediaPresentationDuration="PT12H0M0S"
 timeShiftBufferDepth="PT1H30M0S"

xsi:schemaLocation="urn:3GPP:ns:PSS:AdaptiveHTTPStreamingMPD:
2009 3GPP-MPD.xsd"
 xmlns:xsi="http://www.w3.org/2001/XMLSchema-instance"
 xmlns="urn:3GPP:ns:PSS:AdaptiveHTTPStreamingMPD:2009">
 <ProgramInformation                               moreInfor-
mationURL="http://www.example.com">
  <Title>Example 3: 3GPP SA4 Meeting in Vancouver as Live
Broadcast</Title>
  <Source>3GPP</Source>
 </ProgramInformation>
 <Period start="PT8H22M45S">
  <SegmentInfoDefault duration="PT10S" sourceUrlTemplatePeri-
od="http://www.example.com/Period-2010-04-26T17-07-45/rep-
$RepresentationID$/seg-$Index$.3gs"/>
  <Representation mimeType='video/3gpp; codecs="avc1.42E00C,
mp4a.40.2"' bandwidth="192000" width="320" height="240">
   <SegmentInfo>
    <InitialisationSegmentURL
sourceURL="http://www.example.com/rep-QVGA-LQ/seg-0.3gs"/>
```

```
     <UrlTemplate id="QVGA-LQ"/>
    </SegmentInfo>
   </Representation>
   <Representation mimeType='video/3gpp; codecs="avc1.42E00C,
mp4a.40.2"' bandwidth="384000" width="320" height="240">
    <SegmentInfo>
     <InitialisationSegmentURL
sourceURL="http://www.example.com/rep-QVGA-HQ/seg-0.3gs"/>
     <UrlTemplate id="QVGA-HQ"/>
    </SegmentInfo>
   </Representation>
   <Representation mimeType='video/3gpp; codecs="avc1.64001E,
mp4a.40.2"' bandwidth="512000" width="640" height="480">
    <SegmentInfo>
     <InitialisationSegmentURL
sourceURL="http://www.example.com/rep-VGA-LQ/seg-0.3gs"/>
     <UrlTemplate id="VGA-LQ"/>
    </SegmentInfo>
   </Representation>
   <Representation mimeType='video/3gpp; codecs="avc1.64001E,
mp4a.40.2"' bandwidth="1024000" width="640" height="480">
    <SegmentInfo>
     <InitialisationSegmentURL
sourceURL="http://www.example.com/rep-VGA-HQ/seg-0.3gs"/>
     <UrlTemplate id="VGA-HQ"/>
    </SegmentInfo>
   </Representation>
  </Period>
  <Period start="PT10H45M00S">
   <Representation mimeType='video/3gpp; codecs="avc1.42E00B"'
bandwidth="10000" width="320" height="240">
    <SegmentInfo duration="PT60S">
     <InitialisationSegmentURL       sourceURL="http://www.ad-
server.com/1-day-black/QVGA/0.3gs"/>
     <UrlTemplate     sourceURL="http://www.ad-server.com/1-day-
black/QVGA/$Index$.3gs"/>
    </SegmentInfo>
   </Representation>
  </Period>
 </MPD>
```

The Segments for each representation are encoded according to the Initialisation Segment and Media Segment format as specified in 3GP-DASH. The 'sidx' is provided to permit accurate seeking and time-alignment of media segments.

A typical message flow is aligned with the ones for On-Demand streaming. Updates of the MPD need to be considered. The accessible segment lists for the different times are provided.

At time 2010-04-26T08:53:00-08:00, only one Period and one Representation is available. This is the accessible segment list:

Index	Start Time	URL
1	0s	http://www.ad-server.com/1-day-black/QVGA/1.3gs
2	60s	http://www.ad-server.com/1-day-black/QVGA/2.3gs
3	120s	http://www.ad-server.com/1-day-black/QVGA/3.3gs
...	...	....
7	480s	http://www.ad-server.com/1-day-black/QVGA/7.3gs

At time 2010-04-26T12:26:00-08:00 as the time shift buffer is 90 minutes, media segments back to 2010-04-26T10:56:00-08:00 are available, i.e., media segments from two periods. We present the segment list of the generic Representation in each Period.

For Period starting at <Period start="PT2H01M22.12S">, i.e., at 2010-04-26T10:46:22.12-08:00, the following media segments are available:

Index	Start Time	URL
58	570s	http://www.ad-server.com/15min-Ads/$RepresentationID$/58.3gs
59	580s	http://www.ad-server.com/1-day-black/$RepresentationID$/59.3gs

60	590s	http://www.ad-server.com/1-day-black/$RepresentationID$/60.3gs
...	...	....
90	890s	http://www.ad-server.com/1-day-black/$RepresentationID$/90.3gs

For Period starting at <Period start="PT2H16M22.12S"> i.e., at 2010-04-26T11:01:22.12-08:00, the following media segments are available

Index	Start Time	URL with Base Url http://www.example.com
1	0s	./Period-2010-04-26T11-01-22/rep-$RepresentationID$/seg-1.3gs
2	10s	./Period-2010-04-26T11-01-22/rep-$RepresentationID$/seg-2.3gs
3	590s	./Period-2010-04-26T11-01-22/rep-$RepresentationID$/seg-3.3gs
...	...	....
508	5070s	./Period-2010-04-26T11-01-22/rep-$RepresentationID$/seg-508.3gs

At time 2010-04-26T18:45:00-08:00 the client can access media segments back to 2010-04-26T17:15:00-08:00, i.e., media segments from only one periods. We present the segment list of the generic Representation in this Period.

For Period starting at <Period start="PT8H22M45S">i.e., at 2010-04-26T10:46:22.12-08:00, the following media segments are available due to the NOW constraints

Index	Start Time	URL with Base Url http://www.example.com
44	430s	./Period-2010-04-26T17-07-45/rep-$RepresentationID$/seg-44.3gs
45	440s	./Period-2010-04-26T11-01-22/rep-$RepresentationID$/seg-45.3gs
46	450s	./Period-2010-04-26T11-01-22/rep-$RepresentationID$/seg-46.3gs
...	...	....
583	5820s	./Period-2010-04-26T11-01-22/rep-$RepresentationID$/seg-583.3gs

6. CONCLUSIONS AND OUTLOOK

3GP-DASH defines the first standard on Adaptive Streaming over HTTP. Specific design principles have been taken into account that enables flexible deployments when using the formats defined in 3GP-DASH. Major players in the market, including those that offer proprietary solutions today, participated in the development of the specification. 3GP-DASH also serves as baseline for several other organizations, in particular the Open IPTV Forum and MPEG. Especially MPEG [12] is considering backward-compatible extensions to the 3GP-DASH specification to integrate additional media such as multiview or scalable video coding. Furthermore, initial efforts in interoperability testing have started. Currently there is great hope that the foundations laid in 3GP-DASH build the core package of an industry-standard for Dynamic Adaptive Streaming over HTTP (DASH).

7. ACKNOWLEDGMENTS
Many thanks to all the colleagues in Qualcomm Incorporated and especially in 3GPP SA4 and MPEG DASH for the collaboration on the matter and their contributions to a hopefully successful and widely deployed standard.

8. REFERENCES
[1] 3GPP TS 26.234: "Transparent end-to-end packet switched streaming service (PSS); Protocols and codecs".

[2] 3GPP TS 26.244: "Transparent end-to-end packet switched streaming service (PSS); 3GPP file format (3GP)".

[3] 3GPP TS 26.245: "Transparent end-to-end packet switched streaming service (PSS); Timed text format".

[4] IETF RFC 2616: "Hypertext Transfer Protocol – HTTP/1.1", Fielding R. et al., June 1999.

[5] ISO/IEC 14496-12:2005 | 15444-12:2005: "Information technology – Coding of audio-visual objects – Part 12: ISO base media file format" | "Information tech-nology – JPEG 2000 image coding system – Part 12: ISO base media file format".

[6] IETF RFC 3986: "Uniform Resource Identifiers (URI): Generic Syntax", Berners-Lee T., Fielding R. and Masinter L., January 2005

[7] Cisco White Paper: Cisco Visual Networking Index: Global Mobile Data Traffic Forecast Update, 2009-2014, http://bit.ly/bwGY7L

[8] Apple HTTP live Streaming: http://tools.ietf.org/id/draft-pantos-http-live-streaming-04.txt

[9] DF-Splash Overview: http://www.digitalfountain.com/ufiles/library/DF-Splash-Service-Overview.pdf

[10] Microsoft Smooth Streaming: http://go.microsoft.com/?linkid=9682896

[11] Adaptive Streaming Comparison, http://learn.iis.net/page.aspx/792/adaptive-streaming-comparison

[12] ISO/IEC JTC1/SC29/WG11 N11338, Call for Proposals on HTTP Streaming of MPEG Media, April 2010, Dresden, Germany.

[13] OIPF Specification Volume 2a - HTTP Adaptive Streaming V2.0, 2010/09/07.

Feedback Control for Adaptive Live Video Streaming

Luca De Cicco
Politecnico di Bari
Bari, Italy
ldecicco@gmail.com

Saverio Mascolo
Politecnico di Bari
Bari, Italy
mascolo@poliba.it

Vittorio Palmisano
Politecnico di Bari
Bari, Italy
vpalmisano@gmail.com

ABSTRACT

Multimedia content feeds an ever increasing fraction of the Internet traffic. Video streaming is one of the most important applications driving this trend. Adaptive video streaming is a relevant advancement with respect to classic progressive download streaming such as the one employed by YouTube. It consists in dynamically adapting the content bitrate in order to provide the maximum Quality of Experience, given the current available bandwidth, while ensuring a continuous reproduction. In this paper we propose a Quality Adaptation Controller (QAC) for live adaptive video streaming designed by employing feedback control theory. An experimental comparison with Akamai adaptive video streaming has been carried out. We have found the following main results: 1) QAC is able to throttle the video quality to match the available bandwidth with a transient of less than 30s while ensuring a continuous video reproduction; 2) QAC fairly shares the available bandwidth both in the cases of a concurrent TCP greedy connection or a concurrent video streaming flow; 3) Akamai underutilizes the available bandwidth due to the conservativeness of its heuristic algorithm; moreover, when abrupt available bandwidth reductions occur, the video reproduction is affected by interruptions.

Categories and Subject Descriptors

C.2.5 [**Local and Wide-Area Networks**]: Internet; H.5.1 [**Multimedia Information Systems**]: Video

General Terms

Design, Performance, Experimentation

Keywords

Adaptive Video Streaming, quality feedback control, quality adaptation controller

1. INTRODUCTION

Nowadays, the wide availability of wired and wireless broadband connections is enabling ubiquitous multimedia applications over the Internet, such as video streaming, personal video broadcasting, IPTV, and videoconferencing, at video resolutions that can scale up to full high definition (full HD, 1920x1080) at frame rates up to 30 fps. Such rich video contents require a compressed bitstream in the order of 10 Mbps along with adequate processing resources at the client for decoding. Nevertheless, the Internet is becoming more and more accessible to a wide spectrum of devices: if desktops users are normally equipped with large screens, good processing resources, and wired broadband connections, mobile users typically use small screens devices, with limited processing resources and wireless cellular connections that are characterized by variable link characteristics.

Thus, a key challenge is to provide the user with a seamless multimedia experience at the maximum Quality of Experience (QoE) that can be obtained given the available device and network resources. To this purpose, multimedia content must be made adaptive. It is important to notice that the adaptation process should account take into account a wide set of variables such as user screen resolution, CPU load, network available bandwidth, power consumption, some of which are time-varying. In this paper we focus on adaptation to network available bandwidth.

Adaptive (live) video streaming represents a relevant advancement *wrt* classic progressive download streaming such as the one employed by YouTube.

In classic *progressive download streaming*, the video is delivered as any data file using greedy TCP connections. The video stream is buffered at the receiver for a while before the playing is started so that short-term mismatches between the video bitrate and the available network bandwidth can be absorbed and video interruptions could be mitigated. Nevertheless, if the mismatch persists the buffer could eventually get empty and playback interruptions could occur affecting the user experience.

On the other hand, with *adaptive streaming* the video source is adapted on-the-fly so that the user can watch videos at the maximum bitrate that is allowed by the time-varying available bandwidth and by the device resources.

In this paper we focus on a particular adaptive streaming approach that is the *stream-switching* technique: the server encodes the video content at different bitrates and it switches from one video version to another based on client feedbacks such as the measured available bandwidth. This approach is employed by Apple HTTP live streaming, Microsoft IIS server, Adobe Dynamic Streaming, Akamai HD Video Streaming, and Move Networks. In particular, we present a Quality Adaptation Controller (QAC), which has been designed using feedback control, to drive stream-switching for adaptive live streaming applications. The advantages of using a control theoretical approach to design the controller as opposed to a heuristic-based design is a cleaner design that can be not only experimentally tested but also mathematically analyzed.

The rest of the paper is organized as follows: Section 2 provides a brief review of the different adaptive streaming algorithms proposed in the literature along with the main features of the adaptive streaming algorithms employed in commercial products; Section 3 summarizes the results obtained by an experimental investigation of Akamai HD Video Streaming; in Section 4 we propose the Quality Adaptation Controller (QAC) and in Section 5 we experimentally compare QAC with the Akamai HD Video Streaming; finally, Section 6 concludes the paper.

2. RELATED WORKS

In this Section we provide a review of the relevant literature on adaptive streaming and then we focus on the most known commercial products providing adaptive streaming services.

2.1 Adaptive streaming techniques

In the last decade a vast literature on video streaming has been produced. Main topics that have been investigated are: 1) the design of transport protocols specifically tailored for video streaming, 2) adaptation techniques, 3) scalable codecs.

Concerning the first topic, several transport protocols designed for video streaming have been proposed, such as the TCP Friendly Rate Control (TFRC) [7], Real Time Streaming Protocol (RTSP) [14], Microsoft Media Services (MMS), Real Time Messaging Protocol (RTMP) [3]. Some of the mentioned protocols have been employed in commercial products such as RealNetworks, Windows Media Player, Flash Player. Even though TCP has been regarded in the past as inappropriate for the transport of video streaming protocols, recently it is getting a wider acceptance and it is being used with the HTTP. This is mainly due to the following reasons: i) Internet applications are rapidly converging on web browsers; ii) HTTP-based streaming is cheaper to deploy since it employs standard HTTP servers [17]; iii) TCP has built-in NAT traversal functionalities; iv) it is easy to be deployed within Content Delivery Networks (CDN) [17]; v) TCP delivers most part of the Internet traffic and it is able to guarantee the stability of the network by means of an efficient congestion control algorithm [15].

In [16] the authors develop analytic performance models to assess the performance of TCP when used to transport a live video streaming source without the use of quality adaptation. The theoretical results, obtained considering a constant bit rate (CBR) source and supported by an experimental evaluation, suggest that in order to achieve good performance in terms of startup delay and percentage of late packet arrivals, TCP requires a network bandwidth that is roughly two times the video bit rate. It is important to stress that such bandwidth over-provisioning would systematically waste half of the available bandwidth.

For what concerns adaptation techniques, different ap-

proaches have been proposed in the literature so far. The issue here is how to automatically throttle the video quality to match the available resources (network bandwidth, CPU) so that the user receives the video at the maximum possible quality. The proposed techniques to adapt the video source bitrate to the variable bandwidth can be classified into three main categories: 1) transcoding-based, 2) scalable encoding-based, 3) stream-switching (or multiple-bitrate - MBR). Figure 1 shows a schematic representation of each considered technique. In the figure, the blocks represented in gray are those requiring on-the-fly per-client processing and the (k) index refers to variables pertaining to the k-th client accessing the same video content. In particular, encoders can be considered as the most CPU-consuming function, whereas controllers generally require much less processing capacity.

The *transcoding-based* [12] approach (see Figure 1(a)), consists in adapting the video content to match a specific bitrate by means of on-the-fly transcoding of the raw content. These algorithms can achieve a very fine granularity by throttling frame rate, compression, and video resolution. Nevertheless, this comes at the cost of increased processing load and poor scalability, due to the fact that transcoding has to be done on a per-client basis. Another important issue is that such algorithms are difficult to be deployed in CDNs.

Another important class of adaptation algorithms (see Figure 1(b)) employs *scalable codecs* such as H264/MPEG-4 AVC [9, 10]. Both spatial and temporal scalability can be exploited to adapt picture resolution and frame rate without having to re-encode the raw video content. With respect to transcoding-based approach, scalable codecs reduce processing costs since the raw video is encoded once and adapted on-the-fly by exploiting the scalability features of the encoder. To be used with CDNs, this approach requires specialized servers implementing the adaptation logic. Also this approach is difficult to be used with CDNs since the adaptation logic requires to be run on specialized servers and content cannot be cached in standard proxies. Another issue is that the adaptation logic depends on the employed codec, thus restricting the content provider to use only a limited set of codecs.

Stream-switching algorithms (see Figure 1(c)) encode the raw video content at increasing bitrates resulting into N versions, i.e. *video levels*; an algorithm dynamically chooses the video level that matches the user's available bandwidth; those algorithms minimize the processing costs since, once the video is encoded, no further processing is required in order to adapt the video to the variable bandwidth [17, 1, 11, 2, 8]. Another important advantage of such algorithms is that they do not rely on particular functionalities of the employed codec and thus can be made codec-agnostic. The disadvantages of this approach are the increased storage requirements and the fact that adaptation is characterized by a coarser granularity since video bitrates can only belong to a discrete set of levels.

2.2 Stream-switching adaptive video streaming commercial products

Stream-switching, or Multiple Bit-Rate (MBR) streaming, is gaining momentum since leading commercial media players are preferring it to the other streaming approaches.

IIS Smooth Streaming [17] is a live adaptive streaming service provided by Microsoft. The streaming technology is

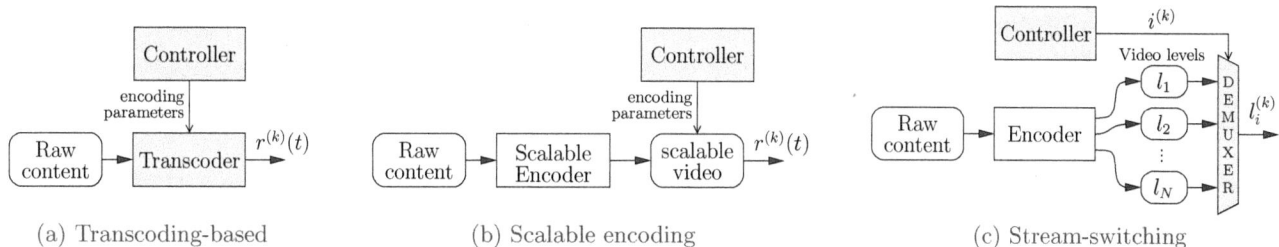

Figure 1: Adaptive streaming techniques

offered as a web-based solution requiring the installation of a plug-in that is available for Windows and iPhone OS 3.0. IIS Smooth Streaming is codec agnostic and employs a stream-switching approach where different video versions can be encoded with configurable bitrates and video resolutions up to 1080p. In the default configuration, the video is encoded in seven layers ranging from 300 kbps up to 2.4 Mbps.

Adobe Dynamic Streaming [8] is a web-based adaptive streaming service developed by Adobe that is available to all devices running a browser with Adobe Flash plug-in. The server stores several streams at different quality and resolution and switches among them during the playback, in order to match user bandwidth and CPU. The service is provided using the RTMP streaming protocol [3]. The supported video codecs are H.264 and VP6, which are included in the Adobe Flash plug-in.

Apple has recently released a client-side *HTTP Adaptive Live Streaming* solution [11]. The server segments the video content into several pieces with configurable duration and video quality. The server exposes a playlist (.m3u8) containing all the available video segments. The client downloads consecutive video segments and it dynamically chooses the video quality by using an undisclosed algorithm. Apple HTTP Live Streaming employs H.264 codec using a MPEG-2 TS container and it is available on any device running iPhone OS 3.0 or later (including iPad), or any computer with QuickTime X or later installed.

Move Networks provides live adaptive streaming service to several TV networks such as ABC, FOX, Televisa, ESPN and others. A plug-in, available for the most used web browsers (Windows and Mac OS X) has to be installed to access the service. Move Networks employs VP7, a video codec developed by On2, a company that has been recently acquired by Google. Adaptivity to available bandwidth is provided using the stream-switching approach. Five different versions of the same video are available at the server with bitrates ranging from 100 kbps up to 2200 kbps.

Hulu[1] offers on demand TV shows and movies in the USA. In 2010 Hulu has launched a new video player that implements adaptivity by employing the stream-switching approach. The adaptation algorithm does not change the video frame rate, whereas it sets the video resolution to match the current user available bandwidth.

3. AKAMAI ADAPTIVE STREAMING

In this Section we summarize and significantly extend the results obtained in a recent experimental investigation of the Akamai HD Video Streaming (AHDVS) service [5].

---

[1]http://www.hulu.com

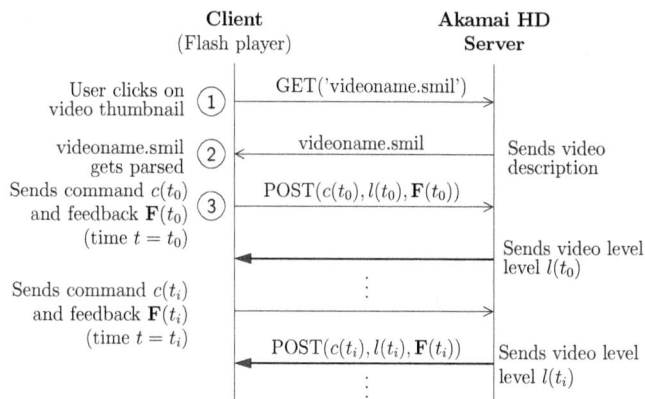

Figure 2: Client-server time sequence graph: thick lines represent video data transfer, thin lines represent HTTP requests sent from client to server

3.1 Client-server protocol

AHDVS employs HTTP connections to stream data from the server to the client. The adaptation algorithm is executed at the client in a Flash application. By analyzing the traffic between the Akamai server and the client we have observed that the client issues a number of HTTP requests to the server throughout all the duration of the video streaming. Figure 2 shows a typical time sequence graph of the HTTP requests sent from the client to the Akamai server.

At first, the client connects to the Akamai server [1], then a Flash application is loaded and a number of videos are made available to the client. When the user clicks on the thumbnail (1) of the video he is willing to play, a GET HTTP request is sent to the server which points to a SMIL[2] compliant file. In the SMIL file the base URL of the video, the available video levels, and the corresponding encoding bit-rates are provided.

After that, the client parses the SMIL file (2) to reconstruct the complete URLs of the available video levels and selects the corresponding video level based on the quality adaptation algorithm. All the videos available on the demo website are encoded at five different bitrates as shown in Table 1. In particular, the *video level* bitrate $l(t)$ can assume values in the discrete *set of available video levels* $\mathscr{L} = \{l_0, \ldots, l_4\}$. Video levels are encoded at 30 frames per second (fps) using H.264 codec with a group of picture (GOP) of length 36, so that two consecutive I frames are 1.2s apart. This means that, since a video switch can oc-

---

[2]http://www.w3.org/TR/2005/REC-SMIL2-20050107/

Video level	Bitrate (kbps)	Resolution (width×height)
l_0	300	320x180
l_1	700	640x360
l_2	1500	640x360
l_3	2500	1280x720
l_4	3500	1280x720

Table 1: Set of available video levels $\mathscr{L}$

	Command	Args	Occurrence (%)
c_1	`throttle`	1	~80%
c_2	`rtt-test`	0	~15%
c_3	`SWITCH_UP`	5	~2%
c_4	`BUFFER_FAILURE`	7	~2%
c_5	`log`	2	~1%

Table 2: Commands issued by the client to the streaming server via the `cmd` parameter

cur only at the beginning of a GOP, video levels can change only each 1.2s. Finally, the audio is encoded with Advanced Audio Coding (AAC) at 128 kbps bitrate.

After the SMIL file gets parsed, at time $t = t_0$ (3), the client issues the first POST request specifying several parameters. Among those, the most important parameters are `cmd`, that specifies a command the client issues on the server, and `lvl1`, that specifies several feedback variables $\mathbf{F}(t)$ such as: 1) the receiver buffer size $q(t)$, 2) the receiver buffer target $q_T(t)$, 3) the received video frame rate $f(t)$, 4) the estimated bandwidth $B(t)$, 5) the received goodput $r(t)$, 6) the current received video level bitrate $l(t)$.

At time $t = t_0$, the quality adaptation algorithm starts. For a generic time instant $t_i > t_0$ the client issues commands via HTTP POST requests to the server in order to select the suitable video level. It is worth to notice that the commands are issued on a separate TCP connection that is established at time $t = t_0$.

Table 2 reports the possible commands c_i that the client can issue on the servers along with the number of arguments and the occurrence percentage. The first two commands are issued periodically, `throttle` with a median inter-departure time of about 2s and `rtt-test` with a median inter-departure time of about 11s. On the other hand, `log`, `SWITCH_UP` and `BUFFER_FAILURE` are commands triggered on the occurrence of a particular event.

In [5] we have shown that the `throttle` command specifies a single argument, the *throttle percentage* $T(t)$, that it is used to control the receiver buffer level $q(t)$ as we will discuss in Section 3.2. The `rtt-test` command is issued to periodically actively probe for the available bandwidth and the round trip time $R(t)$ (RTT) of the connection.

Finally, the two event-based commands `SWITCH_UP` and `BUFFER_FAILURE` are sent from the client to ask the server to respectively switch up or down the video level $l(t)$.

3.2 The control system

Figure 3 shows a block diagram of the control architecture employed by AHDVS. The server is connected to the client through an Internet connection characterized by a forward connection delay τ_f and a backward connection delay τ_b. Figure 3 shows that the three main components of the

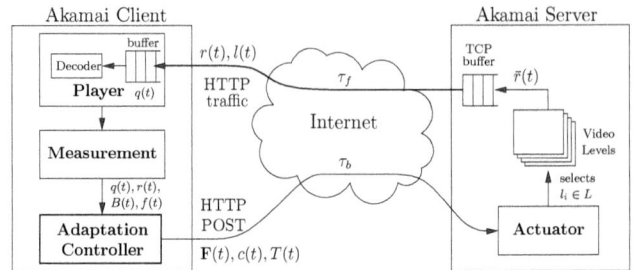

Figure 3: A block diagram of the control architecture employed by AHDVS

control loop, i.e. measurement, adaptation controller, and actuator, are connected through the Internet so that the control loop is affected by an overall delay $\tau = \tau_f + \tau_b$.

The client receives the video flow at level $l(t) \in \mathscr{L}$ over an HTTP connection at a rate $r(t)$. The received video is stored in a playout buffer, whose instantaneous length is $q(t)$, which is drained by the decoder at the current received video level $l(t)$. A *measurement* module feeds the values of the buffer length $q(t)$, the received goodput $r(t)$, the bandwidth $B(t)$, and the decoded frame rate $f(t)$ to the adaptation controller.

The adaptation controller is made of two modules: 1) a *playout buffer level controller* whose goal is to drive the buffer length to a target length; 2) a *stream-switching logic* that selects the appropriate video level to be streamed by the server.

In [5] we have shown that the control law implemented by Akamai to regulate the buffer length $q(t)$ is a proportional controller that takes the error $q_T(t) - q(t)$ as the input and whose output is the throttle percentage $T(t)$:

$$T(t) = \max\left((1 + \frac{q_T(t) - q(t)}{q_T(t)})100, 10 \right) \qquad (1)$$

The throttle percentage $T(t)$ is used to set the rate $\bar{r}(t)$ at which the Akamai server feeds the TCP socket buffer with the current video level $l(t)$ as follows:

$$\bar{r}(t) = l(t)\frac{T(t)}{100} \qquad (2)$$

The rationale of controlling $\bar{r}(t)$ is to induce, on average, a TCP sending rate that is equal to $\bar{r}(t)$. This means that when the throttle percentage is above 100% the server can stream the video at a rate that is above the encoding bitrate $l(t)$. It is important to stress that, in the case of live streaming, it is not possible for the server to supply a video at a rate that is above the encoding bitrate for a long period, since the video source is not pre-encoded.

By looking at (1) we find that when the buffer length $q(t)$ matches the target buffer length $q_T(t)$, the throttle percentage $T(t)$ is equal to 100% and $\bar{r}(t)$ matches $l(t)$. On the other hand, when the error $q_T(t) - q(t)$ increases, $T(t)$ increases accordingly in order to allow $\bar{r}(t)$ to increase so that the buffer can be filled quickly. Since (1) implements a simple proportional controller on the buffer length, the $q(t)$ matches $q_T(t)$ with an offset at steady state [6].

Let us now focus on the stream-switching logic that is a heuristic-based controller that decides which video level $l(t) \in \mathscr{L}$ has to be sent by the server, based on the estimated bandwidth, the current video level, the playout buffer

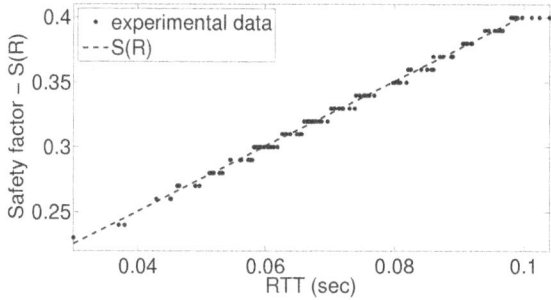

Figure 4: Safety factor vs round trip time.

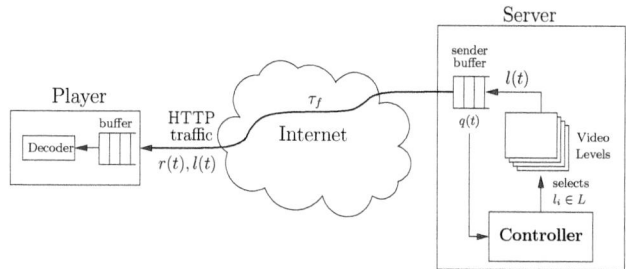

Figure 5: QAC control architecture

length, and the frame rate. In particular, and based on the debug information provided by the Akamai Client and on the experiments we have run, the stream-switching heuristic works as follows.

The client periodically issues `rtt-test` commands that have the effect of setting at the server a throttling percentage of 500%, thus asking the server to periodically send the video in greedy mode. In this way Akamai actively probes for extra available bandwidth and estimates the RTT $R(t)$ under congestion. Based on the estimated value of the RTT, the client computes a *safety factor* S. By parsing the debug information in order to collect the pairs $(R(t), S(t))$ shown in Figure 4, it was possible to run a linear regression over the dataset which yielded to the following static linear model ($R(t)$ is expressed in seconds):

$$f(R(t)) = 2.5R(t) + 0.15$$

We have observed that when $R(t) > 0.1$s the safety factor remains set to 0.4, whereas when $R(t) < 0.02$s, it is set to 0.2. Thus, we can conclude that the complete model for $S(R(t))$ is the following:

$$S(R(t)) = \begin{cases} 0.2 & 0 < R(t) < 0.02\text{s} \\ 2.5R(t) + 0.15 & 0.02\text{s} \leq R(t) \leq 0.1\text{s} \\ 0.4 & R(t) > 0.1\text{s} \end{cases} \quad (3)$$

For each video level $l_i \in \mathscr{L}$ a high threshold L_i^H and a low threshold L_i^L are maintained:

$$L_i^H(t) = l_i \cdot (1 + S(t)) \; ; \; L_i^L = l_i \cdot 1.2 \quad (4)$$

A switch up (`SWITCH_UP`) to a higher video level l_i is enabled only if $B(t) > L_i^H(t)$, which means that if, for instance, the RTT is above 0.1 s and thus $S(R(t)) = 0.4$, in order to switch to level l_i the estimated bandwidth must be at least 40% higher than l_i. This seems to be a conservative approach that leads to network underutilization and, as a consequnece, to a reduced QoE.

The switch down event occurs when:

$$q(t) < q_L(t) \quad (5)$$

where $q_L(t)$ is another threshold that is smaller than the queue target[3] $q_T(t)$. When (5) holds, a `BUFFER_FAILURE` is sent and the new video level $l_i < l(t)$ is selected. In particular, the highest video level $l_i \in \mathscr{L}$ satisfying the following condition:

$$B(t) > 1.2 \cdot l_i = L_i^L$$

---

[3]The identification of $q_L(t)$ has not been carried out.

is selected. Thus, in to select the level l_i, the currently estimated bandwidth $B(t)$ must be at least 20% above l_i. Moreover, in [5] we have shown that when `SWITCH_UP` and `BUFFER_FAILURE` commands are sent from the client, the *actuator*, which is located at the server, takes a delay of $\tau_{su} \simeq 14$s and $\tau_{sd} \simeq 7$s respectively, to actuate these commands.

Finally, it is worth noting that the overall system exhibits a very complex dynamics due to the interaction of two closed-loop dynamics: the stream-switching logic, which has been designed using heuristic arguments, and the buffer level controller. As a consequence, it is very complex to develop a mathematical analysis as well as to tune control variables to satisfy key design requirements such as settling times and steady state errors.

4. QUALITY ADAPTATION CONTROLLER

In this Section we propose a *Quality Adaptation Controller* (QAC) for adaptive live video streaming that aims at pursuing the following goals: 1) *maximize the QoE* by delivering the best quality that is possible given the network available bandwidth while minimizing playback interruptions; 2) *rigorous design of the controller* by employing the control theory; 3) *high scalability* in terms of processing costs; 4) *CDN-friendly design*, i.e. the algorithm can be easily deployed on CDNs; 5) *codec-agnostic*, i.e. the service provider has the freedom to choose any codec.

In order to pursue the goals 3), 4), and 5) we choose the *stream-switching* approach and we employ the standard HTTP streaming over TCP. For what concerns the goals 1) and 2) we employ feedback control theory to design a controller that throttles the video level $l(t)$ to be streamed without using any heuristics. This provides the key advantage of getting a predictable system dynamics that can fulfill required design features such as settling time and steady state errors [6].

4.1 The control system

Figure 5 shows the architecture of the proposed streaming server. The first important difference *wrt* the control architecture employed by Akamai (Figure 3) is that measuring, control and actuation take place at the server so that the control loop is not affected by delays and does not require explicit feedback from the client. This architecture provides the following advantages: 1) *simplicity of the player*: being the control centralized at the server, the player at the client has the only task of decoding and playing the stream; moreover, when a new version of the control algorithm is designed and installed at the server, there is no need to update the

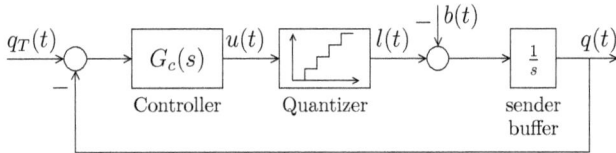

Figure 6: Block diagram of the control loop

player; 2) *effectiveness of the controller*: by avoiding delays in the control loop the controller can provide faster dynamics while retaining stability [6].

The controller works as follows: it takes as input the queue length $q(t)$ of the *sender buffer* that is placed at the server, and it selects the video level $l_i \in \mathscr{L}$. The selected video level is temporally stored at the sender buffer and is then sent to the client via a TCP connection. The received stream is buffered at the client that decodes and plays the video content.

Figure 6 shows a block diagram of the feedback control system designed to throttle the video level $l(t)$. In the following $s \in \mathbb{C}$ denotes the Laplace variable and $F(s) = \mathcal{L}\{f(t)\}$ denotes the unilateral Laplace transform of the real valued function $f(t)$.

The input of the system q_T is the set-point, or threshold value, for the sender buffer length $q(t)$. The controller goal is to track a queue length $q_T > 0$ so that the TCP sender buffer is always full and can fill the communication pipe.

The controller, which can be described by its transfer function $G_c(s)$, takes as input the error $e(t) = q_T - q(t)$ and outputs the control signal $u(t)$ that is the bitrate the encoder should set to match the available bandwidth $b(t)$. In our case, since we employ the stream-switching approach, the video bitrate will belong to the discrete set of available video levels $\mathscr{L}$. This can be modelled through a quantizer, which is a static element that takes as input $u(t)$ and selects the highest video level l_i that is less then $u(t)$. Finally, the sender buffer, which can be modelled by the integrator $1/s$, is filled at a rate $l(t)$ and it is drained by the available bandwidth at the rate $b(t)$. It is worth to notice that the available bandwidth $b(t)$ is modelled as a disturbance [13].

The effect of the quantizer is to add a quantization error $d_q(t) = l(t) - u(t)$ to $u(t)$. This is equivalent to consider $d_q(t)$ as a disturbance acting on $b(t)$ giving the total equivalent disturbance $d_{eq}(t) = b(t) + d_q(t)$. In this way we are able to take the quantizer out of the control loop and we can compute the transfer function from the input q_T to the output $q(t)$ as follows:

$$G_0(s) = \frac{Q(s)}{Q_T(s)} = \frac{G_c(s)\frac{1}{s}}{1 + G_c(s)\frac{1}{s}} \quad (6)$$

We choose a proportional integral (PI) controller:

$$G_c(s) = \frac{U(s)}{E(s)} = K_p + \frac{K_i}{s} \quad (7)$$

since it is able to reject step-like disturbances $b(t)$ and it is very simple to be discretized and implemented in a software module. The integral action of the controller ensures that the video level $l(t)$ matches on average the available bandwidth $b(t)$.

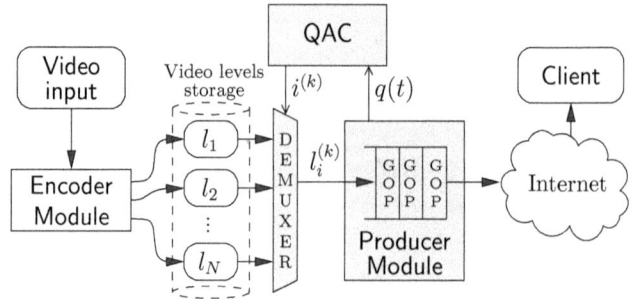

Figure 7: The QAC adaptive streaming server architecture

By substituting (7) in (6) it turns out:

$$G_0(s) = \frac{K_p s + K_i}{s^2 + K_p s + K_i} \quad (8)$$

Thus, the closed loop system is a second order system with one zero. In order to tune the controller, we impose the damping factor of the system (8) to be $\delta = \sqrt{2}/2$ [6] and a natural frequency $\omega_n = \sqrt{K_i} = 0.1886\frac{\text{rad}}{s}$ that corresponds to a system bandwidth of around 0.06 Hz and a 2% settling time of $T_s = \frac{4}{\delta\omega_n} = 30$ s. This choice is made in order to limit the switching frequency between different video levels. The gains of the PI turn out to be $K_i = 0.0356$ and $K_p = 0.2667$.

In the time domain the control law is:

$$u(t) = \mathcal{L}^{-1}\{G_c(s)E(s)\} = K_p e(t) + K_i \int_0^t e(\xi)d\xi \quad (9)$$

In order to implement (9) we need to discretize the control law with a sampling time ΔT:

$$u(t_k) = K_p e(t_k) + K_i \sum_{j=0}^{k} \Delta T e(t_j) \quad (10)$$

We choose a sampling time $\Delta T = 0.5$s that is 1/60th of the settling time T_s. In the following subsection we provide the implementation details of the adaptive streaming server using the QAC.

4.2 Implementation of the adaptive streaming server

The adaptive streaming server is written in Python and developed using the Twisted[4] libraries. A schematic representation of the proposed streaming server is shown in Figure 7. The server contains an audio/video transcoding engine (Encoder Module) developed using GStreamer[5] and FFMpeg[6] libraries. The encoder module takes as input a raw or pre-encoded audio/video file and outputs a set of files transcoded at various bitrates and resolutions. We used the same levels of AHDVS as shown in Table 1 with a frame rate equal to 30 fps. We employ a fixed Group of Picture (GOP) of 30 frames which is equal to 1s of video stream. For each transcoded file, the encoder module stores an index file (.index) containing the file position and the timestamp of each encoded GOP. We used a fixed GOP

---

[4] http://twistedmatrix.com/

[5] http://gstreamer.org/

[6] http://www.ffmpeg.org/

150

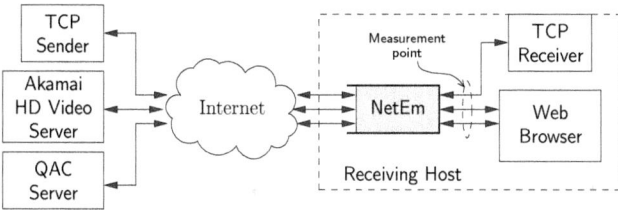

Figure 8: Testbed employed in the experimental evaluation

encoder setting in order to simplify the stream switch between video levels. Moreover, the server integrates also a Producer Module, which is a simple HTTP server. When a client connects to the server, it sends a GET HTTP request specifying the stream unique identifier it wants to play. The producer replies with a HTTP response and starts to send the video stream content reading from the storage at a configured start level[7] $l(0) = \bar{l}$. Moreover, the producer continuously provides the current queue level $q(t)$ to the QAC module. When a video level switch occurs, the producer selects the corresponding input file from the storage, it performs a file seek operation to the current sent time position using the information contained in the .index file and then it feeds the data to the client. The switch operation can be performed only at GOP boundaries in order to ensure the correct decoding by the client.

The adaptive streaming server supports every encoding format provided by GStreamer/FFMpeg libraries. In this paper, in order to make a fair comparison with AHDVS, we encoded the video using H.264 codec and MP3 audio muxed into FLV container.

It is worth noticing that the producer and the QAC modules are independent from the encoding profile used. Finally, we stress that the client can be not only an Adobe Flash applet, but also any video player that supports the same codec employed by the server. A buffering time of 15s at the client side is recommended in order to avoid interruptions.

5. EXPERIMENTAL EVALUATION

In this section we carry out a comparison between the Akamai HD video server and the proposed Quality Adaptation Controller (QAC) by employing the testbed shown in Figure 8. To run the experiments, we have employed the video sequence *"Elephant's Dream"*[8] since its duration is long enough for a careful experimental evaluation. In order to perform a fair comparison, the video sequence streamed with the QAC has been encoded using the x264 codec and the same discrete set of video levels employed by AHDVS (see Table 1). The receiving host is an Ubuntu Linux machine running 2.6.32 kernel equipped with NetEm, which is a kernel module that, along with the traffic control tools available on Linux kernel, allows downlink channel bandwidth and delays to be set. In order to perform traffic shaping on the downlink we have used the Intermediate Functional Block pseudo-device IFB[9].

The receiving host was connected to the Internet through our campus wired connection. It is worth to notice that,

before running any experiment, we carefully checked that the available bandwidth was well above 4 Mbps, which is the maximum value of the bandwidth we set in the traffic shaper. The measured RTT between our client and the Akamai server was in the range 10ms to 30ms. All measurements have been taken after the traffic shaper (as shown in Figure 8) and collected by sniffing the traffic on the receiving host with tcpdump. For what concerns AHDVS, the dump files have been post-processed and parsed using a Python script to obtain the figures that we report in the following.

The receiving host runs an iperf server (TCP Receiver) in order to receive TCP greedy flows sent by an iperf client (TCP Sender).

Four different scenarios have been considered in order to investigate the dynamic behaviour of the two considered quality adaptation algorithms: 1) one video stream over a bottleneck link whose available bandwidth changes following a step function with minimum value of 500 kbps and maximum value of 4000 kbps; 2) one video stream over a bottleneck link whose available bandwidth varies as a square wave with a period of 200s, a minimum value of 500 kbps and a maximum value of 4000 kbps; 3) one video stream sharing a bottleneck, whose available bandwidth is equal to 4000 kbps, with one concurrent TCP flow; 4) two video streams sharing a bottleneck whose available bandwidth is equal to 4000 kbps.

In scenarios 1 and 2 abrupt variations of the available bandwidth occur: such step-like variations of the input signal are often employed in control theory to evaluate key features of a dynamic system response to an external input such as settling time, overshoots and time constants [4]. The third scenario evaluates the dynamic behaviour of a video flow when it shares the bottleneck with a greedy TCP flow, such as in the case of a file download, and it is useful to investigate the inter-protocol fairness.

Since, due to the use of TCP, the loss rate is small, the evaluation of the QoE can be inferred by evaluating the instantaneous video level received by the client, i.e., the higher the received video level $l(t)$ the higher the quality perceived by the user. For this reason we employ the received video level $l(t)$ as the key performance index of the system. In particular, to assess the efficiency of the quality adaptation algorithm, we introduce the following index of utilization:

$$\eta = \frac{\hat{l}}{C} \qquad (11)$$

where $\hat{l}$ is the average value of the video level $l(t)$, $C = \min(l_M, b)$ where l_M is the maximum video level and b is the available bandwidth. The index $0 \leq \eta \leq 1$ is 1 when the average value of the received video level is equal to C, i.e. when the video level exactly matches the bottleneck available bandwidth.

For each considered scenario we will show the dynamics of the following variables: the received video level $l(t)$, the received video rate $r(t)$, the decoded frame rate $f(t)$, and the receiver buffer length $q(t)$.

5.1 Step-like change of the bottleneck capacity

We start by investigating the dynamic behaviour of the two quality adaptation algorithms in a simple scenario. The bottleneck available bandwidth $b(t)$ increases at time $t = 50s$ from a value of $A_m = 500$ kbps to a value of $A_M = 4000$ kbps. It is worth to notice that $A_m > l_0$ and $A_M > l_4$.

[7] In this paper we used a start video level $l(0) = l_1$
[8] http://orange.blender.org/
[9] http://linuxfoundation.org/collaborate/workgroups/networking/ifb

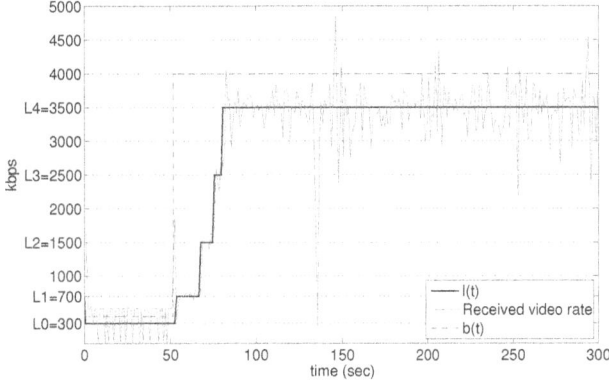

(a) Received rate $r(t)$, video level $l(t)$, and available bandwidth $b(t)$

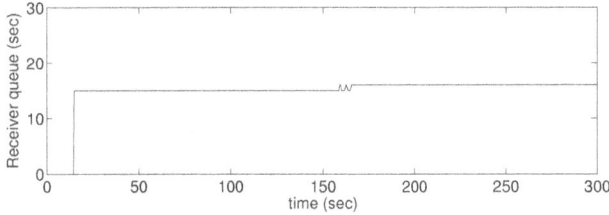

(b) Receiver buffer length

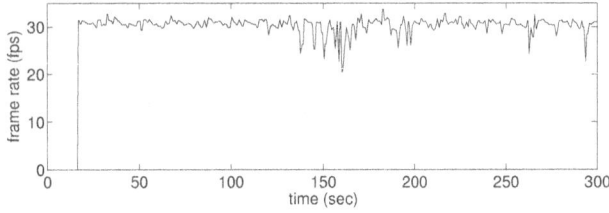

(c) Frame rate $f(t)$

Figure 9: QAC adaptive video streaming response to a step change of available bandwidth at $t = 50$s

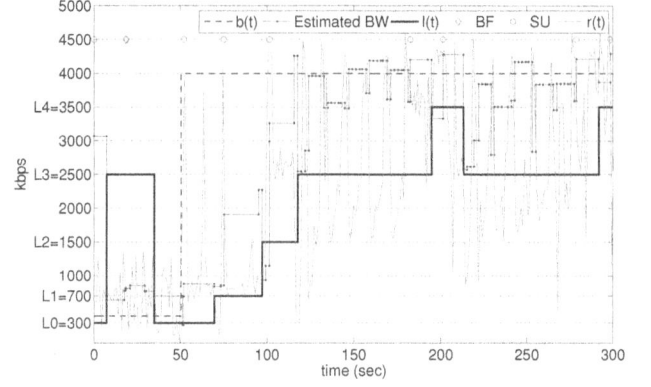

(a) Estimated BW, video level $l(t)$, received rate $r(t)$, BUFFER_FAILURE, and SWITCH_UP events

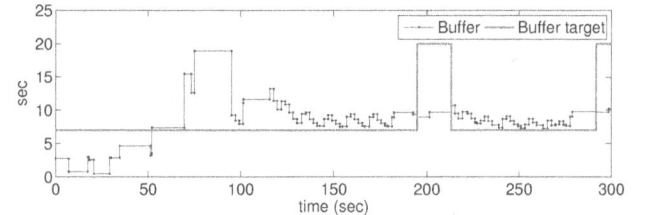

(b) Receiver buffer length and target buffer length

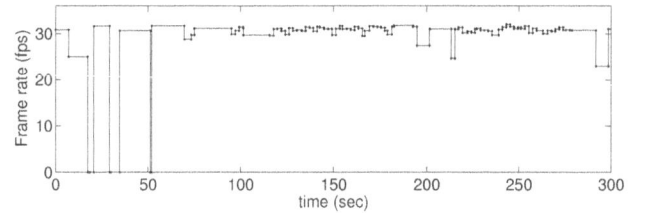

(c) Frame rate $f(t)$

Figure 10: AHDVS response to a step change of available bandwidth at $t = 50$s

In particular, we are interested in assessing the responsiveness of the adaptation algorithms in matching the available bandwidth choosing the adequate video level $l(t)$. Figure 9 and Figure 10 show the dynamics of one QAC and one AHDVS video flow, respectively.

Let us consider Figure 9(a) that shows the received video rate $r(t)$ and video level $l(t)$ in the case of QAC: after that the bandwidth increases at $t = 50$s, the video level increases and eventually reaches, at steady state, the maximum video level l_4 after a transient time of around 30s. It is worth noting that the transient time required for $l(t)$ to match the available bandwidth $b(t)$ is equal to the settling time T_s that was set as requirement when the quality controller was designed (7) (see Section 4). Moreover, Figure 9(b) shows that the received buffer length is 15s throughout all the duration of the connection. The decoded frame rate of the stream oscillates around 30 fps, which proves that there were no video interruptions during the streaming. Finally, the efficiency index (11) is 0.93.

Let us now focus on the Akamai video streaming server. Figure 10(a) shows the dynamics of the video level $l(t)$, the estimated bandwidth reported by the lvl1 parameter, and

the received video rate $r(t)$. In order to show their effect on the dynamics of $l(t)$, Figure 10(a) also reports the time instants at which BUFFER_FAILURE (BF) and SWITCH_UP (SU) commands are issued. The video level is initialized at l_0 that is the lowest available version of the video. Nevertheless, at time $t = 0$ the estimated bandwidth is erroneously overestimated to a value above 3000 kbps and a SWITCH_UP command is sent to the server. The effect of this command occurs after an actuation delay of $\tau_{su} = 7.16$s (see Section 3) when $l(t)$ is increased to $l_3 = 2500$ kbps, which is the video level closest to the bandwidth estimated at $t = 0$. By setting the video level to l_3, which is above the current available bandwidth $A_m = 500$ kbps, the receiver buffer starts to drain and it eventually gets empty at $t = 17.5$s (see Figure 10(b)). Figure 10(c) shows that during the time interval $[17.5, 20.8]$s the playback frame rate is zero, meaning that the video is paused. At time $t = 18.32$s, a BUFFER_FAILURE command is finally sent to the server. After a delay of about $\tau_{sd} = 16$s the server switches the video level to $l_0 = 300$ kbps that is below the available bandwidth A_m. Even though the heuristic to trigger a video level switch down (5) should be able in principle to avoid interruptions, the actuation delay τ_{sd} poses a remarkable limitation to the responsiveness of the quality adaptation algorithm. Moreover, Figure 10(a) shows that the transient time required by $l(t)$ to reach the maximum video level l_4 is around 150s, which is roughly one order of magnitude higher than the transient time exhibited by QAC. Finally, in this case the efficiency index (11) is 0.676 that is well below the value found in the case of QAC. To conclude, the inefficiency of AHDVS is largely due to the conservativeness of the safety-factor $S(t)$ that we discussed in Section 3. In fact, given a minimum safety factor of $S = 0.2$, the available bandwidth required to switch to the level $l_4 = 3500$ kbps according to (4) turns out to be 4200 kbps that is above A_M.

Let us compare the received video rates of QAC and AHDVS shown respectively in Figure 9(a) and 10(a): if on one hand the received video rate of QAC is affected by a moderate burstiness that is typical of a TCP connection, on the other hand the received rate of AHDVS is affected by remarkable and persistent oscillations whose amplitude is more than 2Mbps. This is due to the fact that AHDVS dynamics periodically switches between two states: in the *normal* state the video sending rate is bounded by the maximum sending rate $\bar{r}(t)$ given by (2), whereas each time a `rtt-test` command is issued AHDVS enters the *greedy-mode* state and for a short time interval of around 5s the sending rate is limited by the available bandwidth [5].

In conclusion, this experiment shows that QAC is able to provide the maximum value of the received video level that is possible given the available bandwidth with a transient time of around 30s in accordance with the design requirements given in Section 4. On the other hand, AHDVS exhibits a very large transient of around 150s, remarkable oscillations in the received rate $r(t)$, it is not able to provide the maximum possible QoE to the user, and it is not able to avoid interruptions.

5.2 Square-wave varying bottleneck capacity

In this experiment we consider abrupt drops/increases of the bottleneck available bandwidth $b(t)$ which is shaped as a square-wave function with a period of 200s, a minimum value $A_m = 500$ kbps and a maximum value $A_M = 4000$ kbps. The aim of this experiment is to assess the responsiveness of the two considered adaptive video streaming services in shrinking the video level $l(t)$ in response to an abrupt drop of the available bandwidth and to what extent they are able to guarantee a continuous reproduction of the video content in the presence of this sudden bandwidth reduction.

Figure 11(a) shows the dynamics of the video received rate $r(t)$ and the video level $l(t)$ in response to the available bandwidth $b(t)$. The figure shows that the QAC algorithm is able to control $l(t)$ so that it properly follows step increases and decreases in the available bandwidth. In particular, the transient times required for $l(t)$ to match bandwidth increases/decreases are less than 20s. Moreover, Figures 11(b) and 11(c) show that the receiver buffer length is around 15s and the reproduced frame rate is around 30 fps during all the experiment, so showing a reproduction without interruptions. During the time intervals with bandwidth $A_M = 4000$ kbps, the efficiency index was equal to 0.93.

On the other hand, Figure 10 clearly shows that AHDVS is not able to properly adapt the video level to follow bandwidth variations. By considering the dynamics of the video level $l(t)$ shown in Figure 12(a) we notice two main facts:

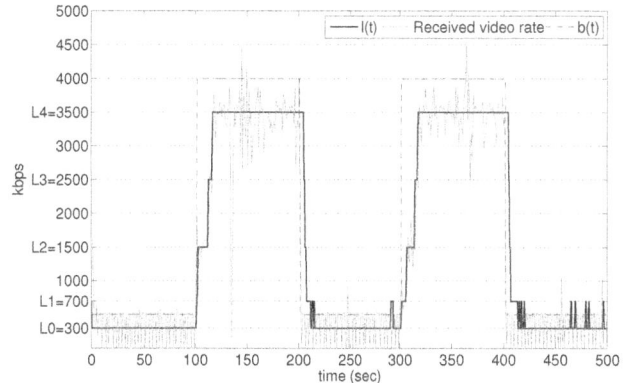

(a) Received rate $r(t)$, video level $l(t)$, and available bandwidth $b(t)$

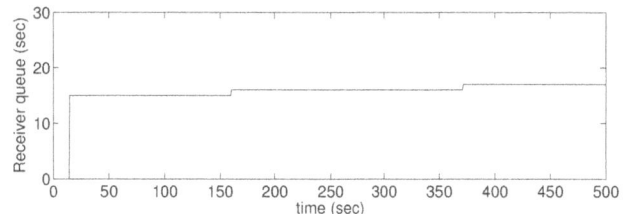

(b) Receiver buffer length

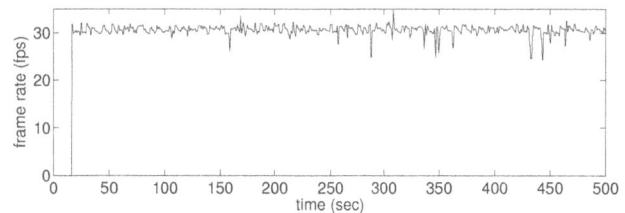

(c) Frame rate $f(t)$

Figure 11: QAC response to a square-wave available bandwidth with period 200 s

1) when the available bandwidth increases to A_M the video level is increased to l_3, which is less than the maximum video level l_4, in around 75s; 2) when bandwidth drops occur the playback is affected by interruptions as it can be inferred by considering Figure 12(b) and Figure 12(c). In particular, when the first bandwidth drop occurs at $t = 200$s, a `BUFFER_FAILURE` is sent to the server after a delay of roughly 7s in order to switch down the video level from l_3 to l_0. After that, a switch-down delay τ_{sd} of 20s occurs and the video level $l(t)$ is finally switched to l_0. Thus, the total delay spent to correctly set the video level $l(t)$ to match the new value of the available bandwidth is 38s. Due to this large delay in setting $l(t)$, the receiver buffer gets empty and the reproduction of the video is blocked for more than 100s. The same situation occurs when the second bandwidth drop occurs. In this case, the total delay spent to correctly set the video level is 26s. Again, 13s after the second bandwidth drop, an interruption in the video reproduction occurs. During the time intervals with bandwidth $A_M = 4000$ kbps, we evaluated a low index of efficiency equal to 0.4, which is less than half the efficiency obtained by QAC in this scenario.

To summarize, this experiment has shown that the pro-

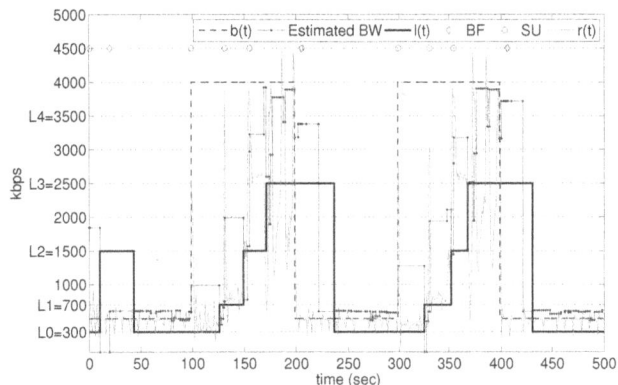

(a) Estimated BW, video level $l(t)$, received rate $r(t)$, BUFFER_FAILURE , and SWITCH_UP events

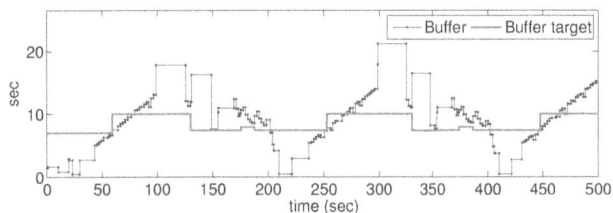

(b) Receiver buffer length and target buffer length

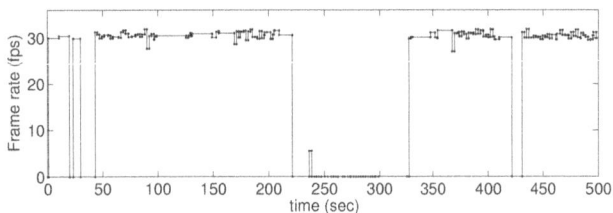

(c) Frame rate $f(t)$

Figure 12: AHDVS response to a square-wave available bandwidth with period 200 s

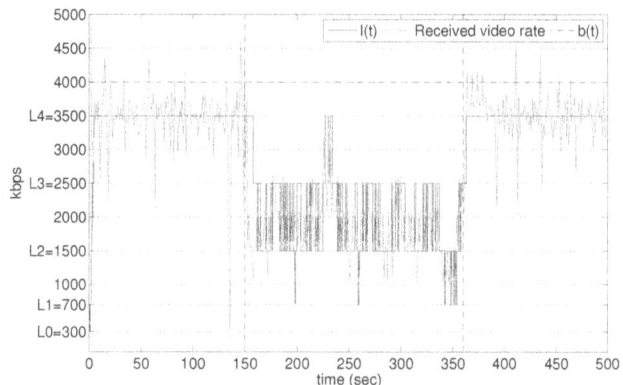

(a) Received rate $r(t)$, video level $l(t)$, and available bandwidth $b(t)$

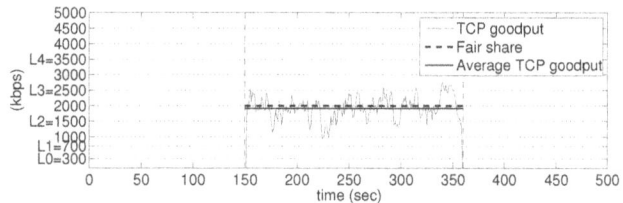

(b) TCP goodput

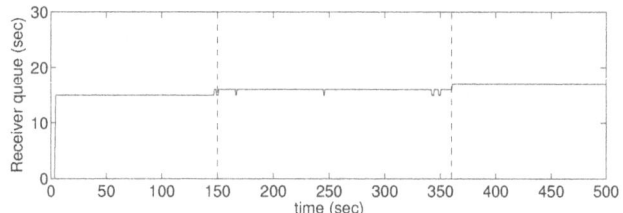

(c) Receiver buffer length

Figure 13: QAC when sharing the bottleneck with one greedy TCP flow

posed QAC is able to control $l(t)$ to follow step increases and decreases of the available bandwidth always providing the user with a continuous reproduction of the video content at the best QoE. In the case of Akamai HD Video Streaming, when the available bandwidth suddenly shrinks, the video reproduction is affected by interruptions.

5.3   One concurrent greedy TCP flow

In this experiment we investigate the performance of the two quality adaptation algorithms when sharing the available bandwidth with one greedy TCP flow, such as in the case of a parallel download session. The available bandwidth has been set to a constant value of 4000 kbps, a video streaming session is started at $t = 0$, a greedy TCP connection is started at $t = 150$s and it is stopped at $t = 360$s.

Figure 13(a) shows the dynamics of the video level $l(t)$ and of the video received rate $r(t)$, whereas Figure 13(b) shows the goodput of the concurrent TCP flow. In the first part of the experiment, for $0 < t < 150$s, $l(t)$ quickly matches the available bandwidth obtaining an efficiency $\eta = 0.98$. After the greedy TCP flow is started at $t = 150$s the video level $l(t)$ is switched down in about 10s and, since the fair share is

2000 kbps, $l(t)$ switches between the two closest video levels $l_2 = 1500$ kbps and $l_3 = 2500$ kbps. In this part of the experiment the efficiency is 0.99 and, the average goodput of the greedy TCP flow is 1930 kbps whereas the goodput obtained by QAC flow is 1910 kbps thus indicating that the two flows share the available bandwidth fairly. When the greedy TCP flow is stopped, the video level $l(t)$ is correctly set to the maximum video level l_4 after a transient of 4s. In this part of the experiment the efficiency of QAC is 0.99. Finally, Figure 13(c) shows that the receiver buffer length is always greater than 15s, meaning that no interruptions occurred during the video reproduction.

Figure 14(a) shows the video level dynamics $l(t)$, the estimated bandwidth and the received video rate $r(t)$ in the case of AHDVS. During the first part of the experiment, i.e. for $t < 150$s, apart from a short time interval $[6.18, 21.93]$s during which $l(t)$ is equal to $l_4 = 3500$ kbps, the video level is set to $l_3 = 2500$ kbps. The efficiency index η in this part of the experiment is 0.74. When the TCP flow joins the bottleneck, it grabs the fair bandwidth share of 2000 kbps. Nevertheless, the estimated bandwidth decreases to the correct value after 9s. After an additional delay of 8s, at $t = 167$s, a BUFFER_FAILURE command is sent (see Figure 14(a)). The

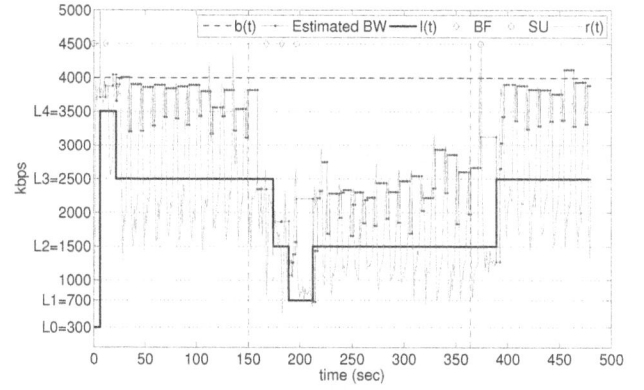

(a) Estimated BW, video level $l(t)$, received rate $r(t)$, BUFFER_FAILURE , and SWITCH_UP events

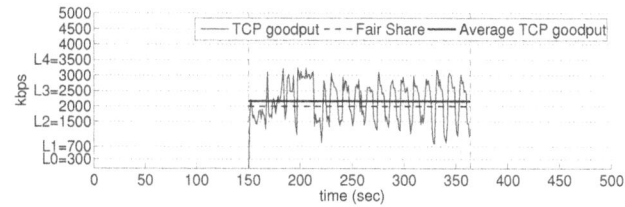

(b) TCP goodput

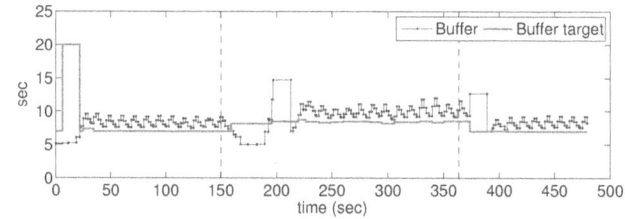

(c) Receiver buffer length and target buffer length

Figure 14: AHDVS when sharing the bottleneck with one greedy TCP flow

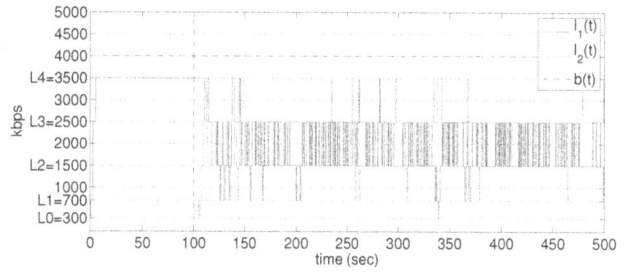

(a) Received video levels $l_1(t)$, $l_2(t)$

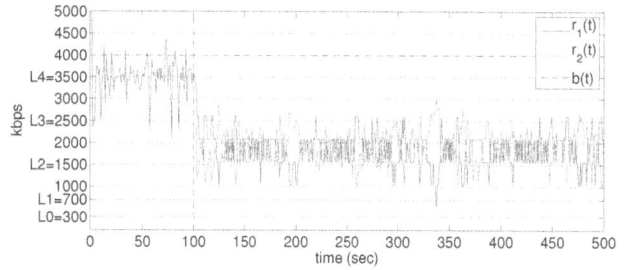

(b) Received rates $r_1(t)$ and $r_2(t)$

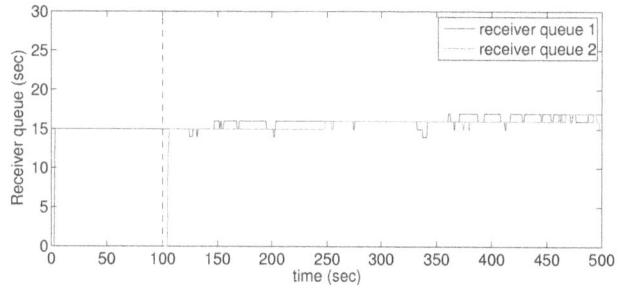

(c) Receiver queue of the two concurrent video flows

Figure 15: Two QAC adaptive video streaming flows sharing a bottleneck

video level is shrunk to the suitable value $l_2 = 1500$ kbps after a total delay of 24s. In this case, this actuation delay does not affect the video reproduction as it can be inferred by considering the receiver buffer dynamics shown in Figure 14(c). However, Figure 14(a) shows that $l(t)$ is further decreased to $l_1 = 700$ kbps and it is set to steady state value of l_2 at $t = 212$s. Thus, the transient time spent to reach the steady state is 62s. In this part of the experiment, the efficiency index is equal to 0.76, the average goodput of the greedy TCP flow is 2170 kbps, whereas the goodput obtained by Akamai flow is 1643 kbps indicating that the available bandwidth is underutilized. In the third part of the experiment, after the TCP flow leaves the bottleneck at time $t = 360$s, the level is switched up to $l_3 = 2500$ kbps with a delay of 26s. In this part of the experiment the efficiency is 0.69. Finally, by considering Figure 14(b), we can observe that the "on-off" dynamics of the sending rate provided by AHDVS affects the dynamics of the TCP received rate that shows remarkable oscillations.

5.4 Two concurrent video streaming sessions

In this scenario we evaluate the behaviour of two video streams that share the same bottleneck whose available band-width has been set to 4000 kbps. The first video streaming session is started at $t = 0$ and after 100s a second video flow is started. This experiment is aimed at assessing to what extent two competing flows are able to share in a fair way the bottleneck. In this experiment the fair share is equal to 2000 kbps.

Figure 15(a) shows the dynamics of the video levels $l_1(t)$ and $l_2(t)$ of the first and the second video flow controlled by QAC. In the first part of the experiment, the first flow behaves as already shown in the other experiments quickly setting $l_1(t)$ to the maximum video level l_4. When the second video flow joins the bottleneck at $t = 100$s, the video level $l_1(t)$ is correctly shrunk to let the second video flow obtain its fair share. After a transient time of 8s the two video levels $l_1(t)$ and $l_2(t)$ start to switch between the two video levels, $l_2 = 1500$ kbps and $l_3 = 2500$ kbps, that are closest to the fair share which is 2000 kbps.

Figure 16(a) shows the dynamics of the two video levels in the case of AHDVS. The figure shows that, when the second flow joins the bottleneck, it takes 210s for the video level $l_1(t)$ to be set to the correct value $l_2 = 1500$ kbps. Thus, during this transient the first video flow experiences a higher video level with respect to the second video flow,

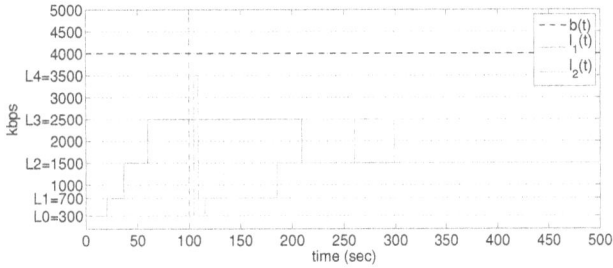

(a) Received video levels $l_1(t)$, $l_2(t)$

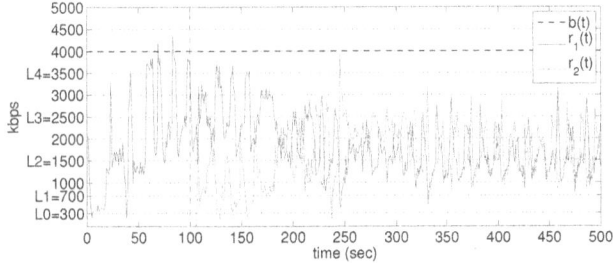

(b) Received video rates $r_1(t)$ and $r_2(t)$

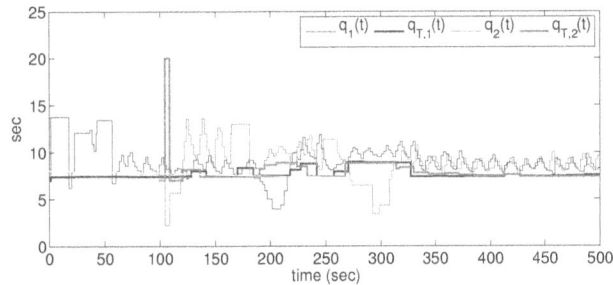

(c) Receiver buffer lengths $q_1(t)$ and $q_2(t)$ and target buffer lengths $q_{T,1}(t)$, $q_{T,2}(t)$

Figure 16: Two AHDVS flows sharing a bottleneck

Server	g_1	g_2	U
QAC	1860	1950	0.95
AHDVS	1815	1612	0.85

Table 3: Goodput g_1 and g_2 (kbps) of the two concurrent flows and channel utilization U

tiveness of its algorithm based on heuristics; 4) moreover, when abrupt reductions of the available bandwidth occur, the video reproduction is affected by interruptions.

7. REFERENCES

[1] Akamai HD Network Demo. http://wwwns.akamai.com/hdnetwork/demo/flash.

[2] Move Networks HD adaptive video streaming. http://www.movenetworkshd.com.

[3] Adobe Systems Inc. Real-Time Messaging Protocol (RTMP) Specification. 2009.

[4] L. De Cicco and S. Mascolo. A Mathematical Model of the Skype VoIP Congestion Control Algorithm. *IEEE Trans. on Automatic Control*, 55(3):790–795, Mar. 2010.

[5] L. De Cicco and S. Mascolo. An Experimental Investigation of the Akamai Adaptive Video Streaming. In *Proc. of USAB 2010*, Nov. 4–5, 2010.

[6] G. Franklin, J. Powell, and A. Emami-Naeini. *Feedback control of dynamic systems*. Addison-Wesley, 1994.

[7] M. Handley, S. Floyd, and J. Pahdye. TCP Friendly Rate Control (TFRC): Protocol Specification. *RFC 3448, Proposed Standard*, Jan. 2003.

[8] D. Hassoun. Dynamic streaming in flash media server 3.5. Available: http://www.adobe.com/devnet/flashmediaserver/.

[9] C. Krasic, J. Walpole, and W. Feng. Quality-adaptive media streaming by priority drop. In *Proc. of ACM NOSSDAV '03*, 2003.

[10] R. Kuschnig, I. Kofler, and H. Hellwagner. An evaluation of TCP-based rate-control algorithms for adaptive internet streaming of H. 264/SVC. In *Proc. of ACM SIGMM conference on Multimedia systems*, pages 157–168, 2010.

[11] R. Pantos and W. May. HTTP Live Streaming. *IETF Draft*, June 2010.

[12] M. Prangl, I. Kofler, and H. Hellwagner. Towards QoS Improvements of TCP-Based Media Delivery. In *Proc. of ICNS '08*, pages 188–193, 2008.

[13] S. Mascolo. Congestion control in high-speed communication networks using the Smith principle. *Automatica*, 35(12):1921–1935, 1999.

[14] H. Schulzrinne, A. Rao, and R. Lanphier. Real Time Streaming Protocol (RTSP). *RFC 2326, Standard track*, Apr. 1998.

[15] V. Jacobson. Congestion avoidance and control. In *Proc. of ACM SIGCOMM '88*, pages 314–329, 1988.

[16] B. Wang, J. Kurose, P. Shenoy, and D. Towsley. Multimedia streaming via TCP: An analytic performance study. *ACM TOMCCAP*, 4(2):1–22, 2008.

[17] A. Zambelli. IIS smooth streaming technical overview. *Microsoft Corporation*, 2009.

indicating that the controller is not able to provide the same QoE to all the users sharing a bottleneck.

Finally, Table 3 collects the average goodputs g_1 and g_2 obtained for $t > 100s$ by the first and the second flow respectively for both QAC and AHDVS streaming systems. The average channel utilization, computed as $U = (g_1 + g_2)/4000$ kbps, obtained by QAC results 10% higer *wrt* the one obtained by AHDVS.

6. CONCLUSIONS

In this paper we have presented a Quality Adaptation Controller (QAC) for a stream-switching adaptive live video streaming system designed by using feedback control theory. Moreover, we have provided a characterization of the adaptation algorithm employed by Akamai High Definition Video Server which also implements a stream-switching system.

The main results of the paper are the following: 1) QAC is able to control the video level $l(t)$ to match the available bandwidth $b(t)$ with a transient time that is less than 30s always providing a continuous video reproduction; 2) the proposed controller is able to share in a fair way the available bandwidth both in the case of a concurrent greedy connection and a concurrent video streaming flow; 3) Akamai underutilizes the available bandwidth due to the conserva-

An Experimental Evaluation of Rate-Adaptation Algorithms in Adaptive Streaming over HTTP

Saamer Akhshabi
College of Computing
Georgia Institute of
Technology
sakhshab@cc.gatech.edu

Ali C. Begen
Video and Content Platforms
Research and Advanced
Development
Cisco Systems
abegen@cisco.com

Constantine Dovrolis
College of Computing
Georgia Institute of
Technology
dovrolis@cc.gatech.edu

ABSTRACT

Adaptive (video) streaming over HTTP is gradually being adopted, as it offers significant advantages in terms of both user-perceived quality and resource utilization for content and network service providers. In this paper, we focus on the rate-adaptation mechanisms of adaptive streaming and experimentally evaluate two major commercial players (Smooth Streaming, Netflix) and one open source player (OSMF). Our experiments cover three important operating conditions. First, how does an adaptive video player react to either persistent or short-term changes in the underlying network available bandwidth? Can the player quickly converge to the maximum sustainable bitrate? Second, what happens when two adaptive video players compete for available bandwidth in the bottleneck link? Can they share the resources in a stable and fair manner? And third, how does adaptive streaming perform with live content? Is the player able to sustain a short playback delay? We identify major differences between the three players, and significant inefficiencies in each of them.

Categories and Subject Descriptors

C.4 [**Computer Systems Organization**]: Performance of Systems

General Terms

Performance, Measurement, Algorithms

Keywords

Experimental evaluation, adaptive streaming, rate-adaptation algorithm, video streaming over HTTP

1. INTRODUCTION

Video has long been viewed as the "next killer application". Over the last 20 years, the various instances

of packet video have been thought of as demanding applications that would never work satisfactorily over best-effort IP networks. That pessimistic view actually led to the creation of novel network architectures and QoS mechanisms, which were not deployed in a large-scale, though. Eventually, over the last three to four years video-based applications, and video streaming in particular, have become utterly popular generating more than half of the aggregate Internet traffic. Perhaps, surprisingly though, video streaming today runs over IP without any specialized support from the network. This has become possible through the gradual development of highly efficient video compression methods, the penetration of broadband access technologies, and the development of *adaptive video players* that can compensate for the unpredictability of the underlying network through sophisticated rate-adaptation, playback buffering, and error recovery and concealment methods.

Another conventional wisdom has been that video streaming would never work well over TCP, due to the throughput variations caused by TCP's congestion control and the potentially large retransmission delays. As a consequence, most of the earlier video streaming research has assumed that the underlying transport protocol is UDP (or RTP over UDP), which considerably simplifies the design and modeling of adaptive streaming applications. In practice, however, two points became clear in the last few years. First, TCP's congestion control mechanisms and reliability requirement do not necessarily hurt the performance of video streaming, especially if the video player is able to adapt to large throughput variations. Second, the use of TCP, and of HTTP over TCP in particular, greatly simplifies the traversal of firewalls and NATs.

The first wave of HTTP-based video streaming applications used the simple *progressive download* method, in which a TCP connection simply transfers the entire movie file as quickly as possible. The shortcomings of that approach are many, however. One major issue is that all clients receive the same encoding of the video, despite the large variations in the underlying available bandwidth both across different clients and across time for the same client. This has recently led to the development of a new wave of HTTP-based streaming applications that we refer to as *adaptive streaming over HTTP* (For a general overview of video streaming protocols and adaptive streaming, refer to [2]). Several recent players, such as Microsoft's Smooth

Streaming, Adobe OSMF, as well as the players developed or used by Netflix, Move Networks and others, use this approach. In adaptive streaming, the server maintains multiple profiles of the same video, encoded in different bitrates and quality levels. Further, the video object is partitioned in *fragments*, typically a few seconds long. A player can then request different fragments at different encoding bitrates, depending on the underlying network conditions. Notice that it is the player that decides what bitrate to request for any fragment, improving server-side scalability. Another benefit of this approach is that the player can control its playback buffer size by dynamically adjusting the rate at which new fragments are requested.

Adaptive streaming over HTTP is a new technology. It is not yet clear whether the existing commercial players perform well, especially under dynamic network conditions. Further, the complex interactions between TCP's congestion control and the application's rate-adaptation mechanisms create a "nested double feedback loop" - the dynamics of such interacting control systems can be notoriously complex and hard to predict. As a first step towards understanding and improving such video streaming mechanisms, this paper experimentally evaluates two commercial adaptive video players over HTTP (Microsoft's Smooth Streaming and the player used by Netflix) and one open source player (Adobe OSMF). Our experiments cover three important operating conditions. First, how does an adaptive video player react to either persistent or short-term changes in the underlying network available bandwidth? Can the player quickly converge to the maximum sustainable bitrate? Second, what happens when two adaptive video players compete for available bandwidth in the bottleneck link? Can they share that resource in a stable and fair manner? And third, how does adaptive streaming perform with live content? Is the player able to sustain a short playback delay? We identify major differences between the three players, and significant inefficiencies in each of them.

1.1 Related Work

Even though there is extensive previous work on rate-adaptive video streaming over UDP, transport of rate-adaptive video streaming over TCP, and HTTP in particular, presents unique challenges and has not been studied in depth in the past. A good overview of multi-bitrate video streaming over HTTP was given by Zambelli [17], focusing on Microsoft's IIS Smooth Streaming. Adobe has provided an overview of HTTP Dynamic Streaming on the Adobe Flash platform [1]. Cicco et al. [3] experimentally investigated the performance of the Akamai HD Network for Dynamic Streaming for Flash over HTTP. They studied how the player reacted to abrupt changes in the available bandwidth and how it shared the network bottleneck with a greedy TCP flow. Kuschnig et al. [9] evaluated and compared three server-side rate-control algorithms for adaptive TCP streaming of H.264/SVC video. The same authors have proposed a receiver-driven transport mechanism that uses multiple HTTP streams and different priorities for certain parts of the media stream [10]. The end-result is to reduce throughput fluctuations, and thus, improve video streaming over TCP. Tullimas et al. [15] also proposed a receiver-driven TCP-based method for video streaming over the Internet, called *MultiTCP*, aimed at providing resilience against short-term bandwidth

fluctuations and controlling the sending rate by using multiple TCP connections. Hsiao et al. [8] proposed a method called Receiver-based Delay Control (RDC) to avoid congestion by delaying TCP ACK generation at the receiver based on notifications from routers. Wang et al. [16] developed discrete-time Markov models to investigate the performance of TCP for both live and stored media streaming. Their models provide guidelines indicating the circumstances under which TCP streaming leads to satisfactory performance. For instance, they show that TCP provides good streaming performance when the achievable TCP throughput is roughly twice the media bitrate, with only a few seconds of startup delay. Goel et al. [7] showed that the latency at the application layer, which occurs as a result of throughput-optimized TCP implementations, could be minimized by dynamically tuning TCP's send buffer. They developed an adaptive buffer-size tuning technique that aimed at reducing this latency. Feng et. al [5] proposed and evaluated a priority-based technique for the delivery of compressed prerecorded video streams across best-effort networks. This technique uses a multi-level priority queue in conjunction with a delivery window to smooth the video frame rate, while allowing it to adapt to changing network conditions. Prangl et al. [13] proposed and evaluated a TCP-based perceptual QoS improvement mechanism. Their approach is based on media content adaptation (transcoding), applied at the application layer at the server. Deshpande [4] proposed an approach that allowed the player to employ single or multiple concurrent HTTP connections to receive streaming media and switch between the connections dynamically.

1.2 Paper Outline

In Section 2, we describe our experimental approach, the various tests we perform for each player, and the metrics we focus on. Sections 3, 4 and 5 focus on the Smooth Streaming, Netflix, and OSMF players, respectively. Section 6 focuses on the competition effects that take place when two adaptive players share the same bottleneck. Section 7 focuses on live video using the Smooth Streaming player. We summarize what we learn for each player and conclude the paper in Section 8.

2. METHODOLOGY AND METRICS

In this section, we give an overview of our experimental methodology and describe the metrics we focus on. The host that runs the various video players also runs a packet sniffer (Wireshark [12]) and a network emulator (DummyNet [14]). Wireshark allows us to capture and analyze offline the traffic from and to the HTTP server. DummyNet allows us to control the *downstream available bandwidth* (also referred to as *avail-bw*) that our host can receive. That host is connected to the Georgia Tech campus network through a Fast Ethernet interface. When we do not limit the avail-bw using DummyNet, the video players always select the highest rate streams; thus, when DummyNet limits the avail-bw to relatively low bitrates (1-5 Mbps) we expect that it is also the downstream path's end-to-end bottleneck.

In the following, we study the throughput-related metrics: 1. The *avail-bw* refers to the bitrate of the bottleneck that we emulate using DummyNet. The TCP connections that transfer video and audio streams cannot exceed (collectively) that bitrate at any point in time.

2. The *2-sec connection throughput* refers to the download throughput of a TCP connection that carries video or audio traffic, measured over the last two seconds.

3. The *running average of a connection's throughput* refers to a running average of the 2-sec connection throughput measurements. If $A(t_i)$ is the 2-sec connection throughput in the i'th time interval, the running average of the connection throughput is:

$$\hat{A}(t) = \begin{cases} \delta \hat{A}(t_{i-1}) + (1 - \delta)A(t_i) & i > 0 \\ A(t_0) & i = 0 \end{cases}$$

In the experiments, we use $\delta = 0.8$.

4. The *(audio or video) fragment throughput* refers to the download throughput for a particular fragment, i.e., the size of that fragment divided by the corresponding download duration. Note that, if a fragment is downloaded in every two seconds, the fragment throughput can be much higher than the 2-sec connection throughput in the same time interval (because the connection can be idle during part of that time interval). As will be shown later, some video players estimate the avail-bw using fragment throughput measurements.

We also estimate the *playback buffer size* at the player (measured in seconds), separately for audio and video. We can accurately estimate the playback buffer size for players that provide a timestamp (an offset value that indicates the location of the fragment in the stream) in their HTTP fragment requests. Suppose that two successive, say video, requests are sent at times t_1 and t_2 ($t_1 < t_2$) with timestamps t_1' and t_2' ($t_1' < t_2'$), respectively (all times measured in seconds). The playback buffer duration in seconds for video at time t_2 can be then estimated as:

$$B(t_2) = [B(t_1) - (t_2 - t_1) + (t_2' - t_1')]^+$$

where $[x]^+$ denotes the maximum of x and 0. This method works accurately because, as will be clear in the following sections, the player requests are not pipelined: a request for a new fragment is sent only after the previous fragment has been fully received.

We test each player under the same set of avail-bw conditions and variations. In the first round of tests, we examine the behavior of a player when the avail-bw is not limited by DummyNet; this "blue-sky" test allows us to observe the player's start-up and steady-state behavior - in the same experiments we also observe what happens when the user skips to a future point in the video clip. In the second round of tests, we apply persistent avail-bw variations (both increases and decreases) that last for tens of seconds. Such variations are common in practice when the cross traffic in the path's bottleneck varies significantly due to arriving or departing traffic from other users. A good player should react to such variations by decreasing or increasing the requested bitrate. In the third round of tests, we apply positive and negative spikes in the path's avail-bw that last for just few seconds - such variations are common in 802.11 WLANs for instance. For such short-term drops, the player should be able to maintain a constant requested bitrate using its playback buffer. For short-term avail-bw increases, the player could be conservative and stay at its current rate to avoid unnecessary bitrate variations. Due to space constraints, we do not show results from all these experiments for each player; we select only those results that are more interesting and provide new insight.

All experiments were performed on a Windows Vista Home Premium version 6.0.6002 laptop with an Intel(R) Core(TM)2 Duo P8400 2.26 GHz processor, 3.00 GB physical memory, and an ATI Radeon Graphics Processor (0x5C4) with 512 MB dedicated memory.

3. MICROSOFT SMOOTH STREAMING

In the following experiments, we use Microsoft Silverlight Version 4.0.50524.0. In a Smooth Streaming manifest file, the server declares the available audio and video bitrates and the resolution for each content (among other information). The manifest file also contains the duration of every audio and video fragment. After the player has received the manifest file, it generates successive HTTP requests for audio and video fragments. Each HTTP request from the player contains the name of the content, the requested bitrate, and a timestamp that points to the beginning of the corresponding fragment. This timestamp is determined using the per-fragment information provided in the manifest. The following is an example of a Smooth Streaming HTTP request.

```
GET (..)/BigBuckBunny720p.ism/
QualityLevels(2040000)/Fragments(video=400000000)
HTTP/1.1
```

In this example, the requested bitrate is 2.04 Mbps and the fragment timestamp is 40 s.

The Smooth Streaming player maintains two TCP connections with the server. At any point in time, one of the two connections is used for transferring audio and the other for video fragments. Under certain conditions, however, the player switches the audio and video streams between the two connections - it is not clear to us when/how the player takes this decision. This way, although at any point in time one connection is transferring video fragments, over the course of streaming, both connections get the chance to transfer video fragments. The benefit of such switching is that neither of the connections would stay idle for a long time, keeping the server from falling back to slow-start. Moreover, the two connections would maintain a large congestion window.

Sometimes the player aborts a TCP connection and opens a new one - this probably happens when the former connection provides very low throughput. Also, when the user jumps to a different point in the stream, the player aborts the existing TCP connections, if they are not idle, and opens new connections to request the appropriate fragments. At that point, the contents of the playback buffer are flushed.

In the following experiments we watch a sample video clip ("Big Buck Bunny") provided by Microsoft at the IIS Web site:

http://www.iis.net/media/experiencesmoothstreaming

The manifest file declares eight video encoding bitrates between 0.35 Mbps and 2.75 Mbps and one audio encoding bitrate (64 Kbps). We represent an encoding bitrate of r Mbps as P_r, (e.g., $P_{2.75}$). Each video fragment (except the last) has the same duration: $\tau=2$ s. The audio fragments are approximately of the same duration.

3.1 Behavior under Unrestricted avail-bw

Figure 1 shows the various throughput metrics, considering only the video stream, in a typical experiment without restricting the avail-bw using DummyNet. t=0 corresponds to the time when the Wireshark capture starts. Note that the player starts from the lowest encoding bitrate and it quickly, within the first 5-10 seconds, climbs to the highest encoding bitrate. As the per-fragment throughput measurements indicate, the highest encoding bitrate ($P_{2.75}$) is significantly lower than the avail-bw in the end-to-end path. The player upshifts to the highest encoding profile from the lowest one in four transitions. In other words, it seems that the player avoids large jumps in the requested bitrate (more than two successive bitrates) - the goal is probably to avoid annoying the user with sudden quality transitions, providing a dynamic but smooth watching experience.

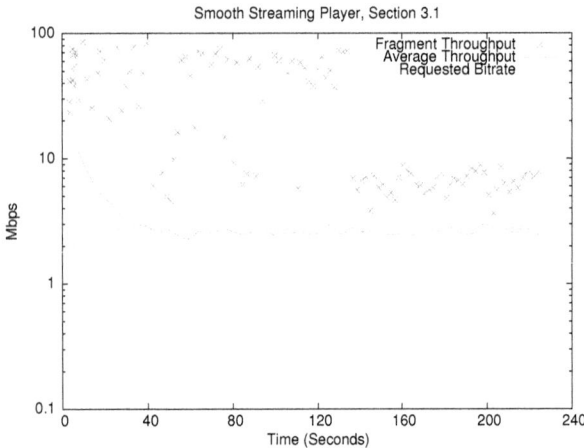

Figure 1: Per-fragment throughput, average TCP throughput and the requested bitrate for video traffic under unrestricted avail-bw conditions. Playback starts at around t=5 s, almost 2 s after the user clicked PLAY.

Another important observation is that during the initial time period, the player asks for video fragments much more frequently than once every τ seconds. Further analysis of the per-fragment interarrivals and download times shows that the player operates in one of two states: Buffering and Steady-State. In the former, the player requests a new fragment as soon as the previous fragment was downloaded. Note that the player does *not* use HTTP pipelining - it does not request a fragment if the previous fragment has not been fully received. In Steady-State, on the other hand, the player requests a new fragment either τ seconds after the previous fragment was requested (if it took less than τ seconds to download that fragment) or as soon as the previous fragment was received (otherwise). In other words, in the Buffering state the player aims to maximize its fragment request rate so that it can build up a target playback buffer as soon as possible. In Steady-State, the player aims to maintain a constant playback buffer, requesting one fragment every τ seconds (recall that each fragment corresponds to τ seconds of

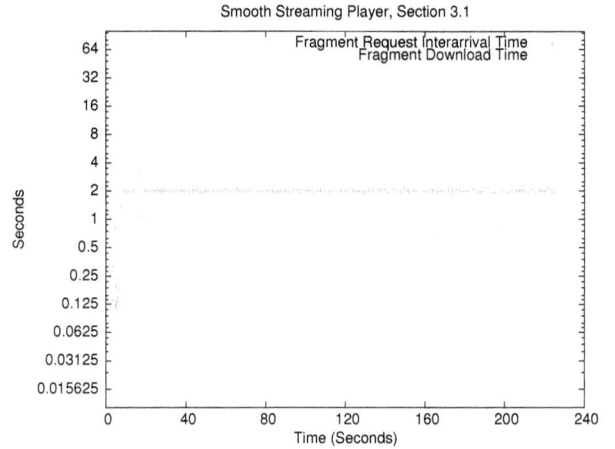

Figure 2: Interarrival and download times of video fragments under unrestricted avail-bw conditions. Each fragment is two seconds long.

content). We estimated the target video playback buffer size, as described in Section 2, to be about 30 seconds. The time it takes to reach Steady-State depends on the avail-bw - as the avail-bw increases, it takes less time to accumulate the 30-second playback buffer. We have consistently observed that the player does not sacrifice quality, requesting low-bitrate encodings, to fill up its playback buffer sooner. Another interesting observation is that the player does not request a video bitrate whose frame resolution (as declared at the manifest file) is larger than the resolution of the display window.

3.2 Behavior of the Audio Stream

Audio fragments are of the same duration with video fragments, at least in the movies we experimented with. Even though audio fragments are much smaller in bytes than video fragments, the Smooth Streaming player does not attempt to accumulate a larger audio playback buffer than the corresponding video buffer (around 30 s). Also, when the avail-bw drops, the player does not try to request audio fragments more frequently than video fragments (it would be able to do so). Overall, it appears that the Smooth Streaming player attempts to keep the audio and video stream download processes as much in sync as possible.

3.3 Behavior under Persistent avail-bw Variations

In this section, we summarize a number of experiments in which the avail-bw goes through four significant and persistent transitions, as shown in Figure 3. First, note that, as expected, the per-fragment throughput is never higher than the avail-bw. Instead, the per-fragment throughput tracks quite well the avail-bw variations for most of the time; part of the avail-bw, however, is consumed by audio fragments and, more importantly, TCP throughput can vary significantly after packet loss events.

We next focus on the requested video bitrate as the avail-bw changes. Initially, the avail-bw is 5 Mbps and the player requests the $P_{2.04}$ profile because it is constrained by the resolution of the display window (if we were watching the video in full-screen mode, the player would request the highest $P_{2.75}$ profile). The playback buffer (shown in Figure

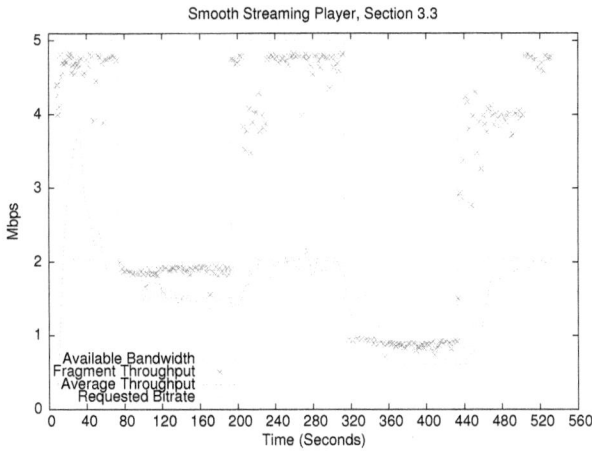

Figure 3: Per-fragment throughput, average TCP throughput and the requested bitrate for the video traffic under persistent avail-bw variations. Playback starts at around t=10 s, almost 3 s after the user clicked PLAY.

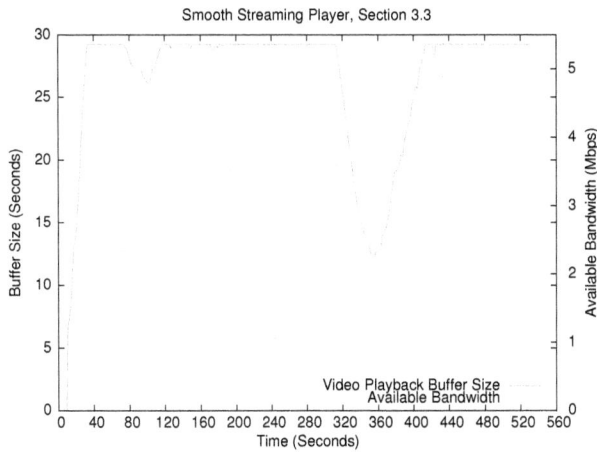

Figure 4: Video playback buffer size in seconds under persistent avail-bw variations.

4) has reached its 30 s target by t=40 s and the player is in Steady-State.

At time t=73 s, the avail-bw is dropped to 2 Mbps - that is not sufficient for the $P_{2.04}$ encoding because we also need some capacity for the audio traffic and for various header overheads. The player reacts by switching to the next lower profile ($P_{1.52}$) but after some significant delay (almost 25 seconds). During that time period, the playback buffer has decreased by only 3 seconds (the decrease is not large because the avail-bw is just barely less than the cumulative requested traffic). The large reaction delay indicates that the player does *not* react to avail-bw changes based on the latest per-fragment throughput measurements. Instead, it averages those per-fragment measurements over a longer time period so that it acts based on a smoother estimate of the avail-bw variations. The playback buffer size returns to its 30 s target after the player has switched to the $P_{1.52}$ profile.

The avail-bw increase at t=193 s is quickly followed by an appropriate increase in the requested encoding bitrate.

Again, the switching delay indicates that the Smooth Streaming player is conservative, preferring to estimate reliably the avail-bw (using several per-fragment throughput measurements) instead of acting opportunistically based on the latest fragment throughput measurement.

The avail-bw decrease at t=303 s is even larger (from 5 Mbps to 1 Mbps) and the player reacts by adjusting the requested bitrate in four transitions. The requested bitrates are not always successive. After those transitions, the request bitrate converges to an appropriate value $P_{0.63}$, much less than the avail-bw. It is interesting that the player could have settled at the next higher bitrate ($P_{0.84}$) - in that case, the aggregate throughput (including the audio stream) would be 0.94 Mbps. That is too close to the avail-bw (1 Mbps), however. This implies that Smooth Streaming is conservative: it prefers to maintain a safety margin between the avail-bw and its requested bitrate. We think that this is wise, given that the video bitrate can vary significantly around its *nominal encoding value* due to the variable bitrate (VBR) nature of video compression.

Another interesting observation is that the player avoids large transitions in the requested bitrate - such quality transitions can be annoying to the viewer. Also, the upward transitions are faster than the downward transitions - still, however, it can take several tens of seconds until the player has switched to the highest sustainable bitrate.

3.4 Behavior under Short-term avail-bw Variations

In this section, we summarize a number of experiments in which the avail-bw goes through positive or negative "spikes" that last for only few seconds, as shown in Figures 5 and 7. The spikes last for 2 s, 5 s and 10 s, respectively. Such short-term avail-bw variations are common in practice, especially in 802.11 WLAN networks. We think that a good adaptive player should be able to compensate for such spikes using its playback buffer, without causing short-term rate adaptations that can be annoying to the user.

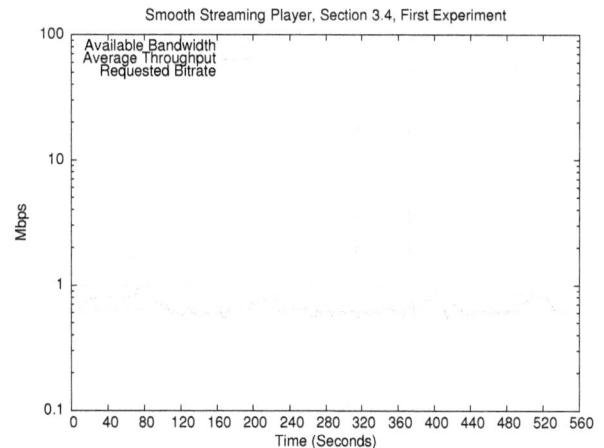

Figure 5: Average TCP throughput and the requested bitrate for the video traffic under positive avail-bw spikes. Playback starts at around t=7 s, almost 4 s after the user clicked PLAY.

Figure 5 shows the case of positive spikes. Here, we repeat the three spikes twice, each time with a different

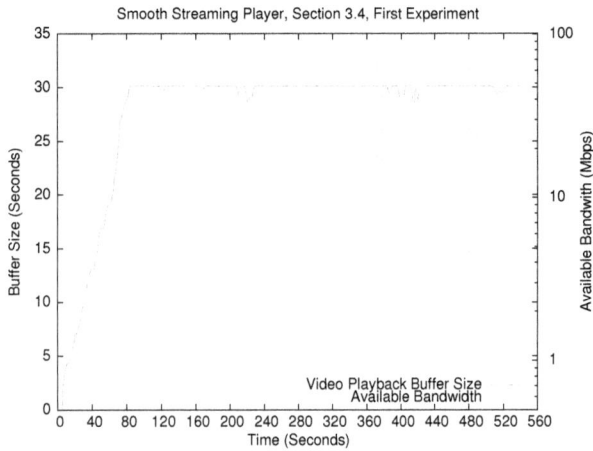

Figure 6: Video playback buffer size in seconds under positive avail-bw spikes.

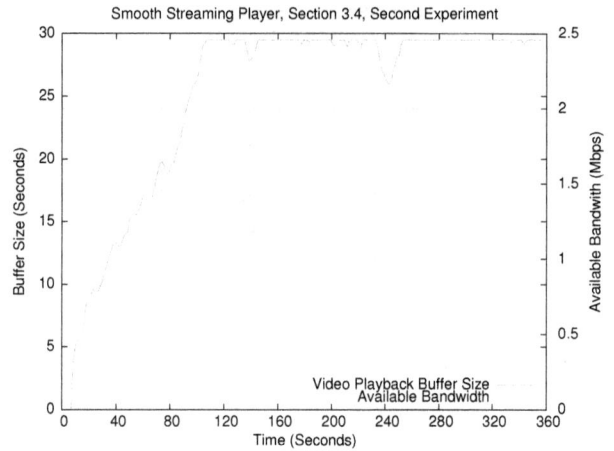

Figure 8: Video playback buffer size in seconds under negative avail-bw spikes.

increase magnitude. The Smooth Streaming player ignores the 2-second spikes and the smaller 5-second spike. On the other hand, it reacts to the 10-second spikes by increasing the requesting video bitrate. Unfortunately, it does so too late (sometimes after the end of the spike) and for too long (almost till 40 s after the end of the spike). During the time periods that the requested bitrate is higher than the avail-bw, the playback buffer size obviously shrinks, making the player more vulnerable to freeze events (See Figure 6). This experiment confirms that the player reacts, not to the latest fragment download throughput, but to a smoothed estimate of those measurements that can be unrelated to the current avail-bw conditions.

Figures 7 and 8 show similar results in the case of negative spikes. Here, the spikes reduce the avail-bw from 2 Mbps to 1 Mbps. The player reacts to all three spikes, even the spike that lasts for only 2 s. Unfortunately, the player reacts too late and for too long: it requests a lower bitrate after the end of each negative spike and it stays at that lower bitrate long for 40-80 s. During those periods, the user would unnecessarily experience a lower video quality.

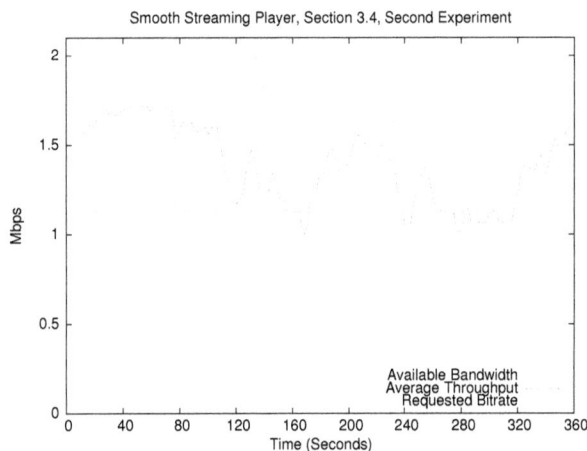

Figure 7: Average TCP throughput and the requested bitrate for the video traffic under negative avail-bw spikes. Playback starts at around t=9 s, almost 3 s after the user clicked PLAY.

4. NETFLIX PLAYER

The Netflix player uses Microsoft's Silverlight for media representation, but a different rate-adaptation logic. The Netflix player also maintains two TCP connections with the server, and it manages these TCP connections similarly with the Smooth Streaming player. As will become clear, however, the Netflix player does not send audio and video fragment requests at the same pace. Also, the format of the manifest file and requests are different. Further, most of the initial communication between the player and server, including the transfer of the manifest file, is done over SSL. We decrypted the manifest file using a Firefox plugin utility called Tamper Data that accesses the corresponding private key in Firefox. Video and audio fragments are delivered in wmv and wma formats, respectively. An example of a Netflix fragment request follows:

```
GET /sa2/946/1876632946.wmv
/range/2212059-2252058?token=1283923056
_d6f6112068075f1fb60cc48eab59ea55&random
=1799513140 HTTP/1.1
```

Netflix requests do not correspond to a certain time duration of audio or video. Instead, each request specifies a range of bytes in a particular encoding profile. Thus, we cannot estimate the playback buffer size as described in Section 2. We can only approximate that buffer size assuming that the actual encoding rate for each fragment is equal to the corresponding nominal bitrate for that fragment (e.g., a range of 8 Mb at the $P_{1.00}$ encoding profile corresponds to 8 seconds worth of video) - obviously this is only an approximation but it gives us a rough estimate of the playback buffer size.

After the user clicks the PLAY button, the player starts by performing some TCP transfers, probably to measure the capacity of the underlying path. Then it starts buffering audio and video fragments, but without starting the playback yet. The playback starts either after a certain number of seconds, or when the buffer size reaches a target point. If that buffer is depleted at some point, the Netflix player prefers to stop the playback, showing a message that the player is adjusting to a slower connection. The playback resumes when the buffer size reaches a target point.

In the following experiments we watch the movie "Mary and Max". The manifest file provides five video encoding bitrates between 500 Kbps and 3.8 Mbps and two audio encoding bitrates (64 Kbps and 128 Kbps).

4.1 Behavior under Unrestricted avail-bw

Figure 9 shows the various throughput metrics, considering only the video stream, in a typical experiment without using DummyNet to restrict the avail-bw. The interarrival of video fragment requests and the download times for each video fragment are shown in Figure 10. In this experiment, the playback started about 13 s after the user clicked PLAY. The playback delay can be much larger depending on the initial avail-bw (even up to few minutes). During this interval, several security checks are also performed before the player starts buffering and the playback begins [11]. For the first few fragments, the player starts from the lowest encoding bitrate and requests a number of fragments from all the available bitrates. Then, the player stays at that highest bitrate for the duration of the experiment.

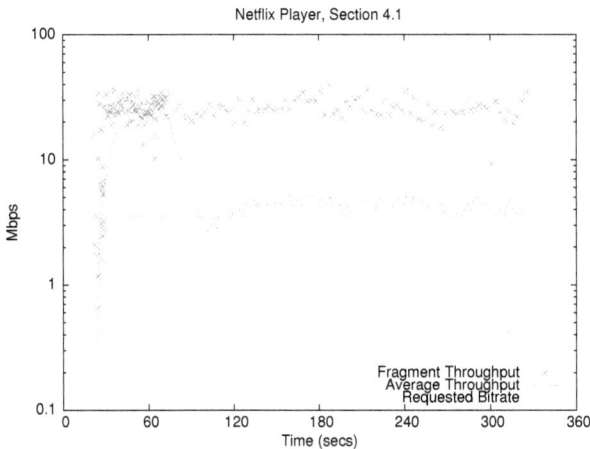

Figure 9: Per-fragment throughput, average TCP throughput and the requested bitrate for video traffic under unrestricted avail-bw conditions. Playback starts at around t=24 s, almost 16 s after the user clicked PLAY.

During the first 55 s of streaming, until t=75 s, the player is clearly in the Buffering state: it requests a new video fragment right after the previous fragment has been downloaded. The achieved TCP throughput in this path is about 30 Mbps, allowing the player to quickly accumulate a large playback buffer. We estimated the size of the playback buffer at the end of the Buffering state (t=75 s) at about 300 s worth of video - this is an order of magnitude larger than the playback buffer size we observed for Smooth Streaming.

When the player switches to Steady-State, video fragments are requested almost every three seconds, with significant variation, however.

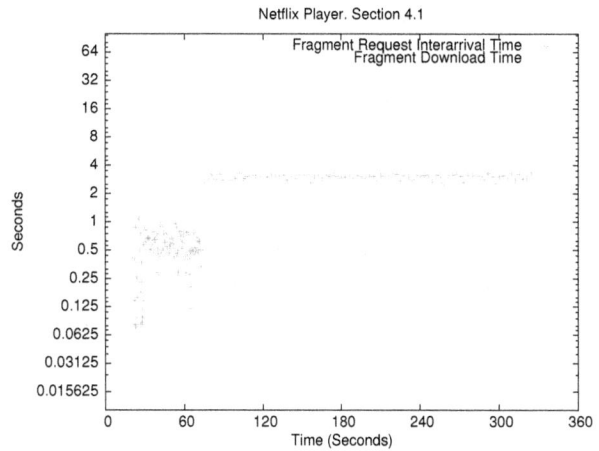

Figure 10: Interarrival and download times of video fragments under unrestricted avail-bw conditions.

4.2 Behavior of the Audio Stream

Audio fragments in the Netflix player are significantly larger than the ones in Smooth Streaming. Specifically, an audio fragment is typically 30 s long. Thus, after the player has reached Steady-State, a new audio fragment is requested every 30 s. Further, it appears that this player does not attempt to keep the audio and video stream download processes in sync; it can be that the audio playback buffer size is significantly larger than the video playback buffer size.

4.3 Behavior under Persistent avail-bw Variations

Figure 11 shows the various throughput-related metrics in the case of persistent avail-bw variations. As in the experiment with unrestricted avail-bw, the player first requests few fragments at all possible encodings. Within the first 40 s it converges to the highest sustainable bitrate ($P_{1.50}$) for that avail-bw (2 Mbps). It should be noted that in this experiment the player never leaves the Buffering state (based on analysis of the video fragment request interarrivals).

When the avail-bw drops to 1 Mbps, the player reacts within about 20 s, which implies that its avail-bw estimator is based on a smoothed version of the underlying per-fragment throughput, as opposed to the instantaneous and latest such measurement. It is interesting that the selected profile at that phase ($P_{1.00}$) is not sustainable, however, because it is exactly equal to the avail-bw (some avail-bw is consumed by audio traffic and other header overheads). Thus, the playback buffer size slowly decreases, forcing the player between 320 and 400 s to occasionally switch to the next lower bitrate. This observation implies that the Netflix player prefers to utilize a certain high bitrate even when the avail-bw is insufficient, as long as the player has accumulated more than a certain playback buffer size. We make the same observation from 450 to 500 s. During that interval, the player switches to a profile ($P_{2.60}$) that is much higher than the avail-bw (2 Mbps). The player can do this, without causing any problems, because it has accumulated a sufficiently large playback buffer size at that point.

In summary, it appears that the Netflix player is more aggressive than Smooth Streaming, trying to deliver the highest possible encoding rate even when the latter is more than the avail-bw, as long as the playback buffer size is sufficiently large.

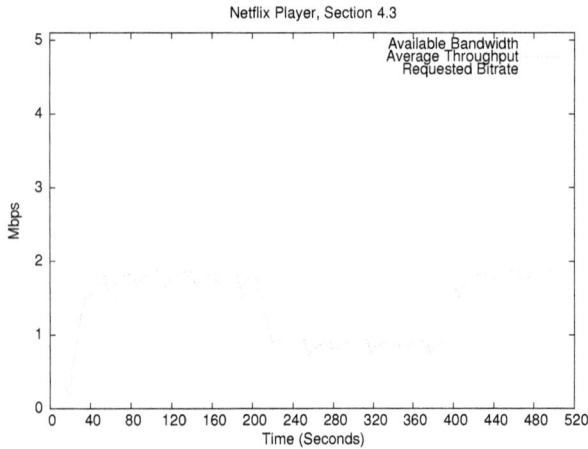

Figure 11: Average TCP throughput and the requested bitrate for the video traffic under persistent avail-bw variations. Playback starts at around t=20 s, almost 13 s after the user clicked PLAY.

4.4 Behavior under Short-term avail-bw Variations

Figure 12 shows how the Netflix player reacts to positive avail-bw spikes, while Figure 13 shows how it reacts to negative avail-bw spikes. We cannot compare directly the results of these experiments to the corresponding experiments with Smooth Streaming, because the video encoding profiles are different between the movies in these two experiments. As in the case of persistent avail-bw variations, we observe that the Netflix player is rather aggressive, reacting to large increases in avail-bw even if they are short-lived. As opposed to Smooth Streaming, which often reacts too late and for too long, Netflix reacts faster, while the spike is still present, even though the reaction can still last much longer after the spike.

On the other hand, in the experiment with negative avail-bw spikes, the Netflix player does not switch to a lower bitrate. It prefers to compensate for the lack of avail-bw using the large playback buffer size that it has previously accumulated.

5. ADOBE OSMF

We have repeated the same set of tests with Adobe's sample OSMF player, using Flash version 10.1.102.64 with player version WIN 10.1.102.64 and OSMF library version 1.0. In the following experiments, we watch a movie trailer ("Freeway") provided by Akamai's HD-video demo Web site for Adobe HTTP Dynamic Streaming:

http://wwwns.akamai.com/hdnetwork/demo/flash/zeri/

Note that the player used in this Web site was not built specifically to showcase HTTP Dynamic Streaming.

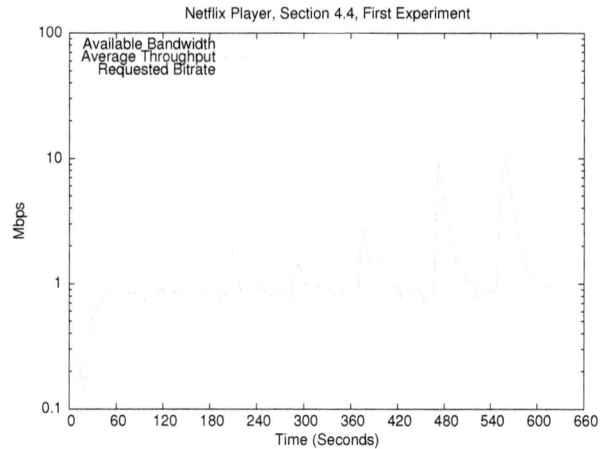

Figure 12: Average TCP throughput and the requested bitrate for the video traffic under positive avail-bw spikes. Playback starts at around t=20 s, almost 16 s after the user clicked PLAY.

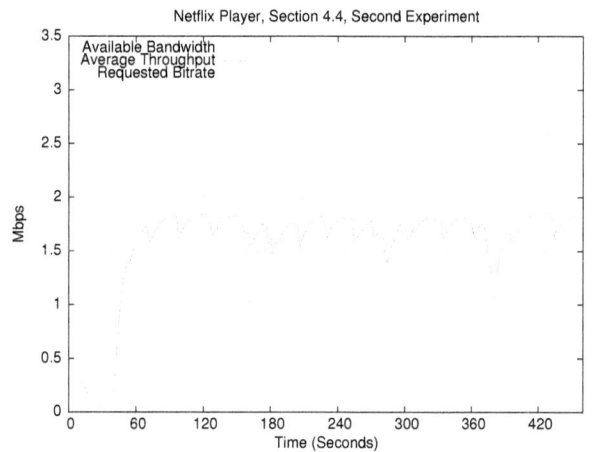

Figure 13: Average TCP throughput and the requested bitrate for the video traffic under negative avail-bw spikes. Playback starts at around t=37 s, almost 31 s after the user clicked PLAY.

The manifest file declares eight encoding bitrates for this trailer between 0.25 Mbps and 3.00 Mbps. In this player, each server file (F4F format) contains one segment of the movie. A segment can contain multiple fragments. The duration of each fragment is determined by the server. The HTTP requests that the player generates include a fragment number instead of a timestamp or a byte range. An example of an OSMF HTTP request follows:

```
GET /content/inoutedit-mbr
/inoutedit_h264_3000Seg1-Frag5 HTTP/1.1
```

Note that the requested bitrate is shown in the request (3000 Kbps) together with the requested segment and fragment numbers. The player maintains one TCP connection with the server and receives all fragments through this connection. The player might shut down the connection and open a new one if the user jumps to a different point in the stream and the connection is not idle.

According to information provided by the player itself, the target playback buffer seems to be less than 10 seconds.

Figure 14 shows that initially the player requests one fragment at the lowest available profile and then quickly climbs to the largest possible one. But, it does not converge to that profile and continues switching between profiles occasionally. When the avail-bw is dropped to 2 Mbps at t=139 s, the player fails to converge to the highest sustainable profile ($P_{1.7}$). Instead, it keeps switching between profiles, often using the lowest and highest ones ($P_{0.25}$ and $P_{3.00}$). The user observes several dropped frames and freeze events, which is an indication of a depleted playback buffer.

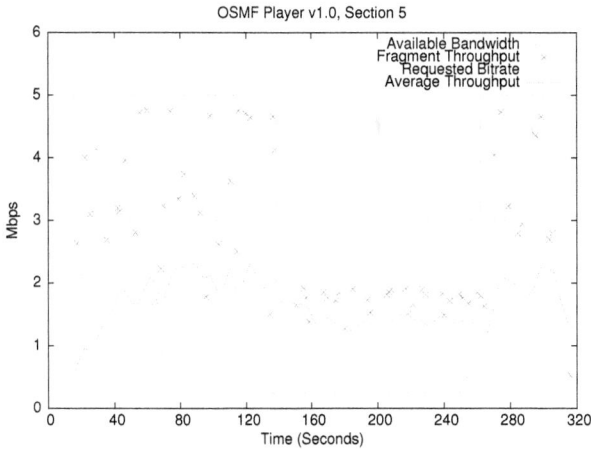

Figure 14: Per-fragment throughput, the requested bitrate for the video traffic and average TCP throughput under persistent avail-bw variations. Playback starts at around t=13 s, almost 3 s after the user clicked PLAY.

We have also conducted the same set of experiments with the latest version of the OSMF player obtained from the following Web site.

`http://sourceforge.net/adobe/osmf/home/`

Figure 15 shows the various throughput related metrics in an experiment with the OSMF player version 1.5 under persistent avail-bw variations. We see a very similar issue here. The player makes similar problematic rate switchings and gets into oscillation.

To summarize, we have observed that the OSMF player fails to converge to a sustainable bitrate especially when the avail-bw is smaller than or very close to the highest available bitrate of the media. Instead, it usually oscillates between the lowest and highest bitrates. The default rate-adaptation algorithm seems to be tuned for short variations in the avail-bw. We do not describe here the rest of the experiments we performed with it, because they simply confirm that the default rate-adaptation algorithm deployed in the OSMF player does not function properly under our test scenarios.

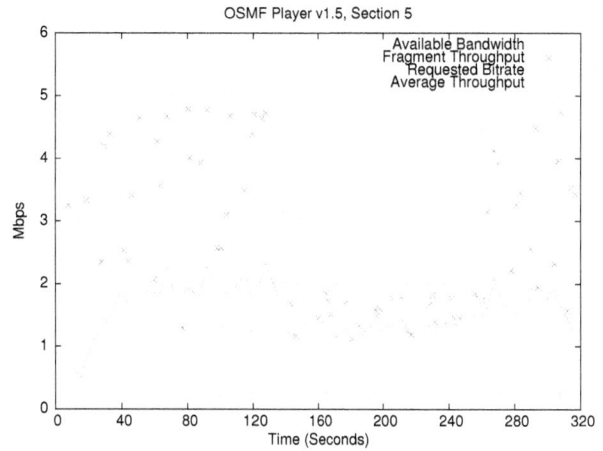

Figure 15: Per-fragment throughput, the requested bitrate for the video traffic and average TCP throughput under persistent avail-bw variations. Playback starts at around t=11 s, almost 4 s after the user clicked PLAY.

6. TWO COMPETING PLAYERS

Suppose that two adaptive HTTP streaming players share the same bottleneck. This can happen, for instance, when people in the same house watch two different movies - in that case the shared bottleneck is probably the residential broadband access link. Another example of such competition is when a large number of users watch the same live event, say a football game. In that case the shared bottleneck may be an edge network link. There are many questions in this context. Can the players share the avail-bw in a stable manner, without experiencing oscillatory bitrate transitions? Can they share the avail-bw in a fair manner? How does the number of competing streams affect stability and fairness? How do different adaptive players compete with each other? And how does a player compete with TCP bulk transfers (including progressive video downloads)? In this section, we only "touch the surface" of these issues, considering a simple scenario in which two identical players (Smooth Streaming) compete at a bottleneck in which the avail-bw varies between 1-4 Mbps. The idea is that, if we observe significant problems even in this simple scenario, we should also expect similar issues in more complex scenarios.

In the following, we present results from two experiments. It should be noted that such experiments are fundamentally non-reproducible: there is always some stochasticity in the way players share the bottleneck's avail-bw. However, our observations, at a qualitative level, are consistent across several similar experiments.

Figure 16 shows the avail-bw variations in the first experiment, together with the requested bitrates from the two players. The second player starts about one minute after the first one. Until that point, the first player was using the highest profile ($P_{2.75}$). After the second player starts, the two players could have shared the 4 Mbps bottleneck by switching to $P_{1.52}$, however, they do not. Instead, the second player oscillates between lower profiles. When the avail-bw drops to 3 Mbps or 2 Mbps, the oscillations continue for both players. The only stable period during this experiment is when the avail-bw is limited to 1 Mbps: in that case both players switch to the lowest profile $P_{0.35}$ simply because there is no other bitrate that is sustainable for both players. Interestingly, when the avail-bw increases to 4 Mbps the two players start oscillating in a synchronized manner: when they both switch to $P_{2.04}$ the shared bottleneck is congested. It seems that both players observe congestion at the same time, and they react in the same manner lowering their requested bitrate at about the same time.

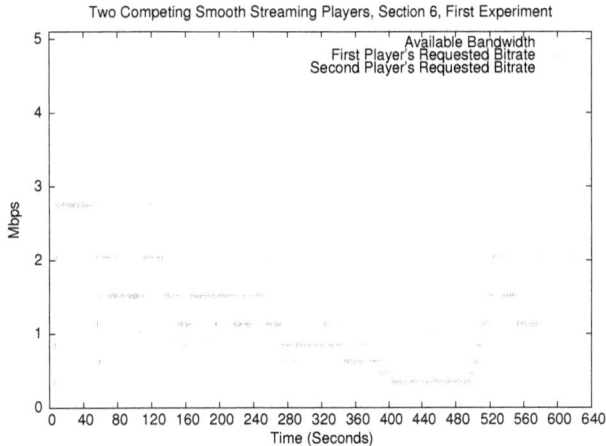

Figure 16: Two Smooth Streaming players compete for avail-bw. The players start the playback at around t=7 s and t=57 s, respectively.

The previous experiment reveals some interesting points about Smooth Streaming. First, it seems that the avail-bw estimation method in that player considers only time periods in which fragments are actually downloaded - there is probably no estimation when the player's connections are idle. So, if two players X and Y share the same bottleneck, and Y is idle while X downloads some fragments, X can overestimate the avail-bw. Second, it appears that the Smooth player does not use randomization in the rate-adaptation logic. Previous studies have shown that a small degree of randomization was often sufficient to avoid synchronization and oscillations [6].

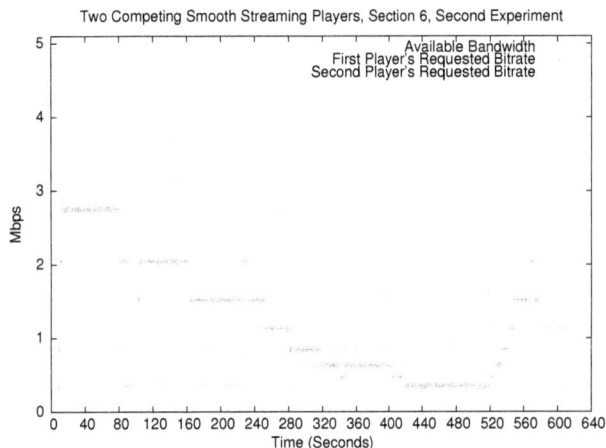

Figure 17: Two Smooth Streaming players compete for avail-bw. The players start the playback at around t=12 s and t=77 s, respectively.

Figure 17 shows the results for another run. Here, the second player stays at the lowest possible bitrate for about 150 s after it starts streaming, while the first player uses the remaining avail-bw with the highest sustainable bitrate. This is clearly a very unfair way to share the bottleneck link. It should be noted that this unfairness is *unrelated* to TCP's well-known unfairness towards connections with large round-trip times (RTT). In this experiment, both connections have the same RTT. The unfairness here is not generated by TCP's congestion control, but by the offered load that each application (video player) requests. The second player estimates the avail-bw to be much lower, and it does not even try to increase its requested bitrate. If it had done so, it would likely be able to obtain a higher bitrate forcing the first player to a lower bitrate. It appears, however, that the Smooth player's rate-adaptation algorithm does not include such bandwidth-sharing objectives.

7. SMOOTH LIVE STREAMING

We are also interested in the similarities and differences between live and on-demand adaptive video streaming. What is the playback delay in the case of live streaming? Does the player react differently to avail-bw variations when it streams live content? And how does the player react when the playback buffer becomes empty? Does it skip fragments so that it maintains a small playback delay, or does it increase the playback delay aiming to show all fragments? We explored these questions with the Smooth Streaming player. In the following experiments, we used the live video feed from the Home Shopping Network (HSN) web site: http://www.hsn.com/hsn-tv_at-4915_xa.aspx?nolnav=1.

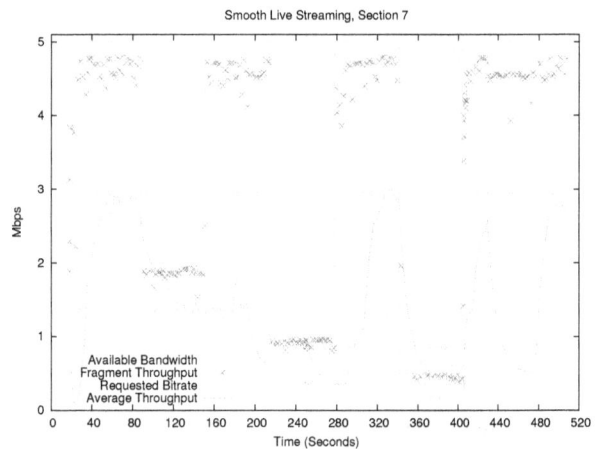

Figure 18: Per-fragment throughput, the requested bitrate for the video traffic and average TCP throughput for live video streaming. Playback starts at around t=20 s.

Figure 18 shows the various throughput metrics and the requested video bitrate, while Figure 19 shows the estimated video playback buffer size (in seconds). A first important difference with on-demand streaming is that the initial playback buffer size is about 8 s; significantly lower than the typical playback buffer sizes we observed in on-demand Smooth Streaming sessions. By the way, even though this playback delay may sound too large for live content,

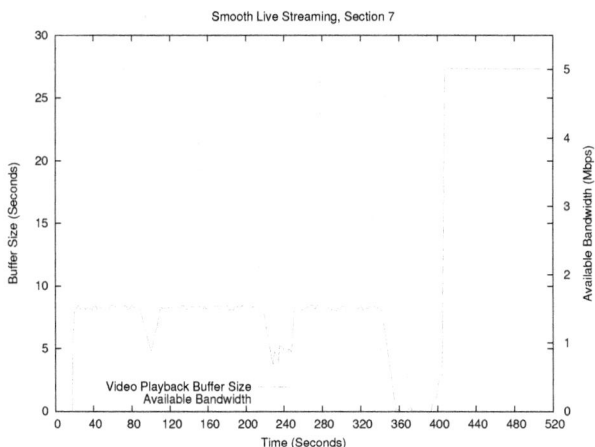

Figure 19: Video playback buffer size in seconds for live video streaming.

note that even cable TV networks usually enforce a similar delay (referred to as "profanity delay") to avoid broadcasting inappropriate scenes.

A second important point, which is not shown in the previous graphs but it can be observed by the timestamps of the HTTP requests, is that the player initially requests fragments that correspond to about 8 s in the past. This way, it can start displaying the video without having to wait for a long initial playback delay; of course, what the user watches then happened at least 8 s ago. As in the case of on-demand streaming, the initial fragment request rate (while the player is in the **Buffering** state) is higher, requesting a new fragment as soon as the last fragment is received.

Other than the previous two points, it appears that the Smooth Streaming player does not react to avail-bw variations any different with live content than with on-demand content. Note that the persistent avail-bw decreases and increases are followed by similar bitrate adjustments as in Section 3.

Another interesting point is what happens when the playback buffer becomes empty. This happened in this experiment at around t=360 s, when the avail-bw was decreased to 500 Kbps. During that event the playback buffer remained practically empty for about 40 s. The player still receives some fragments during that period but they would not increase the playback buffer size by more than a fragment. The player was late to switch to a sufficiently lower bitrate, and so several fragments were requested at bitrates ($P_{1.40}$ and $P_{0.80}$) that were higher than the avail-bw. The end-result was that those fragments took too long to download, the buffer became depleted, and the playback stalled for about 27 s.

Arguably, it is reasonable to expect for live streaming that the player could skip some fragments that take too long to download, jumping to a later point in the video stream. The Smooth Streaming implementation for this particular Web site does not do so, however. It appears that the player aims to show every single fragment. Consequently, the playback delay can increase, gradually staying more and more behind the live broadcast. Indeed, in this case after the avail-bw increased to 5 Mbps, the playback buffer size increased to

almost 27 s, which is comparable to the typical playback delay of on-demand content using Smooth Streaming.

8. CONCLUSIONS

We conducted an experimental evaluation of three commercial adaptive HTTP streaming players, focusing on how they react to persistent and short-term avail-bw variations. Here, we summarize our findings for each player and conclude the paper.

The Smooth Streaming player is quite effective under unrestricted avail-bw as well as under persistent avail-bw variations. It quickly converges to the highest sustainable bitrate, while it accumulates at the same time a large playback buffer requesting new fragments (sequentially) at the highest possible bitrate. This player is rather conservative in its bitrate switching decisions. First, it estimates the avail-bw by smoothing the per-fragment throughput measurements, introducing significant delays in the rate-adaptation logic. Second, it avoids large bitrate changes that could be annoying to the viewer. On the negative side, the Smooth Streaming player reacts to short-term avail-bw spikes too late and for too long, causing either sudden drops in the playback buffer or unnecessary bitrate reductions. Further, our experiments with two competing Smooth Streaming players indicate that the rate-adaptation logic is not able to avoid oscillations, and it does not aim to reduce unfairness in bandwidth sharing. The Live Smooth Streaming player behaves similarly, except that the playback buffer is initially shorter and the player starts requesting fragments from the recent past.

The Netflix player is similar to Smooth Streaming (they both use Silverlight for the media representation). However, we observed that the former showed some important differences in its rate-adaptation behavior, becoming more aggressive than the latter and aiming to provide the highest possible video quality, even at the expense of additional bitrate changes. Specifically, the Netflix player accumulates a very large buffer (up to few minutes), it downloads large chunks of audio in advance of the video stream, and it occasionally switches to higher bitrates than the avail-bw as long as the playback buffer is almost full. It shares, however, the previous shortcomings of Smooth Streaming.

The OSMF player often fails to converge to an appropriate bitrate even after the avail-bw has stabilized. This player has been made available so that developers will customize the code including the rate-adaptation algorithm for HTTP Dynamic Streaming for their use case. We do not summarize any other experiment here.

Overall, it is clear that the existing adaptive HTTP streaming players are still at their infancy. The technology is new and it is still not clear how to design an effective rate-adaptation logic for a complex and demanding application (video streaming) that has to function on top of a complex transport protocol (TCP). The interactions between these two feedback loops (rate-adaptation logic at the application layer and TCP congestion control at the transport layer) are not yet understood well. In future work, we plan to focus on these issues and design improved rate-adaptation mechanisms.

9. REFERENCES

[1] Adobe. HTTP Dynamic Streaming on the Adobe Flash Platform. *Adobe Systems Incorporated*, 2010. http://www.adobe.com/products/httpdynamicstreaming /pdfs/httpdynamicstreaming_wp_ue.pdf.

[2] A. C. Begen, T. Akgul, and M. Baugher. Watching video over the Web, part I: streaming protocols. *To appear in IEEE Internet Comput.*, 2011.

[3] L. De Cicco and S. Mascolo. An Experimental Investigation of the Akamai Adaptive Video Streaming. In *Proc. of USAB WIMA*, 2010.

[4] S. Deshpande. Adaptive timeline aware client controlled HTTP streaming. In *Proc. of SPIE*, 2009.

[5] W. Feng, M. Liu, B. Krishnaswami, and A. Prabhudev. A priority-based technique for the best-effort delivery of stored video. In *Proc. of MMCN*, 1999.

[6] R. Gao, C. Dovrolis, and E. Zegura. Avoiding oscillations due to intelligent route control systems. In *Proc. of IEEE INFOCOM*, 2006.

[7] A. Goel, C. Krasic, and J. Walpole. Low-latency adaptive streaming over TCP. *ACM TOMCCAP*, 4(3):1–20, 2008.

[8] P.-H. Hsiao, H. T. Kung, and K.-S. Tan. Video over TCP with receiver-based delay control. In *Proc. of ACM NOSSDAV*, 2001.

[9] R. Kuschnig, I. Kofler, and H. Hellwagner. An evaluation of TCP-based rate-control algorithms for adaptive Internet streaming of H.264/SVC. In *Proc. of ACM MMSys*, 2010.

[10] R. Kuschnig, I. Kofler, and H. Hellwagner. Improving Internet video streamilng performance by parallel TCP-based request-response streams. In *Proc. of IEEE CCNC*, 2010.

[11] Pomelo LLC. Analysis of Netflix's security framework for 'Watch Instantly' service. *Pomelo, LLC Tech Memo*, 2009. http://pomelollc.files.wordpress. com/2009/04/pomelo-tech-report-netflix.pdf.

[12] A. Orebaugh, G. Ramirez, J. Burke, and J. Beale. *Wireshark and Ethereal network protocol analyzer toolkit*. Syngress Media Inc, 2007.

[13] M. Prangl, I. Kofler, and H. Hellwagner. Towards QoS improvements of TCP-based media delivery. In *Proc. of ICNS*, 2008.

[14] L. Rizzo. Dummynet: a simple approach to the evaluation of network protocols. *SIGCOMM CCR*, 27(1):31–41, 1997.

[15] S. Tullimas, T. Nguyen, R. Edgecomb, and S.-C. Cheung. Multimedia streaming using multiple TCP connections. *ACM TOMCCAP*, 4(2):1–20, 2008.

[16] B. Wang, J. Kurose, P. Shenoy, and D. Towsley. Multimedia streaming via TCP: An analytic performance study. *ACM TOMCCAP*, 4(2):1–22, 2008.

[17] A. Zambelli. IIS smooth streaming technical overview. *Microsoft Corporation*, 2009. http://download.microsoft.com/download/4/2/4/ 4247C3AA-7105-4764-A8F9-321CB6C765EB/IIS_ Smooth_Streaming_Technical_Overview.pdf.

Rate Adaptation for Adaptive HTTP Streaming

Chenghao Liu
Department of Signal Processing,
Tampere University of Technology
Tampere, Finland
+358 5 0934 9231
chenghao.liu@tut.fi

Imed Bouazizi
Nokia Research Center
Tampere, Finland
+358 5 0486 0855
imed.bouazizi@nokia.com

Moncef Gabbouj
Department of Signal Processing,
Tampere University of Technology
Tampere, Finland
+358 3 3115 3967
moncef.gabbouj@tut.fi

ABSTRACT

Recently, HTTP has been widely used for the delivery of real-time multimedia content over the Internet, such as in video streaming applications. To combat the varying network resources of the Internet, rate adaptation is used to adapt the transmission rate to the varying network capacity. A key research problem of rate adaptation is to identify network congestion early enough and to probe the spare network capacity. In adaptive HTTP streaming, this problem becomes challenging because of the difficulties in differentiating between the short-term throughput variations, incurred by the TCP congestion control, and the throughput changes due to more persistent bandwidth changes.

In this paper, we propose a novel rate adaptation algorithm for adaptive HTTP streaming that detects bandwidth changes using a smoothed HTTP throughput measured based on the segment fetch time (SFT). The smoothed HTTP throughput instead of the instantaneous TCP transmission rate is used to determine if the bitrate of the current media matches the end-to-end network bandwidth capacity. Based on the smoothed throughput measurement, this paper presents a receiver-driven rate adaptation method for HTTP/TCP streaming that deploys a step-wise increase/ aggressive decrease method to switch up/down between the different representations of the content that are encoded at different bitrates. Our rate adaptation method does not require any transport layer information such as round trip time (RTT) and packet loss rates which are available at the TCP layer. Simulation results show that the proposed rate adaptation algorithm quickly adapts to match the end-to-end network capacity and also effectively controls buffer underflow and overflow.

Categories and Subject Descriptors
D.3.3 [**Computer-Communication Networks**]: Network Protocols – *Application (multimedia streaming).*

General Terms
Algorithms, Measurement, Standardization.

Keywords
Adaptive HTTP streaming, multimedia streaming over TCP, rate adaptation, 3GPP PSS, TCP congestion control.

1. INTRODUCTION

The current Internet is a best effort network; therefore, the network resources are characterized with varying available end-to-end bandwidth. In order to improve the user experience of multimedia streaming services, rate adaptation is used to prevent the client buffer from under-flowing and to achieve maximum possible playback quality. Rate adaptation may be performed at the sender, the receiver, or both. If the rate adaptation is performed by the server, it is categorized as sender-driven rate adaptation. The proposed algorithms in [6] and [7] can be categorized as a class of sender-driven rate adaptation. In [6], a rate adaptation algorithm over TCP is proposed which estimates the network bandwidth and client buffer occupancy using implicit feedback information built in the TCP congestion control. In [7], the authors propose an adaptive streaming algorithm for streaming of scalable video over UDP based on client buffer feedback. When streaming adaptation is performed by the client, it is classified as receiver-driven rate adaptation. One typical technique of this class is the receiver-driven layered multicast (RLM) [9]. In RLM, the server uses scalable video coding techniques to produce a set of layered bit streams and transmit each layer of the bit stream to a different multicast group. The receiver periodically joins multicast groups to probe the spare network capacity until it detects congestion. When multiple receivers observe packet loss, they conclude the network undergoes a congestion situation. However, the packet loss based congestion detection may not differentiate between losses due to congestion and link layer induced loss. To solve this problem, paper [8] proposes a multi-buffer based congestion control for multicast streaming of scalable video which uses the media time in the client buffer to detect congestion even before packet loss happens. However, the rate adaptation methods presented in [7], [8] and [9] are designed for multimedia streaming over UDP. The authors in [6] discuss the sender-driven adaptive streaming over TCP. Given that HTTP/TCP [1] is used for multimedia streaming, the sender is expected to be an HTTP server or a web cache, thus typically not keeping information about the receiver's connection state. Furthermore the sender-driven rate adaptation method has limitation in supporting the large-scale multimedia delivery since it will dramatically increase the burden on the web server or cache. Hence, it is expected that the rate adaptation in adaptive HTTP streaming will solely be receiver-driven. In this paper we examine the problem of receiver-driven rate adaptation for the application of the adaptive HTTP streaming.

Researchers recently revisited the fundamental question about the suitability of HTTP/TCP for delay-critical applications such as multimedia streaming. The dominant usage of TCP is mainly attributable to the congestion avoidance algorithm, which has so far ensured the scalable growth of the Internet. However, the congestion avoidance algorithm of TCP results in a saw-tooth shaped instantaneous transmission rate. Additionally, the extreme reliability of TCP results in excessive transmission delays and delay jitter due to retransmissions and in-order delivery. As a result, it was widely accepted that TCP is not adequate for multimedia streaming applications, which are delay sensitive but to some extent loss tolerant. Despite this common understanding, a dominant share of multimedia traffic is being delivered using TCP nowadays. HTTP/TCP is easy to configure and is typically granted traversal of firewalls and network address translators, which makes it attractive for multimedia streaming applications.

Recent studies reveal that the instantaneous transmission rate variation of TCP called short-term throughput can be smoothed out by receiver-side buffering. In [5], the authors propose that the receiver side buffer can be used to smooth out the variation effect of TCP transmission rate. Furthermore, paper [4] discusses the receiver buffer requirement and presents an analytic expression of the minimum receiver buffer size to achieve the desired video quality. These research results show that interruption-free multimedia streaming over TCP can be achieved under the assumption that the network resources are not dynamically changing. Most of the current media streaming over web shortly called web streaming uses a similar approach, so called progressive download, to provide streaming services. In the current web streaming, such as provided by popular video portals, a set of pre-defined quality levels of a video clip is offered to the users for manual a-priori selection. Each level represents a specific definition and bitrate, and is henceforth called a representation. If the bitrate of the selected representation turns out to be higher than the available end-to-end bandwidth, then the user will most probably experience playback interruptions and re-buffering events due to buffer underflows. Otherwise, if the bitrate of the representation is lower than the available network bandwidth, then the user will consume the content at a sub-optimal quality. Moreover, as the bandwidth capacity is higher than the representation bitrate, the client will be downloading the content at a faster pace, which could result in bandwidth waste if the user decides to stop watching the content (e.g. when zapping).

To solve the problems in the current web streaming, the 3GPP group recently standardized the adaptive HTTP streaming solution as part of Packet-switched Streaming Service (PSS) [12]. Adaptive HTTP streaming in 3GPP PSS follows a strategy of sequential requesting and receiving of small media chunks of the multimedia content, so-called media segments. 3GPP PSS adaptive HTTP streaming further enables the client to request media segments from different representations to react to varying network resources. Each representation consists of multiple media segments containing certain duration of media data and encoded at a specific bitrate [13]. The research problems in the adaptive HTTP streaming include the following aspects in addition to the common rate adaptation in media streaming. First, the rate adaptation method must deploy a metric to identify if the bitrate of a specific representation matches the available end-to-end bandwidth or not. This metric is expected to distinguish between throughput changes due to network bandwidth variations and those attributable to the congestion control and avoidance algorithm in TCP. To achieve efficient rate adaptation, the metric should identify any mismatch between the representation bitrate and the available end-to-end bandwidth quick enough in order to react promptly and reach the optimum representation level quickly. Second, the rate adaptation algorithm has to manage the client buffer in order to prevent buffer underflows and overflows,

since buffer underflows cause playback interruptions and overflows result in bandwidth waste. Third, the rate adaptation algorithm should be equipped with good convergence property and prevent hopping between neighbor media representations, especially when the available end-to-end bandwidth lies within the bitrate range of two adjacent representations. Fourth, the media segment duration needs to be set appropriately in order to minimize the HTTP overhead, thus minimizing the delay introduced by HTTP request processing and transmission and maximizing the adaptation speed.

In this paper, we propose a receiver-driven rate adaptation algorithm for adaptive HTTP streaming. For deciding switch-up or switch-down operations between different representations, a smoothed HTTP/TCP throughput measurement method is presented that compares the segment fetch time with the media playback time contained in that segment shortly media segment duration. A typical media segment contains 5-10 seconds which is sufficiently long to smooth short-term variations in the TCP throughput. For probing the spare network capacity a step-wise switch-up method is used to switch to a higher representation. Upon detecting network congestion, an aggressive switch down method is deployed to prevent playback interruptions. Possible switch up and switch down operations are assessed each time after receiving a media segment. In order to save network bandwidth and memory resources for the users, a method for determining the idle time between two consecutive GET requests for media segments is deployed, thus limiting the maximum amount of media pre-fetching.

The rest of this paper is organized as follows. Section 2 describes the adaptive HTTP streaming system. The proposed rate adaptation method for HTTP streaming is presented in section 3. Section 4 and 5 show the simulation results and conclusion.

2. ADAPTIVE HTTP STREAMING SYSTEM

In this section, we give an overview of the system specified in the 3GPP PSS Adaptive HTTP streaming solution [12] shortly denoted as 3GPP adaptive HTTP streaming.

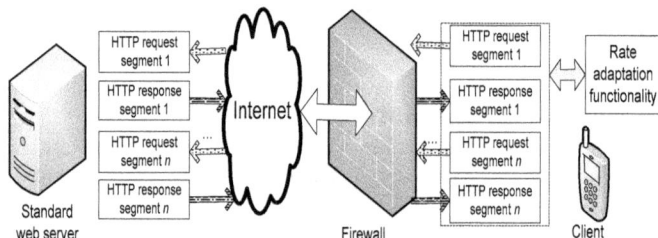

Figure 1. Adaptive HTTP streaming system

Figure 1 shows a 3GPP adaptive HTTP streaming system. As mentioned in the introduction, adaptive HTTP streaming operates as a set of sequential HTTP requests and responses.

The server can be a standard web server with the functionality to create media presentations as specified in 3GPP adaptive HTTP streaming. Creating media presentations may be done offline (static mode) or upon request (dynamic mode). In the static mode, the media presentation description (MPD) and representations are already created before starting any adaptive HTTP streaming sessions. In the dynamic mode, the server creates the media segments based on the received HTTP GET requests [12].

The client may send a series of GET requests, each of which requests a media segment of a representation that is identified through a unique level identifier (ID). In adaptive HTTP streaming, the client performs rate adaptation by identifying the representation that matches as closely as possible the end-to-end network capacity. In 3GPP adaptive HTTP streaming, the adaptation may take place each time before requesting a new media segment.

3. PROPOSED RATE ADAPTATION ALGORITHM

This section presents an advanced rate adaptation algorithm for HTTP streaming. Our algorithm compares the segment fetch time with the media duration contained in the segment to detect congestion and probe the spare network capacity. An effective rate adaptation algorithm is presented which adapts the bitrate by switching up/down between different representations each time after receiving a media segment and before sending the next request.

3.1 Smoothed HTTP/TCP Throughput Measurement

It is well known that the instantaneous TCP transmission rate is dynamically changing hence it is not feasible to measure the network capacity using the instantaneous TCP transmission rate. So instead, the client measures the segment fetch time, which covers a relatively long period of time, to determine if the bitrate of the current representation matches the available end-to-end bandwidth capacity. The segment fetch time (SFT) denotes a period of time from the time instant of sending a GET request for a media segment to the instant of receiving the last bit of the requested media segment.

In order to play media smoothly, the playing rate should be equal to the receiving rate in terms of media time. Thus if the encoded media bitrate of the current representation matches the end-to-end average TCP throughput, then the segment fetch time should be equal to the media segment duration. Otherwise, if the segment fetch time is larger than the media segment duration then it means that the average TCP throughput is lower than the bitrate of the current representation. Otherwise (if the segment fetch time is lower than the media segment duration), it indicates that the average TCP throughput is higher than the bitrate of the current representation. The last situation can occur in HTTP streaming because the TCP sender transmits the available data at the highest possible rate provided by the TCP congestion control and avoidance algorithm. Hence the ratio of media segment duration to segment fetch time denoted as μ is used as metric to detect congestion and probe the spare network capacity.

$$\mu = \frac{MSD}{SFT} \quad (1)$$

where MSD and SFT denote the media segment duration and the segment fetch time. The SFT measures how quickly the current segment is fetched on average.

Then the smoothed TCP throughput measurement can be estimated by multiplying μ with the media bitrate of the currently received segment. The receiver can obtain the encoded media bitrate of each representation from the Media Presentation Description (MPD). To produce the smoothed TCP throughput, the media segment duration shall be selected appropriately. Typically longer period is capable of producing smoother throughput measurement. However the longer period will cause

slower rate adaptation behavior. Based on our observations, media segments of around 10 seconds are basically sufficient to smooth out the varying instantaneous TCP transmission rate, and hence to produce the smoothed HTTP/TCP throughput measurement.

The advantage of using smoothed HTTP/TCP throughput measurement compared to the TCP throughput calculation equation in paper [10] is that our method does not require information from the transport layer (TCP layer). In order to use the TCP throughput calculation equation, the packet loss rates and round trip time (RTT) are required, however, such information is not available at the application layer. By contrast our method only needs to measure the segment fetch time. Therefore our method is feasible for application layer end-to-end rate adaptation.

3.2 Rate Adaptation Algorithm

In this section we present a rate adaptation algorithm based on the proposed smoothed HTTP/TCP throughput measurement presented in section 3.1. The smoothed HTTP/TCP throughput reveals the available network capacity and is suitable to be used as a metric of detecting network congestion and probing spare network resources. Fig. 2 shows the flowchart of the proposed rate adaptation algorithm for the adaptive HTTP streaming. The rate adaptation algorithm determines the representation for fetching the next media segment each time after receiving a media segment. The rate adaptation deploys a step-wise switch up and aggressive switch-down method to change the consumed representation from different bitrates encoded representations.

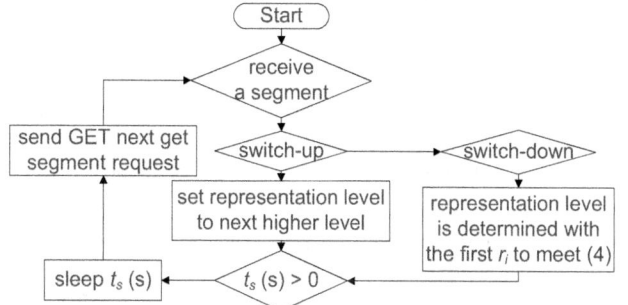

Figure 2. Flowchart of the proposed rate adaptation algorithm of the adaptive HTTP streaming

The switch up/switch down operations are determined as follows:.Switch up: takes place if inequality (2) is met and the buffered media time is larger than the predefined minimum.

$$\mu > 1 + \varepsilon \quad (2)$$

where μ denotes the ratio of the media segment duration to the segment fetch time and ε denotes a switch up factor. In (2), the left term represents the metric to detect congestion and the right term denotes the condition to switch up to the next higher representation level. For determining the switch-up factor, it can be set as

$$\varepsilon = \max \{\frac{b_{r_{i+1}} - b_{r_i}}{b_{r_i}}, \forall i = [0, 1, \ldots, N - 1]\} \quad (3)$$

where b_{r_i} denotes the encoded media bitrate of representation i and N denotes the highest representation level.

As mentioned in section 3.1, the equation 2 is satisfied in the HTTP/TCP streaming scenario when the average TCP throughput for fetching a segment is higher than the encoded media bitrate of the fetched media segment. In case of a decision to switch up, the rate adaptation algorithm selects the next higher representation level. The reason for using a conservative step-wise switch-up strategy is to prevent playback interruptions that might occur in case of aggressive switch-up operations. During the step-wise switch-up, the buffered media time is allowed to accumulate to a safety level in order to prevent buffer underflows that might be incurred by sudden bandwidth drops. So the initial buffering time, spent to reach the protection level of buffered media, is reduced significantly, which improves the user experience.

Switch down: It will be performed if inequality (4) is met.

$$\mu < \gamma_d \qquad (4)$$

where μ represents the ratio of media segment duration to segment fetch time which is used as the rate adaptation metric and γ_d denotes switch down threshold. In case of congestion, the segment fetch time is typically much higher than the media segment duration. Hence, inequality (4) enables to detect network congestion before the media buffer is drained and switches down to a suitable representation as discussed in the following. In the case that (4) fails to detect slight mismatches between the media bitrates and the network capacity, the buffered media time may gradually decrease. Hence, buffered media time can be compared with a pre-calculated minimum, which is used as a complementary switch-down condition to prevent client buffer underflows.

In the switch down, an aggressive switch down will be performed. The selected representation level is determined to be the first representation (in descending order) with level r_i to meet

$$b_{r_i} < \mu b_c \qquad (5)$$

where b_{r_i} denotes the encoded media bitrate of the representation r_i, μ denote the ratio of media segment duration to segment fetch time and b_c denotes the bitrate of current representation.

The idle time calculation algorithm is deployed before sending the next GET request, in order to prevent client buffer overflow. The rate adaptation algorithm will wait a certain period of time after determining the representation level of the next segment and before sending the next request if the buffered media time in the client buffer is large enough to cover the maximum draining of buffered media time during fetching the segment. When the average TCP throughput drops from the bitrate of the current presentation to the bitrate of the lowest representation, the maximum amount of buffered media time will be drained. So the idle time between determining representation level and sending the next request is set as t_s if the inequality (6) is met

$$t_s = t_m - t_{min} - \frac{b_c}{b_{min}} MSD > 0 \qquad (6)$$

where t_s, t_m and t_{min} denote the idle time in seconds, the buffered media time, the predefined minimum buffered media time respectively and b_c and b_{min} denote the current representation bitrate and the minimum representation bitrate respectively, and MSD denotes the media segment duration. The key advantage of the idle time method is to limit the maximum amount of buffered media data; hence, saving network bandwidth consumption and memory resources of the receiver.

4. SIMULATION RESULTS

We implemented the proposed rate adaptation algorithm for adaptive HTTP streaming in ns2 [2]. Fig. 3 shows the network topology used in the simulations. The server and client denote the

HTTP streaming server and client. To simulate the varying delays and bandwidths an exponential traffic generator (Exp_G) and receiver (Exp_R) are used as background traffic with the average "on" time of 500ms, average "off" time of 500ms and the average sending rate during "on" times is set as 1000 Kbits/s during the "on" period hence the overall bitrate of the exponential traffic during whole period is equal to 500 Kbits/s. Both web server and exponential traffic generator start operation at time 0s and end at 1200s. In addition to background traffic a constant bitrate traffic generator (CBR_G) and receiver (CBR_R) are added at time400s to 800s which is used as competitive traffic at the bottleneck bandwidth between node 0 and the proxy. In Fig.3 the bandwidth (Mbits/s) and delay (ms) are given for each link. For media data, 10 sets of representations are provided to perform the rate adaptation wherein the bitrates vary from 100Kbits/s to 1000Kbits/s with a step of 100Kbits/s and representation level 0 to 9 respectively. In the simulation, we set the MSD, t_{min}, , and γ_d to 10s, 9s and 0.67.

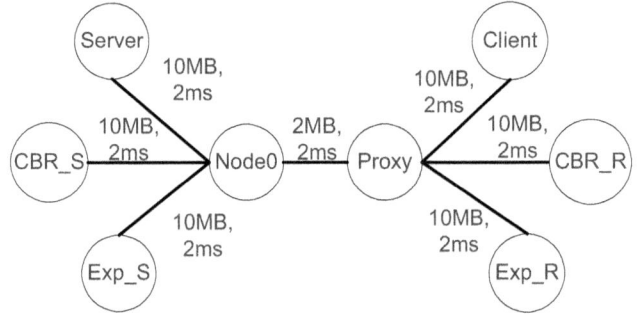

Figure. 3. Network topology

To the best of our knowledge, we haven't found a receiver-driven rate adaptation algorithm for HTTP streaming and only few research works have been conducted in the field of client buffer requirement for media streaming over TCP [4] [5] and TCP-based multimedia streaming performance analysis [11]. Hence, we evaluated the efficiency of the proposed method based on the aspect of rate adaptation accuracy and rate adaptation speed as follows. To identify the impact of the different variations of the bottleneck bandwidths on the proposed rate adaptation algorithm, we vary the bitrates of competitive traffic source, i.e. the CBR traffic generator, from 400 Kbits/s to 1400 Kbits/s at steps of 200 Kbits/s, hence 6 sets of simulation were ran. For evaluating the accuracy, we analyzed the representation level statistics together with the buffered media times after the representation first reaches a stable stage to identify how accurately the rate adaptation algorithm approaches to the network capacity and if it is capable to converge to a stable representation level. If the optimum representation level is n, then reaching representation level n-1 or n+1 is considered as reaching the stable stage. The rate adaptation speed is represented as the time spent to reach the stable representation level starting from the instant of changing the bottleneck bandwidth.

Fig. 4 shows the mean index of the consumed representations at the different CBR traffic bitrates, wherein the x axis denotes the CBR bitrates and y axis denotes the representation level. Here the representation level changes from 0 and 9 corresponding to the media bitrates of 100 Kbits/s to 1000 Kbits/s respectively. We partitioned the whole simulation period into three different periods including 0-400s, 400s-800s and 800s-1200s representing the period before CBR traffic appearing, the period during CBR traffic and after CBR traffic. The mean of representation level in

0-400 is constantly equal to 8.51 for all CBR bitrates since CBR traffic is not added until 400s. In the period of 400-800s, the mean of the representation level drops along with the increase of CBR bitrates. It shows that the rate adaptation effectively switches down to the lower representation level to match the media bitrates to the sharable end-to-end bandwidth. In the period of 800-1200s, when the CBR traffic disappears, the mean of representation level remains relatively constant with the different CBR bitrates and always higher than 8.5. This observation reveals that the performance of the rate adaptation is independent of the change in the bandwidth.

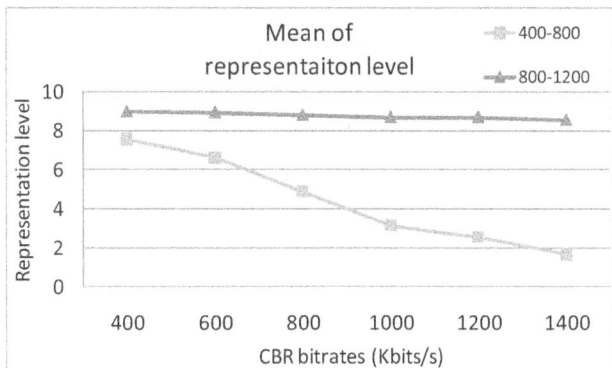

Figure. 4. Mean of representation levels with CBR bitrates in different time periods

In order to show the convergence property of the proposed rate adaptation method after reaching the stable state, the standard deviation (STD) of the representations level at the stable state is depicted in Fig 5. The x and y axes are set similarly to Fig. 4. In the period 0-400s, the STD of the representation level is constantly equal to 0.26. In the period 800-1200s the STD is below 0.26 and during the period 400-800s the STD is below 0.7 except 0.99 for the CBR bitrate of 1000 Kbits/s.

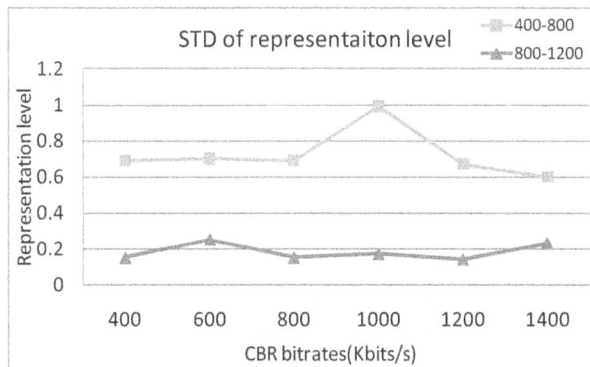

Figure. 5. STD of representation level with different CBR bitrates in different time periods

In adaptive HTTP streaming, the optimum media bitrates can't simply be estimated as the fair share of the end-to-tend bottleneck bandwidth, since the supported media bitrates for interruption free streaming is also affected by the round trip time (RTT) and packet loss rates. To analyze how accurately the rate adaptation algorithm matches the selected representation bandwidth to the optimal level, the STD and the mean of the buffered media time at different CBR bitrates in different time periods are reported in Fig. 6 and Fig. 7 respectively. Here, the x axis denotes the CBR bitrates and the y axis denotes the buffered media time respectively. In HTTP streaming, the server sends the requested

media data at the highest transmission rate allowed by the TCP congestion and flow control algorithms. If the rate adaptation operates in a lower than optimal representation level, then the buffered media time will increase and vice versa. So the lower STD in the buffered media time demonstrates more accurate rate adaptation. In the period 0s-400s, the STD and mean of buffered media time are constant and equal to 9.9s and 65.5s. Fig. 6 shows that the maximum STD for the buffered media time is lower than 9.18s and 12.92s in the periods 400-800s and 800-1200s respectively. In Fig. 7, the minimum mean of the buffered media time is higher than 54s and 90s respectively in the periods 400-800s and 800-1200s respectively. As demonstrated in the simulation results, the STDs for the buffered media time are relatively small compared to the mean of the buffered media time. When the CBR traffic is added to compete on the bottleneck bandwidth, it is important to identify that the rate adaptation algorithm acts appropriately to prevent buffer underflows. In all of the simulation results the minimum buffered media time is higher than 36s, hence ensuring that playback interruptions do not happen.

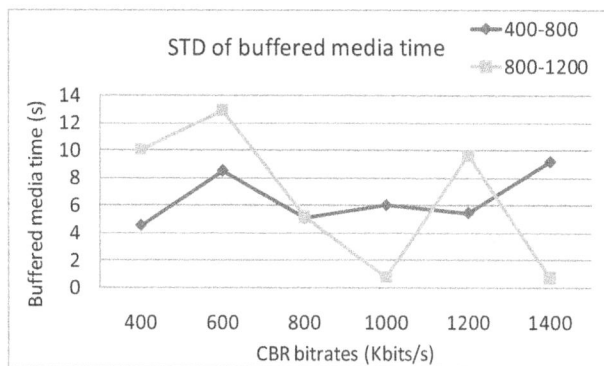

Figure. 6. STD of buffered media time with different CBR bitrates in different time periods

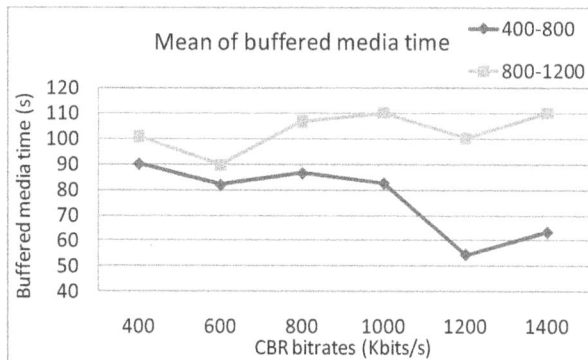

Figure. 7. Mean of buffered media time with different CBR bitrates in different time periods

The rate adaptation speed is another important factor to evaluate the behavior of the rate adaptation algorithm. Fig. 8 shows the rate adaptation speed with different competition CBR bitrates in the different time periods. In the period of 0-400 (s) it takes 44s to switch-up to representation 8 from representation 0. The other switch-up period 800-1200 (s) shows that the rate adaptation speed varies with the amount of competitive traffic between a minimum of lower than 1s and a maximum of 41s. As shown in the period of 400-800 (s), the mean of switch-down speeds are around 30.3s and without showing any correlation with the amount of competitive traffic at the bottleneck. The convergence time in down switching remains within the amount of buffered media time, thus avoiding any buffer underflows. It is worthwhile to note that the major part of the delay is attributable to waiting for the current media segment fetching to finish, which takes significantly longer when the available bandwidth drops.

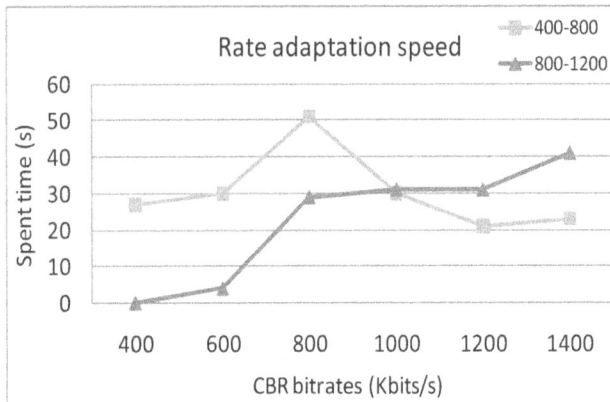

Figure. 8. Rate adaptation speed with different CBR bitrates in different time periods

5. CONCLUSION

In this paper, we propose a novel method for detecting congestion, probing spare network capacity, and measuring the smoothed HTTP/TCP throughput for rate adaptation in adaptive HTTP streaming. The advantage of the proposed smoothed HTTP/TCP throughput measurement compared to the TCP throughput calculation equation used in TCP friendly rate control (TFRC) is that our method does not require the transport layer information such as packets loss rates and round trip time (RTT) to be available at the application layer. Hence, the proposed metric and smoothed TCP throughput measurement method can be used at the application layer. Upon detecting streaming that the media bitrate does not match the current end-to-end network capacity, an algorithm for conservative step-wise up switching and aggressive down switching of representations is presented using the smoothed TCP throughput measurement. In addition an idle time calculation method is used to prevent client buffer overflow and by consequence saving network bandwidth and memory resource at the client. Simulation results show that the proposed metric efficiently detects the congestion and probes the spare network capacity. And the smooth TCP throughput measurement method based rate adaptation method can quickly and accurately reach to the optimum bitrate level.

6. Acknowledgment

This work was supported by the Academy of Finland, (application number 129657, Finnish Programme for Centres of Excellence in Research 2006-2011).

7. REFERENCES

[1] Fielding, R., Getty, J., Mogul, J., Frystyk, H., Masinter, L., Leach, P., Lee, T. Berners. 1999. Hypertext transfer protocol -- HTTP/1.1, RFC 2616. June 1999.

[2] Information Sciences Institute, The University of Southern California. 2006. The Network Simulator - ns-2. (13 July 2006).

[3] Kim, T. and Ammar, M. H.. 2006. Receiver buffer requirement for video streaming over TCP. SPIE VCIP 2006 (San Jose, CA, Jan. 2006).

[4] Kim, T., Avadhanam, N., Subramanian, S. 2006. Dimensioning receiver buffer requirement for unidirectional VBR video streaming over TCP. ICIP 2006 (Atlanta, USA, Oct. 2006).

[5] Krasic, C., Li, K. and Walpole, J. 2001. The Case for Streaming Multimedia with TCP. In Proceedings of IDMS (Lancaster. UK, September 2001).

[6] Lam, L.S, Lee, Jack YB, Liew, S.C, Wang W. 2004. A transparent rate adaptation algorithm for streaming video over the internet. In 18th International conference on advanced information networking and applications (Fukuoka, Japan, March 2004).

[7] Liu, C., Bouazizi, I., Gabbouj, M. 2010. Advanced rate adaptation for unicast streaming of scalable video. IEEE International Conference on Communications 2010 (ICC 2010) (Cape Town, South Africa. May 2010).

[8] Liu, C., Bouazizi, I., Gabbouj, M. 2010. Multi-buffer based congestion control for multicast streaming of scalable video. 2010 IEEE International Conference on Multimedia & Expo (ICME 2010) (Singapore, July 19-23, 2010).

[9] McCanne, S., Jacobson, V., and Vetterli, M. 1996. Receiver-driven layered multicast. In the Proceedings of SIGCOMM'96. ACM Stanford, (CA, Aug. 1996), 117–130.

[10] Padhye,J., Firoiu, V., Towsley, D. and Kurose, J. 2000. Modeling TCP Reno performance: a simple model and its empirical validation. IEEE/ACM Transactions on Networking, vol. 8, no. 2, pp. 133-145, April 2000.

[11] Wang, B., Kurose, J., Shenoy, P., and Towsley, D. 2004. Multimedia streaming via TCP: An analytic performance study. In Proceedings of ACM Multimedia (October 2004), 908 - 915. http://doi.acm.org/10.1145/1352012.1352020.

[12] 3GPP TS 26.234. 2009. Transparent End-To-End Packet-Switched Streaming Service (PSS): protocols and codecs. (Release9).http://www.3gpp.org/ftp/Specs/archive/26_series/26.234/.

[13] 3GPP SP-090710. 2010. Adaptive HTTP Streaming in PSS. (Sophia-Antipolis, France, Jan. 2010.) http://www.3gpp.org/ftp/Specs/html-info/26234-CRs.htm.

Impact of Flash Memory on Video-on-Demand Storage: Analysis of Tradeoffs

Moonkyung Ryu
College of Computing
Georgia Institute of
Technology
Atlanta, GA, USA
mkryu@gatech.edu

Hyojun Kim
College of Computing
Georgia Institute of
Technology
Atlanta, GA, USA
hyojun.kim@cc.gatech.edu

Umakishore
Ramachandran
College of Computing
Georgia Institute of
Technology
Atlanta, GA, USA
rama@cc.gatech.edu

ABSTRACT

There is no doubt that video-on-demand (VoD) services are
very popular these days. However, disk storage is a serious bottleneck limiting the scalability of a VoD server. Disk
throughput degrades dramatically due to seek time overhead when the server is called upon to serve a large number of simultaneous video streams. To address the performance problem of disk, buffer cache algorithms that utilize
RAM have been proposed. Interval caching is a state-of-
the-art caching algorithm for a VoD server. *Flash Memory
Solid-State Drive (SSD)* is a relatively new storage technology. Its excellent random read performance, low power
consumption, and sharply dropping cost per gigabyte are
opening new opportunities to efficiently use the device for
enterprise systems. On the other hand, it has deficiencies
such as poor small random write performance and limited
number of erase operations. In this paper, we analyze trade-
offs and potential impact that flash memory SSD can have
for a VoD server. Performance of various commercially available flash memory SSD models is studied. We find that low-
end flash memory SSD provides better performance than
the high-end one while costing less than the high-end one
when the I/O request size is large, which is typical for a
VoD server. Because of the wear problem and asymmetric read/write performance of flash memory SSD, we claim
that interval caching cannot be used with it. Instead, we
propose using file-level Least Frequently Used (LFU) due to
the highly skewed video access pattern of the VoD workload. We compare the performance of interval caching with
RAM and file-level LFU with flash memory by simulation
experiments. In addition, from the cost-effectiveness analysis of three different storage configurations, we find that
flash memory with hard disk drive is the most cost-effective
solution compared to DRAM with hard disk drive or hard
disk drive only.

Categories and Subject Descriptors

B.3.2 [**Design Styles**]: Mass Storage; D.4.2 [**Storage Management**]: Secondary Storage

General Terms

Design, Measurement, Performance

Keywords

Flash Memory, Solid-State Drive, Video-on-Demand, Interval Caching

1. INTRODUCTION

Video-on-demand (VoD) services like Hulu [2], and Netflix [3] have achieved huge success recently. There are several
technological factors that have contributed to the success of
VoD: (a) high speed networks, (b) data compression algorithms, and (c) powerful CPUs. Due to the success of VoD,
the demand for such services is on the rise both in terms
of the number of requests as well as the quality (i.e., video
bitrate). Larger number of video requests and higher video
bitrate impose a larger bandwidth requirement on the storage subsystem. A pure disk-based storage subsystem is a
serious impediment to meeting this increased bandwidth requirement in a VoD server architecture.

While the capacity of magnetic disks has been steadily increasing over the past few decades, the data access time has
not kept pace with other computing components such as the
CPU and memory. If anything, the speed gap between the
main memory (RAM) and the hard disk has only widened.
This is not very surprising since the data access time for the
disk is limited by the electromechanical delays in the form of
seek time and rotational latency. These delays significantly
degrade the VoD server performance when serving a number of video requests simultaneously. Figure 1 demonstrates
the poor performance of a hard disk drive (HDD) when it
services a large number of sequential streams. In this experiment, we have used *xdd* [4] benchmark on the raw device.
The file cache of the operating system is disabled, and the
I/O request size is 1MB. The disk drive is SEAGATE Cheetah 15K.6, an enterprise class disk with a rotational speed
of 15000RPM and a Serial-Attached SCSI (SAS) interface.
The flash memory SSD is SAMSUNG MMDOE56G5MXP-
0VB, a consumer class one. As shown in the graph, when the
number of streams exceeds 20, the aggregate read throughput of the disk drops significantly. On the other hand, the

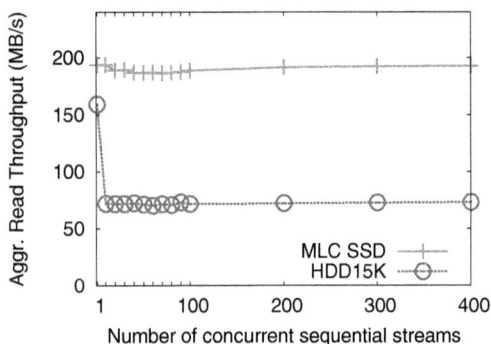

Figure 1: Reading sequential files, 1MB I/O request size. Aggregate read throughput drops quickly from 160MB/s to 70MB/s with 15000RPM hard disk drive. Flash memory SSD provides constant read throughput with a large number of sequential streams.

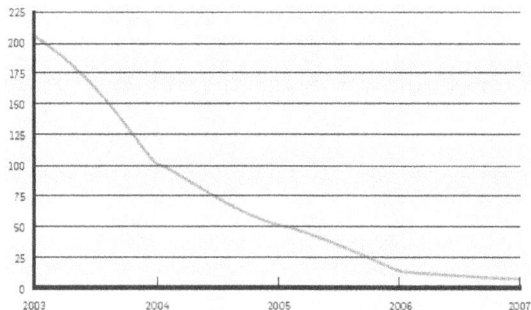

Figure 2: Flash memory $/GB trend

aggregate read throughput of the flash memory SSD remains constant even with 400 streams. When a VoD server services a large number of video streams simultaneously, it generates random read I/O pattern to storage. Therefore, the random read throughput of a storage device determines scalability of the device, i.e., the number of concurrent video streams that the device can serve.

To serve video streams at a cheaper cost, buffer cache algorithms that use RAM as a buffer cache have been proposed. An efficient buffer cache algorithm can reduce the service latency due to the fast access speed of RAM and can serve more video streams compared to the alternative of adding more disks. Interval caching [18, 7, 8, 9], which is a state-of-the-art buffer cache algorithm for a VoD server, exploits temporal locality when independent requests access the same video file by caching intervals between the successive streams. The average size of intervals and the capacity of the buffer determines the number of concurrent streams that can be served by interval caching. Interval caching provides cheaper cost for serving a video stream in certain range of RAM capacity compared to adding more disks depending on the inter arrival time of video requests.

Flash memory SSD opens up new opportunities for providing a more cost-effective solution for a VoD server. Solid-State Drive (SSD) is a new storage device that is comprised of semiconductor memory chips (e.g., DRAM, Flash memory, Phase change memory) to store and retrieve data rather than using the traditional spinning platters, a motor, and moving heads found in conventional magnetic disks. The term "solid-state" means there are no moving parts in accessing data on the drive.

Among various types of SSDs, flash memory SSD nowadays is rapidly penetrating into modern computer systems. NAND flash memory densities have been doubling since 1996 consistent with Hwang's flash memory growth model, and it is expected to continue until 2012 [14]. Figure 2 shows that the cost trend of the flash memory conforms to his estimation [21]. The sharply dropping cost per gigabyte is what has brought flash memory SSD to the forefront in recent years. Flash-based storage devices are now considered to have tremendous potential as a new storage medium for en-

terprise servers [13]. The advantages of flash memory SSD are fast random read, low power consumption, and no vibration or noise due to the absence of the mechanical components. On the other hand, its high cost per gigabyte compared to magnetic disks, poor small random write performance, and wear are major concerns compared to the hard disk [12].

Compared with disks, flash memory SSD boasts excellent features that are appropriate for a VoD storage. First, it has very low latency in retrieving data. The access latency of magnetic disks is 10ms. On the other hand, the read access latency of flash memory SSD is 0.1ms [26]. Lower read latency equates to lower delay users experience when starting a video. Second, its random read throughput can reach the sequential read throughput, which is the maximum read throughput, when the I/O request size is large and a multiple of the block size of the flash memory. A VoD server typically uses a large I/O request size (> 1MB). Larger random read throughput means larger numbers of simultaneous video streams that can be serviced by a VoD server. Third, the video popularity pattern is highly skewed and is modeled by a Zipf distribution [28]. This means only a small fraction of the total video repository is accessed most of the time. The highly skewed access pattern gives an opportunity to the flash memory SSD to be efficiently used even though its cost per gigabyte is more expensive than that of a magnetic disk.

Magnetic disk offers capacity while RAM offers speed of access. The combination has been successful for implementing memory hierarchies to support traditional workload of computer systems including virtual memory and file servers. However, VoD server's requirement is unique in that the storage device needs to provide both capacity and speed. Flash memory fits this requirement since it provides both at a price point that is more favorable than RAM. Therefore, our idea is to use Flash-based SSD as a buffer cache similar to how interval caching uses RAM for the same purpose. The purpose of the paper is to investigate the efficacy of Flash-based SSD as an alternative to RAM as a buffer cache both from the point of view of performance and cost-effectiveness.

The unique contributions of our work are as follows:
(a) We measure and compare performance of various kinds of flash memory SSDs. Surprisingly, we observe that cheap low-end flash memory SSD provides better performance for VoD storage than the expensive high-end flash memory SSD. The low-end flash memory SSD has similar random read throughput to that of the high-end flash memory SSD when

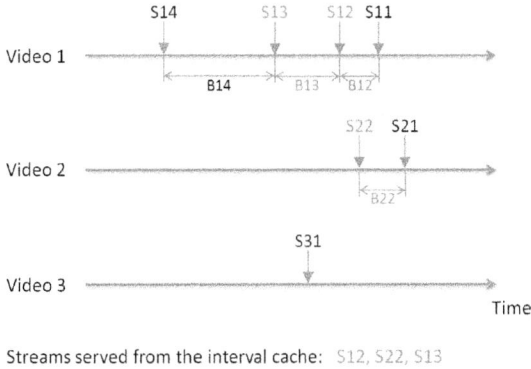

Figure 3: Interval Caching exploits temporal locality accessing the same video and buffers the interval between two successive streams. A preceding stream (e.g., S11) feeds data to a following stream (e.g., S12).

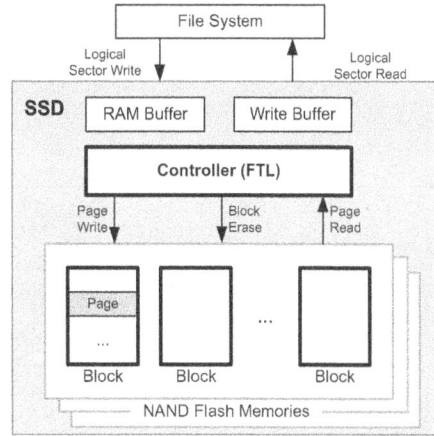

Figure 4: SSD, FTL and NAND flash memory. *FTL emulates sector read and write functionalities of a hard disk allowing conventional disk file systems to be implemented on NAND flash memory*

I/O request size is large as is typical for a VoD server. The low-end flash memory SSD has less variance in the throughput when large random read operations and large sequential write operations co-exist. The low-end flash memory SSD has a lower cost per gigabyte than the high-end one. The reason for this is that high-end flash memory SSD adopts more expensive flash memory cells, a complex FTL algorithm, and a larger RAM buffer to improve small random write performance. Because a VoD server uses a large I/O request size and most of its work is read operations from the storage device, we can avoid small random writes to the flash memory SSD in the VoD server.

(b) Unlike RAM, we observe that flash memory SSD is not an appropriate device for the interval caching algorithm due to the asymmetry of read and write access speeds, the unpredictability of write performance incurred by garbage collection, and the limited number of erase operations. Instead, we propose to use file-level Least Frequently Used (LFU) with the flash memory SSD due to the real-time requirement of video service (i.e., file-level) and the highly skewed access pattern of the VoD workload (i.e., LFU).

(c) We compare the performance of RAM and flash memory SSD over a broad range of device parameters and workload parameters by simulation when interval caching is used with RAM and file-level LFU is used with flash memory SSD. In addition, we analyze the cost-effectiveness of three different storage configurations, which are HDD only, DRAM with HDD, and flash memory with HDD. From the analysis, we find that flash memory with HDD is surprisingly cheaper than other two by a factor of 2.

The rest of the paper is organized as follows. Section 2 explains background about interval caching and flash memory SSD. Section 3 summarizes requirements for a VoD storage device. In Section 4, we measure performance of 3 different SSD models and observe that low-end SSD model meets the VoD storage requirements very well. We discuss how to utilize flash memory SSD for a VoD server in Section 5. Section 6 presents simulation experiment results comparing interval caching with RAM and file-level LFU with flash memory. Moreover, we analyze the cost-effectiveness of flash memory as a VoD storage device. Related work is presented in Section 7 and the final section concludes this paper.

2. BACKGROUND

2.1 Interval Caching

The main idea behind the interval caching algorithm [18, 7, 8, 9] is to choose intervals between two consecutive streams watching the same video. The first stream of an interval is referred to as the *preceding* stream, and the second stream is referred to as the *following* stream. The chosen intervals are cached for serving the "following" streams from the buffer cache. Figure 3 illustrates this. The arrows marked by S_{11} through S_{31} represent the temporal pointers corresponding to the distinct streams on videos 1, 2, and 3. Two streams, S_i and S_j are defined to be consecutive if S_j is the stream that next reads the video blocks that have just been read by S_i. For instance, in Figure 3, (S_{11}, S_{12}), (S_{12}, S_{13}), and (S_{13}, S_{14}) form three consecutive pairs for video 1. The interval caching algorithm orders all intervals according to the memory requirements in an increasing order to allocate memory to as many intervals as possible. The memory requirement of an interval is the length of the interval in seconds times video bitrate of the interval involved. For example, Figure 3 shows intervals B12, B22, B13 can be buffered in the interval cache, while there is no more room to buffer B14. When an interval is cached, the preceding stream writes video blocks to the allocated buffer, and the following streams read the blocks from the buffer avoiding disk access. Therefore, continuous read and write operations are involved in the buffer cache.

2.2 Flash Memory Solid-State Drive

Flash memories, including NAND and NOR types, have a common physical restriction, namely, they must be erased before being written [22]. In flash memory, the amount of electric charges in a transistor represents 1 or 0. The charges can be moved both into a transistor by write operation and out by an erase operation. By design, the erase operation, which sets a storage cell to 1, works on a bigger number of storage cells at a time than the write operation. Thus, flash memory can be written or read a single page at a time, but it has to be erased in an erasable-block unit. An erasable-block consists of a certain number of pages. In NAND flash

Device	Seq. Read Throughput	Random Read Throughput	Cost per Gigabyte
HDD15K	160 MB/s	70 MB/s	$1.23
DRAM	> 20 GB/s	> 20 GB/s	$23
MLC SSD	> 155 MB/s	> 155 MB/s	$1.88

Table 1: Characteristics of different storage devices. SEAGATE Cheetah 15K.6 and RiData NSSD-S25-64-C06MPN are measured for the throughput of HDD15K and MLC SSD by *xdd* benchmark program when I/O request size is 1MB. The throughput of MLC SSD is largely different depending on the vendor and the model. Throughput of DRAM comes from DDR3 SDRAM device specification.

memory, a page is similar to a HDD sector, and its size is usually 2 KBytes.

Flash memory also suffers from a limitation on the number of erase operations possible for each erasable block. The insulation layer that prevents electric charges from dispersing may be damaged after a certain number of erase operations. In single level cell (SLC) NAND flash memory, the expected number of erasures per block is 100,000 and this is reduced to 10,000 in two bits multilevel cell (MLC) NAND flash memory.

An SSD is simply a set of flash memory chips packaged together with additional circuitry and a special piece of software called Flash Translation Layer (FTL) [5, 15, 16, 25]. The additional circuitry may include a RAM buffer for storing meta-data associated with the internal organization of the SSD, and a write buffer for optimizing the performance of the SSD. The FTL provides an external logical interface to the file system. A sector is the unit of logical access to the flash memory provided by this interface. A page inside the flash memory may contain several such logical sectors. The FTL maps this logical sector to physical locations within individual pages [5]. This interface allows FTL to emulate a HDD so far as the file system is concerned (Figure 4).

Agrawal et al. enumerate the design trade-offs of SSDs in a systematic way, from which we can get a good intuition about the relation between the performance of SSD and the design decisions [5]. However, the fact of the matter is that without the exact details of the internal architecture of the SSD and the FTL algorithm, it is very difficult to fully understand the external characteristics of SSDs [6].

More complicated FTL mapping algorithms with more resources have been proposed to get better random write performance [25]. However, due to the increased resource usage of these approaches, they are used usually for high-end SSDs. Even though high-end SSDs using fine grained FTL mapping schemes can provide good random write performances, the effect of background garbage collection will be a problem considering the soft real-time requirements of VoD server systems.

3. VIDEO-ON-DEMAND STORAGE

Video data is classified as *continuous media* (CM) data because it consists of a sequence of media *quanta* (e.g., video frames), which is useful only when presented in time [11]. A VoD server differs significantly from other types of servers

that support only textual data because of two fundamental CM characteristics.

- Real-time retrieval: CM data should be delivered before the data becomes meaningless. Failure to meet this real-time constraint leads to jerkiness or hiccups in video display.

- High data transfer rate and large storage space: A digital video playback demands high bitrate. The size of a video is determined by the bitrate of the video and the length of the video, therefore, a video requires a large amount of capacity from the storage device. In practice, a VoD server must handle playback requests for several streams simultaneously. Even when multiple streams access the same file (such as a popular file), different streams might access different parts of the file at the same time. Therefore, a number of sequential read streams generates random read operations to the storage device. To serve a large number of high bitrate streams simultaneously, the storage device of the VoD server should support a large amount of random read bandwidth. Moreover, the storage device should have a large amount of capacity to store a number of video files that are large in size.

In summary, VoD storage should have both large bandwidth and large capacity for a scalable VoD server. Table 1 shows the random read throughput and cost per gigabyte of three different storage devices, Disk, DRAM, and flash memory SSD. Disk is a capacity optimized device. On the other hand, DRAM is a bandwidth optimized device. Flash memory SSD provides a balanced combination of bandwidth and capacity. This characteristic of the flash SSD gives us an opportunity to efficiently exploit the device for VoD storage.

4. MEASUREMENT OF FLASH SSDS

Different SSDs show very different performance characteristics because SSD manufacturers use different types of NAND flash memories, internal architectures, and FTL algorithms considering design trade-offs and target users [5].

In this section, we show our measurement results with various SSDs. In VoD storage, the workload mainly consists of large but scattered read requests to service multiple streaming clients. Therefore, large random read throughput is the most important metric of SSDs. In addition, when the flash memory SSD is used as a buffer cache, large sequential write throughput is also meaningful because we may want to change the contents of the SSD to accommodate changing popularity of video files. Another important evaluation criterion is deterministic response times. All SSDs have very complicated software layer, which maintains the mapping from logical sectors to physical location within SSDs due to the very nature of NAND flash memory that mandates writing in units of large erasable-blocks rather than individual sectors. The background garbage collection and wear leveling activities can make response time irregular. A desirable SSD for use in a VoD server should have high throughput for large random reads and large sequential writes, and the throughput also needs to be stable.

4.1 Experiment Setting

We have used *xdd* benchmark to measure read/write throughput of SSDs on various request sizes. The benchmark generates random (but aligned) read/write requests with given test size, and reports average throughput. We have compared the performance of three SSDs, which are fairly in-

	A	B	C	D
MODEL	RiData NSSD-S25-64-C06MPN	SAMSUNG MMDOE56G5MXP-0VB	INTEL X25-M G1	Fusion-io ioDRIVE 80GB SLC
CLASS	LOW	LOW	HIGH	ENTERPRISE
TYPE	MLC	MLC	MLC	SLC
CAPACITY	64GB	256GB	80GB	80GB
$/GB	$1.88	$2.34	$2.50	$61.95

Table 2: Characteristics of four flash memory SSDs. SSD A, B, and C are classified as HIGH or LOW based on the small random write performance of the SSDs. We do not measure the enterprise class SSD.

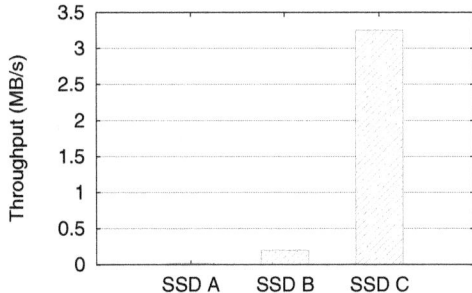

Figure 5: Small random write throughput of different SSDs. 4KB request size is used.

expensive. Intentionally, we do not consider enterprise class SSDs, which are extremely expensive. These enterprise class SSDs provide high reliability and very good random write performance to target enterprise storage server systems. However, such attributes are not important for building a cost-effective VoD server for reasons of the workload characteristics that it has to deal with (see Section 3). Table 2 lists the four SSDs, and some important parameters: cell type, capacity, and price per gigabytes. We classify the three SSDs we experiment with, namely, A, B, and C as HIGH or LOW based on the small random write performance of the SSDs. Figure 5 shows the small random write performance of the three SSDs when the request size is 4KB.

4.2 SSD Throughput Results

Figure 6 shows the throughput measurement results with the three different SSDs for a variety of workloads. Y-axis shows measured average throughput, and higher value means better performance. Test request sizes are shown on the X-axis. As we already explained, large random read and large sequential write are important for the VoD system. In most SSDs and certainly for the ones we experimented with as can be seen from Figure 6, the random read throughput comes close to the sequential read throughput when the request size is more than or equal to 512KB. For SSDs A and C, the random write throughput approaches the throughput of the sequential write workload when the request size is more than or equal to 16MB. However, SSD B has a serious performance problem for random write operations even when the request size is large.

Our real interest in understanding the performance of SSDs for the workload of interest from the point of the VoD server is, namely, large random reads simultaneous with se-

quential writes. Because the flash memory is intended to be used as a buffer cache in the VoD server, write operations will be replacing unpopular video files while read operations serve the video streams. To figure out how the random read performance is affected in the presence of write operations, we measure the throughput of the SSDs for the combined workload (i.e., Random read and Sequential write operations). We use 1MB request size for the measurement, and we run the experiment for 20mins. Figure 7 shows the time series of the random read throughput and the sequential write throughput of SSD A, SSD B, and SSD C respectively. Figure 8 shows the mean and the standard deviation of the random read throughput of the SSDs for the same combined workload as in Figure 7. Surprisingly, the high-end SSD C that has the best small random write performance (Figure 5) and very good random read performance (Figure 6) shows the worst random read throughput for the combined workload, and worse yet it has very large standard deviation from the mean throughput. On the other hand, the low-end SSDs (i.e., SSD A and B) have very small deviation from the mean throughput. This result reveals a very important insight. As we have already mentioned earlier (see Section 2.2), high-end SSDs incorporate sophisticated algorithms for garbage collection and wear-leveling in the FTL layer to boost random (small) write performance. It is impossible to predict from the host side when such algorithms may be invoked internally in the device, and how these algorithms may interact with other requests coming simultaneously to the device. These are the factors most likely adversely affecting the random read performance for SSD C (a high-end SSD) when write operations are requested simultaneously even though the write operations are sequential with large request sizes.

It is not possible to explain the exact reason why the random read performance is heavily influenced by write operations without the internal design details of SSD products. However, we can find probable causes from already published literature. Feng et al. [6] have shown that read response time can be delayed by procrastinated write operations, and STEC [1] has reported that write response time of consumer level SSD can vary significantly due to the background wear leveling and block relocation activities. Based on the good small random write performance of SSD C, we can cautiously guess that SSD C is using fine-grained mapping FTL algorithm internally. Fine-grained mapping scheme may provide good random write performance but requires efficient garbage collection, which can make response time irregular. The result of Figure 8 is well matched with our guess. On the other hand, coarse grained mapping FTL algorithms show poor small random write performance, but

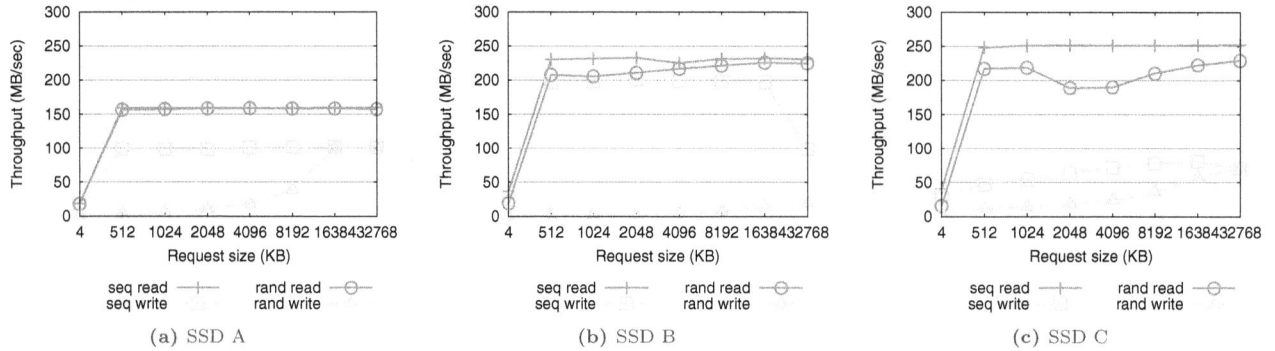

(a) SSD A   (b) SSD B   (c) SSD C

Figure 6: Throughput of various SSDs with different I/O request size

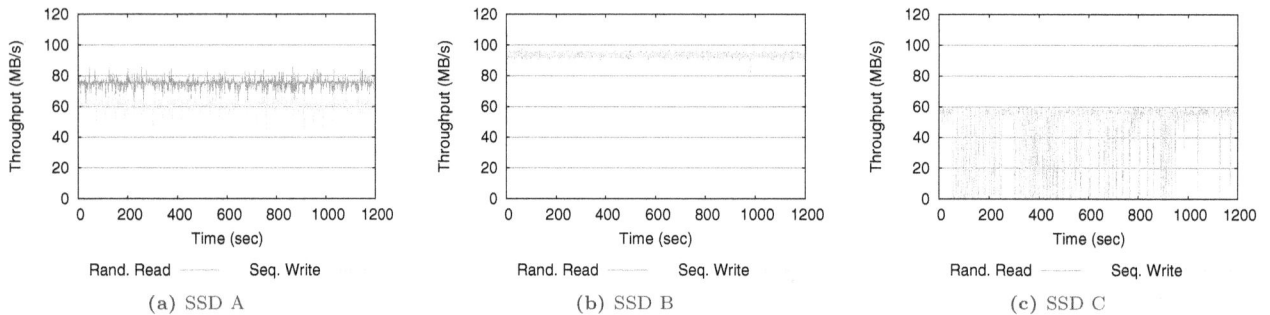

(a) SSD A   (b) SSD B   (c) SSD C

Figure 7: Throughput of SSDs for combined workload: Random read and Sequential write (1MB request size is used). For SSD B and C, red line is overlaid with green line because random read throughput and sequential write throughput vary in similar values.

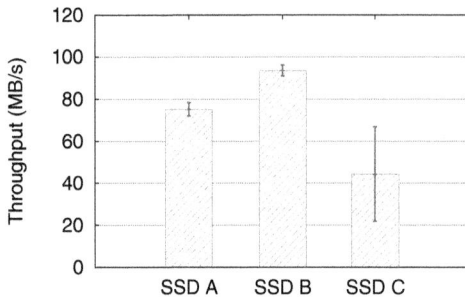

Figure 8: Mean and standard deviation of the random read throughput for the same combined workload as in Figure 7.

do not require background garbage collection process in general. Instead, they may use much simpler merge operations whose overhead is minimal for sequential writes. The stable read performance observed for SSD A and B in Figure 8 can be well explained if SSD A and B (being low-end SSDs) are using coarse grained mapping FTL algorithms.

4.3 Summary of Measurement Results

According to our measurement results, SSD A and B satisfy the performance requirements for VoD storage. These SSDs show high throughput for large random reads and large sequential writes, and the random read throughput is also stable while sequential write operations happen simultaneously. Moreover, they are cheaper than the high-end SSD C, which is an important attribute for building a cost-effective VoD system.

This result is very interesting. Every SSD has its own FTL mapping algorithm, and with the mapping scheme, it hides the physical characteristics of NAND flash memory. NAND flash memory can be written only in large blocks, and thus, small and scattered updates are difficult to handle for an SSD. In general, higher class SSDs show better small random write performance by using more complicated FTL mapping algorithm and more resources. However, in VoD storage, workloads mainly consist of large sized requests, and small random write performance is not very important. Rather, complicated mapping schemes may cause unexpected delays as shown in SSD C due to background garbage collections and wear-leveling operations.

From these results, we can enumerate the flash memory SSD requirements for VoD storage.

1. It should have low cost per gigabyte to be cost-effective.

2. The random read throughput should be able to reach its maximum throughput with a sufficiently large request size.

3. The sequential write operations should not seriously affect the random read performance, and the deviation of the random read throughput should be as small as possible.

4. The garbage collection background process in the FTL layer should be controllable or predictable for the real-time requirement of video service.

5. HOW TO UTILIZE FLASH SSD

Given the measurement results, we now discuss how best to exploit flash-based SSD in a VoD storage. Even though the cost per gigabyte of flash SSD is decreasing, it is expected that flash SSD will have difficulty competing with magnetic disks in terms of capacity. Considering that only a small portion of popular files are requested frequently in VoD services, we claim that buffer cache is the best way to utilize the flash memory SSD, and the magnetic disk is still best for permanent video storage.

Interval caching [8, 9] is a state-of-the-art caching algorithm using RAM as a buffer cache to serve a larger number of video streams for a VoD server. Interval caching exploits both the characteristic of RAM and the characteristic of the VoD access pattern very well, which are symmetric read/write performance of RAM and the short average interval length between requests for popular videos. With these features, interval caching optimizes RAM capacity utilization, and it is more cost-effective than magnetic disks in serving popular videos. On the other hand, we have learned the characteristics of flash memory from the measurement of various flash memory SSDs in Section 4. The prominent feature from the measurement is the asymmetric read/write performance of flash memory SSD. In all SSDs, the write performance is far worse than the read performance. Worse yet is the unpredictable nature of the garbage collection (GC) activity that runs in the background after a number of write operations. The GC activity degrades not only the write performance but also the read performance. In addition, flash memory has a limitation in the number of erase operations, which is a lifetime problem. Suppose that a flash memory SSD is being written with W MB/s, the capacity of the SSD is C GB, and the maximum erase operations of the NAND flash memory cell is N (e.g., N is 10000 for MLC NAND flash memory and 100000 for SLC NAND flash memory). Assuming the erase operations can be distributed perfectly evenly over the cells, the life time of the SSD device is

$$T = \frac{C \times 1024 \times N}{W \times 3600} \text{ hours}$$

For example, if we write data onto a MLC flash memory SSD with 100MB/s and the capacity of the SSD is 128GB, the life time of the SSD is 3641 hours (152 days). Interval caching keeps writing data onto a device to serve the "following" streams, therefore, the flash memory SSD will quickly wear out when we use interval caching with it. Characteristics of flash memory SSD such as asymmetric performance and limited number of erase operations do not match the feature of the interval caching that is continuous write operations.

Traditional caching algorithms employed by various systems (e.g., database buffer manager, operating system memory manager) are LRU or CLOCK [10, 24] that operate at the block-level. These block-level caching algorithms, however, do not make sense for a VoD server for the following reasons. First, the block-level caching algorithm like LRU does not guarantee cache hit. It can impose unexpected load onto disks at inopportune times exactly when cache misses are being serviced from the disk.   Second, a VoD server

---

Algorithm 1 Admission control for interval caching

X ⇐ Disk bandwidth used by existing streams
Y ⇐ Bandwidth required by a new video request
Z ⇐ Maximum disk bandwidth
if X+Y > Z **then**
    {Disk bandwidth is the only criterion for admission. It's because a new stream should read data from disk initially even though the stream can be served from buffer later by interval caching.}
    REJECT the request
else
    ADMIT the request
end if

Algorithm 2 Admission control for file-level LFU

A ⇐ SSD bandwidth used by existing streams
B ⇐ Maximum SSD bandwidth
X ⇐ Disk bandwidth used by existing streams
Y ⇐ Bandwidth required by a new video request
Z ⇐ Maximum disk bandwidth
if A video request hits SSD cache **then**
    if A+Y ≤ B **then**
        ADMIT the request
    end if
end if
if X+Y ≤ Z **then**
    ADMIT the request
else
    REJECT the request
end if

---

should guarantee continuous delivery of a video stream, but it is difficult for the server to guarantee continuous delivery when only some blocks of a video are in the cache buffer. For these reasons, we claim that a file-level caching algorithm should be used with flash memory SSD because SSD has sufficient capacity and can support continuous delivery of streams by caching entire video files. Because popular video files are accessed frequently and it is not trivial to define what is *least recent* for the file-level caching, we propose to use file-level Least Frequently Used (LFU) caching algorithm with flash memory SSD.

Interval caching cannot be used when the VoD server supports fast-rewind or fast-forward functionalities because the interval caching scheme assumes that the viewing streams for the same file are progressing at the same data rate. On the other hand, file-level LFU can support those functionalities because it stores a whole file in the buffer enjoying the cost-effective large capacity of flash memory.

6. EVALUATION

In this section, we will evaluate the performance of two devices, RAM and flash memory, via simulation when they are utilized as a buffer cache in a VoD server. Interval caching is applied for RAM, and file-level LFU is used for flash memory. We define the number of buffered streams as the number of streams served from a buffer cache (e.g., RAM or flash memory). Magnetic disks are used as permanent video storage.

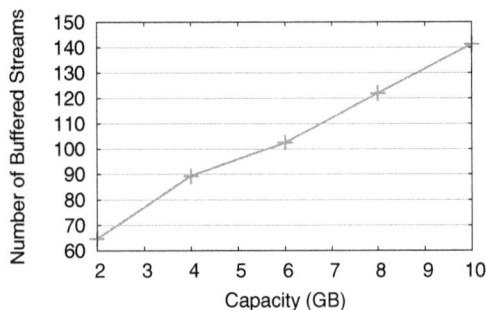

(a) Number of buffered streams increases proportional to the capacity of RAM

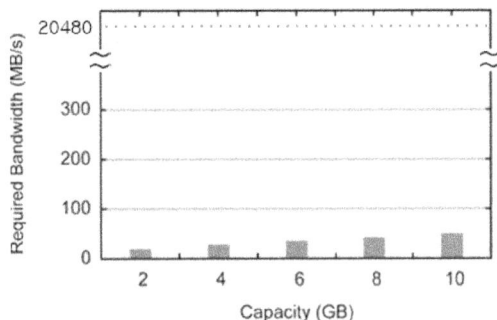

(b) Large unused bandwidth of RAM

Figure 9: Interval Caching with RAM

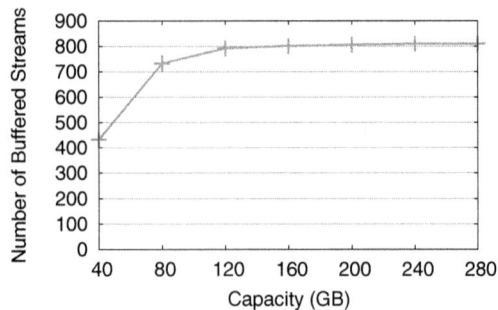

(a) Bandwidth is constant at 200MB/s. Number of buffered streams reaches a plateau due to the bandwidth limitation of flash memory.

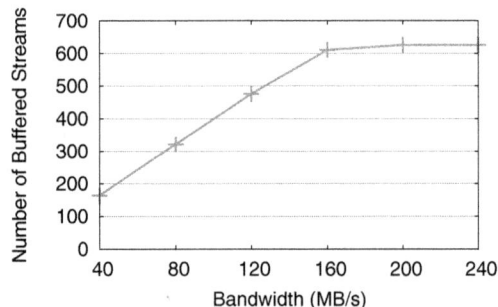

(b) Capacity is constant at 64GB. Number of buffered streams reaches a plateau due to the capacity limitation of flash memory.

Figure 10: File-level LFU with flash memory

6.1 Simulation

We assume all video files have the same and constant bitrate, 245KB/s, which is a typical bitrate for a high-quality video streamed over Internet. All video files have the same length, 60mins, if not mentioned otherwise. Therefore, the size of a video file is 862MB when the length of the video is 60mins. We assume 300 distinct videos are stored on the disks. The capacity and the bandwidth of the disks are 584GB and 100MB/s, respectively. The bandwidth comes from random read throughput measurement with 1MB I/O request size of 4 HDDs striped by RAID0 of our storage server. The HDD is SEAGATE Cheetah 15K.6 146GB and the RAID controller is LSI 1068E. The buffer for interval caching is modeled as a collection of 1MB blocks. We model the user request arrival as a Poisson process and model the video popularity as a Zipf distribution [8, 28]. We assume that the most popular N video files are already staged in the flash memory for ease of implementation.

Control parameters are divided into two sets, device parameters and workload parameters. Device parameters are the capacity and the bandwidth of each device, i.e., RAM and flash memory. Workload parameters include user request arrival rate, the video popularity distribution, and the video length. Performance metrics are average number of buffered streams, rejection probability, and hit ratio. The average number of buffered streams is defined as the number of streams that is served by the buffer cache (i.e., RAM or flash memory) averaged over total simulation duration. Hit ratio is defined as the number of reads served from the buffer cache divided by the total number of reads served by disks and the buffer cache. Rejection probability is defined as the number of rejected requests divided by

the total number of requests that arrive at a VoD server. A VoD server must employ admission control algorithms to determine whether a new stream can be serviced without affecting streams already being serviced. Algorithm 1 shows the admission control for interval caching, and Algorithm 2 is that for file-level LFU. Because both admission control algorithms reject a new request immediately when the request cannot be admitted, the comparison of the two caching polices is fair. The duration of simulation is 10 hours.

6.2 Device Parameters

In this section, we investigate how bandwidth and capacity of a device affect the performance of the caching algorithm used with the device. The performance metric is the average number of buffered streams in this experiment. The Zipf distribution parameter is 0.271, and the arrival rate of the Poisson process is 0.5, which translates to 1 request every 2 seconds on an average.

Figure 9(a) shows the number of buffered streams using interval caching with different RAM capacity, and Figure 9(b) is the required bandwidth to serve the streams at each capacity. For example, when the RAM capacity is 4GB, the interval caching can service 89 streams, and the required bandwidth for that number of streams is 21MB/s. We can see the linear relationship between the number of streams supported by the interval caching and the RAM capacity from Figure 9(a). The available bandwidth of RAM (20GB/s) is plotted as the dashed horizontal line in Figure 9(b). From the figure, We can notice that most of the available bandwidth of RAM is not utilized. This result tells us the scalability of interval caching with RAM is limited by the capacity of RAM, and the bandwidth of RAM is not a limiting factor.

Figure 10(a) shows the number of buffered streams by file-level LFU with different flash memory capacity. In this experiment, the bandwidth of the flash memory is set at 200MB/s. Different from Figure 9(a), the number of streams serviced by the buffer cache reaches a plateau beyond a capacity of 120 GB. At that point, 800 streams are served from the buffer cache and the cumulative bandwidth requirement for these streams from the flash-based SSD is 190MB/s. This means that while the flash memory could store more video files with a larger capacity, there is insufficient bandwidth to accommodate the real-time streaming requirements of the requests. On the other hand, Figure 10(b) demonstrates the number of buffered streams served by file-level LFU with different flash memory bandwidth. In this experiment, the capacity of the flash memory is set at 64GB. Similar to Figure 10(a), the number of buffered streams gets saturated beyond bandwidth of 160MB/s. When the bandwidth is large and the capacity is small, only a limited number of streams can be served by flash memory due to space limitation. In this case, the buffer cache is not able to fully utilize the available bandwidth.

From these results, we can learn the following: First, we do not need to worry about the bandwidth when we use interval caching with RAM. The only concern is the capacity, and we can scale up the number of streams with more capacity. On the other hand, we should worry about both the capacity and the bandwidth when we use file-level LFU with flash memory to scale up the number of streams. Flash memory SSD designer should design the SSD architecture to increase the capacity and the bandwidth both by maximizing the parallelism of flash memory chips to make a flash memory SSD suitable for VoD storage. Agrawal et al. have proposed a couple of possible architectures to achieve maximum bandwidth of the flash memory SSD such as parallel request queuing, individual data path to each flash memory chip, or interleaving [5].

6.3 Workload Parameters

In this section, we investigate how the workload parameters affect the performance of interval caching with RAM and file-level LFU with flash memory. We fix the device parameters as follows. The capacity of RAM is 5.23GB, the capacity of flash memory is 64GB, and the bandwidth of flash memory is 155MB/s. We assume the bandwidth of RAM is infinite because we have learned that it is not a limiting factor from Section 6.2. We use 5.23GB RAM and 64GB flash memory because they have similar cost according to the cost per gigabyte of the devices in Table 1. The bandwidth for the flash memory comes from the measurement of SSD A from Section 4.

Figure 11(a) shows that the number of buffered streams increases proportional to the arrival rate for both interval caching with RAM and file-level LFU with flash memory. With a faster arrival rate, more requests can arrive to the VoD server within the same amount of time, and it makes the inter-arrival time between streams shorter. Therefore, interval caching can serve more streams with a faster arrival rate with a given RAM capacity. On the other hand, we can see that the flash memory cannot serve more than 647 streams limited by the bandwidth (i.e., 155MB/s). Note that 155MB/s bandwidth can accommodate at most 647

video streams when the video bitrate is 245KB/s. For similar reasons, the hit ratio of interval caching increases with a faster arrival rate, and the hit ratio of file-level LFU increases but saturates beyond 0.64 in which flash memory uses its full bandwidth. Figure 11(b) demonstrates this. Figure 11(c) shows the rejection probability as a function of the arrival rate. The rejection probability is 0 initially and then rises approximately linearly. When the arrival rate gets faster, it increases not only the arrival rate of popular videos but also that of unpopular videos. The requests for the unpopular videos that are not served by a buffer cache will go to disks, and they are rejected when the disks bandwidth is fully used. Considering the arrival rates where the rejection probability become non-zero (0.08 for interval caching and 0.16 for file-level LFU), we can see that the effect of interval caching is to increase the system capacity by 23% (hit ratio 0.19), and file-level LFU increases the system capacity by 59% (hit ratio 0.37).

With file-level LFU, 200 streams are served from the flash memory when the arrival rate is 0.16, consuming only 31% (200/647) of the available bandwidth of the flash memory. Therefore, when the arrival rate gets faster than 0.16, the increasing rejection probability is due to the disk bandwidth limitation (i.e., 100MB/s) because the flash memory could have served more streams with unused bandwidth. From this we can learn that much of the flash memory bandwidth would not be utilized if the disk bandwidth is too small.

Figures 11(d), 11(e), 11(f) show the performance of both caching schemes gets better with the increasing Zipf parameter. Larger Zipf parameter means more skewed video popularity. Therefore, the larger Zipf parameter makes the inter-arrival time shorter between streams for popular video files. Then, interval caching can accommodate more streams in the given RAM capacity, and file-level LFU also can serve more streams with the given flash memory bandwidth. This is why the rejection probability of interval caching could be greatly improved with larger Zipf parameters.

Figures 11(g), 11(h), 11(i) show the performance of both schemes as a function of video length. The number of buffered streams of interval caching is independent of the length of a video. It only depends on the length of intervals between streams when the bitrate and the buffer capacity are fixed. However, the buffered streams will hold the buffer space in the interval cache for a longer duration when the video length increases. Therefore, requests that cannot be served by interval cache will go to disks and they can be rejected when the disks bandwidth is fully used. That is why the hit ratio decreases and the rejection probability increases with longer video length for interval cache (Figures 11(h) and 11(i)). For file-level LFU, when the length of video increases, less video files can be stored in the flash memory with a given capacity. Therefore, less video requests hit the buffer cache for a given arrival rate. We can see decreasing hit ratio and increasing rejection probability beyond a video length of 60 mins in Figures 11(h) and 11(i) for file-level LFU.

Note that all streams served by the flash memory can deliver video blocks without hiccups because a whole video file is cached in the flash memory buffer and the VoD server guarantees the streaming rate to be the video bitrate by the admission control mechanism.

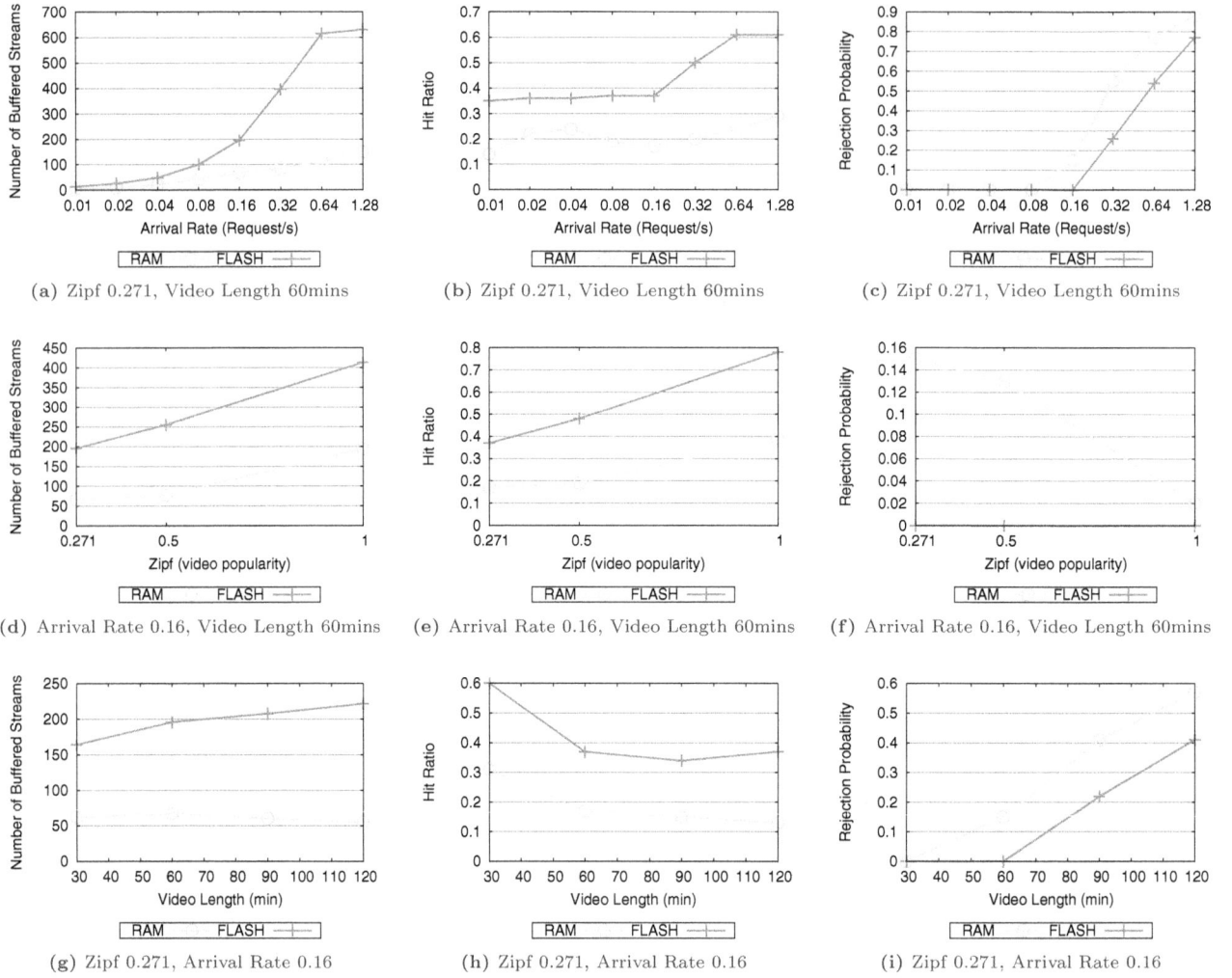

(a) Zipf 0.271, Video Length 60mins   (b) Zipf 0.271, Video Length 60mins   (c) Zipf 0.271, Video Length 60mins

(d) Arrival Rate 0.16, Video Length 60mins   (e) Arrival Rate 0.16, Video Length 60mins   (f) Arrival Rate 0.16, Video Length 60mins

(g) Zipf 0.271, Arrival Rate 0.16   (h) Zipf 0.271, Arrival Rate 0.16   (i) Zipf 0.271, Arrival Rate 0.16

Figure 11: Performance comparison of Interval Caching with RAM and File-level LFU with Flash memory

6.4 Cost-Effectiveness

In this section, we compare the cost-effectiveness of three different storage configurations. First configuration is HDD only. Only hard disk drives are used for storing video files and serving user requests. Second configuration is DRAM with HDD. DRAM is used for a buffer cache, and the interval caching is applied to it. HDDs are used for permanent storage. Third configuration is flash memory SSD with HDD. The SSDs are used for a buffer cache, and the file-level LFU is applied to it. HDDs are used for permanent storage.

The parameters used for the analysis is listed in Table 3: 60 mins video length, 1 request/sec arrival rate, and the 0% rejection probability translates to a peak requirement of 3600 concurrent video streams to be supported by the VoD server. We use a following model for calculating the maximum number of streams that can be served by HDDs or flash memory SSDs.

$$S = \frac{T}{B}, T = R \times N$$

where S is maximum number of video streams, T is total read throughput of devices, B is video bitrate, R is random read throughput of a device, and N is the number of devices.

The number of streams served by DRAM cannot be calculated simply as above, since it is determined by the peak number of concurrent streams that interval caching can serve for a given DRAM capacity for the duration of simulation, which is 10 hours. We assume the bandwidth of DRAM is infinite because the maximum number of streams that can be served by the interval caching is bounded by capacity of the DRAM in most cases.

Using the simulator mentioned in Section 6.1 and the specification of each device listed in Table 4, we calculate the combination of devices for each storage configuration that needs minimum cost and meets the workload requirements of Table 3. From the simulation results, we can see that 13 HDDs are needed for the configuration of HDD only, and its cost is 1.46 streams per dollar. For DRAM with HDD, 2 DRAM modules and 12 HDDs are needed, and its cost is 1.54 streams per dollar. For SSD with HDD, 5 SSDs and 2 HDDs are needed, and its cost is 3.55 streams per dollar. Overall, the storage configuration of SSD with HDD is the most cost-effective solution which meets the workload requirements. It can serve two times more streams than HDD only or DRAM with HDD for the same dollar investment.

Parameters	Values
Video Library	300
Zipf (Video Popularity)	0.271
Video Bitrate	245 KB/s
Video Length	60 mins
Arrival Rate	1 request/sec
Rejection Probability	0 %

Table 3: Simulation parameters used for cost-effectiveness analysis.

Device	Capacity (GB)	Random Read Throughput (MB/s)	Cost ($)
DRAM	1	∞	23
HDD15K	146	70	180
MLC SSD	64	155	120

Table 4: Specification of different devices. DDR3 SDRAM is used as a representative of DRAM. We assume the random read throughput of the SDRAM is infinite. SEAGATE Cheetah 15K.6 is used for HDD15K, and RiData NSSD-S25-64-C06MPN is used for MLC SSD. The random read throughput of HDD15K and MLC SSD is measured by *xdd* benchmark program when I/O request size is 1MB.

6.5 Evaluation Results Summary

From the results, we have learned the following:

1. We need to consider the capacity and the bandwidth when we choose a flash memory SSD for VoD storage. Moreover, flash memory SSD designer should care about the architecture of the device to increase both the capacity and the bandwidth.

2. When we use flash memory SSD with HDD, the capacity and the bandwidth of flash memory should be in balance with those of disks to fully utilize the capacity and the bandwidth benefits of flash memory with a given QoS criterion (e.g., rejection probability),

3. Flash memory SSD with HDD is the most cost-effective solution compared to DRAM with HDD or HDD only.

7. RELATED WORK

Kgil et al. [17] have studied energy efficient web server using flash memory as an extended system memory. By their simulation experiments, using NAND flash incorporated architecture has improved performance by 11% and saved power by 75% for a web server. Lee et al. [20, 19] have researched the application of flash memory SSD to a database server. The authors claim that a single enterprise class SSD can be on a par with or far better than a dozen spindles with respect to transaction throughput, cost effectiveness and energy consumption. Despite the successful research regarding the applicability and effectiveness of flash memory for a web server [17] and a database server [19], flash memory adoption to a VoD server has not been studied yet.

Singleton et al. have shown how much power can be saved

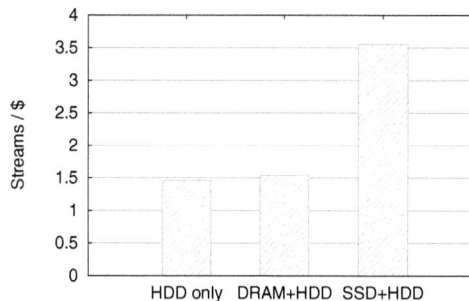

Figure 12: With a given cost, DRAM with HDD can serve slightly more streams than HDD only, but SSD with HDD can support two times more streams than DRAM with HDD.

when flash memory is used as a write buffer along with hard disks for mobile multimedia systems [27].

Narayanan et al. [23] have analyzed the efficacy of using Flash-based SSD for enterprise class storage via simulation. In addition to using Flash exclusively as the permanent storage, they also study a tiered model wherein the SSD is in between the RAM and the disks. In their study they use enterprise class SSD ($23/GB). Their conclusion is that SSD is not cost-effective for most of the workloads they studied unless the cost per gigabyte for SSD drops by a factor of 3-3000. Their results are predicated on the assumption that SSD is used as a transparent block-level device with no change to the software stack (i.e., application, file system, or storage system layers). The results we report in this paper offers an interesting counter-point to their conclusion. In particular, we show that the use of inexpensive SSDs as a buffer cache is a cost-effective alternative for structuring a VoD server as opposed to increasing either the disk bandwidth or RAM capacity to meet a given QoS constraint.

8. CONCLUSIONS

With the increasing demand for high bitrate video, there is a need to rethink the storage architecture of a VoD server. It is not cost-effective to simply rely on disk and RAM alone to scale up the VoD server to meet this increased demand. Disk as the permanent store for video, offers the much needed capacity to store large number of videos. However, a pure disk-based VoD quickly becomes bandwidth limited and cannot meet the latency requirements for real-time playback of video as the workload scales up without a significant investment on the disk infrastructure. RAM as a buffer cache offers the necessary low latency for recently accessed video and has been deployed to address the bandwidth problem in a disk-based VoD. However, RAM technology, due to the prohibitive cost, is feasible only for a modest sized buffer cache. Flash-based SSD is an attractive alternative to consider as a buffer cache instead of RAM since it has much better speed of access compared to a disk, and offers much more capacity for the same dollar investment compared to a RAM. We have explored this alternative by conducting extensive studies in this paper. The studies reveal very interesting insights. The first non-intuitive result was the revelation that low-end SSDs with simple FTLs are better suited for use as a buffer cache in a VoD server given the VoD workload characteristics. Second, we determined that SSD using file-level LFU provides comparable and at times superior performance to RAM as a buffer cache. Third, the cost of engineering a VoD server with flash-based SSD as a buffer cache and HDD as permanent storage will be significantly cheaper than DRAM with HDD or HDD only.

9. ACKNOWLEDGMENTS

We thank our shepherd Prof. Surendar Chandra and the anonymous reviewers for their valuable and constructive comments to improve the quality of this paper.

10. REFERENCES

[1] Enterprise ssds. http://www.stec-inc.com/downloads/whitepapers/Benchmarking_Enterprise_SSDs.pdf.

[2] Hulu. http://www.hulu.com.

[3] Netflix. http://www.netflix.com.

[4] Xdd. http://www.ioperformance.com.

[5] N. Agrawal, V. Prabhakaran, T. Wobber, J. D. Davis, M. Manasse, and R. Panigrahy. Design tradeoffs for ssd performance. In *ATC'08: USENIX 2008 Annual Technical Conference on Annual Technical Conference*, pages 57–70, Berkeley, CA, USA, 2008. USENIX Association.

[6] F. Chen, D. A. Koufaty, and X. Zhang. Understanding intrinsic characteristics and system implications of flash memory based solid state drives. In *SIGMETRICS '09: Proceedings of the eleventh international joint conference on Measurement and modeling of computer systems*, pages 181–192, New York, NY, USA, 2009. ACM.

[7] K. Cho, Y. Ryu, Y. Won, and K. Koh. A hybrid buffer cache management scheme for vod server. In *Proceedings of the IEEE International conference on Multimedia and Expo*, volume 1, pages 241–244, 2002.

[8] A. Dan and D. Sitaram. Buffer management policy for an on-demand video server. Ibm research report rc19347, T.J. Watson Research Center, Yorktown Heights, NY, USA, 1994.

[9] A. Dan and D. Sitaram. A generalized interval caching policy for mixed interactive and long video environments. In *Proceedings of Multimedia Computing and Networking Conference*, San Jose, CA, USA, 1996.

[10] A. Dan and D. Towsley. An approximate analysis of the lru and fifo buffer replacement schemes. In *Proceedings of the ACM SIGMETRICS*, pages 143–152, Denver, CO, USA, May 1990.

[11] J. Gemmell, H. M. Vin, D. D. Kandlur, P. V. Rangan, and L. A. Rowe. Multimedia storage servers: A tutorial. *Computer*, 28(5):40–49, 1995.

[12] G. Graefe. Integrating flash devices. *Communications of the ACM*, 52(4):97–97, April 2009.

[13] J. Gray and B. Fitzgerald. Flash disk opportunity for server-applications. *http://www.research.microsoft.com/~gray*, January 2007.

[14] C.-G. Hwang. Nanotechnology enables a new memory growth model. In *Proceedings of the IEEE 91(11)*, pages 1765–1771, November 2003.

[15] Intel Corporation. Understanding the Flash Translation Layer (FTL) Specification. White Paper, http://www.embeddedfreebsd.org/Documents/Intel-FTL.pdf, 1998.

[16] A. Kawaguchi, S. Nishioka, and H. Motoda. A flash-memory based file system. In *USENIX Winter*, pages 155–164, 1995.

[17] T. Kgil, D. Roberts, and T. Mudge. Improving nand flash based disk caches. In *Proceedings of the 35th International Symposium on Computer Architecture*, pages 327–338, June 2008.

[18] O. Kwon, H. Bahn, and K. Koh. Popularity and prefix aware interval caching for multimedia streaming servers. In *Proceedings of the 8th IEEE International conference on Computer and Information Technology*, pages 555–560, 2008.

[19] S.-W. Lee, B. Moon, and C. Park. Advances in flash memory ssd technology for enterprise database applications. In *Proceedings of the ACM SIGMOD*, pages 863–870, June 2009.

[20] S.-W. Lee, B. Moon, C. Park, J.-M. Kim, and S.-W. Kim. A case for flash memory ssd in enterprise database applications. In *Proceedings of the ACM SIGMOD*, pages 1075–1086, June 2008.

[21] A. Leventhal. Flash storage memory. *Communications of the ACM*, 51(7):47–51, July 2008.

[22] M-Systems. Two Technologies Compared: NOR vs. NAND. White Paper, http://www.dataio.com/pdf/NAND/MSystems/MSystems_NOR_vs_NAND.pdf, 2003.

[23] D. Narayanan, E. Thereska, A. Donnelly, S. Elnikety, and A. Rowstron. Migrating server storage to ssds: Analysis of tradeoffs. In *Proceedings of the ACM EuroSys*, Nuremberg, Germany, April 2009.

[24] V. F. Nicola, A. Dan, and D. M. Dias. Analysis of the generalized clock buffer replacement scheme for database transaction processing. In *Proceedings of the ACM SIGMETRICS*, pages 35–46, 1992.

[25] C. Park, W. Cheon, J. Kang, K. Roh, W. Cho, and J.-S. Kim. A reconfigurable ftl (flash translation layer) architecture for nand flash-based applications. *Trans. on Embedded Computing Sys.*, 7(4):1–23, 2008.

[26] A. R. Rahiman and P. Sumari. Solid state disk: A new storage device for video storage server. In *Proceedings of the International Symposium on Information Technology*, pages 1–8, August 2008.

[27] L. Singleton, R. Nathuji, and K. Schwan. Flash on disk for low-power multimedia computing. In *Proceedings of the ACM Multimedia Computing and Networking Conference*, January 2007.

[28] H. Yu, D. Zheng, B. Y. Zhao, and W. Zheng. Understanding user behavior in large-scale video-on-demand systems. In *Proceedings of the ACM EuroSys*, April 2006.

Watching User Generated Videos with Prefetching

Samamon Khemmarat[†], Renjie Zhou[‡], Lixin Gao[†], Michael Zink[†]

[†] Department of Electrical and Computer Engineering
University of Massachusetts, Amherst, USA
{khemmarat,lgao,zink} @ecs.umass.edu

[‡] College of Computer Science and Technology
Harbin Engineering University, Harbin, China
renjie_zhou@hrbeu.edu.cn

ABSTRACT

Even though user generated video sharing sites are tremendously popular, the experience of the user watching videos is often unsatisfactory. Delays due to buffering before and during a video playback at a client are quite common. In this paper, we present a prefetching approach for user-generated video sharing sites like YouTube. We motivate the need for prefetching by showing that video playbacks of videos on YouTube is often unsatisfactory and introduce a series of prefetching schemes: the conventional caching scheme, the search result-based prefetching scheme, and the recommendation-aware prefetching scheme. We evaluate and compare the proposed schemes using user browsing pattern data collected from network measurement. We find that the recommendation-aware prefetching approach can achieve an overall hit ratio up to 81%, while the hit ratio achieved by the caching scheme can only reach 40%. Thus, the recommendation-aware prefetching approach demonstrates a strong potential for improving the playback quality at the client. We also explore the trade-offs and feasibility of implementing recommendation-aware prefetching.

Categories and Subject Descriptors

C.4 [**Performance of systems**]: Design studies

General Terms

Design, Experimentation, Performance

1. INTRODUCTION

The advent of user-generated video sharing sites such as YouTube, Dailymotion, Metacafe, Tudou, and Daum has provided tremendous opportunities for Internet users to share their personal experiences as well as to conduct business. The astronomical amount of video content uploaded on video sharing sites has made these sites information sources to which Internet users often turn to be informed, entertained, and even educated. For example, YouTube has hundreds of

millions of viewers and delivers billions of videos each month. Unlike the traditional video-on-demand (VoD) systems that typically deliver professionally produced content, video sharing sites typically contain short video clips produced for a particular purpose [5]. The short duration of video clips combined with the huge collection of videos makes it possible for users to browse around for content of interest.

Despite the tremendous popularity of user generated video sharing sites, user experience with watching videos from these sites can vary significantly [18]. As we show in this paper, it is common that a user experiences a pause when watching a video online. These interruptions during video playback can be quite annoying and can potentially discourage users from watching more videos or simply turn users off at the very beginning of a video browsing session. Even a small number of pauses can have a very negative impact since the majority of videos on video sharing sites are usually relatively short (on the order of a few minutes) [22, 11]. Clearly, an increase in network bandwidth and scalable solutions on video sharing sites can solve some of these problems. However, the desire for and the increasing availability of high quality videos (such as high quality or high definition videos) might further exacerbate the experience of browsing video sharing sites.

In this paper, we propose to prefetch video content in order to reduce or eliminate the potential of pauses during video playback and decrease the service delay. We introduce a series of prefetching schemes: conventional caching scheme, search result-based prefetching scheme, and recommendation aware prefetching scheme. Our proposed prefetching scheme conserves bandwidth by prefetching only a *prefix* of a video, since a video clip can playback smoothly if a sufficiently large prefix of the video is prefetched [19]. Furthermore, the prefetching scheme can take advantage of many "idle" periods of a video browsing session by prefetching when the current playback does not saturate the available bandwidth or when users read comments between watching videos.

We evaluate our proposed prefetching schemes with user browsing pattern data collected from a university network. We focus on user browsing patterns on YouTube since YouTube is the most popular video sharing web site in North America. Our measurement results show that the recommendation-aware prefetching approach can achieve an overall hit ratio of up to 81%, while the hit ratio achieved by the caching scheme and search result-based prefetching scheme can reach only 40% and 38%, respectively. Therefore, our study demonstrates a strong potential for improving the playback quality at the client using recommendation-aware prefetching. Although building an effective recommendation system itself is a challenge [2], it can potentially provide sufficient clues for predicting what users are most likely to watch next. We also explore the trade-offs and feasibility of implementing the recommendation-aware prefetching.

Although our evaluation is presented in the context of a proxy cache architecture, the proposed prefetching scheme can potentially be applied to a peer-to-peer architecture or to the servers in content delivery networks (CDNs). Despite the fact that prefetching has been proposed in the context of web and multimedia delivery, demonstrating its effectiveness has been challenging without user browsing traces. To the best of our knowledge, our work is the first to systematically measure and compare the effectiveness of various prefetching schemes based on *actual user browsing activities* and demonstrate the advantage of exploiting the recommendation system for video delivery.

The rest of the paper is organized as follows. In Section 2, we investigate the user experience on YouTube regarding the pauses users experienced in the video playout. Section 3 describes the prefetching schemes and the algorithms to select videos to prefetch. In Section 4, we describe our datasets and measurement of the usage of video referrers. The evaluation of the proposed prefetching schemes is presented in Section 5, and in Section 6, we discuss the trade-offs and feasibility of prefetching. Related work is presented in Section 7. Finally, Section 8 concludes the paper.

2. INVESTIGATING USER EXPERIENCES WITH WATCHING YOUTUBE VIDEOS

Previous work has shown that service delay on YouTube is longer than on other video sharing websites [18]. To further demonstrate the need for prefetching, we perform an experiment to evaluate user experience in watching YouTube videos. In particular, we measure how likely it is that a user experiences pauses during video playback and how long the pauses are. We describe our data collection methodology and how we emulate the playback. Then, we present our results on estimating the possibility and duration of pauses experienced by a viewer.

2.1 Data Collection

We derived the information of pause frequency automatically by analyzing *video download traces*. A video download trace is a trace of incoming and outgoing network traffic captured while a user is watching a video on YouTube. In our case, we asked volunteers to use Wireshark network protocol analyzer [3] on their computers to capture the traffic. We automated the process of detecting pauses in video playbacks to make the process easy for the volunteers and as precise as possible. Instead of asking the volunteers to watch videos and record the number of pauses, the volunteers only had to start the capturing before clicking on the link to a video and stop the capturing after the video playback ends. We then used the trace data from Wireshark to estimate whether pauses in a video playback occurred.

12 volunteers were asked to capture video download traces from various environments representing different locations and network access technologies as shown in Table 1. We believe that the locations chosen for the experiment present a

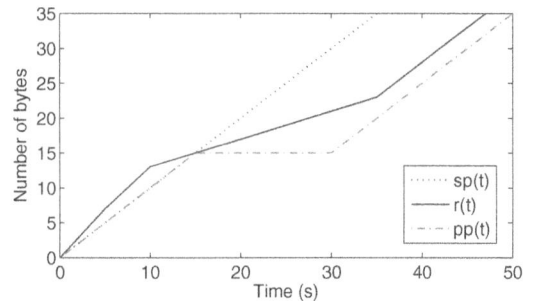

Figure 1: Example plot of $r(t)$, $sp(t)$ and $pp(t)$.

good variety and represent typical places where users would watch YouTube videos.

Environment	Location	Network Technology
E1	University 1	Campus WLAN
E2	Company 1	DSL
E3	Home 1	DSL
E4	Apartment 1	Cable Internet
E5	Dormitory 1	Campus LAN
E6	Dormitory 2	Campus LAN
E7	Apartment 2	Cable Internet
E8	Town Library	Wireless Network
E9	Coffee shop	Wireless Network
E10	University 2	Campus WLAN
E11	Home 2	DSL
E12	Hotel	Wireless Network

Table 1: Environment information.

We asked the volunteers to watch 10 videos from our selection and obtained 10 video download traces from each of them. We selected videos that have different levels of quality (standard quality (SD), high quality (HQ), and high definition quality (HD)). The average bit rate for these videos ranges from 162 to 2150 kbps.

2.2 Modeling a Video Player

The main requirement for a smooth video playback is that each byte of the video arrives at the client before the time it is required to be played. More formally, let $sp(d)$ be the number of bytes needed to play the first d seconds of a video, $r(t)$ be the number of all bytes received at the client at time t, D be the video length in seconds, and t_s be the time the video starts playing. To get a smooth playback, the following condition needs to be satisfied: $r(t) >= sp(t - t_s)$ where $t_s <= t <= t_s + D$.

In the example shown in Figure 1, the video starts playing at $t = 0$. During the first 15 seconds, $r(t) > sp(t)$, thus the video can be played smoothly. However, just after $t = 15$ seconds, the number of bytes received is less than the number of bytes required. At that point the video playback cannot be continued.

To deal with the buffer depletion, video players, including YouTube's video player, pauses to perform buffering whenever there is insufficient data at the client to render the next frame. The video playback is resumed when the player's buffer fills up to a certain level. Based on the data rate at which the video is received at the client, this may lead to one or more pauses during the playback of the video.

To model the video player, we define the function $pp(t)$ as the number of bytes required by a player at time t. The value of $pp(t)$ depends on the length of the video that has

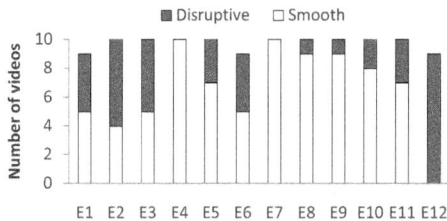

Figure 2: Video playback quality.

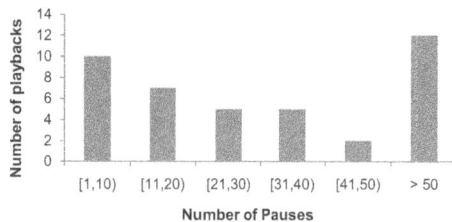

Figure 3: Histogram of number of pauses in disruptive playbacks.

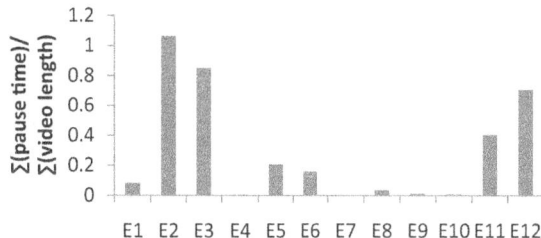

Figure 4: Fraction of time spent in waiting for the videos.

been played at time t. If the player has played up to d seconds of the video at time t, then we have $pp(t) = sp(d)$. In Figure 1, after $t = 15$ seconds, which is the point when the buffer depletion starts, $pp(t)$ remains steady for some period. This period corresponds to a pause in the playback. $pp(t)$ continues to increase after $t = 30$ seconds, corresponding with the player resuming the playback after it has filled up enough data in its buffer.

Based on the previous functions, the video player works as follows. At any time t, the player's state is either 'play' or 'pause'. Let B be the minimum amount of data required to be in the buffer for the playback to resume from pausing. The player changes its state in these two cases:

- 'play' to 'pause': when there is insufficient data to play the video or $pp(t) > r(t)$

- 'pause' to 'play': when the data in the buffer reaches the resume threshold value or $r(t) - pp(t) >= B$, or when the player has received the full video file

2.3 Emulating Video Playback from Video Download Trace

The function $sp(d)$ and $r(t)$ are essential in emulating the video player. In this section, we describe how we derive these two functions from a video download trace.

To derive $r(t)$, we examine the receive time and the TCP sequence number of the packets that contain the video file to get the number of contiguous bytes of the video file we have at each point in time.

To derive $sp(t)$, we analyze the video file which we reassembled from the payload of the packets. Video encoding divides video data into segments. Each segment has its own play timestamp which specifies the time that the segment should be rendered relative to the first segment. From this analysis, we can determine how many bytes are required to render each frame of the video without any delay to allow for an uninterrupted playback.

In addition to the two functions, we need to determine the value of B, the amount of data required to resume from pausing. Since YouTube does not disclose its video player's specification, we let B equal to the amount of data needed to play 2 seconds of a video based on our observation. This means the required buffer size varies for different videos. If we use larger B, the number of pauses in our results will be fewer, but each pause period will also be longer. Thus, although the value of B used in our experiment are not exactly the same as YouTube's video player, we believe our results can reflect the user experience on YouTube well.

2.4 User Experience on YouTube

Using the described model, we emulate video playback from video download traces. First, we determine whether the video was played at the client with a pause or not. Figure 2 shows the number of smooth playbacks and disruptive playbacks for each dataset. Some datasets contain 9 playbacks due to packet capture error. The results show that 10 out of 12 environments contain playbacks with pauses. In addition, 41 of 117 playbacks (35%) contain pauses.

Next, we estimate the number of pauses in the interrupted playbacks. Figure 3 shows the estimated number of pauses in all 41 disruptive playbacks. We find that 31 playbacks, which are 75.6% of disruptive playbacks, contain more than 10 pauses. (Even when we increase B to 5 seconds of videos, 57% of disruptive playbacks contain more than 10 pauses.) Considering that the duration of the videos in our datasets ranges between 3 to 10 minutes, pausing as much as 10 times or more would be extremely unpleasant to users.

Finally, we compute the time that a user had to spend waiting for the videos. We note that since the users's download rate in our datasets is relatively stable, the accumulated pause period is not significantly affected by the size of B. In Figure 4, we show the ratio between accumulated pause time and accumulated video length from all the playbacks in each environment. The user experience varies across different locations. In some locations, like E2, E3, E11 and E12, the time spent waiting for the videos (when the videos were paused), is longer than 40% of the total duration of the videos. In E2, which is the worst sceanario, the time spent waiting is even longer than the total video length.

Our results lead to our conclusion that YouTube users indeed experience disruptive playbacks on YouTube, especially when they watch videos with higher quality. Although a user can choose to wait for a video to buffer before she starts watching, it is undesirable. We expect that this problem will become even more common as high definition videos become increasingly popular on YouTube. The results of this experiment motivated us to devise a video prefetching approach that has the potential to reduce or even eliminate pauses during video playback. The approach is described in the next section.

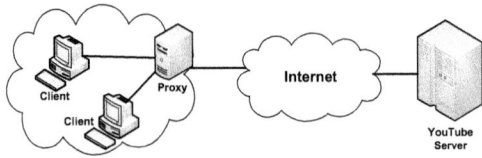

Figure 5: The architecture of prefetching proxy system.

3. VIDEO PREFETCHING SCHEME

The main principle of prefetching is to retrieve content from the source before it is requested by a user and store it in a location that can be accessed by a user conveniently and fast. This is fundamentally different from caching where content is only stored locally if it has already been requested by a client. Prefetching can be applied to various architectures and in different ways. In this section, we describe the settings of the proposed prefetching scheme, followed by the algorithms used to select videos to prefetch.

3.1 Prefetching Agent

Consider a typical network as shown in Figure 5, there are two apparent places where we can implement the prefetch functionality, at the client and the proxy. We call the module that performs prefetching the *prefetching agent* (PA). In this paper, we consider two settings of the prefetching scheme: in the first one, the PA is located at the client (PF-Client), and in the second one, the PA is located at a proxy server (PF-Proxy).

A PA is a module responsible for prefetching. It has a storage to store prefetched prefixes of videos. It determines the videos to be prefetched, retrieves their prefixes from YouTube, and stores them. In addition, the PA can perform caching, i.e., it stores either a whole or a prefix of videos that are requested by clients. Caching YouTube videos at the network edge has been evaluated by Zink et al. and shown to be useful in reducing network traffic and providing faster video access [22].

Every YouTube request from a client is directed to the PA. If the request is a video request, the PA checks if the prefix of the video exists in its storage. If so, it serves the client with the prefix of the video, and at the same time retrieves the remaining part of the video from YouTube and sends it to the client. Note that the video prefix and the remaining part are sent to the client simultaneously. This further helps to decrease the chance of buffer depletion at the client. If the prefix is not in its storage, the PA retrieves the whole video from YouTube and sends it to the client. If the PA also performs caching, it stores the retrieved videos in its storage. Based on the requests received, the PA selects the videos to be prefetched (which have not been requested by any users yet), retrieves their prefixes from YouTube, and stores them in its local storage.

The difference between PF-Client and PF-Proxy is the location of the PA. In PF-Client, every client is connected to its own PA, thus each PA receives requests from only one client. In PF-Proxy, the PA resides in a proxy which is situated between clients and YouTube servers, close to the clients as shown in Figure 5. For example, the proxy may be located at the gateway of a campus network or at the local aggregation point of an ISP network. In this setting, the PA receives requests from all clients in the local network.

The next section describes how the PA selects the videos to prefetch based on the requests it receives.

3.2 Video Selection for Prefetching

In order to perform prefetching, the PA needs to determine the set of videos to be prefetched. Given YouTube requests from clients, the PA needs to predict a set of videos that are likely to be requested in the future. Here, we describe two algorithms that the PA can use to select videos to prefetch.

The first algorithm is based on users' search results. YouTube provides a search box in which a user can enter a query phrase to search for videos of interest. After the search query submission, a list of videos that match the query phrase, or a *Search Result* list is shown in a *search result page*.

To implement this algorithm, the PA detects search result pages sent from YouTube which are the responses to clients' search queries. Then, it extracts the list of videos to determine which videos to prefetch. A search result page can contain up to 20 videos in one page. Prefetching all of those videos may or may not be practical depending on the available bandwidth and storage space at the PA. Therefore, the PA may prefetch only the top N videos of the Search Result list based on their positions on the list. We call this algorithm SR-N.

The second algorithm is based on the YouTube recommendation system. Each YouTube video has its own web page, which we call a *video page*. Each video page contains a *Related Video* list which is a list of videos that have similar content recommended by the YouTube recommendation system. As shown in Section 4.2, besides Search Result lists, a large number of video views originates from Relate Video lists. Thus, videos in Related video lists are also good candidates for prefetching.

A Related Video list contains up to 25 videos. Similar to SR-N, we may prefetch only the top N videos on the Related Video list according to the order they are shown in the list. We call this algorithm RV-N. The PA implements the RV-N algorithm by detecting all the videos pages from the responses it receives from YouTube and parsing the video pages to obtain the Related Video lists.

The advantage of both algorithms, SR-N and RV-N, is that they are simple and not computationally expensive. The PA can obtain the lists of videos to prefetch without requesting or storing any additional data. In the next section, we present the datasets we used to evaluate the two settings of prefetching scheme and video selection algorithms we have described.

4. DATA COLLECTION

In this section, we describe the data collection process and datasets we use to evaluate the prefetching schemes.

4.1 Datasets

Our data collection consists of two phases. In the first phase, we monitored and recorded data traffic between a campus network and YouTube servers. Due to the campus privacy policy, we only recorded fix-length headers of the data packets, so we cannot obtain the Related Video lists and Search Result lists which are essential for our experiments from the traces. In the second phase, we retrieved the two lists from YouTube using YouTube Data API [4].

The details of the two phrases are described in the following subsections.

4.1.1 Network Traces

We obtained three network traces from monitoring You-Tube traffic entering and leaving a campus network. The monitoring device is a PC with a Data Acquisition and Generation (DAG) card [1], which can capture Ethernet frames. The device is located at a campus network gateway, which allows it to see all traffic to and from the campus network. It was configured to capture a fixed length header of all HTTP packets going to and coming from YouTube domain.

The monitoring periods are 1 day, 3 days, and 7 days (T1, T2 and T3 respectively). The general statistics of the traces are shown in Table 2. Since T2 was obtained during the winter break, it has fewer video requests than T1 although the capture period is longer. T3 has the most video requests because it was taken when class was in session and it has the longest capture period.

Trace File	T1	T2	T3
Duration	1 day	3 days	7 days
Start Date	20-Oct-09	8-Jan-10	28-Jan-10
# Request	71,282	7,562	257,098
# Unique Clients	7,914	607	10,511
# Unique Videos	48,978	5,887	154,363

Table 2: Statistics from network traces collected at the campus network gateway.

4.1.2 Search Result Lists and Related Video Lists

In addition to the network traces, to validate the prefetching approach, we need the Search Result lists for every video search query in the traces and the Related Video lists for every requested video. These lists are used by the prefetching agent to determine the set of videos to be prefetched. We retrieved the Search Result lists and the Related Video lists via YouTube Data API.

To retrieve the Search Result lists, we started from identifying all the video search queries in the traces using URI pattern matching. A URI of a video search query on YouTube starts with `results?search_query=`, followed by the query phrase and other parameters. After identifying the search queries in the network traces, we retrieved the Search Result list for each query by sending the same search query to YouTube via YouTube Data API. We retrieved at most 25 videos for each Search result list.

Similarly, to retrieve the Related Video lists, we first extracted video page requests from the traces. A video page request's URI starts with `watch?v=`, followed by a video's ID, which is a 11-character string. With the set of video requests, we then proceeded to fetch the Related Video list for each video through YouTube Data API. We retrieved at most 25 videos for each Related Video lists.

4.2 Usage of Search Result Lists and Related Video Lists

In this section, we present our measurement results on the usage of different view referrers. A referrer of a video is the source that refers a user to the video, for example, a Related Video list of another video, YouTube featured video page, and links on other web sites. The result from this study shows that the two most frequently used referrers are Search

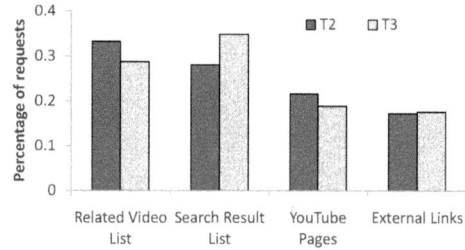

Figure 6: Fraction of requests from each referrer type.

Result lists and Related Video lists, which prompted us to use the two lists in the proposed video selection algorithms.

We perform the study by analyzing the referrer of each video request in our traces. The HTTP referrer fields of the video requests are not contained in our traces due to the limited length of the captured packets. Hence, we employ another method to identify the referrers. The requests coming from certain referrers contain the referrer types explicitly in their URIs. This includes requests generated from users clicking on Related Video lists, which contain the tag `feature=related` in their URIs. Therefore, we can extract the referrers of these video requests from their URIs. However, there are also video requests that contain no referrers information in their URIs, including the requests from Search Results lists and most links from external websites. We use an additional heuristic to infer the referrers of these video requests by analyzing YouTube user sessions. A user's YouTube session is a series of requests sent to YouTube by a user in one visit [14]. We consider that a session ends when a user is idle for 40 minutes, which is the threshold timeout used in [12]. A referrer of a video request without tags is inferred from the previous pages visited in the same session before the request is made. Referrers are then grouped into 4 types: Related Video lists, Search Results lists, other YouTube pages, and external links. The external links category are referrers that are outside YouTube such as video links on blogs and social network sites.

We perform the analysis on trace T2 and T3 because they were captured with longer packet length, so we have complete tags from the URIs. In Figure 6, we show the requests from each referrer type as a percentage of all requests. The results show that the Search Result lists and Related Video lists are major view referrers. There are 28% and 35% of the video requests with the Search Result lists as their referrers (in T2 and T3, respectively), and there are 33% and 29% of the requests with the Related Video lists as their referrers.

From the result, we decided to base the video selection algorithms on the two lists, Search Result list and Related Video list. We note here that although this result might leave the impression that the prefetching approach using the Search Result lists or Related Video lists can only achieve a hit ratio around the same level as the usage rate of the lists, as we show in Section 5, this is not the case since our evaluation of the prefetching approach based on the Related Video lists results in hit ratios up to 81%.

5. EVALUATION

In this section, we present our evaluation of the video prefetching approaches. We compare the performance of the

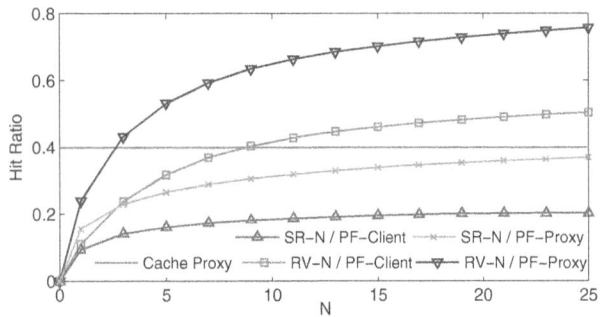

Figure 7: Hit ratios of SR-N and RV-N for T3.

two video selection algorithms and the two settings proposed in Section 3.

5.1 Methodology and Evaluation Metrics

Our evaluation for the prefetching schemes is based on real user usage patterns. This is achieved by performing a trace-driven simulation using the traces captured from a campus network as presented in Section 4.1.1. In the simulation, video requests are issued based on the network traces, which means the videos that are requested and the order of the requests are exactly the same as in the traces. The simulated PA determines the videos to be prefetched based on the requests received and keeps track of the set of video prefixes that are in its storage. Thus, it can determine whether a requested video has been prefetched or not. With this method, we can determine the proportion of video requests from the traces that could have been served faster from the PA if the prefetching system was implemented at the time the traces were captured.

To study the characteristics and compare the performance of different prefetching schemes, we first perform experiments in the cases when the PA always has sufficient storage space, from Section 5.2 to 5.4. Then, in Section 5.6, we explore the case when there is limited storage space. For simplicity, the storage space size is defined by the number of slots, where each slot can hold a prefix of a video. Based on the measurement result in [6], the average video size on YouTube is 8.4 MB. Suppose the prefix size is 30% of a video, then each slot corresponds to about 2.5 MB.

In this study, two metrics are used to evaluate the prefetching schemes. The first metric is the hit ratio, defined as a fraction of the number of requests for a video that can be served from the prefetching storage (called hit requests): $hit\_ratio = hit\_requests/all\_requests$. A higher hit ratio means we can serve more requests from the prefetching agent's storage, resulting in better user experience. The second metric is the precision, which reflects the accuracy of the video selection algorithm. The precision is defined as a number of prefetched videos that are actually requested by users (called the hit videos) over the total number of prefetched videos: $precision = hit\_videos/all\_prefetched\_videos$.

5.2 Performance of Prefetching Using Search Result Lists (SR-N)

We first present the performance of the prefetching scheme which prefetches based on the top N videos on Search Result lists (SR-N). Figure 7 shows the hit ratio of the prefetching scheme using the SR-N algorithm when there is always sufficient space at the PA. We also show the hit ratio of the cache

proxy, which caches all videos that users have requests, as a baseline. From the figure, the maximum hit ratio at $N = 25$ is equal to 20.62% in PF-Client and 36.86% in PF-Proxy. It may be unexpected that the maximum hit ratio achieved in the PF-Client setting is lower than the inferred percentage of video requests from users clicking Search Result lists. This may be attributed to two reasons. The first reason is that a user may click on a video contained in a playlist in a search result, which we cannot retrieved via the API. The second reason is that a user may click on a search result in the position lower than 25. The result here shows that the hit ratio we obtain using the Search Result lists cannot surpass hit ratio of the caching scheme which is 39.96% despite the fact that Search Result lists are one of the the major sources of video views.

5.3 Performance of Prefetching Using Related Video Lists (RV-N)

We now proceed to evaluate the performance of the prefetching scheme that relies on the YouTube recommendation system, or the Related Video lists (RV-N). The hit ratio of the prefetching scheme using the RV-N algorithm is shown in Figure 7. At $N = 25$, the RV-N algorithm results in the maximum hit ratio of 50.38% and 75.68% in the PF-Client and the PF-Proxy setting, respectively. These maximum hit ratios are higher than the hit ratio achieved by the cache proxy. In fact, the PF-Proxy setting can outperform the cache proxy with the value of N as low as 3. As for the PF-Client setting, we need to prefetch at least 9 videos to surpass the cache proxy. From the results, we also observe that as N increases, the increasing rate of the hit ratio is smaller. This suggests that the top videos in the Related Video lists are better predictions of users' future views.

So far, we observe that PF-Proxy yields much higher hit ratio than PF-Client. This suggests that users in the same local network share similar interests, and thus videos from a Related Video list or a Search Result list of a user are also watched by other users in the same local network. PF-Proxy benefits from this fact and achieves about 50% to 100% improvement in the hit ratio compared to PF-Client.

Up to this point, the RV-N algorithm, which is based on the Related Video lists, in combination with the PF-Proxy setting gives us the best hit ratio of up to 75.68%. Consequently, we will focus on the particular prefetching scheme - the combination of the RV-N algorithm and the PF-Proxy setting.

5.4 Analyzing the High Hit Ratios

One interesting observation from previous results is that the maximum hit ratio achieved with the RV-N algorithm is much higher than how often users click on Related Video lists, which is around 30% as analyzed in Section 4.2. This means that the hit requests are not only the requests that come from users clicking on Related Video lists, but also the requests from other referrers. To gain further insight, we conduct an analysis to see how many requests from other referrers are hit requests in the RV-N prefetching scheme.

In Section 4.2, we have identified the referrer of each video request in the traces. Therefore, we can determine how many requests from each referrer are hit when we prefetch using Related Video lists. Figures 8 and 9 show the referrers of the hit requests for the prefetching schemes with the PF-Client setting and the PF-Proxy setting. In PF-Client, only

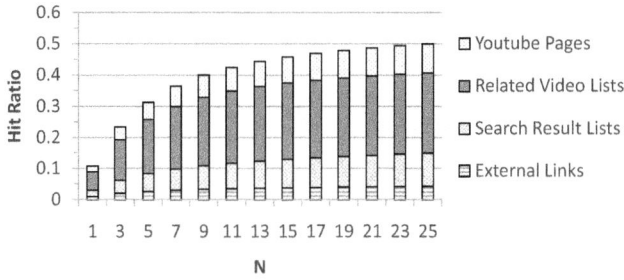

Figure 8: Referrers of hit requests (PF-Client).

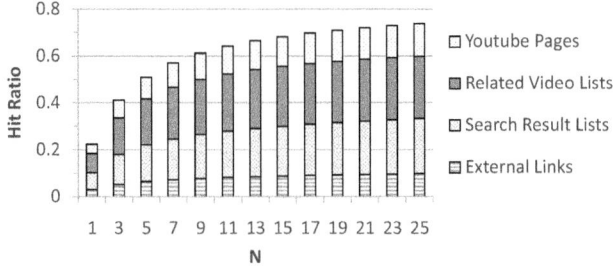

Figure 9: Referrers of hit requests (PF-Proxy).

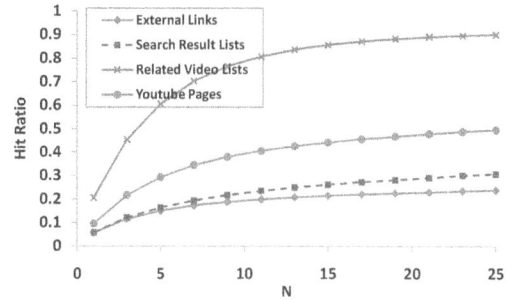

Figure 10: Hit ratios of each request category (PF-Client).

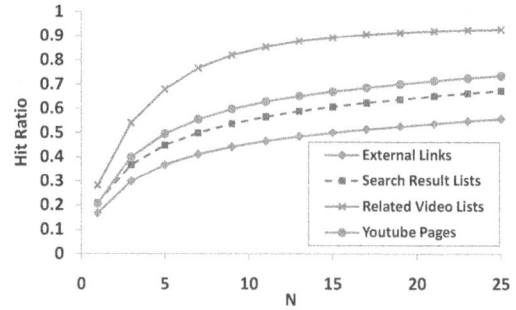

Figure 11: Hit ratios for each request category (PF-Proxy).

about 55% of the hit requests are from the users clicking on Related Video lists. The remaining 45% are the requests caused by users clicking on the Search Result lists and other referrers. This means that, for many videos in the Related video lists, a user may not click on them from the lists, but she eventually watches them through other referrers.

For PF-Proxy, the fraction of the hit requests that are from users clicking on the Related Video lists becomes even smaller, while the requests that come from users clicking the Search Result lists become a significant portion of the hit requests. This means that the additional hit requests in the PF-Proxy setting, which are those requests of a client that can be served by a video prefetched based on another client's request, are mostly the requests that come from a user clicking on Search Result lists.

From both figures, we learn that there is overlap between the videos shown in the Related Video lists, which we prefetch, and video requests that users request through other referrers. This overlap contributes to the high hit ratios when we use the RV-N algorithm. Next, we investigate how large this overlap is for the video requests from each referrer type.

Figure 10 and 11 shows the hit ratios computed separately for the requests from each referrer type. In PF-Client, we can see that the requests from Search Result lists, external links, and YouTube pages, have the hit ratio of up to to 20-50%. Note that the hit ratio for the requests from the Related Video lists is 90%, less than 100% due to the small changes in the Related Video lists when we retrieved them. In PF-Proxy, the hit ratios for these referrers are significantly improved, which makes the aggregated hit ratio in PF-Proxy much higher than PF-Client. Especially, the improvement of the hit ratio of requests from the Search Result lists, from up to 30% in PF-Client to up to 65% in PF-Proxy, is the major contributor because a large number of requests are from Search Result lists.

In sum, the property of the videos in the Related Video list that they largely overlap with the video requests generated from a user clicking on the Search Result lists, which are the large fraction of all requests, and also from other refer-

rers makes them very effective choices for prefetching. The videos in the Search Result lists, on the other hand, do not have this property, and thus the SR-N algorithm does not give as high hit ratio as the RV-N algorithm although the frequency that users use the Related Video list and Search Result list are about the same.

5.5 Combining Caching and Prefetching

Because of the difference in their underlying principals, the prefetching scheme and caching scheme conceptually captures different sets of videos, although there may be some overlapping. Thus, combining these two schemes can potentially result in a higher hit ratio. Figure 12 shows the hit ratio improvement resulting from the combination of caching and prefetching called the cache-and-prefetch mode. The combination of the two schemes increases the hit ratio by 5-20% compared to the prefetch-only mode. The maximum hit ratios we obtain at $N = 25$ increase from 63.47%, 59.85% and 75.68% to 72.30%, 66.83% and 80.88% for trace T1, T2 and T3, respectively. Note that the hit ratio of the cache-and-prefetch mode is not the sum of the cache-only and prefetch-only mode. This is because there is an overlap between the set of cached videos and the set of prefetched videos. As shown in Figure 12, the improvement of the hit ratio induced by the cache-and-prefetch mode becomes smaller as N increases. This means that as we prefetch more videos from the Related Video lists, the overlap between the set of prefetched videos and the set of videos that users have watched becomes larger. Thus, with regards to the hit ratio, the addition of caching functionality is more helpful when we prefetches a small number of videos. In Section 6.4.2, we show another advantage of combining caching and prefetching when we discuss the traffic overhead introduced by the prefetching scheme.

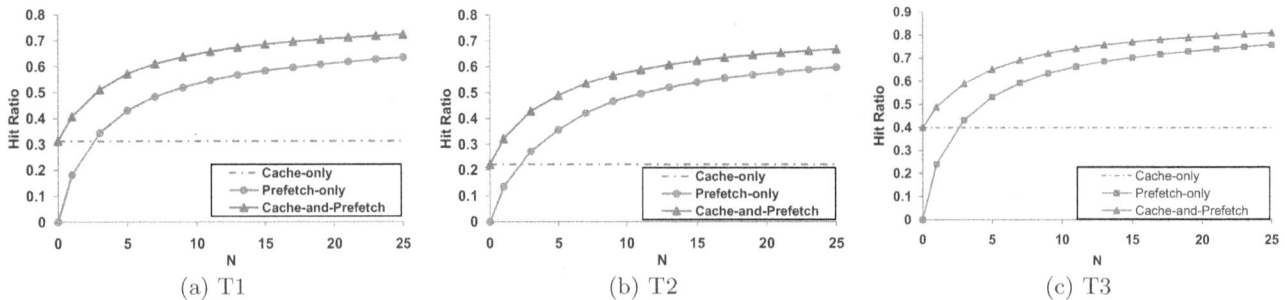

| (a) T1 | (b) T2 | (c) T3 |

Figure 12: Hit ratio improvement from combining caching and prefetching.

5.6 Storage Requirement

So far, the prefetching scheme using the RV-N algorithm and the PF-Proxy setting has yielded the best hit ratio of up to 80% in cache-and-prefetch mode. The presented results are based on the assumption that there is always sufficient storage space to store the prefetched and cached videos. This gives us the highest hit ratio that can be reached. In Figure 13, we show the storage space that is actually required for the case of sufficient storage space. The storage size in the figure is converted from the number of slots to gigabytes where each slot is equal to 2.5 MB, as explained in Section 5.1. The storage space required in cache-only mode is also shown as a baseline.

As shown in Figure 13, when N is larger, which means more videos are prefetched, the required space increases. The required spaces for the three traces are different because of the difference in the number of requests in the traces. The more requests there are, the more space we need. Although prefetch-only mode requires much more space than cache-only mode, the actual space it needs is merely 4.69 TB where it can reach 75.68% hit ratio (in T3). For cache-and-prefetch mode, the storage requirement are very close to prefetch-only mode, while it improves the hit ratio on the order of 5-20%. The maximum space needed is 4.76 TB, which results in a 80.88% hit ratio.

Although the storage requirement given here are specific to our traces with different duration and request volumes, it demonstrates that the storage required to achieve the highest hit ratio with prefetching for a campus-size network is within a feasible range. Later, in Section 6.1, we consider the cases when storage space is insufficient and study how the storage size impacts the performance of the prefetching scheme.

6. DISCUSSION

In this section, we further explore the trade-offs when using the prefetching scheme with the RV-N algorithm and the PF-Proxy setting. We also study certain aspects of the feasibility of prefetching.

6.1 Impact of Storage Space

In reality, the always-sufficient space is not realistic since there are always new video requests and more prefixes to store as the PA continues running. The storage space is fixed, while the storage requirement continues to increase. To investigate the impact of limited storage space on the performance of the prefetching scheme, we ran the simulation with limited storage sizes of 1k, 3k, 5k, 10k, 25k, 50k, and 400k slots. As mentioned in Section 5.1, each slot is about

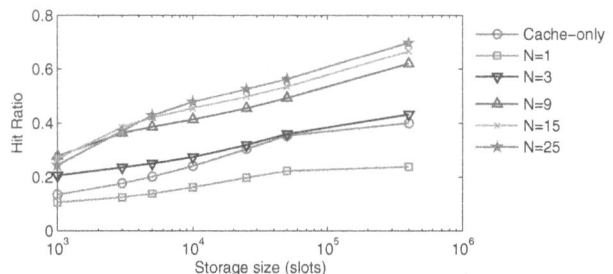

Figure 14: Performance vs. storage size for prefetch-only mode (T3).

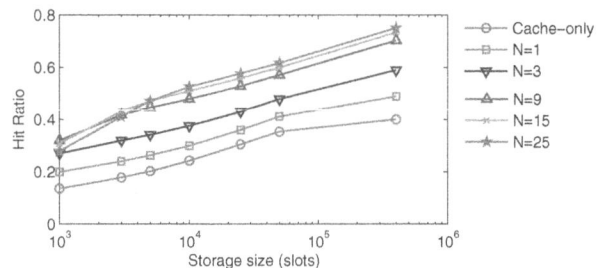

Figure 15: Performance vs. storage size for cache-and-prefetch mode (T3).

2.5 MB. Thus, the maximum slot size of 400k roughly translates to 1 TB. The Least-Recently-Used (LRU) replacement policy is used in our simulation. Figure 14 and 15 show the hit ratio of the prefetch-only and prefetch-and-cache modes with different storage sizes for T3. The results for T1 and T2 are similar but omitted due to space limitation.

The results indicate a correlation between the performance of the prefetching scheme and the storage space size. The hit ratio decreases with the storage space. However, even with a smaller storage space like 125 GB (50k slots), which is less than 3% of space required in the sufficient case, we can still achieve high hit ratios up to 52.59%, 59.36% and 56.26% (for T1, T2 and T3, respectively) with prefetch-only mode and 59.84%, 66.26%, and 61.62% for the cache-and-prefetch mode. In comparison to the caching scheme, the two prefetching schemes can achieve a much better hit ratio using the same storage size. We believe that the hit ratios could even be further improved by applying a smarter cache replacement policy than the LRU policy.

6.2 How large should N be?

In the RV-N algorithm, N is the number of videos we prefetch from each Related Video list. The value of N directly affects the performance of prefetching. To investigate

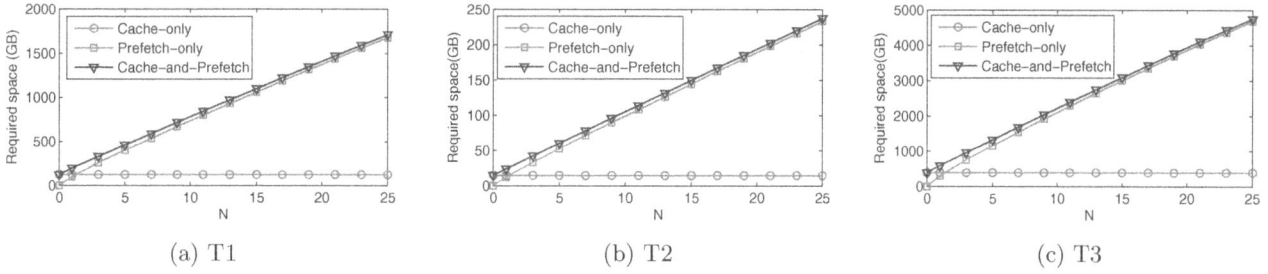

(a) T1   (b) T2   (c) T3

Figure 13: The sufficient storage size for the RV-N prefetching scheme with the PF-Proxy setting.

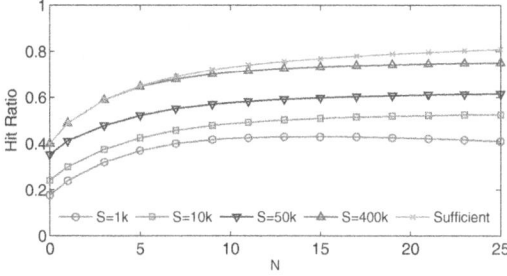

Figure 16: Hit ratio of cache-and-prefetch mode with different storage sizes S and different N (T3).

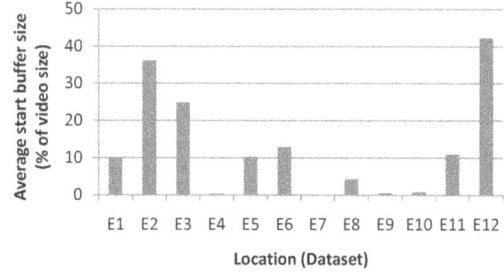

Figure 18: Average minimum start buffer size for smooth playout.

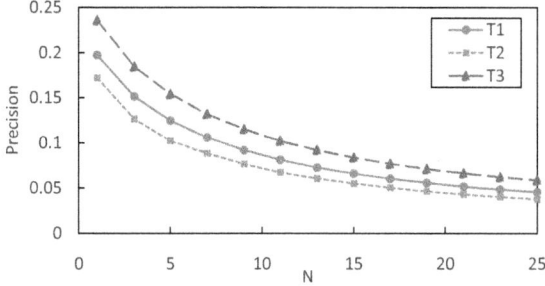

Figure 17: Precision of the RV-N algorithm vs N.

the impact of N, we plot the hit ratio versus N for each storage size for the prefetching scheme with cache-and-prefetch mode, shown in Figure 16. From the figure, with sufficiently large storage space, increasing N always results in a higher hit ratio. However, using small N like 5, we can still achieve a hit ratio up to 65%.

On the other hand, with limited storage size, as N increases, the hit ratio improves up to a certain point and then begins to decline. This effect can also be seen in Figure 14 and 15. When the storage size is small (1k slots), using large N like $N = 25$ results in a lower hit ratio than $N = 9, 15$. In order to explain the cause of this effect, we show the precision of the prefetching scheme for each value of N in Figure 17. From the figure, the precision decreases when N is larger. This means that with larger N the fraction of prefetched videos that are never requested by clients is higher. With limited space, using a too large value of N results in those unused videos taking up the space of the popular videos, giving us lower hit ratios. From Figure 16, a value of N between 5 and 11 seems to be an appropriate range, yielding hit ratios between 65-74% using 1 TB storage space (400k slots). We conclude that when the prefetching scheme is implemented, the value of N should be chosen carefully to avoid the adverse effect when there is limited space and to balance the trade-off between the hit ratio and the additional bandwidth requirement.

6.3 How much should we prefetch?

In the proposed prefetching scheme, only prefixes of videos are prefetched to save storage space and bandwidth. First, we would like to show that we do not need to prefetch the whole video in order to deliver a smooth video playout, thus prefetching only a prefix of a video is sufficient. To demonstrate this, we compute the minimum size of video data that should be buffered before a video starts playing to give a smooth video playout, or minimum start buffer size b_{min}, for each video playout in the datasets from Section 2.

For a video playout with the function $r(t)$ and $sp(d)$ (as described in Section 2), suppose we have video data of size b in the buffer when a video playout starts at $t = t_s$. The total data we have at time t becomes $r(t) + b$. Thus, to get a smooth playout, the start buffer size b must satisfy the condition $\forall t : r(t) + b >= sp(t - t_s)$. The minimum start buffer size b_{min} is then given by $b_{min} = \max \{\max_t(sp(t - t_s) - r(t)), 0\}$.

Using the derived function $sp(t)$ and $r(t)$ from each video download trace in Section 2, we compute b_{min} for every playout. Figure 18 shows the average value of b_{min} as a percentage of the full video size for each dataset collected at different locations. The result shows that b_{min} is much smaller than the full file size; therefore, we do not need to prefetch the whole video file to deliver a smooth playout. The average minimum start buffer size of each location varies from close to 0% to 42% due to the different network condition at each location.

The remaining question is how large should the prefix be. One simple solution is to let the prefix size be a sufficiently large constant percentage of the full video size, but this approach is inefficient since the minimum start buffer size of each playout is actually different. If a prefix is too large, we unnecessarily waste storage space and bandwidth. On the other hand, if a prefix is too small, prefetching would not be useful. For a better solution, the prefetching proxy should choose the prefix size dynamically for each video. The ideal solution is to let the prefix size be equal to b_{min}, which is different for each playout. This solution will give a smooth playout, while using as least storage and bandwidth resource for prefetching as possible. Unfortunately, the computation of b_{min} can only be done after a video is played. Therefore, we propose a mechanism to determine the size of the prefix dynamically.

Our experiment in Section 2 shows that although a video's bit rate is not constant, it usually does not vary significantly. Thus, we assume that a video's bit rate is constant and equal to the average bit rate. We also observe that a video's download rate is usually stable over some short period of time, so we assume that a video download rate is constant as well. These two assumptions greatly simplifies the computation of b_{min}. Let b be a video bit rate, d be a video duration and r be a video download rate. The prefix size is given by $b_{min} = d(b - r)$.

From the equation, we still need to determine the value of b, d and r before we actually download a video. For the future download rate r, the PA can conservatively use the lowest download rate it has seen in some time window as the worst case estimate. In addition, the PA can determine the average video bit rate, b, and video duration, d, from the header of a video file containing video metadata. Therefore, not long after the PA starts prefetching the video, it can determine the value of d, b and r, so it can compute the appropriate prefix size and stop prefetching accordingly. In this manner, the prefix size are adapted according to the network condition and the property of each video.

6.4 Feasibility of Prefetching

One concern about prefetching scheme may be that it will worsen the situation because it requires additional network bandwidth, while interrupted video playouts implies that the network bandwidth is insufficient. Our arguments are as follows. First, users are not watching videos all the time. For example, after watching a video, a user may read or write comments, browse through a list of videos, or replay the video. This provides "idle" time to perform prefetching. Second, since each video's bandwidth requirement is different, we may not have enough bandwidth to accommodate higher bit rate videos, but for lower bit rate videos, we have more than sufficient bandwidth. As shown in our experiments in Section 2, we found both types of playouts, with and without pauses, in the same environment. Thus, we can take advantage of the period where the bandwidth is sufficient to prefetch the videos. Third, by combining caching and prefetching, the bandwidth consumption reduced by caching can compensate the additional bandwidth requirement from prefetching. In the following subsections, we further discuss some aspects about the feasibility of prefetching.

6.4.1 Time to prefetch

In practice, a time gap between video requests may sometimes be short, and thus we may not be able to prefetch some prefixes in time before they are requested. Here we measure the time available to perform prefetching to estimate how this issue will effect the performance of the prefetching scheme. Figure 19 shows the CDF of the time gap between the time that the PA decided to prefetch a video and the time the video was actually requested for every hit requests in trace T3 when N is 5 and 25. When N is larger, the distribution of time to prefetch shifts to a higher value. This means we have longer time to prefetch videos in the lower

ranks of Related Video lists. Comparing the PF-Client to PF-Proxy setting, PF-Proxy has longer time to prefetch. This demonstrates the benefit of sharing prefetched videos in PF-Proxy. Some videos prefetched based on one client's request are requested by another client some time later, and the time gap between the two events is large, allowing more time to prefetch.

Using the result shown in Figure 19, we can estimate the number of hits that are not feasible in practice, i.e., videos that may not be prefetched in time before clients request them. For example, suppose the available bandwidth is 100 KB/s. To download 25 prefixes of video, each with the size of 2.5 MB, we need 11 minutes. Assuming we use a naive scheme where all the prefixes are downloaded in parallel, then, from the CDF, 26% of the hit requests are not feasible, and the hit ratio in the prefetch-only case with N=25 will decrease from 75.68% to 56.00%, yet it is still in a satisfactory level. In practice, the PA can download the prefixes sequentially and employ a smarter scheme, e.g., prefetching the top ranked videos first, to achieve higher hit ratios.

6.4.2 Network traffic overhead of prefetching

To address the concern about additional network bandwidth required for prefetching, we perform a simple calculation of an example case to show how much prefetching will increase the network load. In this example, we prefetch the prefixes of the top 11 videos from Related Video lists using the prefix size equal to 15% of the video size. For cache-only and cache-and-prefetch modes, we assume that videos are cached in full size. Using the hit ratio from T3 to compute the overhead, we show the results of the calculation in Table 3.

Scheme	Hit Ratio	Normalized load
No scheme	0%	1.00
Cache-only	40%	0.60
Prefetch-only	66%	1.44
Cache-and-Prefetch	74%	1.02

Table 3: Normalized traffic load of prefetching schemes.

Table 3 shows the traffic load for prefetching schemes compared with caching scheme, normalized by the case in which no scheme is implemented. Caching has no traffic overhead and helps reduce the traffic. On the other hand, we gain higher hit ratio with prefetching-only mode, but traffic load is also increased by 44%. These extra work comes from prefetching unused prefixes. Finally, cache-and-prefetch mode yields the highest hit ratio and introduces only 2% increase in the network load. Using the combination of caching and prefetching, the extra overhead from prefetching is compensated by the benefit of caching, while we can still maintain the high hit ratio we get from prefetching. In addition, the PA can employ the technique like using TCP Nice [20] to perform prefetching without affecting the peak bandwidth of the network.

7. RELATED WORK

The prefetching technique has its origins in the area of computer architecture. The use of prefetching has been widely studied for web content delivery in early days.

Padmanabhan and Mogul were among the first who applied prefetching within the context of web delivery by proposing the WWW prefetching scheme to reduce latency [15]. In

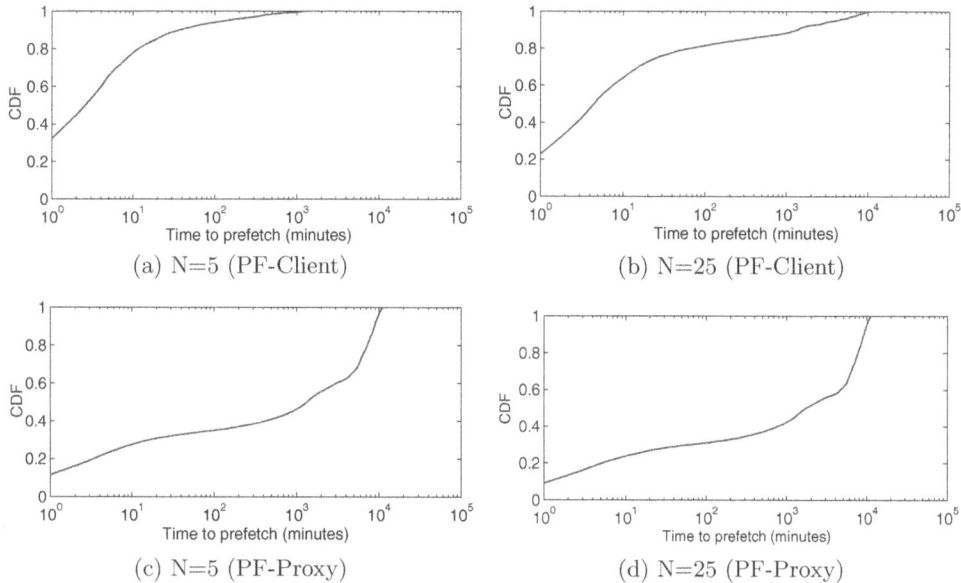

| (a) N=5 (PF-Client) | (b) N=25 (PF-Client) |
| (c) N=5 (PF-Proxy) | (d) N=25 (PF-Proxy) |

Figure 19: CDF of the time to prefetch.

this scheme, a server makes predictions of the links that are likely to be requested next by a client based on past observations. Clients use these predictions to prefetch web documents. In [9], Cunha and Jaccoud proposed two models based on random walk and digital signal processing to model user web access pattern for prefetching. In [10], Fan et al. proposed the proxy-initiated prefetching for web documents. Their approach addresses the low-bandwidth limitation between clients and a proxy by prefetching the cached documents from the proxy to the clients. In this approach, prefetching does not happen between the proxy and the web servers. The use of proxies in VoD systems has been intensively studied in earlier work. We mention the ones that are closest to our approach in the following.

In [19], Sen et al. proposed a prefix proxy caching scheme in which the proxy is used to hide latency, packet loss, and jitter between the local network and server sites. Their proxy caches only a prefix of a video to avoid using a large cache space. They focused on using prefix caching to smooth out the network bandwidth requirement from a proxy to a client and used streaming traces of two videos to demonstrate the benefits of the approach. However, they did not address the issue of how to select videos to prefetch. In [5] and [22], trace-driven simulations were performed to investigate the effectiveness of caching for YouTube videos. Although the traces for both studies were different, the results showed that caching can reduce server and network load significantly. Both studies did not consider prefetching. In addition, there are many existing studies on the use of proxy to improve the quality of media streaming, e.g., [16, 13, 17, 21].

Additional studies have been performed to understand YouTube's characteristics. Cha et al. performed an extensive study of video view statistics on Youtube [5]. Gill et al. studied the usage patterns and video characteristics on YouTube using data from the network edges in [11]. In [12], they further studied user sessions on YouTube. Results from this analysis motivated us to investigate the prefetching approach since they were the first ones who showed that users

spend extended periods of time on YouTube, often watching more than one videos. In [18], Saxena et al. analyzed the service delay for YouTube and other user-generated video sharing sites. Their measurement-based analysis showed that the service delay for YouTube is high, which can lead to a poor playback experience. How often the playback is actually interrupted is not the focus of their study.

Cheng et al. [8] measured the YouTube video graph created by related video links and found that the graph has a large clustering co-efficient and exhibits the small world property. A simulation-based evaluation of a P2P video sharing systems showed that if users use the Related Video list to browse videos, the percentage of source peers that have the requested video in their cache is high.

Cheng and Liu [7] also proposed a P2P video sharing system to reduce YouTube server load and suggested using prefetching based on YouTube's Related Video list at the clients of a P2P system to provide smooth transition between videos. Their evaluation was based on emulated user browsing pattern. The evaluation of their approach showed that it performs significantly better (55% hit ratio) comparing with a random prefetching approach (nearly 0% hit rate).

In contrast to these previous work, we propose and compare various prefix prefetching schemes. Our focus is on user-generated video sharing sites, which are inherently different from VoD systems. We demonstrate the benefit of the prefetching schemes using real user browsing patterns collected from university network traffic. Our study demonstrates that in addition to views from users clicking Related Video lists benefiting from recommendation aware prefetching, other views such as clicking on search results can also benefit from recommendation aware prefetching. Also, the shared interests among network users leads to 50%-100% increase in hit ratios when prefetching is performed at a proxy server at the network edge. This suggests that recommendation aware prefetching is a good heuristic for predicting the interest of viewers both individually and across a community.

8. CONCLUSION

In this paper, we show that currently the user experience in watching videos on video sharing web sites like YouTube is often dissatisfying. In particular, our experiment indicates that many users experience pauses during a video playout. This motivated us to propose a prefetching technique which improves the playback quality and the delay of videos requested from YouTube.

Our proposed prefetching technique works by predicting a set of videos that are likely to be watched in the near future and then fetching the prefixes of those videos before they are requested. If a video has been prefetched, a user can access it faster and the prefetched portion in the buffer can compensate for any insufficient bandwidth and absorb network delay, resulting in a smooth playout of the video.

Our evaluation of the prefetching approach is based on actual network traces which capture real user access patterns. We compare the performance of various prefetching schemes to the traditional caching scheme. We find that applying prefetching at a proxy while using the Related Video lists to select videos to prefetch is the most effective prefetching scheme. Even with limited storage space, prefetching at the proxy results in a hit ratio twice as high as the caching proxy. In addition, the combination of caching and prefetching can further enhance the hit ratio up to 81%.

Finally, we discuss factors that affect the performance of our prefetching scheme including the storage size and the number of videos to prefetch and explore the trade-offs regarding those factors. We also analyze the additional overhead in network traffic that is introduced by prefetching and show that, in the case of caching and prefetching, it is an almost negligible increase of 2%.

9. REFERENCES

[1] Endace DAG Network Monitoring Interface. http://www.endace.com/.

[2] Netflix. http://www.netflixprize.com/.

[3] Wireshark. http://www.wireshark.org/.

[4] YouTube Data API. http://code.google.com/apis/youtube/overview.html.

[5] M. Cha, H. Kwak, P. Rodriguez, Y. Ahn, and S. Moon. I Tube, You Tube, Everybody Tubes: Analyzing the World's Largest User Generated Content Video System. In *Proceedings of ACM Internet measurement Conference(IMC), San Diego, CA, USA*, Oct. 2007.

[6] X. Cheng, C. Dale, and J. Liu. Statistics and social network of youtube videos. In H. van den Berg and G. Karlsson, editors, *IWQoS*, pages 229–238. IEEE, 2008.

[7] X. Cheng and J. Liu. Nettube: Exploring social networks for peer-to-peer short video sharing. In *Proceedings of IEEE INFOCOM*, 2009.

[8] X. Cheng, J. Liu, and H. Wang. Accelerating youtube with video correlation. In *WSM '09: Proceedings of the first SIGMM workshop on Social media*, pages 49–56, New York, NY, USA, 2009. ACM.

[9] C. R. Cunha and C. F. B. Jaccoud. Determining www user's next access and its application to pre-fetching. In *Proceedings of ISCC'97: The second IEEE Symposium on Computers and Communications*, pages 6–11, 1997.

[10] L. Fan, Q. Jacobson, P. Cao, and W. Lin. Web prefetching between low-bandwidth clients and proxies: Potential and performance. In *Proceedings of the SIGMETRICS '99 Conference*, May 1999.

[11] P. Gill, M. Arlitt, Z. Li, and A. Mahanti. YouTube Traffic Characterization: A View From the Edge. In *Proceedings of ACM Internet measurement Conference(IMC), San Diego, CA, USA*, Oct. 2007.

[12] P. Gill, Z. Li, M. Arlitt, and A. Mahanti. Characterizing Users Sessions on YouTube. In *Proceedings of SPIE/ACM Conference on Multimedia Computing and Networking (MMCN), Santa Clara, USA*, Jan. 2008.

[13] C.-M. Huang, T.-H. Hsu, and C.-K. Chang. A proxy-based adaptive flow control scheme for media streaming. In *SAC '02: Proceedings of the 2002 ACM symposium on Applied computing*, pages 750–754, New York, NY, USA, 2002. ACM.

[14] D. A. Menascé, V. A. F. Almeida, R. Fonseca, and M. A. Mendes. A methodology for workload characterization of e-commerce sites.

[15] V. N. Padmanabhan and J. C. Mogul. Using predictive prefetching to improve World-Wide Web latency. In *Proceedings of the ACM SIGCOMM '96 Conference*, Stanford University, CA, July 1996.

[16] R. Rejaie and J. Kangasharju. Mocha: a quality adaptive multimedia proxy cache for internet streaming. In *NOSSDAV '01: Proceedings of the 11th international workshop on Network and operating systems support for digital audio and video*, pages 3–10, New York, NY, USA, 2001. ACM.

[17] R. Rejaie, H. Yu, M. Handley, and D. Estrin. Multimedia proxy caching mechanism for quality adaptive streaming applications in the internet. In *Proceedings of the 2000 IEEE Computer and Communications Societies Conference on Computer Communications (INFOCOM-00)*, pages 980–989, Los Alamitos, Mar. 26–30 2000. IEEE.

[18] M. Saxena, U. Sharang, and S. Fahmy. Analyzing video services in web 2.0: A global perspective. In *Proceedings of NOSSDAV 2008*, 2008.

[19] S. Sen, J. Rexford, and D. Towsley. Proxy prefix caching for multimedia streams. In *Proceedings of IEEE Infocom*, 1999.

[20] A. Venkataramani, R. Kokku, and M. Dahlin. Tcp nice: a mechanism for background transfers. *SIGOPS Oper. Syst. Rev.*, 36(SI):329–343, 2002.

[21] K.-L. Wu, P. S. Yu, and J. L. Wolf. Segment-based proxy caching of multimedia streams. In *WWW '01: Proceedings of the 10th international conference on World Wide Web*, pages 36–44, New York, NY, USA, 2001. ACM.

[22] M. Zink, K. Suh, Y. Gu, and J. Kurose. Watch Global, Cache Local: YouTube Network Traffic at a Campus Network - Measurements and Implications. In *Proceedings of SPIE/ACM Conference on Multimedia Computing and Networking (MMCN), Santa Clara, USA*, Jan. 2008.

Dynamic Codec With Priority for Voice over IP in WLAN

Kewin O. Stoeckigt, Hai L. Vu, P. Branch
kstoeckigt@swin.edu.au

Centre for Advanced Internet Architectures, Faculty of ICT
Swinburne University of Technology, Melbourne, Australia

ABSTRACT

Research on Voice over IP (VoIP) in infrastructure wireless local area networks (WLANs) has shown that, because of the access mechanism, the access point severely limits the number of voice calls a WLAN can support. To address this problem we propose a new scheme based on the IEEE 802.11e quality of service (QoS) mechanism where a tradeoff between codec quality and priority is exploited to improve the number of calls that can be supported. In particular, we propose certain priority settings at the access point (AP) to encourage users to switch to a lower quality codec during periods of high contention and thus enable them to maintain the call. We develop a detailed analytical model to show the benefit of this scheme. Our analytical results are validated by extensive simulation and show that the voice capacity in the network can be significantly improved. Furthermore, by using the ITU-T E-model to assess the voice quality, we show that users with a lower quality codec can still maintain an acceptable level of quality using the proposed scheme.

Categories and Subject Descriptors

C.4 [**Performance of Systems**]: Modeling Techniques, Performance Attributes; C.2.1 [**Computer-Communication Networks**]: Network Architecture and Design—*Wireless communication*

General Terms

Performance

Keywords

VoIP, IEEE 802.11e, EDCA, Multi-queue, Modeling,

1. INTRODUCTION

Voice over IP (VoIP) is one of the fastest growing services on the Internet today [4]. Even though security of such services is still a concern [18], many consumers and businesses now use VoIP to lower their communication costs. As the voice traffic is delivered over the underlying IP network, it can converge with data services, and as such can provide *unified communication*. Mobile and wireless VoIP solutions are an important emerging service as it promises to replace cell phone communication wherever a wireless local area network (WLAN) is available. Decreasing costs for WLAN equipment and improvements to the IEEE 802.11 protocol have led to a widespread deployment of wireless networks. Many places such as cafes, restaurants or airport lounges now offer free WLAN access. However, recent studies [6, 10, 11, 23] have shown that due to the associated overhead of voice traffic, e.g. packet headers, and asymmetric up- and downlink traffic, the access point (AP) is a bottleneck, which limits the number of voice calls a WLAN can support. For example, a G.729 voice codec with a 10 ms sampling rate generates an 8 kbit/s voice stream. Thus a full-duplex (bi-directional) voice calls requires approximately 16 kbit/s of bandwidth. Therefore an IEEE 802.11b WLAN with a data rate of 11 MBit/s should be able to support $11/0.015 \approx 733$ voice calls using that codec. However, it has been shown, that only 5 to 7 calls can be maintained [6, 11]. Even if an IEEE 802.11a/g WLAN with an available bandwidth of 54 MBit/s ($\approx$ five times the bandwidth of 802.11b) is used, the voice capacity does not increase by the same factor [6]. This is because the channel access rather than bandwidth limits the number of voice alls a WLAN can support.

Originally, the IEEE 802.11 protocol [12] was designed to support data services, but with an increasing demand for delay sensitive multimedia applications such as VoIP, more stringent quality of service (QoS) is required. The IEEE ratified the 802.11e protocol [13] in 2005, which has become part of the IEEE 802.11 standard in 2007 [14]. The 802.11e protocol extends the access mechanism in the medium access control (MAC) by allowing adjustment of a number of MAC parameters that were previously fixed. Also, it provides four different access categories (ACs) to provide QoS to different types of traffic.

There have been several proposals in the literature that suggest the use of 802.11e to give different priorities to different traffic in the WLAN. For example, work in [8, 20] assign different access categories to voice and data traffic, respectively. Independent of that research, the access mechanism in 802.11e can also be used to resolve the AP bottleneck problem as proposed in [7, 23]. In particular, in [7] the authors propose the use of different contention windows for upstream and downstream traffic which increase the voice capacity by approximately 30%. In our previous work [23], we showed that using a similar approach the number of voice calls can be doubled (i.e. 100% increase) when the adjustable transmission opportunity ($TXOPLimit$) parameter is utilized.

On the other hand, recent development in VoIP introduce the use of *dynamic* voice codecs which are designed to adapt to changes in network condition. For example, SILK [25] used in Skype V.4 or SPEEX [3] used in Google Talk, monitor the call quality and adjust the codec parameters accordingly. The idea here is to maintain the call with reduced quality during the congestion period of the network. In this context mixed codecs can be seen in some of the previous work. In particular, the authors in [9] considers two type of voice traffic using different codecs. Also in [21] a dynamic adaptation of the voice codec is proposed to suit the change in transmission rate of the WLAN.

In this paper we propose a novel scheme based on the IEEE 802.11e mechanism to exploit the tradeoff between the codec quality and priority to maintain the call during periods of high contention without compromising the individual call quality. At the same time the proposed scheme also improves the overall number of calls that can be supported by the WLAN. The novel idea is to give incentive to users who are willing to use a lower quality codec and thus reduce the overall contention when there is a high traffic load in the medium. The incentive is implemented by way of giving priority at the AP to traffic originated from low quality codec users. Note that this scheme can be easily implemented because the priority is only applied at the AP where the network bottleneck is. Also, users can voluntarily choose the codec by monitoring their own call quality as done in [2].

In order to understand the benefits of the above proposed scheme, we develop a detailed analytical model based on our previous work [23]. In particular, we extend the existing model to accommodate multi-codec voice streams and to include a so-called internal collision caused by the use of priority at the AP. Note that in [8, 20] the authors investigated the use of multiple queues based on IEEE 802.11e, however, they did not consider the effect of internal collisions. We will show in this paper through our analytical model that the impact of this internal collision is not negligible. Furthermore we assess the quality of calls in the WLAN using the proposed scheme using the ITU-T E-model [15]. Although the analytical model has been developed to analyze the scenario outlined above, the proposed model is sufficiently versatile to study a range of scenarios such as the interactions between voice and video traffic in an IEEE 802.11e WLAN. Additionally, the model can be used to obtain a range of network parameters such as collision probability and queue utilization at a station, and different network metrics, i.e. throughput, can be derived.

To this end, our main contributions can be summarized as follows.

- a novel scheme to reduce the overall contention in a highly congested WLAN,

- an improved voice capacity while maintaining an acceptable quality for all individual calls that is evi-

denced by results obtained from the ITU-T E-model, and

- a detailed analytical model to obtain the voice capacity in a multi-codec environment that also takes into account the AP's internal collision.

The rest of the paper is organized as follows. In Section 2 we describe in details the proposed scheme with dynamic codecs and priority at the AP. The analytical model is then developed in Section 3. We validate our analytical results by simulation in Section 4, and conclude the paper in Section 5.

2. DYNAMIC CODEC WITH PRIORITY SCHEME

Consider a scenario where multiple voice calls are initiated simultaneously in an IEEE 802.11e infrastructure wireless LAN, as depicted in Fig. 1.

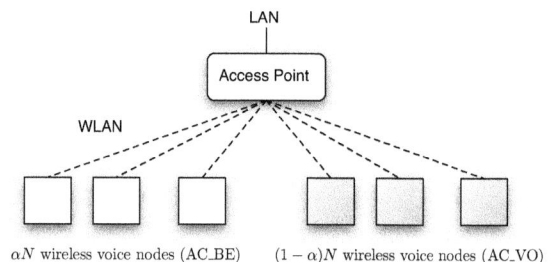

Figure 1: WLAN topology

The IEEE 802.11e protocol can provide QoS in WLANs using four access categories, each with different and adjustable MAC parameter settings as defined in the enhanced distributed channel access (EDCA) mechanism [13]. The first two access categories, *best effort* (AC_BE) and *background* (AC_BK) can be understood as *data* categories, whereas *video* (AC_VI) and *voice* (AC_VO) are specifically designed for real-time multimedia traffic. In this paper, we propose the use of dynamic voice codecs where users can choose to switch to a lower quality codec to maintain their calls in a congested WLAN. To this end, both the sampling rate and the payload of the packet can be adjusted to form a low quality codec. Similar to existing VoIP implementation, e.g. Skype [2] or Google Talk [1], users can monitor their own call quality and make the switching decision when appropriate. However, this action can lead to a lower perceived voice quality as sometimes observed in existing VoIP applications. To compensate the reduction in voice quality and to give incentive to users who are willing to switch to a lower quality codec, higher priority is then given at the AP to traffic originated from those users. Thus placing traffic in the higher priority queue at the AP will encourage a less aggressive behavior from users in a highly congested medium. As a result not only users can maintain their call at an acceptable quality level using a lower quality codec, but the overall number of calls is also increased.

In this paper our proposed dynamic voice codec with priority is implemented as follows. Every voice user will content for a channel access using the MAC parameters defined in the AC_BE category. Users will continue to use the same MAC parameters independent of the codec used. At the

200

AP, however, different traffic originated from users equipped with different quality codecs will be placed into different access categories. In particular, traffic from users with high quality codecs will be assigned to the AC_BE category, while other voice traffic will be mapped into the AC_VO category. Note that only contention windows (CW_{min}, CW_{max}) are used in these two categories to differentiate different traffic at the AP. Although other MAC parameter such as $TXOPLimit$ or the arbitrary interframe space ($AIFS$) can also be used, the use of contention window is the simplest way to prioritize traffic and to demonstrate the benefit of the scheme proposed in this paper.

Herein we consider the voice capacity to be the maximum (total) number of voice calls a WLAN can support with an adequate level of quality. We define κ as a packet loss threshold, beyond which a user-perceived quality of a call can no longer be maintained. Additionally, we will also consider an end-to-end delay bound of 60 ms [22]. Even though the ITU-T G.114 specification [16] allows a 150 ms end-to-end delay before the call quality is no longer considered to be good, this delay however, is the total delay from the sender to the receiver. In this work, we do not consider the path outside the WLAN, and as such, the experienced delay in the one-hop infrastructure WLAN should be well below the 150 ms. We make use of the ITU-T E-model [15] which uses delay and loss to obtain a measure (the R-value) that estimates the user-perceived voice quality. In the next section, we develop a detailed analytical model to evaluate the performance gain of our proposed scheme.

3. ANALYTICAL MODEL

In this paper we consider an IEEE 802.11 infrastructure WLAN, consisting of one AP and N wireless nodes. The AP has two *queues* (access categories), one best effort (AC_BE) and one voice (AC_VO). The two access categories carry only voice flows using a specific codec, i.e. G.711 with a 10 ms sampling rate in AC_BE and G.729 with a 20 ms sampling rate in AC_VO. We refer to wireless nodes served by the AC_BE queue of the AP as *standard* wireless nodes, whereas we refer to *priority* wireless node, whenever a node is served by the AC_VO queue of the AP. In this WLAN, there are αN standard wireless nodes and $(1 - \alpha)N$ priority wireless nodes. Each wireless node maintains a full-duplex voice call to a node outside the WLAN. In this scenario we assume EDCA basic access is used over an ideal channel without interference or hidden terminals. Unless otherwise stated, the indices a and n correspond to the AP and a wireless node, respectively. Also, to differentiate between the two access categories, the voice access category is tagged using the asterisk (*).

Let λ denote the packet arrival rate at a wireless node. The arrival rate at the AP is a superposition of all the individual rates per access class from the wireless nodes. Thus, the packet arrival rate at the AC_BE queue at the AP is $\lambda_a = \alpha N \lambda_n$. Similarly for the voice access category, the packet arrival rate is given by $\lambda_a^* = (1 - \alpha)N\lambda_n^*$. The packet service rate is denoted by μ for each *station* (wireless node and/or AP). Assuming that the traffic flows arrive at a node according to a Poisson process, the AP and a wireless node can be modeled using an $M/G/1/K$ queueing model, where K is the number of packets that can be queued at a station and can take different values for the AP, and the wireless nodes. Even though the assumption of packet arrival as a

Poisson process is coarse, it can partly model the superposition of multiple periodic streams at the AP, which, in turn, is the bottleneck determining the voice capacity in this network, as shown in our previous work [23].

The queue utilization is expressed as $\rho = \lambda/\mu$, where ρ is also the probability that a station has a packet to send. Consequently, the system will be idle with probability $1 - \rho$. Our analysis is built around a fixed-point formulation between the collision probability c, seen by a packet transmitted on the channel, and the attempt rate per slot $\rho\tau$, of a station, where τ is the conditional attempt rate per slot (i.e. number of transmission attempts over the total duration of the backoff of a station). The latter is conditioned such that a queue is nonempty, i.e. $\rho > 0$. In the following we establish the fixed-point equations and derive the average service times associated with the AP and the wireless nodes. We will split our analysis into three parts. In the first part we will calculate the average service time of the AP. In the second part, we will derive the average service time of a standard wireless nodes, before we obtain the average service time of a priority node in the third part.

Because the IEEE 802.11 protocol defines different access categories with different priorities, the collision probability of the AP depends on two parts: 1) the internal collision probability, 2) the external collision probability. Because the AP has multiple traffic categories, an internal collision can occur if the backoff process in at least two ACs reaches zero simultaneously. The IEEE 802.11e protocol defines an internal collision resolution mechanism to handle these collisions. In case of an internal collisions, the internal collision handler will grant access to the wireless medium to the higher access category; in this scenario AC_VO. The packet of the lower access category (AC_BE) is rescheduled for transmission after an additional backoff. If no internal collision occurs, the packet can still collide on the wireless medium (referred to as external collision). If an external collision occurs, the packet is scheduled for retransmission in its respective access category, as outlined above.

Let δ denote the internal collision probability at the AP. Because an internal collision between a lower and a higher access category only occurs if a packet of AC_VO is ready to be sent, the internal collision probability is defined as

$$\delta = 1 - (1 - \rho_a^* \tau_a^*), \tag{1}$$

whereby $\rho_a^* \tau_a^*$ is the conditional attempt probability of AC_VO. Thus, with probability $1 - \delta$ no internal collision occurs. If no internal collision occurs, the packet can still collide externally with packets transmitted by either, a standard or a priority wireless node. The external collision probability for packets sent by the AP of either traffic categories is equal. This is because both packet types can only collide with packets transmitted by both, a standard or a priority wireless node. Therefore the external collision probability (=collision probability of an AC_VO packet) is given by

$$c_a^* = 1 - (1 - \rho_n \tau_n)^{\alpha N}(1 - \rho_n^* \tau_n^*)^{(1-\alpha)N}. \tag{2}$$

Using (1) and (2), an AC_BE packet will be transmitted successfully by the AP with probability $(1 - \delta)(1 - c_a^*)$, or be discarded if the retry limit R has been reached. Thus for $R \to \infty$, we can establish a recursive formula to obtain the collision probability c_a, which is given by

$$R = 1 \rightarrow c_{a,1} = \delta + (1 - \delta)c_a^*$$
$$R = 2 \rightarrow c_{a,2} = \delta c_{a,1} + (1 - \delta)c_a^* c_{a,1}$$
$$R = 3 \rightarrow c_{a,3} = \delta c_{a,2} + (1 - \delta)c_a^* c_{a,2}$$
$$\vdots$$
$$R = n \rightarrow c_{a,n} = \delta c_{a,n-1} + (1 - \delta)c_a^* c_{a,n-1}, \quad (3)$$

and therefore, for a maximum retry limit R $(R > 1)$, the collision probability of a standard packet send by the AP is given as

$$c_a = \delta c_{a,i-1} + (1 - \delta)c_a^* c_{a,i-1}, i = 2, ..., R. \quad (4)$$

The above recursive concept is illustrated for $R = 1$ and $R = 2$ in Figs. 2 and 3.

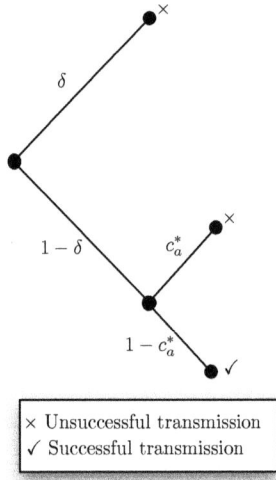

Figure 2: Collision probability c_a for $R = 1$

Following our previous work [23] we decompose the average service time for the AP $(1/\mu_a)$ into three parts: 1) the successful transmission and collision of the packet itself, 2) the interruptions to the backoff due to successful transmissions and collisions of the other stations, 3) the average backoff of the station itself. For the first part, the successful transmission time of a standard and a priority packet is defined as

$$T_s = T_{AIFS} + T_p + T_{SIFS} + T_{ACK}, \quad (5)$$
$$T_s^* = T_{AIFS} + T_p^* + T_{SIFS} + T_{ACK} \quad (6)$$

where T_p, T_p^*, T_{ACK} are the transmission times of a standard packet, a priority packet and the acknowledgement. Note that T_p and T_p^* can be different, depending on the sampling rate and used voice codec. Additionally, T_{AIFS} and T_{SIFS} are the duration of the arbitrary interframe space (AIFS) and the short interframe space (SIFS) in microseconds, respectively, as defined in the IEEE 802.11 protocol.

The collision times are the durations during which the channel is seen busy due to collisions, and are given by

$$T_c = T_{AIFS} + T_p + T_{ACK_{TO}}, \quad (7)$$
$$T_c^* = T_{AIFS} + T_p^* + T_{ACK_{TO}}, \quad (8)$$

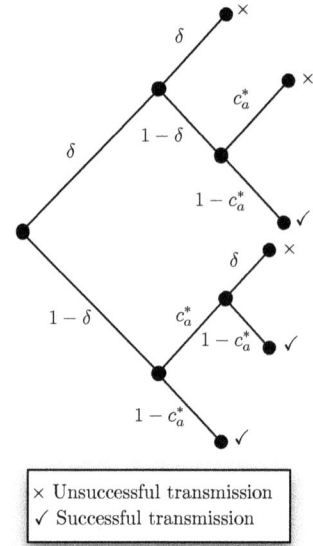

Figure 3: Collision probability c_a for $R = 2$

where $T_{ACK_{TO}}$ is the ACK timeout period of an unsuccessful transmission. As a packet can collide multiple times before its successful reception, the average collision time depends on the packet itself, and whether it collides with a standard or priority packet. As the average collision time also depends on T_p and T_p^*, the average collision time of a standard and a priority packet transmitted by the AP is defined as

$$\frac{\bar{t}_a}{2} = \frac{1}{2} \sum_{i=1}^{R} c_a^i (1 - c_a^i) i (\gamma T_c + (1 - \gamma) T_c^*)$$
$$\approx \frac{\gamma T_c c_a + (1 - \gamma) T_c^* c_a}{2(1 - c_a)}, \quad (9)$$

$$\frac{\bar{t}_a^*}{2} = \frac{1}{2} \sum_{i=1}^{R} c_a^i (1 - c_a^i) i T_c^* \approx \frac{T_c c_a^*}{2(1 - c_a^*)}. \quad (10)$$

Note that the $1/2$ factor in the aforementioned expressions is based on the assumption that a collision is due to simultaneous transmission from two stations only, and thus the average collision time caused by a packet is half of the total collision time experienced by all stations. Also note that γ is the probability of transmitting a standard packet, which is given as follows

$$\gamma = \frac{\alpha N \lambda_n}{\alpha N \lambda_n + (1 - \alpha) N \lambda_n^*}. \quad (11)$$

The second component of the average packet service time of the AP is the interruption to the backoff process due to successful transmission and collisions of packets, and depends on three factors: 1) the interruption caused by an internal collisions conditioned such that an AC_BE packet collides with an AC_VO packet, 2) the interruption caused by an external collision when an AC_BE packet is send, and 3) the interruption caused by an external collision if an AC_VO packet is send. Note that the interruption to the backoff is given in backoff slots, each of length $\sigma[\mu s]$. Then, for the first part, the backoff process, on average, will be interrupted for

$$\delta \left((1-\alpha)N\frac{\lambda_n^*}{\mu_a}\left(T_s^* + \frac{\bar{t}_a^*}{2}\right)\right)\sigma \tag{12}$$

slots. The external collision of an AC_BE packet, will, on average, interrupt the backoff process by

$$(1-\delta)\gamma N\left(\alpha\frac{\lambda_n}{\mu_a}\left(T_s + \frac{\bar{t}_n}{2}\right) + (1-\alpha)\frac{\lambda_n^*}{\mu_a}\left(T_s^* + \frac{\bar{t}_n^*}{2}\right)\right)\sigma \tag{13}$$

slots. This is because, the AC_BE packet can collide with αN standard packets and $(1-\alpha)N$ priority packets, sent by the respective wireless nodes. Finally, the collision of an AC_VO packet with packets from both types of wireless nodes, will further interrupt the backoff of the AP by

$$(1-\delta)(1-\gamma)N\left(\alpha\frac{\lambda_n}{\mu_a}\left(T_s + \frac{\bar{t}_n^*}{2}\right)\right.$$
$$\left.+ (1-\alpha)\frac{\lambda_n^*}{\mu_a}\left(T_s^* + \frac{\bar{t}_n^*}{2}\right)\right)\sigma \tag{14}$$

slots.

The third component for the average packet service time of the AP is the average backoff. The IEEE 802.11 protocol [14] specifies that a station has to wait for a random period of time measured in backoff slots before attempting to transmit its packet. The backoff is uniformly and randomly selected from $[0, CW-1]$, where CW is the current contention window with the initial value of $CW_{min} = W$. A collision occurs if more than one station transmits in the same slot. If a collision occurs, the contention window of the sender is doubled unless the maximum value ($CW_{max} = 2^m CW_{min}$, $m \geq 1$) has been reached, and the packet is scheduled for retransmission. The contention window is reset to CW_{min} when the packet has been successfully transmitted or discarded when the retransmission limit R ($R \geq m$) is reached. In this paper we assume a constant and independent collision probability, denoted as c for a station. From the time a packet is ready to be sent until a packet is successfully transmitted, the average backoff experienced by a station is given by [23]

$$\overline{w} = \sum_{i=0}^{R-2}(1-c)c^i\frac{\left(\prod_{j=1}^i \phi_j W\right)-1}{2}$$
$$+ c^{R-1}\frac{2^m W - 1}{2}, \tag{15}$$

where $\phi_j = 2$ if $j \leq m$ and 1 otherwise. By replacing c in (15) with c_n, c_n^*, c_a and c_a^*, the average backoff window for a standard and priority wireless voice node, as well as the two accesses categories of the AP can be obtained.

Given that a station has a packet to send, the conditional attempt probability τ that a station is attempting to transmit in any given slot is

$$\tau = \frac{\sum_{j=0}^R c^j}{\overline{w}}, \tag{16}$$

and thus, the probability that a station is attempting to transmit in a slot is given by $\rho\tau$ [24].

To obtain the total average backoff of the AP requires the average backoff of each access category, and the probability of transmitting an AC_BE or an AC_VO packet. Then using (15) with c_a and c_a^* as well as (11), the total average backoff of the AP is given as

$$\overline{w}_a' = \gamma\overline{w}_a + (1-\gamma)\overline{w}_a^*. \tag{17}$$

However, as shown in [23], the average backoff is not simply $\overline{w}_a'\sigma$ because the backoff counter is differently managed in EDCA [5]. In particular, after every channel activity, the backoff counter in EDCA is resumed one slot time before the AIFS timer elapses. Thus an adjustment of the backoff time is required. Let ϵ_a denote this adjustment, then ϵ_a can be devised based on the average number of successful transmissions and collisions during the backoff given in (12), (13) and (14). Furthermore, according to the EDCA mechanism, a station has to wait either an additional slot when the medium is idle or an additional AIFS period when the medium is sensed busy, before attempting to transmit. Depending on the access category, the former occurs with probability $1-c_a$ or $1-c_a^*$, while the latter is with probability c_a or c_a^*. Thus the total average backoff of the AP is then calculated using

$$(\overline{w}_a' - \epsilon_a)\sigma + \gamma((1-c_a)\sigma + c_a T_{AIFS})$$
$$+ (1-\gamma)((1-c_a^*)\sigma + c_a^* T_{AIFS}). \tag{18}$$

Based on (2), (4)-(6), (9)-(14), and (18), the total average packet service time of the AP is then given by

$$\frac{1}{\mu_a'} = \gamma\left(T_s + \frac{\bar{t}_a}{2}\right) + (1-\gamma)\left(T_s^* + \frac{\bar{t}_a^*}{2}\right)$$
$$+\delta\left((1-\alpha)N\frac{\lambda_n^*}{\mu_a}\left(T_s^* + \frac{\bar{t}_a^*}{2}\right)\right)$$
$$+(1-\delta)\gamma N\left(\alpha\frac{\lambda_n}{\mu_a}\left(T_s + \frac{\bar{t}_n}{2}\right)\right.$$
$$\left.+ (1-\alpha)\frac{\lambda_n^*}{\mu_a}\left(T_s^* + \frac{\bar{t}_n^*}{2}\right)\right)$$
$$+(1-\delta)(1-\gamma)N\left(\alpha\frac{\lambda_n}{\mu_a}\left(T_s + \frac{\bar{t}_n^*}{2}\right)\right.$$
$$\left.+ (1-\alpha)\frac{\lambda_n^*}{\mu_a}\left(T_s^* + \frac{\bar{t}_n^*}{2}\right)\right)$$
$$+(\overline{w}_a' - \epsilon_a)\sigma + \gamma((1-c_a)\sigma + c_a T_{AIFS})$$
$$+ (1-\gamma)((1-c_a^*)\sigma + c_a^* T_{AIFS}). \tag{19}$$

To obtain the collision and attempt probability as well as the average packet service time for the αN and $(1-\alpha)N$ wireless nodes, we follow a similar approach to the AP. Note that we assume that each wireless node only carries one type of traffic, and thus, does not experience any internal collisions. Hence, a wireless node attempting to transmit a packet can only collide with the remaining nodes in its traffic class, with all nodes of the other traffic class, as well as packets of either traffic class sent by the AP. Then, the collision probability for a standard wireless node is given as

$$c_n = 1 - (1-\rho_n\tau_n)^{\alpha N-1}(1-\rho_n^*\tau_n^*)^{(1-\alpha)N}(1-\rho_a'\tau_a'), \tag{20}$$

where $\rho_a'\tau_a'$ is the conditional attempt probability of the AP transmitting a packet in any slot, irrespective of its traffic class. Hence ρ_a' is the probability that the AP has packet to send and is defined by

$$\rho_a' = \frac{\alpha N\lambda_n + (1-\alpha)N\lambda_n^*}{\mu_a}. \tag{21}$$

Similar to (16), the attempt probability τ_a' is given by

$$\tau_a' = \frac{\sum_{i=0}^R c_0^i}{\overline{w}_a'}, \tag{22}$$

whereby $c_0 = \gamma c_a + \gamma c_a^*$ with γ as in (11).

The average packet service time of a standard wireless voice node $(1/\mu_n)$ can also be decomposed into the aforementioned three parts: 1) the successful transmission and collision time of the packet itself, 2) the interruptions to the backoff due to successful transmissions and collisions by the wireless voice nodes of both traffic classes as well as the AP, 3) the average backoff of the station itself.

The first part, the successful transmission time of a standard packet is given in (5), and replacing c_a with c_n in (9) the average collision time for a standard packet can be obtained.

For the second component, the backoff process of a standard wireless voice node will be interrupted by

$$(\alpha N - 1)\rho_n \left(T_s + \frac{\overline{t_n}}{2}\right)$$
$$+(1-\alpha)N\frac{\lambda_n^*}{\mu_n}\left(T_s^* + \frac{\overline{t_n^*}}{2}\right)\sigma \qquad (23)$$

slots, due to the successful transmission and collision of packets sent by the $\alpha(N-1)$ remaining standard wireless voice nodes, as well as the $(1-\alpha)N$ priority wireless voice nodes. Additionally, successful transmissions and collisions of packets of both access categories sent by the AP, will further interrupt the backoff process by

$$\frac{\Lambda}{\mu_n}\left(\gamma\left(T_s + \frac{\overline{t_a}}{2}\right) + (1-\gamma)\left(T_s^* + \frac{\overline{t_a^*}}{2}\right)\right)\sigma \qquad (24)$$

slots, where $\Lambda = \alpha N \lambda_n + (1-\alpha)N\lambda_n^*$.

The third component, the average backoff, can be calculated using (15) and appropriately replacing c with c_n. The average backoff on a standard wireless node also requires the adjustment of the calculated backoff time as previously outlined for the AP. Therefore ϵ_n is given by

$$\epsilon_n = 2\left((1-\alpha)N\frac{\lambda_n^*}{\mu_n}\right) + \frac{\lambda_n}{\mu_n}(2\alpha N - 1), \qquad (25)$$

Note that (25) can be derived from the successful transmission and collisions given in (23) and (24). Then, the total average backoff of a standard wireless node is given by

$$(\overline{w}_n - \epsilon_n + (1 - c_n))\sigma + c_n T_{AIFS}. \qquad (26)$$

Using (5), (9), (20), (23), (24), and (26), the average packet service time of a standard wireless voice node can be calculated using:

$$\frac{1}{\mu_n} = \left(T_s + \frac{\overline{t_n}}{2}\right)$$
$$+(\alpha N - 1)\rho_n\left(T_s + \frac{\overline{t_n}}{2}\right)$$
$$+(1-\alpha)N\frac{\lambda_n^*}{\mu_n}\left(T_s^* + \frac{\overline{t_n^*}}{2}\right)$$
$$+\frac{\Lambda}{\mu_n}\left(\gamma\left(T_s + \frac{\overline{t_a}}{2}\right) + (1-\gamma)\left(T_s^* + \frac{\overline{t_a^*}}{2}\right)\right)$$
$$+(\overline{w}_n - \epsilon_n + (1 - c_n))\sigma + c_n T_{AIFS}. \qquad (27)$$

The process to calculate the average service time of a priority wireless node is similar compared to a standard node, and it also requires the collision probability, transmission and collision times, the duration of the backoff, the interruptions to the backoff and the compensation for the different backoff

in EDCA. Homologous to (20), the collision probability of a priority wireless node is given as

$$c_n^* = 1 - (1 - \rho_n\tau_n)^{\alpha N}(1 - \rho_n^*\tau_n^*)^{(1-\alpha)N-1}(1 - \rho_a'\tau_a'). \qquad (28)$$

Similar to (23) and (24), the backoff process of a priority wireless voice node will be interrupted by

$$\alpha N \frac{\lambda_n}{\mu_n^*}\left(T_s + \frac{\overline{t_n}}{2}\right)$$
$$+(1-\alpha)(N-1)\frac{\lambda_n^*}{\mu_n^*}\left(T_s^* \frac{\overline{t_n^*}}{2}\right)\sigma \qquad (29)$$

$$\frac{\Lambda}{\mu_n^*}\left(\gamma\left(T_s + \frac{\overline{t_a}}{2}\right) + (1-\gamma)\left(T_s^* + \frac{\overline{t_a^*}}{2}\right)\right)\sigma \qquad (30)$$

slots, where (29) is the interruption due to the successful transmission and collision of the αN standard wireless voice nodes and the $(1-\alpha)(N-1)$ priority wireless voice nodes. The interruptions to the backoff caused by the AP is given in (30).

The compensation, ϵ_n^*, for the different backoff mechanism in EDCA is given as

$$\epsilon_n^* = 2\left(\alpha N\frac{\lambda_n}{\mu_n^*}\right) +$$
$$(1-\alpha)(N-1)\frac{\lambda_n^*}{\mu_n^*} + (1-\alpha)N\frac{\lambda_n^*}{\mu_n^*}, \qquad (31)$$

and can be derived from (29) and (30). Thus

$$(\overline{w}_n^* - \epsilon_n + (1 - c_n^*))\sigma + c_n^* T_{AIFS} \qquad (32)$$

is the total backoff of a priority wireless node.

Then, using (6), (10), (28), (29), (30), and (32), the average packet service time of a priority wireless voice node $(1/\mu_n^*)$ is then given as

$$\frac{1}{\mu_n^*} = \left(T_s^* + \frac{\overline{t_n^*}}{2}\right)$$
$$+\alpha N\frac{\lambda_n}{\mu_n^*}\left(T_s + \frac{\overline{t_n}}{2}\right)$$
$$+(1-\alpha)(N-1)\frac{\lambda_n^*}{\mu_n^*}\left(T_s^* + \frac{\overline{t_n^*}}{2}\right)$$
$$+\frac{\Lambda}{\mu_n^*}\left(\gamma\left(T_s + \frac{\overline{t_a}}{2}\right) + (1-\gamma)\left(T_s^* + \frac{\overline{t_a^*}}{2}\right)\right)$$
$$+(\overline{w}_n^* - \epsilon_n + (1 - c_n^*))\sigma + c_n^* T_{AIFS}. \qquad (33)$$

Using the aforementioned set of equations to iteratively obtain the collision and attempt probability of a station, as well as the queue utilization, we can now determine the maximum number of voice calls (C) a wireless LAN can support. To determine C, we require that the average packet loss (κ) to be less than 2% to have an acceptable level of quality [19]. Because the average packet loss seen at the AP is also the average packet loss of an individual call of that class, the packet loss at the AP can be approximated by

$$p_a' \approx \frac{(1 - \rho_a')\rho_a'^K}{1 - \rho_a'^{K+1}}. \qquad (34)$$

Note that (34) is the blocking probabilities of an $M/M/1/K$ queue [17] by assuming exponential service time at the AP, and thus, is only an approximation of the packet loss probability.

4. RESULTS AND DISCUSSION

In this section we validate our model by comparing the analytical results with simulation. Simulation is performed using NS-2 (version 2.28) with the EDCA extension from the TU-Berlin [26]. The voice streams are generated as periodic streams of packets for a given voice codec. Table 1 provides an overview of the parameters used in our analysis and simulation.

Table 1: Network parameters for an 802.11 WLAN

Channel rate	11MBit/s
Basic rate	1MBit/s
Backup Slot length σ	20 μs
CW_{min} (AC_BE)	32
CW_{max} (AC_BE)	1024
CW_{min} (AC_VO)	8
CW_{max} (AC_VO)	256
T_{SIFS}	10 μs
T_{AIFS}	50 μs
Max. backoff stage (m)	5
Retry limit (R)	7
Buffer size (K)	50 packets
Traffic/Data details	
PLCP & Preamble	192 μs
MAC Header + PCS	24.7 μs
RTP/UDP/IP Header	29.1 μs
Voice payload	7.27 μs (G.729, 10 ms)
	14.54 μs (G.729, 20 ms)
	58.18 μs (G.711, 10 ms)
	116.36 μs (G.711, 20 ms)
	14.54 μs (G.723, 30 ms)
ACK frame	112 μs

In the following we will use different *VoIP call configurations*, denoted by $S_i(\alpha N, (1-\alpha)N), i = 1, ..., 5$, shown in Table 2. The configurations indicate the number of voice calls served by each access category. For example, $S_1(5, 2)$ is scenario 1, where 5 voice calls use a G.711 voice codec with a 10 ms sampling rate served by the AC_BE category, and 2 voice calls use the same codec but are served by the AC_VO category at the AP. In Figs. 4 we show the packet

Table 2: VoIP call configuration overview

i	Voice codec used in	
	AC_BE	AC_VO
1	G.711, 10 ms	G.711, 10 ms
2	G.711, 10 ms	G.729, 10 ms
3	G.711, 10 ms	G.711, 20 ms
4	G.711, 10 ms	G.729, 20 ms
5	G.711, 10 ms	G.723, 30 ms

loss probability at the AP for G.711 and G.729 voice calls, each with a 10 ms and 20 ms sampling rate. It can be seen that the WLAN can maintain 6 or 7 voice calls using either a G.711 or a G.729 voice codec with a 10 ms sampling rate. It can also be observed that the number of voice calls is increased to 13 or 14 calls if the voice codec uses a sampling rate of 20 ms. The results shown here have previously been

reported in [6, 10, 11, 23]. These results are the baseline for our analysis, and we will compared them with results obtained from our proposed scheme to highlight the voice capacity gain that can be achieved.

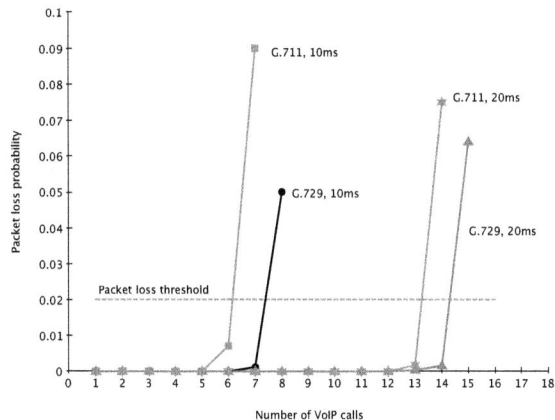

Figure 4: Packet loss probability obtained using equation (34) for a G.729 and a G.711 voice codec with 10 ms and 20 ms sampling rate, where packets are served by the AC_BE queue at the AP.

In Figs. 5 and 6 we show the packet loss probability at the AP for scenarios 1 and 2. It can be observed that the simulation matches the analytical results well in terms of the number of voice calls the WLAN can support. In some cases there is a one call difference between the analytical results and simulation. This discrepancy is due to the use of the $M/M/1/K$ model rather than a model with periodic arrivals and deterministic service time.

In scenario 1, each call uses a G.711 voice codec with a 10 ms sampling rate, irrespective of its access category at the AP. In Fig. 5 it is shown that for a number of configurations, the observed packet loss exceeds the threshold of $\kappa = 0.02$ (= 2% packet loss). Yet, for the two configurations $S_1(1, 6)$ and $S_1(0, 7)$ the observed packet loss is below that threshold, hence increasing the number of voice calls a WLAN can support. This increase of voice capacity is because of a) several calls are transferred to the high priority queue, thus reducing the queue utilization of AC_BE, and b) calls served by AC_VO have an increased frequency with which they can attempt to access the channel, thus maintaining a lower queue utilization compared to AC_BE with the same number of calls. However, even if all calls are served by the AC_VO queue, the maximum number of calls in this scenario is limited to 7.

In scenario 2, several VoIP user switch to the lower quality G.729 voice codec, however, the sampling rate is set equal to 10 ms for calls served by both access categories. Even though the payload size of a G.729 voice packet is much smaller than the payload of a G.711 voice packet, the results shown are comparable to those in scenario 1. This is because the sampling rate for all calls in both scenarios is equal and fixed to 10 ms. Thus an equal number of channel accesses are required to transmit the packets, irrespective of the codec used. The difference in payload size has only a marginal effect, as shown for configuration $S_1(2, 5)$. In scenario 1 the observed packet loss (analytical) is above the threshold, whereas in scenario 2 this is not the case for the

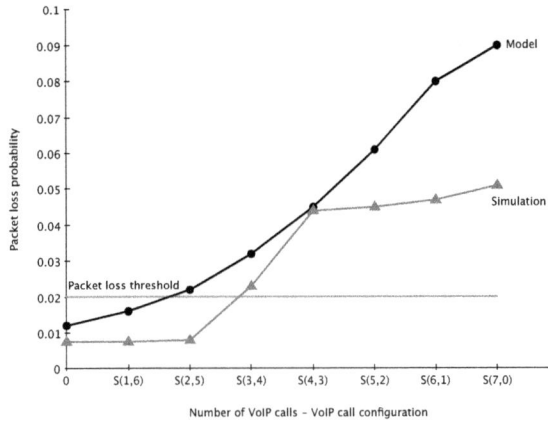

Figure 5: Packet loss probability at the AP for scenario 1 obtained using (34) and NS-2 simulation

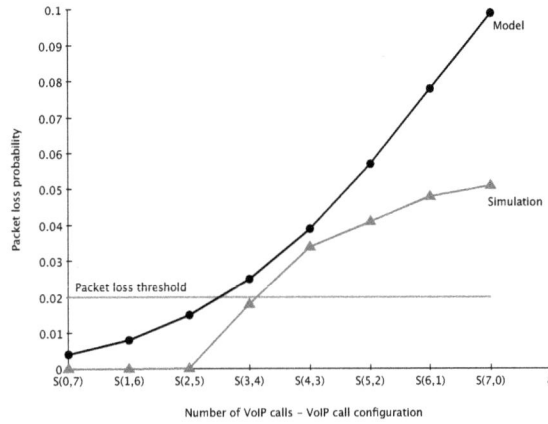

Figure 6: Packet loss probability at the AP for scenario 2 obtained using (34) and NS-2 simulation

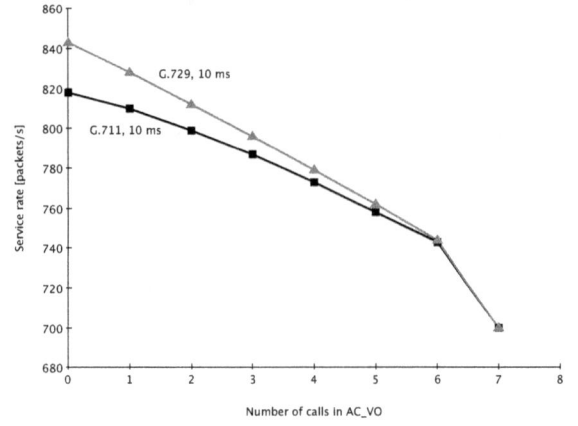

Figure 7: Service rate of he AP when a G.711 or a G.729 voice codec is used with a 10 ms sampling rate and calls are served by AC_VO

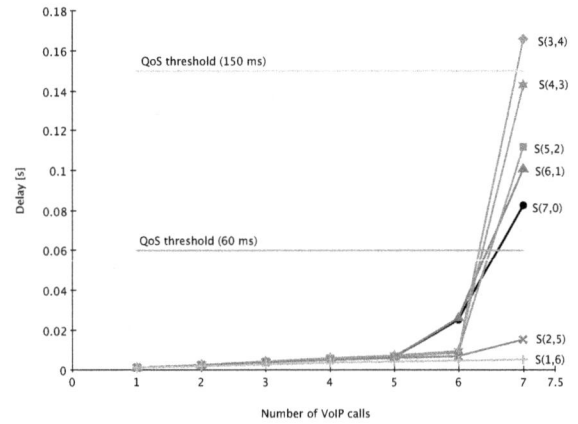

Figure 8: Experienced delay of voice calls in the the AC_BE queue for scenario 1 (NS-2 simulation)

same configuration. This is because the G.729 voice packets have a smaller payload size. This reduces the average packet service time of a packet, which results in an increased service rate, as shown in Fig. 7.

Even though the packet loss at the AP is reduced as the number of AC_VO calls increases, the delay for AC_BE calls is increasing, as shown in Fig. 8. This increase in delay is because the AC_BE calls have to wait an extended period of time before gaining access to the channel. This increased delay is caused by a) the number of calls in AC_VO with its higher channel access frequency, and b) internal collisions. Note that the experienced delay for AC_BE calls in scenario 2 is equivalent to scenario 1 and is thus omitted.

The experienced packet loss and delay at the AP is also reflected in the measured user-perceived voice call quality, obtained using the ITU-T E-model. The E-model defines a measure of call quality called the R-value. The R-value is selected from a range of 0 to 100, where 0 represents the lowest and 100 the highest quality. As shown in Table 3, in ideal conditions, a G.711 voice codec has an *excellent* voice call quality with an R-value of 93, whereas a G.729 voice codec can only maintain a *good* quality ($R = 84$).

As shown in Table 4, the G.711 voice calls in the best

effort access category can maintain an "excellent" level of quality ($R = 93$) as long as there is only a light load in the WLAN. Once the WLAN reaches saturation, e.g. 6 or 7 calls, the voice call quality of standard voice calls is severely reduced. For example, the experienced delay and packet loss for configuration $S_1(7,0)$ has an impact on the voice quality such that the overall quality is considered "*bad*" ($R = 52$). It is shown that for scenario 1 and 2 there exists a configuration ($S_{1,2}(2,5)$) with which calls in either access categories can maintain a "good" or "excellent" voice call quality, depending on the codec used (marked **bold** in Table 4). Note that irrespective of the codec used, the user perceived voice quality is maximum for all users who switch to a new codec setting. This shows that our proposed dynamic codec with priority scheme allows users to maintain a high level of quality when there is a high level of contention in the WLAN (i.e. the WLAN reaches saturation).

In the previous two scenarios VoIP users switch to a lower quality voice codec without changing the sampling rate. In the following two scenarios we demonstrate the effect of a sampling rate change on the observed packet loss, the delay as well as the user perceived call quality.

Table 3: Voice quality level and R-values of the ITU E-model

R-value	Quality level
90	Excellent
80	Good
70	Fair
60	Poor
50	Bad

Table 4: ITU E-model R-value for different VoIP call configurations (Scenario 1 and 2)

$S(\alpha N,(1-\alpha)N)$	AC	Total number of VoIP calls						
		1	2	3	4	5	6	7
$S_1(7,0)$	BE	93	93	93	93	93	84	52
	VO	-	-	-	-	-	-	-
$S_1(6,1)$	BE	93	93	93	93	93	83	49
	VO	-	93	93	93	93	93	93
$S_1(5,2)$	BE	93	93	93	93	93	93	45
	VO	-	-	93	93	93	93	93
$S_1(4,3)$	BE	93	93	93	93	93	93	41
	VO	-	-	-	93	93	93	93
$S_1(3,4)$	BE	93	93	93	93	93	93	43
	VO	-	-	-	93	93	93	93
$S_1(2,5)$	BE	93	93	93	93	93	93	**87**
	VO	-	-	-	93	93	93	**93**
$S_1(1,6)$	BE	93	93	93	93	93	93	**93**
	VO	-	-	-	93	93	93	**93**
$S_1(0,7)$	BE	-	-	-	-	-	-	-
	VO	93	93	93	93	93	93	93
$S_2(7,0)$	BE	93	93	93	93	93	84	52
	VO	-	-	-	-	-	-	-
$S_2(6,1)$	BE	93	93	93	93		93	49
	VO	-	84	84		84	84	84
$S_2(5,2)$	BE	93	93	93	93	93	93	45
	VO	-	-	84	84	84	84	84
$S_2(4,3)$	BE	93	93	93	93	93	93	41
	VO	-	-	-	84	84	84	84
$S_2(3,4)$	BE	93	93	93	93	93	93	43
	VO	-	-	-	84	84	84	84
$S_2(2,5)$	BE	93	93	93	93	93	93	**87**
	VO	-	-	-	84	84	84	84
$S_2(1,6)$	BE	93	93	93	93	93	93	**93**
	VO	-	-	-	84	84	84	84
$S_2(0,7)$	BE	-	-	-	-	-	-	-
	VO	84	84	84	84	84	84	84

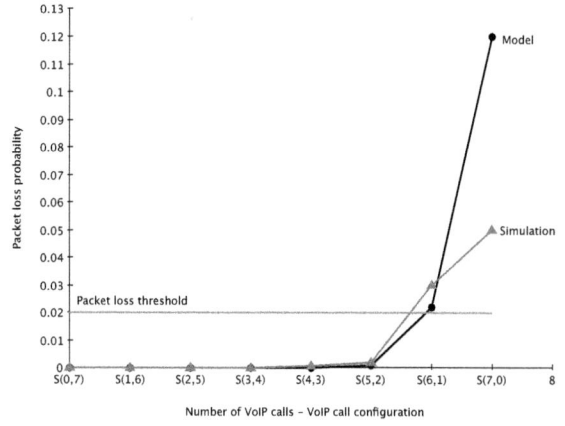

Figure 9: Packet loss probability at the AP for scenario 3 obtained using (34) and NS-2 simulation

load size can be neglected, and that the sampling rate has a higher impact on the voice capacity.

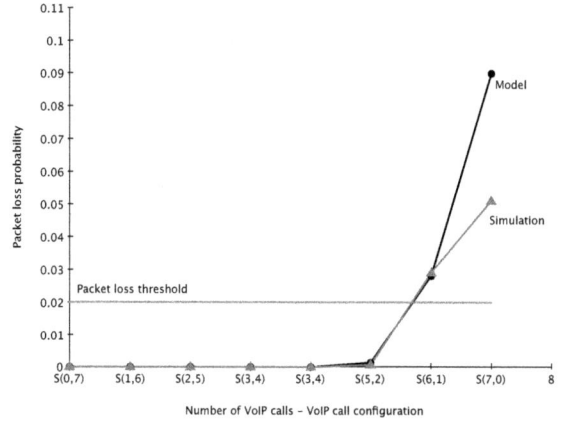

Figure 10: Packet loss probability at the AP for scenario 4 obtained using (34) and NS-2 simulation

In Fig. 9 we show the packet loss probability at the AP for scenario 3. In this scenario all calls use a G.711 voice codec. However, all calls served by the AC_BE queue use a 10 ms sampling rate, while calls served by the AC_VO queue use a 20 ms sampling rate. As shown, the observed packet loss at the AP is significantly reduced if a single user switches to a different codec sampling rate. Observe that there is no loss if at least two user adjust their codec sampling rate. This is because the packet arrival rate at the AV_VO queue (λ^*) is half of the arrival rate at the AC_BE queue (λ). As a result, the lower arrival rate reduces the overall contention in the WLAN, which subsequently improves the voice capacity.

The observed packet loss at the AP for scenario 4 is shown in Fig. 10. In this scenario, a VoIP user who is willing to switch to a lower quality codec will switch to a G.729 voice codec with a 20 ms sampling rate. As shown, in this scenario, there is no packet loss if a least two users adapt their voice codec. The results show that the difference in pay-

The downlink delay for calls served by the AC_BE queue in scenario 3 is shown in Fig. 11. It can be seen that the delay for the configurations $S(7,0)$ and $S(6,1)$ exceeds the delay bound of 60 ms, while the delay for all other VoIP call configurations is well below the threshold. This is because the change in sampling rate of at least two calls is sufficient to significantly reduce the congestion in the WLAN.

The reduced contention on the channel, and therefore the reduced packet loss and delay is also reflected in the voice call quality measurement, given in Table 5. It can be observed, that only for the configurations $S_i(7,0)$ and $S_i(6,1), i \in \{3,4\}$ the voice calls of the lower priority access category experience a degraded voice call quality ("bad") when the WLAN becomes saturated (marked **bold** in Table 5). The voice calls in the higher priority access category, however, can maintain a high voice quality in all scenarios.

In Fig. 12 we show the observed packet loss at the AP when several users switch to the low quality G.723 voice codec (scenario 5). The G.723 voice codec supports two different bit rates, 5.3 kbps and 6.3 kbps. In this scenario the 5.3 kbps bit rate was used, hence the codec has a sampling

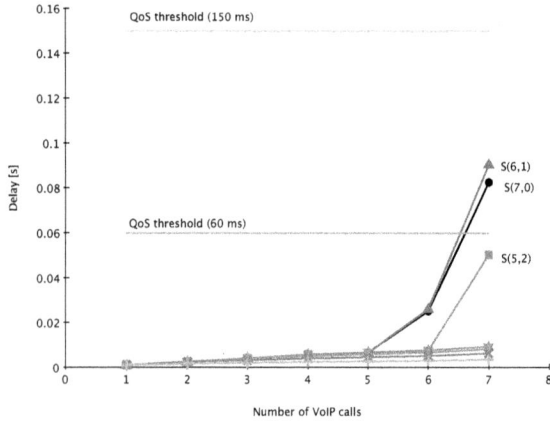

Figure 11: Experienced delay of voice calls in the the AC_BE queue for scenario 3 (NS-2 simulation)

rate of 30 ms with a voice payload size of 20 bytes. Note that the voice call quality for this codec is low. The maximum R-value for this codec is $R = 79$, and as such, the user perceived call quality is only *fair* to *good*. Observe that only a single user needs to switch to this low quality codec, before the packet loss at the AP drops below the threshold of 2%. Even though the payload size of a G.723 voice packet is equivalent to a G.729 voice packet (20 ms sampling rate), the results emphasize that the sampling rate of a voice codec is an important factor for the maximum number of voice calls a WLAN can support. Note that the delay in this scenario is equivalent to the one shown for scenario 4 and is thus omitted.

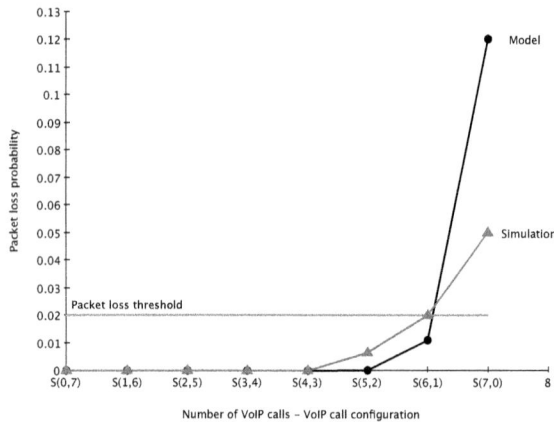

Figure 12: Packet loss probability at the AP for scenario 5

As we have shown, our proposed scheme allows users who are willing to adjust their codec parameter to maintain their call with a lower quality voice codec. Even if there are several users willing to use a lower quality voice codec, the total number of voice calls is still limited. Using different combinations for $S_i(\alpha N, (1-\alpha)N), i = 1, ..., 5$ it can be shown that the maximum number of voice calls is reached for the $S_i(0, (1-\alpha)N), i = 1, ...5$ configuration. Thus the maximum number of calls a WLAN can support varies between 6 for a G.711 voice codec with a 10 ms sampling rate and 22 for

Table 5: ITU E-model R-value for different VoIP call configurations (Scenario 2)

$S(\alpha N, (1-\alpha)N)$	AC	Total number of VoIP calls						
		1	2	3	4	5	6	7
$S_3(7,0)$	BE	93	93	93	93	93	83	**50**
	VO	-	-	-	-	-	-	-
$S_3(6,1)$	BE	93	93	93	93	93	93	**62**
	VO	-	93	93	93	93	93	**93**
$S_3(5,2)$	BE	93	93	93	93	93	93	93
	VO	-	-	93	93	93	93	93
$S_3(4,3)$	BE	93	93	93	93	93	93	93
	VO	-	-	-	93	93	93	93
$S_3(3,4)$	BE	93	93	93	93	93	93	93
	VO	-	-	-	93	93	93	93
$S_3(2,5)$	BE	93	93	93	93	93	93	93
	VO	-	-	-	93	93	93	93
$S_3(1,6)$	BE	93	93	93	93	93	93	93
	VO	-	-	-	93	93	93	93
$S_3(0,7)$	BE	-	-	-	-	-	-	-
	VO	93	93	93	93	93	93	93
$S_4(7,0)$	BE	93	93	93	93	93	84	**52**
	VO	-	-	-	-	-	-	-
$S_4(6,1)$	BE	93	93	93	93	93	83	**51**
	VO	-	84	84	84	84	84	**84**
$S_4(5,2)$	BE	93	93	93	93	93	93	93
	VO	-	-	84	84	84	84	84
$S_4(4,3)$	BE	93	93	93	93	93	93	93
	VO	-	-	-	84	84	84	84
$S_4(3,4)$	BE	93	93	93	93	93	93	93
	VO	-	-	-	84	84	84	84
$S_4(2,5)$	BE	93	93	93	93	93	93	93
	VO	-	-	-	84	84	84	84
$S_4(1,6)$	BE	93	93	93	93	93	93	93
	VO	-	-	-	84	84	84	84
$S_4(0,7)$	BE	-	-	-	-	-	-	-
	VO	84	84	84	84	84	84	84

a G.723 voice codec with a 30 ms sampling rate. In Fig. 13 we show the minimum and the maximum number of voice calls that the WLAN can support for our dynamic codec with priority scheme. As shown, a performance gain of between 16% to approximately 200% can be achieved with our proposed dynamic codec with priority scheme. Note that even though the voice capacity can be improved when several users switch to a different codec, the call quality for each individual call is different, depending on the codec used.

4.1 Impact of CW_{min} parameter for the high priority access category

In this section we evaluate the impact of different CW_{min} parameter settings for the higher priority access category on the number of calls a WLAN can support. In the previous section, the contention window size were set according to the voice access category (AC_VO) of the IEEE 802.11e protocol. Here we study if different settings can provide an additional gain. In Figs. 14 and 15 we show the observed packet loss at the AP for different settings of the CW_{min} parameter for scenario 1 and 2. Note that the CW_{max} parameter was adjusted accordingly. It can be seen that for $CW_{min} = 4$, a marginal gain can be achieved. In both scenarios, packet loss already drops below the threshold for the $S_i(3,4)$ VoIP call configuration. This shows that by setting a smaller than default CW_{min} parameter, fewer users have to switch to a lower quality voice codec. The results also show for larger values of CW_{min}, i.e. 16, the observed packet loss

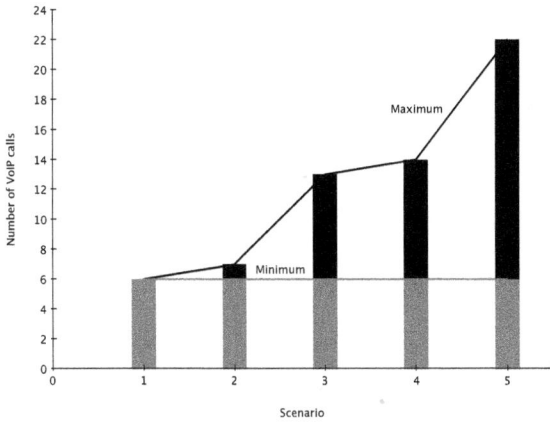

Figure 13: Minimum and maximum number of voice calls for each scenario

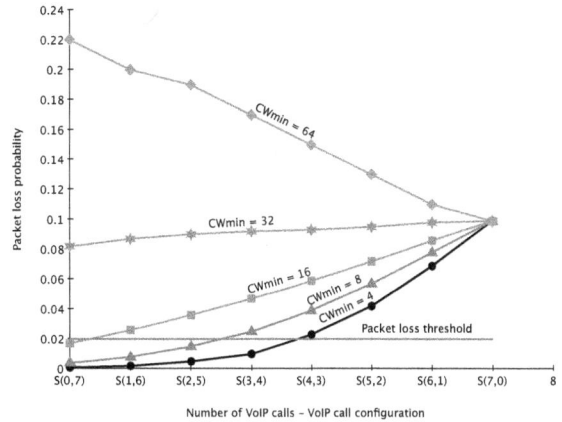

Figure 15: Packet loss at the AP for different values of CW_{min} for AC_VO (scenario 2)

exceeds the threshold for all configurations. This is because a larger than default contention window size increases the average packet service time, and queue utilization resulting in larger packet loss.

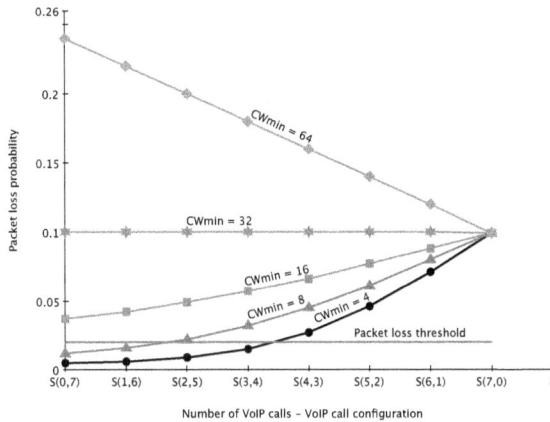

Figure 14: Packet loss at the AP for different values of CW_{min} for AC_VO (scenario 1)

A change in contention window size for scenario 3 and 4 has no significant impact, and the voice capacity is not increased beyond the one shown in the previous section. Even with different values of CW_{min}, only two users are required to adapt their codec, before the packet loss at the AP is below 2%. This shows that the sampling rate of a voice codec has a higher impact on the number of voice calls a WLAN can support, than the setting of the contention window size.

5. CONCLUSION

In this paper, we proposed a novel scheme to exploit a tradeoff between codec quality and priority. In this scheme, users are encouraged to switch to a lower quality codec during periods of high contention and thus enable them to maintain the call. To compensate for the reduction in voice quality, and to give incentive to users to switch to a lower quality codec, a higher priority is given at the AP for those users. As a result of users using a lower quality codec the overall con-

tention is reduced allowing more voice calls to be supported. We have developed a detailed analytical model to demonstrate the benefits gained from the proposed scheme. Our model offers important insights on the behavior of multi-codec voice streams and the impact of the AP internal collisions. We showed that depending on the codec setting, a capacity gain of between 16% and approximately 200% can be achieved. This significant capacity improvement is without compromising the individual call quality. By analyzing the observed packet loss and delay, we also showed, using the ITU-T E-model that in most cases the voice calls can maintain a high level of voice call quality. Specifically, we observe that adjusting the sampling rate has a more profound impact on the voice capacity than changing the payload of the voice packet. Furthermore, results obtained from our analytical model matched closely with simulation in term of the number of voice calls a WLAN can support (i.e. when the loss threshold is not exceeded). We also showed that some priority settings using different contention window values can result in a better performance compared to others, and thus optimal design can be achieved in future work for the proposed dynamic codec with priority scheme.

6. ACKNOWLEDGEMENTS

This work was supported by the Australian Research Council grant DP1095103.

7. REFERENCES

[1] Google Talk. http://www.google.com/talk/.
[2] Skype. https://www.skype.com.
[3] SPEEX: A free codec for free speech. http://www.speex.org/.
[4] Australian Government - Australian Communication and Media Authority. The Australian VoIP Market - The supply and take-up of VoIP in Australia. 2008.
[5] G. Bianchi, T. Vergata, I. Tinnirello, and L. Scalia. Understanding 802.11e Contention-based prioritization mechanisms and their coexistence with legacy 802.11 stations.
[6] L. X. Cai, X. Shen, J. W. Mark, L. Cai, and Y. Xiao. Voice capacity analysis of WLAN with unbalanced

traffic. *IEEE transactions on vehicular technology,* pages 752–761, 2006.

[7] D. Gao, J. Cai, C. H. Foh, C.-T. Lau, and K. N. Ngan. Improving WLAN VoIP capacity through service differentiation. *IEEE Transactions on Vehicular Technology,* 57(1):465–474, January 2008.

[8] S. Harsha, A. Kumar, and V. Sharma. An Analytical Model for the Capacity Estimation of Combined VoIP and TCP File Transfers over EDCA in an IEEE 802.11e WLAN. *Quality of Service, 2006. IWQoS 2006. 14th IEEE International Workshop on,* pages 178–187, June 2006.

[9] S. Harsha, A. Kumar, and V. Sharma. Analytical model for an IEEE 802.11 WLAN using DCF with two types of VoIP calls. *National Communications Conference (NCC) New Delhi,* 2006.

[10] N. Hedge, A. Proutiere, and J. Roberts. Evaluating the voice capacity of 802.11 WLAN under distributed control. *The 14th IEEE workshop on Local and Metropolitan area networks (LANMAN2005),* 2005.

[11] D. Hole and F. Tobagi. Capacity of an IEEE 802.11b wireless LAN supporting VoIP. *Communications, 2004 IEEE International Conference on,* 1:196–201, June 2004.

[12] IEEE. Part 11: Wireless LAN Medium Access Control (MAC) and Physical Layer (PHY) Specification, 1999.

[13] IEEE. Part 11: Wireless LAN Medium Access Control (MAC) and Physical Layer (PHY) Specification, Amendment 8: Medium Access Control (MAC) Quality of Service Enhancements, 2005.

[14] IEEE. Part 11: Wireless LAN Medium Access Control (MAC) and Physical Layer (PHY) Specification, 2007.

[15] ITU-T. G.107: Transmission Systems and Media, Digital Systems and Networks, International telephone connections and circuits - General definitions, The E-model, a computational model for use in transmission planning, March 2005.

[16] ITU-T. G.114: Transmission Systems and Media, Digital Systems and Networks, International telephone connections and circuits - General Recommendations on the transmission quality for an entire international telephone connections - One-way transmission time, May 2005.

[17] L. Kleinrock. *Queueing Systems,* volume 1. John Wiley & Sons, 1975.

[18] R. Kuhn, T. J. Walsh, and S. Fries. Security Considerations for Voice over IP Systems. Technical Report 800-58, National Institute of Standards and Technology - Technology Administration - U.S. Department of Commerce, 2005.

[19] K. Medepalli, P. Gopalakrishnan, D. Famolari, and T. Kodama. Voice capacity of ieee 802.11b, 802.11a and 802.11g wireless lan.

[20] M. Narbutt and M. Davis. Experimental tuning of AIFSN and CWmin parameters to prioritize voice over data transmission in 802.11e WLAN networks. In *IWCMC '07: Proceedings of the 2007 international conference on Wireless communications and mobile computing,* pages 140–145, New York, NY, USA, 2007. ACM.

[21] A. Sfairopoulou, C. Macian, and B. Bellalta. VoIP Codec Adaptation Algorithm in Multirate 802.11 WLANs: Distributed vs. Centralized Performance Comparison. *Lecture Notes in Computer Science,* 4606:52–61, 2007.

[22] S. Shin and H. Schulzrinne. Experimental Measurement of the Capacity for VoIP Traffic in IEEE 802.11 WLANs. *INFOCOM 2007. 26th IEEE International Conference on Computer Communications. IEEE,* pages 2018–2026, May 2007.

[23] K. Stoeckigt and H. Vu. VoIP Capacity Analysis in IEEE 802.11 WLAN. In *Proceedings of the 34th IEEE Conference on Local Computer Networks (LCN2009),* 2009.

[24] O. Tickoo and B. Sikdar. Queueing analysis and delay mitigation in IEEE 802.11 random access MAC based wireless networks. 2:1404–1413 vol.2, March 2004.

[25] K. Vos, S. S. Jensen, and K. V. Soerensen. SiILK Speech Codec, 2009.

[26] S. Wiethoelter, M. Emmelmann, C. Hoene, and A. Wolisz. TKN EDCA Model for ns-2. Technical report, Technische Universitaet Berlin, 2006.

Adaptive Encoding of Zoomable Video Streams based on User Access Pattern

Ngo Quang Minh Khiem, Guntur Ravindra, Wei Tsang Ooi
Department of Computer Science
National University of Singapore
Singapore 117417
E-mail:{nqmkhiem,ravindra,ooiwt}@comp.nus.edu.sg

ABSTRACT

Zoomable video allows users to selectively zoom and pan into regions of interest within the video for viewing at higher resolutions. Such interaction requires dynamic cropping of RoIs on the source video. In this paper, we consider how the bandwidth needed to transmit the RoIs can be reduced by carefully encoding the source video. The key idea is to exploit user access patterns to the RoIs, and encode different regions of the video with different encoding parameters based on the popularity of the region. We show that our encoding method can reduce the expected bandwidth by up to 27%.

Categories and Subject Descriptors: H.5.1 [Multimedia Information Systems]: Video H.4.3 [Communications Applications]:Video Streaming

General Terms: Algorithms, Design, Experimentation, Performance

Keywords: Zoomable Video, Region-of-Interest Streaming, Monolithic Streaming, Tile Streaming, Optimal Tiling, Bandwidth Efficient, Encoding

1. INTRODUCTION

Two opposing trends in digital video capture and display have emerged. On one hand, consumers are increasingly capable of capturing high resolution digital video using off-the-shelf cameras. On the other hand, it is increasingly common for consumers to play back digital video on portable devices with limited screen size and resolution. Such impedance mismatch between captured and displayed video resolutions leads to introduction of zoom and pan as two new interaction primitives during video playback.

We are interested in enabling zoom and pan interaction in a video streaming setting, a paradigm we call *zoomable video streaming*. A video server stores multiple high resolution videos. Remote clients can request for these videos to be transmitted for playback at a smaller resolution. A lower resolution version of the video is streamed to the client for playback. The client may zoom into a region of interest (RoI) in a video, i.e., to view a cropped region in the video at a high resolution. The RoI coordinates are sent to the server. The server then sends the RoI at a higher resolution to the client for playback. The client may also pan around the video, i.e., to view a different region but at the same resolution. The server in this case crops a different RoI and streams the RoI to the client.

There are several ways the server can support dynamic cropping of RoIs at different resolutions. The server can pre-compute different versions of the same video at different resolutions and switch between these different versions when different zoom levels are requested. This approach is known as *bitstream switching*. Alternatively, scalable video coding can be used to encode the video at different resolutions.

The key challenge for zoomable video streaming is dynamic cropping of RoI, which can be implemented in a few ways. A naive way is to pre-encode each possible RoI as an independent video stream and serve the requested RoI to the client when requested. Such approach results in huge storage requirements. One could reduce the pre-encoded RoIs to only the popular ones, but this reduces the flexibilities of user interactions. The other naive method is to encode the RoI on the fly. The video server crops the RoI from the video with appropriate resolution, encodes the RoI into a video stream, and transmits. Such implementation, while is flexible enough to support any RoI, is not scalable to large number of clients.

We have previously [16] proposed two scalable schemes in which the server only encodes the video once, but can flexibly support multiple clients with any RoI. Our first scheme is called *tiled streaming*. Tiled streaming divides each video frame into a grid of tiles, and encodes each tile as an independent video stream, called tiled stream. When an RoI is requested, the server sends the tile streams that overlaps with the RoIs. Figure 1 illustrates how tiled streaming works.

The second scheme we proposed is called *monolithic streaming*. Here, each video is encoded as a single monolithic video. When the server needs to send an RoI, the server sends all macroblocks that overlap with the RoI, as well any other macroblocks that are needed in order to decode the macroblocks in the RoI. The server needs to parse through the encoded video and build a data structure that identifies the dependencies (including motion vector dependencies and VLC dependencies) among the macroblocks. This data structure is looked up during streaming to decide whether a

MMSys'11, February 23–25, 2011, San Jose, California, USA.
Copyright 2011 ACM 978-1-4503-0517-4/11/02 ...$10.00.

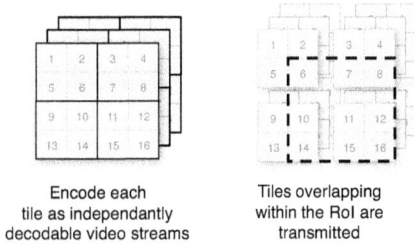

Figure 1: Tiled Streaming. Macroblocks at the same position in different frames are grouped into tiles. Each tile is independently encoded and thus can be independently decoded. Tiles overlapping with the requested RoI are sent.

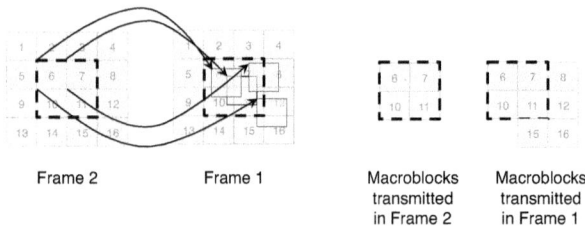

Figure 2: Monolithic Streaming. Macroblocks belonging to the RoI (box with dash line) are sent, along with any other macroblocks outside of the RoI that are dependent (curved arrows) on by macroblocks in the RoI in subsequent frames. We show only motion vector dependencies for simplicity.

macroblock needs to be sent given the current RoI. Figure 2 illustrates the monolithic streaming scheme.

Unlike the naive schemes, however, both monolithic streaming and tiled streaming pay the price of sending additional bits outside the RoI that are not displayed by client. In the case of tiled streaming, region of a tile that falls outside of RoI will not be displayed, but is sent anyway to the clients. To reduce the wasted bits, one can reduce the dimension of the tiles. But since each tile is encoded independently, small tiles lead to lower compression ratio, increasing the number of bits needed for the RoI. In the case of monolithic streaming, macroblocks outside of the RoI that are depended upon (either directly or indirectly) by the macroblocks inside the RoI are sent. To reduce these macroblocks, we can reduce the amount of dependencies in the video stream by tuning the encoding parameters (such as motion vector search range and number of B-frames). Reducing dependencies, however, lead to lower compression ratio, and increases the number of bits needed for the macroblocks in the RoI. Our previous paper has carefully study the trade-offs in different encoding parameters and tile sizes for these two schemes [16].

This paper presents our investigation into how we further reduce the wasted bits when transmitting an RoI. We exploit the fact that not every possible RoI is equally interesting to the users – some RoIs are requested more frequently than others. For instance, in a lecture video, the RoIs centering on either the lecturer or the projector display tends to be more popular. Our user study on viewing behavior [3] has revealed that the user interest tends to be consistent, i.e., the

access frequency to the RoIs is highly skewed and popular regions are spatially clustered.

Given historical traces of how users access the RoIs, we can adapt the encoding parameters for both tiled streaming and monolithic streaming such that, more popular RoIs (i.e., RoIs with higher probability of being requested) require fewer bits to transmit. As a result we can expect that the *expected* bandwidth needed to transmit the RoIs will be reduced. Specifically, we can adapt the motion vector search range for monolithic streaming, to reduce the expected amount of motion vector dependencies from within an RoI to outside of RoI and to increase the expected amount of motion vector dependencies within an RoI. For tiled streaming, we adapt the tile size, such that the tiles that overlap with the RoIs have a smaller region falling outside of these RoIs. Although the two approaches seem to be unrelated, both of them rely on a common technique, namely, to restrict motion search range by different amount for every macroblock in the video.

We evaluate our proposed approaches using user access patterns that we have collected on four standard test video sequences exhibiting different scene complexity and motion. We find that by adapting the motion vector search range of monolithic streams, we can reduce the expected bandwidth by up to 21%; by adapting the tile size in tiled streams, we can reduce the expected bandwidth by up to 27%. Our results are encouraging and shows the efficacy of our approach.

We organize the rest of the paper into six sections. Section 2 discusses the existing literature on encoding videos with RoIs. Section 3 describes a web-based zoomable video system and how we obtained access patterns from users. Section 4 presents the exploitation of user access pattern to adapt the tile size for tiled streaming. Section 5 presents how we exploit the user access pattern to reduce the expected bandwidth when monolithic streaming is used to transmit RoIs. We evaluate both schemes and present our results in Section 6. Finally, we conclude in Section 7.

2. RELATED WORK

There has been significant study in the field of what constitutes a RoI, its characteristics, and how users interact in the context of video and image viewing [11, 18, 20, 15, 4]. We focus this related work section on issues related to encoding of videos with considerations to RoIs.

In the context of zoomable video streaming, bitstream switching has been proposed as a possible solution to multi-resolution representation [6, 9, 8]. Video is encoded at multiple resolutions, with the lowest resolution being streamed by default. Users can zoom into the video by selecting a region from the low resolution video. The corresponding region is cropped from a higher resolution video and transmitted. In essence, the video server switches between (and crops from) different resolution videos when users zoom in and out.

Different approaches have been proposed to encode videos with bit-stream switching. In the context of viewing a selected RoI from a high-resolution panoramic video stream [6], a grid-based approach is proposed. The panoramic view is broken into rectangular tiles of size 512×512 pixels, where each tile is an independently decodable entity. All tiles falling within and intersecting with the RoI boundary are streamed. Tiling creates independence among regions as unnecessary tiles can be dropped and new tiles included into the scene as and when the RoI changes.

A practical approach to adaptive bit rate streaming of panoramic video with tiling is proposed recently in [8]. The proposed approach exploits the fact that MPEG4 multi-view coding standard provides inherent synchronization among tiles when tiles are encoded as separate streams. Video frames are broken into tiles, and each tile is encoded as a separate stream at three different qualities. The lowest resolution stream along with meta-data representing the tile identifiers is streamed. The viewer can select a region, and tiles corresponding to that region are selected and streamed from the highest resolution panoramic video. Each selected tile from the panoramic stream is selected at a quality matching available bandwidth. This approach supports only two resolutions, but handles cropping with bit rate scaling well.

In the context of H.264 video, special frames [9], called SI and SP frames, can be used for bit-stream switching. These frames allow switching between video streams encoded with different parameters at non-GoP boundaries. This feature is possible only when the two video streams are of a single video sequence. The SP frames are transmitted whenever there is a need to switch the bit-stream. In the context of zoomable video, SP frames can be transmitted when the zoom level of the RoI changes. The display area of the RoI itself is handled by RoI cropping.

Another approach to efficiently encode videos in the context of zoomable video using scalable video, is to use background extraction [14]. In this approach, considering the case where the camera is static, the authors construct an intracoded *background frame* using temporal median operator. There are two reference choices for inter-coded blocks: either refer to the background frame or upsampled base-layer. Motion-compensated prediction is limited to long-term memory motion-compensated prediction only, while motion-compensation among consecutive frames is avoided.

As RoI-based streaming involves cropping rectangular regions, Feng et al. suggested an encoding approach that breaks the frame into tiles by constraining motion estimation [5] to within the tile area. All tiles falling within the RoI or intersecting with the RoI boundary are selected for streaming. This approach allows composition of rectangular RoIs of any dimension. An important issue to be addressed in this approach is the size of the tile and the impact of the size on bandwidth efficiency. In the context of H.264 encoding, Mavlankar et al. showed that using a slice (tile) of dimension 4×4 macroblocks [13] is optimal for RoI cropping.

The related work discussed above changes motion compensation in video encoding to allow for random access to RoIs. This approach often sacrifices compression efficiency, increasing file size and transmission bandwidth. To further reduce the bandwidth, methods that vary the quantization scale based on the RoIs have been proposed. The idea is simple: non-RoI areas are accessed less often and thus can be encoded with bigger quantization scale and lower quality.

One such proposal exploits flexible macroblock ordering (FMO) [19] in H.264 video streams. RoIs are encoded as single FMO and all macroblocks falling within this FMO are quantized using a fixed quantization scale. Every time the RoI changes, FMO is redefined for the new RoI. Macroblocks falling outside the FMO use a quantization scale that results in significantly lower bit allocation for this region. The quantization scale for the FMO region is determined by empirical evaluation. Although the bandwidth of the video reduces and the PSNR for the RoI increases, this approach results in an abrupt quality transition between RoI and non-RoI regions.

To handle the issue of abrupt quality transition, Huang and Lin propose a transition region [7], encoded with a quantization scale different from the RoI region and the non-RoI region. A more formal way to choose quantization scale while handling the case where a RoI can have varying degree of viewership is described by Lai et al. [10]. A rate-distortion optimization formulation is used to determine the quantization scale. All macroblocks in a RoI have a viewership weight assigned. One can view this weight as an access probability. The distortion metric for each macroblock is a product of the weight, variance in the macroblock region with respect to the reference, and exponentially weighted bit rate for that macroblock.

All quantization-scale based approaches attempt to maintain a fixed bit rate while improving upon the PSNR. Nevertheless, Reingold and Loschky [17] have shown that continued perceptual variations caused by changing quality in RoI-based encoding results in perceptual distraction. Loschky and Wolverton also [12] found that using a higher quality encoding at the point of gaze/attention when compared to the peripheral areas, results in reduced saliency when users try to identify other RoIs. Besides distraction, another problem with quantization scale-based rate-distortion optimization is that of reduced quality when users select a non-RoI region. These approaches assume that once a RoI is defined users are likely to access that RoI alone. This is not true in interactive RoI access systems and in systems where there can be multiple RoIs all of which cannot be guessed apriori.

Our approach in this paper differs from the two major approaches above, and can be viewed as a loose hybrid of the two approaches. On one hand, we play with the motion compensation component of video encoding by defining a per-macroblock motion vector search range for monolithic streaming, and by constraining motion vectors to within a tile for tiled streaming. On the other hand, we distinguish between popular RoI and non-popular RoIs, and encode them differently. Our approach, however, can encode each region with the same quality, avoiding distraction caused by variations in perceptual quality.

3. ROI ACCESS PATTERNS

In this section, we describe a web-based system that was used to log users' interaction with a zoomable video. The interaction log provides us with a map of RoI accesses along with the access frequency, from which we model the probability of access of each macroblock.

The web-based system consists of a HTML5 interface that provides users with abilities to zoom and pan in a video during playback. An interaction area displays the video corresponding to the user's current region-of-interest (RoI) in a window of size 320×192 pixels. The entire video frame is visible in a smaller 160×90 pixel thumbnail display, showing the context of the RoI. One can use the arrow buttons on the keyboard to pan, or zoom/unzoom using the $(+,-)$ buttons. The mouse can also be used to zoom/unzoom using the scroll wheel, or pan by clicking and dragging.

The highest resolution video has a resolution of 1920×1080, from which six levels of zooming (0-5) corresponding to six bitstreams with different resolutions are derived. At Level 0, users see the whole video at 320×192 resolution. At higher zoom level, the RoI is cropped and scaled down to 320×192

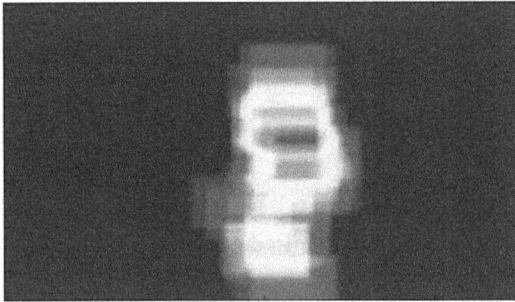

Figure 3: RoI Access Pattern

for display. All interactions are done locally at the client after the original video is downloaded. Thus, the response time for zooming and panning is negligible as the data to display is already available at the client.

We recorded four videos at resolution of 1920×1080, consisting of magic shows and gymnastic competitions. User's interactions with these videos were logged as *sessions*. A session consists of a sequence of interaction activity on a video by a user, starting from the time the user loads the video to the time the user leaves the page. There were a total of 53 users whose interactions were logged over a period of two weeks, with a total of 11183 interaction events (zoom, pan, play, and stop), averaging about 13 users per video. Each video was seen to have between 800-1300 RoI changes, out of which about 66-375 RoI transitions are at zoom level 5. Once users zoom into the video (an RoI transition) they tend to view the video at that zoom level for consecutive frames.

The frequency of access of a RoI is computed as the number of times the RoI has been viewed by all users. The RoI is allowed to change only at a GoP boundary, and depending on motion and user interest, RoIs can be spread about in a frame. Figure 3 shows one such access pattern. The figure shows that many RoIs are clustered around specific regions. The bright red regions have a higher probability of access when compared to the paler regions. The probability of access of a RoI is computed as the normalized frequency of occurrence of the RoI in a GoP. Hence, the probability of access of a region/macroblock is the sum of probabilities of all the RoIs that the region/macroblock is a part of.

4. ADAPTIVE TILING

4.1 Tiled Streaming

Tiled streaming is one of the RoI streaming methods we introduced in [16]. It is inspired by how Web-based map services work, where huge maps are divided into smaller grids of images. Only the images that overlap with the RoI are sent to users for display. In the context of RoI streaming, video frames are divided into a grid of tiles. Tiles of the same (x, y) co-ordinates from all frames in a GoP are grouped together and encoded to form an independent tiled stream. Motion vectors and other dependencies are constrained to within the tile area. For each RoI requested, the server transmits a minimal set of tiled streams that cover the RoI. As such, tiled streaming introduces simplicity at the server side. Besides, publish-subscribe paradigm can be applied

to this method. The server can multicast each tiled stream to a channel. A client that is interested in some RoI may subscribe to channels which have tiles necessary for the decoding that RoI.

One major drawback of tiled streaming is that data outside the RoI may be transmitted to users. Since the RoI is not always aligned with tile boundaries, some tiles may partially overlap with the RoI. These tiles are transmitted in whole and hence, some bandwidth is wasted in transmitting regions outside the RoI. Our previous study [16] has shown that tile size is one of the most influential factors to the performance of tiled streaming in terms of compression and bandwidth efficiency. Small tile size helps reduce bandwidth wastage but reduces compression efficiency due to the fact that motion estimation is constrained within a tile. On the contrary, large tile size helps achieve better compression efficiency but leads to more redundant data being transmitted for partially overlapped tiles.

We previously limited our study to *regular tiling*, i.e., covering the frames with tiles of the same size (except at the boundary of the frames). Removing this limitation, by allowing tiles of different sizes, can further reduce the transmission bandwidth of RoIs. To get an intuition of why this is the case, consider the following simple scenario, where every user is interested in viewing the same RoI. Assume that we start with a regular tiling. All tiles that completely fall inside the RoI can be merged into a single larger tile. Since larger tiles have better compression efficiency, the overall bandwidth needed to transmit the RoI reduces. Further, tiles at the boundary of the RoI that partially overlap with the RoI can be split into smaller tiles. This reduces the area of the region from outside of RoIs that has to be sent. Note that in this case, splitting a larger tile into smaller ones is not always beneficial, since smaller tiles may consume more bandwidth due to reduced compression efficiency.

We now extend the above extreme case to a more general case, where different users may be interested in viewing different RoIs. Now, each macroblock has some probability of belonging to an RoI. Suppose that the access probability to each macroblock is known, we would like to find the best way to tile the video such that the expected bandwidth to transmit the set of RoIs is minimum. We refer to this problem as Adaptive Tiling Problem. The formulation of this problem is discussed below.

4.2 The Adaptive Tiling Problem

In this section, we will formally describe the adaptive tiling problem studied in our paper as well as some definitions and notations related to the problem.

We abstract the problem of tiling a video into tiling of rectangles. A rectangle is always identified by its top-left coordinates (x, y) and its width and height (w, h), where $x, y, w, h \in \mathbb{Z}$. We write a rectangle r as (x, y, w, h). A rectangle r_i is *contained* in another rectangle r_j if and only if the four corners of r_i are either on or within the boundary of r_j. We write $r_i \sqsubseteq r_j$ if r_i is contained in r_j. We say $r_i \cap r_j \neq \phi$ if the rectangles r_i and r_j overlap.

We denote the rectangle that we are interested in *tiling* as R. A tile map T of R consists of a set of non-overlapping rectangles, called *tiles* and denoted $t_1, t_2, \ldots t_n$, with each of t_i contained in R and collectively covering exactly R. Each tile t is assigned a cost $c(t)$, which is given by a cost function c.

The *heat map* for a rectangle R is a function p that maps any rectangle r contained in R to a non-negative real number $p(r)$. Given an rectangle r, we denote $\Omega(r, T)$ as a set of tiles in T that overlap with r.

Adaptive Tiling Problem: Given a rectangle R, a heat map function p, a cost function c, find a tile map $T(R)$ such that

$$\sum_{r \sqsubseteq R} p(r) \sum_{t \in \Omega(r,T)} c(t) \qquad (1)$$

is minimized.

It can be shown that Expression 1 is equivalent to

$$\sum_{t \in T(R)} c(t) \sum_{r \sqsubseteq R, r \cap t \neq \emptyset} p(r) \qquad (2)$$

Proof: Let the expression in 1 be E. Then,

$$E = \sum_{r \sqsubseteq R} \sum_{t \in T} c(t) f_t(r) \qquad (3)$$

$$where\ f_t(r) = \begin{cases} p(r) & \text{if } t \in \Omega(r,T) \\ 0 & \text{if } t \notin \Omega(r,T) \end{cases}$$

$$\Rightarrow E = \sum_{t \in T} c(t) \sum_{r \sqsubseteq R} f_t(r)$$

$$\Rightarrow E = \sum_{t \in T} c(t) \sum_{r \sqsubseteq R, r \cap t \neq \emptyset} p(r) \text{ (Shown)}$$

The relationship between the above formulation and adaptive tiling for zoomable video streaming is as follows: The rectangle R is the video frame. The heat map function p maps an RoI to its access probability. The cost function is the compressed size (in bytes) of the tile. Expression 1 and 2 therefore compute the expected amount of data transmitted for an RoI. Equivalently, our goal is to minimize the *expected data rate* or *expected bandwidth*. Note that in adaptive tiling, we are given a set of RoIs and its access probability, while Expression 1 sums over all possible rectangles contained in the video frames. These two are equivalent if we set $p(r)$ to 0 for any r that is not an RoI (i.e., r has a different dimension than an RoI).

4.3 A Greedy Heuristic

Finding the optimal tile map that minimizes the expected bandwidth is likely to be NP-complete. We therefore use a greedy heuristic to find a tile map that reduces the expected bandwidth. We present our heuristic in this section.

Let's first define a few more notations and terms. Given two tiles $t_i = (x_i, y_i, w_i, h_i)$ and $t_j = (x_j, y_j, w_j, h_j)$, t_j is said to be *right neighbor* of t_i if $x_i + w_i = x_j$ and $y_j \leq y_i \leq y_j + h_j - 1$. t_i is *right mergeable* with its right neighbor t_j if $y_i = y_j$ and $h_i = h_j$. We similarly define *bottom neighbor* and *bottom mergeable*.

We can merge a tile (x, y, w, h) with its right mergeable neighbor (x', y, w', h), creating a new tile $(x, y, w + w', h)$. Similarly, we can merge a tile (x, y, w, h) with its bottom mergeable neighbor (x, y', w, h'), forming a new tile $(x, y, w, h + h')$.

Figure 4(a) shows some examples of neighbors and mergeable neighbors. t_1 has bottom neighbors t_3 and t_4 and right neighbors t_5. t_2 is not a right neighbor of t_1. Only t_3 and t_4

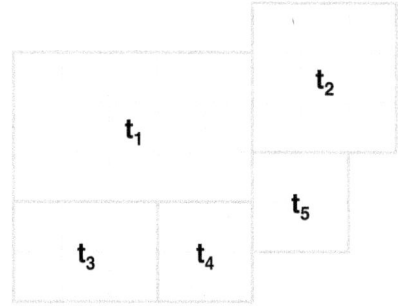

(a) Example of neighbors and mergeable neighbors.

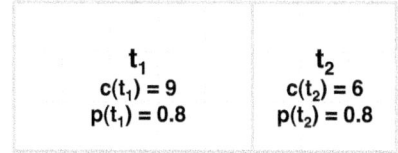

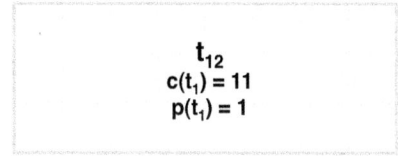

(b) Example of a good merge.

Figure 4: Example of Neighbors and Merge Conditions

are right mergeable. After merging, however, t_1 is bottom mergeable with the merged tile.

We abuse the notation of heat map function p for the *access probability $p(t)$* of a tile t. *Access probability* of a tile t is the sum of access probabilities of RoIs overlap with t. Accordingly, Expression 2 can be written as:

$$\sum_{t \in T} c(t)p(t) \qquad (4)$$

We are using Expression 4 in our algorithm to compute the expected bandwidth. We say that two tiles t_i and t_j form a *good merge* if the new tile t_k formed by merging t_i and t_j helps reduce expected bandwidth, i.e.,

$$p(t_i)c(t_i) + p(t_j)c(t_j) \geq p(t_k)c(t_k) \qquad (5)$$

Note that the compressed size of the new tile stream $c(t_k)$ is likely to reduce ($c(t_k) \leq c(t_i)+c(t_j)$), while its access probability $p(t_k)$ may increase ($p(t_k) \geq p(t_i) + p(t_j)$). As such, even if the expected data rate remains the same, merging is performed if it helps to reduce size of the newly formed tiled stream. Figure 4(b) shows an example of a good merge.

Given the above introduction, we are now ready to present our heuristic. We start with a tile map consisting of regular 1×1 tiles. The idea underlying our heuristic is to repeatedly merge a tile with its neighbor (right or bottom neighbors) as long as it is a good merge (and update the tile map with the merged tile). This step is repeated for each tile in the tile map until no good merge is possible. In our algorithm, we encode that tile on the fly to obtain the compressed size of a tile. This helps our algorithm make better decision when growing tile.

The pseudocode to merge a tile with its neighbors is shown in Algorithm 1. The methods RIGHT and BOTTOM returns the right- and bottom-mergeable neighbors of a tile respectively, if such neighbor exists. The methods IsMERGEABLE checks if the conditions for mergeable are satisfied. Finally, the method TRYMERGE checks if the given tiles form a good merge. If so, it merges the tiles, updates the tile map, and returns the reduction in the expected bandwidth due to the merge. Otherwise, it returns 0. Algorithm 1 does not show error handling cases for simplicity.

The method, called GROW, basically considers first the basic cases of merging with the right neighbor and bottom neighbor. Then it checks if there is a diagonal neighbor (bottom neighbor of right neighbor) that is mergeable with both the tile's right neighbor and bottom neighbor. If so, this means that the tile can potentially merge with its right, bottom, and diagonal neighbor to form a larger tile. Here, the method tries all possible merging configurations. Finally, it picks the configuration that maximizes the reduction in expected bandwidth, and updates the tile map accordingly.

The method GROW is applied for every tile in the tile map to further reduce expected bandwidth. Tiles are sequentially traversed in the increasing order of y-coordinate followed by x-coordinate of their top-left corners. If a tile is merged with its neighbors at the end of GROW, this method is again applied for the newly-formed tile to greedily grow it further if possible. Otherwise, the next tile will be traversed. After the last tile has been reached, more passes are made through the tile map to find other possible merges until no further reduction in expected bandwidth is achieved. This step is necessary since after every loop, the tile configuration changes, resulting new mergeable neighbors.

Algorithm 1 GROW(tile t, tile map T)

1: {create some temp tile maps}
2: $T_h \leftarrow T$
3: $T_v \leftarrow T$
4: $T_{hv} \leftarrow T$
5: {try to merge with right neighbor}
6: $t_r \leftarrow$ RIGHT(t)
7: $c_h \leftarrow$ TRYMERGE(t, t_r, T_h)
8: {try to merge with bottom neighbor}
9: $t_b \leftarrow$ BOTTOM(t)
10: $c_v \leftarrow$ TRYMERGE(t, t_b, T_v)
11: **if** IsMERGEABLE(t, t_r) and IsMERGEABLE(t, t_b) **then**
12: $\quad t_d \leftarrow$ BOTTOM(RIGHT(t))
13: $\quad$ **if** IsMERGEABLE(t_r, t_d) and IsMERGEABLE(t_b, t_d) **then**
14: $\qquad$ {a "diagonal" neighbor forms a rectangle}
15: $\qquad c_h \leftarrow$ TRYMERGE$(t_b, t_d, T_h) + c_h$
16: $\qquad c_v \leftarrow$ TRYMERGE$(t_r, t_d, T_v) + c_v$
17: $\qquad c_{hv} \leftarrow$ TRYMERGE$(t, t_r, t_b, t_d, T_{hv})$
18: $\quad$ **end if**
19: **end if**
20: {find the merge with largest reduction in cost among the possibilities and use that as the new tile map}
21: $i \leftarrow \arg\max_{i \in \{h,v,hv\}} c_i$
22: $T \leftarrow T_i$

4.4 Resulting Tile Maps

Figure 5 shows some example inputs and outputs from our heuristic. The top row shows three heat maps from three different GoPs. The color spectrum indicates the popularity of regions (i.e., probability that it will fall within an RoI), with red being popular and blue being not popular. The bottom rows show the output tile maps from our heuristic.

There are several interesting observations we would like to point out here. First, un-popular regions tend to be covered by huge tiles. Such huge tiles contribute to better compression efficiency of the video. Note that this does not help in reducing the expected bandwidth. On the contrary, in the rare event that a user selects an RoI that intersects with such huge tiles, the tiles need to be transmitted, increasing the transmission bandwidth.

Second, the center area of popular regions (such as the yellow region in the left most heat map and green region in the middle heat map) tend to be encoded with tiles slightly smaller than a RoI. These regions typically show interesting contents that users tend to zoom into and are contained in the many requested RoIs. Encoding these regions with such tiles leads to better compression compared to using regular, small, tiles. Since these regions are requested often by the user, good compression in the regions leads to lower expected transmission bandwidth. Further, since such regions are contained within many RoIs, there is less chance that they partially overlap with the RoIs, hence less chance of wastage.

Finally, the boundaries of the RoIs tend to be coded with long thin tiles. Such tiles are used to encode regions surrounding popular regions with interesting content. Since different users select their RoIs at slightly different positions, such thin tiles neatly cover the boundary of the RoIs, reducing the wasted out-of-RoI areas in tiles that partially overlap with the RoI.

One final point to note regarding adaptive tiling. By integrating the cost of a tile into our model, our tiling can adapt to characteristics of the video content. For instance, if a video has much horizontal motion, then our heuristic tends to create more horizontal tiles, since such tiles can be better compressed compared to vertical ones.

5. MONOLITHIC STREAMING WITH ROI-AWARE CODING

Monolithic streaming (MS) refers to streaming videos encoded with a conventional standards compliant video encoder. Raw video frames are encoded as a sequence of GoPs and macroblocks are organized as slices while being encoded as intracoded or predictively coded. Predictively coded macroblocks have motion vectors that are forward/backward referencing or coded in direct mode.

RoI is streamed by transmitting all macroblocks within the RoI along with macroblocks referenced as a result of motion vectors. Referenced macroblocks may fall within the RoI or may lie outside the RoI. Referenced macroblocks falling within the RoI would anyway be transmitted when the reference frame is streamed. Macroblocks referenced from outside the RoI need to be transmitted before the referencing frame is transmitted. A single motion vector may refer to at most four other macroblocks in the reference frame. In turn, these four macroblocks may refer to four others. This form of motion vector dependency can result in a large

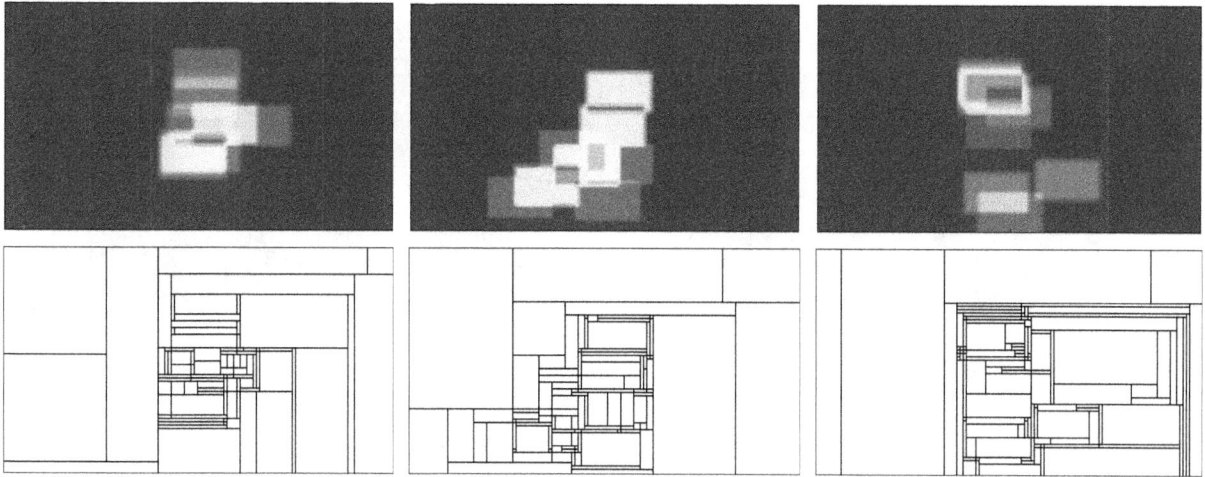

Figure 5: Top row: Heat maps from three different GoPs. Bottom row: Tile maps produced by our algorithms using the corresponding heat maps in the same column.

region outside the RoI to be transmitted. Figure 6(a) shows a rectangular RoI with colored area around it. The colored area is the motion vector dependency that needs to be transmitted in order to decode the RoI. The colored area outside the RoI represents the extent of spatial spread of motion vector dependency. The color itself represents the extent of spread in the temporal direction. Bright red regions represent macroblocks which are referenced many more times compared to the blue regions. One of the test videos that we used in our evaluation showed that macroblocks in the last few frames of the GoP need macroblocks from the first few frames. One of the factors contributing to larger effective RoI is the nature of content in the video, as a result of which, macroblocks may be encoded with long motion vectors. One option is to force the encoder to limit the motion search range. But, it has been shown [16] that using short motion vectors is less bandwidth efficient, and also results in larger video files.

5.1 Limiting Motion-Based Dependency

In this section we describe an approach to statistically limit the spread of motion vector dependency in MS. We refer to this approach as Probabilistic Boxing (PB), and the encoder which uses this approach will be referred to as MS-PB. Probabilistic boxing involves constraining or "boxing" motion vector search to within pre-determined rectangular region. Unlike tiling, probabilistic boxing limits the motion vectors to regions based on access probability and regions can be non-rectangular.

MS-PB uses a two pass encoding approach. In the first pass, the raw video is encoded in a standard format and made available to users. Once user interactions have been logged, the encoder analyzes the motion vector dependency of macroblocks in the encoded video with reference to the RoIs viewed by users. The result of the analysis step is a series of instructions specifying the motion search range for every macroblock in every frame of the video. The specified motion search range would allow the encoder to run a second pass encoding, such that, the motion vector dependency

is confined to the expected regions-of-interest. As a result of confining motion vectors, the amount of data sent from outside the regions-of-interest is minimized.

Confining motion search has a negative impact on the size of encoded video. The first pass encoding would have determined the optimal reference macroblocks for predictively coded macroblocks. Limiting motion search may result in the reference macroblocks that are less than optimal. Hence the prediction error is higher there by increasing the size of predictively coded macroblocks. To account for this problem, MS-PB uses the probability of access of RoIs as well. If the expected size of macroblocks after the second pass encoding is lower than the expected size in the first pass, then, motion search for macroblocks may be constrained. As the expected size cannot be determined without actually encoding the video, MS-PB uses heuristics.

Figure 7 depicts how the RoIs are expanded to account for the variations in access pattern. The top left corner of each RoI from the user interaction log is quantized by a constant factor. The quantized co-ordinates are clustered in a fixed sized grid, the elements of which are squares with dimension corresponding to the variance of the distribution. Probabilistic boxing is performed by taking the smallest rectangular boundary of the grid elements enclosing all the RoIs for each cluster. In our implementation, we choose grid elements to be 2×2 macroblocks in dimension. In paragraphs to follow, we describe how the motion search range is determined when the regions-of-interest and access probabilities are known.

5.2 Problem Formulation

Figure 8 illustrates a case where two RoIs (R_1, R_2) have different probability of access (p_1, p_2) with motion vector based dependency of R_1 spreading into R_2. Macroblocks in R_1 contributing to the spread are labeled A, and macroblocks in the spread are labeled B. In this particular example, boxing of motion vectors to within the region common to R_1 and R_2, would result in all macroblocks in the overlap area to have dependencies within the overlap region.

(a) Effective RoI with 0 B-Frames

(b) Effective RoI with 2 B-Frames

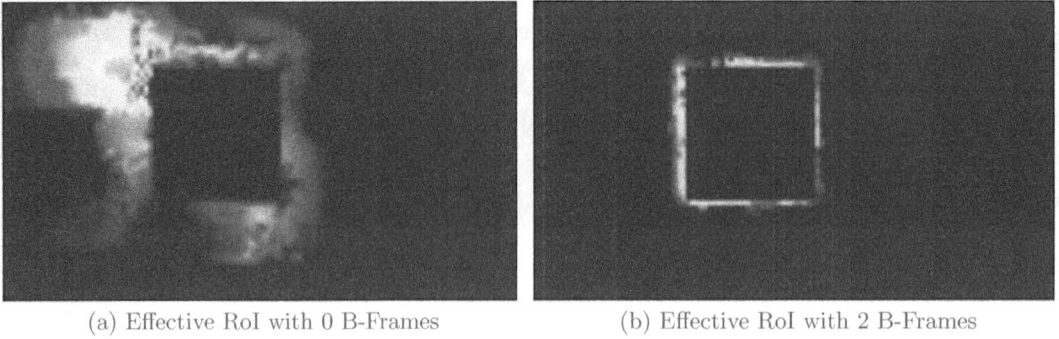

Figure 6: Motion Vector Spread and Effective RoI

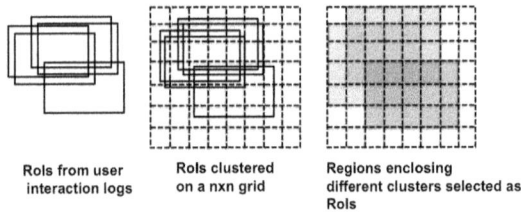

RoIs from user interaction logs   RoIs clustered on a nxn grid   Regions enclosing different clusters selected as RoIs

Figure 7: RoIs Fitting the User's Interactions

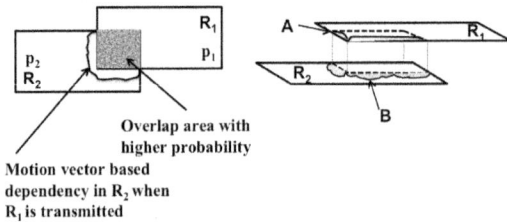

Figure 8: Example of Motion Vector Spread in Overlapping RoIs

In the default encoding case, predicted macroblocks are chosen based on error minimization. As a result, choice of any other predicted macroblock would invariably result in increasing the size of encoded macroblocks. As a result, boxing can result in a higher expected bandwidth. On the other hand, PB accounts for the probability of transmission of the dependency, estimate for the size of the dependency, and estimate for the increase in size due to boxing.

Let $p(A)$ and $p(B)$ be the probability of transmitting A and B respectively. Let $p(A|B)$ be the probability of transmitting A, when B is not the region from which motion vectors of A are estimated. Hence $p(A|B)$ is nothing but the probability that A and B are transmitted together as a result of being co-located in the same region. Hence the probability of transmitting A independent of B is $p(A) - p(A|B)$. If the condition $p(B) \geq p(A) - p(A|B)$ is satisfied, then it implies that the region which A depends on, is more likely to be transmitted than A itself. As motion vector prediction reduces the size of encoded macroblocks, prediction from a higher probability region should be allowed. Hence probabilistic boxing constrains motion search of A only if the condition

$$p(A) - p(A|B) > p(B) \qquad (6)$$

is satisfied. As mentioned earlier, constraining motion search results in a larger encoded macroblock size. The increase in size should not counter the benefit of reduction in motion vector related spread. Hence (6) is modified to

$$[p(A) - p(A|B)]\,\overline{S(A)} > p(B)S(B) \qquad (7)$$

where $\overline{S(A)}$ is the size of A after boxing motion vectors of A, and $S(B)$ is the size of B.

5.3 Intuition

During encoding, allowing longer motion vectors results in better compression. As a result the data rate while transmitting a RoI is also lower. On the other hand, the amount of motion vector dependency increases resulting in transmitting macroblocks from outside the RoI. Figure 6(a) shows a case where there is a large region outside the RoI that is need to decode the RoI. If the size of dependency is larger than the benefits due to better compression with longer motion vectors, the purpose of using longer motion vectors is defeated. If we reduce motion search range (use shorter motion vectors) macroblocks are predicted from less optimal references. Hence the size of macroblocks increases. Now let us refer back to Figure 8. If we constrain the motion vectors in the overlap area, R_1 will be transmitted with a larger size for the overlap area but without motion vector dependency. On the other hand, R_2 will be transmitted with a larger size corresponding to the overlap area, but does not have any benefits of reduced motion vector dependency. If R_2 is accessed significantly more number of times than R_1, the expected bandwidth would have increased instead of decreasing.

5.4 Determining Motion Search Range

The encoder performs motion search for every macroblock. Hence we need to specify the motion search boundary for every macroblock that is likely to be predicted from outside the RoI. Algorithm 2 shows the steps involved in determining the bounding box for every macroblock $x \in A$.

In step-2, the boundary of RoI overlap $(R(x))$ in which x is present is determined. Then, in step-3, all the macroblocks that are needed to decode x and falling outside $R(x)$ are determined. Boxing x alone does not guarantee that the

Figure 9: Motion Vector Spread Constrained to Within RoI Boundaries after Encoding with MS-PB

Algorithm 2 Steps in probabilistic boxing

1: **for** $x \in A$ **do**
2:   $R(x) \leftarrow$ region bounding x
3:   $C(x) \leftarrow$ MBs required to decode x and lying outside $R(x)$
4:   $p(x) \leftarrow$ sum of probabilities of RoIs in which x is present
5:   **if** $|C(x)| == 0$ **then**
6:     box the search range for x to $R(x)$
7:   **else**
8:     find $Z \in R(x)$ and sharing MBs from $C(x)$
9:     $C(Z) \leftarrow$ MBs required to decode each $z \in Z$
10:    $\overline{S(x)} \leftarrow |Z|$
11:    $S(B) \leftarrow |C(Z)|$
12:    $p(B) \leftarrow$ smallest probability in C(Z)
13:    $p(x|B) \leftarrow$ smallest probability in C(Z) and in a region shared with x
14:    **if** $\overline{S(x)}(p(x) - p(x|B)) > S(B)p(B)$ **then**
15:      box the search range for x to $R(x)$
16:    **end if**
17:   **end if**
18: **end for**

existing dependency $C(x)$ will vanish. Other macroblocks in the same region as x may refer to the same dependency. To eliminate the macroblock dependency of x, all macroblocks in $R(x)$ sharing $C(x)$ have to be boxed as well. In step-8, Z is the set of macroblocks in $R(x)$ sharing $C(x)$ and the size of the dependency that will be eliminated if x is boxed is $|C(Z)|$. Hence $S(B)$ in Inequality (7) is set to $|C(Z)|$ in step-11.

In steps 10-11, the size of a motion constrained macroblock x is set to the number of macroblocks that would have been constrained as a result of sharing the same motion vector based dependency as x. The size of dependency removed is set to the total number of macroblocks in the dependency. All macroblocks needed to decode x need not be present in the same RoI overlap. Hence each of these macroblocks can have a different probability. In steps 12-15, the lowest probability macroblock $y \in C(Z)$ is chosen, and its probability is selected as the probability of the dependent region. The sum of probabilities of all RoIs common to y and x is assigned to $p(x|y)$.

In our video encoder, we set the motion search range to 72 for all four directions by default. Once motion search range is constrained by boxing, macroblocks may have smaller search range that is different in four directions.

Figure 9 helps visualize the impact of constraining motion vectors to within RoI boundaries. The figure was generated by applying MS-PB to one of the test videos, and by plotting the motion search range for each macroblock. RoIs used during encoding are shown as rectangular boxes. To visualize the modified motion search range, we count, for each macroblock m, the number of other macroblocks whose motion vector cannot fall into m due to modified motion search range. We then plot this value in Figure 9, with higher values shown in reds and lower values in blues.

From Figure 9, we observe that motion vectors tend to be constrained at the boundary of RoIs, where the probability of access is low, as can be seen from the red and yellow bands around the RoIs. We also observe that, in regions where there are many overlapping RoIs, the motion vectors are not constrained, since the probability of access to such regions and regions around it tends to be high.

6. EVALUATION

The bandwidth efficiency of adaptive tiling (AT) and probabilistic boxing (MS-PB) was verified using four 1080p non-interlaced HD video clips [1, 2]. The clips used in our experiments are *Rush-Hour, Tractor, Bball,* and *Rainbow.*

Figure 10: Thumbnail Images of Frames from Test Videos

Rush-Hour is a 500-frame clip of a street scene during rush hour captured with a fixed camera. *Tractor* is a 688-frame clip showing a tractor ploughing a field. The camera tracks the tractor's motion, producing both foreground and background motion. Further, there is a gradual zoom-out at the end of the clip. *Bball* is a 200-frame clip of a basket ball match with camera tracking the play area along with zoom. *Rainbow* is a 350-frame clip of colorful objects on a rotating table. The camera is in a fixed position and gradually zooms into the objects at the end of the clip. Figure 10 shows a thumbnail of the four test sequences used.

FFMPEG encoder version 0.5 was used to encode these clips into MPEG-4 videos. The motion search range was set to 72 with motion vector scaling. The encoder was modified to scale motion search range r for P-frames and B-frames to $r \times (1 + d)$, where d is the distance to the reference frame in terms of number of frames. The quantization scale was set to 2 and full motion search was employed. The encoder was configured to arrange macroblocks into slices of length 64 bytes, and there were 25 frames per GoP.

Evaluation of AT and MS-PB was conducted by a training-testing framework. The two methods use one set of RoIs (training set) to guide the encoding parameters, and use another set of RoIs (test set) to verify the bandwidth efficiency of the encoding. The test set is derived from the same distribution as the training set.

6.1 Generating Training and Test RoI Sets

To evaluate the merits of the encoding methods proposed in this paper, we pick user interactions from one specific video viewed via the web-based interface. This video is of a magic trick where the performance is always within the camera view and centered around the middle of the frame.

Note that in order to evaluate the efficiency of our proposed adaptive encoding method, we choose to use access patterns from one of our own video but test the encoding efficiency of a range of standard test video sequences. The rationale is that the standard test video sequences contain a variety of motions and complexity, and is good for evaluating video encoders. These test video sequences, however, are boring to watch over a zoomable video interface and are not suitable to gather realistic user interaction patterns.

We now explain how we generate the training sets and test sets from user interaction patterns. We generate one training set and one test set for each 25-frames GoP. Since RoI changes occur at the GoP boundary, the access patterns (and thus, the encoding parameters) can be different across different GoPs. Further, the access patterns can be different across different zoom levels. We focus our evaluations on Zoom Level 5, since this is the most challenging in terms of video resolutions (1920×1080) and most interesting in terms of RoI viewing patterns.

For each GoP at Zoom Level 5, we compute the frequency of access f_i of a RoI i as the number of frames for which i is viewed multiplied by the number of users who viewed i.

In our traces, there are 12 - 30 unique RoIs per GoP, which comprise of the training set. The video frame is divided into a grid of macroblocks organized in the x and y directions. The RoI is macroblock-aligned and are of size 20×12 macroblocks (same dimension as the viewing interface, 320×192 pixels). We use only 11 GoPs worth of training sets to match the length of the test video sequences (our user traces is much longer).

These training set is used as input to our encoding algorithm for both monolithic streaming and tiled streaming. To evaluate the expected bandwidth, however, we cannot use the same set since it is unrealistic that future users would access exactly the same set of RoIs. We thus need to generate another sets of RoI access patterns to mimic new users. The user access patterns, however, are expected to be the same as we have shown in [3].

To generate the test set, we approximate the distributions of the RoI, and generate a new set of RoIs following the same distribution. To do so, we create bins of RoIs locations by quantizing the top left corner of each RoI. All RoIs with top-left corners falling into the same bin are grouped as a cluster. We use a bin size of 2×2.

The frequency of occurrence of a cluster is the sum of frequencies of occurrence of all RoIs in that cluster. From this frequency of occurrence, we can derive the probability that a requested RoIs fall into a cluster. We can now generate the test set by randomly choosing an RoI according to the cluster probability, once a cluster is chosen, the exact position of RoI is uniformly and randomly chosen from the four possible positions within the cluster.

With the generated RoIs in the test sets, we can now evaluate the performance of our encoding algorithms.

6.2 Per-RoI Encoding

We compare the performance of our algorithms to a reference encoding approach we denote as *PerRoI*. This method crops the RoI from the raw video and re-encode it as a standard MPEG-4 video before transmission. In essence, PerRoI encodes videos exactly to the RoI dimensions and position within a frame. It is not scalable when there are large number of users. Nevertheless, PerRoI serves as a benchmark when we want to evaluate our encoding algorithms, since PerRoI transmits zero bytes from outside a specified RoI.

6.3 Comparison of Encoding Approaches

We compare the performance of the proposed encoding approaches in terms of their ability to compress a video file as well as the bandwidth efficiency while streaming RoIs. We compute the expected bandwidth as the total number of bits transmitted for a given RoI, multiplied by the probability of occurrence of the RoI. Every GoP has a different set of RoIs. If the number of test set RoIs are less than the total number of GoPs in the test video, we re-use the same set of RoIs in a round-robin fashion. The expected bandwidth of each RoI in a GoP is added to give the expected bandwidth for that GoP. Bandwidth across GoPs is added and averaged to give the expected bandwidth for the entire video clip. We use PerRoI along with MS-PB and AT for comparison purposes. We also use two tiled steams encoded with 16x16 tiles (TS16x16) and 4x4 tiles (TS4x4) for benchmark purposes. We compared the PSNR values for MS-PB, AT, MS and found that the difference was insignificant.

6.3.1 Compression Efficiency

Figures 12 and 11 show a comparison of encoded video files using AT and MS-PB. We observe that PerRoI is the most efficient in compression. In fact, it is unfair to compare the file size of PerRoI with other methods, as PerRoI compresses cropped frames while other methods compress the full frame. The size of the RoI in our experiments is 20x12 macroblocks. This size is significantly less than the frame dimensions of 120x67 macroblocks. Nevertheless, we do show PerRoI's file size for completeness. Monolithic streaming is the most efficient in compressing the video file, since the video is encoded using standard encoder without constraints of motion compensation. MS-PB and AT result in increased size as a result of constraining motion vector search. This trend is seen in all the test videos.

A point to highlight is the comparison between AT and TS16x16. Among the several regular tiling configurations we evaluated, TS16x16 achieves the best compression. AT is found to be comparable to TS16x16 (no more than 2.5% larger).

Another observation is that the compression efficiency is better when B-frames are not used in spite of using an increased motion search range for P-frames in the presence of B-frames. All the test videos have reasonably high motion. When we encode B-frames we do not have the option of choosing intracoded macroblocks if the variance between the macroblock and its reference is high. In P-frames, macroblocks can be intra-coded when the variance between the macroblock and the best reference macroblock is high.

6.3.2 Expected Data Rate

We compare the expected data rate for the case where there are two B-frames between P-frames and the case where

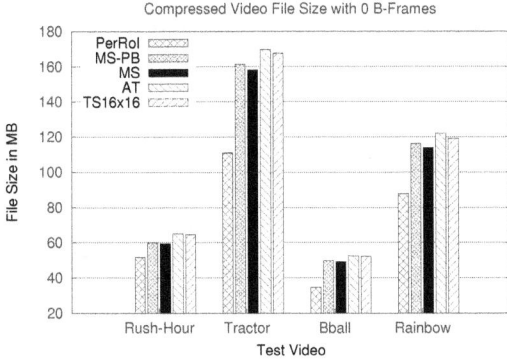

Figure 11: File Size Without B-Frames

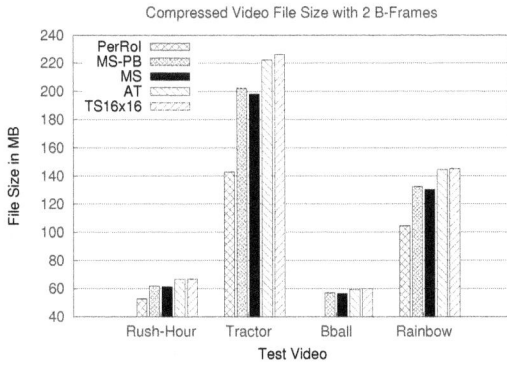

Figure 12: File Size With 2B-Frames

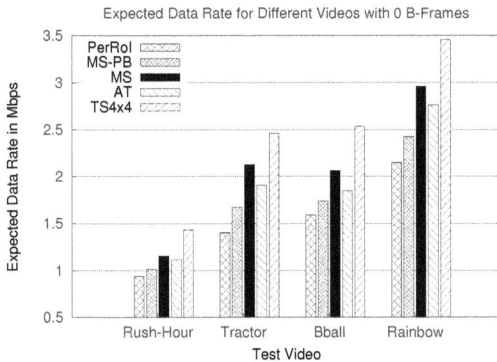

Figure 13: Data Rate Without B-Frames

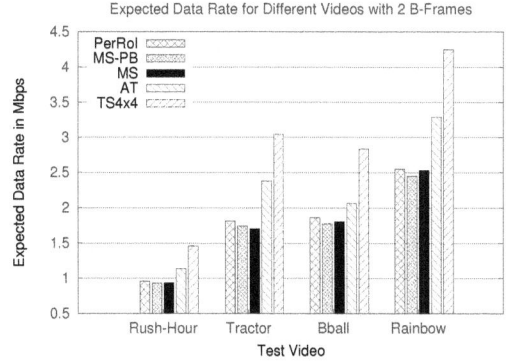

Figure 14: Data Rate With 2B-Frames

the video is encoded without B-frames in Figures 6.3.1 and 6.3.1. We use TS4x4 as a benchmark because smaller tiles result in less wasted bits in the case of tiled streaming.

Comparing AT and TS4x4, we see that AT's expected bandwidth are about 20% - 27% smaller than TS4x4 with or without B-frames for all four test sequence. Comparing MS-PB with MS, we found that MS-PB only perform significantly better than MS in the case without B-frames (12% - 21%). With B-frames, MS-PB is comparable with MS.

The presence of B-frames also affects the relative performance of PerRoI and MS-PB. Without B-frames, PerRoI requires 7% - 16% less bandwidth than MS-PB. With B-frames, however, PerRoI requires 3% - 5% more bandwidth than MS-PB. The latter is surprising to us, since intuitively we expect PerRoI to have smaller data rate, as it only transmit data within the RoIs.

We explain the surprising effects of B-frames in the following section.

6.4 Discussion

We found that, with the presence of B-frames, the motion vectors tends to spread less (see Figure 6(b)) in the temporal dimension. Without B-frames, the motion vectors spread more widely (see Figure 6(a)) and plays to the advantage of MS-PB's capabilities. With B-frames, the motion vector dependency is tightly packed around the RoI, MS-PB can do as best as MS.

The wide spread of motion vectors without B-frames also explains why PerROI is significantly better than MS-PB without B-frames. With wide spread of motion vectors, MS-PB has to transmit more data outside of the RoI due to dependencies (albeit less than MS). With B-frames, however, MS-PB needs to transmit much less due to the much smaller spreads. MS-PB now has an advantage over PerRoI – the macroblocks near the boundary of RoIs has more options during motion compensation, since the motion search range can extend outside of the RoIs. On the other hand, the PerROI motion compensation is limited within the RoIs. The fall in compression efficiency in PerRoI causes the overall bandwidth to transmit RoI to increase.

The same rational causes difference in the performance of AT compared to MS and MS-PB as well. AT is better than MS when there are no B-frames. Adaptive tiling allows for the creation of areas within which the motion search is constrained. In some sense it is very similar to MS-PB. As the motion vector spread is high when B-frames are absent, AT is able to limit the spread at the expense of increased macroblock size and file size. Hence AT is more bandwidth efficient. On the other hand, AT is less bandwidth efficient when compared to MS and MS-PB when there are B-frames. As the motion vector spread is not high in this case, limiting motion search by tiling does not play a significant role.

7. CONCLUSION AND FUTURE WORK

This paper proposes an adaptive encoding approach in the context of a zoomable video streaming systems. Based on historical user access patterns, we compute the probability of each RoIs being requested, and encode the source video considering the RoI access probability. We adapt the motion vector search range in the case of monolithic streaming, and tile size in the case of tiled streaming. We show that by adapting the encoding parameters to RoIs request probability, we are able to reduce the bandwidth by up to 21% and 27% for monolithic streaming and tiled streaming respectively.

There are several practical issues that needs to be further looked into. The first is the computation time required. Both adaptive encoding methods are expensive and requires multiple passes of encoding. The fact that this is done offline in-frequently alleviate the problem but can still be an issue for large-scale video-on-demand systems with many video content. The second issue is frequency of adaptation. Our study over 53 users show that user interests tends to be stable over a short period of time, but it is possible for user interests to evolve over time. For instance, in a lecture video, users interest may be different when they view the video the first time (to copy notes from blackboard) and when they view it subsequently (just for revisions) The third issue is that different user profiles can have diverse user interest. For instance, in a sport video, supporters for different teams tend to zoom in to different players. In this case, the users need to be categorized, with the system providing multiple different versions of videos to cater for different access patterns. Prompt adaptation to changes of user interest over time and clustering of user behaviors into different profiles remain as open questions.

Acknowledgment

This research is supported by National University of Singapore Academic Research Fund R-252-000-368-112.

8. REFERENCES

[1] http://media.xiph.org/video/derf/.
[2] http://www.cdvl.org/.
[3] A. Carlier, G. Ravindra, and W. T. Ooi. Towards characterizing users' interaction with zoomable video. In *Proc. of International Workshop on Social, Adaptive, and Personalized Mutlimedia Interaction and Access (SAPMIA 2010)*, Florence, Italy, October 2010.
[4] L.-Q. Chen, X. Xie, X. Fan, W.-Y. Ma, H.-J. Zhang, and H.-Q. Zhou. A visual attention model for adapting images on small displays. *Multimedia Systems*, 9(4):353–364, 2003.
[5] W. Feng, T. Dang, J. Kassebaum, and T. Bauman. Supporting region-of-interest cropping through constrained compression. In *Proc. of ACM MM'08*, pages 745–748, Vancouver, British Columbia, Canada, 2008.
[6] S. Heymann, A. Smolic, K. Mueller, Y. Guo, J. Rurainsky, P. Eisert, and T.Wiegand. Representation, coding and interactive rendering of high-resolution panoramic images and video using MPEG-4. In *Proc. Panoramic Photogrammetry Work-shop PPW'05*, Feb 2005.
[7] C. M. Huang and C. W. Lin. Multiple-priority region-of-interest H.264 video compression using constraint variable bitrate control for video surveillance. *Optical Engineering*, 48(4):047004, 2009.
[8] M. Inoue, H. Kimata, K. Fukazawa, and N. Matsuura. Interactive panoramic video streaming system over restricted bandwidth network. In *Proceedings of the international conference on Multimedia*, MM '10, pages 1191–1194, New York, NY, USA, 2010. ACM.
[9] M. Karczewicz and R. Kurceren. The SP- and SI-frames design for H.264/AVC. *IEEE Transactions on Circuits and Systems for Video Technology*, 13(7):637–644, 2003.
[10] W. Lai, X.-D. Gu, R.-H. Wang, W.-Y. Ma, and H.-J. Zhang. A content-based bit allocation model for video streaming. In *Multimedia and Expo, 2004. ICME '04. 2004 IEEE International Conference on*, volume 2, pages 1315 –1318, jun 2004.
[11] H. Liu, X. Xie, W.-Y. Ma, and H.-J. Zhang. Automatic browsing of large pictures on mobile devices. In *Proc. of ACM MM'03*, pages 148–155, Berkeley, CA, USA, 2003.
[12] L. C. Loschky and G. S. Wolverton. How late can you update gaze-contingent multiresolutional displays without detection? *ACM Trans. Multimedia Comput. Commun. Appl.*, 3(4):1–10, 2007.
[13] A. Mavlankar, P. Baccichet, D. Varodayan, and B. Girod. Optimal slice size for streaming regions of high resolution video with virtual pan/tilt/zoom functionality. In *Proc. of EUSIPCO'07*, 2007.
[14] A. Mavlankar and B. Girod. Background extraction and long-term memory motion-compensated prediction for spatial-random-access-enabled video coding. In *PCS'09: Proceedings of the 27th conference on Picture Coding Symposium*, pages 61–64, Piscataway, NJ, USA, 2009. IEEE Press.
[15] A. Mavlankar, D. Varodayan, and B. Girod. Region-of-Interest prediction for interactively streaming regions of high resolution video. In *Proc. of International Packet Video Workshop, PV2007*, Lausanne, Switzerland, Nov. 2007.
[16] N. Quang Minh Khiem, G. Ravindra, A. Carlier, and W. T. Ooi. Supporting zoomable video streams with dynamic region-of-interest cropping. In *Proc. of MMSYS '10*, Phoenix, Arizona, USA, 2010.
[17] E. M. Reingold and L. C. Loschky. Reduced saliency of peripheral targets in gaze-contingent multi-resolutional displays: blended versus sharp boundary windows. In *ETRA '02: Proceedings of the 2002 symposium on Eye tracking research & applications*, pages 89–93, New York, NY, USA, 2002. ACM.
[18] A. Santella, M. Agrawala, D. DeCarlo, D. Salesin, and M. Cohen. Gaze-based interaction for semi-automatic photo cropping. In *Proc. of ACM CHI '06*, Montréal, Québec, Canada, 2006.
[19] P. Sivanantharasa, W. Fernando, and H. K. Arachchi. Region of interest video coding with flexible macroblock ordering. In *Industrial and Information Systems, First International Conference on*, pages 596 –599, aug. 2006.
[20] X. Xie, H. Liu, S. Goumaz, and W.-Y. Ma. Learning user interest for image browsing on small-form-factor devices. In *Proc. of ACM CHI '05*, Portland, Oregon, USA, 2005.

On the Impact of Quality Adaptation in SVC-based P2P Video-on-Demand Systems

Osama Abboud*
Multimedia Communications
Lab, TU Darmstadt, Germany
abboud@kom.tu-
darmstadt.de

Thomas Zinner
Chair of Communication
Networks, University of
Wuerzburg, Germany
zinner@informatik.uni-
wuerzburg.de

Konstantin Pussep
Multimedia Communications
Lab, TU Darmstadt, Germany
pussep@kom.tu-
darmstadt.de

Sabah Al-Sabea†
Internet Services Group
NEC Europe Ltd.
Heidelberg, Germany
al-sabea@neclab.eu

Ralf Steinmetz
Multimedia Communications
Lab, TU Darmstadt, Germany
steinmetz@kom.tu-
darmstadt.de

ABSTRACT

P2P Video-on-Demand (VoD) based on Scalable Video Coding (SVC) (the scalable extension of the H.264/AVC standard) is gaining momentum in the research community, as it provides elegant adaptation to heterogeneous resources and network dynamics. The major question is, how do the adaptation algorithms and designs affect the overall perceived performance of the system? Better yet, how can the performance of an SVC-based VoD system be defined? This paper explores the impact and trade-offs of SVC-based quality adaptation with focus on the SVC layer selection algorithms, which are performed at different streaming stages. We carry out extensive experiments to evaluate the performance in terms of session quality (start-up delay, video stalls) and delivered SVC video quality (layer switches, received layers), and find out that these two metrics exhibit a trade-off. Our analysis and conclusions give multimedia providers insights on how to design and fine-tune their VoD system in order to achieve best performance.

Categories and Subject Descriptors

C.2 [**Computer-Communication Networks**]: Distributed Systems

---

*This work was funded by the Federal Ministry of Education and Research of the Federal Republic of Germany (Support code 01 BK 0806, GLab). The authors alone are responsible for the content of the paper.
†Work done before joining NEC Europe Ltd.

General Terms

Algorithms, Design, Performance

Keywords

Peer-to-Peer, Overlay Networks, Scalable Video Coding, Quality Adaptation, Video-on-Demand, Content Distribution.

1. INTRODUCTION

Demand for multimedia applications has witnessed enormous growth recently [9]. To catch-up with this growth, various service architectures ranging from client/server to distributed cloud approaches have been developed. One promising architecture is the peer-assisted delivery, which relies on a delicate balance between client/server and Peer-to-Peer (P2P) delivery techniques. Peer-assisted[1] Video-on-Demand (VoD) systems utilize the idea of peers assisting the servers by uploading chunks they have already downloaded. Thereby, peer-assisted VoD allows for either a higher number of supported peers, or a higher bit-rate for the same number of peer and server resources.

Nonetheless, peer-assisted VoD is still challenging. In current systems, video bit-rates typically range from 300 Kbps to 2 Mbps [11]. While lower bit-rates are still preferred by the content providers in order to support a wider spectrum of end-user devices, higher bit-rates are increasingly getting popular. Additionally, there is a need to support the heterogeneity of Internet devices, e.g. PCs, tablet computers, and mobile devices, within the same video delivery system.

Prominent approaches to achieve this goal are: Multiple Descriptor Coding (MDC) and Scalable Video Coding (SVC). In this paper, we focus on the latter as it exhibits a lower complexity, and allows for adaptation to resources with three degrees of freedom. Receivers can have different screen resolutions, heterogenous link capacities, and different processing capabilities [1].

Combination of P2P VoD and SVC with full-fledged adaptation features raises many challenges and questions: Does SVC really help in systems with heterogenous resources?

---

[1]We use the terms peer-assisted VoD and P2P VoD interchangeably in this paper.

How should the layer selection algorithm choose the layer to be fetched? How often should these algorithms be executed? What is the impact these adaptation algorithms have on the perceived system quality? And also, how to measure the quality of the VoD system?

These questions are not only posed by current developments of VoD applications [3], but also by content providers that have to embrace adaptation techniques for delivering multimedia to devices with a diverging resource spectrum.

In this paper, we address these questions using extensive simulations. We not only present performance metrics that assess the tradeoffs of an SVC-based VoD system, but also investigate the impact of adaptation and how it can be tweaked to reach best performance. We base our analysis on the VoD system presented in [1], while further elaborating the architecture and algorithms behind our VoD system.

This paper is structured as follows, Section 2 provides related work. Background on SVC is given in Section 3. Our proposed architecture for P2P VoD is presented in Section 4. Section 5 gives an overview on our used methodology. In Section 6, we present our simulative analysis and then conclude the paper in Section 7.

2. RELATED WORK

The research community has put substantial effort into investigating P2P VoD [16]. This includes different aspects such as prefetching policies [12], theoretical models [14], replication techniques [6], network-awareness [10] and impact of server allocation [23]. It was early recognized that prefetching and coding techniques are crucial for a high streaming experience [4], while Chi *et al.* proposed to combine network coding techniques with deadline awareness [7].

However, in scenarios with heterogeneous user devices, media coding techniques such as SVC allow to operate in the presence of devices with varying resources, from desktop computers to handhelds [8]. Furthermore, quality can be switched during playback to adapt to changing network conditions and system load. To support a wide spectrum of resources within the same system, various adaptation techniques were considered [5, 17, 20, 22, 25]. For example, PALS [25] is a receiver driven P2P video streaming system with quality-adaptive playback of layered video. However, PALS only considers single dimensional scalability (as the case for many layered streaming systems) and, therefore, cannot adapt to heterogeneous characteristics of peers with different degrees of freedom.

Different live video streaming approaches have been developed and discussed in research in recent years. Baccichet *et al.* [5] use prioritization of packets and multicast trees to distribute SVC sub-streams with a bound on the introduced delay. Lee *et al.* focus in [15] on challenges for segment seeding and scheduling while deploying a live P2P streaming system using SVC. In [20], Nguyen *et al.* present and analyze a streaming system designed to incorporate network coding and SVC to facilitate deployment of adaptation techniques in streaming systems.

In contrast to the mentioned pieces of work, we present our P2P VoD system with focus on the impact of adaptation and layer selection algorithms. Therefore, we use three dimensional scalability as defined by the H.264/SVC standard [26] to adapt to different peer resources and network conditions.

Regarding P2P-based VoD systems that combine P2P and SVC, several architectures have been recently proposed. For instance, [19] proposes and evaluates a system that aims at achieving quality adaptation and a smooth playback. However, the authors do not investigate a real P2P system, but rather focus on a local view (simple download of content from several peers). Mokhtarian *et. al* present in [18] an analysis of peer-assisted VoD systems with scalable video streams. They provide analytical models that estimate the number of peers that can be admitted into the system in case of flash crowds. Their results can be integrated into our analysis to better match server and peer resources.

Another approach, introduced by Oechsner *et. al* [21] is similar to ours. However, the authors investigate only temporal scalability and evaluate the mean played-out layers and stalling times. This differs from our approach, since we additionally investigate the trade-off between SVC video quality and session quality. We also investigate performance metrics per peer. This is of special interest, since then we can better assess the impact of adaptation on the system as a whole as well as on individual peers.

SVC allows adaptation to be performed at the receiving peers by simply requesting parts of the stream that match their resources. Nonetheless, the existence of more powerful peers enables approaches where those peers can actively re-encode the video file to match resources of the receiving peers as done in [13].

3. SCALABLE VIDEO CODING

The video codec H.264/SVC (Scalable Video Coding) [26] is based on the H.264/AVC (Advanced Video Coding) standard, a video codec widely used in the Internet, for instance by video platforms (e.g., YouTube, GoogleVideo) and video streaming applications (e.g., Zattoo). H.264/AVC is a single-layer codec, which means that different copies of the same video streams have to be encoded to support different end-user devices. Using the scalable video coding extension of H.264/AVC, a video file can be encoded at different qualities within the same layered bitstream. This includes different resolutions, different frame-rates and different picture qualities with respect to the Signal-to-Noise Ratio (SNR). These three dimensions of scalability are denoted by spatial, temporal and quality respectively.

Figure 1 gives an example on the different possible scal-

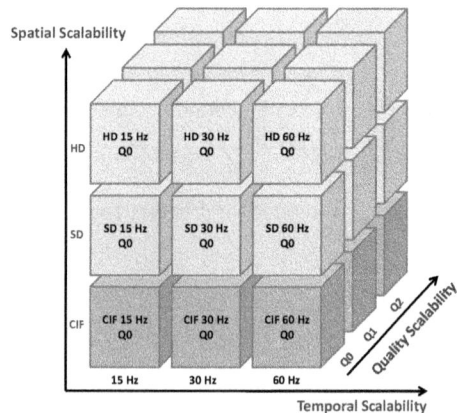

Figure 1: SVC cube model, illustrating the possible scalability dimensions in an SVC video file

abilities offered by an SVC file. This scalable video can be viewed in three different spatial resolutions (CIF, SD, HD), three different temporal resolutions (15Hz, 30Hz, 60Hz), and three different quality resolutions (Q0, Q1, Q2). The left bottom sub-cube, CIF resolution with 15 Hz and quality Q0, is called the base layer and is essential for playback. Based on this base layer, different enhancement layers permit a better video quality with a higher resolution, higher frame rate and/or better SNR. The more sub-cubes along any of the three axes are included, the higher the quality is in the respective dimension. If all sub-cubes are available, the video can be played back with highest quality. The possibility to switch seamlessly between different qualities enables an adaptation of the video quality to device resources and capacity of the system. Thus, it is possible to skip some enhancement layers in case of insufficient resources while enabling a continuous playback of the video.

To allow for multi-source streaming, an SVC file is divided into many chunks, which can be played independently. Usually, a chunk is worth 0.5 up to 2 seconds of video playback. Each chunk can be streamed with different qualities following the SVC model. A chunk is further divided into multiple blocks each contributing to a different quality level. A block will be used as basic unit for fetching and distributing video data across the network.

4. THE QUALITY-ADAPTIVE SYSTEM

In this section, we present our SVC-based quality-adaptive VoD system. We assume a mesh-based pull approach for VoD as presented in [1]. We further assume having a tracker that keeps track of all peers in the network. To ensure a certain quality of service, servers with modest resources are deployed, which additionally inject the initial content. Figure 2 depicts the basic architecture of our quality adaptation workflow.

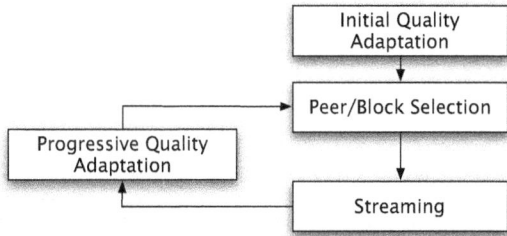

Figure 2: The quality adaptation workflow

Quality adaptation is achieved by adjusting quality according to the different peer resources and network dynamics. It is performed by two modules: the Initial Quality Adaptation (IQA) and the Progressive Quality Adaptation (PQA). Both modules form the algorithms that match the layers with resources available at the peer. On the one hand, the IQA is used for determining the highest possible layer that a peer can retrieve and play, and is performed at session start. On the other hand, the PQA is performed periodically to adjust the layer according to the changes of the network environment.

After the playback is initiated, the IQA is first called to make a decision on the feasible quality level based on local resources. Based on this decision, peer selection and block

selection are performed. Peers are selected in such a way that they are able to provide the selected layer. After the neighboring peers have been contacted and upload slots have been reserved, block selection is done. To ensure continuous playback, the PQA is performed regularly, and if required, it may increase or decrease the selected layer accordingly.

Next, we give the details of the quality adaptation modules and their role in the VoD system.

4.1 Initial Quality Adaptation

Initial Quality Adaptation (IQA) is typically invoked only once at the beginning of the playback session. It is designed in such a way that each peer can determine its highest SVC quality level before starting to download the SVC video. The architecture of the IQA is depicted in Figure 3.

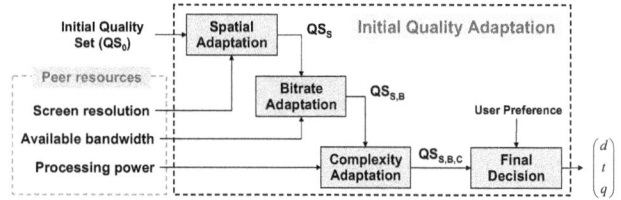

Figure 3: Initial quality adaptation [1]

The basic idea of IQA is to compare the requirements of each layer of the video stream with the local resources[2] of a peer so that the layers that are not supported are left out of the decision process. The subtle property of the IQA, is that it has to make a decision on the quality level without having any information about system throughput and dynamics.

According to the three dimensions of scalability in the SVC model, we have identified the following relevant local resources of a peer:

- *Screen resolution.* The resolution of the user's display determines the picture size of the video to be downloaded. Therefore, the screen size will be used to restrict the spatial quality-level of a video.
- *Bandwidth.* The download bandwidth of a peer corresponds to the maximal bit-rate of the video stream it can receive. Therefore, bandwidth sets limits on the bit-rates of the streamable SVC layers.
- *Processing power.* Decoding SVC streams requires more processing power compared to non-scalable streams. Additionally, the more processing power a peer has, the more layers it can decode. Therefore, it is necessary to take the available processing power into consideration, which would set limits on the decoding complexity of the SVC layers.

Using the three types of local resources, we can filter out those SVC layers that are not compatible by cross-checking them with local resources. The IQA starts off from an initial quality set QS_0 that contains all possible layer combinations. This set is passed through the spatial, bit-rate, and complexity adaptation sub-modules to generate the lists QS_S, $QS_{S,B}$, and $QS_{S,B,C}$ respectively. Each sub-module filters out all incompatible layers. For example, if the bandwidth of a certain peer is BW, then all layers with bit-rates larger

---

[2]Local resources here mean hardware resources that do not change dynamically.

than *BW* are filtered out. The same is also done for the screen resolution and processing power.

Final Decision. The *final decision* algorithm continuously receives a list of feasible layers from the previous adaptation algorithms. It is then up to this module to make a final decision on the layer to be fetched in the next round. The straight-forward decision is to choose the highest layer in order to give the user the best possible video quality. However, it is sometimes difficult to choose the best one from a number of SVC layers. For example, given a $2 \times 2 \times 3$ SVC video file, we could have the layer $(1, 1, 2)$ (higher SNR quality) and $(1, 2, 1)$ (higher frame rate) as candidates for the best layer after the IQA or PQA. Here one cannot tell which layer is better. In this case, the final decision of which one to choose depends on the user's preference (for example, configured by the user in the application settings).

4.2 Progressive Quality Adaptation

The Progressive Quality Adaptation (PQA) module is the dynamic part of the quality-adaptive system. The PQA is invoked regularly during the video playback, with configurable time intervals to adjust the SVC layer according to the different system dynamics. Thus, potential stalls can be avoided and a smooth playback is ensured. The architecture of the PQA is depicted in Figure 4.

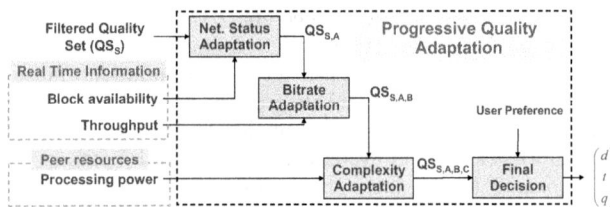

Figure 4: Progressive quality adaptation [1]

In addition to using complexity adaptation, as for the IQA, the PQA uses real-time information of network status measured through the *block availability* in the neighborhood and the active *download throughput*. It takes the current SVC layer as input, then adjusts it according to the real-time network information. This layer is processed by the different stages of the PQA to produce a new layer that fits the current network conditions.

The three adaptation stages of the PQA form together the decision-making process. Since the screen size of the user does not change during the video playback, the PQA adjusts only the temporal and SNR dimensions. The spatial layer will not be changed by the PQA.

We now give more details about the three PQA adaptation algorithms.

Net-status Adaptation. This part of the PQA keeps track of the block availability of all connected peers. Its objective is to check whether the current layer can be supported by the available blocks from current neighbors. Here "support" means that all the blocks in the high priority or buffering window can be downloaded without changing the currently connected peers. If this cannot be guaranteed, the SVC layer of the local peer will be decreased to avoid performance degradation until new peers have been contacted. The adaptation process can be briefly described in the following steps:

1. The local peer uses the information of all available blocks at its connected peers acquired through the so-called buffer-maps.
2. Then, the local peer can calculate a neighborhood availability map for the blocks in its high priority window.
3. The availability map is then compared with the current layer of the local peer. If the map covers all blocks to be downloaded for this layer in the high priority window, the current layer will not be changed. Otherwise, the layer will drop to the level that is covered by the availability map. In addition, if the availability map contains additional blocks of a higher layer, the PQA then switches to this layer.

Using PQA, the SVC layer of a peer can be adapted according to the real-time resources of its connected peers, so that the playback does not need to stop and wait for unavailable blocks. Consequently, the number of stalls can be reduced during the playback.

Bit-rate Adaptation. This stage of PQA affects the SVC layer by analyzing the change of download throughput during the buffering process. The goal of the bit-rate adaptation is to predict possible buffer-underflows due to slow block supply, then adapt the layer so that the bit-rate fits the throughput, therefore, avoiding potential stalls.

To realize this goal, we first have to answer this question: How can we efficiently measure a peer's download throughput of the high priority set of the current layer? To do this, we have observed the following: The buffering state, which means how full the buffer is, reflects the recent download throughput for the current layer. Based on this observation, we can measure the throughput by monitoring the buffer state. Therefore, a nearly full buffer indicates a high throughput, while an almost empty buffer indicates a low throughput. With the above observation, we realize throughput adaptation as follows:

1. We measure how much the buffer is full with video data for the current layer.
2. If this portion is very low (say, less than 10%), then we decrease by one the SNR or temporal level of the current layer.
3. If the state of the buffer is good (e.g. more than 80% is filled), and the current layer is below the initial level determined by the IQA, then we increase the current SNR or temporal layer by one level towards its IQA upper bound.

Complexity Adaptation. The complexity adaptation algorithm is responsible for checking whether the currently available processing power of the local peer is sufficient for decoding the selected SVC layer. Therefore, this part of the PQA would increase or decrease the selected layer according to the current processor load of the device.

Finally, if the different adaptation algorithms result in more than one layer possibility, the predefined user preference is again used to make the final decision.

4.3 Peer Selection

The quality level of each peer has to be taken into consideration during peer discovery and selection. Since each peer in the VoD system has its own SVC layer, not all peers registered at the tracker can support this quality level. Therefore, more information is needed at the tracker in order to match the layer offer and demand. Thereby, the *current layer* of the peer is included into the *peer-discovery request* sent to the tracker. The tracker can then return only those peers that can support the given quality level. The tracker further stores this quality level in its local database for further peer discovery requests. Later on, each peer would announce its current layer with each keep-alive message sent to the tracker to keep the information there as fresh as possible.

The idea behind the modified peer selection algorithm is to have neighborhood peers whose layer is possibly equal to or higher than that of the requesting peer. Therefore, it is more probable that any of the contacted peers can potentially provide any block needed by the downloading peer.

4.4 Connection Management

Algorithms for managing connections are divided into downloader and uploader side algorithms:

Downloader Side. Dowloader peers periodically send connection requests to other peers. If the reply is positive, then the downloader peer requests the blocks it needs, which are further transmitted. If the reply is negative, then the downloader peer degrades the rank of the remote peer to avoid keeping useless connections. Unused connections will be eventually replaced by new ones.

Uploader Side. After an uploader peer receives a new connection request, it checks whether it still has free slots to accept the request. If it does, then a slot is assigned and the request is served. If there are no free slots, the peer evaluates the urgency of the request. If the request is more urgent than one of the existing connections, then it assigns the new connection to the slot whose connection has the lowest priority. Then, this connection is dropped gracefully.

4.5 Block Selection

Block selection has the main role of assigning each block a certain priority. In addition, it is sometimes required to skip some blocks to allow for continuous playback. With the information of the current layer, a peer does not need to download every block of the original video stream, but only those that belong to the selected quality level.

We still follow the idea of dividing the remaining video data into two zones according to the priority: high priority video blocks and low priority video blocks [16]. The partition of these two priority zones is similar to that of a general video streaming system (namely using the buffering window as high-priority zone and the rest of the video as low-priority zone). To calculate the download priority for each block, we have to consider not only its position in the temporal domain, but also its quality level in the SVC model.

High-Priority Zone. The download-priority of each block in the high-priority zone is determined by considering two factors: its distance to the current playback position and its quality level in the SVC model. Therefore, a block n is assigned a certain priority as follows:

$$Priority(n) = -A\frac{n - P}{HP\_Size} - B(W_d d + W_t t + W_q q). \quad (1)$$

The left part of Equation 1 represents the temporal priority by taking the distance between the playback position (P) and the block number (n) into account. The right part of the equation generates the SVC priority: a value which sinks with an increased quality level in any dimension. With the coefficients W_t, W_d and W_q, the speed of the priority-drop in any dimension of the SVC model can be controlled. Finally, the two parts are added together with the weights A and B so that a balance between temporal urgency and SVC quality is ensured.

Low-Priority Zone. For the low-priority zone, we use an algorithm that favors prefetching blocks that will soon be needed by peers downloading from the local peer as presented in [2]. Prefetching is started once the high priority set is full. Therefore, only peers with excess resources would actually perform the following strategies.

The local peer sends a request to all the peers in its upload neighborhood querying for votes on their most wanted blocks. On receiving such a request, each peer places its votes starting from the first non-received block. Those votes are decreasing with increasing block number. The local peer then sums up the votes for each block and then sorts those blocks according to their vote values, i.e. importance. The block with the highest vote, which is not yet available at the local peer, will be prefetched and made available to the neighboring peers. The local peer filters out those blocks that do not belong to its IQA layer. The last step ensures that the selected blocks for prefetching should also be possibly playable by the peer itself, so that unnecessary downloads can be avoided. More details about this prefetching algorithm can be found in [2].

5. METHODOLOGY AND METRICS

Before we can evaluate the performance of the VoD system and the impact of quality adaptation, we first need to define relevant metrics that reflect the key features of perceived video quality. These metrics can be divided into two main categories: *session quality* and *SVC video quality* metrics.

5.1 Session Quality

In this category, we consider the most important factors that affect the users' watching experience in any VoD system. These are the *start-up delay* and *video stallings* that occur during the playback.

- *Start-up delay*. With this metric we measure how long the user waits until the playback begins. The shorter this time interval, the better is the session quality.

- *Stalling events per peer*. This metric reflects the frequency of stalling events taking place during the video playback, i.e. video freezes due to empty buffer. Therefore, in order to improve the session quality, the total number of stalling events should be minimized.

- *Average stalling duration*. In addition, we are also interested in the average duration of stalling events that happen during video playback. Again the shorter the stalling event, the better is the session quality.

- *Relative playback delay per peer*. For simplicity, sometimes we would like to have one metric that summarizes the above mentioned metrics. Therefore, we define the total playback delay as the sum of the start-up delay and all the stalling time. The relative delay is the total playback delay normalized by the total playback time, as shown in Equation 2.

$$Relative_{delay} = \frac{Delay_{init} + \sum_{i=1}^{n} Stall_i}{Time_{playback}} \quad (2)$$

5.2 SVC Video Quality

In addition to the session quality metrics, we are also interested in assessing the respective SVC video quality. This enables us to better judge the overall performance of the VoD system. Here the metrics of interest are:

- *Number of layer changes during video playback.* Some studies [27] have reported that having too frequent layer variations might be more annoying for users than watching the lowest quality. Therefore, we measure the average number of SVC layer variations as an indictor of SVC video quality. A smaller number of layer changes indicates a better VoD system.
- *Relative Received Layer.* In addition, the level of the SVC layer received by each peer during the playback is important. Since each peer has different local resources and thus can retrieve only a certain range of SVC layers, we cannot directly use the *absolute* layers received by the peers to compare their performance. Instead, we define the *relative layer* to assess whether the peers are receiving the highest quality they can actually get given their resources. The relative layer of each received video chunk is equal to the received layer divided by the initial SVC layer calculated by the IQA, as follows:

$$Quality_{rel}(d,t,q) = \frac{d+t+q}{D_{init} + T_{init} + Q_{init}}, \quad (3)$$

where d, t, q are the received layers in spatial, temporal and SNR-dimension respectively as chosen by the PQA, while $D_{init}, T_{init}, Q_{init}$ are the initial SVC layers as chosen by the IQA.

Since the layer selected by the PQA can never be higher than that selected by the IQA (which is determined by physical resources), the relative received layer calculated by Equation 3 falls into the interval [0,1] for all peers. Using this metric, we can better compare the received SVC layer for peers with different local resources. A higher value of the relative received layer indicates that the peer is better able to maintain the quality supported by local resources. Having a lower value, on the other hand, means that although there are enough local resources, the P2P network itself is not able to provide the highest layer to the peer.

This can be due to network congestions or to weak server resources.

6. EVALUATION

Here we present our simulative evaluation of the P2P VoD system. The goals of this study are: to assess the importance of quality adaptation using SVC, to measure the impact of adaptation, as well as to identify the tradeoffs of our system.

We focus mainly on three points: first, we want to see the impact of quality adaptation on the performance in comparison to a non-adaptive VoD system, i.e. a media agnostic one. Second, we are interested in the impact of the different quality adaptation algorithms. Finally, we are going to investigate how having different invocation intervals of the PQA affects the performance.

6.1 Scenario

Table 1 gives an overview on the used SVC video file. This model has 3 spatial levels (d), 4 temporal levels (t), and 1 SNR level (q), with a total of 12 SVC layer combinations. The rightmost column represents the total bit-rate of the respective quality level. The data in Table 1 was extracted from a real 5-minute SVC video file, which was encoded using the JSVM SVC Reference Software [24].

Parameter	Value
Simulation duration	200 minutes
Number of peers	90
Peer arrival pattern	Exponential
Number of servers	4
Server upload capacity	6 Mbps
Play-out buffer size	7 seconds
Neighborhood size	10
Video length	5 minutes

Table 2: Simulation setup

Our simulation setup is depicted in Table 2. We run simulations for 200 minutes during which 90 peers arrive based on an exponential distribution. To ensure a certain quality of service, we consider having 4 servers each with 1Mbps upload capacity. The playout buffer was chosen to be 7 seconds to ensure a small startup time and acceptable playback delay. The peers maintain a neighborhood of 10 peers.

Peer resources are configured as shown in Table 3. The

SVC layer (d,t,q)	Picture size	Frame rate (fps)	Partial Bit-rate (Kbps)	Total Bit-rate (Kbps)
0,0,0	176×144	3.75	60	60
0,1,0	176×144	7.5	30	90
0,2,0	176×144	15	30	120
0,3,0	176×144	30	30	150
1,0,0	352×288	3.75	180	240
1,1,0	352×288	7.5	90	330
1,2,0	352×288	15	60	390
1,3,0	352×288	30	60	450
2,0,0	352×288	3.75	270	510
2,1,0	704×576	7.5	150	660
2,2,0	704×576	15	180	840
2,3,0	704×576	30	160	1000

Table 1: SVC video structure with respective quality levels, partial bit-rates, and total bit-rates

	Set 1	Set 2	Set 3
Number	30	30	30
Screen size	176×144	352×288	704×576
Upload speed	128 Kbps	320 Kbps	800 Kbps
Download speed	256 Kbps	560 Kbps	1200 Kbps

Table 3: Resource configuration for the peers

given values help us to assess the impact of heterogenous resources in terms of bandwidth and screen sizes. Therefore, there are 3 groups of peers each with different bandwidth and local resources.

6.2 Results and Analysis

6.2.1 Quality Adaptative Versus Media Agnostic VoD

Now we evaluate how our proposed adaptation algorithms improve the performance of the P2P VoD system. We simulate our streaming system in three different cases: with no adaptation at all i.e. all peers try to retrieve the highest layer possible as in any media agnostic system, with adaptation algorithms utilizing first only IQA and then with both IQA and PQA.

The results are presented in Figure 5. The left sub-figure illustrates the average number of stalls while the right sub-figure illustrates the total playback delay for each peer in the network. The x-axis refers to the peer IDs in the VoD network. For better comparability, we present the per-peer results in an increasing order and further divide the results into three groups according to the bandwidth capacities of the peers, starting from slowest (on the left) to the fastest (on the right). The horizontal lines present the average values for each group.

Looking at the session quality performance of the three groups when no adaptation is used, we see strong variations in performance. Starting from left to right: the weak, medium and strong peers, had an average of 43, 35, and 23 stalling events respectively. This performance gap is even

more visible for total delay, where the maximum delay of 200 seconds indicates that the peers left the system without watching the whole video due to bad performance. What we see here is the natural effect of correlated performance-resources usually evident in media agnostic VoD systems. This usually leads to excluding peers with weak resources from the system, forcing them to leave the system.

However, already with the addition of the IQA, the slow peers can take part in the system and even have good performance. The slow, medium and fast peers had only 9, 14 and 15 stalling events respectively. The total delay mounted to 25, 37, and 43 seconds for the three groups respectively.

Another interesting improvement gained when using the IQA, is the homogeneous performance for the three groups. We see that having less resources does not affect the session quality, but rather only reduces the video quality. Although the group with lower bandwidth can only receive low quality video, it can nevertheless enjoy continuous playback.

IQA is essential to adapt the system to static resources, however it is not enough as it cannot predict system dynamics. As can be seen from the lowest curves in Figure 5, the performance when using both IQA and PQA was the best. Each peer, irrespective whether slow, medium or fast, witnessed on average 2 stalling events and had 3 seconds of total delay. The PQA, therefore, helps in achieving better session quality and more homogeneous performance across heterogeneous peers.

6.2.2 Session Quality versus SVC Video Quality

From the previous evaluation we see the need to have both initial and progressive quality adaptation. For the PQA, the question arises: how often should it be invoked? i.e. how often should each peer adapt to system variations? To better understand the effects of this parameter and to also understand the trade-offs regarding adaptation dynamics, we evaluate the system for different PQA intervals, namely: 5, 10, 20, 30, 45, 60, and 90 seconds.

To assess the effect of having different PQA intervals, we

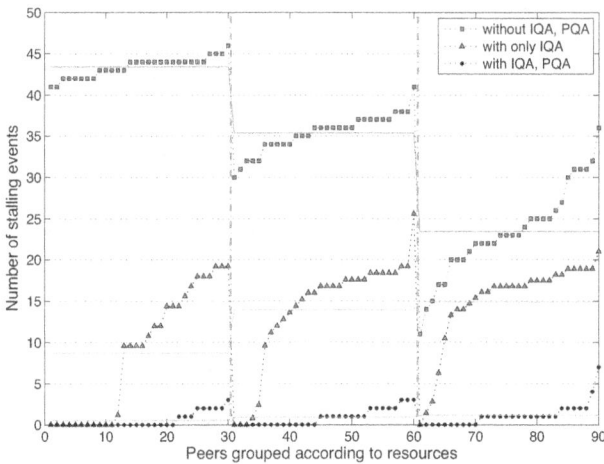

(a) Number of stalling events per peer

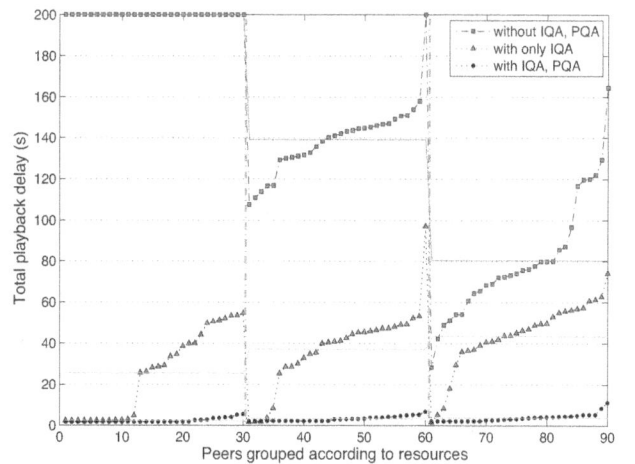

(b) Average playback delay per peer

Figure 5: Quality-adaptive streaming using SVC versus streaming using a media agnostic system (no IQA, no PQA). The peers are divided into three groups according to their resources (slow, medium, fast). For each group, the peers are sorted according to the performance metric in the Y-axis

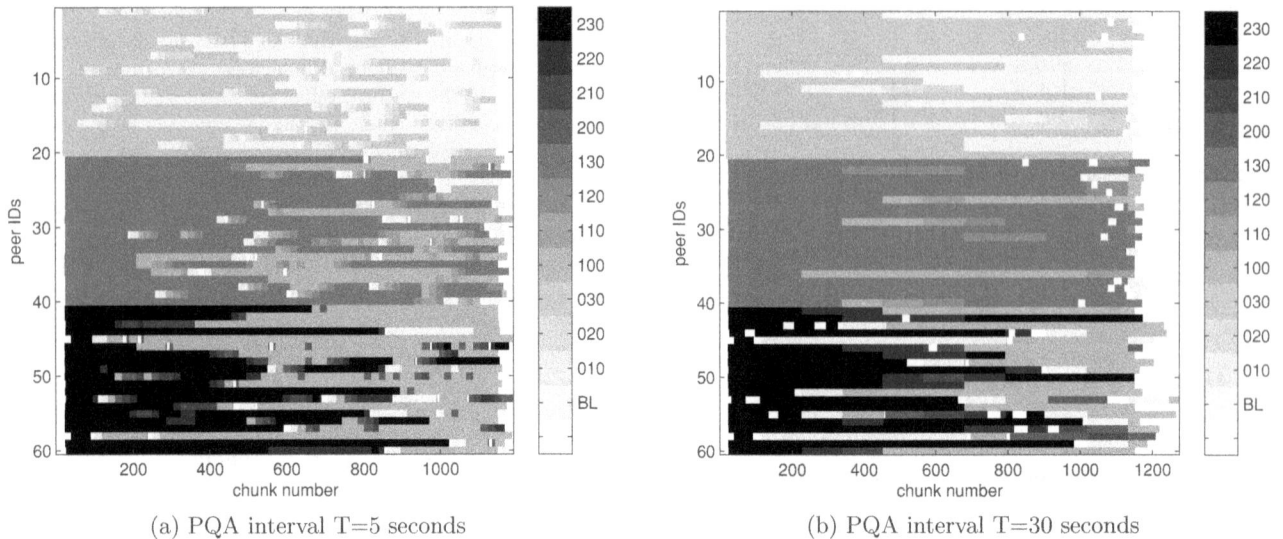

(a) PQA interval T=5 seconds

(b) PQA interval T=30 seconds

Figure 6: Visualization of the layer selection decision for different PQA intervals

present in Figure 6, a visualization of the received layers for the peers when having PQA interval of 5 (Figure 6a) and 30 (Figure 6b) seconds. The peers are grouped according to their resources with strong peers in the bottom (ID range: 40-59), medium peers in the middle (ID range: 20-39), and weak peers in the top (ID range: 1-20). The darker color indicates a higher received layer. For clarity, we present only 20 peers per resource group. We can nicely observe the effect of having different adaptation frequencies on the overall layer decision at the peers.

To better quantify this effect, we now go into more detailed simulation results using the metrics defined in Section 5. Session quality performance (number of stalls, average stall duration, and total relative delay) is presented in Figure 7, while SVC video quality (layer changes, relative received layer) is presented in Figure 8. To further assess the importance of having IQA, we run two sets of simulations, one with IQA and PQA, and one with only PQA. Each scenario is repeated 8 times to exclude any random effects. Standard deviations are shown.

Through the comparison of the session quality for the different PQA intervals, we can see that the more frequently PQA is invoked, the fewer stalls will happen (see Figure 7a). Additionally, the shorter are the stall durations (Figure 7b) and total relative delays (Figure 7c). The reason behind this is that with a larger PQA interval, the peers will be slower to react to system dynamics. Based on this observation, we can conclude that the performance, i.e. the session quality, decreases with an increase of PQA invocation interval. Furthermore, when the IQA is not used, the adaptation behavior is no longer predictable. In the range of 5-45 seconds, the total relative delay is almost the same and then strongly increases for higher values. Therefore, the IQA is necessary, since it already prepares the peer from the beginning for better adaptation to system dynamics.

We have also investigated the received SVC video quality. What we desire is a high relative layer level that changes as less as possible, since too frequent layer changes tend to frustrate users [27]. From Figure 8(a) we can see that as the PQA interval grows, the number of layer changes becomes

fewer. When the interval is infinitely large, the number of layer changes becomes zero, since the layer selected by the IQA will be used throughout the streaming session. On the other hand, Figure 8(b) shows that the average relative received layer increases with a larger PQA interval. The reason for this is that the PQA usually tends to decrease the layer level to avoid potential stalls during the playback (which explains the better session quality). The more frequently the PQA is invoked, the more layer drops it may cause. Consequently, the average layer level throughout the playback will also decrease. From the results of Figure 8, we can conclude that the SVC video quality for the peers increases with a larger PQA invocation interval.

In summary, the relation between session quality and SVC video quality exhibit a trade-off for the different PQA intervals. Therefore, one has to carefully address this trade-off to achieve a compromise between the performance metrics when choosing the PQA interval. Depending on which aspect is more important for the users, the adaptation interval can be adjusted accordingly to meet the given requirements or can be even chosen dynamically depending on how dynamic the system is.

7. CONCLUSION

In this paper we have explored the performance, trade-offs, and impact of adaptation on SVC-based P2P Video-on-Demand. The use of P2P technology to support content delivery is very appealing since it enhances the capacity of the P2P network and thus either increases the achievable bit-rate or allows the system to support more peers. In order to support a plurality of different end-user devices and heterogeneous network resources, we propose to use the H.264/SVC standard with full scalability support.

Our investigations revealed that additional control algorithms are needed to enable an efficient provisioning of resources with good video quality. First, Initial Quality Adaptation (IQA) has to be performed for defining the highest video quality, which can be played back on a device. Further, Progressive Quality Adaptation (PQA) has to be performed

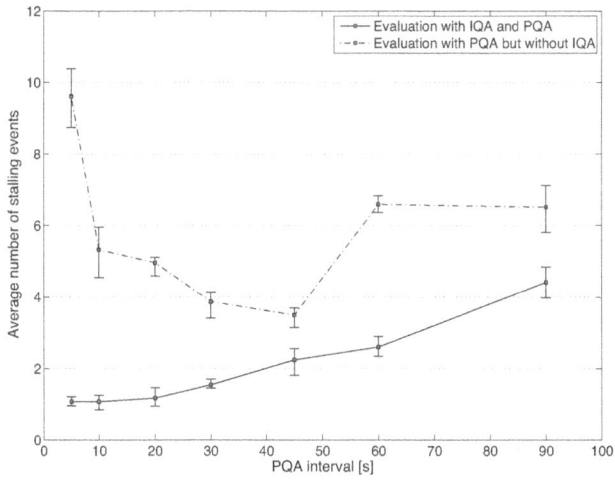

(a) Average number of stalls

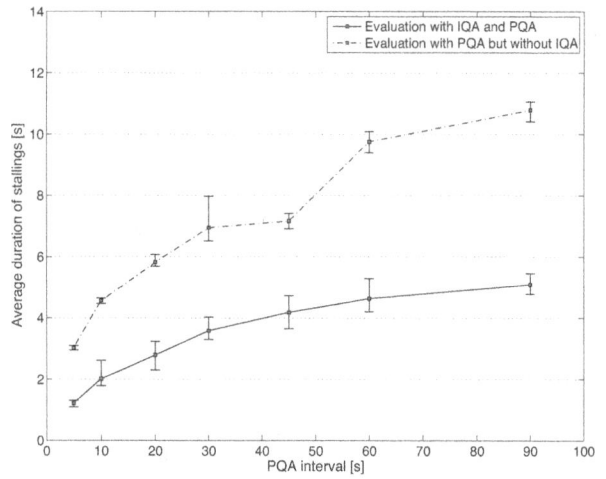

(b) Average duration of stalling events

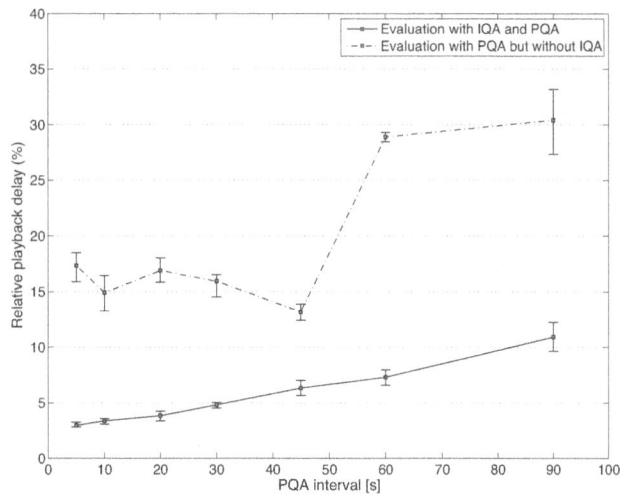

(c) Relative playback delay

Figure 7: Session quality with different PQA intervals

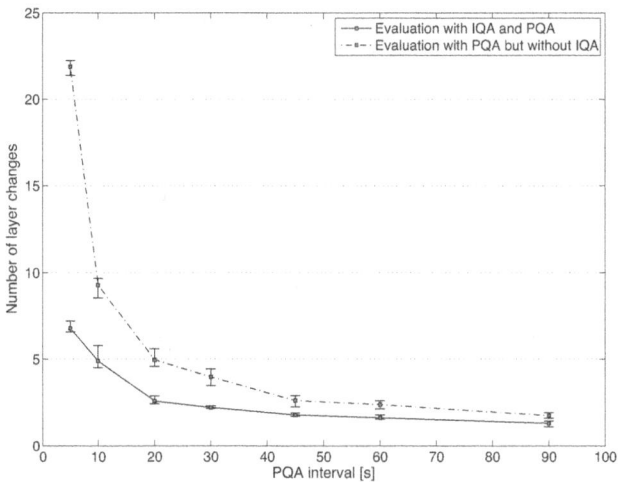

(a) Number of layer changes

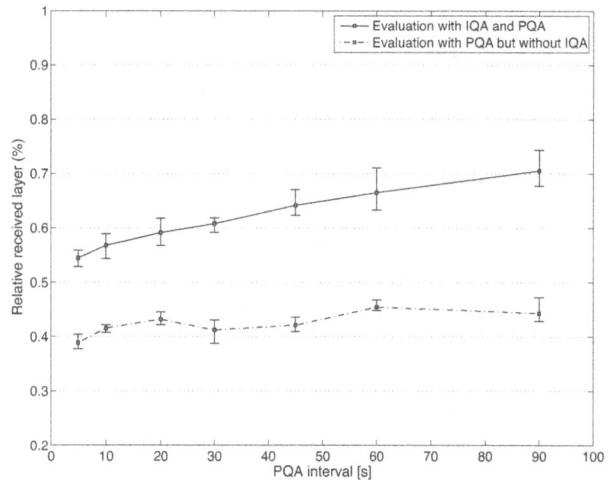

(b) Relative received layer

Figure 8: SVC video quality with different PQA intervals

in constant intervals in order to adjust the video quality to the network conditions. An investigation of the length of this interval revealed interesting insight. The longer the PQA interval, the better is the quality of the played out video and the less are quality changes during video playback, but the higher are stalling times, number of stalls and the total delay.

These results are very interesting for providers of VoD services, since they have to take these trade-offs into consideration in order to optimize their system. Further, service providers may offer their customers better quality with longer stalling times if acceptable. These gaps could be filled e.g. with commercial spots in order to increase the revenue of the providers.

Further work will deal with an extended investigation of the system as outlined above. Additionally, we want to map our session and SVC quality metrics to user quality of experience, for example using user surveys. Then, session and SVC video quality indicators would be merged into one, easy-to-optimize quality of experience metric.

8. REFERENCES

[1] O. Abboud, K. Pussep, A. Kovacevic, and R. Steinmetz. Quality Adaptive Peer-to-Peer Streaming Using Scalable Video Coding. In *MMNS 2009: 12th IFIP/IEEE International Conference on Management of Multimedia and Mobile Networks and Services*, 2009.

[2] O. Abboud, K. Pussep, M. Müller, A. Kovacevic, and R. Steinmetz. Advanced Prefetching and Upload Strategies for P2P Video-on-Demand. *ACM Workshop on Advanced video streaming techniques for peer-to-peer networks and social networking*, Oct 2010.

[3] O. Abboud, T. Zinner, K. Pussep, S. Oechsner, R. Steinmetz, and P. Tran-Gia. A QoE-Aware P2P Streaming System based on Scalable Video Coding. In *IEEE P2P 2010: 10th IEEE International Conference on Peer-to-Peer Computing*, Aug. 2010.

[4] S. Annapureddy, C. Gkantsidis, P. Rodriguez, and L. Providing Video-on-Demand using Peer-to-Peer Networks. *Proc. Internet Protocol TeleVision (IPTV) workshop*, 2006.

[5] P. Baccichet, T. Schierl, T. Wiegand, and B. Girod. Low-delay Peer-to-peer Streaming Using Scalable Video Coding. In *Packet Video*, 2007.

[6] B. Cheng, L. Stein, H. Jin, and Z. Zhang. A Framework for Lazy Replication in P2P VoD. In *18th International Workshop on Network and Operating Systems Support for Digital Audio and Video*, NOSSDAV '08. ACM, 2008.

[7] H. Chi, Q. Zhang, J. Jia, and X. Shen. Efficient Search and Scheduling in P2P-based Media-on-Demand Streaming Service. *IEEE Journal on Selected Areas in Communications*, 25(1):119–130, Jan. 2007.

[8] Y. Cui and K. Nahrstedt. Layered Peer-to-Peer Streaming. In *13th international workshop on Network and operating systems support for digital audio and video*, NOSSDAV '03. ACM, 2003.

[9] Dissecting the Gap Between Downloading and Streaming Video. Online: http://www.ipsos-ideas.com/article.cfm?id=3804.

[10] M. Hefeeda, B. Bhargava, and D. Yau. A hybrid architecture for cost-effective on-demand media streaming. *Computer Networks*, 44(3):353–382, 2004.

[11] X. Hei, C. Liang, J. Liang, Y. Liu, and K. W. Ross. A Measurement Study of a Large-scale P2P IPTV System, year = 2007. *IEEE Transactions on Multimedia*.

[12] C. Huang, J. Li, and K. W. Ross. Can Internet Video-on-Demand be Profitable? In *SIGCOMM '07*. ACM, 2007.

[13] R. Iqbal and S. Shirmohammadi. DAg-stream: Distributed Video Adaptation for Overlay Streaming to Heterogeneous Devices. *Peer-to-Peer Networking and Applications*, 2009.

[14] R. Kumar, Y. Liu, and K. Ross. Stochastic Fluid Theory for P2P Streaming Systems. *Infocom*, 2007.

[15] T.-C. Lee, P.-C. Liu, W.-L. Shyu, and C.-Y. Wu. Live Video Streaming Using P2P and SVC. In *MMNS*, 2008.

[16] Y. Liu, Y. Guo, and C. Liang. A Survey on Peer-to-peer Video Streaming Systems. *Peer-to-Peer Networking and Applications*, 1(1):18–28, March 2008.

[17] N. Magharei and R. Rejaie. Adaptive Receiver-driven Streaming from Multiple Senders. *Multimedia Systems*, 11:1–18, 2006.

[18] K. Mokhtarian and M. Hefeeda. Analysis of Peer-assisted Video-on-Demand Systems with Scalable Video Streams. In *MMSys '10: ACM Conference on Multimedia systems*, pages 133–144. ACM, 2010.

[19] M. Mushtaq and T. Ahmed. Smooth Video Delivery for SVC based Media Streaming over P2P Networks. In *IEEE CCNC*, 2008.

[20] A. T. Nguyen, B. Li, and F. Eliassen. Chameleon: Adaptive Peer-to-Peer Streaming with Network Coding. In *IEEE INFOCOM'10*, 2010.

[21] S. Oechsner, T. Zinner, J. Prokopetz, and T. Hoßfeld. Supporting Scalable Video Codecs in a P2P Video-on-Demand Streaming System. In *21th ITC Specialist Seminar on Multimedia Applications - Traffic, Performance, and QoE*, Mar. 2010.

[22] V. N. Padmanabhan, H. J. Wang, and P. A. Chou. Supporting Heterogeneity and Congestion Control in Peer-to-Peer Multicast Streaming. In *IPTPS*, 2004.

[23] K. Pussep, O. Abboud, F. Gerlach, R. Steinmetz, and T. Strufe. Adaptive Server Allocation for Peer-assisted Video-on-Demand. In *24th IEEE International Symposium on Parallel and Distributed Processing IPDPS 2010*, 2010.

[24] J. Reichel, H. Schwarz, and M. Wien. Joint Scalable Video Model JSVM-9. Doc. JVT-V202, Joint Video Team (JVT) of ISO/IEC MPEG & ITU-T VCEG, Jan. 2007.

[25] R. Rejaie and A. Ortega. PALS: Peer-to-Peer Adaptive Layered Streaming. In *ACM NOSSDAV '03*.

[26] H. Schwarz, D. Marpe, and T. Wiegand. Overview of the Scalable Video Coding Extension of the H.264/AVC Standard. *IEEE Transactions on Circuits and Systems for Video Technology*, 17(9), 2007.

[27] M. Zink, O. Kuenzel, J. Schmitt, and R. Steinmetz. Subjective Impression of Variations in Layer Encoded Videos. In *International Workshop on Quality of Service*, 2003.

Error-Resilient Live Video Multicast using Low-Rate Visual Quality Feedback

David Varodayan and Wai-tian Tan
Hewlett-Packard Laboratories
1501 Page Mill Rd.
Palo Alto, California 94304
{varodayan, wai-tian.tan}@hp.com

ABSTRACT

Effective adaptive streaming systems need informative feedback that supports selection of appropriate actions. Packet level timing and reception statistics are already widely reported in feedback. In this paper, we introduce a method to produce low bit-rate visual quality feedback and evaluate its effectiveness in controlling errors in live video multicast. The visual quality feedback is a digest of picture content, and allows localized comparison in time and space on a continuous basis. This conveniently allows detection and localization of significant errors that may have originated from earlier irrecoverable losses, a task that is typically challenging with packet level feedback only. Our visual quality feedback has low bit overhead, at about 1% for high-definition video encoded at typical rates. For live video multicast with 10 clients, our experimental results show that the added ability to detect and correct large drift errors significantly reduces the resulting visual quality fluctuations.

Categories and Subject Descriptors

I.4.2 [**Image Processing and Computer Vision**]: Compression (Coding); C.2.4 [**Computer-Communication Networks**]: Distributed Systems

General Terms

Design, Performance

Keywords

Error-resilient video, video quality monitoring, video conferencing

1. INTRODUCTION

Controlling the effects of packet losses in real-time video applications like video conferencing is a challenging task. Central to the challenge is the low-latency requirement, which limits the effectiveness of general data resilience methods

such as retransmissions and forward error correction (FEC). Specifically, retransmission can add significant delay if round-trip delay is large, and FEC needs added latency for interleaving to be effective against burst losses. Consequently, a practical streaming system often needs to operate under the condition that parts of the transmitted video are irrecoverably lost. To this end, the general solution is to employ live encoders that reactively adapt to losses based on receiver feedback. The effectiveness of such methods depends fundamentally not only on the merits of available encoding adaptations, but also on the usefulness of feedback information.

Packet level timing and reception statistics are already widely reported in feedback. Standard protocols such as RTCP and its extensions [4], in particular, provide average loss rates and individual packet reception statistics that can support adaptive use of FEC and retransmissions. Nevertheless, when irrecoverable losses become inevitable, packet level statistics are often less useful. This is because they offer little direct guidance in determining where corrective measures are needed without resorting to full emulation of decoder error tracking operations.

A survey of feedback-based error resilience techniques can be found in [6]. In the simplest technique, the encoder codes the entire current frame as an intra-frame whenever a decoder signals that some prior frame has suffered a loss. Intra-coding in this way worsens the rate-distortion performance excessively if losses are frequent. This can happen in a large multicast, where aggregate loss can become large even if loss for individual client remains small. Intra-frame coding is supported by packet level statistics. Reference picture selection (RPS) is a more efficient technique [5, 13] whereby error propagation is stopped by selectively performing predictive encoding using only pictures known to be reconstructed correctly. As the number of decoders grows, the aggregate loss becomes more frequent. The reference pictures selected at the encoder become distant from the current frame to be encoded and, thus, rate-distortion performance suffers significantly. RPS is supported by packet level statistics.

Both intra-coding and RPS reject an entire picture as corrupt even if only a portion is impacted by loss. Such an assumption is reasonable for low bit-rate video, where one compressed picture is often carried in a single transport packet. For high-definition video where one compressed picture is often carried in multiple packets, such a conservative approach is inherently inefficient. Instead, it is desirable to selectively correct only the regions impacted by loss. One such method that relies only on packet level feedback is error tracking, which requires the encoder to duplicate the operation of the decoders whenever a loss is experienced [3, 12]. In this way, the encoder can correct (e.g., by intra-coding) precisely the parts of the video that would continue to be distorted. This method has two disadvantages. Firstly, the encoder must know the error concealment techniques used by the decoders and, secondly, the encoder's computational burden scales linearly with the number of decoders.

In this paper, we propose a low-complexity error tracking method that relies on low-rate visual quality feedback from the decoders instead of burdening the encoder to duplicate each of the decoders. Specifically, the encoder performs light-weight tracking of severe errors at the decoders using their respective visual quality feedback to take corrective action, such as intra-coding or RPS, for the affected regions only. Compared to traditional intra-frame coding and RPS, the proposed method offers two advantages. Since errors are tracked, mild or imperceptible errors do not need to be corrected unless they propagate into severe errors. Moreover, corrective action taken at the encoder can be targeted to the regions where the errors lie. Both of these advantages translate to less degradation in overall rate-distortion performance.

Our error resilience technique is based on low-rate visual quality feedback, an active area of research for a variety of applications. The term reduced-reference video quality monitoring encompasses techniques for estimating video quality metrics. One such reduced-reference method proposed in [14] extracts spatiotemporal features from edge-enhanced versions of the video. Another technique specified in the ITU-T J.240 standard uses a block-wise pseudorandom projection to create a low-rate signal [1, 7]. In both cases, features or projection coefficients from several frames of the received video are compared with the corresponding coefficients of the original video to obtain a single estimate of the video quality. A single metric can be used to perform adaptive encoder rate control as in [10], but it does not offer the localization of errors required by our system.

A projection capable of localization is explored in [8]. The authors propose a video thumbnail be created (using a block-wise mean operation) to assist in location-specific retransmission and error concealment. Another work exploring the use of thumbnails for the dual purpose of error localization and concealment is given in [15], where robustly compressed thumbnails are combined with past full resolution pictures for concealment purposes. In the current paper, by concentrating on error localization alone, we achieve an overhead of only 1% compared to about 10% in [15].

The work in [8] also suggests binning the quantized projection coefficients to further reduce bit-rate; in effect, quantization is performed using non-contiguous quantization regions. Related to compression by binning is Slepian-Wolf coding [11] of J.240 coefficients for video PSNR estimation [2, 9].

In Section 2, we argue using illustrative examples that our proposed error resilience technique based on low-rate visual quality feedback improves performance of live video multicast compared to several existing techniques. Section 3 concerns the design of the visual quality feedback; we discuss design considerations and develop the video projection. In Section 4, we incorporate the visual quality feedback technique into a live multicast system and show comparative experimental results.

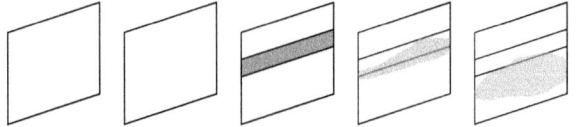

Figure 1: Spatiotemporal error propagation. Depending on content, uncorrected error in frame 3 can migrate and expand over time. Intra-coding of a later frame is guaranteed to stop error propagation but is expensive. Light-weight method of tracking error propagation is desirable.

2. ILLUSTRATIVE EXAMPLES

Error resilience is a challenging problem because video is coded in a motion-compensated predictive manner. In the typical mode of operation, a block of pixels is encoded as a residual with respect to a block in a previously reconstructed picture at some motion vector offset. This means that, when a slice of video is lost, errors can propagate spatiotemporally as illustrated in Fig.1. A packet loss in the third frame causes error confined to the slices that were lost. But blocks in these slices serve as predictors for motion-offset blocks in the fourth frame. Likewise, block in error in the fourth frame serve as predictors for the fifth frame.

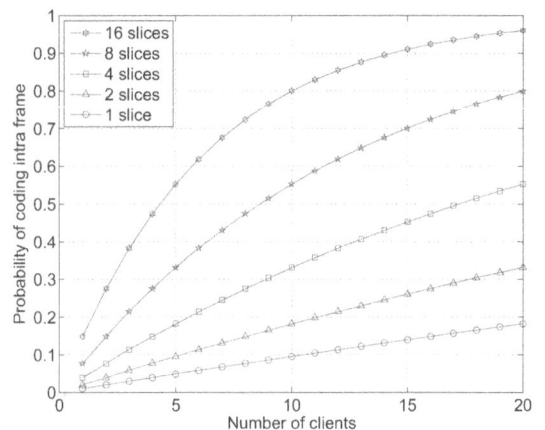

Figure 2: In error resilience by intra-frame coding, the probability of coding an intra-frame does not scale well as the number of decoders grows.

The intra-frame coding technique, discussed in the previous section, guarantees that error propagation stops, but becomes costly in terms of rate-distortion performance if used too frequently. Assuming that all decoders suffer independent and identically distributed slice losses with probability p, then the probability of coding an intra-frame is $1 - (1 - p)^{kn}$, where k is the number of slices per frame, and n is the number of decoders. Fig. 2 plots this probability when the slice loss probability $p = 0.01$. Since intra-coding is expensive, this technique does not scale well as the number of decoders grows. Even a probability of coding an intra-frame of 0.1 is excessive for applications that demand tens of consecutive frames to be predictively coded.

Intra-slice coding is a less costly but more opportunistic variant of the above technique. Instead of coding the entire frame as intra upon the receipt of a NACK, only the slices corresponding to the NACK are intra-coded. This method often work well but fails spectacularly when motion propagates the error beyond the spatial region of the lost slices. Fig. 3 shows an example, for which the encoder reaction time is 4 frame intervals. The lower slices of frame 120 are lost and error concealed by frame copy. The slice boundary, intersecting the words "Februari 2002," is apparent. The lost slices are intra-coded 4 frames later in frame 124, but by this time the words "Februari 2002" have moved out of the intra-coded region. Therefore, the error continues to propagate to frame 138 and beyond.

Fig. 4 shows the corresponding frames when we use the proposed error resilience technique based on visual quality feedback. Frame 120 is identical to its counterpart in Fig. 3 because the loss and error concealment are the same. After the 4-frame reaction time, the encoder intra-codes the same slices as in the intra-slice coding approach, because those are the slices which displayed errors in frame 120. For this reason, frame 124 is also identical to its counterpart. But the encoder continues to use the visual quality feedback to track and correct the propagating errors. Thus, frame 138 is displayed at much better quality than its counterpart.

3. VISUAL QUALITY FEEDBACK

We now delve into the design of the quality feedback signal sent back to the live video encoder. With the target application of multi-party video conferencing in mind, we first enumerate several design constraints and opportunities. Then we step through the process of designing and tuning the video projection.

3.1 Video Projection Design Considerations

The video projection is a dimensionality-reducing operation applied to the reconstructed received video at a decoder. The decoder feeds back the projection symbols to the encoder as a quality feedback signal. Meanwhile, the encoder applies the same video projection to the local reconstructed video to create a set of local projection symbols. The encoder compares the two sets of projection symbols, marks some portions of the video as severely degraded, and takes corrective encoding action at those locations. We now outline the main design considerations for this video projection.

3.1.1 Low Bit-Rate

The quality feedback signal must have a bit-rate that is insignificant compared to that of the primary video stream. In a video conferencing system, video travels both into and out of each terminal. Therefore, the quality feedback for a given stream can piggyback on the packets of the reciprocal stream. We target a bit-rate for the quality feedback of approximately 1% of the primary video stream. We will design a video projection that is transmitted at around 20 kbps for HD video at resolution 720×1280 and frame rate 30 Hz. This level is below 1.35% of the primary video bit-rate as long as the video is encoded above 1.5 Mbps.

3.1.2 Localization

The quality feedback signal must provide sufficient information for the encoder to localize quality degradations within received video frames. In this way, the encoder can take corrective action (such as intra-coding) only in the regions where necessary. We will produce independent quality feedback for each 64×64 block of pixels. At this block size,

(a) frame 120 (loss)

(b) frame 124 (recovery)

(c) frame 138

Figure 3: Example of failure of the intra-slice coding variant of intra-frame coding. Frame 120 (a) suffers from slice losses in the bottom portion of the frame and is concealed via frame copy. After an encoder reaction time of 4 frames, the lost region is intra-coded in frame 124 (b). But imperfections in error recovery propagate to future frames such as frame 138 (c), even when there is no further loss.

the bit-rate target corresponds to 3 bits per block. Any smaller square block size would allow less than 1 bit per block.

3.1.3 Perceptibility

The quality feedback signal must enable the encoder to distinguish between mild (close to imperceptible) degradations and severe degradations in the received video. The encoder can, thus, take corrective action (and incur additional primary bit-rate) where it is needed most. This requirement

(a) frame 120 (loss)

(b) frame 124 (recovery)

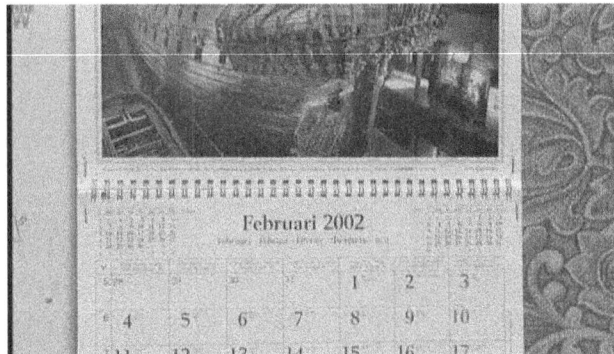

(c) frame 138

Figure 4: Example of error recovery by the visual quality feedback technique. Frame 120 (a) suffers from slice losses in the bottom portion of the frame and is concealed via frame copy. After an encoder reaction time of 4 frames, the lost region is intra-coded in frame 124 (b). The system continues correcting imperfections in the error recovery, so that there are no perceptible errors by frame 138 (c).

is subjective and difficult to evaluate. We simplify our design task by setting the threshold between mild and severe degradations at mean square error of the luma equal to 25.

3.1.4 Robustness

The quality feedback signal must not suffer from error propagation in case of packet loss. This requirement precludes inter-frame compression of the quality feedback signal.

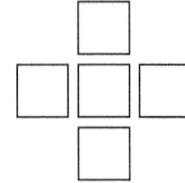

Figure 5: Structuring element for dilation and erosion of map of blocks marked as severely degraded.

3.1.5 Zero Added Delay

The quality feedback signal must enable the encoder to take corrective action for a given received frame immediately on receipt of the feedback. For this reason, we impose a requirement for zero added delay beyond propagation time. This is another reason for avoiding inter-frame compression the quality feedback signal.

3.1.6 Detection Error Ratios

Each symbol of the quality feedback signal is compared with the corresponding local symbol at the encoder. A block is marked as severely degraded if the two symbols do not match; otherwise, the block is marked as not severely degraded, a term which encompasses undegraded and mildy degraded. The figures of merit for our design experiments are two different detection error ratios. The undetection ratio is the fraction of severely degraded blocks that are not marked as severely degraded. Conversely, the false detection ratio is the fraction of undegraded or mildly degraded blocks that are marked as severely degraded. Both of these ratios are calculated only for frames in which errors are known to exist; that is, frames which have suffered a packet loss or frames predicted from them. The undetection ratio should be made as small as possible because uncorrected severely degraded blocks are visually disturbing. The false detection ratio, on the other hand, need not be made extremely small since it corresponds to the amount of unnecessary corrective action taken by the encoder. We target a false detection ratio of less than 10%.

3.1.7 Spatial Processing

Severe video degradations due to packet losses and error propagation tend to be spatially coherent. We can exploit this property to improve the overall detection performance. Within a frame, we take the map of blocks marked as severely degraded and fill holes by applying binary morphological operations. Specifically, we dilate and then erode the map with the cross-shaped structuring element shown in Fig. 5. This spatial operation switches the marking of some blocks from not severely degraded to severely degraded. Consequently, the lower undetection ratio is traded for increased false detection ratio.

3.1.8 Temporal Processing

Video degradations are also coherent in the temporal direction. But filling holes temporally in the map of blocks marked as severely degraded may be wasteful. This is because the encoder's corrective action soon after a severe degradation is marked is often sufficient to mitigate the propagation of that degradation. For the purpose of designing the video projection, we consider a severely degraded block to be undetected if the corresponding block is not marked as severely degraded in any of the 4 frames starting from (and including) the current frame. This has the effect of decreasing the undetection ratio, while keeping the false detection ratio fixed.

3.2 Video Projection Design

The video projection is designed with reference to training data derived from 3 HD (720×1280) video sequences, named "jeff", "shields" and *Mobile Calendar* ("mobcal") with respective frame rates of 30 Hz, 30 Hz, and 25 Hz. The "jeff" sequence is a typical head-and-shoulders video conferencing scene with stationary background. The "shields" sequence is a panning scene with a walking person on highly textured background. The "mobcal" sequence is a complex scene with multiple objects in complex motions.

We encode the first 250 frames of each sequence to a constant bit-rate of 1.5 Mbps using the JM-15.0 H.264/AVC encoder. The frames are coded into I-P-P-P frame structure with 6 slices of 900 macroblocks each per frame. The video reconstructed at the encoder from the 3 sequences forms the encoder-side training data.

The decoder-side training data is composed of 72 reconstructed sequences derived from the 3 encoded bit streams. In each case, a single slice is dropped from the encoded bit stream and the sequence is reconstructed using frame-copy error concealment. The location of each dropped slices is in one of the frames numbered 50, 100, 150 and 200.

In the development of the video projection presented next, the projection is applied to each reconstructed sequence at the decoder and the corresponding sequence reconstructed at the encoder without loss. The detection error ratios are calculated only on the frames which are known have errors or propagated errors. In the remainder of this section, each figure depicts 3 receiver operating characteristic (ROC) curves, showing the unprocessed ratios, the ratios after spatial processing, and the ratios after spatial and temporal processing.

3.2.1 Mean Projection

We consider the mean projection because it is intuitively the most sensitive to perceptually significant distortions in the decoded video. For every 64×64 block, we take the mean of the luma values and quantize them with respect to a given step size. From this quantized symbol, we extract the 3 least significant bits as the projection coefficient. This binning operation constrains the quality feedback signal to the desired low bit-rate.

Fig. 6 plots the mean projection's ROC curves for the 3 input sequences, "jeff", "shields" and "mobcal." Each curve is traced from left to right by varying the quantization step size from 2^5 to 2^{-1} by factors of 2. Observe that the ROC curves are usually (but not always) monotonic; in particular, reducing the step size usually decreases the undetection ratio and increases the false detection ratio. This behavior is not guaranteed because the 3-bit binning operation results in (non-contiguous) non-embedded quantization regions. Notice also that at the target false detection ratio of 10%, the undetection ratio is best for the "jeff" sequence, but remains above 1%.

3.2.2 Horizontal Difference Projection

The horizontal difference projection also produces 3 bits from each 64×64 block of pixels, but is orthogonal to the

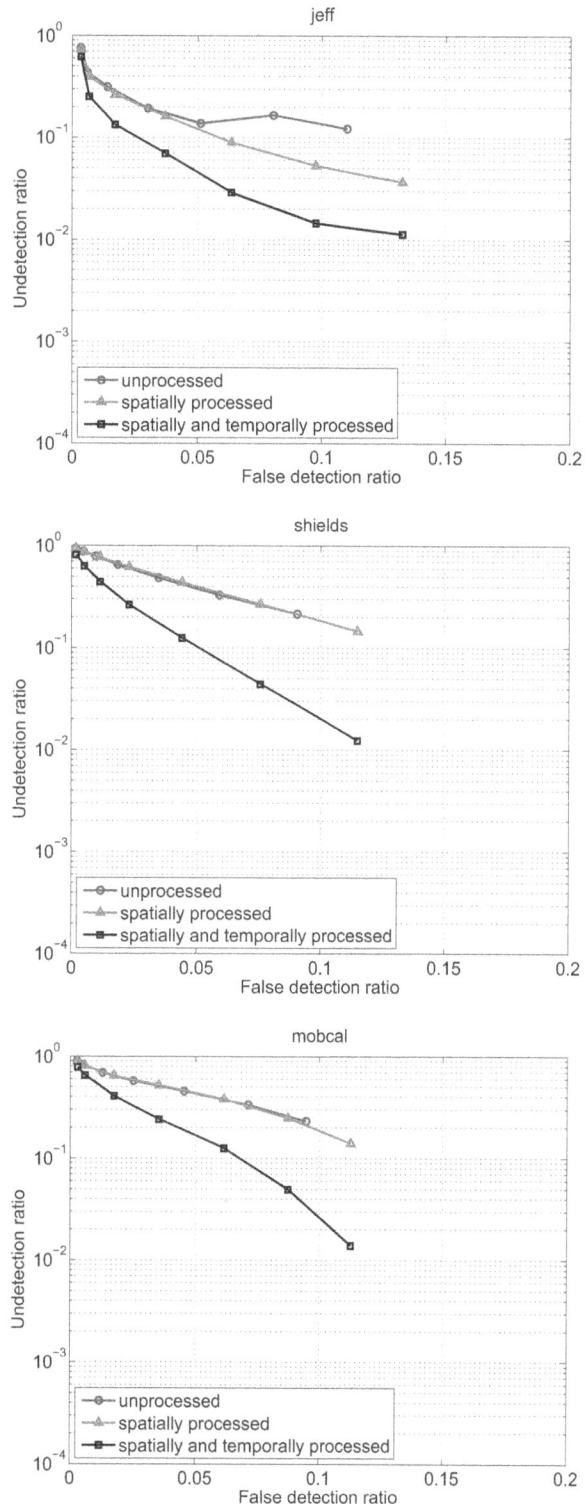

Figure 6: Detection performance ROC curves for the mean projection applied to "jeff", "shields" and "mobcal." Each curve is traced from left to right by varying the quantization step size from 2^5 to 2^{-1} by factors of 2.

mean projection. We divide the block into a left and a right subblock, each of size 64×32 pixels, and compute the mean of the left luma values minus the mean of the right luma values. This symbol is quantized with a certain step size and the 3 least significant bits are extracted as the projection coefficient. In this way, the horizontal difference projection is more sensitive than the mean projection to horizontal misalignment errors due to frame copy under horizontal motion.

Fig. 7 plots the ROC curves, each of which is traced from left to right by varying the quantization step size from 2^4 to 2^{-2} by factors of 2. With spatial and temporal processing, the horizontal difference projection underperforms the mean projection for "jeff" and outperforms it for "shields" and "mobcal." This is because "shields" and "mobcal" are predominantly composed of textured regions, while "jeff" mainly consists of flat regions. These flat regions do not suffer as much from misalignment errors. At the target false detection ratio of 10%, the undetection ratio is best for the "shields" sequence, at around 0.5%.

3.2.3 Vertical Difference Projection

The vertical different projection also produces 3 bits from each 64×64 block, in a way orthogonal to both the mean and horizontal difference projections. Lile the horizontal difference projection, we compute the difference of means of luma values of two subblocks. In this case, the two subblocks are the top and bottom halves, each of size 32×64 pixels. As before, each symbol is quantized and the 3 least significant bits are extracted as the projection coefficient. Thus, the vertical projection is sensitive to vertical misalignment errors caused by frame copy under vertical motion.

Fig. 8 plots the ROC curves, each of which again is traced from left to right by varying the quantization step size from 2^4 to 2^{-2} by factors of 2. The vertical projection performs best on sequences that contain a lot of textured regions, for the same reason as the horizontal projection does. But at the target false detection ratio of 10%, the undetection ratio is best for the "mobcal" sequence, at around 0.8%.

3.2.4 Combined Projection

Observe that the choice of the best projection among the three above depends very much on the video content. For sequences with flat regions, such as "jeff", the mean projection is best. For sequences with texture and horizontal motion, such as "shields", the horizontal projection is best. For sequences with texture and vertical motion, such as "mobcal", the vertical projection is best.

We therefore combine these projection types to create a combined projection that is appropriate for different types of video content. One of the three projections is chosen for each 64×64 block according to its spatiotemporal position in the video sequence. Fig. 9 shows the patterns of projections that cycle every 4 frames. Within a frame, the pattern is Bayer-like, with the mean projection occupying one checkerboard color and the horizontal and vertical difference projections sharing the other. As can be seen readily, any block will have a projection different from the projections of its adjacent neighbors. The reason for spatial hole filling with the cross-shaped structuring element in Fig. 5 now becomes clearer. When one of the projection types does not mark severe degradations but the others do, then this structuring element fills the resulting holes. The temporal processing

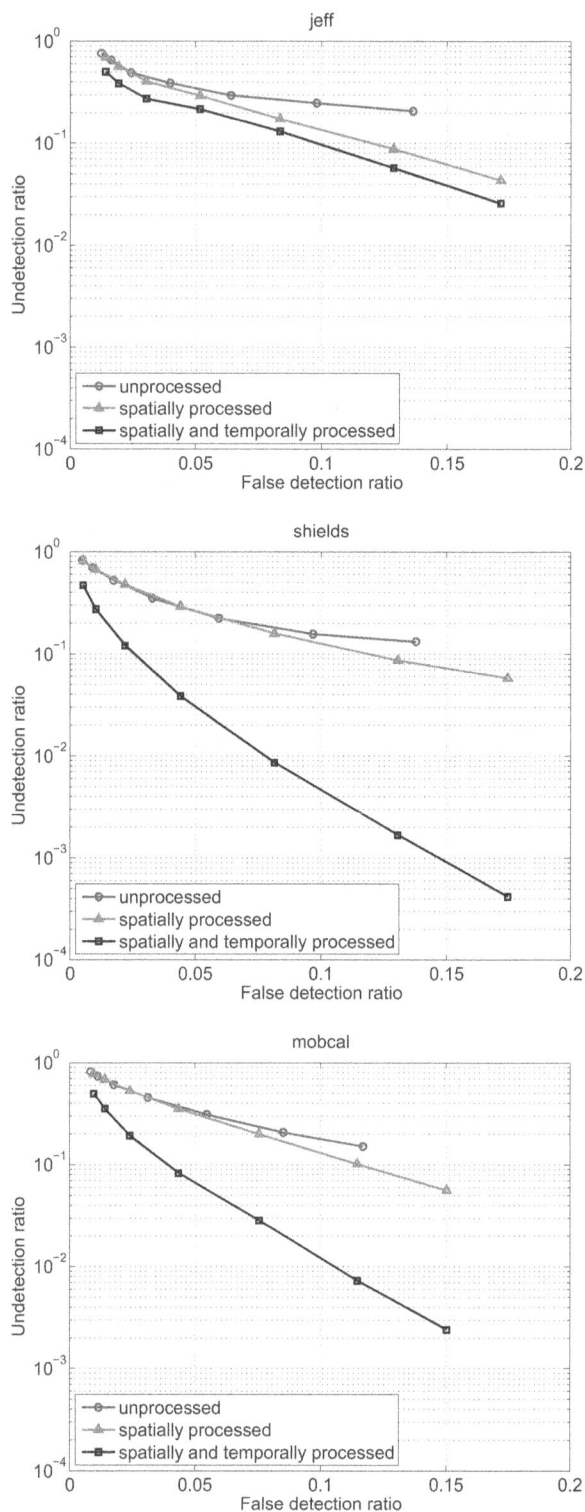

Figure 7: Detection performance ROC curves for the horizontal difference projection applied to "jeff", "shields" and "mobcal." Each curve is traced from left to right by varying the quantization step size from 2^4 to 2^{-2} by factors of 2.

Figure 9: Bayer-like patterns of projection types. The patterns cycle every 4 frames.

over windows of 4 frames similarly takes advantage of the cycling patterns.

Fig. 10 shows ROC scatter plots for the combined projection. Each point is generated by choosing a pair of quantization step sizes drawn from 2^5 to 2^{-1} for the mean projection and from 2^4 to 2^{-2} for the other blocks. The performance of the combined projection, after spatial and temporal processing, exceeds that of the other projections for all sequences. Consider the following pair of quantization step sizes: 2^3 for the mean projection and 2^{-2} for horizontal and vertical difference projections. At this setting, the false detection ratios are 10%, 9.5% and 8.3% for "jeff", "shields" and "mobcal", respectively, and the corresponding undetection ratios are 0.2%, 0.4% and 0.5%. Thus, the combined projection with quantization step sizes 2^3 and 2^{-2} provides for very effective low-rate visual quality feedback.

4. LIVE VIDEO MULTICAST SYSTEM

In this section, we present evaluation results of our proposed visual quality feedback in a live streaming multicast setting, where one live encoded video stream is distributed to multiple clients with independent loss patterns. We seek to compare the video quality achievable using visual quality feedback and schemes that only exploit packet level loss statistics such as sequence number of lost packets.

Our focus is to evaluate the advantage of visual quality feedback in a practical and reasonable setting rather than developing a state-of-the-art multicast system. As such, we do not attempt to employ and optimally combine multiple error recovery tools such as retransmissions, error correcting codes, resilient source coding and peer-to-peer error recovery structures. Instead, we will focus our attention on a single effective error recovery measure: intra-coding.

4.1 System Description

We perform the following three experiments using the setup in Fig. 11:

- *intra-frame*: the feedback from each client contains sequence numbers of its lost packets . The *adaptation agent* signals the encoder to intra-code all slices of the

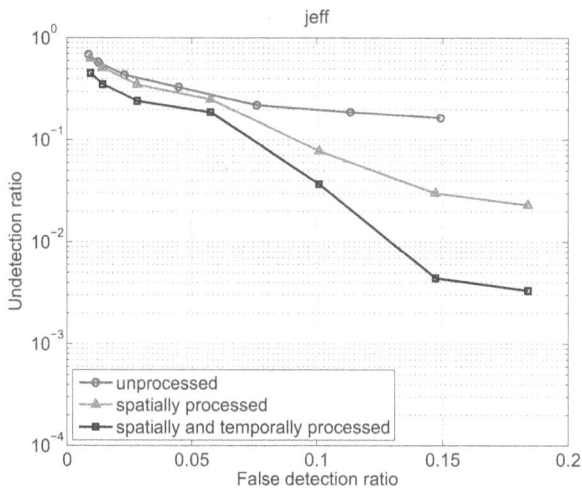

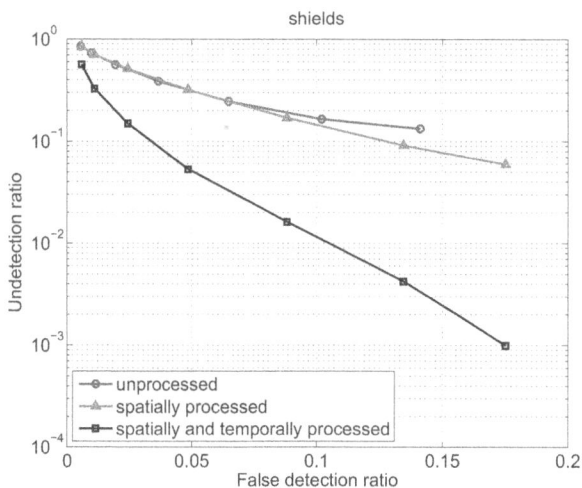

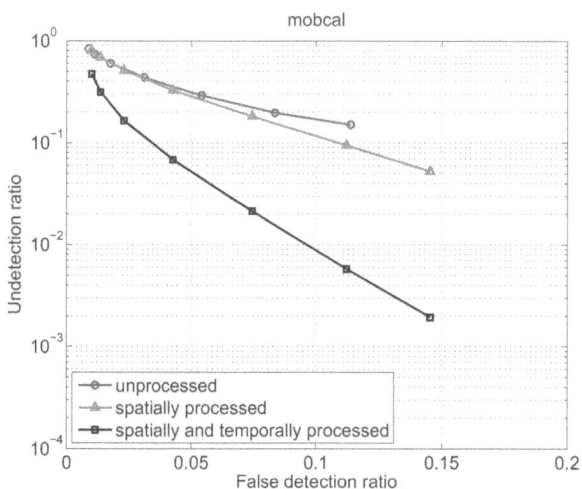

Figure 8: Detection performance ROC curves for the vertical difference projection applied to "jeff", "shields" and "mobcal." Each curve is traced from left to right by varying the quantization step size from 2^4 to 2^{-2} by factors of 2.

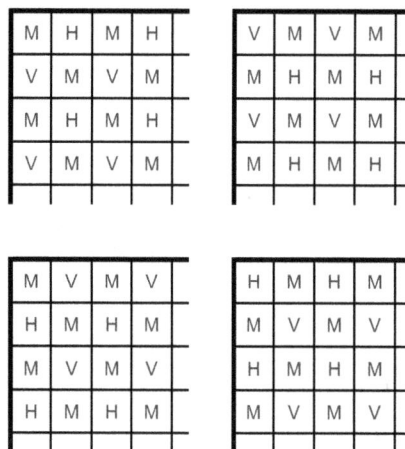

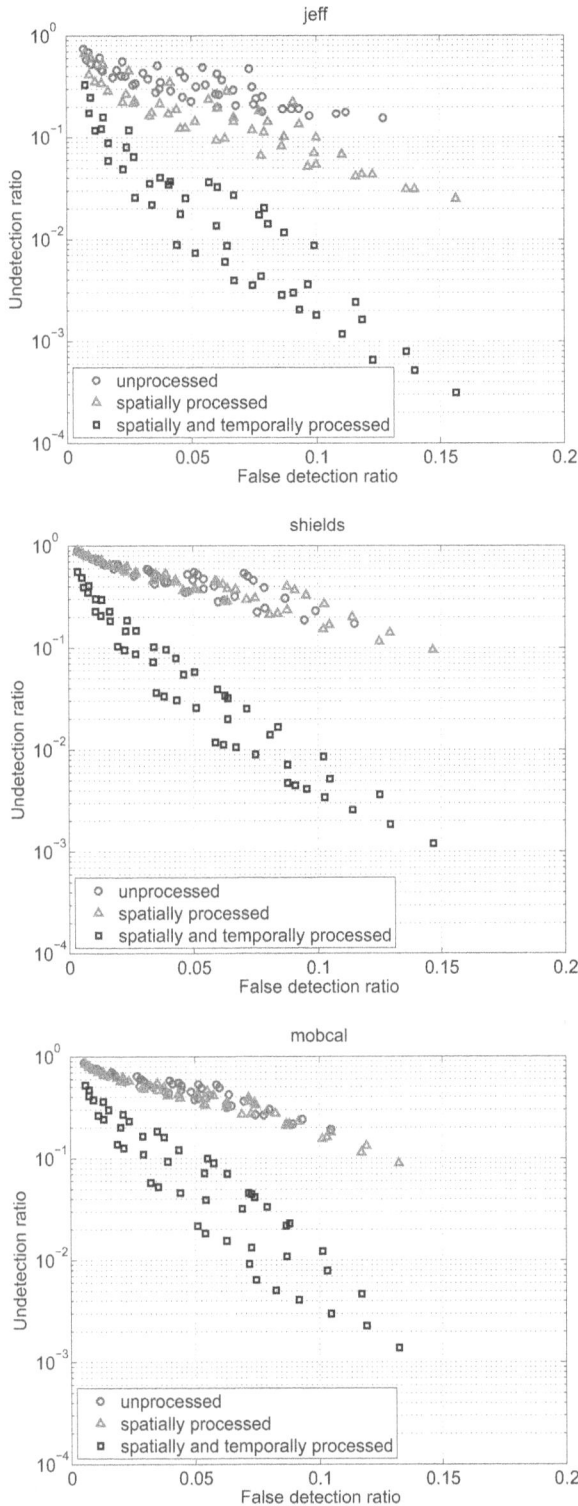

Figure 10: Detection performance ROC scatter plots for the combined projection applied to "jeff", "shields" and "mobcal." The points represent quantization step sizes drawn from 2^5 to 2^{-1} for the mean blocks and from 2^4 to 2^{-2} for the other blocks.

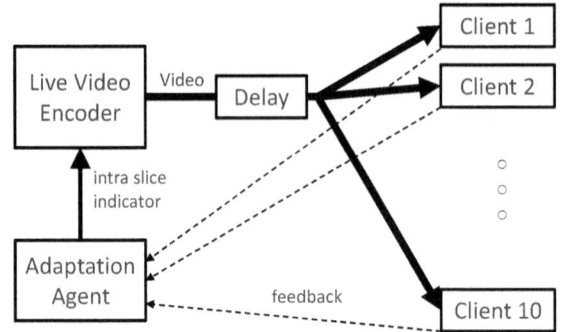

Figure 11: Experimental setup for live video multicast. Depending on the experiment, *feedback* can contain sequence number of lost packets, or visual feedback to determine which slices, if any, need to be intra-coded by the live encoder in the next frame.

next frame if *any* client experience a loss since the last intra-coded frame.

- *intra-slice*: same feedback as *intra-frame*. The *adaptation agent* locates the slice corresponding to the sequence number of lost packets for all clients, and singal all slices with losses to be intra-coded in the next frame.

- *visual*: the feedback contains visual quality feedback described in Section 3. The *adaptation agent* performs the same projection on the loss-free video (not shown) to determine which slices contain errors for each client. All slices with errors for at least one client is intra-coded in the next frame.

For live video encoding, we employ the H.264 encoder from Intel Performance Primitive v6.1, which we have modified to support signalling of intra-slice coding. For video source, we employ the 250 frame *Mobile Calendar* sequence at 720×1280 and 25 frames per second, which we cropped to a size of 704×1280 so that both dimensions are a multiple of 64, our chosen block size in Section 3. The source is repeatedly transmitted in a loop to support longer experiments. Each frame is coded using 11 slices, each with size 64×1280. In all experiments, the encoder is configured to produce a constant bit-rate of 1.7 Mbps, and each coded slice is broken into one or more packets with maximum size 1400 bytes. As discussed in Section 3, the feedback overhead of *visual* is 3 bits per 64×64 block, or 16.5 kbps, which is about 1% of the video bit-rate.

Packet losses are simulated using trace files that are generated independently for the 10 clients. The loss model is random loss with a low packet loss rate of 0.05%. For fair comparison among the experiments, the same set of trace files are used for all experiments.

The simulated delay in our experiment is 10 ms for all clients, which is less than half the inter-frame time of 40 ms for video at 25 Hz. This means a loss in frame N can be reported to *adaptation agent* in time to effect corrective measures at frame $N + 1$. In a general multicast system, the clients may have widely varying delays. Nevertheless, a more uniform and low delay is of practical interest in many settings such as school and corporate campuses.

4.2 Experimental Results

We examine the video quality of the schemes *intra-frame*, *intra-slice*, and *visual* in terms of average Peak Signal-to-Noise Ratio (PSNR)[1]. We first show the per-frame PSNR averaged over all clients for the various schemes in Fig. 12. The apparent 10-second periodic structure is a direct result of transmitting a 10 seconds clip repeatedly in a loop. We see that *intra-frame* achieves the lowest average PSNR, at 31.25 dB, with large quality fluctuation over time despite the low packet loss rate of 0.05%. This is due to the aggressive bit usage of an intra-coded frame when only one packet is lost. Specifically, with 11 slices commonly mapped to 11 packets, the probability of coding an intra-frame due to losses from *one* client becomes about 0.5%. With 10 clients, the overall probability of intra-coding a frame increases to about 5%. The resulting frequent usage of intra-coding causes average PSNR to be low. Furthermore, these intra-coded frames are created in response to random losses, and may occasionally cluster in time, causing the need to produce very low quality video in order to maintain average bit-rate, resulting in high volatility in quality over time.

In contrast, by trading off the guarantee in error recovery for lower bit cost, *intra-slice* avoids the two problems of low and volatile quality. It achieves an average PSNR of 33.33 dB. Similar *average* performance is obtained by *visual*, achieving a PSNR of 33.24 dB. Nevertheless, while the average PSNR reported in Fig. 12 is a good way to summarize experience of all clients, the averaged result is not indicative of the actual experience of any one client.

The individual PSNR traces for all 10 clients using the *visual* and *intra-slice* schemes are shown in Fig. 13. Notice that the traces for *visual* and *intra-slice* are similar with a few notable exceptions. For client 1, *intra-slice* suffers from a severe 7-second drop in PSNR of about 10 dB relative to *visual*. Clients 5 and 7, when using *intra-slice*, also experiences long bouts of error propagation of about 5 and 3 seconds in duration, respectively. In contrast, the noticeable PSNR drops encountered by using *visual* are limited to individual frames. These brief errors can be visually masked by momentarily freezing the previous frame. Under *intra-slice*, there is error indication only at the frame where losses occur. There is no provisions for error tracking to determine subsequent error propagation. The support for *continuous* error checking is one key advantage of using visual quality feedback over simple loss indicators like sequence number of lost packets.

The current implementation of *visual* performs intra-coding at a slice level. The slices are of size 64×1280, which contains 20 64×64 blocks. As discussed in Section 3, the 1% bit overhead allows for error detection on a granularity of 64×64 block. As a result, greater improvement over *intra-slice* may be possible by adopting intra-coding on a per 64×64 rather than 64×1280 basis. This is a subject of future investigation.

---

[1]computed as $10 \times \log_{10} \frac{255 \times 255}{MSE}$, where MSE is the pixel-wise mean square error. Generally a PSNR of about 35 dB is considered excellent, 32 dB is considered good, and below 30 dB is considered poor.

5. CONCLUSIONS

In this paper, we argue that providing useful feedback is an important task for feedback adaptive streaming applications. While typical feedback schemes exploit only packet level statistics, we show that it is possible to construct visual feedback that allows error tracking and localization with a low overhead of about 1%. In such a way, selective correction of necessary portions can be realized without the complex task of emulating decoders. We also demonstrate in a live video multicast setting how such visual feedback can be exploited to allow more intelligent use of a specific adaptation method, namely intra-coding of slices. With visual quality feedback, we achieve over 2 dB gain compared to intra-frame coding, and achieves significantly less quality fluctuation than an intra-slice scheme.

There are several aspects of the current work that can be further improved. The encoder should match the region where intra-coding is applied to the detection granularity of 64×64 rather than one slice. Slepian-Wolf coding of feedback should provide more efficient compression, which would allow lower overhead or more reliable feedback. A broader study should investigate the impact of conflicting uses of the network (such as other applications and video streams) on the proposed error resilience system.

6. REFERENCES

[1] ITU-T Recommendation J.240: Framework for remote monitoring of transmitted picture signal-to-noise ratio using spread-spectrum and orthogonal transform, Jun. 2004.

[2] K. Chono, Y.-C. Lin, D. P. Varodayan, and B. Girod. Reduced-reference image quality estimation using distributed source coding. In *Proc. IEEE Internat. Conf. Multimedia and Expo*, Hannover, Germany, Jun. 2008.

[3] N. Faerber, E. Steinbach, and B. Girod. Robust H.263 compatible video transmission over wireless channels. In *Proc. Picture Coding Symp.*, Melbourne, Australia, 1996.

[4] T. Friedman, R. Caceres, and A. Clark. RTP control protocol extended reports (RTCP XR). *RFC 3611*, November 2003.

[5] S. Fukunaga, T. Nakai, and H. Inoue. Error resilient video coding by dynamic replacing of reference pictures. In *Proc. IEEE Global Commun. Conf.*, London, United Kingdom, 1996.

[6] B. Girod and N. Faerber. Feedback-based error control for mobile video transmission. *Proc. IEEE*, 87(10):1707–1723, Oct. 1999.

[7] R. Kawada, O. Sugimoto, A. Koike, M. Wada, and S. Matsumoto. Highly precise estimation scheme for remote video PSNR using spread spectrum and extraction of orthogonal transform coefficients. *Electronics Commun. Japan (Part I)*, 89(6):51–62, Jun. 2006.

[8] Z. Li, Y.-C. Lin, D. P. Varodayan, P. Baccichet, and B. Girod. Distortion-aware retransmission and concealment of video packets using a Wyner-Ziv-coded thumbnail. In *Proc. IEEE Internat. Workshop Multimedia Signal Process.*, Cairns, Australia, Oct. 2008.

[9] Y.-C. Lin, D. P. Varodayan, and B. Girod. Video quality monitoring for mobile multicast peers using distributed source coding. In *Proc. Internat. Mobile Multimedia Commun. Conf.*, London, United Kingdom, Sept. 2009.

[10] X. Lu, S. Tao, M. El Zarki, and R. Guerin. Quality-based adaptive video over the internet. In *Proc. Commun. Networks Distrib. Syst. Conf.*, Orlando, Florida, 2003.

[11] D. Slepian and J. K. Wolf. Noiseless coding of correlated information sources. *IEEE Trans. Inform. Theory*, 19(4):471–480, Jul. 1973.

[12] E. Steinbach, N. Faerber, and B. Girod. Standard compatible extension of H.263 for robust video transmission in mobile environments. *IEEE Trans. Circuits Syst. Video Technol.*, 7(12):872–881, Dec. 1997.

[13] Y. Tomita, T. Kimura, and T. Ichikawa. Error resilient modified inter-frame coding system for limited reference picture memories. In *Proc. Picture Coding Symp.*, Berlin, Germany, 1997.

[14] S. Wolf and M. Pinson. Spatial-temporal distortion metrics for in-service quality monitoring and any digital video system. In *Proc. SPIE Symp. Voice Video Data Commun.*, Boston, Massachusetts, 1999.

[15] C. Yeo, W. Tan, and D. Mukherjee. Receiver error concealment using acknowledge preview (RECAP) - an approach to resilient video streaming. In *Proc. IEEE Internat. Conf. Acoustics, Speech and Signal Process.*, Taipei, Taiwan, 2009.

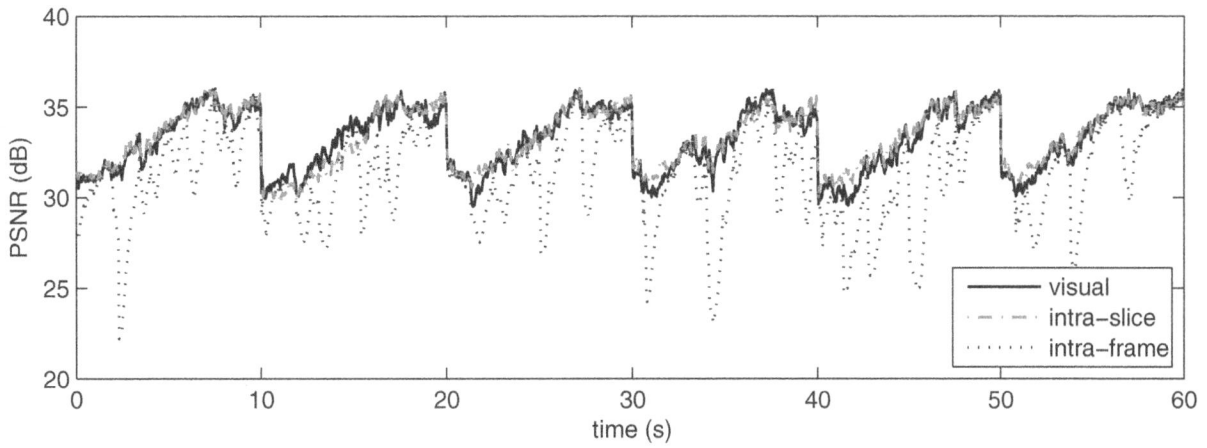

Figure 12: Per-frame PSNR, averaged over all clients. The traces for *visual*, *intra-slice* and *intra-frame* are shown as solid black, dashed red and dotted black curves, respectively.

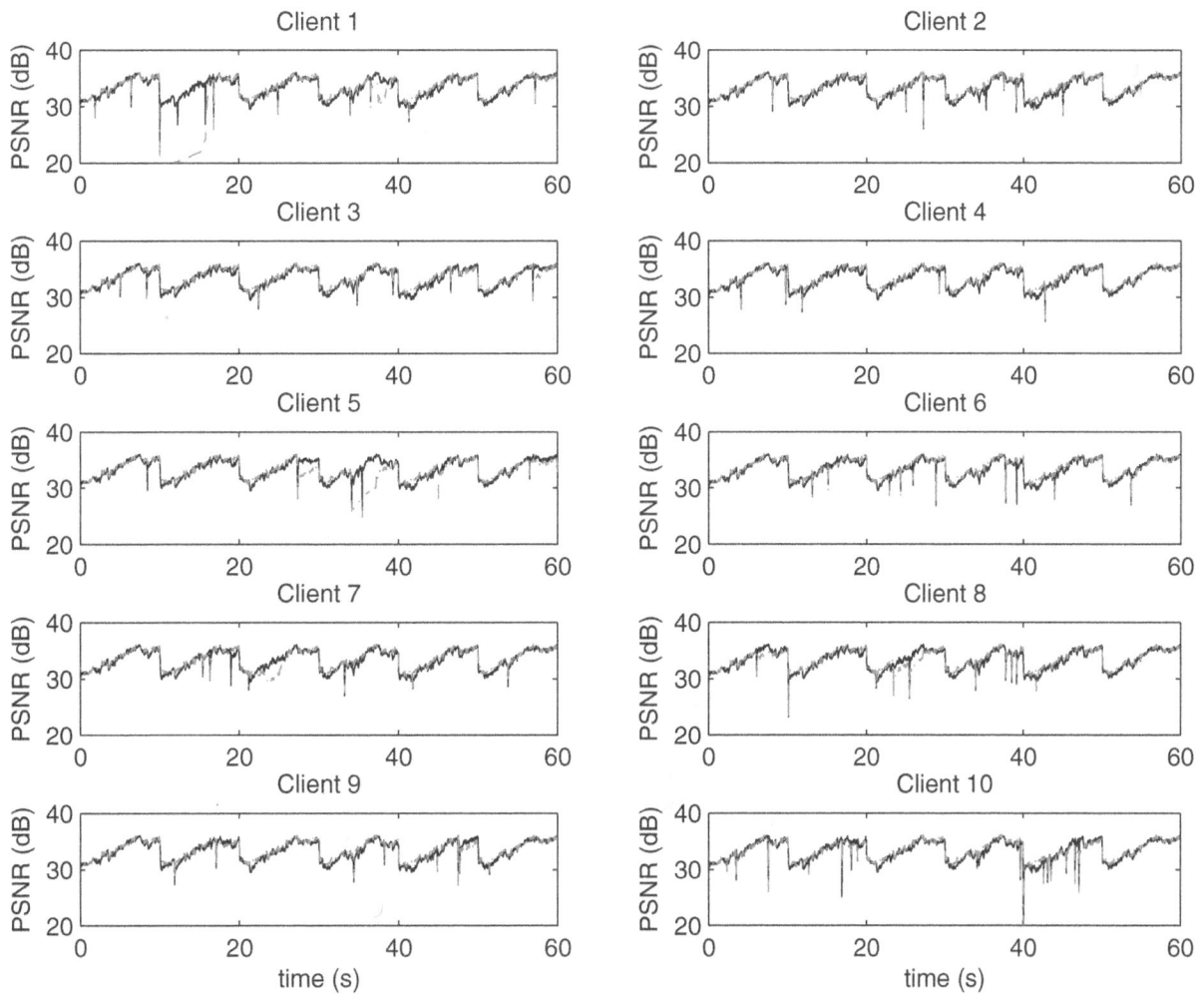

Figure 13: PSNR traces for all 10 clients. The traces for *visual* and *intra-slice* are shown as solid black and dashed red curves, respectively.

Evaluation of HTTP-based Request-Response Streams for Internet Video Streaming

Robert Kuschnig, Ingo Kofler, Hermann Hellwagner
Institute of Information Technology (ITEC)
Klagenfurt University, Austria
{firstname.lastname}@uni-klu.ac.at

ABSTRACT

Adaptive video streaming based on TCP/HTTP is becoming popular because of its ability to adapt to changing network conditions. We present an in-depth experimental analysis of the use of HTTP-based request-response streams for video streaming. In this scheme, video fragments are fetched by a client from the server, in smaller units called chunks, potentially via multiple parallel HTTP requests (TCP connections). A model for the achievable throughput is formulated. The model is validated by a broad range of streaming experiments, including an evaluation of TCP-friendliness.

Our findings include that request-response streams are able to scale with the available bandwidth by increasing the chunk size or the number of concurrent streams. Several combinations of system parameters exhibiting TCP-friendliness are presented. We also evaluate the video streaming performance in terms of video quality in the presence of packet loss. Multiple request-response streams are able to maintain satisfactory performance, while a single TCP connection deteriorates rapidly with increasing packet loss. The results provide experimental evidence that HTTP-based request-response streams are a good alternative to classical TCP streaming.

Categories and Subject Descriptors

H.5.1 [**Multimedia Information Systems**]: Video

General Terms

Design, Experimentation, Performance

Keywords

HTTP video streaming, TCP-friendliness, H.264/SVC, adaptive video streaming

1. INTRODUCTION

The Internet and its applications are starting to play a main role in consumer electronics. To be able to connect a

MMSys'11, February 23–25, 2011, San Jose, California, USA.
Copyright 2011 ACM 978-1-4503-0517-4/11/02 ...$10.00.

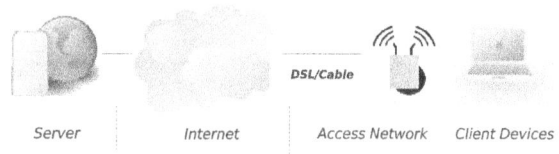

Figure 1: Use case

growing number and variety of devices, the network infrastructure has to be enhanced. As a result of ongoing investments, last-mile bandwidths increased considerably in recent years [4]. This also gave Internet video streaming, which heavily relies on network bandwidth, a lot of momentum. Video-on-Demand (e.g., online video rental), Live Video (TV broadcasts) or social video sharing are only some of the popular video streaming applications.

The Internet imposes new challenges on video streaming since it offers best-effort service only and lacks admission control and quality of service (QoS) mechanisms. Although the Internet does not provide admission control, some mechanisms have to be deployed to avoid network congestion. The transport protocol TCP is responsible for avoiding congestion by continuously adjusting the transmission rate at the sender based on feedback from the network. An example for TCP-based video streaming in the Internet is the video portal YouTube, which streams the content to consumers all over the world. The delivery of YouTube videos is almost centralized [15], which leads to round trip times (RTTs) of up to 200 ms and more. In this context, coping with packet losses which may occur due to congestion or packet corruption, becomes a challenge [8].

In our use case (see Figure 1), we focus on access networks which are assumed to form the bottleneck links. Currently the adaptation to different network conditions is done by the user who chooses from different qualities of the content, ranging from low resolution video to HD (e.g., 720p). Having the user select the video quality based on his/her experience may be cumbersome and error-prone, because the available bandwidth is in general not constant. *Adaptive* video streaming aims to simplify this process by continuously adapting the content bit rate to the available bandwidth of the network. Consequently, adaptive video streaming over TCP gained a lot of attention in recent years [19, 7, 23, 1].

In this paper, we analyze TCP/HTTP-based adaptive video streaming for use in the Internet (see Section 2). In particular, we investigate the performance of multiple parallel HTTP-based request-response streams for video streaming. Previous work [13] showed that multiple streams show favorable characteristics in case of packet loss and mitigate the effects of TCP connection timeouts or stalls, while maintaining TCP-friendliness. In Section 3 we will present a refined analytical model (as compared to [13]) for the achievable throughput of a request-response streaming system. After giving a short introduction of H.264/SVC and priority streaming in Section 4, we present an HTTP-based request-response H.264/SVC video streaming system in Section 5. We will investigate how the system parameters of the request-response streaming system influence the system performance under diverse network conditions. The evaluation methodology, the investigated system, network parameters, and the evaluation setup will be described in Section 6. In Section 7, our findings on the throughput performance and TCP-friendliness are presented. A comparison in terms of video quality of using multiple HTTP request-response streams vs. a single TCP connection will show the actual benefit of the request-response streams. Section 8 concludes the paper.

2. TCP-/HTTP-BASED VIDEO STREAMING

While there are dedicated protocols for video streaming in IPTV networks (like RTP/UDP [16]), TCP (and HTTP over TCP) gained a lot of attention in the area of Internet video streaming due to its reliable end-to-end transport, the ability to adapt to changing network conditions, and easy deployment. Since TCP's reliability and adaptive behavior are based on acknowledgments and retransmissions, the performance of TCP depends a lot on the network conditions. Dynamically changing RTTs or packet losses lead to a degradation of the performance of TCP.

The throughput rate of TCP depends on the maximum segment size (MSS) and the round trip time (RTT). If we consider a packet loss pattern such that after the successful transmission of $1/p$ packets (of size MSS) one packet is lost, the *estimated TCP throughput rate* r_{tcp} for TCP Reno would be [9]:

$$r_{tcp} = \frac{MSS}{\sqrt{p}} \cdot \frac{1}{RTT} \qquad (1)$$

With Equation 1 it becomes evident that the maximum throughput of TCP is limited by the packet loss rate p for a given RTT. The additive-increase/multiplicative-decrease (AIMD) behavior of the congestion control algorithm leads to an additional variation of the throughput. Thus TCP has been considered unsuitable for video streaming for many years. The streaming performance of TCP for constant-bit-rate content was investigated in [19], which stated that the TCP throughput should be at least twice the media bit rate in order to avoid jerky playback of the video. With increasing bandwidth of the last-mile networks (a significant number of users own DSL/cable connections with downlink bandwidth greater than 4 Mbps [4]), this kind of over-provisioning is now feasible for low resolution videos. However, high-definition videos have in general higher bandwidth requirements (> 2 Mbps), so over-provisioning may not be sufficient to prevent transmission stalls and therefore jerky playback. In this case, adapting the video content may be required to be able to cope with changing network conditions.

In the last couple of years, adaptive video streaming using TCP/HTTP has become quite popular. Microsoft introduced HTTP-based adaptive streaming with their Smooth Streaming System [23]. The idea is to use small HTTP progressive downloads (of so-called fragments) instead of a single one. Each fragment comprises several seconds of video data and is usually aligned with the GOP boundaries of the video [23]. In general, the fragments are downloaded consecutively and the video can be decoded and displayed on the client. With this approach, it is possible to switch the media bit rate (and hence the quality) after each download and adapt to the current network conditions. Move Networks [10] also uses similar mechanisms like Microsoft Smooth Streaming [23] for the media transport, and so does Apple's HTTP Live Streaming [11]. The 3GPP Adaptive HTTP Streaming standard [1] defines methods for adaptive media streaming. The Akamai HD Network [3] also features adaptive streaming of media content.

The adaptation system of all mentioned approaches works in a similar manner. Different video fragments are supplied which represent various qualities of the media. The video fragments are downloaded sequentially. If the available bandwidth does not allow to download the fragments of high quality, lower quality fragments are selected for download. The main difference between the approaches lies in the metadata for describing the media content, the container format for the media [14], and the adaptation decision taking algorithm, which decides when to switch from one media quality to another. Most of the streaming systems restrict their adaptiveness to stream switching (like shown in [17] for H.264/AVC), without taking advantage of the most recent scalable video codec H.264/SVC [22] which enables fine-grained adaptation. The transport of the video fragments is mainly based on HTTP's request-response paradigm, because using HTTP allows easy deployment in existing network infrastructures.

In our work we call a single HTTP connection transporting video fragments an *HTTP-based request-response stream*. While the streaming systems mentioned above are mainly based on a single request-response stream, we investigate the behavior of *multiple* concurrent HTTP request-response streams. In the next section, the HTTP-based request-response streams will be described in detail.

3. HTTP-BASED REQUEST-RESPONSE STREAMS

In classical TCP streaming, the media data is continuously streamed from the server to the client using a long-lived TCP connection. Because HTTP is based on the request-response (rr) paradigm, *HTTP-based request-response streams* have to request the media data to initiate their transmission. Request-response streams behave differently also in that the responses are in general small chunks of media data. While it is possible to emulate the behavior of a long-lived TCP connection in a request-response streaming setting by using very large chunks, the use of small chunks leads to short responses, which may experience unfairness in congested networks [8].

In general, TCP connections share the available bandwidth in a fair manner [8]. Aggregating multiple TCP streams for a single use is potentially unfair to concurrent single connections. We observed that it is possible to control the TCP-friendliness of request-response streams by introducing temporal gaps between requests (inter-request gap t_{gap}), which emulate an increased RTT [13]. Because TCP features no throughput fairness between connections with different RTTs [8], it is possible to aggregate multiple submissive request-response streams for a single purpose, while still providing TCP-friendliness. In addition, multiple request-response streams are not as prone to packet losses as a single TCP connection [13].

To get an of idea of the achievable throughput of such a request-response streaming system, we created a simple model describing the upper bound of the throughput. Assuming that a chunk (of size l_{ch}) is transferred within a single RTT and n_c concurrent streams are used for transmitting the media data, the upper bound for the throughput without packet loss $r_{rrsimple}$ can be calculated as follows [13]:

$$r_{rrsimple} = n_c \left(\frac{l_{ch}}{RTT + t_{gap}} \right) \quad (2)$$

Equation 2 shows that we are able to control the throughput by means of n_c, l_{ch} and t_{gap}. In addition, TCP-friendliness has to be supplied, so a trade-off has to be found between the throughput and the TCP-friendliness. The goal is to stabilize and enhance the overall throughput and to be more robust to changing network conditions than a single TCP connection, but also to be fair to other concurrent TCP connections in case of congestion.

Because the assumption that a chunk can be transferred within a single RTT is not valid for large chunk sizes, we extend our model by taking the network configuration into account. This extension allows us to explore the limitation of the request-response streams under certain network conditions. For that reason, we assume to know the bottleneck bandwidth BW and the maximum queueing delay t_q of the bottleneck router. Using BW and t_q we can calculate the queue size $l_q = BW * t_q$. Because the n_c concurrent TCP connections are competing on the network link, we assume that the router queue is shared between all request-response streams ($l_{rr} = l_q/n_c$). Taking into account that each request-response stream can transfer at most l_{rr} bytes per RTT, we can define the number of round trips needed to transmit the chunk as $n_{rt} = l_{ch}/l_{rr}$.

Because the underlying TCP connection tries to maximize the throughput, we can assume that the router queue will be fully utilized. For a single request-response stream, the AIMD algorithm of TCP leads to a saw tooth shaped queue utilization (see Figure 2), which results in a queuing delay of $t_q/2$ on average. Because multiple TCP streams tend to self-synchronize [2], we assume that the average queuing delay is also valid for multiple TCP streams. A request-response stream may not be able to fully utilize the network queue, if small chunk sizes and a low number of concurrent streams are used. In this case, we reduce the estimated queuing delay in our model, if n_{rt} is below one. So the average queuing delay of a request-response stream can be defined as $t_{qav} = min(n_{rt}, 1) \cdot t_q/2$. Using this information the *estimated transfer duration of one chunk* t_{ch} can be defined as:

$$t_{ch} = \lceil n_{rt} \rceil (RTT + t_{qav}) \quad (3)$$

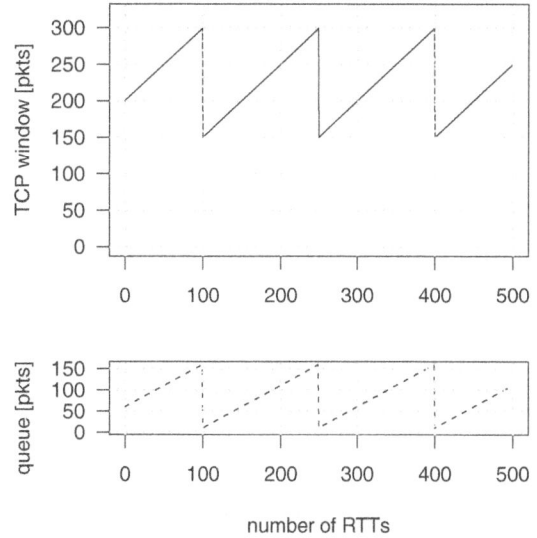

Figure 2: TCP window size and router queue utilization for a TCP flow through a router with a queue size of $l_q = BW * MAXRTT$ **[2].**

The *average achieved throughput* r_{rr} of the request-response streams can be defined as:

$$r_{rr} = n_c \left(\frac{l_{ch}}{t_{ch} + t_{gap}} \right) \quad (4)$$

Like in the initial model, we are able to tune the throughput by means of n_c, l_{ch}, and t_{gap} (see Equation 4). The main difference is now that this model takes the characteristics of the network into account (except packet loss).

A direct result of Equation 1 is that the data which TCP can transport within a single RTT is limited by the packet loss rate. So in case of packet loss, we have to define l_{rrloss}, which is the amount of data which can be transported by a request-response stream within one RTT. This is now either restricted by the router queue or the behavior of TCP in case of packet loss. Note that we are now using the same packet loss pattern as used in the TCP throughput estimation (see Equation 1).

$$l_{rrloss} = min(l_{rr}, \frac{MSS}{\sqrt{p}}) \quad (5)$$

The queuing delay is also affected by the packet loss, because the packet loss restricts TCP's window size and therefore the router queue utilization. Our model makes the simplifying assumption that if the utilized queue size in the router sinks below a certain level, the queuing delay begins to decrease. For that reason, we define the *average queuing delay under packet loss* $t_{qavloss}$ as:

$$t_{qavloss} = \begin{cases} \frac{l_{rrloss}}{l_{rr}} \cdot t_q/2 & \text{if } l_{rrloss} < \frac{l_{rr}}{2} \\ min(n_{rt}, 1) \cdot t_q/2 & \text{otherwise} \end{cases} \quad (6)$$

Because the number of round trips needed to transmit the chunk is also affected by the packet loss, we redefine it as $n_{rtloss} = l_{ch}/l_{rrloss}$. As a result, we can calculate the estimated transfer duration of one chunk under packet loss t_{chloss}:

$$t_{chloss} = \lceil n_{rtloss} \rceil (RTT + t_{qavloss}) \quad (7)$$

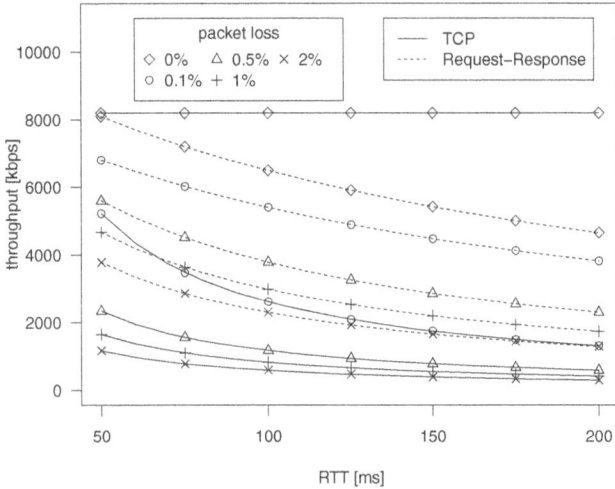

Figure 3: *Model* for throughput performance of a single TCP connection (TCP) r_{tcp} and for the request-response streams r_{rr} (MSS = 1460 *bytes*, l_{ch} = 160 kB, n_c = 5, t_{gap} = 210 ms) at a fixed bottleneck bandwidth BW = 8192 $kbps$ and packet loss rate p.

The throughput under packet loss for the request-response streaming system r_{rrloss} can be defined as follows:

$$r_{rrloss} = n_c \left(\frac{l_{ch}}{t_{chloss} + t_{gap}} \right) \qquad (8)$$

This refined model for request-response streams jointly takes the packet loss and the queuing delay on the bottleneck router into account, by using the throughput estimation for TCP and the knowledge about the bottleneck router. In general, increasing the number of request-response streams or the chunk size leads to an increased throughput, but obviously also affects the TCP fairness and the computational effort needed to manage the multiple streams. In Figure 3, the upper bounds for a single TCP connection and the request-response streams (RR) according to Equations 1 and 8, respectively, are shown. While the performance of the single TCP connection highly depends on the packet loss and the RTT, the decline of the throughput of the request-response streams with increasing RTT and packet loss is significantly reduced. In Section 6, we will discuss the pros and cons of the request-response system parameters in detail and present a comparison of our model with real measurements. In the next section, we will briefly introduce the scalable video codec H.264/SVC and priority streaming, which will be used in our HTTP-based request-response streaming system (see Section 5).

4. H.264/SVC AND PRIORITY STREAMING

To investigate the video streaming performance of request-response streams in terms of video quality, we choose priority streaming based on H.264/SVC scalable content because this does not require an estimation of the available bandwidth and therefore makes additional buffer management at the server obsolete [12]. This simplifies the interpretation of the evaluation results on the streaming performance.

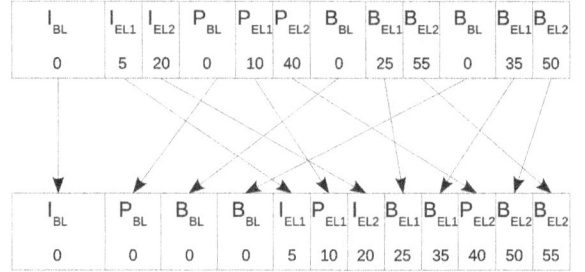

Figure 4: PRID-based NAL unit reordering

The H.264/SVC video coding standard [22] was recently standardized as an extension to the well-known H.264/AVC standard. H.264/SVC introduces scalability in three dimensions. *Temporal scalability* is the property of a bit stream that video sequences with different frame rates can be extracted. *Spatial scalability*, which allows the extraction of video sequences with different spatial resolutions, is also realized in a layered fashion. Finally, *quality scalability* is supported, which enables the adaptation to certain quality levels or bit rates. An H.264/AVC bitstream is structured into NAL (Network Abstraction Layer) units, which start with a one byte header. In order to signal the scalability information in the bit stream, SVC extends the NAL unit concept of H.264/AVC [20] (NAL unit header and types). Among others, the SVC header contains a *priority id (PRID)* field which can be used to define a suggested adaptation path. This adaptation path specifies in which order the NAL units should be discarded in case of adaptation. The assignment of the PRID to NAL units is not further specified in the standard and can be allocated based on the needs of a certain application or use case. The Quality Level Assigner tool that is included in the JSVM [6] reference software can be used to assign priority values to NAL units contained in the bit stream. The assignment is done in a way that the extraction based on the PRID is optimal w.r.t. rate-distortion. Using the PRID, we are able to extract up to 64 different qualities of the video content.

Unlike traditional buffering at the receiver, which tries to overcome bandwidth shortages, *priority streaming* [18, 7] levels the quality of the video over a period of time. For that reason, the video is split into fragments, each comprising the same play-out duration. In a next step, the video syntax elements (e.g., slices, frames, layers) are rearranged in order of priority. For example, using a non-scalable video codec, the I-frames would precede the P-frames and the B-frames. A reordered video fragment is called *video segment*. In priority streaming with H.264/SVC, the NAL units of each video fragment are rearranged according to their priority. In our case, a lower numerical value of the PRID signals a higher priority of the NAL unit according to [21]. The basic principles of this reordering are illustrated in Figure 4. For the sake of simplicity, the figure shows a GOP consisting of only four pictures (I, P, B, B) in decoding order. Each of the pictures is represented by one NAL unit carrying the base layer (BL) and two NAL units representing enhancement layers (EL1, EL2). The numerical values in the boxes represent the PRID value of each NAL unit; in our configuration, all NAL units of the base layer have the highest priority. For transmission, the NAL units are ordered according to their priority. As a result of the scalable property of H.264/SVC,

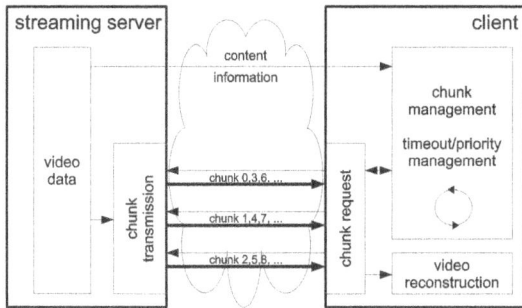

Figure 5: Request-response-based client-driven streaming system

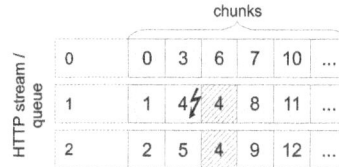

Figure 6: Three HTTP streams/queues on the client with priority management

the quality of the decoded bit stream at the client monotonically increases with the amount of data (NAL units) received by the client.

In the next section our HTTP-based request-response streaming system based on priority streaming and H.264/SVC will be explained in detail.

5. HTTP-BASED REQUEST-RESPONSE STREAMING SYSTEM

To investigate the video streaming performance of request-response streams, we designed a streaming system based on HTTP. The ability of the request-response streams to avoid transmission stalls and therefore jerky playback makes them a good candidate for video streaming. Multiple request-response streams are able to reduce quality fluctuations, while providing fairness to a single TCP connection. In addition, priority streaming is used to ensure timeliness of delivery.

The architecture of the *HTTP-based request-response streaming system* can be seen in Figure 5. Since the system uses HTTP, easy deployment, reuse of existing infrastructure (HTTP server, client, encryption, etc.) and application-layer multicast through HTTP proxies are possible. Persistent connections (as defined in HTTP/1.1 [5]) are used for establishing the TCP connections, in order to reduce the overhead of connection setup. Before streaming, the video is split into fragments, each comprising the same play-out duration. Each video fragment is rearranged according to the video quality / priority, resulting in a *video segment* (see Section 4).

The streaming system is characterized by three different parameters, namely the *chunk size* l_{ch}, the *number of concurrent streams* n_c and the *inter-request gap* t_{gap}. A video segment is split into *chunks* of size l_{ch}, which are served by a standard HTTP server. The download of the video chunks is coordinated by the client. For that purpose, the client maintains n_c HTTP-based request-response streams and schedules the downloads of the different chunks by using a separate queue for each stream as shown in Figure 6. Each chunk is retrieved by the client according to the order within the queue. Between consecutive chunk download requests, an inter-request gap t_{gap} is inserted to provide TCP-friendliness. On the client, the time used for downloading a segment is monitored. If the maximum time allocated for downloading a segment is reached (normally the the play-out duration of the segment), the client stops downloading chunks of the segment and switches to chunks of the next

segment. The client reconstructs the video from the received (and possibly truncated) video segment.

The streaming client coordinates the in-order transmission of the chunks and attempts to maximize the in-order throughput. To prevent transmission stalls, *timeout management* is used. A chunk is considered stalled if it is not retrieved within a timeout duration which can vary between 1000 ms and 5000 ms. Assuming that the maximum RTT is about 200 ms, which is common in Internet video streaming [15], at most 25 "attempts" ($25 * 200\ ms \approx 5000\ ms$) should be needed to transmit the video chunk. Very large chunks may exceed this limit, but we regard using such chunk sizes as unreasonable for video streaming. The lower bound of the transfer timeout is set to 1000 ms, to allow retransmissions on congested network links. The timeout is initialized as 3000 ms. The *transfer duration*, i.e., the time needed to download a chunk, is monitored for each chunk. A moving average over the last 20 transfer durations plus a tolerance of 30% is used for the calculation of the current transfer timeout. Expired transfers are considered (with a penalty) in the moving average as well, in order to supply the timeout management with early feedback on stalled transfers.

Priority management tries to improve the timeliness of the delivery by prioritizing video chunks required in the near future. In our case, the chunks will be needed by the client in priority order (as shown in Figure 6). If the transmission of a chunk is stalled (see original chunk 4 in Figure 6), it will be re-inserted into two queues (see hatched chunks), in order to increase the probability of a successful download. The priority management does not change the TCP-friendliness of the streaming system, because the number of concurrent HTTP streams is kept constant. Only the queues at the client used for fetching the chunks are updated, while the congestion control is ensured by the underlying TCP implementation of each single HTTP stream.

6. EVALUATION

In Section 5, we presented an HTTP-based video streaming system which makes use of request-response streams. The system offers many parameters to configure the HTTP-based streaming process, so it allows for an in-depth analysis of the streaming performance. Therefore, we will use this request-response streaming system as a basis for the evaluation of the streaming performance regarding the achievable throughput and the TCP fairness in different congestion scenarios.

Content

The test sequences used for evaluation were created by means of the H.264/SVC codec provided by the Joint Scalable Video Model (JSVM) [6] 9.18 software. The *soccer* sequence was encoded in 4CIF resolution at 30 fps and the

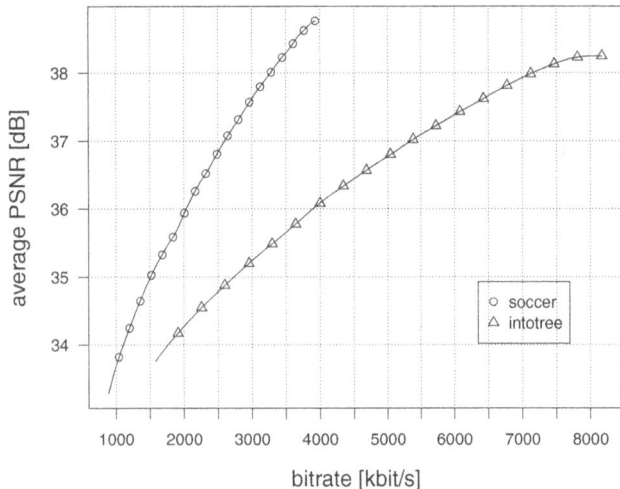

Figure 7: Rate-distortion curves of the test sequences

in to tree sequence in 720p resolution at 50 fps. Each sequence features an H.264/AVC backward compatible base layer and one MGS quality enhancement layer. Within the MGS quality enhancement layer, the transform coefficients are uniformly partitioned into four NAL units. The Quality Level Assigner tool (JSVM) was used to assign 64 different PRIDs to the NAL units based on rate-distortion values. In Figure 7, the rate-distortion values of the test sequences are shown, ranging from the lowest bit rate (highest priority) to the full bit rate (lowest priority). The video quality is evaluated at a fixed bottleneck bandwidth of $BW = 8192kbps$ and two different test sequences. To show the influence of over-provisioning on the video quality, the sequences have a different maximum bit rate (see Figure 7). It can be observed that the maximum bit rate of the *in to tree* sequence is roughly twice the maximum bit rate of the *soccer* sequence. Each test sequence has a play-out duration of 10 seconds, which is also considered as the video fragment size. For the streaming experiments, the content is streamed 50 times in a loop.

Evaluation Setup

For the emulation of the Internet and the last-mile network, we use a test setup consisting of six Linux boxes. As shown in Figure 8, two servers are streaming the media data to two clients. Two routers are responsible for network emulation. The operating system is Ubuntu Linux (kernel 2.6.27) and on all computers the *TCP Reno* variant is used. On the routers, *Netem*[1] is used for the emulation of network characteristics like delay, jitter, and packet loss. The symmetric end-to-end delay of the Internet and the provider network is emulated by Router 1. Router 2 acts as the access network and limits the up- and downstream bandwidths (BW), allowing a maximum queuing delay of 200 ms. In addition, the packets are dropped in a random fashion to emulate packet loss on the transmission channel. Our implementation of the streaming system is based on Python and the HTTP library *libcurl*[2]. In the evaluation, Server 1 streams the media data

---

[1] http://www.linuxfoundation.org/en/Net:Netem
[2] http://curl.haxx.se

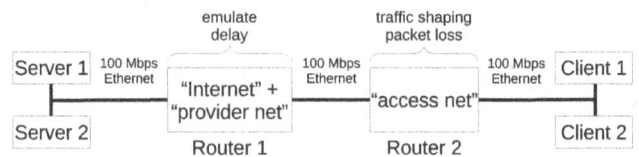

Figure 8: Evaluation setup

to Client 1. Congestion is emulated by concurrent HTTP downloads from Server 2 initiated by Client 2. The Apache HTTP Server[3] was used for serving the video chunks and the concurrent downloads.

System Parameters

The performance of the system is measured for the different system parameters (see Equation 4) and network scenarios. Different chunk sizes l_{ch} are used for the evaluation, namely 20, 40, 80, 160 and 320 kBytes (kB). The number of concurrent request-response streams n_c used is varied in a range of 1 to 5. The fairness of the request-response streaming system can be controlled via the inter-request gap parameter t_{gap}, as shown in [13]. On the other hand, the inter-request gap increases the transmission latency, therefore we choose it to be 220 ms at maximum. Each streaming evaluation run lasts for 500 seconds.

Network Scenarios

Because HTTP-based request-response streaming targets the Internet streaming use case, two different network scenarios are considered. First, we start the evaluation with an *uncongested network link*, where the streaming system should be able to make use of all the bandwidth. Second, we look at *congested network links* with different congestion levels, which are emulated by 1 to 4 concurrent TCP downloads. Two different bottleneck network bandwidths (4096 and 8192 kbps) and four different RTTs (ranging from 50 to 200 ms) were investigated. Given all the possible network and system parameters, a single evaluation run varying all parameters consists of 8000 streaming experiments. Each streaming experiment was repeated three times and the average performance values were used for the presentation of the results.

Performance Metrics

For the characterization of the streaming system, we use the *average throughput* which is measured for each video fragment (in our case every 10 seconds) and the *average download duration of the chunks*. We decided to use the average performance value of the different RTTs for presentation, because we want to show a single performance value for each system parameter set.

$$\frac{RR}{TCP} = \frac{r_{rr}}{\frac{1}{n_{tcp}} \sum_{i=1}^{n_{tcp}} r_{tcpi}} \qquad (9)$$

The *TCP fairness ratio* RR/TCP of the request-response streams (see Equation 9) in a congested network should give us a good idea of how to choose the system parameters to achieve TCP fairness for a given bottleneck bandwidth of

---

[3] http://httpd.apache.org

the last-mile link. A fairness ratio value $RR/TCP = 1$ indicates that the request-response streams only use their fair share of the available bandwidth. The request-response streams are potentially unfair to concurrent TCP streams if the ratio is larger than one ($RR/TCP > 1$), while a ratio of $RR/TCP < 1$ indicates that the request-response streams are only using less than their fair share. For the presentation of the fairness ratio, we average the values for the different congestion levels (number of competing downloads), in order to get a single value for a specific system parameter set. In addition, we will show how our model of Section 2 correlates with the measured results for the averaged performance values and a specific system parameter set ($l_{ch} = 160\ kB$, $n_c = 5$, $t_{gap} = 210\ ms$ at a fixed bottleneck bandwidth $BW = 8192\ kbps$), which provides TCP fairness.

In the next section, the results of our evaluation are presented.

7. RESULTS

In our evaluation of video streaming with HTTP-based request-response streams, we conducted a broad range of experiments. We measured the average throughput, the average download duration of the chunks, and evaluated the fairness of the streaming solution. To show our findings in a concise manner, we choose to average the results over the different RTTs.

In the first part of this section, we discuss the influence of the three system parameters, namely the chunk size l_{ch}, the number of concurrent request-response streams n_c and the inter-request gap t_{gap}. Figures 9 and 10 show the average throughput performance and the average download duration of a chunk for the bottleneck bandwidths $BW = 4096\ kbps$ and $BW = 8192\ kbps$, respectively. The evaluation took place in an uncongested network. In general, it can be noticed that a single request-response stream cannot make full use of the available bandwidth, because of the nature of the request-response paradigm and the inter-request gap. The influence of the system parameters under consideration is discussed as follows.

Chunk size: Larger chunk sizes use the available network bandwidth more effectively. This can be noticed in Figure 10, when comparing the chunk sizes 20 kB and 160 kB. While the 20 kB chunks cannot fully utilize the network link with 5 streams, the 160 kB chunks are able to make good use of the available bandwidth with even 3 streams. Request-response streams with very large chunks behave similarly to single TCP connections. This leads to an increased throughput performance, but also to congestion in case of multiple streams. Because of the fixed bandwidth limit BW, in uncongested networks the download duration increases linearly with the chunk size (e.g., with a single stream $t_{dur} = l_{ch}/BW$). Yet, if the available bandwidth is exhausted, enlarging chunks will not lead to an increased throughput anymore.

Number of streams: The number of request-response streams shows a behavior similar to the chunk size. In Figure 9, at a chunk size of 20 kB, a higher number of streams leads to higher throughput. Multiple streams are also more error resilient (see Section 3), but tend to generate self-congestion, because each request-response stream is based on TCP which tries to maximize the throughput. If

increasing the number of streams does not lead to a substantial throughput increase, we can assume that self-congestion takes place (see chunk size 320 kB in Figure 9). As a result of this, also the download duration increases with the number of streams. We observed that one can safely increase the number of streams as long as the download duration does not increase in a linear fashion.

Temporal gap: The inter-request gap parameter has obviously no positive effect on the throughput or download durations. Because of the artificial gap between the requests, the time the request-response streams are not transporting data is increased. Therefore, smaller inter-request gaps lead to higher throughput. In general, the inter-request gap has no influence on the download duration, because the inter-request gap is applied between the downloads. In addition, Figure 9 shows that the inter-request gap has a higher influence on small chunks, because the inter-request gap is applied between consecutive downloads of chunks and larger chunks need longer to be transferred.

In Figures 9 and 10 we also show the values of our model for the estimated throughput. The model shows a good correlation with the measured values and can give a good hint on the achievable throughput. At large chunk sizes and heavy self-congestion, the model seems to increase its error, but can predict the upper bound of the throughput. The same behavior can be noticed for the download duration.

For the evaluation of TCP fairness, we start 1 to 4 concurrent HTTP downloads to the request-response streaming system. By changing the number of concurrent downloads, we are able to adjust the network congestion to different levels. For the HTTP downloads and the streaming system, the throughput values are recorded and the *TCP fairness ratio RR/TCP* is calculated (see Equation 9). We choose to average the fairness ratios for the different RTTs and congestion levels, to get a single value for the fairness of a specific parameter set. In Figure 11, the TCP fairness of the request-response streaming system for the three system parameters is shown. The value $RR/TCP = 1$ is marked, because it shows under which conditions TCP fairness can be achieved. It can be seen that all three parameters have an influence on the TCP fairness. While the fairness decreases (RR/TCP increases) with the number of streams and the chunk size, an increasing inter-request gap is able to increase the fairness. For very large chunks (e.g., 320 kB at $BW = 4096\ kbps$), it becomes increasingly difficult to find a fair parameter set with multiple streams. This is because the inter-request gap has in general an upper bound defined by the use case envisioned (in our case 220 ms).

Another interesting finding can be noticed when directly comparing the fairness ratio plots for $BW = 4096\ kbps$ and $BW = 8192\ kbps$. The fairness ratio values of a certain chunk size in $BW = 4096\ kbps$ behave similarly to the fairness ratio values of the doubled chunk size in $BW = 8192\ kbps$. In our opinion, this may be an indicator for the scalability of the request-response streaming system. If more bandwidth is available, using larger chunk sizes may lead to a better link utilization without hurting TCP fairness. Further work will look into that presumption in more detail to explore the scalability of request-response streams.

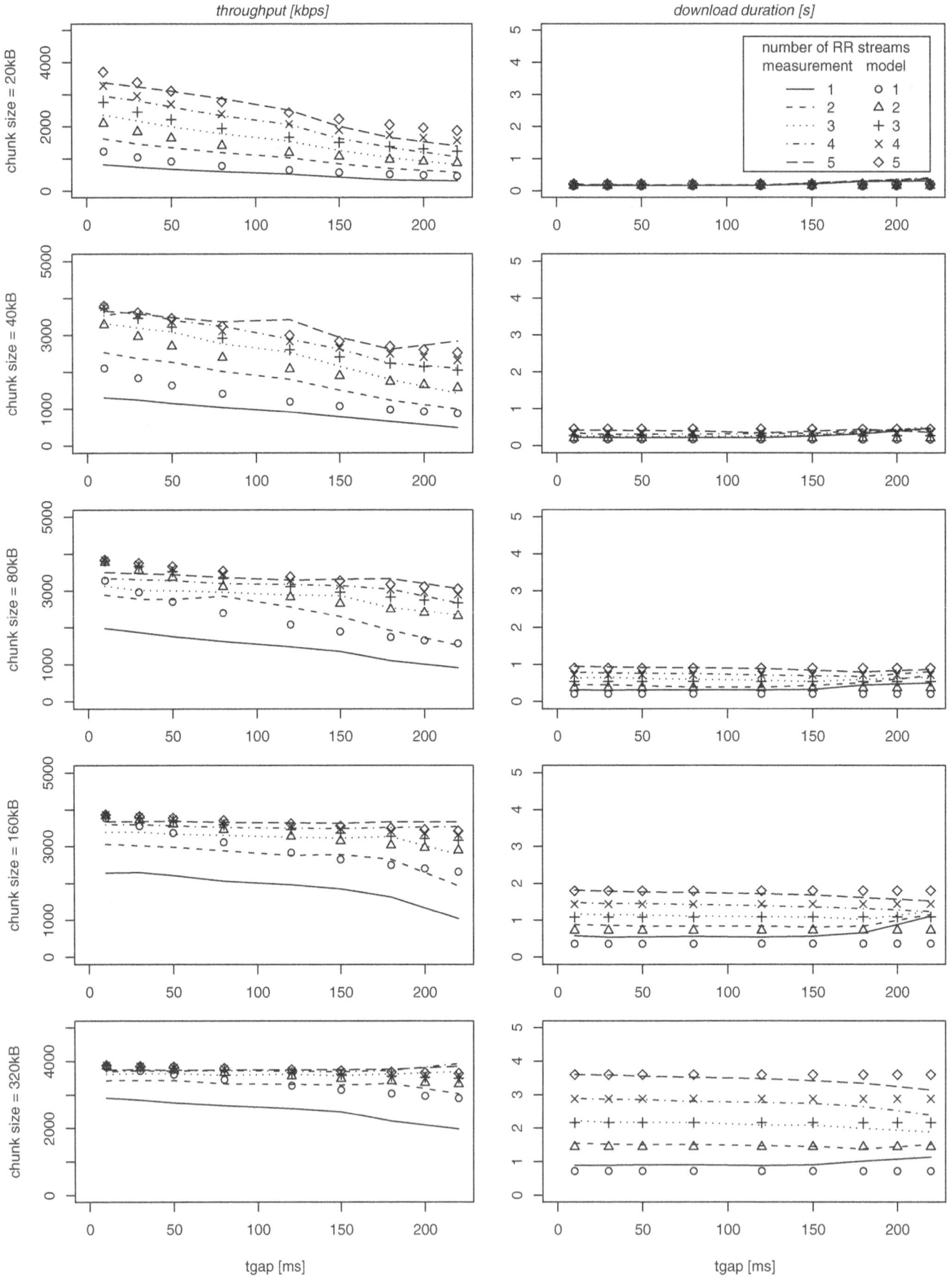

Figure 9: Measured and modeled throughput performance r_{rr} and download duration of a chunk t_{ch} for the request-response streams. The results are shown for a fixed bottleneck bandwidth of $BW = 4096$ $kbps$, a maximum queuing delay of $t_q = 200$ ms and averaged over the RTTs to provide a single performance value.

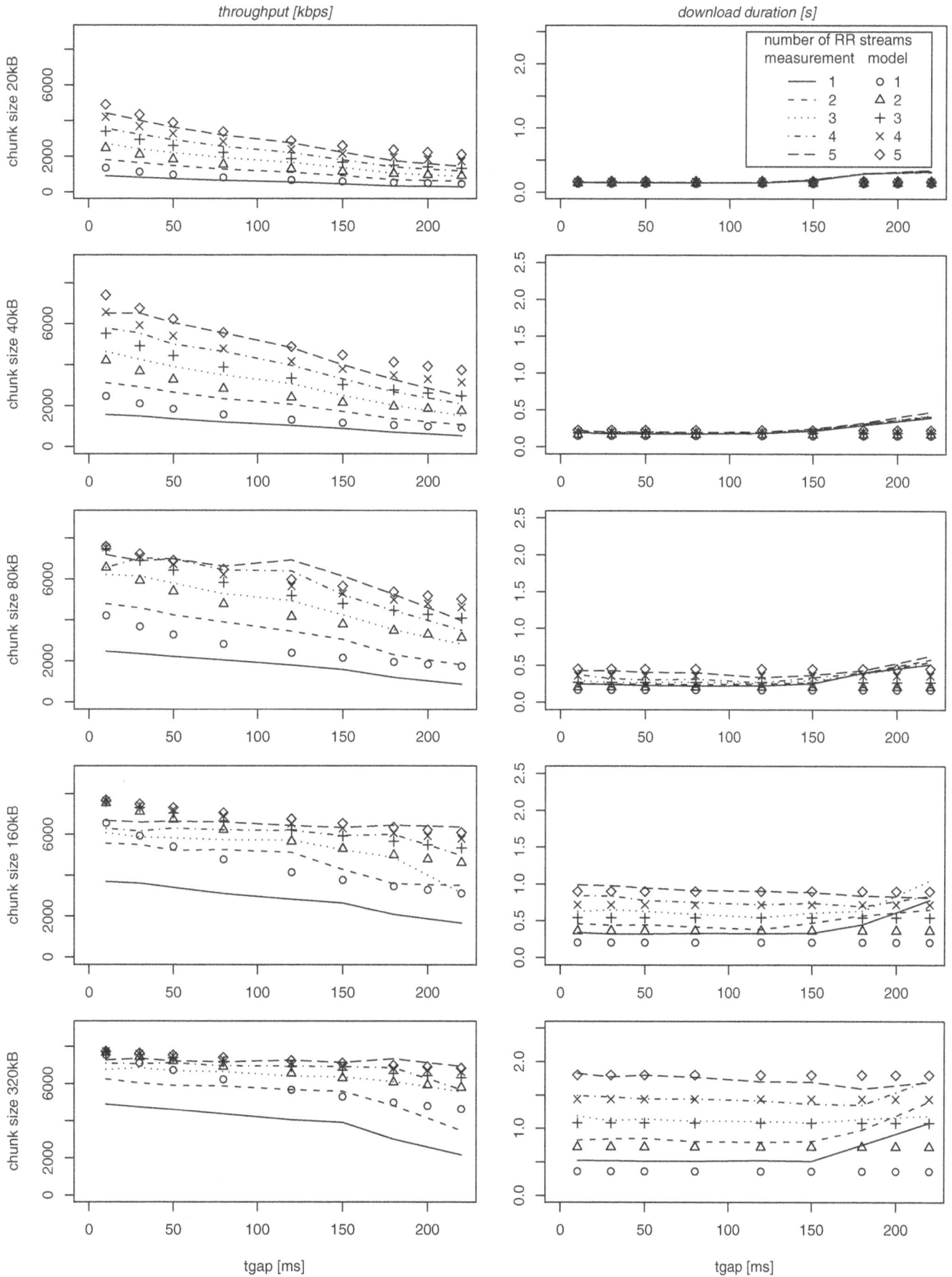

Figure 10: Measured and modeled throughput performance r_{rr} and download duration of a chunk t_{ch} for the request-response streams. The results are shown for a fixed bottleneck bandwidth of $BW = 8192$ $kbps$, a maximum queuing delay of $t_q = 200$ ms and averaged over the RTTs to provide a single performance value.

253

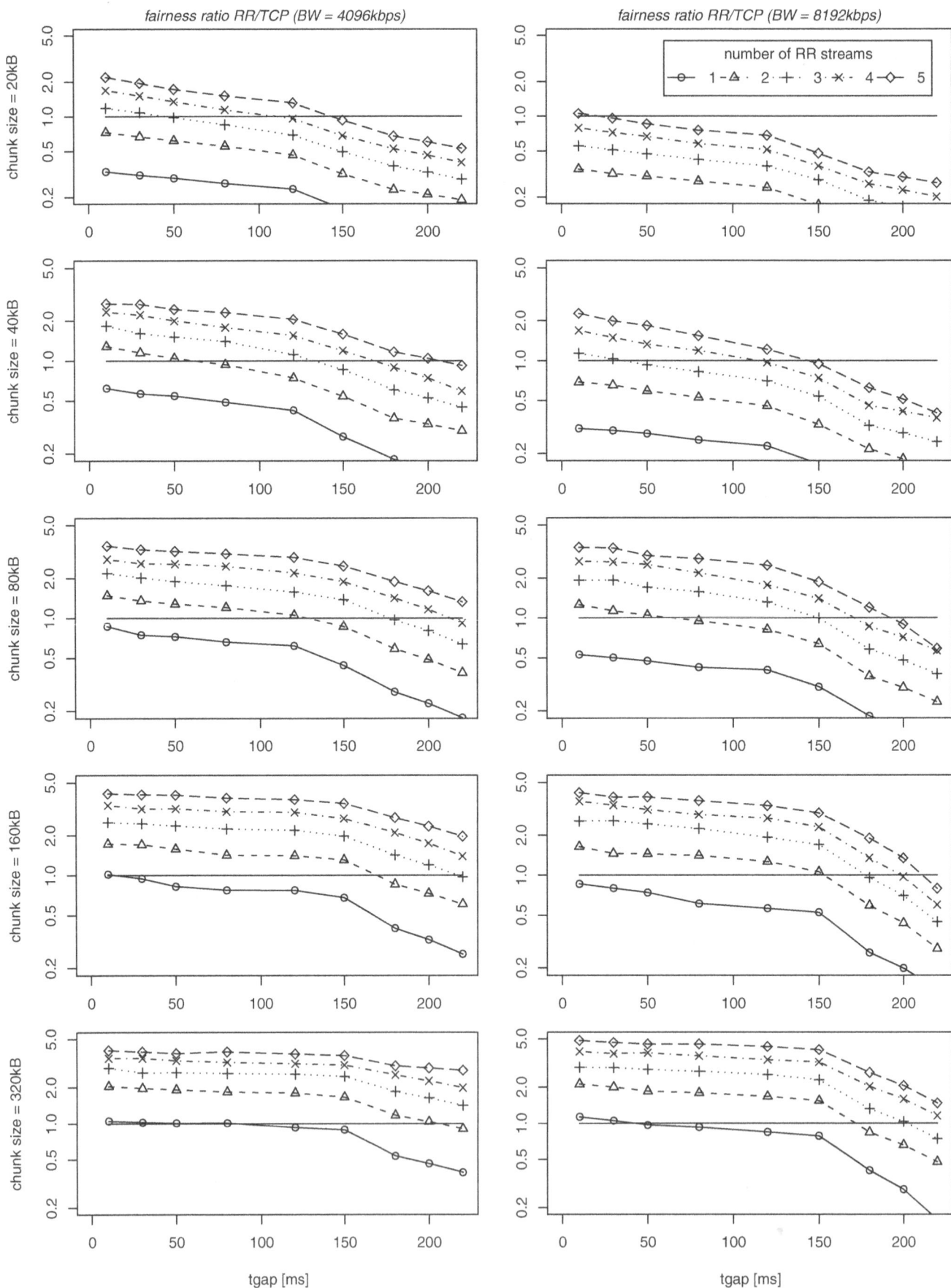

Figure 11: **Measured TCP fairness ratio** RR/TCP **of the request-response streams compared to 1 ... 4 concurrent HTTP downloads. The results are shown for two bottleneck bandwidths (** $BW = 4096$ *kbps* **and** 8192 *kbps* **and maximum queuing delay of** $t_q = 200$ *ms* **and averaged over the RTTs and different congestion levels to provide a single performance value.**

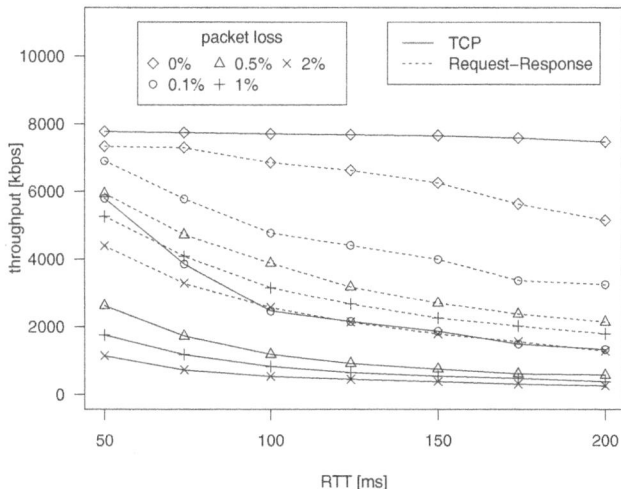

Figure 12: *Measured* throughput performance of a single TCP connection (TCP) r_{tcp} and for the request-response streams r_{rr} using the same conditions as used in Figure 3.

When using request-response streaming systems in the Internet, the streaming system should provide TCP fairness ($RR/TCP = 1$). Because there is more than a single parameter set which provides TCP fairness, a good trade-off between throughput performance and TCP fairness has to be found. The number of request-response streams also directly impacts the performance in case of packet loss or transmission stalls. Therefore, we propose to use a parameter set with a large number of streams which offers good throughput.

In Figure 12, the performance of such a parameter set for a fixed bottleneck bandwidth of $BW = 8192\ kbps$ is shown. The chunk size was set to 160 kB and 5 request-response streams with an inter-request gap of 210 ms were used for the transmission of the video data. In direct comparison with the performance of a single TCP connection, the benefit of the multiple streams becomes evident. While the throughput of the single TCP connection rapidly decreases with increasing packet loss, the request-response streams are able to mitigate the effect. Also, the performance in an uncongested network with no packet loss ($p = 0\ \%$) is quite good, but of course not as good as TCP, because of the fixed inter-request gap value. When comparing the values of the measurement with the model (see Figures 12 and 3), it can be noticed that the correlation between the model and the real measured values is good. We know that our model is only a simplification of the real world problems, but we think it can be used for an estimation of the throughput performance of the request-response streams (with and without packet loss).

The impact of the streaming performance on the video quality shows a behavior similar to the throughput performance. Figures 13 and 14 present the video quality in terms of PSNR for the test sequences *soccer* and *in to tree*, respectively. In case of no packet loss and stable network conditions, TCP and the request-response streams perform well, with an advantage for TCP in terms of network utilization. If packet loss is present, then this fact changes dramatically.

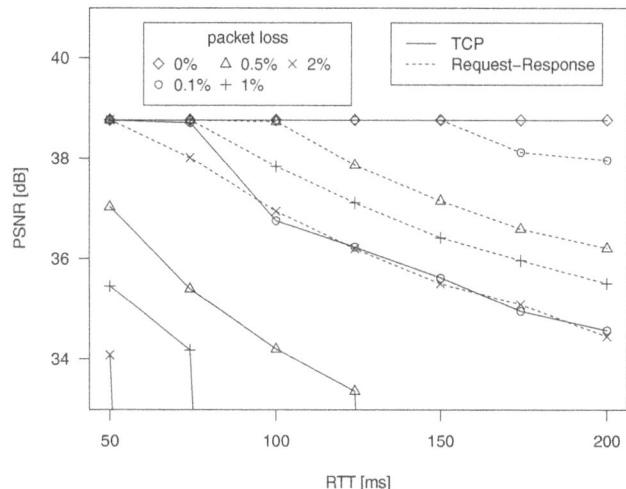

Figure 13: Measured video quality of the streamed test sequence *soccer* in terms of PSNR of a single TCP connection (TCP) and for the request-response streams ($MSS = 1460\ bytes$, $l_{ch} = 160\ kB$, $n_c = 5$, $t_{gap} = 210\ ms$) at a fixed bottleneck bandwidth $BW = 8192\ kbps$ and packet loss rate p.

For high packet loss rates, the single TCP connection cannot even transmit the base layer of the video, because of insufficient TCP throughput. High RTTs and the HD video *in to tree* present difficulties for the request-response streams as well. It is quite evident, though, that the request-response streams can make better use of the available bandwidth, while the performance of the single TCP stream is stuck (see Equation 1). Unfortunately, the difference in PSNR values can only be calculated for a packet loss rate of $p = 0.1\ \%$ and the test sequence *soccer*, which is at average 2.04 dB. In the other network scenarios with packet loss and for the sequence *in to tree*, TCP cannot deliver the video at every given RTT. So the main advantage of the request-response streams compared to a single TCP connection is that it can deliver the video, while TCP may not be capable of delivering the video at all.

8. CONCLUSION

Internet video streaming has gained popularity mainly due to social video portals and video-on-demand applications. Because of the dynamic nature of the Internet, constant bit rate video streaming based on TCP is only possible with high over-provisioning [19]. Adaptive video streaming based on TCP/HTTP is certainly the key to Internet video streaming and a lot of systems were proposed [23, 10, 3, 1, 11].

HTTP streaming using video fragments is usually more robust against network fluctuations and is basically stateless on the server-side, because it is in general fully client-driven. Compared to a single TCP connection, request-response streams can mitigate the effects of packet loss and TCP connection timeouts or stalls. In our work, we analyzed the basic properties of HTTP streaming. By introducing HTTP-based request-response streams, we were able to identify the system parameters of HTTP-based streaming. Using knowledge about the bottleneck router led us to a model for the estimated throughput of the request-response streams.

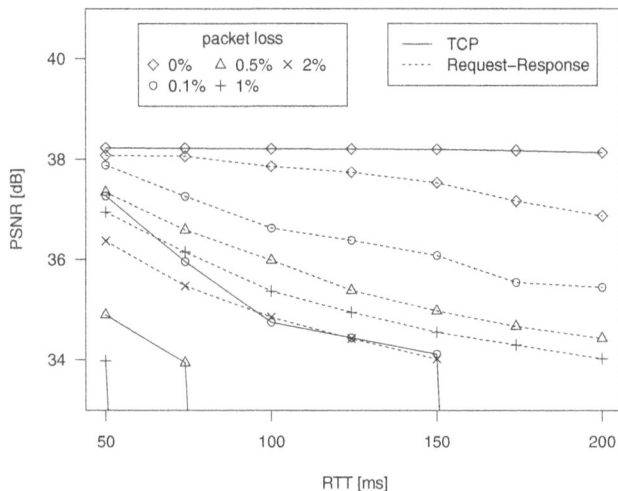

Figure 14: Measured video quality of the streamed test sequence *in to tree* in terms of PSNR of a single TCP connection (TCP) and for the request-response streams ($MSS = 1460$ *bytes*, $l_{ch} = 160$ *kB*, $n_c = 5$, $t_{gap} = 210$ *ms*) at a fixed bottleneck bandwidth $BW = 8192$ *kbps* and packet loss rate p.

An in-depth evaluation of the performance of request-response streams was presented in this paper. It revealed that request-response streams are able to scale with the available bandwidth by increasing the chunk size or the number of concurrent streams. The system parameters have to be carefully chosen, however, based on the bandwidth of the bottleneck router in order to avoid self-congestion. Our proposed model for the throughput shows a good correlation with the experimental results. Regarding TCP-friendliness, we were able to show that there are several combinations of system parameters which exhibit TCP-friendliness. By means of a temporal inter-request gap, we were able to adjust the fairness of a certain chunk size / number of streams combination to a fair level. For such a fair system parameter set, we evaluated the video streaming performance in terms of video quality in the presence of packet loss. While the single TCP connection performs better than the request-response streams if no packet loss is present, the performance of the single TCP connection deteriorates rapidly with increasing packet loss.

In this paper, we provided experimental evidence that multiple HTTP-based request-response streams are a good alternative to classical TCP streaming. Additionally, we presented several system parameter sets featuring TCP-friendliness, which can be used in the design of TCP-friendly streaming systems. Currently the performance of the request-response streams is limited by their fixed parameter settings. Future work will cover an investigation of dynamic parameter sets and their TCP-friendliness.

9. ACKNOWLEDGMENT

This work was supported in part by the European Commission in the context of the Integrated Project ALICANTE (FP7-ICT-248652; http://www.ict-alicante.eu).

10. REFERENCES

[1] Transparent End-to-end Packet-switched Streaming Service; Protocols and codecs. ETSI TS 126 234, V9.3.0, June 2010.

[2] G. Appenzeller, I. Keslassy, and N. McKeown. Sizing router buffers. *SIGCOMM Comput. Commun. Rev.*, 34:281–292, August 2004.

[3] L. De Cicco and S. Mascolo. An Experimental Investigation of the Akamai Adaptive Video Streaming. In *Proceedings of the 6th Symposium of the Workgroup Human-Computer Interaction and Usability Engineering (USAB)*, pages 447–464, Nov. 2010.

[4] M. Dischinger, A. Haeberlen, K. P. Gummadi, and S. Saroiu. Characterizing Residential Broadband Networks. In *Proceedings of the 7th ACM SIGCOMM Conference on Internet Measurement (IMC '07)*, pages 43–56, 2007.

[5] R. Fielding, J. Gettys, J. Mogul, H. Frystyk, L. Masinter, P. Leach, and T. Berners-Lee. Hypertext Transfer Protocol – HTTP/1.1. RFC 2616 (Draft Standard), June 1999.

[6] Joint Video Team (JVT) of ISO/IEC MPEG and ITU-T VCEG. Joint Scalable Video Model. *Doc. JVT-X202*, 2007.

[7] C. Krasic, J. Walpole, and W.-C. Feng. Quality-adaptive Media Streaming by Priority Drop. In *Proceedings of the 13th International Workshop on Network and Operating Systems Support for Digital Audio and Video (NOSSDAV '03)*, pages 112–121, 2003.

[8] M. Hassan and R. Jain, editor. *High Performance TCP/IP Networking: Concepts, Issues, and Solutions*. Pearson Prentice Hall, 2004.

[9] M. Mathis, J. Semke, J. Mahdavi, and T. Ott. The Macroscopic Behavior of the TCP Congestion Avoidance Algorithm. *ACM SIGCOMM - Computer Communication Review*, 27(3):67–82, 1997.

[10] Move Networks. Move Adaptive Stream - Product Sheet. http://www.movenetworks.com. Last accessed on 2010-12-07.

[11] R. Pantos. HTTP Live Streaming. Internet Draft draft-pantos-http-live-streaming-04, 2009.

[12] R. Kuschnig, I. Kofler, and H. Hellwagner. An Evaluation of TCP-based Rate-Control Algorithms for Adaptive Internet Streaming of H.264/SVC. In *Proceedings of ACM Multimedia Systems (ACM MMSYS 2010)*, February 2010.

[13] R. Kuschnig, I. Kofler, and H. Hellwagner. Improving Internet Video Streaming Performance by Parallel TCP-based Request-Response Streams. In *Proceedings of the 7th Annual IEEE Consumer Communications and Networking Conference (IEEE CCNC 2010)*, January 2010.

[14] H. Riiser, P. Halvorsen, C. Griwodz, and D. Johansen. Low Overhead Container Format for Adaptive Streaming. In *Proceedings of ACM Multimedia Systems (ACM MMSYS 2010)*, pages 193–198, Feb. 2010.

[15] M. Saxena, U. Sharan, and S. Fahmy. Analyzing Video Services in Web 2.0: A Global Perspective. In *Proceedings of the 18th International Workshop on Network and Operating Systems Support for Digital Audio and Video (NOSSDAV '08)*, pages 39–44, 2008.

[16] H. Schulzrinne, S. Casner, R. Frederick, and V. Jacobson. RTP: A Transport Protocol for Real-Time Applications. RFC 3550, July 2003.

[17] T. Stockhammer, G. Liebl, and M. Walter. Optimized H.264-AVC-based bit stream switching for mobile video streaming. *EURASIP J. Appl. Signal Process.*, 2006:1–19, 2006.

[18] W. Feng, M. Liu, B. Krishnaswam, A. Prabhudev. A Priority-Based Technique for the Best-Effort Delivery of Stored Video. In *Proceedings of the SPIE/IST Multimedia Computing and Networking 1999 (MMCN'99)*, 1999.

[19] B. Wang, J. Kurose, P. Shenoy, and D. Towsley. Multimedia Streaming via TCP: An Analytic Performance Study. *ACM Transactions on Multimedia Computing, Communications and Applications*, 4(2):16:1–16:22, 2008.

[20] Y. Wang, M. Hannuksela, S. Pateux, A. Eleftheriadis, and S. Wenger. System and Transport Interface of SVC. *IEEE Transactions on Circuits and Systems for Video Technology*, 17(9):1149–1163, 2007.

[21] S. Wenger, Y.-K. Wang, T. Schierl, and A. Eleftheriadis. RTP Payload Format for SVC Video. Internet Draft draft-ietf-avt-rtp-svc-19, 2009.

[22] T. Wiegand, G. Sullivan, H. Schwarz, and M. Wien, editors. *ISO/IEC 14496-10:2005/Amd3: Scalable Video Coding*. International Standardization Organization, 2007.

[23] A. Zambelli. IIS smooth streaming technical overview. Technical report, Microsoft Corporation, March 2009.

iDASH: Improved Dynamic Adaptive Streaming over HTTP using Scalable Video Coding

Yago Sánchez, Thomas Schierl,
Cornelius Hellge, Thomas Wiegand
Fraunhofer HHI, Germany

Dohy Hong
N2N Soft, France

Danny De Vleeschauwer,
Werner Van Leekwijck
Bell Labs - Alcatel Lucent, Belgium

Yannick Le Louédec
Orange-FT, France

ABSTRACT

Abstract—HTTP-based delivery for Video on Demand (VoD) has been gaining popularity within recent years. Progressive Download over HTTP, typically used in VoD, takes advantage of the widely deployed network caches to relieve video servers from sending the same content to a high number of users in the same access network. However, due to a sharp increase in the requests at peak hours or due to cross-traffic within the network, congestion may arise in the cache feeder link or access link respectively. Since the connection characteristics may vary over the time, with Dynamic Adaptive Streaming over HTTP (DASH), a technique that has been recently proposed, video clients may dynamically adapt the requested video quality for ongoing video flows, to match their current download rate as good as possible. In this work we show the benefits of using the Scalable Video Coding (SVC) for such a DASH environment.

Categories and Subject Descriptors

C.4 [**performance of systems**]: Modeling techniques.

General Terms

Performance, Experimentation, Verification.

Keywords

HTTP streaming, Video on Demand, Adaptive, SVC.

1. INTRODUCTION

HTTP-Streaming has been gaining popularity in recent years. Contrary to the past tendency of relying on RTP over UDP for multimedia communications due to the higher end-to-end delay imposed by TCP connections, many content providers have resorted to using HTTP transport for media delivery when the delay constraints allow it. In fact, [1] shows that HTTP/TCP is widely used to stream media to clients. The main reasons for that are first that HTTP is not affected by firewall and NAT traversal issues that exist in traditional streaming scenarios which typically rely on RTP over UDP and second that using HTTP for the file delivery can substantially relieve the load on the video server by re-using

existing HTTP cache infrastructures on the Internet, therefore reducing the overall traffic at the cache feeder link.

Some additional evidence of the increasing interest of the market in HTTP-Streaming is the standardization processes lead by the standardization organization IETF [2], 3GPP [3], OIPF [4] and MPEG [5].

Dynamic Adaptive Streaming over HTTP (DASH) as defined in [5] refers to a video transport methodology where the clients adapt their requests based on some estimates of their available download rate at every time instant of the streaming service. For DASH a video is offered in a various (typically 4 to 10) versions. Each terminal can choose which version to download depending on its capabilities and the network congestion level. This choice is not only made at the beginning of the flow, but at frequently dispersed time instant during the streaming of the video, at which the DASH client can switch from one version to another (for example to alleviate the onset of congestion). Typically this is achieved by segmenting each version in chunks such that the segment boundaries are aligned in time. All the DASH clients need to do is to consecutively download the most appropriate chunks, based on the information obtained by monitoring recently downloaded chunks of the ongoing movie.

One possibility to provide DASH is to encode multiple representations of each of the videos with H.264/AVC [6] at the server and offer them side-by-side. Another is offering all these representations embedded in one file via Scalable Video Coding (SVC) [7]. Offering all these representations side-by-side does not only put a high burden on the storage requirements at the origin server, but might also result in a decrease in cache performance in comparison to SVC. In this paper we discuss the potential gain of using SVC to offer the different versions. Furthermore, as explained in [8], due to its layered nature, SVC provides flexibility to DASH, since it allows dividing media content both per SVC layers and per time intervals, and thus prioritizing very accurately the different elements of the media content according to their importance. Therefore, a higher responsiveness and better playback quality under adverse network conditions is obtained since a request for a time interval is diluted into multiple requests (HTTP_GET requests) performed subsequently, one for each of the layers, and when congestion is detected, requests for higher layers may be omitted. Conversely, for the AVC case a unique request is issued for the whole data of a given interval, having to wait longer for the requested data to be downloaded until witching to a lower representation can be performed.

This work describes the effects of congestion in the network, as well as the effects of caching multiple representations of the same content in DASH systems. Indeed the dynamic adaptation leads to a situation where the clients may request a different representation of a same video content. This paper aims to show the benefits of using SVC over AVC encoded streams in this respect. We will evaluate and show the improvement on the caching efficiency, which is a key factor for reducing the amount of transported data from the server, due to the use of SVC in an environment with requests for multiple content representations as a consequence of different client connectivity situations due to congestion.

The remainder of this paper is organized as follows. Section 2 summarizes some previous work. In section 3 SVC is introduced as well as how different representations can be obtained in order to preserve an efficient encoding. Sections 4 and 5 describe the simulation carried out and the obtained results, respectively. The paper is concluded in section 6.

2. RELATED WORK

There has been some previous work on the topic of combining caching and layered video codec, as [9] or [10], where the benefits of caching layered video codec have been shown. These previous works focused on a service where users selected a representation among a variety of possibilities based on their equipment capabilities.

Both studies focus on a system as the one depicted in Figure 1. This figure schematically shows a network over which a video library is offered by a Video on Demand (VoD) service. The operator of the access network (i.e., the cloud in the figure), offers connectivity to its customers via access links (e.g., DSL-links) and connects to the Internet (where the content library is offered on an origin server by a third party) over a "transit" link, in this paper referred to as the cache feeder link. In that way the customers of the access network operator can access video content, in particular the movies on the origin server. The network operator deploys a proxy and a cache in its network to minimize the amount of transmitted data through the "transit" link relieving the server of having to send an extremely high amount of video data. Since the cache is usually too small to host the complete video library and the content library on the origin video server often changes, the video files that are stored in the cache at every moment need to be carefully selected. This is accomplished by an appropriate caching algorithm.

In [10] the advantage of using SVC for better usage of the cache resources/capability is shown. In this work the improvement on cache-hit-ratio as well as traffic within the cache feeder link are presented. In fact, it is shown that storing different representations of the same video side-by-side with independently encoded streams with AVC leads to a spoilage of the cache capacity, while showing that doing it similarly with layer of SVC lead to a much better solution.

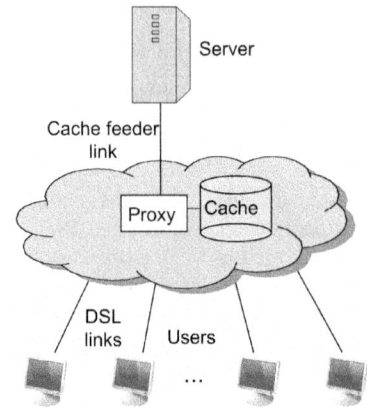

Figure 1: DASH network environment

There are many different cache replacement algorithms that have been proposed over the last years that optimize the caching performance based on some special criteria, as summarized in [11][12]. Most algorithms make decisions based either on how recently an object has been requested (e.g., Least Recently Used - LRU) or on how frequently an object has been requested (e.g., Least Frequently Used - LFU) over a time period or a combination thereof. In [13] the chunk-based delivery (video files downloaded in smaller parts thereof, i.e. chunks/segments) is exploited in a caching context. In this work the chunks that will be consumed in a near future with a high probability are predicted, assuming that it is very likely that a user playing chunk n of a given video file at the current moment will play chunk $n+k$ of the same video file k time instants later.

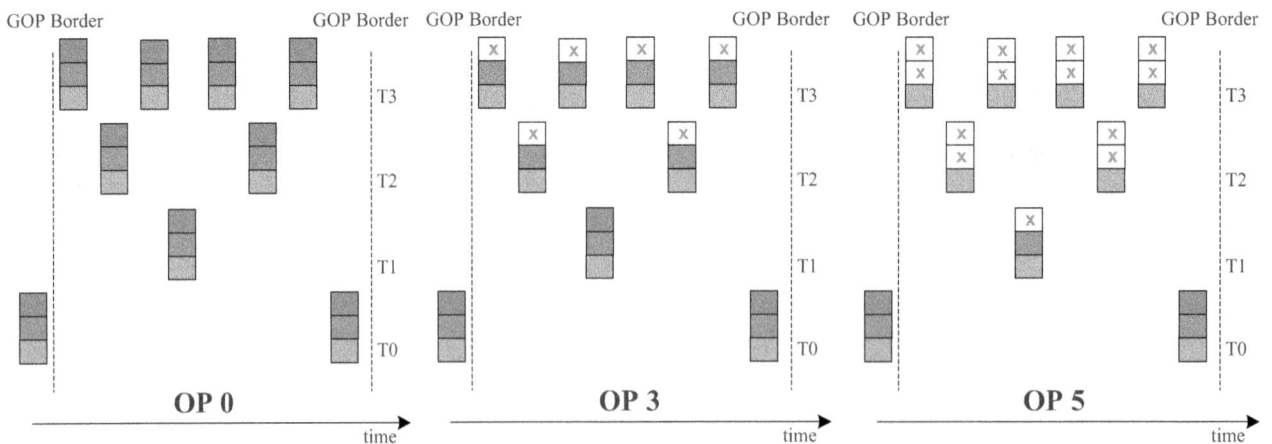

Figure 2: SVC coded pictures of temporal and quality layer combinations for OP 0, 3 and 5.

3. EFFICIENT ENCODING WITH SVC

The scalable extension of H.264/AVC (SVC) [7] provides features to represent different representations of the same video within the same bit stream by selecting a valid sub-stream. SVC is divided into layers, which correspond to different quality, spatial or temporal representations. It is composed by a base layer, which corresponds to the lowest representation, and one or more enhancement layers, which increase the quality, spatial and/or temporal representation when added to the base layer.

The main advantages of SVC are the possibility of serving a great number of users with different equipment capabilities with a single bit stream and the fact that it facilitates coping with congestion by applying on-the-fly adaptation, performed by adding or subtracting layers to match the capabilities of the network at every time instant.

SVC allows for multiple Operation Points (OP) within the same bit stream. An OP refers to a valid sub-stream at a certain quality level and a corresponding bit rate. In this work we only focus on quality scalability since we considered that all users have the same equipment capabilities and we take advantage of SVC in order to cope with congestion.

One way is to encode multiple quality layers either with Coarse-Grain Scalability (CGS) or Medium-Grain Scalability (MGS), and select each layer as an OP. Each integrated quality layer additionally reduces the coding efficiency of the SVC stream to some extent. However, if addressed properly the overhead can be kept below 10 % as shown in [14].

CGS and MGS differ basically in the fact that for the former the stream switching (from one OP to another OP) can only be performed on a layer basis, while the later has more flexibility. Hence, for CGS, the number of OPs is the same as the number of layers. However, when MGS is considered switching can be perform on a NAL unit basis, leading to a much higher number of possible OPs. As a result MGS can have more OP at less overhead than CGS.

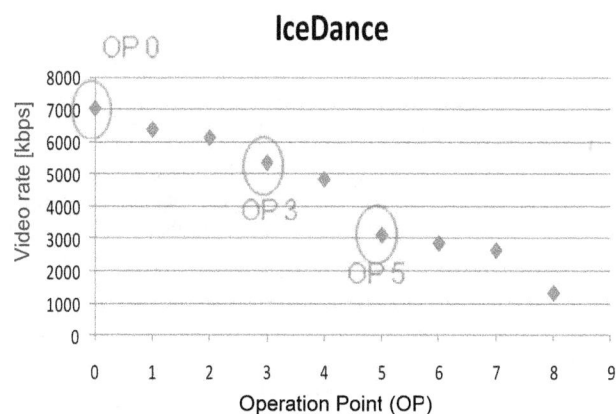

Figure 3: Operations points

Consequently, foreseeing that having so many layers as the number of desired OPs results in an increase in coding overhead, in order to achieve multiple OPs we encode a reduced number of quality layers with MGS and select a sub-stream of the original data not only selecting whole layers but an smaller part of them. This allows keeping the overall coding overhead within an acceptable range. Figure 2 illustrates how to obtain different OPs in this way. In the example, the SVC stream is comprised of the base layer (green parts of the rectangle), and two quality enhancement layers (red, blue parts of the rectangle) for the coded pictures (rectangles in the figure). The different OPs are obtained by dropping enhancement layer packets from the highest temporal levels. Figure 3 shows the bit rates of 9 OPs for the ITU-T test sequence "IceDance". It can be seen that dropping the quality layer parts Q2 (blue) of the coded pictures in temporal levels T2 and T3 reduces the video rate from 7Mbps to 5.3Mbps (OP3). Further, dropping the quality layer Q2 of all temporal levels and pictures from Q1 (red) of temporal levels T2 and T3 results in a video rate of 3.1Mbps (OP5). In general, several OPs can be selected for bit rate optimization. In Figure 3, we show different PSNR/bitrate combinations corresponding to the selection of different OPs. However, the OPs must be selected in such a way, that users experience smooth quality degradation. The selection of OPs is out of the scope of this work.

4. MODEL

4.1 User demand and network set up

The simulations are based on real data statistics. The requests have been extracted from the observation of a deployed VoD service. The statistics have been measured within the time period of one month. The provided VoD service offers a wide variety of movies (more than 5000) among which the users can make their selection from. In these statistics an average of about 3400 requests of movies per day is reported.

Figure 4 shows more in detail the pattern of the requests during 31 days. It shows the number of request aggregated over one hour for each hour of the period of 31 days. Clear diurnal and weekly patterns can be observed. We define "busy hours" or peak hours as hours where the number of requests per hours is larger than a certain threshold.

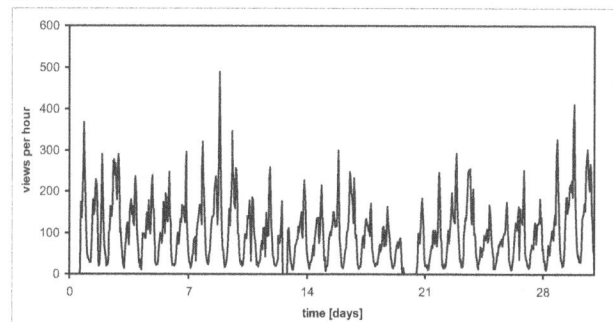

Figure 4: Requests statistics

The requests extracted from the real data are distributed among the users connected to the service, and congestion is simulated as described below in section 4.3. These users are connected over access links (e.g., DSL-links) to a proxy hosting a cache. The origin server is connected to the proxy hosting the cache by a transit link. The latter link is referred to in this paper as the cache feeder link. We consider two cases: only congestion on the access links and only congestion on the cache feeder link. The case where both the access links and the feeder link are simultaneously congested is outside the scope of the paper, since even though it could be easily handled and simulated the aim of this paper is to show the effects of congestion separately in cache feeder and access links for clarity. Both cases are detailed below.

4.2 Caching algorithms

The performance of the cache is here analyzed for two different caching algorithms (operating on chunks):

- LRU: where the most recently requested chunks are kept in the cache.

- CC: An algorithm described in [13] that takes into account the number of guaranteed hits of chunks (if the DASH client keeps on selecting the same version as it currently does), which uses an improved movie content scoring algorithm that combines the LRU and LFU basics.

In case of considering SVC there are n chunks per time interval, where n corresponds to the number of layers. In other words, the layers are transmitted and stored in the cache separately and therefore count as different objects for the cache-hit-ratio evaluation. In case of offering the n version side by side via AVC, each time interval has n independent versions, in the sense that if one version is cached and another is requested no cache hit can be counted.

4.3 Congestion Control

Clients (on the same access network) of a multimedia service typically share (transport and caching) resources with other multimedia clients and/or users downloading any type of data from the Internet, which produces some cross-traffic in the network causing congestion. This results in a temporarily reduced available download rate for the clients of the service.

These clients (DASH-clients) detect these variations in the connection rate available to them and adapt the bit rate at which they download their ongoing video stream, by requesting the following chunks/segments in an appropriate version. Therefore, every time a user requests a new chunk of a video an additional decision has to be made with respect to which version it will download. This choice depends on:

- the capability of the terminal of the user.

- the congestion state of the link between the server and the cache (feeder link) and congestion state between the cache and the end user (i.e., the access link (e.g., DSL-link)). If requesting the version that a user wants to download would congest the link, this request is downgraded as many times as needed to alleviate congestion.

The main contribution in this paper is to analyze the performance of the cache and transmitted rate, as well as the quality at the DASH-clients under different congestion situations within the network that are described below.

4.3.1 Modeling Congestion at the cache feeder link

Since the cache is not large enough to host the complete content library (and this content library regularly introduces new content) there is still considerable traffic on the feeder link towards the cache. Moreover, Figure 4 shows that the traffic demand is several times more important during peak hours than during off-peak hours. Therefore, the traffic on the cache feeder link due to cache misses and caches updates is expected to be higher during peak hours. Consequently, even though cache infrastructures are placed in the network to relieve the load on the server and reduce the overall traffic at the cache feeder link, this may not be sufficient at peak hours. A huge amount of data might be transmitted across the cache feeder link, resulting in congestion within this link.

This would disrupt the streaming service if nothing were done. Therefore, the DASH video clients of the users detect congestion, by e.g. noticing that the requested data is received with an additional delay, they adapt their requests, and this results in a lot of users switching to a lower quality, i.e., requesting the next chunk inline in a lower quality. In this paper the downgrading of the requests is done such that the congestion on the feeder link is alleviated.

If congestion disappears, the DASH video clients will try to grab more capacity, i.e., they will request future chunks in a higher quality. In this paper, the quality adaptation policy for switching-up is performed as follows. A waiting timer is set after switching to a lower quality. If during a time interval equal to this timer, no congestion is detected, DASH-clients switch to a higher quality. If this leads to congestion the quality is quickly downgraded again. If not, the clients keep on downloading the quality they have switched to.

The above behavior will approximate the behavior of real DASH clients very closely. We opted for simulating this coarse behavior without actually modeling a detailed DASH algorithm in each client for two reasons. First, DASH client algorithms are not standardized. Some implementations are known, and these aim for a behavior as we described above. Second, in this paper we are not interested in the time scales at which DASH clients see the packets trickling in, but we concentrate on the time scale at which cache decisions are made. Not simulating at the finest time scale allows us to simulate a month's worth of world time in a reasonable amount of computational time (simulations run typically for a couple of hours), but introduces some errors, which we argue, will be negligible.

4.3.2 Modeling congestion in the access links

In this subsection we consider congestion on the access link. On this access link other services run (i.e., a user may be downloading a large file, may be browsing the web, etc.) beside the DASH video streaming. This type of congestion can occur any time of the day and is not necessarily restricted to peak hours. The model for this type of congestion that we have simulated in this paper is shown in Figure 5. This figure illustrates a Markov-chain with four states corresponding to four possible download rates and selected OPs.

In fact we assume that the cross traffic on the access link (e.g., DSL link) which is the result of sharing this link with one or more DASH clients or any other client requesting data from the Internet is such that the DASH client requesting the version in the next slot, can be described by a Markov chain.

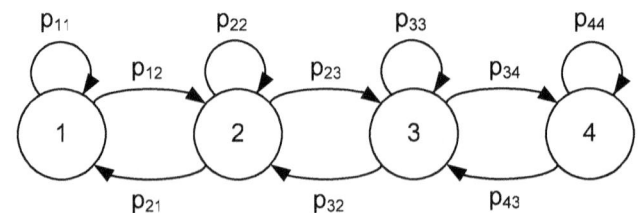

Figure 5: Model for congestion due to cross-traffic

As seen in Figure 5 this Markov chain consists of four states where the transition probabilities p_{ij} of the transition matrix $P=[p_{ij}]$ with

| j - i | > 1 are set to zero, i.e. it is only possible to go from a state to its neighbor sates. The rest of the parameters (represented in the figure) have been set to values that lead to realistic situations.

The most important parameters to take into account to consider whether the selected values correspond to a realistic situation or not are the mean state sojourn time (mean duration of being in a state: $E[t_i]$) and average percentage of time in each of the states (p_i), which can be derived easily from the transition probabilities, as shown in Eq.(1) and Eq.(2).

$$E[t_i] = \sum_{t_i=0}^{\infty} (t_i + 1) * p_{ii}^{t_i} * (1 - p_{ii}) = \frac{1}{1 - p_{ii}} \qquad (1)$$

$$p_i : \pi * P = \pi \qquad (2)$$

where, $\pi = \{p_1, p_2, p_3, p_4\}$ is the left eigenvector of P (associated with eigenvalue 1), a.k.a. steady state vector, which fulfils

$$\sum_{i=1}^{4} p_i = 1 \qquad (3)$$

The simulation time step in the presented Markov-chain model corresponds to the selected chunk size, since the adaptation is performed by the DASH clients on a chunk basis.

4.4 Performance targets

In order to compare the system where the different version of a video are offered encoded in AVC side by side with the system in which the versions are embedded in one SVC stream, we consider three performance targets:

- The cache-hit-ratio: calculated on a chunk basis, or when SVC is considered on smaller objects, corresponding to each of the layers of each of the chunks. It represents the percentage of these objects that can be served from the cache and do not need to be transported over the (possibly congested) cache feeder link.

- Not downgrading clients: percentage of users that do not need to downgrade the requested quality for the video session, i.e. percentage of users that received the maximum quality for the whole service.

- D/R: this introduced measure represents the relation between the desired (D) rate and the received (R) video rate. High values (close to 100 %) correspond to users receiving the highest possible quality, while low values correspond to users receiving a much lower quality than that which would be desirable.

These parameters are either averaged over the complete duration or over the "peak/busy hours". Note that all these performance targets are defined in that way that higher values correspond to a better quality of service.

5. Results

The results presented in the following show the performance of the system comparing both multiple representations encoded with AVC (MR-VoD) offered side-by-side and multiple representations encoded with SVC (SVC-VoD). The rate distribution for the different video representations is summarized in the table:

Table 1: Rate distribution for the video representations

Codec	Rep. 1	Rep.2	Rep.3	Rep. 4
AVC	500 kbps	1000 kbps	1500 kbps	2000 kbps
SVC	500 kbps	1066 kbps	1633 kbps	2200 kbps

As aforementioned, in the performed simulations we studied separately two main cases for congestion: 1) DASH clients requesting too many data in peak hours (resulting in congestion in the cache feeder link) and 2) cross-traffic due to DASH clients sharing resources with other user downloading any type of data (resulting in congestion in the access link).

The videos that are considered for the following simulations have a duration of 90 minutes and are divided in chunks of 10 seconds length.

5.1 Congestion in the cache feeder link

We have simulated a cache feeder link with a bit rate capacity of 250 Mbps and have run the simulation with the data extracted from the deployed real VoD system. Whenever the needed data from the server exceeds the capacity of the cache feeder link, congestion arises, which results in many users adapting the video streaming quality. Table 2 and Table 3 summarize the performance observed in this simulation.

Table 2: Cache-hit-ratio for congestion in cache feeder link

Cache capacity (media units)	LRU		CC	
	AVC	SVC	AVC	SVC
500	52.8 %	57.0 %	59.9 %	64.3 %
1000	64.0 %	66.2 %	67.0 %	70.2 %
2000	73.8 %	73.9 %	74.1 %	75.8 %

The cache capacity is measured in media units, which are equivalent to the size of a video clip of 90 minutes at 500 kbps (1 media unit=337.5 MB).

The results shown in Table 2summarize the cache-hit-ratio for different values of cache capacity and the two different caching algorithms. It can be seen that there is a slight difference between the use of AVC and SVC, where the adoption of SVC as codec results in a small gain in terms of cache-hit-ratio in comparison with AVC. Furthermore, the CC algorithm outperforms the LRU algorithm by up to almost a 7 % for low cache capacity values (similar to what was observed in [13]).

Table 3: Percentage of users not downgrading quality

Cache capacity (media units)	LRU		CC	
	AVC	SVC	AVC	SVC
500	26.7 %	26.1 %	45.4 %	48.0 %
1000	47.5 %	43.5 %	58.9 %	61.0 %
2000	70.3 %	63.7 %	74.4 %	74.0 %

The results in Table 3 show that SVC and AVC perform similarly, although MR-VoD results in an almost equal but lower percentage of users downgrading their quality. This is the result of the slightly lower coding efficiency of SVC. Since we are considering that all users are requesting the same quality, this negative effect appears. However in the conclusion we will discuss what would happen in the reality where users may request for different representations due to congestion also in the access link or different equipment capabilities.

Table 4: Avg. D/R over the whole VoD service

Cache capacity (media units)	LRU		CC	
	AVC	SVC	AVC	SVC
500	63.6%	68.6%	72.2%	77.4%
1000	76.3%	79.5%	81.0%	84.8%
2000	88.6%	89.2%	89.9%	91.8%

Table 4 shows the results of the obtained average D/R over the whole simulation time. The results for SVC are better than for AVC for both LRU and CC caching algorithms. The values are also higher for the presented CC algorithm than for LRU. The gain for SVC comes from the fact that switching to a higher quality only results in having to request the additional layers from the servers while re-utilizing the already cache video content (lower layers). However, when intended to perform that with MR-VoD, it is necessary to download the complete video data directly from the server, ignoring the lower representations of the video stored in the cache, resulting in a suboptimal usage of the available network resources.

Table 5: Avg. D/R over the peak hours (congested feeder link)

Cache capacity (media units)	LRU		CC	
	AVC	SVC	AVC	SVC
500	57.8%	64.8%	66.5%	73.2%
1000	69.3%	75.1%	74.8%	79.9%
2000	81.4%	84.6%	83.4%	87.0%

In Table 5 similar results as for Table 4 are presented but only focusing on the period of time when congestion happens. It can be seen how the D/R values are lower than the ones presented in Table 4, which is logical, but the results are coherent with the ones of Table 4. SVC-VoD outperforms MR-VoD and the usage of CC results in a better performance.

5.2 Congestion in the DSL-links

The results shown in Table 6 correspond to the case where the bottleneck is the access link, as a consequence of some cross-traffic produced by other users on the Internet. The transition probabilities can be found in the following transition matrix.

$$P = \begin{bmatrix} 0.996 & 0.004 & 0 & 0 \\ 0.004 & 0.992 & 0.004 & 0 \\ 0 & 0.004 & 0.992 & 0.004 \\ 0 & 0 & 0.004 & 0.996 \end{bmatrix}$$

The shown transition probabilities correspond to an $E[t_i]$ of approximately 40 minutes (for the selected chunk length of 10 s) and DASH clients that spend on average an equal percentage of time in each state of 25%.

In order to show the D/R value as done for the previous simulations, with congestion in the cache feeder link, we can compute this value easily based on the π vector. In fact, the components of this vector correspond to the average time receiving a video rate of 25%; 50%, 75% and 100%. Eq. (4) shows how to compute this value by multiplying the π with the column vector [0.25 0.5 0.75 1] that corresponds to the receiving video rate:

$$D/R = \pi * \begin{bmatrix} 0.25 & 0.5 & 0.75 & 1 \end{bmatrix}^T \qquad (4)$$

For the presented transition matrix the D/R value is equal to 0.625 for both MR-VoD and SVC-VoD.

Table 6: Cache-hit-ratio for congestion in access links

Cache capacity (media units)	LRU		CC	
	AVC	SVC	AVC	SVC
500	30.9%	45.6%	42.9%	56.6%
1000	42.1%	58.2%	52.0%	64.5%
2000	54.6%	69.0%	61.5%	72.0%

It can be seen that these results show much higher differences between the use of AVC and SVC, since different versions of the requested videos are stored in the cache and this leads to a spoilage of the available storing capacity of the cache when a single layer codec is considered, whereas when SVC is used the available resources are much more efficiently used. A similar effect was observed in [10]. Furthermore, the hit-ratio increases due to the fact that many users make requests for the same data since, even though they may be interested in different version of the same video, their requests are split into multiple request, one associated with each layer that they are requesting. Since the layers built on top of each other, a user requesting layer k, needs to request layer 1 to k-1 too. In particular the base layer is requested by everyone.

Since the difference between both AVC and SVC are more disparate for this case we have conducted the simulations for a higher range of values for cache capacity (C) only focusing on the LRU caching algorithm, leading to the results shown in Figure 6.

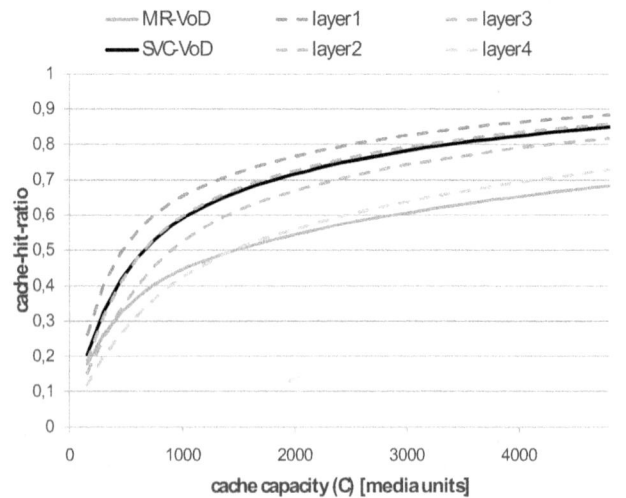

Figure 6: Congestion due to heavy cross traffic

In this figure, the cache-hit-ratio over cache capacity is depicted. It can clearly be seen how the use of SVC improves the performance of the system in terms of cache-hit-ratio compared to the use of MR-VoD. It is also noticeable that the cache-hit-ratio for the AVC case is even lower than for the highest layer (layer 4) when SVC is used almost for all cache capacity values, since the storage capacity at the cache runs out faster with the higher diversity in requested files due to using the MR-VoD approach. Furthermore, the caching performance for the base layer is significantly higher compared to the other files and layers as the number of request for this is higher than for the other layers or different representations when AVC is considered.

Figure 7 shows the results for a different set up of the simulation, for a situation with less heavy cross traffic, resulting in the DASH client residing in the highest state (4) more often. In this case the percentage of time in each state is unequal with p={9.1%, 9.5%, 19.1%, 62.3%}, as well as the mean state sojourn time $E[t_i]$=(approx.){2min, 2min, 10min, 40min}, which may be closer to that which may happen in the reality. The correspondent transition matrix is shown below:

$$P = \begin{bmatrix} 0.9 & 0.1 & 0 & 0 \\ 0.096 & 0.9 & 0.004 & 0 \\ 0 & 0.002 & 0.985 & 0.013 \\ 0 & 0 & 0.004 & 0.996 \end{bmatrix}$$

In this case, for the selected transition matrix the average D/R expected for the DASH-clients is equal to 0.84, noticeably higher than in the case before, which is expected for an environment with lighter cross-traffic.

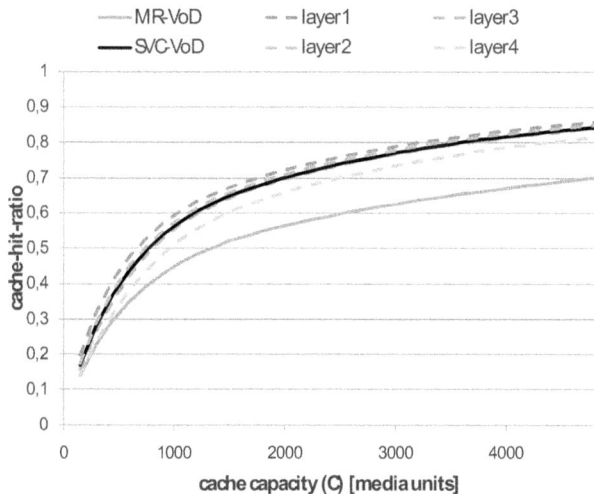

Figure 7: Congestion due to light cross traffic

Although the variety of versions requested for this set up is supposed to be lower than in the case before, the gains of SVC-VoD compared to MR-VoD are still noticeable. Due to this reduced variability the MR-VoD performs slightly better than before but still quite poorly when compared to SVC-VoD. It can be also clearly seen how the cache-hit-ratio for the base layer is reduced (layer 1) and the cache-hit-ratio for the highest layer is increased (layer 4). If we keep on reducing the congestion all lines would converge. An important interpretation of these results

is that even though the network is not heavily congested, SVC-VoD outperforms MR-VoD and to make this effect negligible there should not be congestion in the access links, which is far away from the reality.

6. Conclusions

DASH is a promising technique for video delivery in VoD services, since first transmission is not affected by firewall and NAT traversal issues that are typical in traditional streaming over UDP, and second network caches contribute to a reduction in the load on the servers and the transit links. However, providing a wide variety of files at different encoding rates, in order to be able to cope with congestion within the network may result in a suboptimal performance of the network caches, especially if the congestion arises in the access links next to the clients, since they may request same videos but at different representations.

The adoption of SVC as a media codec enhances the efficiency of the network caches in comparison to the use of AVC at multiple encodings, significantly reducing the load on the video server. This would counter the effect of the low overhead of SVC that lead to a higher number of clients having to downgrade to a lower video quality, when the cache feeder link was considered as the single bottleneck. If both congestion cases (at cache feeder link and access links) are considered simultaneously, as would be expected in the reality, or clients with multiple equipment characteristics are considered, the worse performance of the cache with AVC would lead to more traffic within the cache feeder link, contributing to congestion faster than when SVC-VoD is considered leading to higher number of users downgrading quality. Thus, using SVC would lead a better experience for the users and a higher number of satisfied users.

7. ACKNOWLEDGMENTS

The research leading to these results has received funding from the European Union's Seventh Framework Programme ([FP7/2007-2013]) under grant agreement n° 248775.

8. REFERENCES

[1] K. Sripanidkulchai, B. Maggs, and H. Zhang, "An Analysis of Live Streaming Workloads on the Internet", In Proc. of the 4th ACM SIGCOMM conference on Internet measurement, 2004.

[2] R. Pantos, and W. May, "HTTP Live Streaming" Draft V04, IETF, June 5, 2010, http://tools.ietf.org/html/draft-pantos-http-live-streaming-04.

[3] 3rd Generation Partnership Project; Technical Specification Group Services and System Aspects; Transparent end-to-end Packet-switched Streaming Service (PSS); Protocols and codecs (Release 9); 3GPP TS 26.234 V9.3.0 (2010-06), Section 12: Adaptive HTTP Streaming.

[4] Open IPTV Forum – Release 2 Specification, HTTP Adaptive Streaming, Draft V0.06 - June 7, 2010.

[5] ISO/IEC JTC 1/SC 29/WG 11 (MPEG), "Dynamic adaptive streaming over HTTP", w11578, CD 23001-6, Guangzhou, China, Oct 2010.

[6] T. Wiegand, G. J. Sullivan, G. Bjøntegaard, and A. Luthra, "Overview of the H.264/AVC video coding standard," IEEE

Trans. Circuits Syst.Video Technol., vol. 13, no. 7, pp. 560–576, Jul. 2003.

[7] H. Schwarz, D. Marpe, and T. Wiegand, "Overview of the scalable video coding extension of the H.264/AVC standard," IEEE Transactions on Circuits and Systems for Video Technology, vol. 17, no.9, pp 1103–1120, 2007.

[8] T. Schierl, Y. Sanchez, R. Globisch, C. Hellge, and T. Wiegand, "Priority-based Media Delivery using SVC with RTP and HTTP streaming", Multimedia Tools and Application, 2010

[9] F. Hartanto, J. Kangasharju, M. Reisslein, and K. Ross, "Caching video objects: layers vs. versions?", Multimedia Tools and Applications, vol. 1, n. 2, 221-245, 2006.

[10] Y. Sánchez, T. Schierl, C. Hellge, T. Wiegand, D. Hong, D. De Vleeschauwer, W. Van Leekwijck, Y. Le Louedec. "Improved caching for HTTP-based Video on Demand using Scalable Video Coding", Proceedings of the 8th Annual IEEE Consumer Communications and Networking Conference - Special Session IPTV and Multimedia CDN - (CCNC'2011 - SS IPTV)", Las Vegas (NV), January 9-12, 2011.

[11] H. Bahn, K. Koh, S. H. Noh, and S. Lyul Min, "Efficient Replacement of Nonuniform Objects in Web Caches", IEEE Computer magazine, vol. 35 no. 6, p.65-73, June 2002.

[12] S. Podlipnig, L. Böszörményi, "A survey of Web cache replacement strategies", ACM Computing Surveys, vol. 35 (2003), pp. 331-373, 2003.

[13] D. Hong, D. De Vleeschauwer, F. Baccelli, "A Chunk-based Caching Algorithm for Streaming Video", Proceedings of the 4th Workshop on Network Control and Optimization, Ghent (Belgium), November 29 – December 1, 2010.

[14] H. Schwarz and T. Wiegand, "Further results for an rd-optimized multi-loop SVC encoder", JVT-W071, JVT Meeting San Jose, USA, 2007, ftp://avguest@ftp3.itu.int/jvt-site/2007_04_SanJose/JVT-W071.zip.

Usages of DASH for Rich Media Services

Cyril Concolato   Jean Le Feuvre   Romain Bouqueau

Telecom ParisTech; Institut Telecom; CNRS LTCI

46, rue Barrault

75634 PARIS CEDEX 13

{concolato, lefeuvre, bouqueau}@telecom-paristech.fr

ABSTRACT

In recent years, audio-visual distribution over Internet has witnessed the growing usage of HTTP based delivery systems. While these systems have their drawbacks for some use-cases, they also have many advantages, the most important one being reusing the existing delivery infrastructure such as HTTP servers, proxies and caches. The MPEG group has started the standardization of the Dynamic Adaptive Streaming over HTTP (DASH) of major transport formats, MPEG-2 TS and ISO Base Media File, and mostly focuses on audio, video and subtitle formats. We believe Rich Media services have a role to play in this landscape, as a presentation layer for the audio-visual content first, but also as a dedicated media in the DASH content for real-time media-synchronized interactive services. In this paper, we present a study on usages of DASH for Rich Media Services.

Categories and Subject Descriptors

C.2.2 [**Computer-Communication Networks**]: Network Protocols – *Applications.* H.3.2 [**Information Storage and Retrieval**]: Information Storage – *file organization.* H.5.4 [**Information Interfaces and Presentation**]: Hypertext/Hypermedia – *architectures.*

General Terms

Design, Experimentation, Languages, Standardization.

Keywords

Adaptive Streaming, HTML 5, HTTP, Interactivity, MPEG, Rich Media.

1. INTRODUCTION

In the past few years, new types of multimedia devices have emerged, in particular smartphones, tablet PC or connected SetTop Boxes and TV sets. These new devices have brought new usages for the consumption of audio visual services. Indeed, users now want to view the same audiovisual service either at home, in front of their TV or on their tablet PC in their bedroom, or on the move, with 3G services. These changes imply that methods for the efficient delivery of audiovisual services to a large number of

users and devices have to be found. The number of audiovisual providers has drastically increased with the upcoming of Web videos, and technologies such as broadcast, which assumes that a return channel is not available, or RTP in unicast or multicast, which assumes that UDP traffic is available, are no longer appropriate for all providers. Recent developments in the industry [1] or in standardization bodies such as 3GPP [2] or MPEG [3] have defined new technologies for streaming of audio-visual resources over HTTP.

In the meantime, users' expectations with IP-based applications have risen. They are now used to consume audiovisual services as part of larger rich media services providing additional resources with the content. The upcoming HTML 5 standard is a good example of how video content can be enriched with graphics, animations, textual meta-data or community services.

At the same time, content providers need to ensure that their meta-data can be tightly synchronized with the content, as is usually the case in traditional broadcast environment for DTV systems for various use cases such as advertisements, voting, or annotations.

In this paper, we are interested in the usage of DASH in this environment. DASH [3] stands for Dynamic Adaptive Streaming over HTTP and acts as a superset of existing streaming technologies defined by other standardization bodies. We study how DASH can be useful to rich media technologies and how rich media technologies can be useful to DASH.

The remainder of this paper is organized as follows. Section 2 presents several scenarios where DASH and rich media technologies coexist. Section 3 describes what the state-of-the-art work in this area can achieve. Section 4 presents our study on the use of DASH and our proposals to improve DASH or existing rich media technologies. Section 5 presents some implementation considerations. Finally, Section 6 concludes this paper and presents future work.

2. SCENARIOS

In this paper, rich media services are defined as services that feature multiple media elements (audio, video, images, text, graphics) organized in a specific 2D/3D manner, with some dynamicity either in the organization of the media elements or in the content of the media elements (e.g. changing text, animated graphics) and with an interactive part. Such dynamicity may need to be finely synchronized with media elements.

With that definition, we can envisage the following types of scenarios: some where the rich media service is static and does not need to be streamed per se; and some where the rich media data (e.g. graphics, layout) changes rapidly. In the first scenario presented in this paper, we consider the usage of DASHed media in a rich media service. In the second one, we consider that the rich media data can be DASHed. The third scenario is a combined approach of the first two scenarios, where only the dynamic part of the rich media content is DASHed.

2.1 Controlling a session from a Web page

In this scenario, we consider that a presentation is available with multiple video streams, one for each different camera angle, multiple audio streams for each language, and multiple subtitles streams. We envisage that an author wants to use a Media Presentation Description (MPD), defined by DASH, within a rich media document, for example an HTML 5 page. This page features some controls to enable the selection of a camera angle, the selection of a sound track, the activation/deactivation and selection of a subtitle track, and the ability to seek into the media presentation time line.

2.2 Visual Web Radio

In this scenario, we envisage an extension of traditional Web radios. Indeed, Web radios deliver their audio content over HTTP using Ice cast, Shout cast or over similar protocols. The extension of Web Radio into Visual Web Radio consists in adding a visual (non video) component to the audio component. The visual component carries additional visual information associated with the audio component. Some information can be synchronized and change more or less rapidly (lyrics, news headlines, quiz items). Some information can be quite static for example the weather forecast, the stock quotes. In this scenario, we consider that the service is integrated, in the sense that there is only one application/one window handling the visual and audio parts, as this is easier to ensure synchronization.

Figure 1 - Visual component of a Web Visual Radio when the speaker speaks about President Obama

We can illustrate the concept of visual radio with the following figures. During the news report, when the speaker speaks about President Obama, the visual component will show Figure 1. When he reports about the weather, the visual component will show Figure 2. At any time, the user can interact on the left-side text to display some non-synchronized information (e.g. horoscope, program grid).

2.3 Interactive Service Design Switching

In this scenario, we consider a TV program consisting of audio and video streams delivered in DASH with an associated interactive application, for example an SVG file. In order to avoid overloading the bandwidth by resending the SVG content on a regular basis, as it would be done in traditional broadcast application, the SVG content is made available on a Web server and downloaded by each user upon connection to the TV channel.

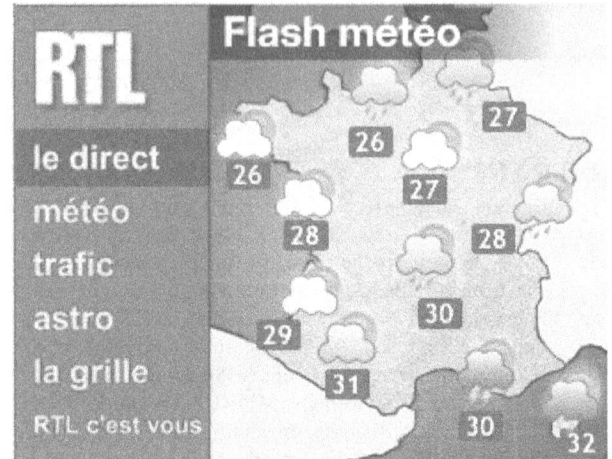

Figure 2 - Visual component of a Web Visual Radio when the speaker reports about the weather

The broadcaster wants to synchronize parts of the interactive application with the audio-visual content, such as active speaker name and biography in a talk show, as seen in the previous scenario. This requires tight synchronization between the interactive application and the DASH streams.

Although the DASH session is well structured into pre-identified periods, each corresponding to a single show and its associated interactive application, the content provider wants to be able to handle unpredictable events in its live broadcast:

- Red Alert Codes triggered by government agencies, for which the broadcaster wants to present an interactive application allowing fast phone call dialing or emailing,

- Failure of the contribution network, in which case the broadcaster may have to switch to a different program and change the current interactive application.

For these reasons, the broadcaster needs to be able to switch at any time between interactive programs during the lifetime of the DASH session.

3. RELATED WORKS

The WhatWG has started drafting some thoughts around the usage of Adaptive Streaming technologies in HTML5 [4], using the M3U8 format [1]. Their work is focusing on the control of quality of service at the player, including video layer switching or buffer management. Specific JavaScript APIs are proposed to handle stream switching at the browser level, based on various live parameters such as download rate, media buffer levels or frame drops. It does not take into account the possibility that a single session can be composed of many resources such as one video, several audio and several meta-data tracks (e.g. subtitles), all of them available in different resolutions, viewpoints and/or quality. Therefore, the proposed interaction with the underlying adaptive streaming subsystem is not sufficient to cover our scenario 1. The 3GPP group has also standardized a mapping between the MPD syntax and the SMIL syntax, but this syntax does not provide ways for an upper presentation layer, such as an HTML <video> element, to select media representations based on user criteria such as language or viewpoint.

In the broadcast world, several technologies already offer the possibility to deliver interactive applications to the end user, including audio/video-synchronized events. Most are based on MPEG-2 Transport streams carrying either the application as files in object carrousels, such as in DVB-MHP [6] or HBBTV; or as rich media streams in MPEG-4 BIFS format, such as in T-DMB. Other technologies rely on an IP layer for transport [7], and carry the applications as a collection of files (using FLUTE) and data streams (using RTP) in SVG/3GPP DIMS format, such as DVB-H or ATSC-M/H. One key notion in all these systems is the carousel of media files. It allows users to download an application over a broadcast link in a reasonable time, but it is bandwidth costly. It also allows changing the complete application in all connected terminals if the broadcaster needs to.

In the Internet world, many technologies exist to allow dynamic modifications of a multimedia document such as HTML or SVG. We can classify these technologies in two categories. Pull techniques allow the client to request new data from the Web server; the most known example is AJAX-based technologies using the XmlHTTPRequest JavaScript object. Push techniques allow the server to send new data to the client. For a long time, these techniques were relying on script, either through progressive download or long-polling HTTP request from the client, and are often referred to as COMET [5] technology. Rich Media standards such as MPEG-4 BIFS, MPEG-4 LASeR or 3GPP DIMS, and more recently HTML 5 with its EventSource interface [8], have the ability to define data streams used by the server to send updates to the client. All these techniques are suitable for our Rich Media use cases, but we should keep in mind that AJAX, COMET or HTML5 techniques are heavier as they require scripting support even for simple operations such as text replacement and have no support for audio-video synchronization.

4. STUDY OF DASH FOR RICH MEDIA

4.1 Linking MPD from a Rich Media Document

In DASH, a given media resource as delivered by the network is called a representation. A representation can be a multiplexed MPEG-2 TS or ISO Base Media File, for example containing video and audio tracks, or can be a single-media file, for example containing only audio in a given language. Single-media representations can be assigned to a given group. A group is a set of alternate media representation, and a DASH player is expected to play at most one representation from each group; therefore, groups have to be carefully defined. The possible combinations can be restricted by defining subsets, for instance to disallow a particular audio track when playing the Director's cut version of a movie. For our scenario, it must be noted that only groups and representations have associated identifiers.

We consider in this paper that the MPD we want to manipulate is made of single-media representation, since multiple-media representations do not offer any flexibility regarding audio or subtitle track selection, as they are all part of the same representation. We also only consider the use case where the MPD file is the same for all users and is not negotiated based on

user preferences: although this later case may offer a pre-selection of tracks, it does not solve the case of interactive switching between tracks unless a renegotiation for a new MPD occurs, which is precisely what we want to avoid.

One simple approach for media selection in DASH would be to identify representations to be played from the HTML content. However, this would force the DASH player to select one given representation and we will lose the capability of DASH to switch between representations when bandwidth conditions change. In other words, the HTML author would have to manage the stream switching logic in its content, which is a real burden and requires monitoring many real-time parameters of the network stack.

A better approach would be to identify groups, as each group constitutes the set of alternative representation for a media. However there are scenarios for which this is not sufficient. Let us consider the case of language selection for audio tracks. If all tracks are set in the same group, there is no way for the HTML document to select one particular language by using only the group id. One solution could be to group audio tracks by language, therefore defining as many groups as they are languages, and defining subsets in the MPD to avoid playing together two audio tracks. Each group can then be referenced through its ID in the HTML document. However, if the HTML document wants to switch the quality of selected audio track, the group id is no longer sufficient to identify the possible representations. Let us now consider the case of multiview video: a DASH session offers two views at two different resolutions, each of the videos being encoding at two bitrates. The HTML user interface needs to be able to select the view, and may need to switch the resolution when displaying the video at a lower resolution. The DASH player may not always know the target resolution of the video, e.g. when the video is used for visual effects in an HTML 5 Canvas object; only the HTML presentation layer may hint this. In such a case, either the MPD describes each representation as a group, restricting their combinations with subsets, or another selection mechanism should be used for HTML. If the HTML layer wants to select representations based on another criteria (e.g. frame rate), more groups would have to be defined and subsets and selection processing becomes cumbersome. One final consideration is that the HTML browser would need to be aware of group and representation identifiers, which makes designing a generic HTML UI for any MPD harder. We therefore propose to identify a sub-set of selection criteria from the MPD schema and expose them to the HTML layer. The set of criteria is presented in Table 1.

Not all of the various criteria defined in MPD have been exposed. We assume that bandwidth-related criteria are handled directly by the DASH player for adapting to bandwidth variation. We assume that in most cases, the DASH player will automatically handle the TrickMode criterion, used in slow/fast motion forward/backward, when the HTML object modifies the playback rate of the content; in other words the HTML Web author should not have to touch it. We however expose this parameter to allow non-linear viewing of video content in HTML, for example when displaying video key frames when moving the mouse over the media timeline bar. In such a case, the playback rate of the overlaid video is null (video is paused) but the DASH player has to be instructed to select a representation where random access is faster.

Table 1 – MPD Selection Criteria exposed in HTML

Criteria	HTML Selection Action
width, height	Specifies the desired video resolution
lang	Specifies the desired language
frameRate	Specifies the desired frame rate
qualityRanking	Specifies the desired quality
viewpoint	Specifies the name of the desired viewpoint
TrickMode	Specifies maximum playback rate desired for fast forward or rewind

Currently, the typical way to embed video/audio resources within a rich media document is through the use of dedicated elements and attributes such as the HTML 5 <video> or <audio> elements and the 'src' attribute, or the SVG <video> or <audio> element and the 'xlink:href' attribute, or the BIFS MovieTexture or AudioSource elements and the 'url' attribute. The use of DASHed media should not deviate from this current practice, but additional tools are needed to enable scenario 1. It should be possible for Web page authors to pass parameters to the DASH player, in an interoperable way. We can envisage three complementary methods to extend existing documents and achieve scenario 1.

The first method is to define fragment identifiers. Fragment identifiers are appended to the URL and have the advantage of being language independent. An example is as follows:

```
<video src="dash.mpd#viewpoint=1
&width=176&height=144">
```

The second method is to define specific attributes for the selection of a particular resource in the MPD. These attributes may be defined in the host language and namespace or in a DASH namespace. This is illustrated below.

```
<video src="dash.mpd">
  <track kind=subtitles src="dash.mpd"
   dash:qualityRanking="1" srclang="en"
   label="English">
</video>
```

The third method is to define an Application Programming Interface (API), typically, using a generic Interface Definition Language (IDL), which can then be mapped onto concrete languages such as JavaScript. Here we present a possible HTML5 API to create a new TimedTrack object from an MPD representation.

```
<script>
 var videoElement =
document.createElement('video');
var track =
createTrackFromDASH('subtitles','lang','
en');
videoElement.addTrack(track);
</script>
```

Given the novelty of DASH and HTML5, there are currently no available implementations of DASH players in an HTML5 environment, and it is quite hard to predict how close the HTML5 browser and the DASH player will be integrated. This makes it difficult to choose one of the proposed method rather another. Our preference goes to the first method, using fragment identifier, as it is language independent and may therefore be used in non-HTML5 environment such as CE-HTML-based, SVG-based or MPEG-4 BIFS. This approach avoids defining extensions in the host language (new attributes or elements).

4.2 Using MPD to carry Rich Media Services

When the techniques mentioned in Section 3 are used in a broadcast channel, they require sending the entire service has in a carousel on regular basis, but take advantage of the tight synchronization between audio-visual data and the service updates in the broadcast. When transposed in an on-demand context over HTTP, the service updates provided by these technologies are usually carried in a dedicated channel, for instance HTTP for AJAX or COMET based technologies, or RTP for BIFS or DIMS. This channel follows a different path than the audio-visual data presented in the service, and may even originate from a different server; this introduces important delays in service update acquisition, such as RTP buffer and transmission times or HTTP round-trip delay. Such solutions are therefore not suited for tight synchronization of service data with audio-visual data. In this section, we investigate how the service updates can be carried in DASH to guarantee this synchronization while being bandwidth-friendly. We will take the example of a BIFS service, but our approach is more generic and can be used for any timed data.

4.2.1 Example of a T-DMB Digital Radio Service

We take the example of a complex service, stored in an MP4 file, which has duration of 6:40 minutes and is composed of:

- An audio stream, here an AAC sound track

- An MPEG-4 BIFS stream, used to display a visual scene synchronized with the audio track. The scene uses text, graphics and images. The scene features a live screen and some non-live information like the last weather forecast, the last horoscope, or the EPG.

- An MPEG-ODF stream used to describe when images are used.

- 41 images, not displayed all at the same time.

The BIFS stream is a continuous stream, hence meaningful for DASH applications. It is a bit different from typical video stream, as it is made of only 69 access units, very sparse. The original sequence contains only one Random Access Point at time 0.

4.2.2 Using DASH to deliver the example content

Our first approach in using DASH for the transport of this interactive service is to embed BIFS media data in the DASH session. The DASH session uses ISO Base Media File Format as a container, and each track is setup to use track fragments. The segment duration is selected to be 10 seconds. The initialization segment of the session conforms to the DASH specification and only contains track declaration with no media data.

To enable random access in the presentation, we recreate a carousel at the beginning of each segment by generating random access points in BIFS and OD streams and reinserting images used during the segment duration. In our tests, the impact of this content modification on the BIFS bitrate is quite important as can be seen in Table 2. The image bitrate is of course much more important but this is not really problematic as images could be moved outside the DASH session, as explained in next example.

Our second approach, which fits our third scenario, is to extract the static part of the presentation (of the BIFS stream) from the DASH session and only convey the scene modifications in the DASH session. This avoids carouseling most of the presentation, and therefore leads to a BIFS bitrate close to that of the original file with the initial random access point omitted. Images in the BIFS scene are referenced through HTTP links rather than using the OD framework, which allows simple image replacement in the DASH session by carrying only one link rather than the entire image. This also greatly reduces the bandwidth of the OD stream as can be seen in Table 2. This slight increase is due to the fact that image links to OD are replaced with image links to http resources, which are larger text strings.

Table 2 – Bit rate of a BIFS Visual Web Radio over DASH

	Average bit rate (kbps)	Peak bit rate (kbps)
Original bit stream	0.168	27
Dashed bit stream (Approach 1)	7	147
Dashed bit stream (Approach 2)	0.195	28
Dashed bit stream (external RAPs)	0.098	5

In summary, what we learn from this experiment is that delivering an interactive application, initially designed for broadcast and carousels, using DASH requires actual modification of the way the application is structured. Static elements and dynamic synchronized elements need to be delivered separately.

4.2.3 Optimizing DASH for Rich Media

The previous experiment showed that it is possible to use DASH to deliver continuous and dynamic interactive applications, but a problem remains. The requirement in the DASH specification that the initialization segment shall not contain any media data forces the content provider to insert the Rich Media service in a segment. Since users may start playing at any segment, this implies that the Rich Media service has to be repeated often in the segments, which is bandwidth costly as shown previously. If the Rich Media service structure is the same throughout the DASH session and only modifications to the content (text data changing, animation triggering…) are streamed in DASH, such repetition is awkward. The same remark applies for any meta-data format stored as media tracks in the file (XML, JPEG files…). We therefore propose to allow non-empty initialization segments in DASH to carry the static media data used in the DASH session in order to save bandwidth. This allows the content to be delivered with the original bitrate as described in Table 2.

One additional limitation we faced to fulfill our third scenario is that the ISO Base Media File Format does not provide many tools to reference external, remote resources that may change over time. We investigated using the capability of the file to define an external data source for the track using the DataReferenceBox, which may point to an HTTP URL; however we faced a new limitation in DASH that forces all data offsets to be relative to the

start of the movie fragment. This makes external data references for tracks unusable in DASH. We propose to remove this constraint on relative data offset for track fragments using external data references, thereby allowing a client to fetch sample data on a given server outside of the DASHed file. This method gives us the result presented in Table 2, with a much lower bitrate for the DASHed part of the Rich Media service.

Finally, as explained in our third scenario, the Rich Media scene has to be sent, or at least signaled, on a regular basis. We explained that we reduce the size of this scene by placing its static content outside the DASH session, but still there remains a minimal scene. In scenario 3, we want the possibility to completely replace its content, as in a classical carousel. This is achieved by sending periodical random access points (RAP), for example, at the beginning of a segment. However, we must have the ability to signal that a RAP can be discarded in normal playback, otherwise a client will reload the scene at each RAP and loose all the current interactivity (user input, scripting context).

The SampleDependencyBox tool available in the file format is a good candidate for our needs. This tool allows signaling whether a media sample depends on another on, whether other samples depend on this one and is depended on and whether the sample has redundant. The notion of redundant coding depends on the coding type, and is not defined for meta-data or scene descriptions (BIFS, SVG). Our proposal is to define that a sample tagged as redundant, not depended on and not depending on other samples can be discarded if a RAP or another such redundant sample has already been processed. An alternative way could be to add a new flag in the track fragment header box indicating all samples in the fragment can be discarded under the same conditions.

This signaling may be redundant with existing features in some languages, such as the RefreshScene command in MPEG-4 LASeR. However, such signaling would require the client to first download the sample data and then discard it. Our proposal simplifies this process by saving some bandwidth and can be used with any meta-data streams.

Figure 3 illustrates the various cases enabled by our solution. The BIFS track in the DASH initialization segment uses two data references, one pointing to the DASH file itself, one referring to a Web server through HTTP. The figure shows that the DASH server and the BIFS random access server do not have to be at the same location. The first segment received in the DASH session contains a regular BIFS RAP conveying the interactive service associated with the audio. Its data is contained in the segment and the client must process it. The ith segment is a simple service update. The jth segment is a discardable BIFS RAP, which is ignored by connected clients and processed only by clients connecting at this time in the session. The data of this RAP is not included in the segment but made available on an HTTP server, thereby saving bandwidth in the DASH session even when inserting the RAP at high frequencies. The kth segment is a regular BIFS RAP which must be processed by all clients, however the RAP data is stored on the server rather than in the segment. This covers the use case of our third scenario where the broadcaster decides to unexpectedly switch interactive services for all connected clients.

Our proposal is not restricted to BIFS, it may be used with other description languages such as LASeR or SVG; it may also be used

269

with AJAX-based solutions querying a meta-data stream in the DASH session, as used in DTV environments such as HBBTV.

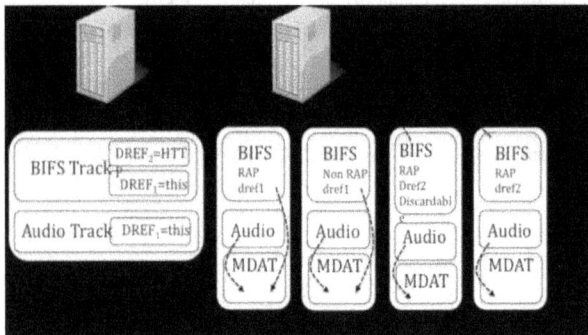

Figure 3 - Example of BIFS Carousel in DASH

5. IMPLEMENTATION

We have implemented our proposal in GPAC [9], an open-source multimedia framework supporting many interactive languages (BIFS, LASeR, SVG, X3D...) and delivery formats (MPEG-2 TS, ISO Base Media File...). Our implementation concerns both DASH media generation and playback.

We have extended the MP4Box tool to include a MP4/3GP fragmenter to generate segments of a given duration. The fragmenter may truncate the file at RAP boundaries to simplify content access in the DASHed file. The tool was also modified to generate random access points in BIFS and OD streams at a given frequency, in order to estimate the bandwidth overhead of using BIFS in DASHed without our proposed modifications.

We also have implemented DASH support in Osmo4, the GPAC player. A description of the implementation is given in Figure 4. We have validated support of both live sources using MPEG-2 TS as the DASH transport format, and on-demand sources using ISO Base Media File as the transport format. It supports both M3U8 formats and a subset of MPD files as defined in DASH.

In our implementation, the DASH player is in charge of parsing the MPD or M3U8 fetched from the server. It then selects the representation based on bandwidth criteria and other parameters set by the browser through the Selection API. The current implementation uses fragment identifiers in the MPD URL to configure the DASH player. The DASH player is then in charge of scheduling the segment downloads and sending them to the MPEG-2 TS or ISO File readers. We have extended our ISO reader to support external data references and redundant sample signaling for scene description.

Our implementation, released under the LGPL license, is available on the GPAC Web site http://gpac.sourceforge.net.

6. CONCLUSION

In this paper, we have investigated how Rich Media languages can be used with adaptive streaming over HTTP technologies, especially MPEG DASH. We have shown the need to provide standard ways to identify parts of a DASH session for track selection. We have also presented how Rich Media services can be carried in a DASH session along with audio and video data to ensure tight synchronization between the media data and the interactive service. Finally, we have proposed some light modifications to DASH and

ISO Base Media File to allow building a smart, bandwidth-friendly data carousel of interactive services and meta-data in a DASH session.

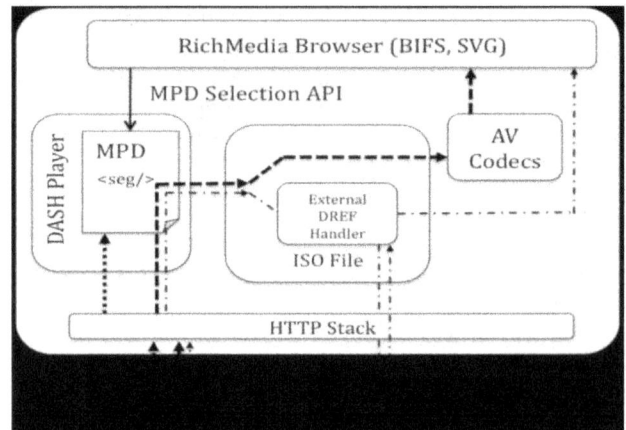

Figure 4 - DASH Implementation in GPAC

In future works, we will investigate implementation of real-time, live DASH services including interactive ones. We will evaluate how Rich Media adaptation to terminal characteristics and user preferences can be used in DASH, especially in live services.

7. ACKNOWLEDGMENTS

Part of the work presented in this paper has been funded by the French ANR projects Radio+ and HybRadio.

8. REFERENCES

[1] HTTP Live Streaming RFC,
    http://tools.ietf.org/html/draft-pantos-http-live-streaming-04
[2] 3GPP Adaptive HTTP Streaming, TS 26.234
    http://www.3gpp.org/ftp/specs/html-info/26234.htm
[3] MPEG DASH, ISO/IEC 23001-6 CD (N11578)
[4] WhatWG Adaptive Streaming
    http://wiki.whatwg.org/wiki/Adaptive_Streaming
[5] E. Bozdag, A. Mesbah, A. van Deursen *"A Comparison of Push and Pull Techniques for AJAX"*, WSE 2007. 9th IEEE International Workshop on Web Site Evolution. DOI: http://dx.doi.org/10.1109/WSE.2007.4380239
[6] DVB DSM-CC Data Broadcasting, ETSI TR 101 202
[7] P.Leroux, V.Verstraete, F.De Turck, P.Demeester, *Synchronized Interactive Services for Mobile Devices over IPDC/DVB-H and UMTS*, 2nd IEEE/IFIP International Workshop on Broadband Convergence Networks, 2007. BcN '07. DOI= http://dx.doi.org/10.1109/BCN.2007.372743
[8] HTML 5 Server-sent Events,
    http://dev.w3.org/html5/eventsource/
[9] Le Feuvre, J., Concolato, C., and Moissinac, J. 2007. GPAC: open source multimedia framework. In *Proceedings of the 15th international Conference on Multimedia* (Augsburg, Germany, September 25 - 29, 2007). MULTIMEDIA '07. ACM, New York, NY, 1009-1012. DOI= http://doi.acm.org/10.1145/1291233.1291452

A Test-Bed for the Dynamic Adaptive Streaming over HTTP featuring Session Mobility

Christopher Müller and Christian Timmerer
Klagenfurt University, Multimedia Communication
Universitätsstraße 65-67
9020 Klagenfurt am Wörthersee, Austria
+43 (0)463 2700 3600

{firstname.lastname}@itec.uni-klu.ac.at

ABSTRACT

In this paper, we present a multimedia test-bed enabling session mobility in the context of the emerging ISO/IEC MPEG standard, Dynamic Adaptive Streaming over HTTP (DASH). In general, session mobility is defined as the transfer of a running streaming session from one device to another device where it may need to be consumed in an adaptive way. The two main challenges are: (1) taking into account the new context of the device (e.g., capabilities) to which the session is transferred and (2) performing the actual transfer in a seamless and interoperable way. Our system addresses both challenges supported by a prototype implementation integrated into VLC. In anticipation of the results we can conclude that interoperability is achieved adopting existing standards while the performance of the system does not depend on these standards. That is, the modules responsible for the performance are usually not defined within such standards and left out for competition. However, our system is designed in an extensible way and is able to accommodate this fact.

Categories and Subject Descriptors

H.5.1 [**Multimedia Information System**]: Video

General Terms

Documentation, Design, Standardization.

Keywords

Dynamic Adaptive Streaming over HTTP, MPEG-21 Digital Item Declaration, MPEG-21 Session Mobility, Test-bed.

1. INTRODUCTION

The streaming of media resources over the Hypertext Transfer Protocol (HTTP) is nowadays omnipresent and has become a de-facto standard on the Internet for two reasons. First, reasonable Internet connectivity (i.e., in terms of bandwidth for media content) is nowadays available anywhere, anytime, and almost on any device. Second, the usage of HTTP does not cause any

NAT/firewall issues as it is the case with other media transport protocols like RTP/RTSP. In order to provide interoperability among vendor implementations, standards developing organizations such as MPEG have recognized the need for an international open standard in order to reduce the number of already existing proprietary solutions (cf. Section 5 for details). The MPEG standard which is used in this paper is referred to as ISO/IEC 23001-6 entitled Dynamic Adaptive Streaming over HTTP (DASH) [1]. It is based on 3GPP Adaptive HTTP Streaming (AHS) which has been also adopted by the Open IPTV Forum (OIPF) as a baseline standard.

In this paper we address – in the context of DASH – the need for leveraging existing media repositories (and their representation formats) and enabling session mobility in an interoperable way. Therefore, we have developed a test-bed for DASH which enables session mobility in an interoperable way and may be added on top of existing media repositories. In particular, existing media repositories utilize XML data formats in order to describe the content and the relationship among the assets within the repository. One well-known example is Universal Plug and Play's (UPnP) Content Directory which specifies DIDL-Lite [2] that is derived from a subset of MPEG-21 Digital Item Declaration Language (DIDL) [3]. Both DIDL-Lite and DIDL provides means to describe the relationship among various information assets that may be consumed as such by a user and which are collectively referred to as Digital Item (DI). In this paper we leverage the fact that media resources are described by existing formats such as DIDL(-Lite) and introduce a method that enables its usage within the emerging DASH standard. Additionally, we demonstrate the use case of session mobility which enables the seamless session transfer from one device to another per user request, everything fully interoperable by utilizing existing as well as emerging (MPEG) standards. We have uploaded a demo video to YouTube (http://www.youtube.com/user/timse7) in order to demonstrate our system in action.

The remainder of the paper is organized as follows. Background about the technology standards used in this paper is presented in Section 2. Section 3 defines the system architecture and Section 4 provides the details about our implementation. Section 5 provides an overview of related work and the paper is concluded in Section 6 including future work items.

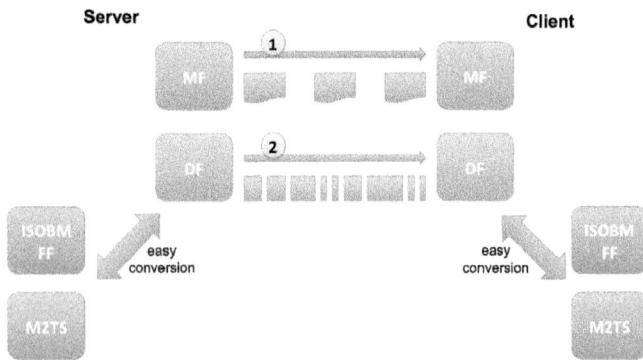

Figure 1. MPEG-DASH System Architecture.

2. BACKGROUND

2.1 Dynamic Adaptive Streaming of HTTP

During its 93rd meeting, MPEG evaluated 15 submissions from 20 organizations (including companies, research institutions, and universities). The submissions provided technologies for the HTTP streaming of MPEG media in the following areas:

- Manifest File (MF), i.e., playlist, media presentation description, etc. which is mostly based on XML.

- Delivery Format (DF) as extensions/specializations of ISOBMFF and M2TS.

The system architecture is depicted in Figure 1 and based on that MPEG started a new work item called Dynamic Adaptive Streaming over HTTP (DASH) which will be Part 6 of MPEG-B (i.e., ISO/IEC 23001-6).

On request, the manifest file will be provided to the client in order to initiate the session (cf. step-1 in Figure 1). The client will parse the manifest file and request individual segments compliant to the delivery format using HTTP and according to the information found in the manifest file (cf. step-2 in Figure 1). For the manifest file, DASH adopted the Media Presentation Description (MPD) as defined by 3GPP AHS [4] as a starting point. The MPD follows a data model comprising a sequence of one or more consecutive non-overlapping periods for which one or more representations may be available. A single representation refers to a specific media following certain characteristics such as bit rate, frame rate, resolution, etc. Furthermore, each representation consists of one or more segments that actually describe the media and/or metadata to decode and present the included media content. The actual delivery format is also based on 3GPP files which are derived from the well-known ISO base media file format. Additionally, extensions to the MPEG-2 Transport Stream (TS) will be also defined within DASH in order to support its transport over HTTP.

2.2 MPEG-21 Digital Item Declaration

The aim of the MPEG-21 standard (ISO/IEC 21000), the so-called Multimedia Framework, is to enable transparent and augmented use of multimedia resources across a wide range of networks, devices, user preferences, and communities, notably for trading (of bits). That is, to support the transaction of Digital Items among Users.

A Digital Item is a structured digital object with a standard representation, identification, and metadata. The standard representation of Digital Items is defined by a model which describes a set of abstract terms and concepts and is expressed by the XML Schema based Digital Item Declaration Language (DIDL) [3]. The resulting XML document conformant to DIDL is called Digital Item Declaration (DID). The DID may contain several building blocks as defined in DIDL which defines the structure of the Digital Item. A brief overview of the most important building blocks is given in this paper, for further details the reader is referred to [3][5].

The *Item* comprises a grouping of sub-items or components. In general, an item can be considered as a declarative representation of a Digital Item. Note that an item without sub-items can be considered a logically indivisible work and an item that does contain sub-items can be considered a compilation.

The *Component* defines a binding of a multimedia resource to a set of descriptors which provides information related to all or parts of the resource. These descriptors will typically contain control or structural information about the resource such as bit rate, character set, start points, or encryption information.

A *Descriptor* associates information with the enclosing element, i.e., its parent (e.g., item) or following sibling (e.g., component). The information can itself be a component (e.g., thumbnail of an image) or a textual statement.

A *Resource* is defined as an individually identifiable asset such as a video, audio clip, image, or textual asset. Note that the resource must be locatable via an unambiguous address.

Digital Items are configurable through the so-called choice/selection mechanism. A *Choice* describes a set of related *Selections* which can affect the configuration of an item. As such it provides a generic and flexible way for multimedia content selection based on certain criteria defined by the Digital Item author. Such criteria may include rights expressions and/or usage environment constraints.

Finally, DIDL allows to associate annotations and assertions to its building blocks using the equally named elements, i.e., *Annotation* and *Assertion* respectively.

2.3 MPEG-21 Digital Item Adaptation

Part 7 of MPEG-21, entitled Digital Item Adaptation (DIA) [6], addresses issues that are related to Universal Multimedia Access (UMA) [7] which refers to the ability to seamlessly access multimedia content from anywhere, anytime, and with any device. Due to the heterogeneity of terminals and networks and the existence of various coding formats, the adaptation of the multimedia content may be required in order to support the requirements of the consuming user and his/her environment. Therefore, MPEG-21 DIA specifies description formats (also known as tools) to assist with the adaptation of Digital Items. In the context of this paper, the MPEG-21 DIA Session Mobility (SM) tool is adopted which enables the interoperable transfer of a session from one device to a second device. Therefore, one needs to capture the configuration state of a Digital Item (i.e., the instantiation of the choices and selections) as well as the DASH application state (i.e., the representation and the segment as well

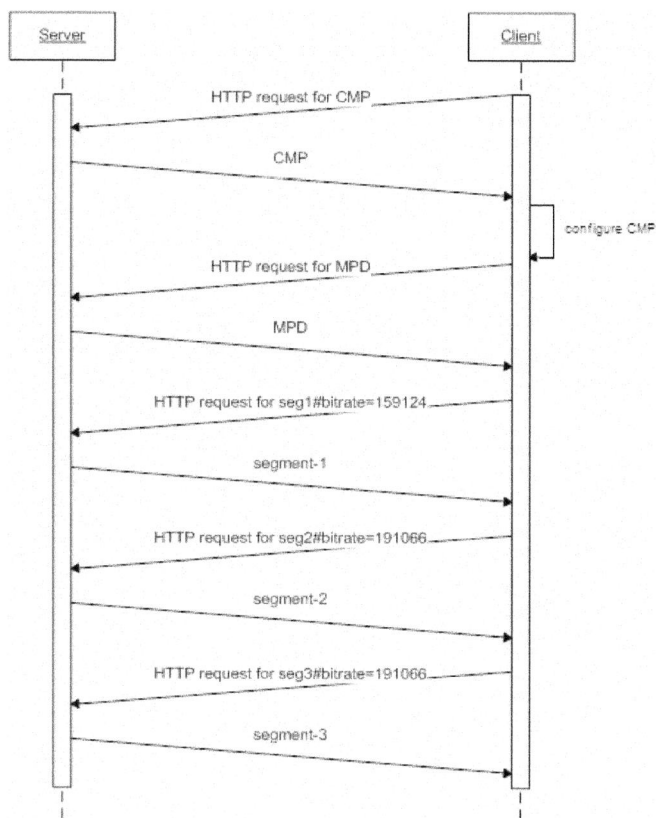

Figure 2. Sequence Diagram for CMP-enabled DASH.

as the time position within the segment) and transfer this information to the second device.

3. SYSTEM ARCHITECTURE

3.1 Composition of Media Presentation

The Composition of Media Presentation (CMP) description comprises another layer that is added on top of the MPD and provides means for the selection of a specific configuration (e.g., codec selection, subtitles, different views, etc.) prior to the delivery of the actual MPD. In particular, a CMP description is an XML document which specifies initial user and device options like camera angel, audio language, subtitle language, resolution, decoding algorithm, and any other possible choice that the user or the device may decide. The CMP is very flexible and, thus, overlaps with the MPD are possible but not advisable.

The CMP description is compliant to MPEG-21 DID and utilizes its choice/selection mechanism to allow a runtime configuration of the DI which makes the static XML dynamic [5]. A full example of such a CMP can be found at [8]. Upon receipt of a CMP description the DI is configured according to the usage environment which may be accomplished manually by the user, automatically by the device, or semi-automatically (i.e., some choices may be presented to the user whereas some are resolved by the device). A more detailed walkthrough of CMP-enabled DASH is provided in the next section.

3.2 CMP-enabled DASH

The sequence diagram of CMP-enabled DASH is shown in Figure 2. At the beginning the client requests the CMP from the server.

In this case the request/response of the CMP is based on HTTP but any other protocol or mechanism could be used. After the successful download of the CMP the client configures the DI based on the CMP in such a way that it fulfills the requirements of the device and the user. This configuration typically includes the elimination of choices and selections that are not supported by the capabilities of hardware or software modules of this device (e.g., decoding or decryption algorithm). Furthermore, the user may select her/his preferred configuration that fulfills his/her needs. For example, the user is able to choose between different movies, different camera angles (e.g., of a football game), different languages, or if subtitles and in which language should be used. In this sense, the configuration of the CMP comes close to a DVD menu where it is also possible to configure several options as mentioned before.

Such a configuration of a DI may contain several iterations as some selections may affect other/subsequent choices (and vice versa). However, this kind of functionality is fully supported by the CMP based on MPEG-21 DID. After the client has successfully configured the CMP according to its needs, the corresponding MPD is requested in the same way as the CMP. The MPD is used to perform the dynamic adaptive streaming (over HTTP) of the media resources which is associated to the CMP configuration. The MPD is an XML document compliant to DASH and may describe different bitrate representations of the media resource enabling dynamic adaptive streaming over HTTP. Each representation is divided into small parts called segments. These segments are located on a regular Web server and accessible per HTTP.

The MPD contains fully qualified URLs to these segments and it expresses the relationship between the segments and the corresponding representation. Some examples for MPDs can be found at [9]. After the download of the MPD the client is able to start with the download of the first segment at a lower bitrate as shown in Figure 2, e.g., to reduce the start-up delay. At segment boundaries, the client is able to switch to segment of different representations, e.g., to higher or lower bitrates depending on the actual download rate of the segments. In this way dynamic adaptive streaming over HTTP is achieved.

3.3 Session Transfer during DASH

3.3.1 General Considerations

At some point in time during a DASH session the user may decide to transfer the session from one device to another device. Obviously, the session should be started with the same configuration and the same point in time where the user has initiated it on the first device. Additionally, the user should also be able to reconfigure the initial setup from the first device at the start of the session on the second device where the session is transferred. An example case for such a user reconfiguration is that the user decides that it is not necessary to display the subtitles on a mobile device because they are not readable on such a small screen. On the other hand, an automatic reconfiguration may become necessary in cases where the second device does not fully support the requirements of the configuration on the first device (e.g., different decoding or decryption algorithm). One common reconfiguration may concern the spatial resolution when transferring the session from a TV screen to a mobile device and vice versa.

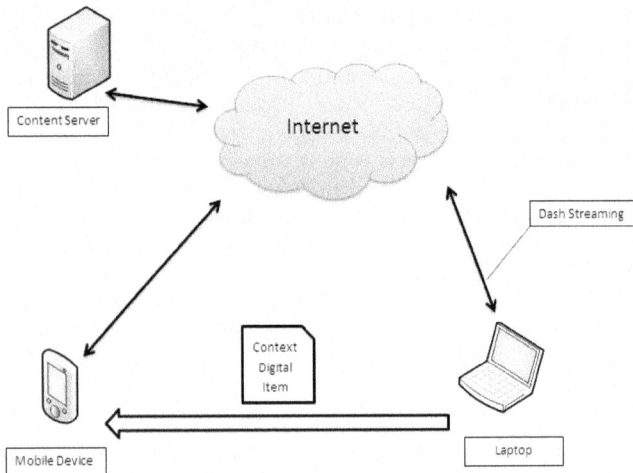

Figure 3. Session Mobility Architecture.

3.3.2 Session Transfer with MPEG-21

Our approach is based on the session mobility tool specified in MPEG-21 DIA as introduced earlier and now described in more detail for DASH.

The session mobility architecture based on MPEG-21 DIA is depicted in Figure 3. In this scenario, the user decides during the DASH session to switch to another device (i.e., from the laptop to the mobile device). Therefore the client on the laptop has to save the current state of the CMP, the media play time and the state of the video player. For this purpose MPEG-21 has introduced the Context Digital Item (CDI). It is based on XML and it describes the user's current state of interaction with a Digital Item (DI) and it is also possible to describe application-specific information [5] (i.e., the DASH context with respect to the segment which is currently decoded/displayed).

In our system the CDI describes the state of the CMP which is based on a DI. The play time and play state is stored in the CDI as application-specific information as mentioned before. Also the path to the CMP which is a fully qualified URL is stored as application-specific information in the CDI. Thus, a CDI contains all information that is required to reconstruct a session at another device. Like shown in Figure 3 the laptop generates the CDI upon user request and transfers it over the network to the mobile device. The next step is that the mobile device has to extract the information from the CDI that is important to reconstruct the session. At this point the most important information of the CDI is the path to the CMP, because the CDI contains only the selected configuration of the CMP which is useless without the actual CMP.

Therefore, the mobile device needs to download the CMP and configure it with the information of the CDI. Please note that the user and also the device are able to reconfigure the CMP as discussed in the previous section. This is not really a problem because the same will be done during the startup of DASH. The only thing that we had to change was the initial configuration of the CMP. Another important thing is the play time and play state. This information will be used after the download of the MPD. As also mentioned in the previous sections the MPD contains the bit rate representations of the media and the corresponding segments. The MPD describes also the length of the whole media and the length of each individual segment. With that information and the play time of the CDI it is possible to calculate the offset and to select the appropriate segment, so that the session could start at the same position where the user has stopped on the other device.

4. IMPLEMENTATION

This section describes our implementation of CMP-enabled DASH and the session transfer based on the MPEG-21 DIA. As indicated before our implementation consists of two applications: (a) playback of CMP-enabled DASH content and (b) session mobility.

Our first application, the playback of CMP-enabled DASH content is based on the well-known VideoLan Client (VLC) [10]. We have used a common application like VLC as basis because it should be easier for the user to accept DASH within a known environment. However, VLC does not support DASH out of the box and, thus, we had to include this functionality into VLC. At the beginning of writing this paper we were not aware of any other player supporting DASH like specified by MPEG (cf. Section 5 for more details).

4.1 VLC Architecture

This section describes the VLC architecture in general. VLC is built in a highly modular way around the VLC core library called LibVLC. At each layer it is very easy to build an own module, because modules always follow the same structure. In general one could say that a module consists of two major parts.

The first part of a module consists of a module description that is made out of macros which describe the behavior and the capabilities of a module. Also the priority of the module will be specified in this part including some other functionality like variables that are specific to the module. These variables are also important for our system because we use them to add a command line parameter named *contextDI*. This command line parameter will be used to start the application with a CDI, for the pre-configuration of the CMP.

The second part of a module is the callback part. A module always has to implement two callback functions named *open(vlc_object_t *)* and *close(vlc_object_t *)* that are specified in the module description part. The *open(vlc_object_t *)* function will be called by the VLC core to initialize the module. The *close(vlc_object_t *)* function should basically uninitialize the module and free all memory that has been allocated by the *open(vlc_object_t *)* function.

The main layers of VLC:

- *Interface*: Contains all modules that have something to do with the user interaction like stop, play, forward and backward key presses or mouse events and playlist management.

- *Access*: Modules that are able to open files or streams are located at this layer. The access modules supply the demux modules with data.

- *Demux*: At this layer different formats will be demultiplexed such as MP4, AVI, MKV, etc.

- *Decoder*: This layer provides modules that are able to decode the demultiplexed data from the demux layer.

- *Output*: This layer simply displays the decoded data on the screen and it is also possible to stream to another device from this layer.

4.2 CMP-enabled DASH support for VLC
In this subsection we will describe the modifications of VLC in order to support our architecture described in the previous section.

4.2.1 Interface layer
At the interface layer we have added a new tab called DASH. The tab is fully written with the common graphical library QT [11]. The main class of the tab is located at the *open_panles.cpp* file which also contains the other tabs. The class manages the whole user interaction with the DASH tab. After the user has entered the URL of the CMP into the textfield on the top of the tab, the main class of the DASH tab initializes a new *CMPManager* class that is able to parse the CMP. The DASH tab provides the user the information about the choices that he or she can make. After the user has selected a configuration that fulfills his/her needs the DASH tab generates a CDI and passes this with the selected path of the MPD to the access plugin. Another modification that we have made at this layer is the session transfer menu. If the user right clicks on the video a menu appears that provides the user some options that relate to the media that is currently playing. We have added a new submenu called session transfer to this menu. The session transfer submenu presents the user the devices to which VLC could transfer the session.

4.2.2 Access Layer
At the access layer we have written our own plugin called MPD plugin that is able to handle DASH streams. The plugin gets the information where the MPD is located and the CDI from the DASH tab. Thus, at the beginning the plugin starts to download the MPD and after the parsing it begins with the download of the segments. It is also responsible for the representation change, i.e., when the plugin detects that more bandwidth is available it selects the next higher representation of the media and downloads the segments that relate to this representation, and the other way around if the bandwidth decreases.

4.2.3 Demux Layer
It was also necessary to make some small changes at the demux layer because VLC did not support the DASH delivery format out of the box. In our approach we have used the avformat library which is able to demultiplex MP4 and the DASH delivery format is also similar to MP4. But we had to change some things inside of the library because the offset of the second track would be false interpreted by the library. However, after this little modification it was no problem to demultiplex the DASH delivery format.

4.3 Session Transfer
This section describes the session transfer in the context of DASH with VLC.

As described before the user has to select a device from the session transfer submenu. After that the VLC variable will be changed to the hostname or address of the selected device. The change of this variable triggers the callback function that is located in the MPD plugin. The callback function gathers now the required information like play state and play time. After that it inserts this information to the CDI that the MPD plugin has received during the startup from the DASH tab. Thereafter the CDI will be send through a TCP

connection to the selected device. On the selected device a service is running which waits for incoming connections. If it receives a CDI it starts VLC with the parameter *contextDI* and the path that points to the received CDI. The DASH tab perceives that VLC has been started with the parameter *contextDI*. After that it parses the CDI and downloads the CMP that is described by the CDI. Now the user could change some of the available choices within the CMP like the language or the subtitles. Probably also the device makes some changes because it needs a different decoding algorithm or resolution. Afterwards DASH starts as usual with the only difference that the play state and the play time of the received CDI will be passed to the MPD plugin. With that information the MPD plugin could than start the stream at the point where the user has stopped the stream on the other device.

5. RELATED WORK
To start with we provide an overview of related work in the area of HTTP streaming.

Recently, 3GPP already specified Adaptive HTTP Streaming (AHS) [4] which defines a Media Presentation Description (MDP) and extensions to the well-known ISO Base Media File Format (ISOBMFF) [12]. The former is an XML document providing a manifest/session description which enables the client to request individual media segments via HTTP. The media segments are compliant to a delivery format that has been derived from the ISOBMFF.

Adobe's Dynamic HTTP Streaming [13] is based on their own Flash media manifest and F4F file format. The former is an XML document similar to 3GPPs' MPD and the latter are MP4 fragment files, i.e., also based on ISOBMFF. However, the solution is proprietary and not compliant to 3GPP AHS.

Apple's HTTP live streaming [14] is well known for quite some time and implemented on the iPhone and similar devices. It makes use of a M3U playlist file which serves as the manifest and each media file must be formatted as an MPEG-2 Transport Stream (M2TS) [8].

Finally, Microsoft's Smooth Streaming [16] is also around for a while which utilizes a server manifest file (i.e., SMIL document) and a client manifest file (i.e., proprietary XML document). Furthermore, this approach defines a smooth streaming format (ISMV) as an extension of the ISOBMFF. Additionally, they have also provided a comparison with the solutions provided by Apple and Adobe [17].

Recently, another implementation has been provided within the GPAC project on advanced content [18][19]. It ships with a similar functionality to our implementation with respect to DASH. Furthermore, it is open source and comes with its own player, i.e., no integration with VLC or any other existing player and no support for CMP. There is also an early version of reference software – not yet publicly available – which comprises command line tools for creating segments and requesting segments based on the MPD.

We respect to pure research results, a few papers are worth to mention in this context. Riiser et al. defined a low overhead container format for adaptive streaming [20] that proposes an alternative to the MPEG family of delivery formats (i.e., M2TS, ISOBMFF, and derivations thereof) for the streaming over HTTP. Kuschnig et.al. has performed an evaluation of rate-control algorithms in the context of dynamic adaptive streaming over

HTTP, specifically when using scalable media resources. Finally, Rong et al. [22] and De Keukelaere et al. [23] (and related publications) provide first publications in the area of MPEG-21 session mobility and have been used as an inspiration for starting this work item in the context of DASH.

6. CONCLUSIONS AND FUTURE WORK

In this paper we have described our test-bed for DASH featuring session mobility. It is based on international open standards and fully integrated into the well-known VLC. In particular, it facilitates MPEG-21 Digital Item in order to leverage existing media repositories such as UPnP and provides a testing framework for actual dynamic adaptive streaming algorithms including the possibility for transferring a running session from one device to another.

Future work includes the integration and comparison of various algorithms for the dynamic adaptive streaming such as [20] and [21] as well as those that will pop up at MMSys'11. Additionally, we plan to implement the actual connector to the UPnP repositories in order to be used in a home entertainment environment. Finally, once our code is stable enough and DASH is technically frozen we will consider submitting our implementation to the VLC developers in order to become open source.

7. ACKNOWLEDGMENTS

This work was supported in part by the EC in the context of the ALICANTE project (FP7-ICT-248652).

8. REFERENCES

[1] ISO/IEC CD 23001-6. 2010. Information technology -- MPEG systems technologies -- Part 6: Dynamic adaptive streaming over HTTP (DASH) (Guangzhou, China, Oct. 2010)

[2] UPnP Forum. 2006, ContentDirectory:2 Service Template Version 1.01 (May 2006) Available: http://www.upnp.org/specs/av/UPnP-av-ContentDirectory-v2-Service-20060531.pdf (last access: Dec. 2010)

[3] Burnett, I.S., Davis, S.J., Drury, G.M. 2005. MPEG-21 Digital Item Declaration and Identification – Principles and Compression. IEEE Transactions on Multimedia. 7, 3 (Jun. 2005), pp. 400-407.

[4] 3GPP TS 26.234. 2010. Transparent end-to-end packet switched streaming service (PSS); Protocols and codecs.

[5] Burnett, I.S., Pereira, F., Van de Walle, R., Koenen, R. 2006, The MPEG-21 Book, Wiley & Sons.

[6] Vetro, A, Timmerer, C. 2005. Digital Item Adaptation: Overview of Standardization and Research Activities. IEEE Transactions on Multimedia. 7, 3 (Jun. 2005), pp. 418–426.

[7] Vetro, A., Christopoulos, C., Ebrahami, T., Eds. 2003. Special Issue on Universal Multimedia Access. IEEE Signal Processing Magazine. 20, 2 (March 2003)

[8] Composition of Media Presentation (CMP) examples: http://www-itec.uni-

[9] Media Presentation Description (MPD) examples: http://www-itec.uni-klu.ac.at/~cmueller/adaptivestreaming/mpd/ (last access: Dec. 2010).

[10] VLC: open-source multimedia framework, player and server, http://www.videolan.org/vlc/ (last access: Dec. 2010).

[11] QT: cross-platform application and UI framework, http://qt.nokia.com/products/ (last access: Dec. 2010).

[12] ISO/IEC 14496-12:2008. Information technology -- Coding of audio-visual objects -- Part 12: ISO base media file format.

[13] Adobe HTTP Dynamic Streaming, http://www.adobe.com/products/httpdynamicstreaming/ (last access: Dec. 2010).

[14] Pantos, R., May, W. 2010. HTTP Live Streaming, IETF draft (Jun. 2010) http://tools.ietf.org/html/draft-pantos-http-live-streaming-04 (last access: Dec. 2010).

[15] ISO/IEC 13818-1:2007. Information technology -- Generic coding of moving pictures and associated audio information: Systems.

[16] Microsoft Smooth Streaming, http://www.iis.net/download/smoothstreaming (last access: Dec. 2010).

[17] Adaptive Streaming Comparison, http://learn.iis.net/page.aspx/792/adaptive-streaming-comparison (last access: Oct. 2010).

[18] Le Feuvre, J., Concolato, C., Moissinac, J.-C. 2007. GPAC: Open Source Multimedia Framework. In Proceedings of the ACM Multimedia 2007 (Augsburg, Germany, Sep. 2007)

[19] GPAC Project on Advanced Content, http://gpac.sourceforge.net/ (last access: Oct. 2010).

[20] Riiser, H., Halvorsen, P., Griwodz, C., Johansen, D. 2010. Low overhead container format for adaptive streaming, In Proceedings of the First Annual ACM SIGMM Conference on Multimedia Systems (Scottsdale, Arizona, USA, Feb. 2010), pp. 193–198.

[21] Kuschnig, R., Kofler, I., Hellwagner, H. 2010. An Evaluation of TCP-based Rate-Control Algorithms for Adaptive Internet Streaming of H.264/SVC. In Proceedings of the First Annual ACM SIGMM Conference on Multimedia Systems (Scottsdale, Arizona, USA, Feb. 2010), pp. 157–167.

[22] Rong, L, Burnett, I. S. 2004. Dynamic multimedia adaptation and updating of media streams with MPEG-21, In Proceedings of the First IEEE Conference on Consumer Communications and Networking (Jan. 2004) pp. 436-441.

[23] De Keukelaere, F., De Sutter, R., Van de Walle, R. 2005. MPEG-21 session mobility on mobile devices. In Proceedings of the 2005 International Conference on Internet Computing. (Las Vegas, NV, USA, May 2000)

DRM Protected Dynamic Adaptive HTTP Streaming

Frank Hartung   Sinan Kesici   Daniel Catrein

Ericsson GmbH
Research Multimedia Technologies,
Ericsson Allee 1, 52134 Herzogenrath

frank.hartung@ericsson.com   sinan.kesici@gmail.com   daniel.catrein@ericsson.com

ABSTRACT

Dynamic adaptive HTTP streaming (DASH) is a new concept for video streaming using consecutive downloads of short video segments. 3GPP has developed the basic DASH standard which is further extended by the Open IPTV Forum (OIPF) and MPEG. In all versions available to date, only very simple content protection use cases are enabled. Extensions are needed to enable important advanced use cases like pay-per-view and license change in an ongoing video channel.

In this publication, we analyze what is missing in the current DASH standards with regards to content protection, and propose changes and extensions to DASH in order to enable the application of DRM. This includes changes to the Media Presentation Description (MPD), and the file format. With a suitable key and license structure used together with DASH, even complex use cases like pay-per-maximum-quality are possible.

Besides the analysis of required changes to DASH for content protection, and the description of suitable key and license structures applied to DASH, we also present a proof-of-concept implementation of the proposed concepts.

Categories and Subject Descriptors

H.3 [**Information Storage and Retrieval**]: Systems and Software - distributed systems, information networks; J.7 [**Computers in Other Systems**]

General Terms: Security, Standardization

Keywords: Adaptive HTTP streaming, content protection, digital rights management, encryption

1. INTRODUCTION

Digital video has become so popular that it nowadays constitutes the majority of Internet traffic. Different protocols and principles for video transport have been developed and are in use. Previously, the idea was widely accepted that streaming video, in contrast to e.g. file transfer, can cope with packet losses, and that lossless transmission should be avoided in order to keep transmission delays due to re-transmissions low. The transport mechanism that was developed in that spirit is based on RTP transport and RTSP control

commands. An example for an end-to-end streaming system that builds on RTP is the 3GPP Packet-switched Streaming Standard [1], PSS, which is implemented in virtually all mobile phones sold today. A drawback of RTP based streaming is however that special streaming servers are needed that support the RTP stack and RTSP based control. Recently, the idea of using off-the-shelf and possibly cloud based web servers for video delivery gained popularity. This implies the use of HTTP/TCP, instead of RTP/UDP, based transport. The requirements of trick play control and adaptivity directly lead to the concept of segmentation into small video segments which are concatenated for playback. The family of methods that use these ideas are called "dynamic adaptive HTTP streaming" (DASH) methods. DASH methods have other advantages too: DASH provides reliability through the use of TCP; content can be delivered through firewalls without problems; and DASH is congestion-controlled and can adapt to it. The first representatives of the DASH family were proprietary schemes proposed by Apple [7] and Microsoft [8]. Meanwhile, standards bodies have also developed standards for adaptive HTTP streaming. Interestingly, like in the case of RTP-based PSS streaming, again 3GPP was the pioneer, with their adaptive HTTP streaming specification described in [1]. The Open IPTV Forum (OIPF) adopted the 3GPP solution as baseline and extended it, most notably with support for MPEG-2 transport stream transport encoding [2]. Meanwhile, MPEG and IETF are also working on adaptive HTTP streaming standards, partly based on 3GPP DASH [1] as starting point.

If DASH methods shall be used for commercial high-definition video content, they must satisfy the relevant technical and commercial requirements. A major requirement of video content providers and the media industry is the support for protection, that means for encryption and key management, together also commonly called Digital Rights Management (DRM). In this paper, we investigate concepts and needed extensions for the application of DRM protection to DASH.

This paper is organized as follows: first, we briefly review the concepts of DASH and DRM systems. Then, we discuss and identify gaps in the standards that are missing for connecting DRM and DASH. We explain how the gaps can and should be filled to get a functional end-to-end system for DRM protected DASH. Finally, we present a proof-of-concept implementation that we developed to demonstrate the feasibility of protected DASH. We used Marlin DRM, but this should be regarded as an example; the use of other DRMs is equally possible.

In the following, when talking about DASH, we refer to 3GPP DASH [1], unless otherwise expressed.

2. BACKGROUND

2.1 Dynamic Adaptive HTTP Streaming (DASH)

The DASH standard is composed of two main parts. One part defines the Media Presentation Description (MPD) that is used by the server to describe, and by the client to access content using HTTP requests. The other part defines the format of the media segments as extensions to the 3GPP File Format (3GP).

The purpose of the MPD is to give location and timing information to the client to fetch and playback the media segments of a particular content. The MPD syntax is defined in XML. Typically the MPD file is fetched using HTTP at the start of the streaming session.

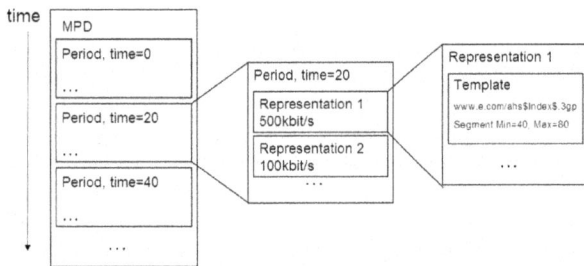

Figure 1 Media Presentation Description (MPD) layout

The MPD consists of three major components, namely Periods, Representations and Segments (Fig. 1). Period elements are the outermost part of the MPD. Periods are typically larger pieces of media that are played out sequentially. Inside a period, multiple different encodings of the content may occur, called representations. These alternative representations can have, for example, different bitrates, frame rates or video resolutions. Finally, each representation describes a series of segments by HTTP URLs. Those URLs are either explicitly described in the representation (similar to a playlist) or described through a template construction, which allows the client to derive a valid URL for each segment of a representation. The MPD format is flexible and can support other media container formats such as MPEG-2 TS.

The 3GP file format is based on the ISO base media file format. A 3GP segment is either an initialization segment or a media segment. An initialization segment contains configuration data (formatted as so-called 'ftyp' and 'moov' boxes of the file format), whereas a media segment is a concatenation of one or more movie fragments of media pointers and samples ('moof' and 'mdat' boxes). Concatenation of the initialization segment and one or more media segments of the same representation results in a valid 3GP file (Fig. 2).

The 3GP file format was extended for the specific HTTP streaming requirements.

The optional Segment Index box ('sidx') helps a client to seek and switch in large or overlapping media segments by locating random access points and parts of a media segment suitable for partial download. It also provides absolute timing information for time recovery after seeking. Another extension is the Segment Type box ('styp') which includes brand (i.e., type) information for media segments and enables compatible usage between standards, for segments that comply with multiple DASH standards.

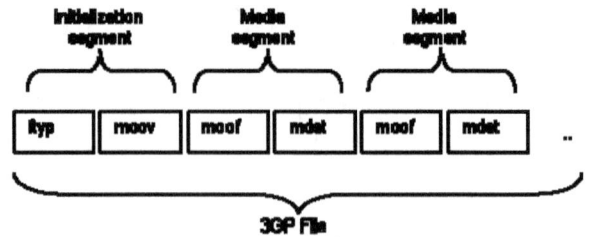

Figure 2 3GP based HTTP streaming segments

Media segments are identical to all users; adaptivity is obtained simply by switching between segments of alternative representations. This property makes DASH HTTP cache and Content Delivery Network (CDN) friendly. The media segments, uniquely identified by their URLs can be served from intermediate HTTP Proxy/Caches in the same way as any other web content.

The Open IPTV Forum has extended DASH to also be usable with MPEG-2 Transport streams (MPEG-2 TS). The MPD indicates through MIME Types that the format of the media segments is MPEG2-TS. Only restrictions, but no extensions, on the MPEG2-TS format have been defined in OIPF. This makes it possible to create a compliant MPEG2-TS stream by concatenating the media segments fetched by the client. The Program Specific Information (PSI) tables may be either contained in an initialization segment or in the media segments.

2.2 Digital Rights Management (DRM)

Digital Rights Management denotes technologies that shall prevent unauthorized use and duplication of digital media. Conceptually, this is achieved using specification and expression of usage permissions pertaining to the data, and ensuring that the data is only rendered in accordance with those permissions. Technically, this requires encryption of the data. The key used for decryption, called content key, is itself encrypted and bundled with the permissions, into a "license" or "rights object" (Fig. 3).

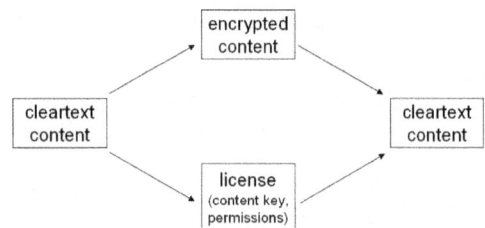

Figure 3 Basic DRM principle: license and encrypted content together give content access

Encrypted data and the corresponding licenses are typically associated to each other using unique content identifiers. The hardest problem of DRM is ensuring that only the intended single receiver can access and use the license, and thus the content key, and thus the content. This is typically achieved by encrypting the license with a key that is only known to the sender and the intended receiver. This can conveniently be done by deploying a public-key infrastructure and surrounding trust ecosystem. Thus, it is ensured that only the authorized and trusted device can decrypt the license, thus get access to the content key, and thus get access to the content. As far as it is publicly known, most of the widely used DRM systems in use today follow the described principles, for example Open Mobile Alliance (OMA) DRM [19], Marlin DRM [5][6], or

Microsoft Playready DRM. For a more in-depth introduction to DRM please refer to [20].

3. DRM PROTECTED DASH

In the previous section, we briefly reviewed plain DASH, without protection. Now we discuss extensions for the support of DRM protection.

3.1 Requirements

First, we need to be clear what we want to achieve. The main goal is to enable encryption of DASH video and to signal the required information for license and key acquisition to the receiver. This shall work with any DRM system, e.g. OMA DRM 2.1 [19], or Marlin Broadband (Marlin BB) [5][6], and not be DRM system specific. It shall also be possible to use different DRM systems for key management in parallel. It shall be possible to use MP4 file based or MPEG-2 TS based DASH.

For television or IPTV use cases, we adopt the concept of video channels, as known from classical TV channels. In conjunction with DASH, each channel is available in multiple representations. It is desirable to be optionally able to bundle video channels into a channel group (often also called channel bouquet), that can then be purchased as an entity and be accessed with one common license. Also, it shall be optionally possible to have pay-per-view (PPV) parts within a channel, in other words be able to use a different key for certain parts of a video channel.

It shall further be possible to grant access to individual representations, i.e., quality levels. This is called pay-per-quality. An additional optional requirement is that access to a certain quality/bit-rate, i.e. representation, of a video also enables access to lower representations, but not to higher representations. This allows for different subscriptions to video services at different (maximum) quality representations, in other words, pay-per-maximum-quality.

3.2 Gap analysis: what is missing in the current standards

Both 3GPP and OIPF have already included some provisions for content protection or DRM, but only in a rudimentary way.

In 3GPP DASH [1], some fields in the MPD are defined that can carry basic content protection information. This is restricted to the specification of one or more content protection systems in the form of a *schemeIdUri*, per representation. The choice of DRM systems is left open, however, if OMA DRM is used, the used file format must be the OMA non-streamable Packetized DRM Content Format (PDCF), which is a special version of the ISO file format with additional OMA DRM specific boxes for OMA DRM parameters and metadata. Besides the fact that no DRM specific content identifiers are included, as they are typically used to associate content and license, no segment-specific DRM information can be conveyed. The file format used in [1] is the 3GP file format [17], except, as said, if OMA DRM is used.

In OIPF DASH [2], it is clarified that the *schemeIdUri* shall carry the same type of DRM system identifier used elsewhere in the OIPF specification. For MPEG-2 TS, [2] supports the Marlin Broadband Transport Stream (BBTS) format [16], which is an extension of the original MPEG-2 TS specification [18] with some added crypto metadata. It is required that a file that concatenates initialization segment and a set of media segments is a BBTS compliant file. This may be achieved by using the same crypto-period boundaries and keys across different representations. The TS carries DRM related metadata. General metadata e.g. indicating the used protection system and crypto parameters are included in the Program Map Table (PMT) containing conditional access (CA) descriptors and the Conditional Access Table (CAT). Multiplexed with the media elementary streams are key streams. So called Entitlement Management Message (EMM) streams contain long-lived keys; so-called Entitlement Control Message (ECM) streams contain short-lived keys. The DRM metadata in relation to a certain elementary stream are delivered as part of either the initialization segment or the media segments that carry the samples of the elementary stream. The ECM stream of a protection system in relation to a certain elementary stream has the same packet identifier (PID) in all segments in which it is included. [2] supports two protected MP4 file formats: OMArlin PDCF [14], which is an extension of OMA DRM PDCF [19], and the so-called Marlin MIPMP format [15]. It is required that a file that concatenates initialization segment and arbitrary media segments of any complete representation or the set of partial representations are stored as either a PDCF compliant file or MIPMP compliant file. Additional DRM metadata, besides the metadata in the MPD, can be stored in the file, specifically in the initialization segment.

Thus, it is possible with the existing standard to encrypt DASH segments; for example by using the encrypted OMA PDCF flavor of the ISO file format, or by using the encrypted Marlin BBTS flavor of the MPEG-2 TS format. However, in both cases, since adequate signaling in the MPD is missing, the client will only know after downloading and parsing of the segments whether it has a suitable license and is able to decrypt them.

In order to enable all requirements outlined above, some components need to be added.

First of all, a more sophisticated MPD signaling is required. A content identifier, *DRMContentID*. and a URL to the license server are needed in the MPD in order to allow checking for availability of licenses, and acquisition of missing licenses, even before the initialization segment is downloaded. Further, the granularity of these content identifiers should be per segment, not per representation. Another missing attribute is a pay-per-view (PPV) indicator which is not technically mandatory, but would allow signaling of PPV content to the end user.

Secondly, the key and license hierarchy should enable subscription to channel groups and PPV services, and quality-dependent access to media. However, this can be regarded to be "on top of" DASH, as it superimposes a license structure, but uses DASH as it is.

In order to enable PPV and fine-grained access, and enhance security in general, we introduce (possibly) separate keys per segment. This is similar to short-term keys as known in TV encryption.

We describe these extensions in more detail below.

3.3 Proposed Extensions to DASH for Content Protection

In order to fulfill the requirements and use cases outlined above, we propose the following additions to the DASH standard, and the following way of structuring keys and licenses. Please note that both parts are independent from each other.

3.3.1 MPD extensions

We propose to place a child element *ContentProtection* with additional attributes into each MPD, on representation or alternatively on segment level. The first additional attribute is the rights issuer URL, *RIURL*, which gives an absolute URL to the license server or rights issuer of the content. This URL can be used to request a license from license server, using the protocol defined for the respective DRM system (please note the DRM system is also signaled in the MPD). The *ContentProtection* element further includes a *DRMContentID* attribute to allow license matching before data streaming. A *PPV* attribute is also placed into *ContentProtection* to indicate whether the user needs special per-view licenses for a program. The necessity of the *PPV* attribute will be explained below in section 3.3.2. Further, an extension mechanism holding DRM system specific metadata should be added. In our case, this was not necessary, so we did not implement such an extension.

The proposed MPD extensions allow early license acquisition, and thus help avoiding delays when starting the DASH streaming session. The merit of the *PPV* attribute is mainly enhanced usability, as pay-per-view media can be signaled to the user.

3.3.2   Architecture of Key Hierarchy

For TV delivery, the use of a key hierarchy is an old and known concept. A long-lived key (with a lifetime of e.g. a day) is used to encrypt short-lived keys (with a lifetime of e.g. 10 seconds) which are used to encrypt the data. Initially it seems redundant to encrypt an encryption key; the idea behind it is however to a.) change the content key frequently to make its sharing difficult, b.) disallow access to the broadcasted content key, c.) being able to give access to the broadcasted content key to individual users by issuing targeted individual keys giving access to the content keys. In that spirit, ITU Recommendation 810 [12] proposed in 1992 a three-level key hierarchy. The keys are called Control Word (CW), Authorization Key (AK) and Distribution Key (DK) respectively, from upper level to lower level. The CW is used as short term key to scramble the content, the AK is used to encrypt CWs, and the DK is used to transmit AK in a secure way. The DK is common to all users. The scheme is however not used anymore, because it is vulnerable to piracy: once the DK is compromised, the service provider has to change all security modules. In 1996, Lee et al. [10], in 1999 Tu et al. [9] and in 2004, Huang et al. [11] proposed advanced four level key hierarchies which solved the above problem. The group oriented key distribution scheme of Huang et al. builds different channel groups. Each channel group is a subgroup of another channel group so that if a user registers for any channel group, he or she can access the subgroups as well. We used thus concept as a basis for our proposed key and license system for DASH.

In this section, we propose an efficient key distribution scheme based on a three-level key hierarchy which makes the use cases mentioned in section 3.1 possible for DASH and can be combined with any DRM system. We call the keys in the respective layers Segment Key (SK), Representation Key (RK) and Channel Group Key (CGK). The key for each level is used to encrypt/decrypt the keys for the previous level.

Figure 4 shows an example of a channel group. The channel group is composed of multiple channels with three quality representations. Each representation has one initial segment and multiple media segments. SK is the short term key and is used to encrypt/decrypt segments. To increase the security, each segment is encrypted with a different SK.

RK is used to encrypt/decrypt SK. Each representation of any channel has a unique RK.

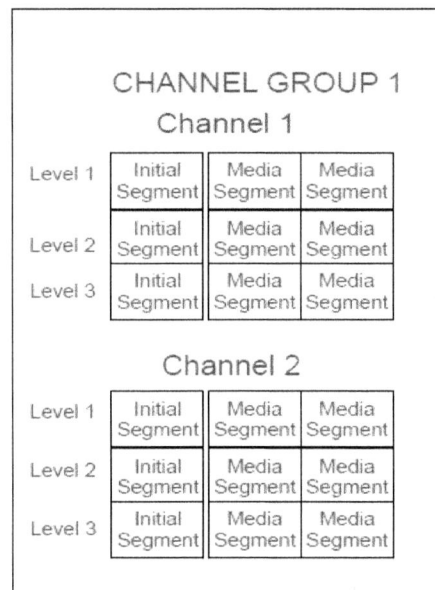

Figure 4 Example channel group

The service provider encrypts the SK using the RK and than transmits the encrypted SK within the segments as:

$$\{SK_{ijkl}\}_{RK_{ijk}} \text{---}> Segment_{ijkl}$$

where i is the channel group index, j is the channel index, k is the representation index and l is the segment index. That means the lth segment in k^{th} representation of channel j of channel group group i is encrypted with the RK of this representation and embedded to the lth segment.

The RKs are updated per program because the service provider may offer PPV services where the RKs are delivered to the users within a license.

Each channel group has different CGKs per representation in order to encrypt/decrypt the RK of the corresponding representation. The encrypted RK is transmitted within the initial segment of the same representation as:

$$\{RK_{ijk}\}_{CGK_{ik}} \text{---}> InitialSegment_{ijk}$$

and the CGK is distributed to the users in a DRM license which needs to be acquired according to the license acquisition process and protocol for the used DRM system. As an example, CGKs are updated once a month, for monthly subscription. The CGK of the highest representation of any channel group is created randomly and the successive CGKs are derived from the previous one with a one-way hash function as:

$$CGK_{i,k} = H(CGK_{i,k-1})$$

where $H()$ is the one way hash function based on any cryptographically-secure hash algorithm. With this scheme, users can subscribe to any representation of a channel group by purchasing the CGK corresponding to that representation and also can access to lower representations by deriving the CGKs with one-way hash function H(). However, they do not have access to higher qualities than purchased. The use of the one-way hash function thus enables the pay-per-maximum-quality use case.

In the case of subscription to a group of channels, the service provider has to make sure that channel groups are disjoint.

In the PPV case, the MPD should inform the user that the program is PPV and give the necessary information for temporary license acquisition (the user may have to interactively order the license and confirm payment). The RKs are created in the same way as the CGK by using a one-way hash function $H()$ in order to let the users only access the purchased and lower representations, i.e., qualities.

The described key architecture allows pay-per-view and key change, as well as pay-per-quality and pay-per-maximum-quality use cases. Further, it allows bundling of channels into channel groups that can be accessed through a common license.

3.4 Encryption

In the proposed key distribution scheme, encryption is applied in three different steps: Encryption of segments (i.e., content), encryption of SKs and encryption of RKs.

The encryption algorithm deployed is the Advanced Encryption Standard (AES) with 128 bits block size and 256 bits key size in cipher-block chaining (CBC) mode, which is the most widely used encryption algorithm for DRM systems, but other kinds of encryption algorithms ca be applied as well. Selective encryption is not used in our scheme.

In general, switching between quality representations is done at segment boundaries. Therefore, encryption of a segment as a whole is not a problem in terms of quality representation switching. By assuming that switching between quality representations within segments can be applied in the future, segments are encrypted sample by sample in our scheme.

Encrypted SKs and RKs are delivered to the users within a special box called 'imif' of media and initial segments respectively. This box is a sub-box of 'sinf' located inside the 'ipro' box which is a sub-box of the 'meta' box. This means four extra boxes are created for delivering encrypted keys. More information about MPEG-4 based file boxes can be found in [4].

3.4.1 Effect of Encryption on Data Size

The encryption algorithm increases the size of the initialization segment and the media segments because of padding (insertion of dummy values to fill up the ciphertext to block boundaries) and inclusion of extra DRM/crypto related boxes.

If the program is not PPV, the initial segment of each representation of the program contains an encrypted RK. The four additional empty boxes increase the size 256 bits (64 bits per box). After encrypting with CGK, the size of the RK increases from 256 bits to 384 bits because of the Initialization Vector (IV) that is placed in front of the encrypted RK. As a result, the size of the initial segments expands by 640 bits. If the program is PPV, the RK is delivered to the users within a DRM license, hence out-of-band for the media data. Thus, the size of the initial segment does not change.

Embedding the encrypted SK into a segment increases the size of the segment by 640 bits as in the case of the initial segment. Each segment is encrypted sample by sample with the same SK, but with different initialization vectors (IVs). In our system, the IV of the first sample is created randomly and the other IVs are derived from the first IV. Therefore it is sufficient to just signal the first IV. This results in another 128 bits expansion in a media segment. Totally, there is a data expansion of 768 bits in a media segment. However, sample by sample encryption requires padding for each sample unless the sample size is a multiple of 128 bits. This results in a random data expansion between 0-127 per sample, i.e. around 64 bits on average.

3.4.2 Effect of Encryption on Segmentation Time

In order to get an impression of the effect of encryption on the segmentation time, we segmented, with and without encryption, an example video with three representations. Each representation of the content is divided into 10 segments with equal duration of 12 seconds. The segmentation times are given in Figure 5.

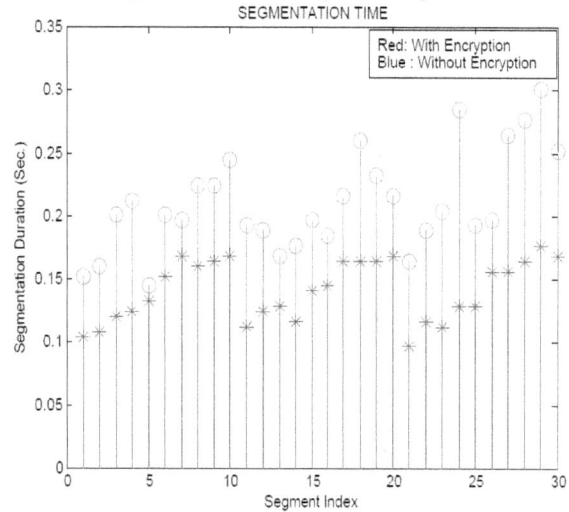

Figure 5 Server Segmentation Time

Figure 5 shows the segmentation time of 30 segments on the content creation server, with and without encryption. The red circles indicate the segmentation duration with encryption, while blue stars represent the segmentation time without encryption, of the same segments. As can be seen from the figure, the delay stemming from encryption is comparable to the segmentation time but relatively small compared to segment duration which indicates that encryption will not cause any problem, even in the live streaming case. Encryption time is not a significant delay factor.

4. PROOF-OF-CONCEPT: MARLIN BB PROTECTED DASH

We chose Marlin Broadband (BB) as DRM system for a proof-of-concept implementation that incorporates the concepts outlined above. Marlin BB has been developed by the Marlin Developer Community (MDC). MDC is an industry forum, mainly from the consumer electronics industries, that has developed a state-of-the art family of DRM systems. Marlin BB is conceptually similar to e.g. OMA DRM or proprietary DRMs like Windows Media DRM.

The *DRMSystemID* element the in MPD is set to "urn:dvb:casystemid:19188", using the value for Marlin DRM defined in the DVB forum.

Our proof-of-concept system is mainly composed of six components: Key Database, Content Rendering, HTTP Server, Marlin BB Server, HTTP Client and Marlin Client, Figure 6 shows the interaction between the different components.

The content rendering component is responsible for off-line media segmentation and encryption using the keys in the key database. It produces the MPD, the unencrypted initialization segment per representation and encrypted media segments, which are all stored at the HTTP Server.

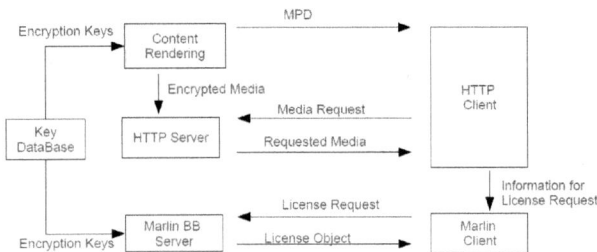

Figure 6 Proof-of-Concept Architecture

The HTTP client first downloads and interprets the MPD. Using the protection information in the MPD, the Marlin Client checks for the availability of a suitable license for the content. If necessary, a license is requested by the Marlin client from the Marlin BB server. The Marlin BB server checks the request and returns the license object which includes the key, *DRMContentID*, license expiration date and possibly other information. If the program is PPV, the requested license is a temporary license, otherwise, the requested license is a channel group license. Subsequently, the HTTP client requests media segments from the HTTP Server via the segment addresses in the MPD. As the license and thus the content key is available at the Marlin client, the Marlin client delivers the key to the HTTP client, which decrypts and renders the received media segments.

Marlin Client and Marlin Server both perform the Marlin protocols as specified in [6] which are Marlin registration, Node acquisition, Link acquisition, Marlin License acquisition, and, if necessary, Marlin de-registration.

Figure 7 Example Electronic Program Guide Detail

The proposed scheme has been implemented as part of a DASH client and server test system. In an example service, two channel groups are offered to the user. Each channel group has multiple channels with three quality levels/representations: *HD TV, Standard TV and Mobile TV,* which are composed of multiple segments. Figure 7 is a snap-shot of the user interface, in TV terms Electronic Program Guide (EPG), that is offered to the user.

Channel group I has three channels (channel 1, channel 2, channel 3). In an example case, the user has registered to the standard TV level of channel group I. Thus, the user can access standard TV and mobile TV levels of all channels in channel group I as shown by the green "OK" signs in Fig. 7. Channel 3 is an exception because the program running on this channel at this time is pay-per-view, and thus not included in the channel group license. In this case, the EPG guides the user to buy an additional temporary PPV license.

The license that the user bought for channel group I is not valid for channel group II. Thus, if the user wants to access the only channel of group II, he has to buy another license which was the HD license in the example case. Using that license, the user can access all three representations of channel group II, as shown in the Figure.

5. SUMMARY AND CONCLUSIONS

Dynamic adaptive HTTP streaming (DASH) is a new concept for video streaming using consecutive downloads of short video segments. 3GPP has developed the basic DASH standard which is further extended by OIPF and MPEG. In all versions available to date, content protection is not properly enabled. Extensions are needed to enable important use cases like pay-per-view, license change in an ongoing video channel, and pay-per-maximum-quality.

In this publication, we have examined which extensions are needed, in order to use DASH for DRM protected content. This comprises required changes in the DASH standard, namely MPD metadata extensions, as well as changes in the used transport file formats, namely the inclusion of a ISO file format box carrying a segment key, and finally a suitable key and license structure applied to the underlying DASH concept. All those changes have been proposed and explained in the paper. With these changes and additions, which do not change the core idea of DASH, even more complex use cases like pay-per-view and pay-per-maximum-quality are possible.

As a proof-of-concept, we have implemented the proposed changes and integrated them with a real DRM key and license management system. For the proof-of-concept, we have used Marlin DRM, but any other similar DRM would be equally usable.

6. REFERENCES

[1] 3GPP TS 26.234: Transparent end to end packet switched Streaming Service (PSS), Protocols and codecs, v9.4.0

[2] Open IPTV Forum. HTTP Adaptive Streaming. Technical report, V2.0

[3] Open IPTV Forum, Authentication, Content Protection and Service Protection. V2.0

[4] ISO/IEC International standard 14496, Information technology – Coding of audio-visual objects, Part 12 : ISO base media file format

[5] Marlin Developer Community. Marlin Architecture Overview

[6] Marlin Developer Community. Marlin Broadband Architecture Overview for Marlin Adopters

[7] Apple. HTTP Streaming Overview. Technical report

[8] Microsoft Corporation. ISS Smooth Streaming Technical Overview. Technical report

[9] F. K. Tu, C. S. Laih, and S. H. Toung, "On key distribution management for conditional access system on pay-TV system," *IEEE Trans. Consumer Electron.,* vol. 45, no. 1, pp. 151–158, Feb 1999

[10] J. W. Lee, "Key distribution and management for conditional access system on DBS" in *Proc. Int. Conf. Cryptology and Information Security,* pp.82-86, 1996

[11] Y. L. Huang and S. Shieh, "Efficient key distribution schemes for secure media delivery in pay-TV systems," *IEEE Trans. Multimedia,* vol. 6, no. 5 , pp. 760–769, October 2004

[12] Conditional-Access Broadcasting systems, ITU-R Recommendation 810, 1992

[13] Open IPTV Forum, "Release 2 specification, Volume 2 – Media Formats", V2.0

[14] Marlin Developer Community, OMArlin Specification, Version 1.0.3

[15] Marlin Developer Community, Marlin – File Formats Specification, Version 1.1.2

[16] Marlin Developer Community, Marlin Broadband Transport Stream Specification. Version 1.0.2

[17] 3GPP TS 26.244, Transparent end-to-end packet switched streaming service (PSS); 3GPP file format (3GP)

[18] Information technology – Generic coding of moving pictures and associated audio information: Systems, ISO/IEC 13818-1:2000(E)

[19] Open Mobile Alliance, OMA Digital Rights Management V2.2

[20] E. Becker, W. Buhse, D. Günnewig, N. Rump (Eds.), "Digital Rights Management - Technological, Economic, Legal and Political Aspects", Springer, 2nd edition, 2004

Author Index